A HINDUSTANI-ENGLISH LAW AND COMMERCIAL DICTIONARY

A HINDUSTANI-ENGLISH LAW AND COMMERCIAL DICTIONARY

BY

S. W. FALLON, Ph. D. Halle.

GYAN

Published by

GYAN

Gyan Publishing House
5, Ansari Road
Daryaganj, New Delhi-110002
Phone: 011-47034999, 9811692060
E-mail: books@gyanbooks.com

Distribution Network
gyanbooks.com
India, USA, Canada, UK, Australia, France

ISBN : 978-81-212-4319-3 (PB)
First Published, 1879

2nd Impression 2020

Printed at: Gyan Press, Delhi.

A HINDUSTANI-ENGLISH LAW AND COMMERCIAL DICTIONARY,

BY

S. W. FALLON, Ph. D. *Halle.*

PRINTED AT THE MEDICAL HALL PRESS, BANĀRAS.

MAY BE HAD, FOR CASH ONLY, OF

E. J. LAZARUS AND CO., BANĀRAS.—TRUBNER AND CO., LONDON.

1879.

PREFACE.

The present work is the Compiler's English-Hindustani Law and Commercial Dictionary reversed, with a large number of additions. The authorities for the law technicalities are the Urdu translations of the Acts and Regulations published in the *Government Gazette* and the authorized translations of the Chief Court.

Besides the practical purpose for which it has been compiled, as an aid to persons who have to deal with Courts of law and to translators of law papers, this work will serve to show at a glance that the language of the Law Courts of the Provinces in which Hindustani is spoken is made up almost entirely of foreign Arabic phrases. In a great many instances the Hindi equivalents, given in this work by the side of these Arabic phrases, clearly show that Arabic has been drawn upon without the slightest excuse, simply because Arabic is esteemed a learned language while Hindi is only the vulgar vernacular of the people of the country. And then it serves to keep up that mystification which is the nefarious advantage of the few, and a wrongful injury to the many.

Thus the Plaint, Answer, Reply, and Rejoinder, or the 'four papers' of the Civil Code, was, in the authorized phraseology of the Courts, *kāgazāt-i-arba,* as though the Arabic *arba* conveyed any more precise idea than the common Hindi *chār* four. And so of a host of words. For the well-known H. *dharoṛ* a deposit we have A. *amānat, drishṭ-bandhak* hypothecation is A. *rahn bil-kafālat,* H. *jhuṭlānā* to make null, from *jhūṭ* false, is A. *ibṭāl.* The Hindi terms for near relations also must be transformed into Arabic. Thus H. *beṭā* is A. *ibn,* H. *gailaṛ bahn* step-sister (different fathers) wears the equally occult form P. A. *hamshīrah-i-akhyāfī,* H. *byāh* marriage must be replaced by A. *izdivāj,* lineal descendants H. *ek bāp ke* by A. P. A. *aulād-i-rishta-i-mustaqīmah,* H. *beṭyaṅ* daughters (female issue) by A. *aulād-i-anās,* H. *mā kā peṭ* mother's womb by A. *batn-i-mādar, garbh girānā* causing miscarriage by A. *isqat-i-hamal.* And then we have such commonly used phrases as H. *sūkha* drought metamorphosed into A. P. *imsāk-i-bārāṅ,* H. *marghaṭ* a burning ground for Hindu corpses into the elaborated phrase, A. P. *muqām-i-ātish-zanī-i-nāsh.*

The common native name *dhartī* for land, soil, must be superseded by A. *arāzī,* A. *qābil-i-zarāat* culturable has thrust out the universally-used H. *khetī-jog,* and A. *mazāra,* the familiar H. *jota* a cultivator, H. *chorī* theft is A. *sarqa,* H. *baiyar-bānī* women is A. *mastūrāt,* H. *sājhā* is A. *sharākat, batwāṛā* partition is A. *taqsīm* and *inqisām, sahāēta* help is A. *isteānat,* H. *bartāo* use is A. *istemāl, khānā pīnā* food is A. *akl o shurb, roṭī kapṛā* a maintenance is P. A. *nān-o-nafqa*, H. *bastu*, P. *chīz* things is A. *ashyā*, H. *gāhak* purchaser is A. *mushtarī*, H. *bharat* a load is A. *māl-i-mahmūla*.

Even for the common Hindi particles, adverbs, etc. have been substituted elaborate Arabic phrases. Thus H. *or se* on the part of is P. A. *az jānib*, H. *un sab me se* out of the whole is A. P. *az ān jumla*, H. *jorāvarī se* by force is A. *bil-jabr*, *nae sire se* anew is *az sar-i-nau*, H. *alag alag* severally is A. *al al infirād*, H. *sada* is A. *al-ad-davām*, *aur aisā hī* and so on is A. *alā hāza*, *bīch meṅ* between is A. *mā-bain*.

The very sign boards in the streets of Dehli bear witness to the foreign Persian and mystic Arabic which rules our Courts and public offices with such despotic sway. Thus *Lāl kūā* the red well has been transmogrified into *Lāl chāh* لعل چاه, *baṛā darība* into *darība-i-kalāṅ*, *chhoṭā darība* is *darība-i-khurd*, *jūte-vālā* seller of shoes is *juft-farosh*, *ṭopī-vālā* seller of caps is *kulāh-farosh*, *sunār* goldsmith is *zar-gar*, *dhunyā* carder is A. *naddāf*.

The Hindi *Behar Gazette* in which the laws of the country were to have been given in the vernacular Hindi of the people would, under its present Editor, Rāē Sohan Lal, have demonstrated beyond a doubt the practicability of rendering legal technicalities in the indigenous tongue. But its projector, Sir G. Campbell, had left the country long before the project was sanctioned by the Government of India, and the *Behar Gazette* is published indeed in the Hindi character but the technicalities are still Arabic, pure but not simple. The Editor's strong predilection for the simple and natural, joined to his command of popular Hindi makes him especially fitted for the accomplishment of a task so important as that of enabling the people of India to read and understand the laws under which they live. The admirable Hindi translation of Sir G. Campbell's Educational Despatch by this writer may be cited as an example of a successful rendering into simple Hindi of the abstract ideas and refinements of European thought, and the frequently complex constructions of a highly cultivated language.

S. W. FALLON.

Delhi, 1st February, 1880.

FALLON'S
LAW AND COMMERCIAL
DICTIONARY.

ا أ آبا

P ا S. and H. अ, *a.*

1. (*Arith.*) The number one.

2. (*Sanskrit almanacks and astrology*) for *ādityavāra* or *arkvār* Sunday, and Aries.

3. The initial letter in ओम् the Hindu triad; Vishnu.

P آب *āb*, n. m. Z. آب, S. अप.

Water (پاني). [fields.

آب پاشي *āb-pā'shī*, n. f. Irrigation; watering There are two modes of irrigation. 1. *tor* consists in simply breaking away the ridges of fields to let the water in. 2. *ḍāl*, Throwing the water out of a small bucket or basket into the field.

آب خيز *āb-khez*, Ped. adj. used substantively. Moist or wet soil; springy ground where water is found by digging a little below the surface. *Rare.*

آب دار *āb-dār*, n. m. P. آب water, دار keep. A servant in charge of the drinking-water, etc.

آب رواں *āb-i-rav'āṅ*, n. m. *lit.* Running water.

A kind of very fine muslin.

آب شور *āb-i-shor*, n. m. Sea-water; salt-water.

abūr-i-āb-i-shor, Transportation beyond seas.

آبکار *āb-kār*, n. m. P. آب water, کار work. A distiller or seller of spirituous liquors.

آبکاري *āb-kā'rī*, n. f.

1. The business of a distiller.

2. A distillery; a tavern; liquor shop.

3. A duty on the manufacture and sale of spirituous liquors, as *tāṛī* or toddy, *pachwāī*, *arrack*, etc., and on intoxicating drugs, whether in substance, infusion, or extracts, as opium, *bhaṅg*, *charas*, etc. It is levied on certain licenced distilleries, or in fees for licences granted by the Collector to retailers.

ābkārī-daroǧā, n. m. The head officer appointed to superintend distilleries, spirit-shops, etc.

ābkā'rī-mahāl', n. m. The department or office of *ābkārī*; the excise department; a distillery.

آبي *ā'bī*, adj. Ped. Aquatic; irrigated; blue.

A إباحت *ibā'hat*, n. f. Giving permission.

(In. *Mah. Law.*) Authority; permission.

A آباد *ābā'd*, adj. Z. āvād, S. आवास, P. *būdan* to be.

(*In Comp.*) A city; village, etc. The opposite of *wīrān* waste.

1. Inhabited; populous; full of buildings and inhabitants.

2. Cultivated; peopled.

3. Applied to a village or lands from which revenue may be levied.

ābād' kar'nā, v. a.

1. To build and plant; cultivate; make a place habitable; people; found; settle in.

2. To extend cultivation, buildings, or population.

آباد بيشي *ābād-besh'ī*, n. f. First, or increased assessment of newly settled or cultivated land. [waste land.

آباد کار *ābād'-kār*, n. m. The first settler on

آباد کاري *ābād'-kā'rī*, n. f. The right derived from first clearing away and occupying land. Hence a claim to property by descent from the *ābād-kār*.

آبادي *ābā'dī*, n. f.

1. Cultivation; a cultivated place.

2. Extended or improved cultivation.

3. The inhabited portion of the village lands, opp. of *ujāṛ*.

4. Population; number of people; an inhabited place; a colony. [sessment.

5. Enhancement of rent; increased as-

E اِبالش کرنا *ebā'lish kar'nā*, v. a. To abolish.

A آباؤاجداد *ā'bā o ajdād*, n. m.

1. Forefathers; (our) fathers (باپ دادا); ancestors; progenitors.

2. Family ; race ; stock ; generation (گهرانا).

3. Lineage ; line ; extraction (کُل).

P آبائي *ābā'ī*, adj. Ped.

Belonging to, or descending from paternal ancestors ; paternal ; direct ; lineal ; hereditary ; ancestral ; patrimonial.

A اِبتدا *ibtidā'*, n. f. A. بَدَأَ he began.

1. Beginning ; commencement; exordium ; introduction ; outset ; inception (H. آد). [(نکاس).

2. Birth ; bud ; source ; origin ; rise *ibtidā-i-tārīkh-i-nālish lagā yat tā rīkh-i-adā, yā wasūl'.* From the date of institution of the suit to the date of payment, or realization of the claim.

اِبتداءً *ibtidā'an*, adv. Ped. for *pahle.*

At or in the beginning ; at first ; *imprimis ;* firstly ; in the first place ; originally ; *in limine ;* in the first instance ; first and foremost.

اِبتدا سے *ibtidā se*, adv.

Ab initio ; from the beginning (پرم پراسے).

ibtidā' se intihā' tak. H. *ād se ant tak.*

From beginning to end; from first to last.

اِبتدا کرنا *ibtidā' kar'nā*, v. a. Ped.

1. To originate ; open ; usher in. [going.

2. To broach ; set on foot ; launch ; set a

3 To begin ; to commence (شروع کرنا). Ped.

اِبتدائي *ibtidā'ī*, adj. [introductory.

1. Prefatory ; preliminary ; preparatory ;

2. Prior ; anterior ; primary.

ibtidā'ī imtihān', Ped. G. G.

A preliminary examination. [gation.

tahqīqāt-i-ibtidā'ī', Ped. Preliminary investi-

P اَبتَري *abtar'ī*, n. f.

1. Disorder ; derangement ; disorganization ; irregularity ; confusion ; disarrangement.

2. Deterioration ; decay ; falling off.

3. Mal-administration ; mismanagement.

A اِبدال *ibdāl'*, n. m. Ped. for بدل change.

A اَبدال *abdāl'*, n. m.

1. A religious person ; a devotee ; an enthusiast ; a class of wandering Mahomedan saints ; a religious fraternity.

2. The successors of the prophets.

H اَبدهوت अवधूत *abdhūt'*, n. m. S. अव down, off, धू to shake.

A perfect *(sidh) Jogī ;* a Hindū *faqīr* who professes to have "shaken off" the infirmities of humanity ; one who devotes himself to God alone, rejecting all ceremonies and worship ; a Hindū devotee ; a worshipper of *Shiva* who indulges in intoxicating drugs, as *Shiva* (Mahādeo) is said to have done.

A اِبراے ذمّه *ibrā'ē-zim'ma,* Ped. for *barī-uz'-zim'ma*, q. v.

A اَبرق *ab'raq*, Pop. *ab'rak*, n. S. अभ्रक Talc ; mica (بهوڈل)

P آبرو *ābrū'*, n. f. آب brightness, رو face.

Honour ; character ; reputation.

ābrū' utār'nā,—bigāṛ'nā,—lenā, v. a.

1. To disgrace ; abuse ; call names ; put to shame ; to destroy one's good name ; take away one's character (بے عزّت کر).

2. To debauch ; violate ; commit rape ; commit an indecent assault ; dishonor.

P اَبري *ab'rī,—kāġaz*, n. f. ابر a cloud, *lit.* Clouded ; mottled. Variegated or marble paper.

P اَبريشم *abre'sham*, n. m. Raw silk, the cocoon (کویه) of which is given with other medicines by *hakīms.* [Ped.

S اَبشیک अभिषेक *abishek', abhishek',* n. m.

1. Sprinkling with Ganges water ; purification by the sprinkling of water and utterance of certain prayers.

2. Baptism ; initiation.

3. Royal unction ; installation.

A اِبطال *ibtāl'*, n. m. بطل became false, null.

Rendering null ; abrogation ; repeal.

ibtāl-i-qarār dād, n. m. Impeachment of a contract.

ibtāl kar'nā, v. a. Ped. H. *jhuṭlā'nā.*

To make null ; abrogate (منسوخ کر).

A اِبن *ibn, bin,* used in *Comp.* only. A son ; child.

H اُبنا उबना *ub'nā, ug'nā,* Rus. *upaj'nā,* v. n. S. उत up, गम, वज् to go (?) [grow.

To spring ; germinate ; shoot ; sprout ;

P آبنوس *āb'nūs*, n. m.

Ebony ; *Diospyros ebenum,* Wat. [chapter.

A اَبواب *abwāb'*, n. m. pl. of باب door, Z. *babā*

1. Chapters ; sections. (Rare).

2. Taxes imposed by the Mahomedan government in excess of the original assessment; cesses; heads or subjects of taxation.

3. Miscellaneous cesses, imposts, and charges, levied by *zamīndārs* and public officers. These cesses were either abolished or consolidated with the land revenue, and are no longer payable to the British Government; but such as existed before the perpetual settlement, and were not specially abrogated, or not consolidated, are still claimed sometimes by the *zamīndārs*.

abwāb-i-be-jā,—nā-jāiz, n. Ped. Illegal or unauthorized cesses.

abwāb-i-zamīndā rī, Ped. *Zamīndārī* cesses.

abwāb-i-sā'biqā, Ped. Old established cesses.

abwāb-i-shā dī, Ped. An imposition levied to defray the marriage expences of landholders.

H ابيج **अबीज** *abīj'*, Pop. *ab'bī*, E. n.m.

Seed that will not germinate; bad seed.

H أبير **अबीर** *abīr'*, n. m. S. **अभक**. Probably from A. عبير.

A white powder mixed with *gulāl* (red powder) used by Hindus in the Holi festival.

H اُپاڑ **उपाड़** *upāṛ'*, n.m. *lit.* peeling off the skin.

An irritating composition for peeling off the skin of the male organ, held by natives to be a cure for impotency.

H اُپاس **उपास** *upās'*, n. m. Māṛ. **बास**, S. **वस्** to live, dwell.

A fast; fasting (برت); hunger; thirst.

upās'nā, n. m. Offerings; sacrifice; worship.

S اُپاسک **उपासक** *upā'sak, upā'sī*, n. m.

1. One who fasts.

2. A worshipper; devotee.

H اَپاهج **अपाहज** *apā'haj*, W. *apā'hij*, E. n.m. S. **अप** not, **आ** + **हिडि** to go. A cripple.

H اَپت **अपत** *apat'*, *ā'pat*, n. f. S. **पद्** dignity. Loss of credit; disgrace; dishonor; insult.

H اُپج **उपज** *upaj'*, n.f. S. **उप** up, **जन** to spring up. Produce; crops; yield.

اُپجاؤ **उपजाऊ** *upjā'ū, upjanhār'*, adj.

Fertile; culturable; productive; rich.

H اُپجنا **उपजना** *upaj'nā*, v. n.

To spring up; grow; to be produced; shoot; germinate; sprout; yield. [touch.

H اَپرس **अपरस** *apras', abras*, n. m. A. *bars*. Leprosy (کوڑ).

H اُپرس **उपरस** *upa'ras*, n.m. A kind of red chalk; bitumen.

H آپس **आपस** *ā'pas*; Māṛ. *māhomāh*, pron. Each other; one another; reciprocal; mutual.

āpas, āpas-dārī, n. f. Fraternity; brotherhood; kindred.

āpas dārī kā muāmla, āpas kā māmlā, —n. m. A family or caste affair.

āpas meṅ, adv. Among themselves; mutually; in concert; together.

āpas meṅ tasfīa, Amicable adjustment; private arbitration; mutual settlement.

āpas meṅ rahn'ā, v. n.

1. To live together; to live together as man and wife.

2. To cohabit; to live in adultery.

3. To live in incest.

āpas-nāma, n. m.

A voluntary deed of adjustment.

H اُپلا **उपला** *up'lā, up'rā, go'sā, go'hā, kan'ḍā*, W, *go'iṭhā*, E n. m. *lit.* What floats.

Dried cakes of cow-dung used for fuel.

S اُپنشد **उपनिषद्** *upa'nishad*, n.m. S. **उप** + **नि** + **सद्** sitting at one's feet.

Sacred texts or extracts from the Veds.

S اُپنَے **उपनय** *upanya*, n. m. S. **उप** + **नी** to lead.

The initiation of the first three classes of *Hindūs*; investiture with the *janeū* or sacred thread, worn over the left shoulder and under the right armpit.

H اَپهيم **अफीम** *aphīm'*, Rus. *phīm, afīm*. Illit. *afyūṅ*, Ped. S. **अहिफेन**, P. *shīr-i-khash khāsh*.

Opium; the concrete juice of the *Paver somniferum*. Wat.

—denā, v. a. To give opium; to poison; kill by poison.

E اَپيل *apīl'*, n. m. Cor. of the word Appeal.

apīl ba-nā-rāzī-i-faisla.

appeal from the decision of a lower court.

apīl-i-khās. Special appeal.

apīl-i-sarsarī. Summary appeal.

apīl-i-āām, apīl-i-lambarī. Regular appeal.

apīl ke sīge meṅ. In appeal.

apīl-i-muta-khālif. A cross appeal.
apīl-i-mutafariqa. A miscellaneous appeal.
apīl-i-manzūr. Admitted appeal.
apīl-i-nā-manzūr. Rejected appeal.

اپیلانٹ *apīlānt,* n. An appellant.
Apīlāt'-i-apīl-i-muta-khālif. A cross appel- [lant.

P. H. آتا *ātā, atā,* The wild custard apple; *Anona squamosā.* Wat. [pass.

H اُتار उतार *utār',* n. m. S. उत + तृ to cross, [across.
1. Descent; slope; declivity; dip; fall; depression; down-hill; declension; declination.
2. Subsidence; ebb-tide; low water.
3. Decrease; diminution; abatement falling off; wane; decline.
4. A fall or reduction in price. Remission of revenue.
5. Scale of decrease in the rate of revenue levied from different qualities of soil.
6. A quarrelsome person. [character.
7. A bad or shameless woman; a bad
8. A copy; a duplicate (A. مثنّى).
9. A ford or ferry; charge for ferrying

آتارا उतारा *utā'rā,* n. m.
1. Deduction; remission.
2. The cooked rice, flour, etc. moved an odd number of times from the head to the foot of a sick person under the belief that the evil spirit is thus removed from the sick person into the rice, etc.
3. An offering made to *Masān,* an evil spirit believed to haunt cross-roads.
4. Station; halting place for travellers; temporary residence (پڑاؤ).
5. A *ghat;* ferry; wharf; quay.
6. A copy; duplicate (نقل).
7. *Rus.* An answer; reply; response (اُتّر).
8. House rent; ferry toll.
9. Land given to a temple.
10. Land given by Government to an individual as a reward for services at a quit-rent.

A آتالیق *atālīq',* T. *atābīk, atābuk.* n. m.
A private tutor; an instructor.

A اِتّباع *ittebāā,* n. m. Ped. *for* تابعداري q. v.

H اُتپات उत्पात *ut'pāt,* n. m.
Violence; injury; injustice (اَپدر).

H اُتپت ہونا उतपत होना *ut'pat ho'nā, ut pan ho'nā,* v. n.
1. To be born or produced; to come into the world.
2. To yield; produce.

H اُتپن उत्पन *ut'pan, utpann, ut'pati,* n. m.
1. Birth; creation; production.
2. Extraction; descent; family.
3. Appearance; phenomenon; portent.
4. Produce; proceeds (پیدا).
5. The realized rents (of a village); produce of the harvest; profits.

A اِتّحاد *ittehād',* n. m. احد one. Ped. for (ایکا).
1. Union; combination; friendship; amity; concord.
2. Covenant; league; compact; treaty of alliance; convention.

S اُتّر उत्तर *ut'tar,* n. m. S. उत् high?
1. An answer; reply; rejoinder; defence.
2. The north.

ut'tar de'nā, v. n. To answer; to make, or give answer; reply.

اُتّرلکشن उत्तर लक्षण *ut'tara-lak'shan,* n. m. Ped.
The characteristics of a reply, viz. that it be applicable to the whole charge; that it be maintainable by law; that it be not equivocal or evasive; that it be consistent with itself; and that it be perspicuously expressed.

اُترا دهکاري उत्तर अधिकारी *ut'tar-adhikārī,* n. m. Ped.
An heir; one who inherits; a successor.

اترانتر उत्तरान्तर *uttar-āntar,* n. m. Ped.
A reply which is irrelevant to the charge; an evasive reply.

اُتراوتر उत्तरोत्तर *uttar-ottara,* n. m. Ped.
Rejoinder; replication.

اتر بهاس उत्तर भास *ut'tara bhā'sa,* n. m. Ped. आभास.
What seems like an evasive or prevaricating reply; the semblance, not the soundness, of an answer; evasion; equivocation; shift.

اُتر پرتي اُتر उत्तरप्रत्युत्तर *ut'tar-pratī'uttar,* n. m. Ped. Defence and rejoinder; pleadings in a law suit.

اُتر ساکشي उत्तर साक्षी *ut'tar sāk'shī,* n. m. Ped.
A witness for the defendant.

اُتر بهادر پد उत्तर भाद्रपद, *ut'tara-bhādr-pad,* n. m
The twenty-sixth lunar mansion, figured by a couch and comprehending two stars, of which one is *Andromedæ.*

اُتر پهالگني उत्तर फालगुनी *ut'tara-phāl'gunī,* n. f.

The twelfth lunar mansion, containing two stars figured by a bed.

H **أُترائي** **उतराई** *utrā'ī*, n. f. Coming down, alighting.
1. Requital; grateful return; retribution.
2. The toll paid at a ferry.

H **اِتر جانا** **इतर जाना** *it'ar jā'nā*, v. n. *Ṭhagī*.
To be forewarned (a traveller) against robbers.

H **أُترن** **उतरन** *ut'ran*, n. f. A medicinal lactescent plant, *Cynanchum extensum*. Wat.

H **اِتري پهل** **इत्रीफल** *itrī-phal*, *tir-pha'lā*, A. *tirīfal*, *itrīfal*, (اطریفل). n. m.
An electuary composed of three sorts of Myrobalans, with coriander seed and honey.

H **أتسي** **अत्सी** *at'sī*, *tī'sī*, E. n. m. Flax. See السي

P **آتش باز** *ā'tish-bāz*, n. m. A maker of fire works; pyrotechnist.
آتش بازي *ā'tish-bā'zī*, n. f. Fireworks; pyrotechnics.
آتش پرست *a'tish-parast'*, n. m. A fire worshipper; a guebre; one of the Magi; a disciple of Zoroaster.
آتش خانه *ā'tish-khā'na*, n. m. A fire temple; fire place; grate.
آتش دان *ā'tish-dān*, n. m. Any receptacle for fire; a grate (انگیٹھي).
آتش زدگي *ā'tish-zad'gī*, — *zan'ī*, n. f. Arson; conflagration; the firing of houses, etc. whether accidentally or by design.
ā'tish-zanī-i-khafīf, n. f. Incendiarism.
āt'ish-zanī-i-shadīd, n. f. Arson.

H **أُتشب** **उतशब** *ut'shab*, *uch'chhāo*, Mār. *uchhav*, n. m. S. **उत्सव**, S. **उत्+सु** to perform a sacrifice, Pr. *ussava* a feast.
A public demonstration of joy; jubilee; festival.

A **اِتّصال** *ittisāl'*, n. m. Ped. for ميل
1. Contact; connection (لگاو).
2. Adhesion; union (جوڑ).
3. Contiguity; attachment.

A **اِتّفاق** *ittifāq'*, n. m. وفق agreeing.
1. Agreement; concurrence; coincidence; correspondence; accordance; accord.
2. Unison; conformity; consonance (ملاپ).
3. Union; unity; concord; harmony (ایکا).
4. Assent; consent; acquiescence.
5. Combination; concert; co-operation.
6. Collusion; conspiracy (سازس).
7. Friendship; amity; affection; brotherhood (بهائی چارا).
8. Circumstance; event; case; contigency; incident; adventure.
9. Affair; proceeding; particular.
10. Opportunity; chance; accident; lot (سنجوگ).

—*kar'nā*, v. a.
1. To agree; co-operate; conspire; combine.
2. To form an alliance, friendship, intimacy.

—*ho'nā*, v. n.
1. To agree; to be agreed; concur; be in accord or of one mind; to agree together.
2. To correspond; tally; harmonize; chime in; conform to.
3. To become fast friends; to grow intimate.
4. *Ped.* To accede to; comply with.

—*se*, Ped. *bil-ittifāq*, adv.
1. In communication with; concurrently; together; jointly.
2. By chance; accidentally; incidentally; by the way.
3. Rarely; scarcely (اِتّفاقاً).

اِتّفاقات *ittifāqāt*, n. m. Ped. Pl. of اِتّفاق q. v.

اِتّفاقي *ittifā'qī*, *ittifāqīy'ā*. adj. Accidental; casual; occasional; fortuitous; incidental.

A. **اِتمام** *itmām'*, n. m. Ped. Perfection; completion (پورا پن).
itmām kar'nā, To complete; perfect (پورا کر).

S **آتم گهات** **आत्मघात** *ā'tm-ghāt*, — *hat'yā*, — *badh*, P. خود کشي n. f. Suicide; self-murder.
آتم گهاتي **आत्म घाती** *ā'tm ghā'tī*, P. خود کش A suicide; a self-murderer; *a felo de se.*
آتم گیان **आतमग्यान** *ā'tam-gyān'*, n. m. S. **आत्मज्ञान**. Knowledge of the soul; self-knowledge.

H **آتمل** **आत्मल** *āt'mal*, n.
Swallow wort; *Asclepias asthmatica*. Wat.

P **آتو** *ā'tū*, *ā'tūn*, *ā'tūn jī*, n. f. A female teacher; a governess.

S **آتوشا** **अतिविषा** *ativishā*, n. m. S. **विष** poison,
A medicinal root. *Aconitum feror.* Wat.

A **اِتّهام** *ittihām'*, n. m. Ped. for *tohmat*, q. v.

ittihām be-jā, A false accusation or charge.

S اِتي इति *iti*, Pr. *ia*, thus. A particle signifying, thus, therefore, lo, behold.

iti, n. f. Finis; the end; as زيادہ-چہ-فقط in Persian, and تَم in Arabic, at the end of a book, letter, etc.

S اِتيادی इत्यादि *ityādi*,' n. m. S. इति thus, आदि beginning. [(وغيرہ).

Et cetera; and so forth; and so on

H اَتيت अतीत *atīt'*, n. m. S. अतिथि a traveller.

A Hindu *faqīr;* ascetic; devotee; a *sannyāsī*; pilgrim.

S اَتيس अतीस *at'īs*, n. m. A root used in medicine. *Aconitum heterophyllum*. Wat.

H آٹا आटा *āṭ'ā*, n. m.

Flour; meal; anything ground to powder.

H اَٹالا अटाला *aṭā'lā*, n. m. S. अट्टालक a tower.

1. Accumulation; heap; pile; mass; store; stock; a large quantity; abundance.

2. A stack of corn, grass, etc; a heap; pile; a rick.

3. Goods; provision; effects; chattels; baggage; materials; articles; commodities; rubbish.

4. Furniture; household goods.

aṭālā kar'nā,—lajā'nā, v. a.

To pile; heap; stack.

aṭālā banā'nā, v. a. E.

To erect a lofty building.

aṭālā lād'nā, v. a. To overload (a cart).

H اٹکا अटका *aṭ'kā*, n. m. The vessel in which victuals are dressed for the public at the door of the temple of *Jagarnāth*.

H اٹکلنا अटकलना *aṭkal'nā, aṭkal kar'nā*, v. a. S. अट to wander, कल to reckon.

1. To guess; to make a rough guess; conjecture.

2. To estimate; make a rough estimate; value; assess (آنکنا).

3. To find out; to see through one; to take one's measure; to make out.

اٹکلي अटकली *aṭ'kal'ī*, adj.

Conjectural; probable; presumptive.

H اُٹنگن उटंगन *uṭangan'*, n. m.

A species of nettle or stinging plant, the seed of which is used in Indian practice, by the natives as an aphrodisiac; nettle seed. Wat.

H اُٹھائي گيرا उठाईगीरा *uṭhā'ī-gī'rā, uchak'kā*, n. m. H. *gir* fall, *uṭhā* take up. *lit*. One who takes up what has fallen.

A pilferer; shop-lifter; a petty thief.

H اَٹھ پہري अठ पहरी *aṭh pah'rī,—pah'īrā,—pahr'yā*.

One who is always on duty. Applied to a servant employed to collect rents, or set to watch the crops and to take messages for the rest of the villagers.

H اٹھ کونسل अठ कौंसल *aṭh kaunsal*, n. f. (Cor. of the Eng. Council.)

Council; meeting; assembly.

H اٹھ ماسا अठ मासा *aṭh mā'sā, aṭhwān'sā*, n. m.

1. An eight months' child.

2. Lands constantly ploughed for eight months for sugar-cane; or, from *Asāṛh* to *Māgh*, both inclusive.

H اٹھ ماشي अठ माशी *aṭh-mā'shī*, n. f.

1. A weight weighing eight *māshas*.

2. A gold mohur weighing eight *māshas*, worth ten rupees.

H اُٹھنگن उठंगन *uṭhan'gan, tek'an*, n. A prop; support; buttress.

A اِثبات *is bāt*, n. Ped for ثبت A. ثبوت fixed.

1. Permanence; maintenance; establishment.

2. Affirmation; confirmation; corroboration (تصديق). [(ثبوت)

3. Proof; verification; demonstration.

isbāt-i-jurm ko mustarad karnā.

To annul a conviction.

isbāt-i-haqīyat.

Establishment of a right or interest.

isbāt-i-nālish-i-haq.

Suit to establish a right.

A P اثرپزير *as'ar pizīr'*, adj.

Taking effect; efficacious; of effect efficient; effectual; effective.

A اَثناے تجويز *asnā'-i-tajwīz'*,

In course of investigation; during the proceedings; while the negotiations were pending.

A اِجارہ *ija'rāh*, n. m.

A lease or farm of land held at a stipulated rent, whether from Government direct or from an intermediate payer of the public revenue.

ijārah paṭṭā, ijārdārī paṭṭā.

A deed or lease for a farm, giving

authority to the holder to occupy and cultivate, or receive the rents of an estate.
ijārah-dār shikmī. Under-farmer; under-lessee, sub-tenant.
ijārah-dārī, n. f. [revenue.
1. Farming; contracting, for rent or
2. An *abwāb* or cess formerly levied on lands or districts let out in farm for the benefit of the farmer or contractor.
ijārah dene-wā'ā, A lessor.
ijārah-shikmī, Sub-divisions of a piece of land; sub-farm.
ijāre kī sar'had, n. Boundaries of a farm.

A أَجر *ajr, ajar, uj'rat, ajū'rah*, n. أجر compensated.
1. Remuneration; compensation; reward; recompense; return; consideration; equivalent; a *quid pro quo*.
2. Cost; price; hire; fare; fee.
ajr-i-jāiz, n. m. Legal remuneration.
ajr-denā, ujrat—, v. a. [pay.
1. To remunerate; give an equivalent;
2. To repay; compensate; reward; recompense.
ajr-i-nā-jāiz, n. m. An illegal remuneration.
ujrat amī'nī,—ta'khmīnī, Amīn's remuneration; assessor's fees. [*de'nā.*
ujrat par chalā'nā, v. a. Unid. for *kirāë ko* To let on hire; hire out.
zar-i-ujrat, n. m. Fees.

A إِجراء *ijrā'e*, n. m. جري Passed.
1. Giving currency or circulation; putting in execution.
2. Issue; execution; service; enforcement; carrying into effect; performance.
—*i'khtyār nā-jāiz.* [authority.
Unlawful authority; abuse of power or
—*haq*, The exercise of a right. [*wālā.*
—*hukm jiskī m'arfat ho, hukm jārī karne-*
Executive officer; the officer who serves the writ; bailiff.
—*hukm-nāmah*, The issue of a warrant.
—*ḍigrī*, Execution of a decree.
—*ḍigrī se bachnā*, To avoid judgment; to evade an execution.
—*saman*, The issue of a summons.
—*faislā-i-sāl'sī*, The enforcement of an arbitration award.
—*kāmil*, Complete execution.
—*kar'nā*, v. a.
1. To pass; execute; carry into execution; carry out or through; to make current.
2. To proclaim; publish; promulgate.
—*kamīshan*, The issue of a commission.
bilā ijrā-i-safīnā, Without issue of process or subpœna.

kharcha ijrā-i-saman, Cost of serving the summons.

A أَجزاء *ajzā*, n. m. pl. of جز a part.
Parts; portions; ingredients; component parts; constituents; members; elements.
b'az ajzā, Some parts or portions.
sazā kī mīāādoṅ ke ajzā, G. G.
Fractions of terms of punishment.

A آجل *ājil*, Procrastination, or suffering such interval to elapse as to render complaint inadmissible (statute of limitation).

H اُجلا उजला *uj'lā*, adj. S. ज्वल् to shine.
White; clean.
ujlā bhaṅgrā, n. m. *Verbesina prostrata.* Wat.
ujlā jāmūn, Calyptranthes caryophyllifolia. Wat. (A white variety of the fruit).
ujlā chandan, n. m. *Santalum album.* Wat.
ujlā hulūl, Cleome viscosa. Wat. The *viscid cleome*, the seeds of which, called *chhorī ajwān*, are regarded by the native practitioners as anthelmintic and carminative.
ujlā dhatūrā, n m. *Datura metel.* Wat.
ujlā kaddū, The long white pumpion or pumkin. *Lagenaria vulgaris.* Wat.
ujlā kaner, n. m. *Nerium odorum.* Wat.
ujle pān kī jar, Galangal; root of *Alpinia galangā.* Wat. [basil.
ujlī tulsī, n. f. *Ocymum album.* Wat. White
ujlī kā āzār, Fluo albus; the whites; *leucorrhœa*, a discharge of white yellowish or greenish mucus from the vagina.
ujlī kāchkūrī, n. f. *Dolichos pruriens;* a variety of cowhage or cowitch, a leguminous plant which produces on the outside of its pods an irritating substance used in medicine as vermifuge. [pepper.
ujlī mirch,—mirchī, n. f. *Piper album;* White

A إِجلاس *ijlās'*, n. f. A. جلس he sat.
1. The act of sitting (of a court of justice); sitting; sessions; a court.
2. (Under the Mahomedan government) An assembly of jurists or learned men for the decision of an intricate or important cause.
ijlās-i-kāmil, A full bench.
ijlās-i-kaunsil, A meeting or sitting of the Supreme Council. [judges.
ijlās-i-vāhid, A court held by one of several
ba-ijlās, ijlās meṅ, At the sitting; in court; in council; in the presence of; before.

A إِجمال *ijmāl'*, n. m. Ped. جمل many strands of a rope put together, aggregate.
1. An abstract; summary; compendium;

precis; abridgement; epitome; digest; synopsis.
2. Joint occupancy or possession. [resumè.
2. Sum and substance; recapitulation;

A اِجمالی *ijmālī*, adj. Ped. [cinct.
1. Gross; compendious; abridged; suc-
2. Held in common, as an estate settled in common with two or more parties; undivided; unpartitioned.
ijmālī-gumāshtah, An agent or factor for persons holding property conjointly; a manager of property so held.
ijmālī mahāl, An undivided estate; an estate held in co-parcenership by the heirs of a common ancestor.

A اَجناس *ajnās'*, n. f. pl. of جِنس
1. Kinds; sorts; various sorts.
2. Commodities; wares; effects; articles; goods; chattels (Ped. for اسباب).

E اَجنت *aj'ant*, n. m. An agent.

E اجنتي *ajan'tī*, n. f. Agent's office; agency; the office of a Political Agent, or Resident in a native court; the residency. [n. f.

H اَجوان अजवान *ajwān,' ajwāin*, Rus. *jawāin*.
A kind of aniseed; *Ligusticum ajowan*; species of lovage or bishop's weed with the flavour of carraways, used medicinally by natives; *Ptychotis ajowan*. Wat.
aṭh-pahrī ajwāin, Dill seed steeped in water for twenty-four hours, believed to be a cure for fever.
chhorī ajwān, n. f. *Cleome viscosa*. Wat.
khurāsānī ajwāin, n. f. *Hyoscyamus niger*. Wat. Black Henbane seeds. [land.

H اَجوت अजोत *a jot'*, adj. Untilled land; waste

A اَجُورہ *ajū'ra*, n. m. A. اَجر compensated.
1. Remuneration; compensation.
2. Wages; hire; fare.
ajūra-dār', n. m. A laborer for hire; a hireling, not a regular servant.
ajūra-dā'rī, n. f. Hire; wages; payment by the job or piece.

H اجوري अजौरी *ajau'rī, agau'ṛī*, n. f. H. *agā-ṛī, āge* before. [laborers.
Advances, particularly to agricultural

H اَجولي अजौली *ajau'lī* E Rus., *anj'lā, anj'lī*,
Pop. n. f. *lit.* As much as will come in the two hands spread out together.

Perquisites of the lower castes from the threshing floor.

H اُچاپت उचापत *uchā'pat*, n. m. S. उ + चप to grind, cheat, H. *uṭhāo* credit.
1. Taking goods on credit; a credit transaction; tick *(slang)*; credit. W.
2. Sharp practice; roguery; fraud. E.

H اُچھاؤ उछाओ *uchhā'o, uṭhā'o, ut'shab*, n. m.
Festival, jubilee; a public demonstration of joy; a grand procession of an image.

H اَچھت अच्छत *ach'chhat, ā'khat, a'khad*, n.m.
S. अ not, क्षत broken, Pālī. *akkhatam*.
1. Whole or unbroken rice used in oblations. [*pūjā*).
2. A pinchful of rice (just enough for
ach'chhat tilak, The ceremony of putting a few grains of rice on the forehead of an image when addressed, or of a *Brāhman* when invited to an entertainment.

H اَچھواني अछवानी *achhvā'nī*, n. f. from *ajwān* a kind of aniseed. An aromatic decoction given to women after child-birth.

A اَحاطہ *ahā'tah, ehā'tāh*, Pop. *hā'ta*, n. m.
1. Compass; limit; boundary.
2. Precincts; premiss; area.
3. Enclosure; an enclosed place; fence; compound; court-yard (آنگن); field.
4. Fold; pound; pen (کھڑک).
5. Zone; belt; circle; province; territory; tract; domain; presidency (حلقه).
—*i-ikhtyār*, Limits of jurisdiction; extent of authority; jurisdiction.
hā ta kar'nā, yā gher nā, v. a. [circle.
1. To surround; hem in; hedge in; en-
2. To enclose; rail in; wall in.
3. To bind; confine; limit; determine.
4. To define (boundaries); appoint limits; bound (حدباندھنا).

A اِحتمال *ehtemāl'*, n. m. حَمَل he bore.
1. Reasonable chance; fair chance; probability; likelihood; presumption.
2. Conjecture; guess; supposition.
3. Doubt; suspense; uncertainty. [peace.
—*i-fasād'*, Apprehension of a breach of the
—*i-qānū'nī*, A presumption of law.
—*kar'nā*, v. n. To doubt; distrust; mistrust; suspect; call in question.
—*i-mʿāqūl'*, Reasonable apprehension.
—*i-nuqsān, yā zarar*, Apprehension of loss or injury.

—*honā*, v. n.
1. To be likely or probable; to expect.
2. To be open to doubt, or question; to be doubtful.
—*hai*, It is likely; it is probable.
احتمالي *ehtemā'lī*, adj.
1. Presumable; presumptive; likely.
2. Hypothetical; problematical; conjectural.
3. Doubtful; dubious; ambiguous; questionable; suspicious.
4. Contingent; precarious.

A إحتياج *ehteyāj'*, Ped. for *hā'jat*, q. v. حوج needed.
Need; want; urgency.
—*i-muqad'ama*, Exigency of the case.

A إحتياط *ehtyāt'*, n. f. حوط guarded.
1. Caution; care; attention (هوشياري); heed; wariness; vigilance.
2. Circumspection; precaution; deliberation.
ehtyāt aur' khabar dārī-i-munāsib.
Proper care and attention.
—*o imti hān*, Ped. Care and examination.
—*kār'nā,—rakh'nā*, v. a.
1. To heed; attend, or see to; look to.
2. To look after; watch; keep watch over; take care; to be careful (خبرداري كرنا).
3. To take precautions.
ehteyāt-i-munā'sib, Proper care.

A إحتياطا *ehteyā'tan*, adv. Carefully; cautiously; with care or circumspection; warily; with caution.

A أحد *a'had*, n. m. P. يک S. एकः H. एक.
Unity; one; an individual.
a'had-ut-tarfain,—ut-muta' khās'imain.
One of the two parties (in a law suit).
ahad-ul-mudd'a-'alaihim, One of the defendants or accused persons.

A إحرام *ehrām'*, n. حرم was forbidden, *lit.*
Making or determining any thing to be unlawful.
1. Abstinence from sensual enjoyment during the month of *Moharram.*
2. The period of pilgrimage at Mecca.
3. A coarse dress worn by pilgrims on entering Mecca.
—*bāndhnā*, v. a. To make a vow as a pilgrim at a certain stage from Mecca appointed for the purpose, preparatory to entrance into the holy city.

A إحصان *ehsān'*, Ped. Rare حصن was inaccessible.
In *Mah. law*, a person who is a free sane adult, of chaste reputation, and of the Mahomedan faith, and who is therefore entitled to demand punishment for adultery committed with respect to him or her so characterized.

A إحضار *ehzār'*, n. m. حضر was present.
Causing to be present; summoning; a summons; causing one's attendance or appearance.
'adam-i-ehzār. Default of appearance.
ehzār-i-farīqain, yā garāhān.
Attendance or appearance of the parties in the suit, or their witnesses.

A إحقاق *ehqāq'*, n. m. Rare حق was just.
Restoring or determining any one's *haq*, or right; the establishment of a right; the act of proving or establishing the truth of a doctrine.

A أحكام *ahkām'*, n. m. pl. of حكم order.
1. Orders; commands; decrees.
2. Mandates; injunctions; ordinances; statutes; judicial decisions, or decrees; letters patent.
3. A summons, or injunction.
—*i-dīn,—shar'a*, The ordinances or precepts of the Mahomedan religion.
—*i-nujūm*. Astrological predictions.

A P أحمقانه *ahmaqā'na*, n. m.
1. Money to be paid in returning a purchased thing.
2. The money which an *āmil* is obliged to pay to make good the deficiency of the revenue.

A أخبار *a'khbār'*, n. m. pl. of خبر news, خبر.
A newspaper; gazette; journal.
—*navīs*,' n. m. A news-writer; "our own correspondent;" an editor (مهتمم اخبار).

A إختتام *i'khtitām'*, Ped. for *'khatam*, n. m.
End; conclusion; completion.
i'khtitām karnā, v. a. To complete; finish.
i'khtitām-i-nīlām, Conclusion of an auction or sale.

A إختراع *i'khtir'āā*, Ped. for *ījād'*, n. m.
1. Invention; discovery; device.
2. Propagation; publication.

A إختصار *i'khtisār'*, n. m. خصر became intensely cold.

1. Conciseness; brevity; condensation.
2. Summary; abstract; epitome; synopsis; *precis.*

—*kar'nā*, v. a.
1. To abridge; summarize; epitomize; to draw up a *precis.*
2. To curtail; cut short. [a word.

bil-ikhtisār, Ped. adv. In short; briefly; in

A إختفا *ikhtifā'*, n. m. Rare. The act of withdrawing or concealing; concealment.

A إختلاط *ikhtilāt'*, n. m. خلط mixed. The act of mixing; mixture; union; amalgamation (ميل).
1. Acquaintance; intimacy; familiarity.
2. Attachment; friendship; attachment between the sexes.

—*i-muhālāt*, Union of estates.

A إختلاف *ikhtilāf*, Ped. for *khilāf'*, A. خلف came after.
1. Contrariety; contradiction; opposition; discrepancy; difference. [ment.
2. Incongruity; incompatability; disagree-
3. Rupture; variance; schism.

ikhtilāf bayā'nī, n. f. Contradiction; discrepancy; inconsistency.

ikhtilāf sābit kar'nā, v. a. To prove the contrary; to refute.

ikhtilāf-i-rāī, Difference of opinion.

ikhtilāf rakh'nā,—ho'nā, v. n. To disagree; differ; clash.

ikhtilāf-i-mazhab, H. *jāt parekhā.* Difference of religion. [good.

A إختيار *ikhtyār'*, n. m. خير What is chosen,
1. Choice; option; election.
2. Will; discretion; pleasure. [chise.
3. Liberty; privilege; immunity; fran-
4. Control; disposal; management.
5. Right; charter (استحقاق).
6. Competency; authority; power; prerogative; patronage.
7. Jurisdiction; cognizance; province; rule; sway; government; administration.
8. Office; function; charge; commission. (*Rare*).

ikhtyārāt-i-band o bast rakh'nā. To be invested with settlement powers.

اختيار ابتدائي *ikhtyār-i-ibtidāī, samāāt-i-ibtidāī*, Primary jurisdiction.

اختيار آمد و رفت *ikhtyār-i-āmad o raft*, Right of way.

اختيار انفكاك الرهن—*infikāk-ul-rahn*, Equity of redemption of a mortgage; equity of redemption.

اختيار تجويز قانون—*tajvīz-i-qānūn*, Legislative power. [power.

اختيار تجويز مقدمه —*i-muqadma* Judicial

اختيار جايز — *jāiz* Legal power; lawful authority; a right.

اختيار حاصل شده — *hāsil-shudā* Accredited; authorized; empowered.

—*hāsil hogā*, It shall rest with.

— *hifāzat apne jān o māl kī.* (Penal Code). Right of private defence.

—*khās*, Special powers; privilege.

اختيار خاص بادشاه — — *bādshāh*, Royal prerogative.

اختيار سرسري — *sarsarī*, Summary jurisdiction, or power.

— *sam'āāt aur tajvīz-i-dāwī-ī-zar-i-qarzā*, Power to hear and determine actions of debt.

— *se*, Voluntarily; of one's own accord; a will; at pleasure; *ad libitum;* freely.

— — *bāhar ho'nā*, To exceed, or pass the limits of one's authority.

اختيار شوهري *ikhtyār shauharī*, Marital authority; authority of a husband over his wife.

— *āām*, Ordinary jurisdiction; general power.

اختيار عدالت — *ādālat*, Jurisdiction; judicial power, or authority.

اختيار عمل ميں لانا *ikhtyār āmal meṅ lānā, ikhtyār nāfiz kar'nā*, v. a. To exercise (certain) powers, functions, or authority.

اختيار احدالامرين — *i-ahad-ul-amarain*, Right of election. G. G.

اختيار فوجداري — *faujdārī*, Criminal jurisdiction; magisterial power.

اختيار قانون — *qānūn*, Legal power.

— *kāmil*, Plenary powers; full powers.

— *kar'nā*, v. a.
1. To choose; elect; adopt; fix upon. [on.
2. To determine to do; to resolve or decide
3. To undertake; assume; take up; espouse; take upon one's self.
4. To effect; have recourse to; resort to.

اختيار مطلق — *mut'laq* Absolute authority.

— *mil'nā*, To be invested with power or authority.

اختيار مناسب — *munāsib* Due authority; sufficient power.

— *mun'sifī,—hākimā'nā*, Judicial power, or authority.

— *meṅ ho'nā*, v. n. To be in one's power; to be subject to one's will or discretion.

— *nā-jāiz.* Unlawful authority ; illegal power.
— *hai.* Has the power to act ; is competent ; may do (an act). [authority.

حاکم ذي اختیار *hākim-i-zī i̊khtyār*, Competent

nåkhwat se i̊khtyār lā-hāsil apne ūpar lenā, To arrogate any power or authority ; undue assumption of authority. G. G.

اختیاري *i̊khtyārī*, adj. Competent ; discretionary, optional.
— n. f. One invested with power ; a deputy ; assignee ; agent.

A أَخذ *åkh'az*, n. m. Ped. أخذ taken.
1. Taking ; seizing ; intercepting.
2. Seizure ; exaction ; appropriation.
— *kar'nā*, v. a.
1. To seize ; take away ; deprive.
2. To claim ; exact ; appropriate.

اخذ بالجبر *åkh'az bil-jabr.* Compulsory exaction ; extortion ; forcible seizure.

lābat åkhaz-bil-jabr. On account of the illegal exaction of rent.

åkh'az-i-be'jā, n. m. Unjust requisition; unlawful demand. [adj.

A آخر *ā̊'khir, ā̊kh'rī, åkhīr'*, H. *pichh'lā*,
1. Last ; final ; ultimate ; extreme.
2. Late ; latter ; last-mentioned. [clusive.
3. Decisive ; positive ; definitive ; con-
— *tak le jā'nā.* To bear or carry through ; carry out to the end.

اخیر جمع طوماري *åkhīr' jamā tūmārī*, Improved revenue from that fixed originally, applied especially to the revenues of Bengal, Behar, Orissa, Allahabad, etc. in the time of Mahammad Shāh, as contrasted with those fixed in the time of Akbar.

اخیر جمع واصل باقي — *jamā vā'sil bā'qī.* Final settlement of the accounts of a Zamīndārī, or a village, crediting profits and receipts, debiting all disbursements and payments of revenue, and adjusting the balance.

اخیر نکاس *åkhīr nikās.*
1. Final settlement of an account.
2. Final adjustment of demand for revenue to be levied on a village or an estate.
3. Annual account of collections duly balanced, furnished by an Assistant Collector or subordinate revenue officer. *Nikās* is properly the settlement of an account or payment of rent by the cultivating ryots to the Zamīndār.

ڈگري اخیر *ḍigrī-i-åkhīr.* Final decree.

A إِخراج *i̊khrāj'*, n. m. Ped. خرج passed out opp. of دخل entered.
1. Expulsion ; evacuation ; ejection ; banishment ; turning out of possession ; deportation ; extradition.
2. Elimination ; exclusion ; exception.
3. Extraction ; derivation.

اخراج بلد *i̊khrāj i-balad*, H. *des nikā'lā.* Banishment ; expatriation ; extradition.

A إِخراجات *i̊khrājāt'*, Illit. *̊kharājāt'*, pl. of اخراج n. m. [costs.
1. Expenses ; disbursements ; charges ;
2. Produce ; assignments of revenue to public servants employed in management and collection.

اخراجات دیہي —*i-de'hī*, Village expenses.

اخراجات عدالت — *i-ādā'lat*, Court costs ; judicial costs.

اخراجات مرض الموت —*i-mar'az-ul-maut.* Death-bed charges.

اخراجات مقدمه — *muqad'mah*, Law charges.

اخراجات نالش — *i-nā'lish*, Costs of court ; law charges.

اخراجات واقعي — *i-wā'qāī*, Actual expenses.

A آخري *ā̊kh'rī*, adj. Of or belonging to the end ; latter.
—*chahār' sham'bā*, n. m. The last Wednesday that falls annually in the month of *Safar*, a festival observed by the Mahomedans of India, their prophet having on that day found himself well enough to walk abroad for the first time after a very severe illness.

آخري حساب خرچ *ākhrī hisāb kharch*, Adjustment with the cultivators at the end of the year, shewing the amount of revenue assessed, paid, and in arrears, with the items of deduction for expenses.

A إِخفاء *i̊khfā'*, n. m. Ped. خفي was hidden. Concealment.
— *i-izdiwāj'*, Concealment of marriage.

اخفاے بالعمد — *i-bil-āmd*, — — *qasd*
— — *irā'dah*, Wilful concealment. [birth.

اخفاے تولد — *i-tawal'lud*, Concealment of
— *az taraf-i-mā'dar*, Concealment of birth by the mother.

اخفاے جرایم — *i-jarā'yam*, — *jurm*, Concealment of crimes or crime.
—*i-jarāyam-i-sangīn'*, Wilful concealment of heinous offences.

—*kar'nā*, Ped. for H. *chhupā'nā*, v. a. [bury.
1. To hide ; conceal ; secrete ; cover ;
2. To smother ; suppress ; hush up.

A آخيافي *a^khyā'fi*, adj. Ped. for H. *saute'lā*.
A step-brother or sister by the same mother, but by a different father ; of half blood. G. G.

hamshī'ra-i-a^khyāfi, Ped. for H. *saute'lī bahn*.
Sister of half blood ; step-sister.

H أد अद *ad, adh, ādh, ād*, adj. S. अर्ध Used in composition for آدھا half.

ادبٹائي *ad-baṭāī* n. f. Division of produce in equal shares.

ادھکپاري अध कपारी *adh-kapā'rī*,—*kapālī*. E. n. f. S. कपाल् skull.
Two areca nuts partially attached, and hence believed to be an effective cure for *hemicrania* (آدھاسيسي). [कर tax.

ادھکر अधकर *adh-kar*,—*kari*, n.f. S. अर्ध half,
1. Half the collections; half the tax or rent.
2. An instalment of eight annas in the rupee, or half the government *jamā*.

ادھيا अधया *adh'yā*, n. f.
1. Division into two equal parts.
2. Division of produce between two parties in equal proportions, one furnishing the land, seed, etc. and the other, the labour.
3. The payment of half the annual assessment for the revenue at the spring and autumnal harvests.

ادھيار अधयार *adhyār'*, W. *dohalbār'*, E. n. m.
1. A man who spends half his time in one village, half in another, cultivating land in both.
2. A cultivator who assists in cultivating land, on condition of receiving half the crop.

ادھياري अधयारी *adhyā'rī*, n. f. A half-share; an eight-anna share.

A أدا *ad'a*, n. f.
1. Bringing to completion, perfection.
2. Performance ; observance ; execution ; fulfilment; accomplishment. [satisfaction.
3. Payment (of a debt) ; discharge ;

adā-bandī, qist bandī, Fixing a term for the payment of a debt, or the performance of a contract ; liquidation of a debt by instalments.

adā-i-^khidmat Performance of service ; execution, or discharge of a duty.

اداے دين—*i-dain*, Ped. The payment of a debt.

اداے زر—*i-zar*, Ped. Payment of money.

اداے زرڈگري—*zar-i-ḍigrī*, Satisfaction of a judgment debt ; payment of the sum decreed.

اداے شہادت—*i-shahādat*, The act of giving evidence. [dence.

— — *se inkār' kar'nā*, To refuse to give evi-

adā karne par mustaid honā, To be ready to pay one's debt.

—*karne-wāla*, n. m. Payer ; one who pays or liquidates his liabilities. [revenue.

اداے مالگزاري—*i-māl guzarī* Payment of

A أدب *ad'ab*, n. m. Politeness ; good manners ; good breeding ; civilities ; courtesy ; urbanity.

حرکت خلاف ادب *harkat ^khilaf-i-adab*, Undutiful act. G. G.

^khilaf-i-usūl-i-adab, Contrary to morality. G. G.

A إدخال *id^kh-al'*, n. m. Ped. دخل entered.
1. Admission ; entrance ; penetration ; thrusting or putting in.
2. Record ; entry ; registry ; insertion.
3. Import ; importation (goods).

—*i nām* Entry of a name.

bilā id^khāl rupae qist-i-avval.
Without having paid the first instalment.

A إدعا *iddeaā'*, n. m. Ped. for دعوے کرنا q. v.

ادعاي خريدار اصلي.—*i-^kharīdār-i-aslī*,
Claim to be held to the real purchaser.

—*i-milkyat*, Claim to proprietorship.

H أدمرجائي अदमरजाई *admarjā'ī*, n. f. S. मृ to die. A term used in leases, signifying failure from drought.

A آدمي *ad'mī*, n. m.
1. An individual ; person ; man.
2. Mankind ; the human race, nation ; people ; souls ; inhabitants ; population ; community ; folk.
3. Husband ; lord ; consert ; wife.
4. A servant ; retainer ; follower ; attendant.
5. A grown-up person ; an adult.

kā'lā ād'mī, n. m.
1. A black man ; a negro. [peans).
2. A native ; an Indian (used by Euro-

S أدھکار अधकार *adhkār'*, n. m. S. अधि over, कृ to make.
Right of possession ; occupancy.

—*karat'nā*, v. a. Rare.

1. To exercise powers or authority; to use a right; put in force; enforce. [jection.

2. To bring under control; hold in sub-

—*tyāg'nā*, v. a. To give up one's authority; to abdicate an office; resign.

S ادهکاري अधिकारी *adhikā'rī*, n. m.

1. The state of holding office; incumbency; possession of a right, title, or privilege.

2. One invested with power, or authority; an executive officer; minister; functionary; officer; official.

3. Owner; proprietor; heir; master.

4. Deputy; agent; factor; attorney; man of business; plenipotentiary.

5. A privileged person.

grām-adhikā'rī, n. m. Ped. for *gāoṅ kā chaudhrī*, The head man of a village.

H اَدھکچّا अध कच्चा *adh-kach'cha*, n. m. A soil lying between the land named *Pahāṛā* and the *Tarāī* in the district of *Sahāranpūr*.

H اَدھیلیا अधेलया *adhel'yā*, n. m. Proprietor of a half share.

H اَدھیلی अधेली *adhelī'*, *dhe'li*, n. f. A half share in any property.

H اَڈّا अड्डा *aḍ'ḍa*, n. m. S. अट्टाल H. *aṭa'rī*, Rus. *aṭ'ṭā*, house, upper-room.

1. A stand; a station or place where persons of the same profession, as porters, bearers, labourers, carters, gamblers, tiplers, etc. congregate; any place where people congregate for business or pleasure.

2. A police station (in the country); an outwork of a factory.

3. A post, or *dāk* station, or office.

4. The quarter where prostitutes reside.

5. A division of the land watered by a common well; a division of the land attached to the well, usually two—one to each *harath*.

6. A fixed measure; standard.

H اَڈَتیا अड़तया *aḍat'yā*, *āṛhat'yā*, n. m. A mercantile correspondent; an agent; a broker.

H اَڈسٹّا अडसट्टा *aḍsaṭ'ta*, *arsaṭṭa*, A rough estimate or calculation.

A إذن *izn*, n. m.

1. Permission granted by a master to a slave to engage in business, or trade.

(The word is laxly used for bequests, or distribution of property).

2. The consent of the parties to a marriage contract.

اذن عام —*i-ām*, n. m. Among Mahomedans, permission to depart, given after the reading of prayers over the dead.

اذن نامه *izn-na'mah*, P. نامه a document.

A will, a distribution of property by a testator, whether Mahomedan, or Hindū.

A أراضى *arā'zī*, n. f. Ped. for H. *dhartī* pl. of ارض land, S. धरा earth, अर to plough.

1. Lands; landed estates; acres; grounds; detached portions of land.

2. Real assets; real property.

—*bāġ*, Garden land.

—*bāsgat*, Portions of land which have been built upon, and on which revenue is not levied; homestead.

—*bi'han, yā bihnaur'*, Lands in which plants are grown for transplantation; nurseries for rice plants.

—*paṛ'tī*, Waste, or uncultivated lands.

—*tawāg'*, Lands to which rice plants are transplanted.

—*jalkar, yā jalkhāta*, Lands in which rain water is allowed to accumulate for the purpose of irrigation.

—*jaṅg'al*, Forest lands.

اراضي خالصه —*khāl'sa*. *Khālsa* lands; lands held immediately from Government.

—*dār*, The holder of a plot at a fixed rent with power to alienate the land. [*barār*.

—*dar'yā bar-āmad*,—*nau bar-āmad*,—*nau-*

1. Alluvial increment. G. G.

2. Alluvion; land reclaimed by recess of water; new formations; alluvial lands; new lands gained by alluvion; new alluvial soil.

—*daryā burd*,—*gaṅg shikast*.

Lands destroyed by a river; diluvion.

—*dyā'rā*, The dry bed of a river, or the adjacent lands which are flooded in the rains, but left dry and fit for cultivation in the dry weather; an island left in the channel of a river, or nullah, liable to be flooded when the water rises but cultivable in dry weather.

اراضي سکني —*sakanī*. Sites for building.

——*qadīm'*, Old building sites.

—*sīr*, *Sīr* lands cultivated by the hereditary proprietors, or village zamīndārs themselves as their own special share, either by their own labourers and at their own cost, or by tenants-at-will, not being let in lease, or farm.

These lands were sometimes allowed to be held at a favourable assessment, or were unassessed so as to provide *Nānkār*, or subsistence for the proprietor. The term is also sometimes applied to lands cultivated on account of the State, or to those in which the revenue is paid by the cultivators without any intermediate agent.

اراضي شاملات—*shā'milāt*, Lands held in common.

—*shor*, Saline unproductive soil; land impregnated with saltpetre.

اراضي ضبطي معافي—*zab'tī muā'fī*, Resumed rent-free lands.

اراضي قابل زراعت—*qa'bil zirā'ăt*, Arable land; culturable land; land capable of being cultivated.

اراضي كاشت—*kasht*, Cultivated holdings.

اراضي كرشن آرپن—*krishn ār'pan*, Lands granted to a *Brāhman*, or temple for the propitiation of the Hindū god, Krishna.

—*gauṅ wādh*, Lands given in perpetuity, as it were, for some consideration and creating a sort of proprietary right in the holder.

—*goner*, Cultivated lands adjoining the inhabited parts of villages.

—*lā-khirāj'*,—*muāfī*, Rent-free lands; lands exempt from revenue.

اراضي مالگزاري—*māl-guzā'rī*, Lands paiyng revenue to Government; revenue paying lands. [lands.

اراضي متّصله—*muttas'ilah*, Ped. Contiguous

اراضي نوتردد—*nau-tarad'dud*, Ped. for *nau-tor*, Newly cultivated lands.

—*nīlām' shudā'*, Ped. Land sold by auction.

—*ham qism o ham-munja'ăt*, Ped. Lands of similar character and yielding like profits.

P آرام *ārām'*, n. m. S. रम, Z. *ram*, *rām* to rest.

Rest; quiet; repose; quietude. [G. G.

بنظر آرام خلايق *ba-nazar ārām-i-khalāyaq*. Respect being had to the public convenience.

A أرباب *arbāb'*, n. m. pl. of رَب Possessors; lords; masters; members; officers.

—*māl*, Officers of the treasury.

S آرپن अर्पण *ar'pan* n. m. S. अर्पय Caus. of ऋ to fall to one's share.

1. Offering; gift; sacrifice.
2. A sum set apart for religious, or charitable purposes.

—*kar'nā*, v. a.

1. To sacrifice; offer sacrifice; make an oblation, or libation; give alms.
2. To consecrate; dedicate to; devote to.
3. To offer; present; give; make over.

—*nā'mā*, n. m. A deed of gift, especially to a temple, or idol.

H آرتا आरता *ār'tā*, n. m. S. आरात्रिक The light waved before an idol, Ped. आर to praise.

A marriage ceremony. On the arrival of the bridegroom at the house of the bride, he is received by her relations carrying a tray with some rice and powder for *tilak*, and a four-wicked lamp made of flour in the middle. [mounted.

A اِرتكاب *irtikāb'*, n. m. Ped. رَكَب rode,

Perpetration, or commission (of a crime).

ارتكاب جبر—*i-jabr*, Coercive treatment; compulsion; force.

ارتكاب جرم - *i-jurm*, Attempt to commit an offence, or crime; commission of an offence.

ارتكاب زنا—*zin'ā*, Commission of adultery.

ارتكاب فعل—*f'el*, Doing an act.

—*kar'nā*, v. a. To commit, or perpetrate.

H آرتي आरती *ār'tī*, n. f. A ceremony performed in adoration of some god by waving, in a circle before the image, a platter containing a five-wicked burning lamp, flour, and incense.

The same rite, only substituting a bridegroom for the idol, is called *ārtā*, q. v.

A اِرث *irs*, n. See. وِرثه

mahjūb-ul-irs, One not allowed to share in an inheritance (*Mah. law*).

E اَردلي अरदली *arda'lī*, n. m. Cor. of orderly.

1. A sepoy, or native soldier in attendance on a military officer for conveying messages, carrying letters, orders, etc.
2. An attendant who runs before a *pālkī*, or other conveyance of his master.

A اَرزال *arzāl'*, n. m. pl. of *razīl*, *arzal*, base.

Low castes located on the estates of Zamīndārs in some parts of Hindustān, as tenants at will, partly paying rent and partly rendering personal services considered in some measure as *adscripti glebæ*, and not entitled to quit except at the landlord's pleasure.

A اَزرق *ar'zaq*, H. *nī'lā*, adj. Sky-blue, blue; azure; cerulean.

—*chashm'*, Ped. for *kanjā*, Blue-eyed; cat-eyed.

H أَرس **अरस** *ar'as*, E. *pār'chā*, W. n. m. S. **रस्** water. The reservoir in which the water from a well is collected.

A إرسال *irsal'*, n. m. رسل he brought a message, sent.
1. Despatch; remittance; supplies.
2. Monthly collections of rents forwarded to head quarters by the subordinate revenue authorities.

irsāl kar'nā, Ped. for H. *bhej'nā*, v. a.
1. To remit; transmit; despatch; forward.
2. To commit; consign (*saunpnā*).

—*nāmah*,—*paṭṭī*, Statement of remittances despatched; an invoice.

عرض‌ارسال *arz-i-irsāl*, Invoice; particulars of the despatch of treasure.

H أَرس پرس **अरस परस** *ar'as par'as*, n. m. S. **स्पर्श** to become wet.
1. Sprinkling; immersion; partial bathing; throwing a little water on the head with the hand.
2. Impurity from touch; pollution.

H أرسٹّا **अरसट्टा** *arsaṭ'ṭā*, n. m.
1. A monthly account of receipts and disbursements, otherwise called *jamā-kharch*; cash account; debit and credit.
2. Guess; rough estimate.
3. A broker; mediator.

—*navīs*, The clerk, or accountant who keeps the monthly accounts.

H A آرسي مصحف *ār'sī mas'haf*, Pop. *ārsī mus'haf*. Mah.
The marriage ceremony among Mahomedans, when the bridegroom reads a chapter in the *Korān*, and for the first time sees his wife's face in a glass.

H أرگھ **अरघ** *ar'agh*, *ar'ag*, n. m. S. **अर्घ** to worship, Pr. and Pālī. *aggho*.
A mode of worship; a libation; a libation of eight ingredients made to a god or a *brāhman*.

aragh de'nā,—*chaṛhā'nā*, v. a. To pour libations to the sun, moon, etc.; to make an offering to a god (Jain).

ar'ghā, *ar'gā*, n. m. A copper vessel shaped like a boat, used by Hindūs in pouring out their libations.

H أرنا **अरना** *ar'nā*, W. n. m. S. **आरण्यक** Forest-born.
1. A wild buffalo (*arnā bhaiṅsā*).
2. E. *kaṇḍā*, Cowdung dried in the jungles, used as fuel by natives, and by physicians in the preparation of medicines (*arnā-uplā*).
3. Name of a plant.

H أرنڈ **अरनड** *ar'aṇd*, Rus. *aṇḍī*, *aṇḍā*, *an-ḍauvā*, W. *reṅṛ*, E. n. m. S. **एरण्ड**.
The tree from the fruit of which castor-oil is extracted; *Ricinus communis*. Wat.

araṇḍ kharbū'za, W. *papī'tā*, E. n. m. *Carica papaya*. Wat.

aran'ḍī, W. Rus. *aṅḍolī*, E. *reṅ'ḍī*, *reṅṛī*, Tir. *aṅ'ḍī*, n. f.
1. The fruit of the *Ricinus communis*.

aranḍī kā tel, n. Castor-oil, used medicinally and for burning.

H أروا **अरवा** *ar'wā*, *arwā chā'wal*, E. *ārab*, Tir. n. m. Cleaned rice, not boiled.

H أروي **अरवी** *ar'wī*, W. *a'rui*, E. *arī*, Māṛ. n. f.
An edible vegetable root, called also *ghuīyāṅ*, and *kachchū; Colocasia antiquarum*. Wat.

H أرهٹ **अरहट** *ar'haṭ*, E. *ra'haṭ*, E. and W. *har'anṭ*, Sah. *ar'aṭh*, Māṛ. *a'haṭ*, Tir. n. f. S. **अरघट्ट**. A revolving wheel for drawing water; the Persian wheel.

H أرهر **अरहर** *ar'har*, *har'har*, *ar'haṛ*, *aṛ'haṛ*, W. *ra'har*, *rah'rī*, E. n. f. S. **आढकी**. A species of pulse; *Cytisus cajan*, Wat. *Cajanus flavus*.

H ارهنت **अरहन्त** *ar'hant*, n. m. S. **अरि** enemy, **हन्** to kill, Pālī. *arham*, *lit.* One who destroys his enemies (passions).
An appellation of *Jain* gods.

H أرئي **अरई** *ar'aī*, n. f. A kind of grass for cattle and thatching. *Mimosa rubicaulis*. Wat.

H آري **आरी** *ā'rī*, n. f.
1. A small saw.
2. A shoe-maker's awl.
3. (*Brij*) Friend; dear (*ālī*).

H آري **आरी** *ārī*, n. f. The low ridge of land which separates and forms the boundary between two fields; the bank of a river.

H آريا **आरया** *ār'yā*, n. m. A plant of the gourd species resembling a cucumber.

H أڑ **अड़** *aṛ*, n. f.
1. Contention; dispute; controversy; strife.
2. Obstinacy; contrariety; opposition.

3. Constipation; costiveness (*qabz*).
4. E. A dam or weir thrown across running water for catching fish; boom; barricade.

H آراڑا **अड़ाड़ा** *arā'ṛa*, E. Rus. *kaṛā'ṛā*, E. and W. n. m. The high steep bank of a river.

H آڑت **आड़त** *āṛ'at*, W. *āṛ'haṭ*, E. *āḍat*, W. Rus. n. f. H. *āṛ* what comes between.
1. Commission; allowance; fee; percentage.
2. Brokerage; sale by commission.
3. Agency; mercantile correspondence.

آڑتیا **आड़तीया** *āṛ'tyā*, Pop. *āṛ'tī*, *āṛat-wālā*, Rus. *aḍatyā*, n. m.
1. An agent; factor; saleman; consignee.
2. A commercial correspondent; a commission agent.
3. A jobber; broker; one who sells on commission.
4. A banker who grants and accepts bills on other bankers or correspondents.

H اُڑد **उड़द** *uṛ'ad*; Rus. *uṛdī*; Tir. *uridī*; n. m. A pulse; *Dolichos pilosus*, or *Phaseolus radiatus*. Wat. [Rus. *thū'nī*, n. m.

H اڑوار **अड़वाड़** *aṛwāṛ'*, *āṛ*, Māṛ. *thob'lī*, W.
1. A prop; support; joist; tie-beam.
2. A buttress; abutment. [n. m.

H اڑہایا **अड़हाया** *aṛhā'yā*, *aṛ'hā*, W. *akrā*, E. Weeds; oats; tares.

H آڑو **आड़ू** *ā'ṛū*, Sah. *aṛū*, n. m. A peach; *Prunus domestica*. Wat.
chak'aī āṛū, *chapḷā āṛū*, n. m. A flat peach.

H اڑواڑی **अड़वाड़ी** *aṛwā'ṛī*, E. n. f. The mullet.

H اُڑوالا **उड़वाला** *uṛwā'lā*, (*Ṭhagī*), n. m. A stone.

H اَڑوس پَڑوس **अड़ोस पड़ोस** *aṛaus' paṛaus'*, *ag'ar paṛaus*, *aṛos paṛos*, Tir. *arāsā parosā*, n. m. H. *vare* this side, *pare*, (S. पर) the other side, S. वस, H. *basnā* to dwell.
Neighbourhood; vicinity (*paṛaus*).
aṛaus' paṛaus', adv. About; around; near.
aṛausī paṛausī, n. Neighbours.

H اَڑھائی **अढ़ाई** *aṛhā'ī*, *ḍhāī*, adj. S. अर्द्ध + तृतीय, Pāli. *aḍḍhateyyo*. Two and a half.

اڑھیّا **अढ़ैया** *aṛha'īyā*, Pop. *ḍhaī'yā*, *ḍhāī-serā*, Rus. *aḍhaī'yā*, n. f.
1. A measure of two and a half seers.
2. The multiplication table (*pahāṛā*) of 2½ times. E. (*ḍhauṅchā*). [n. f.

H اُڑھری **उढ़री** *uṛh'rī*, *udh'lī*, E. *ka'rī lugāī*, W. A mistress; a kept woman; concubine.

H اُڑھیکن **उढ़ीकन** *uṛhī'kan*, n. m. See *uṭhgan*.

H اڑیوا **अड़ेवा** *aṛe'wā*, W. Hin. n. f. Wealth; property; assets; chattels.

P اَز *az*, H. *se*, prep. From; than; by; with; out of.
azāṅ-jā-ke, Whereas; seeing that; inasmuch as; since. [from among.
az-āṅ-jumla, adv. Out of the whole; out of;
az-āṅ-i-khās, Belonging to.
az-bas-ke, Inasmuch as; insomuch that.
az jā'nib, adv. On the part of; in behalf; on the side of; for; from; by.
az had', adj. Indefinite; boundless; unlimited; immeasureable; infinite; unutterable; unapproachable; unspeakable; beyond expression; unrestricted; surprising.
az had', adv. In a high degree; highly; deeply; strongly; mightily.
az khud, adv. Of one's own accord; himself; of one's own will or act; voluntarily; *suo motu*.
az khud-raf'tah, n. Out of one's mind; beside oneself; *non compos*.
az-rāh-i-tajwīz, Judicially.
az-rāh-i-ta'līf, Vexatiously; with the intent to disress or annoy.
az-rūë-hukm-i-ādālat, By the order of the court according to the law.
az rū e, adv. From the face or appearance of; by reason of; according to; by; in consequence of; by virtue of; under the circumstances.
az rū'e iske, By these presents.
az rūë alfaz-i-sarīhī, Expressly by; according to the exact words.
az rū'e haq, Ped. Equitably; justly.
az rūe shumār' ruqūm-i-āmdanī o khkarch, According to the aggregate items of receipts and disbursements. G. G.
az rū'e qānūn', Legally; according to the law.
az rūë hibā, By gifts.
az sar tā pā, Ped. for H. *sir se pāoṅ tak*.
1. From head to foot; from top to toe; from head to heel.
2. *In toto*; altogether; wholly.
3. Throughout; through; *en masse*.
4. Perfectly; completely; totally; entirely; thoroughly; *cap-a-pie*; every inch; wholesale.
Phr. From end to end; from beginning to end; from first to last.
az sar-i-nau, Ped. for H. *naë sire se*. Anew; afresh; over again.
az taraf, adv. On behalf of; on the part of; on the side of; from; in the interest of; in favor of.
az gaibī, adj. Hidden; mysterious.
az kī az, Ped. for H. *joṅ kī toṅ*. Exactly; precisely; neither more nor less; just the thing; the very thing; to a hair.

az īn jā, From this place ; hence.

P آزاد *āzād',* n. m.

1. A freeman ; freedman ;

2. A Mohamedan devotee who shaves his beard and eyelashes and takes a vow of continence, but considers himself exempt from the usual observances of religion ; a free thinker.

3. An impudent or shameless person (*āzād kā sonṭā*).

āzād', adj.

1. Acquitted ; at large ; loose ; scot free ; unrestrained ; emancipated ; set free ; manumitted ; unchecked ; released ; set at liberty.

2. Let go ; let out ; discharged ; ransomed.

3. Independent ; uncontrolled ; free born ; unenslaved.

4. Disencumbered ; freed ; disburdened ; unburdened. [at home.

5. At ease ; free from care ; light hearted ;

āzād kar'nā, v. a.

1. To set at liberty ; set free ; deliver ; untie ; disenthrall ; manumit ; release ; emancipate ; liberate.

2. To dismiss ; absolve ; enfranchise ; let off ; free ; extricate.

āzād ho'nā, v. a.

1. To gain, obtain, have, or acquire one's liberty, freedom, etc ; deliver oneself from ; be scot free ; be liberated ; set free ; be discharged or released.

2. To break prison ; get clear off ; shake off the yoke.

3. To be free, independent, unconfined, unrestrained.

PHR. To have one's one way ; to have a will of one's own.

4. To become an *āzād.*

5. To care for no man ; be indifferent or unconcerned ; care nothing ; stand on one's legs (*apne hāth pair pe kūdnā*) ; to be free as air.

6. To hold cheap ; hold in contempt ; think nothing of ; snap one's fingers at ; make light of.

آزادي *āzā'dī, azā'dī, āzād'gī,* n. f.

1. Release ; enlargement ; deliverance ; emancipation ; liberation ; discharge.

2. Freedom of action ; power ; liberty ; full play ; latitude ; freedom ; independence.

P اِزار *izār',* H. *sut'nā, sut'tan* ; W. Rus. *tam'bā* (Cor. of T. تنبان), n. f. Drawers ; trousers (*paijāmā*).

ازار بند *izār-band,* n. m. The strings with which drawers are tied ; trouser-strings (*nārā*).

P آزار *āzār',* Ped. for *bīmārī,* n. m. [firmity.

1. Sickness (*rog*) ; disease ; disorder ; in-

2. Injury ; trouble ; affliction ; outrage.

āzār'denā, v. a.

1. To trouble ; injure ; vex ; torment ; cause, produce, give, or inflict pain ; molest (*dukh denā*).

2. To persecute ; oppress ; hurt, or wound one's feelings (*dil dukhānā*). [etc.

3. To cause grief, uneasiness, or trouble,

H ازالة *izā'la,* n. m. Ped. A. زول. It departed, ceased to be.

Removal ; abolition.

izā'la-i-amān, Ped. n. m. Forfeiture.

izāla-i-bikr kar'nā, Ped. for H. *kuār-pat utār-nā,* v. a. To take away one's virginity ; to commit a rape.

izāla-i-haisy'at-i-urfī, Ped. for H. *lālī bigāṛ'-nā.* Defamation.

izālā kar'nā, v. a. To remove ; put away.

H اِزدواج *izdiwāj',* Ped. n. m. زاج coupling.

Marriage ; nuptials ; wedding (*biyāh*).

—*jāiz,* Lawful marriage.

—*ke zarye se,* Ped. By marriage. G. G.

ādam izdiwāj, Ped. Unmarried.

P آزمايش *āzmā'ish, āzmūd'gī,* n. f. P. آزمودن to try. [(*kasauṭī*).

1. Examination ; trial ; essay ; test

2. Tentative proof ; experiment ; verification ; *experimentum crucis* ; criterion.

آزمانا आज़माना *āzmā'nā, azmā'nā* ; P. H. *āzmā'-ish kar'nā, āzmū'dā lenā,* v. a. [(*kasnā*).

1. To examine ; try ; essay ; subject to trial

2. To test ; prove ; make trial of ; to put, bring, or submit to the test or proof ; verify.

آزموده كار *āzmū'dah-kār,* adj.

1. Experienced ; practised.

2. Clever ; wise ; intelligent.

āzmū'dah-kār, n. m. A veteran ; an experienced person ; a master.

P اِزدهام *izhdihām', ambok,* n. m. Cor. of A. ازدحام Multitude ; crowd (*bhīṛ*).

H اُس उस *us,* Pop. *vis,* Rus. *oh, o, ū, wā, wū* ; Tir. *vaīha, unā,* Māṛ. ऊं, उण, adj. pro. S. अदस्, असौ, Pr. *aha,* Pr. and Pālī. *asu,* That.

us par, E. *oh par.* The other side (of the river).

us-ke nām se, Under his name. [sake.

us-ke nām kā, For his name's sake ; for his

H اِس इस *is.* Rus. *yā, ih, e, yeh, yū, je, jū,* Māṛ. *īn,* इण. Tir. *yaīha,* adj. pro. S. इदम्, Pr.

iha, ima, inam, इयम् S. एतद्, एष, Pr. *esa, esā, eso.* This.

is baras, is sāl, E. *asoṅ, e'soṅ,* P. *im-sāl,* adv. This year.

is pār, Rus. *i-pār,* adv. The near bank of a river; the hither side; this side.

is sire se us sire tak,—chhor se us chhor tak. Through; from end to end; from this side to that.

is se, adv. From this; on this account; upon this; wherefore; hereupon; therefore; hence.

is shart se, On this condition; provided that; with the proviso.

is sū'rat meṅ,—ha'lat meṅ, adv. Inasmuch as; in this case; under these circumstances.

is tar'ah se,—taur se, adv. In this manner; thus; for example.

is ibā'rat se, To this effect; in form and manner following.

is garz se,—murād se, To this effect; with intent; to this intent; to this end; with this view; in this sense.

is martab'e tak,—had ko, Insomuch; to this extent or degree; in so far as; to this limit.

is mazmūn' se,—mā'nī se, To this effect; with this intent; in this sense.

is muqad'me meṅ, In this suit; in this case.

is meṅ, pro. S. अस्य मध्ये or अस्मिन्, Pr. *assim.*
1. In it; in this.
2. Meanwhile; meantime; by the way.

is wās'ie, adv. On this account; hence; therefore; for this reason; because; owing to; forasmuch as.

is waqt, isī waqt, adv.
1. Now; at present.
2. Just now; immediately; at once; forthwith.

S اسادھ असाध *asàdh',* n. f. S. अ not, साध् effect. Any chronic disease which terminates fatally; mortal disease; desperate illness.

asā'dhya, adj. Very weak; confined to one's bed; dangerously ill.

H آسادھارنا आसाधारना *āsā-dhārnā,* n. m. In Hindu law, the property held by one person without the participation of another, as opposed to co-heirship or coparcenary.

H أسارا उसारा *usār'ā;* Tir. *usāral;* Sah. *asvārā,* n. m. S. अपसतम्, Pr. *avasariam* gone out. A thatched porch; portico or a verandah, or sun-shade.

H اساڑھ असाढ़ *asāṛh', āsāṛh;* Rus. *asāḍh', sāṛh, sāḍh,* n. m. S. आषाढ, Pālī *āsālhā.* The fourth Hindu solar month (June—July) during which the sun is in Geminī; the first month of the rainy season, and consequently of cultivation.

اساڑھی असाढ़ी *asāṛ'hī, sāṛhī;* Rus. *asāḍ'hī, sāḍ'hī,* n. f.
1. The day of the full moon in *āsāṛh,* used for the *rabi* (spring harvest).
2. The harvest of *asāṛh.*

S آساگوترا असागोत्रा *āsāgot'rā,* n. m. In Hindu Law, a kinsman by the female line only; one not of the same lineage or descent.

A أسامي *āsā'mī,* Pop. *asā'mī,* n. f. Pl. of اسم name.
1. Name; office *(ohdah)*; appointment; post *(jagah)*; situation; berth; employment.
2. A person; individual; party; substitute.
Asāmī came to signify an individual from A. *āsām* (names), the heading of the register in which the names of the cultivators, etc. are recorded. Each item or entry thus became *asāmī.*
3. *(In law).* An inhabitant; a tenant *(raīyat)*; cultivator *(boā jotā).*
4. A debtor; witness; culprit; defendant; client. *Asāmī ko hāzir karo.*
5. A customer; purchaser.
6. People; souls; community; population.

asāmī banānā, v. a. To pigeon; bilk; chouse; chisel; fleece; to make a fool of; palm upon.

asāmī pāhī, asāmī pāhī kāsht, n. Non-resident cultivator; one who cultivates lands in a village to which he does not belong by birth or hereditary claim, or holds his lands either for a stipulated term, or at the pleasure of some member or members of the proprietary body; one who cultivates land in a village different from that in which he resides.

asāmī jamā-bandī, n. f. Settlement with individual cultivators; the *rayatwārī* system.

asāmī-i-chhapar-band, n. A resident cultivator; one who occupies his own *chhappar* or thatched house.

—i-shikmī, shikmī raīyat, shikmī kāshtkār. A sub-tenant; a subordinate cultivator; a holder of part of the village lands as a subordinate or dependent occupant, occupying his portion and paying his quota of the Government revenue through the representative of the community.

—i-gair mustaqil, Tenant-at-will; an acting post.

—i-gair maurū'sī, Non-hereditary tenant.

asāmī khajjar. A class of cultivators in the district of Cawnpore. They may be classified thus:—
1. Those who cultivate *sīr* land of proprietors with the stock and assistance of the owners
2. Those who cultivate the *sīr* land on

their own account, paying for the same in money or in kind.

3. Those who cultivate either a portion or the whole of the fields of recorded tenants at a profit to the latter. Government records. N. W. P. New series.

—i-mustaqil, A tenant with right of occupancy.

—i-maurū'sī, Hereditary cultivator.

asāmī-wār, adv. The phrase includes all the names usually applied to statements and revenue settlements made with proprietors in detail; the *rayatwār* individually according to name; severally.

āsāmī wārī muqattā.

The rent or revenue payable by each individual cultivator; an account shewing the distribution of the above.

ḍūbī asāmī, A bankrupt; an insolvent.

sarkārī āsāmī, n. f. A post or office under Government.

kharī asāmī, n. One who pays cash; a good paymaster; a reliable or credible person.

līchar asāmī, n. f. Opp. of *kharī asāmī*, One who is slow in paying his debts.

moṭī asāmī, n. A rich man; a wealthy person; a man of fortune (*sone kī chiṛyā*); a catch.

yāft kī asāmī.

1. A lucrative office.
2. An office in which perquisites or bribes are to be had.

H اُسانا उसाना *usā'nā, use'nā, usev'nā, uso'nī kar'nā* E.; *barsānā* W. v. a. S. अव away, स to flow. To winnow; to separate the husk from the corn; drive the chaff with the fan.

H آساوری असावरी *asāv'rī*, E. n. f.

1. A kind of pigeon (*nisāore*, W.).
2. The name of a tune (*Jogyā-asāvrī*); a musical mode.
3. A kind of silken and silver cloth.

P آسایش *āsā'ish*; H. *sukh*, n. f. Convenience; comfort; ease.

A اَسباب *asbāb'*; n. m. pl. of A. سبب.

1. Means; substance; resources.
2. Tools; instruments; implements (*okhar*); apparatus; materials; raw materials.
3. Furniture; commodities; articles; property; things; appliances; machinery.
4. Provision; stores; funds; necessaries; stock; supplies.
5. Cargo; lading; equipment.
6. Luggage; baggage; traps.
7. Goods; chattels; effects; (*In law*) personal assets.

—i-peshā, n. Implements of trade.

—i-jang,—harb, n. m. Military stores; arms and ammunition; munitions of war.

asbāb-i-khānā-dārī, n. Household furniture.

asbāb-i-zarāat,—i-khetī, Ped. for *khetī ke okhar*. Implements of husbandry; agricultural implements.

—i-safar, n. m. Luggage or provisions for a journey; travelling requisites.

P اِسبند *isband', ispand*; H. *kālā dānā*, n. m. *Peganum harmala*. Wat. A species of mustard seed burnt at marriages and births to drive away evil spirits.

H اِسپات इसपात *ispāt'*; P. *faulād*, n. m. Steel.

H اسپرش असपर्श *asparsh*; Ped. *spursh*, n. m. S. स्पर्श to touch.

The state of a Hindū after bathing, previous to worship or eating, during which it is unlawful for him to touch any one.

P اِسپغول *isp'aġol, asp'aġol, isb'aġol*; Pop. *is'abgol*; W. Rus. *sabgol'*; E. Rus. *sapgol'*, n. m. P. اسپ horse, A. غول ear, the shape of the leaf resembling that of a horse's ear.

Seed of the fleawort; *spogel seed*. Wat.

P اَسپینا *aspī'nā*, n. (Horse dealer's idiom) One.

H اَست असत *as'at*, adj. S. अ not, सत्य true.

1. False (*jhūṭ*); not true; untrue; unfounded.
2. Unholy; ungodly; impious; irreligious.
3. Not genuine; spurious; fictitious (*banā huā*). [terfeit.
4. Illusory; delusive; deceptive; coun-
5. Wrong; sinful; evil (*burā*).
6. Unjust; unfair; inequitable.

P آستان *āstān', āstā'nā, astā'nā'*, n. m. S. स्था H. *asthān* place.

1. Threshold; door; entrance.
2. The abode of a *faqīr*.
3. The entrance to a shrine.

H اَستُت अस्तुत *as'tut, astu'tī*, n. f. S. स्तुति from स्तु to praise.

1. Worship; adoration; devotion. [tion.
2. Prayer; invocation; praise; glorifica-
3. Psalmody; psalm; hymn.

A اِستثنا *istis'nā*, n. m. A. ثني Doubled.

1. Exception; bar; exclusion.
2. Rejection; non-admission.

—i-chand rozā, A temporary bar.

—i-khās, A special bar.

istisnā kar'nā, v. a. To exclude; bar; except; leave out.

—*i-mudām'*, A perpetual bar.
ba-istisnā, Exclusive of; excepting; excluding.

A إِستحسان *istehsān'*, n. m. حسن was, or became good. Taking or considering as a favor; approving or praising.

A favorable construction or interpretation of a point of law; deviating from the strict letter of law from kindness either to the suitor or to the community; equity.

A إِستحصال *istehsāl'*, n. m. حصل was extracted. Profit; the act of gaining or acquiring property.
—*bil-jabr*, Extortion; exaction.
—*i-nā-jāiz*, Wrongful gain.
iqrār kā istehsāl bil-jabr karnā, To extort a confession. G. G.
māl kā istehsāl bil-jabr, Extorted property.

A إِستحقاق *istehqāq'*, n. m. حق It was, or became right. A claim; demand; right (*haq*); title; privilege.
—*istisnāī*, An exceptional title.
—*i-e'ada-i-wirāsat*, A reversionary title.
—*i-infikāk-i-rahn*, Equity of redemption of a mortgage.
—*ba-zar'ye hibā*, A title by gift.
—*i-ta'khfīf-i-lagān*, Claim for reduction of rent.
—*tarka*, Right of succession or inheritance; right to the estate of a deceased person.
—*tarka bilā wasīyat*, Title to intestate property.
—*i-tash'khīs-i-jam'a*, Right of assessment.
—*taqdīm 'kharīdārī*, Right of pre-emption.
—*i-taqsīm*, Right of partition.
—*i-jāiz*, A valid title.
—*i-hīfāzat-i-'khud i'khtyārī*, Right of private defence, or self-defence.
—*i-hīn-i-hayāt'*, A life interest.
—*'kharīdā'rī-i-nīlām*, Right or title acquired by purchase at an auction.
—*i-dāimī*, Permanency of tenure.
—*i-dāimī taqsīm*, A right to claim partition.
—*i-da'khl*, Right of entry or possession.
—*i-darbāb-i-haqīat*, A legal title as to tenure.
—*i-dāwā*, Preferential claim.
—*i-dāwa-i-ibtidāī*, An original right of action.
—*i-zātī*, Personal privilege.
—*i-rahn*, A mortgage right.
—*i-shufā*, A pre-emptive title.
istehqāq-i-usūbat, Residuary title.
istehqāq-i-qānūn', A valid title at law.
—*qāim-bil-wajūd*, An inchoate right.
—*qāim-bil-wajūd-shartī*, An inchoate and conditional right.
—*i-qāim muqāmī*, Right of representation; the right to represent another.
istehqāq-i-qāima, A vested interest.
—*i-qabza*, Right of possession.
—*i-qadā'mat*, A title by prescription; prescriptive right.
—*kāmil*, An absolute interest; a complete right.
—*karnā*, v. n. To claim; demand as due; to sue; lay claim to; assert a right.
—*i-mālikānā*, Proprietory title.
—*i-mālkyat*, A title of ownership.
—*i-mālkyat pesh karnā*, To set up a title of ownership.
—*i-mālkyat mukhālifānā*, An adverse title.
—*i-murtahnī*, A mortgage title.
—*muzāreā'na*, A cultivating title.
—*mustaqil'*, A permanent right or interest.
—*mashrūt'*, A conditional right.
—*maurūsī*, An hereditary right.
istehqāq-i-nāqis, An imperfect title.
—*nifāz*,
1. Right of way. G. G.
2. The exercise or use of a right.
—*i-nālish bāqī na rahā*, Loss of right to sue.
—*i-nīlām-dārī*, Unid. An auction title.
—*wā'qaī*, A right; an actual right.
—*wirāsat*, Right of heirship.
—*wirāsat-āin'dah*, A reversionary title.

A إِستحکام *istehkām'*, n. m. حکم he gave judgment.

1. Confirmation; corroboration; ratification; verification.
2. Strength; firmness; support.

istehkām de'nā, v. a. Ped. for H. *pakkā kar'nā*.
1. To corroborate; strengthen; confirm; support.
2. To ratify; sanction; make valid, or legal.
3. To certify; attest; verify; endorse.

A إِستحلاف *istehlāf'*, n. m. حلف he swore.

Causing to swear, applied especially in law to cases in which the oath of a wife is necessary for the establishment of the fact relating to her marriage.

A إِستحلال *istehlāl'*, n. m. حلال making lawful.

In law, the cry of a new born child, the occurrence of which is a necessary proof, in a peculiar case of inheritance, as that of a man leaving a widow pregnant, and a brother; in which case proof being given that the cry of the child was heard, the widow, as its mother, will inherit on the death of the child. If no cry has been heard, the brother is heir.

A إستخاره *isti'khā'rah*, n. m.

Divination by the book or by the Bible; stichomancy; bibliomancy. [boon.

A إستدانت *istidā'nat*, n. m. دان he sought a

1. Borrowing; contracting a debt; suing for a debt.

2. *(In law)*, any transaction which the manager in a partnership, where one finds the capital and the other the management, may undertake, but for which, if not concluded in, or consonant to the terms of his contract with the proprietor of the share, he alone is responsible, and the profits of which he alone is entitled to, unless his partner had given his previous sanction.

A إستدعا *istidā'ā'*, n. m. Ped. for H. *chāhnā*. A. دعا asking; supplicating. [tion.

1. Request; desire; application; requisi-
2. Claim; demand (*dāwā*).
3. Supplication; prayer; humble petition; entreaty.

A إستدلال *istidlāl'*, n. m. See. *dalīl*.

P أستر *as'tar*, n. m. Lining; priming; mordant.

استرکاری *as'tar-kā'rī*, n. f. Plastering; work done in plaster.

P أسترا *usta'rā*, W. *as'turā*, E. n. m. A razor.

A H إسترداد کرنا *istirdād' kar'nā*, v. a. Ped. for *rad k.* to send back.

1. To repeal; supersede; annul.
2. To set aside; disannul; abrogate; rescind; overrule; nullify; do away with; declare null and void.

istirdād-i-nīlām, n. m. Reversal of a public sale.

A إسترضا *istir'zā*, n. f. رضي he was pleased,

Assent; consent. (*razā-mandī*).

H أستري इस्त्री *is'trī*, *tiriyā* Old H.; *nā'rī*, *tir'yā*, *nār* (Poet); *bai'yar-bā'nī*, *bai'yar*, *bīr* Rus; *tī'ā*, *tī'mat*, *tīmī* Panj.; *khel'nī* (in jest); *'au'rat* A.; *ran'ḍī*, *lugā'ī*, *log'nī*, *rāṅḍ*. W.; *mehrā'rū* E.; *māū*, *mau'gī* Mag.; *māug* Tir.; *laṭyālī*, *janānī* (Cor. of P. *zan*) Gaṛh.; *bām* (in *Bulandshahar*); *astarī*, Māṛ. n. f. S. स्त्री from स्त्यै to conceive, Pr. *tiryā*, *tyā*, *itthī*.

1. A woman (*lugāī*).

2. Wife (*jorū*). [kind.

is'trī barg,—*jāt*, n. f. The female sex; woman-

is'trī dhan. Jointure; settlement made on a wife by her father or husband; paraphernalia.

is'trī kar'nā, v. a. To marry; wed (*biyāh k.*).

is'trī gāmī, n. m. An adulterer (*ranḍī-bāz*).

H إستري इस्तरी *is'tarī*, n. f.

A tailor's goose; a smoothing iron. [iron.

istrī kar'nā, v. a. To iron; to smooth with the

A إستسقا *istis'qā*, H. *jā'landar*, *jilan'dar*, n.m.

سقي gave to drink. The dropsy.

—*i-ziqqī*, Anasarca; dropsy of the whole body.

—*i-tablī*, Tympanites.

A إستصواب *istiswab'*, n. m. A. صواب a thing that is right.

1. Enquiring what is the right thing to be done; asking; interrogating; questioning; inquiry; asking one's opinion.
2. Consultation; reference.

istiswāb' kar'nā, v. a.

1. To refer; inquire; submit. [opinion.
2. To consult; take advice; ask one's

ba nazar-i-istiswāb, With the view of consultation.

A إستعانت *iste'ā'nat*, n. f. A. عون seeking aid.

Aid; assistance; help (*madad*).

ba-iste''aānat. By aiding or abetting; by the aid of.

A إستعداد *iste'dād'*, n. f. A. عد preparing.

1. Capacity; abilities; talents (*lyāqat*).
2. Intellect; genius (*ukat*); mental power; endowments.
3. Parts; wit; headpiece; aptitude.
4. Proficiency; accomplishments; acquirements; tact; knowledge; art; science.

ist'edād arāzī, ——*ba-haq-i-paidāvāri*. G. G. Productive power of land.

A إستعفا *ist'e'fā*; Pop. *istī'fā*, *astī'fā*, n. m. A. عفو begging to be released from an obligation.

Asking forgiveness; resignation.

istīfā de'nā, v. a. To resign an office; tender one's resignation; give up an appointment.

istīfā qubūl kar'nā, v. a. To accept one's resignation.

A إستعمال *ist'emāl'*, n. m. عمل causing to work.

1. Use ; practice (*rabt*) ; exercise.
2. Usage; custom; observance; fashion (*chāl*) ; vogue ; run. [(*kām*).
3. Employment ; operation ; play ; work
ba-istᵉemāl zarᵉye-i jāiz. By lawful means. G.G.
istemāl kar'nā, istemāl meṅ lā'nā, v. a.
1. To exercise ; use ; employ ; put to use ; practise ; make use of ; apply (*kām meṅ lānā*).
2. To turn to account ; press or enlist into service ; put in requisition ; call, or bring into play or operation ; utilize.
3. To wear ; work up ; consume ; expend ; turn to use.
PHR. To put in action ; set in motion ; put in practice ; ply one's task ; discharge an office ; put in execution.
istemāl meṅ ānā, istemāl meṅ honā, v. n.
To be used ; to be in use.
استعمالي *istemā'lī,* adj.
1. Used ; worn ; old.
2. Customary ; usual ; practical.
istemālī, n. m. The best kind of rice.

A إستغاثة *istiᵉgā'sah,* n. f. غاث calling for help.

1. Demanding justice ; moving a court for justice.
2. Complaint (*faryād*) ; a suit (*nālish*).
—*kar'nā,* v. a. To demand, sue, or seek redress (*nālish k.*).

A إستغراق *istiᵉgrāq'* n. m. Ped. غرق taking the whole.

Lien ; hypothecation ; mortgage (*girvī*).

A إستغفار *istiᵉgfār',* n. m. غفر asking forgiveness.

1. Begging mercy ; craving grace.
2. The Mohamedan prayer for forgiveness or defence against *Shaitān* (Satan).
3. Deliverance ; riddance.
استغفر الله *astagfir ullāh,* intj. May God forgive me! I entreat forgiveness of God! God forbid!

A إستفراغ *istifrā'g',* n. m. Ped. for *qaë,* q. v.

A إستفسار *istifsār',* n. m. فسر enquiry.

1. Question ; interrogatory ; interrogation (*pūchh*).
2. Enquiry ; investigation ; search.
3. Reference ; sending or asking for information.
istifsār kar'nā, v. a. Ped. for *pūchhnā.* To call for information ; question ; demand an explanation ; make a reference.

A إستفهام *istifhām',* n. m. فهم desiring to know.

Seeking or asking for an explanation ; desiring to know or understand ; enquiry (*daryāft*).

A إستقالة *istiqā'la,* n. m. From قال Requiring any one to cancel an agreement or to give up a bargain.

A إستقامت *istiqā'mat,* n. f. قام remaining.

1. Firmness (*mazbūtī*) ; constancy. [*rāo*).
2. Rectitude ; stability ; stagnancy (*ṭha-*

A إستقبال *istiqbāl',* n. m. قبل going forth to meet.

Welcome ; reception (*agvā'nī*).
istiqbāl kar'nā, v. a.
1. To go forward to meet one ; to greet, receive, or welcome a person.
2. To proceed any distance to meet one and escort him to one's house (*agwānī k.*).

A إستقرار *istiqrār',* n. m. قر resting. Demanding settlement or affirmation ; declaration ; confirmation ; recognition ; examination ; ratification.
istiqrār'-i-haqī'at. Declaration or recognition of title.
istiqrār-i-haqīat ᵉkhālis. A declaration or recognition of sole title.

A إستقلال *istiqlāl',* n. m.

1. Constancy ; stability ; resolution ; determination ; firmness ; fortitude.
2. Steadiness ; persistence ; perseverance.
istiqlā'lī, adj. Unid. for مستقل Invested with authority ; having absolute power.

A إستماع *istimāᵉa,* Ped. for *samāᵉat,* From سمع giving ear, *lit.* That which is heard.
Hearsay ; evidence ; indirect testimony, receivable only in particular cases and under certain restrictions.

A إستمداد *istimdād',* n. f. مدّ asking help.

1. Desiring or begging assistance ; craving aid ; asking for supplies or subsidies.
2. Application for protection.

A إستمرار *istimrār',* n. m.

1. Permanence ; perpetuity ; preservation.
2. Uninterrupted possession. [teration.
3. *In law,* a fixed rent not liable to al-

istimrār-dār, n. The holder of a farm or lease in perpetuity. [never-ceasing.

استمراري *istimrā'rī*, adj. Perpetual; continuative;

istimrārī, n. f. A piece of land on a fixed lease; land permanently settled; the permanent settlement of Lord Cornwallis.

istimrārī paṭṭā, A lease or farm granted at a fixed rent; a lease in perpetuity.

—*paṭṭe-dār*, n. m. Holder of a lease of land at a fixed rent.

istimrārī jamā. A fixed assessment or revenue.

istimrārī dehāt,' Permanently settled villages; villages held at a fixed rent under a permanent settlement.

istimrārī māl guzārī. Permanent revenue.

istimrārī muqarrar karnā, v. a. To fix in perpetuity.

istimrārī band o bast, band o bast-i-istimrārī, n. m. Permanent settlement.

A اِستمزاج *istimzāj'*, n. m. مزاج disposition. Ped. for صلاح.

1. Desiring or asking one's opinion; striving to discover one's purpose or intentions.

2. Enquiry; reference. [lution.

A اِستنجا *istin'jā*, Pop. *istan'jā*, n. m. نجا ab-

1. Making water; pissing (*mūtnā*).

2. Purification after alvine evacuation (*hāth pānī lenā*).

P اُستوار *ustuvār'*, adj.

1. Strong; firm (*pakkā*).

2. Level; equal (*iksāṅ*); even (*hamwār*); straight (*sīdhā*). [prop.

ustuvār karnā, v. a. To strengthen; support;

استواري *ustuvā'rī*, n. f.

1. Firmness; stability; permanence.

2. Corroboration; confirmation; support.

S استھ अस्थि *as'thi*, Pālī. *aṭṭhī*, H. *haḍ'ḍī*, *hāṛ*, n. m. A bone.

asthi bhaṅg, n. m. A plant of supposed efficacy in resetting a fracture; *Cissus quadrangularis*. Wat.

H اَستھاپن अस्थापन *asthā'pan*; Rus. *thā'pan*, n. m. S. स्थापन from स्था to place.

Establishment; the act of establishing; appointment.

asthā'pan kar'nā, v. a. [*rānā*).

To establish; dedicate; fix; set (*padh-*

H اَستھان अस्थान *asthān'*, *thān*, *asthal*, n. m. S. स्थान from स्था to place, P. *āstān*.

1. Locality; receptacle; situation (*ṭhāṅo*); position; spot; point; post; seat; station (*jagah*).

2. Abode; residence; home (*ghar*).

3. Temple; shrine (*mandar*).

asthān' de'nā, v. a. To lodge; place; locate (*jagah denā*).

H اِستھر इस्थिर *isthir'*; *thir*; Bhoj. *astir*; Tir. *asthir*, adj. S. स्थिर from स्था to place.

Stable; stagnant; immovable.

H اَستھل अस्थल *as'thal*, *astal*, n. m. S. स्थल a place. See *asthān*.

1. A kind of free monastery in which communities of religious mendicants reside together under a *Mahant* (a chief or abbot).

2. A stand or station of a *faqīr*.

E اِسٹام *isṭām'*, *ishṭām'*, n. m. Stamp (*ṭikaṭ*).

isṭām-farosh, n. m. Stamp vender.

isṭām kā kāgaz, n. m. Stamped paper.

isṭām lagā huā, pospid (Post paid), Ped. *ṭikaṭ chaspāṅ*, adj. Bearing stamp; stamped.

isṭām musannā, Ped. adj. Stamped.

E اِسٹنٹ *isṭanṭ'*, n. m. An assistant.

E اِسٹیشن *isṭe'shan*; Rus. *isṭe'kan, isṭeṭan, isṭe san, ṭesan*, n. m. Railway or Police station.

A اَسد *as'ad*, S. सिंह n. m. *Leo*.

H اَسدھ असुध *a-sudh'*, *a-sud*, *a-shudh*, adj. S. अ not, शुद्ध pure; Pālī. *asuddho*.

Impure; unclean; polluted; defiled (*nāpāk*). [make impure.

—*kar'nā*, v. a. To defile; spoil; pollute;

H اَسدھ असिध *a-sidh'*, E adj. S. अ not, सिद्ध completed. Raw; not properly cooked; unripe (*kach'chā*).

H اِسر इस्सर *is'sar* E.; *ī'sar, ī'shar, īs'var* W.; Mag. *is'var*, n. m. S. ईश्वर from ईश to rule, Pr. *issaro, īsaro* God.

1. The Almighty God; Lord; the Supreme Being. [Divinities.

2. One of the three presiding Hindū

H اُسّر उस्सर *us'sar*, *ū'sar*, E. *banj'ar*, W. *reṛ'hā*, Mag. adj. S. ऊषर, ऊष salt ground.

Impregnated with salt, or saltpetre; barren (land).

H اَسر असुर *a'-sur*, n. m. Opp. of *sur* a god· S. असु spiritual life. [goblin.

Devil; demon; an evil spirit; monster;

H آسِر आसिर *ā'sir*, n. f. Cor. of A. عشر Ten rupees (idiom of butchers).

A اِسرار *isrār', asrār'*, n. m.
1. The act of concealment.
2. Secret; mystery.
3. The influence of an evil spirit

A اِسراف *isrā̂f'*, n. f. سرف wasting.
Abuse of wealth; extravagance; lavish expenditure; excess of expenditure (*fazūl-kharchī*).

H آسرباد आसिर्बाद *āsirbād'*, n. f. See *asīrbād*.

H آسَرت आस्रत *ās'rat, ās'rī, āsrī-bhūt*, n. m.
1. A dependant; parasite; hanger on; sycophant; courtier.
2. Subject; follower; servant; retainer.
3. A Brahman who assists in the performance of marriage ceremonies.

آسرتای आस्रताई *āsrata'ī*, n. f.
1. The office of an *āsrat*.
2. The privileges of an *āsrat*.

H آسرم आस्रम *ās'ram*, n. m. Pālī. *assamo*, S. आश्रम from आ + श्रम to make effort, perform austerities.
1. Abode, residence (of a religious man).
2. A religious order, called also *baran* whereof the Hindūs reckon four, viz. the *Brahmachārī*, who devotes his life to religious exercises, austerity and celibacy; 2nd *Grihī* or *Grihastha*. who lives in the world and rears a family; 3rd *Vānaprastha*, one who retires from the world with his family, and passes his life in devotion in the forest; 4th *Bhikshū, Bhichchhū* or *Sannyāsī*, one who lives on alms.

A اُسطوخودوس *ustu-khudūs'*, n. m. French lavender; *Lavendula stœchas*. [Wat.

A اِسقاط *isqāt'*, n.m. سقط it fell. Causing to fall; casting her young (a camel).
isqāt-i-hamal, n. m. Causing to miscarry; procuring an abortion; miscarriage; abortion (*peṭ girānā*).
bilā razāmandī isqāt-i-hamal kar'nā.
Causing miscarriage without consent.

H اَسگن असगुन *as'gun, ku-sugan'*, Pop. *kuson'*, Māṛ. अपसुगण, n. m. S. अ not, शकुन good omen. A bad omen.

S اَسگند असगुन्ध *as'gund*, n. m.
Physalis somnifera. Wat.

S اَسگندھ असगन्ध *as'gandh, isgand, āskand*, n. m. A medicinal plant; *Physalis flexuosa*. Wat.

A اِسلام *islām'*, n. m. سلم he became secure.
The religion of *Mohammad*; orthodoxy according to Mahomedans.
islām lānā,—qubūl k., v. n. To be converted to Mahomedanism; to profess the Mahomedan faith.
اِسلامي *islā'mī*, adj.
Faithful; orthodox (according to the Mahomedans).
islāmī, n. m. A follower of the Mahomedan [religion.

A اَسلحه *aslah'*, n.m. pl. of سلاح Arms (*hatyār*).
Weapons; armour; implements of war.
aslah-khānah, salah—, H. *hatyār-ghar*, n. m. A magazine; armoury; arsenal.

A اِسم *ism*, n. m. H. *nām*.
1. Name; denomination; appellation.
ism-i-āzam, The name of the Almighty; one of the ninety-nine attributes of the Divinity, the utterance of which is an irresistible spell over demons. Mah.
ism-i-farzī, H. *dharā nām*, Feigned name; assumed name; fictitious name.
ism-navīsī, n. f.
1. The office of registering names; the act of enrolling.
2. Roll or register of names; muster roll.
3. A list of names, as of witnesses in a suit.
ism-navīsī-i-gavāhān, n.
1. A petition to summon witnesses.
2. A list of witnesses.
ism-wār, H. *nām pīchhe*, An entry in the order of individual names.

P آسماني *āsmā'nī*, adj.
Heavenly; celestial; divine.
āsmānī ba'lā,—thape'ṛā,—gaz'ab,—go'lā,—tīr, n.
A calamity from Heaven; Divine visi- [tation.
āsmānī farmā'nī, E. n. f. *lit.* Heavenly decree.
1. Unforeseen disasters arising from drought or excessive rain, as failure of crops in a bad season.
2. A term used formerly in deeds and leases, providing for any incidents or injuries arising from calamitous seasons or unjust exactions of the Government, which, if affecting the Zamīndārs, the ryots were compelled to make good.
3. In Gaṛhwāl, estimated fines and forfeitures, as part of the revenue.

H آسن आसन *ā'san*; Mag. *āsnī*, n. m. Pālī. *āsanam*. S. आस् to sit.
1. Posture; attitude; position; the mode of sitting.

2. The mode of sitting of jogīs at their devotional exercises, of which they enumerate eighty-four.

3. The driver's seat; the rider's seat (on a horse); the fork.

4. A small carpet on which Hindūs sit at prayer, also called *āsnī*.

5. One of thirty-six postures described in *Kok Shāstar*—branded as carnal and unmentionable; the thigh.

āsan lagā'nā, v. n.

To sit obstinately in one place till one's demands are satisfied.

H آسن आसिन *ā'sin* E.; *asauj'*, *kuār'*, W. n. m. S. आश्विनः from अश्विनी the first of the twenty-eight constellations in the moon's path.

The seventh month of the Hindū luni-solar year (Sept.-Oct.) when the moon is full, near the stars in the head of Aries.

H اُسنّا उसना *usan'nā*, *osan'nā*; Gaṛh. *omāl-nā*, v. a.

1. E. To boil; simmer (*ubālnā*).

2. W. To knead the flour (*māṅḍnā*).

us'nā chāur, E. *se'lā chāwal*, W. n. m. The rice separated from the husk after being boiled.

A أسناد *asnād'*, n. m. pl. of سند A. سند he leaned upon it.

1. Grants; deeds; documents; charters; law papers in general; warrants. [*sanads*.

2. Credentials; testimonials; certificates;

H P أسوار *asvār'*; Pop. *sawār*, Opp. of *paidal*, n. m. S. अश्व horse. [rider.

A cavalry man; horseman; trooper;

اسواري *aswā'rī*, *sawā'rī*, n. f.

1. The act of riding or driving.

2. Carriage; vehicle; horses; *ḍolī*; palanqueen, etc.

3. A cavalcade; retinue; procession.

4. The occupant of a carriage, etc.

5. The descent of some god, or evil spirit on a person.

H أسوامی بکری अस्वामी बिकरी *aswāmī-bik-rī*, n. f. S. अ not, स्वामी master, विक्रय sale; Pālī. *assāmiko*. Sale without ownership; illegal sale.

H أسوانسي अस्वांसी *aswāṅ'sī*, n. f. S. अंश, H. अन्स a part. A lineal land measure; $\frac{1}{20}$ of a *kachwāṅsī*. [q. v.

H آسوج असौज *asauj*, *āsauj*, n. m. *kuār*, W. *āsin*, E.

P آسودگي *āsūdg'ī*, n. f. P. آسودن to be at rest.

1. Quiet; peace; tranquility; ease; calm.

2. Comfort; contentment; convenience; competency; tranquil enjoyment; well-being; easy circumstances; affluence.

آسوده *āsū'dah*, *āsūdah-hāl*, adj.

1. Comfortable; affluent; possessing a competency; independent. [*souci*.

2. Cosy; in clover; easy in mind; *sans*

S أسوگ असोग *a-sog'*, E. n. m. S. शुच to be grieved, Pālī. *asoko*.

1. Ease; tranquility; comfort.

2. A tree, called also *Devādārū*; *Guattëria longifolia*. Wat. [fortable.

aso'gī, adj. Unmolested; undisturbed; com-

H اسوني असविनी *as'winī*, n. f. S. अश्व horse.

The first lunar mansion resembling a horse's head (the three stars in the head of Aries).

A إسهال *is hāl'*, n. m. Ped. for *dust*. Loosening of the bowels; purging.

P آسيب *āseb'*, n. m.

1. Mischief; misfortune; trouble; calamity—generally from the shadow of a demon having fallen on one.

2. Ped. Damage; injury; hurt.

3. Ped. Fear (*ḍar*); apprehension; care; concern.

āseb pahuṅchānā, v. a. To injure; damage; hurt.

āseb pahuṅchnā, v. n. To be injured, hurt.

āseb dūr kar'nā, *āseb utārnā*, v. a.

1. To expel any disease caused by the shadow of a demon or evil spirit.

2. To expel an evil spirit; exorcise.

H أسير उसीर *usīr'*, n. f. S. उशीर A grass, the scented roots of which are used for making *tatties*; *Andropogon muricatum*. Wat.

H اسيرباد असीर्वाद *asīr'bād*, *ā'sirbād*, *ashīr-bād*, n. m. S. आशिस् benediction, वद् to speak.

Blessing; benediction.

H اسيس असीस *asīs'*, Māṛ. *āsīs*, n. f. S. आशिस् benediction.

1. Blessing; benediction; return of compliments from a (Hindū) superior.

2. Prize; reward; present.

اسيسنا असीसना *asīs'nā*, *asīs denā*, v. a.

1. To bless; call blessings for, or on; pray for.

E اسيسر *ase'sar*, n. m. An assessor; a juryman.

A إشارہ *ishā'rah*, n. m. شار he exhibited.
1. Sign; pointing; touch; nudge; nod; beck; wink; gesture; shrug; gesticulation.
2. Cue; hint; inkling; clue.
3. Dumb-shew; by-play. [(*slang*).
4. Love glances; ogling; sheep's eyes
5. Mark; trace; direction; indication.
6. Allusion; implication; reference.
7. Innendo; hint; insinuation.

ishārā kar'nā, v. a.
1. To make a sign; to beckon.
2. To wink; nod; beck; nudge.
3. To cast amorous, or side glances.
4. To hint; give the cue or sign; to tip the wink (*slang*).
5. To refer; allude to.
6. To direct; induce; command.

A إشتباہ *ishtibāh'*, n. m. Ped. for *shubah*, q. v.
1. A vague conception; doubt; suspicion; ambiguity; scruple.
2. A vague likeness; a bad resemblance.

A إشترا *ishtir'ā*, Ped. for خرید q. v.

A إشتراک *ishtirāk'*, n. m. شرک he shared in it. Ped. for H. *sājhā*, q. v.
1. Entering into partnership; partnership; coparcenary.
2. Fellowship; association.

A إشتعال *ishteāāl'*, *ishteāālak*, n. f. Ped. for *bharak*, q. v.
1. A small flame.
2. Fomenting or instigating a quarrel; incendiarism; sedition; outbreak.

ishteāāl denā, *ishteālak* —, v. a.
1. To kindle a light.
2. To foment or instigate a quarrel; to encourage bad or unlawful acts; excite.

A إشتہار *ishtehār'*, n. m. شہر he made it commonly known. [lic notice.
1. Announcement; publication; pub-
2. Publicity; declaration; proclamation.
3. Advertisement; notice; circular; notification.
4. A poster; bill; placard.

ishtehār ibtidāī. A preliminary notification.
*ishtehār ba tahdīd-i-infisā*kh-i-band o bast.* A notification threatening annulment of a settlement
*ishtehār-i-da*khl.* Notice of delivery of possession.
ishtehār denā, v. a. [set forth.
1. To promulgate; announce; notify;
2. To give notice; spread abroad. [lish.
3. To disseminate; make known; pub-
4. To circulate; propagate; give out.

PHR. To send round the crier; to announce with beat of drum (*ḍhaṅḍorā piṭwānā*); to publish in the Gazette.

ishtehār-i-ādam-intiqāl. Notice prohibiting the transfer (of a property).
ishtehār-i-qur'qī. Notice of attachment or confiscation.
ishtehār-nāmah. A written or printed proclamation for public notice.
ishtehār-i-nīlām. Notice of sale or auction.
ishtehārī, n. m. A person who has absconded.

H إشٹ इष्ट *ishṭ*, n. S. इष् to desire, यज् to worship.
1. Faith; trust; belief.
2. One chosen or favoured of a god or goddess. [Eight.

S اشٹ अष्ट *ashṭ*, H. *āṭh*, *aṭh*; P. *hasht*, adj.

اشٹانگ अष्टाङ्ग *ashṭāṅg*, H. *āṭhoṅ aṅg*, n. m. The eight members of the body.
ashṭāṅg pranām,—*parnām*, *sāsh'aṅg daṅḍvat*, n. m. Prostration or adoration so as to touch the ground with the eight principal members, viz., with the hands, thighs, breast, eyes, and head.

اشٹ دھات अष्ट धातु *ashṭ dhātu*; H. *āṭh dhāt*; P. ہشت دھات n. m. *lit.* The eight metals. Bell metal; mixed metal.

اشٹ سدھ अष्टसिद्धि *ashṭ siddhi*, n. m. [beings).
1. The eight *siddhis* (perfect or superior
2. A personification of the powers and laws of nature, when they are subjected to the will by holiness and austerities.

☞ Whatever the fancy desires, may, it is said, be obtained; universal sovereignty may be acquired, and implicit obedience to any command enforced; the magnitude, weight, or levity of the body may be increased or diminished at will, and the body be transported in an instant to any part of the universe.

اشٹ منگل अष्ट मंगल *ashṭ maṅg'al*, n. m.
1. A horse with a white face, tail, breast, and hoofs.
2. A collection of eight lucky objects to be got together on occasion, as a lion, a bull, an elephant, a water-jar, a fan, a flag, a trumpet, and a lamp.

اشٹمی अष्टमी *ashṭ'mī*; H. *āṭ'hen*; Rus. *āṭhe*, *āṭhain*; Bhoj. *aṭhmī*, n. f. The eighth day of the increase or decrease of the moon.
janam ashṭ'mī, n. f. The eighth day of the dark half of *Bhādoṅ* (August); the birthday of *Krishna*.

A أَشَدّ *ash'add, ashad,* adj. More or most vehement; severe; violent; excessive; difficult.

A اشراف *ashrāf',* n. m. شَرُفَ he became eminent. pl. of. شريف

1. Nobles; noblemen; persons of rank; grandees; gentlemen; men of high extraction; gentry; gentle folk; squirearchy; magnates.

2. *Preux chevaliers*; honorable men.

3. In Rohilkhund, Oude, and Benares, a class of cultivators who claim certain privileges.

A إِشراق *ishrāq',* n. m. شَرَقَ the sun rose. H. *ude,* q.v.

namāz-i-ishrāq, n. f. Prayer at sunrise; morning prayer. [n. f.

P اشرفي *ash'rafī,* Ped.; *ashar'fī*; Rus. *sar'phī,*

A gold coin; a gold mohar, equivalent to about 16 rupees.

P آشكاره *āshkā'rah,* Ped. for A. *zā'hir,* adj.

1. Conspicuous; open; broad; bald; plain (*sāf*).

2. Manifest; patent; revealed.

H اشلوك अश्लोक *ashlok', shlok,* Ped.; *aslok', ishlok', salok, shilok,* Pop. n. m. S. श्लोक to versify.

1. Poetry; verse.

2. A couplet; distich.

ashlok' kahāī, gazal parhvāī, n. f. A present from the female relatives of the bride to the bridegroom for repeating some verses called *chhan.*

S آشليكها अश्लेषा *ashle'khā, ashleshā,* n. m. The ninth *Nakshattra* or lunar mansion (five stars near the southern claw of Cancer).

P آشنا *āsh'nā*; Rus. *asnā,* n.

1. Friend; companion; acquaintance; crony; intimate friend; bosom friend; familiar.

2. A lover; mate; paramour; sweetheart; *cavalier servente*; *cicisbeo*; flame; beau; *amoroso.*

3. A kept mistress; *inamorata*; concubine.

4. A woman's dog (a lover).

5. (*asnāo*). Rus. A son-in-law.

sūrat āshnā, n. m.

One known by sight only; a formal acquaintance.

آشنائي *āshnā'ī,* Illit. *ashnāī*; Rus. *asnāī,* n. f.

1. Friendship; intimacy; familiarity; acquaintance; intercourse.

2. Relationship; connexion; relation through marriage.

3. Carnal knowledge; illicit love; unlawful attachment.

H أَشنان अश्नान *ashnān', asnān', nahān'*; Ped. and Rus. *sinān,* n. m. S. स्ना, P. *shinā* to bathe. Bathing; ablution; purification.

ashnān dhyān, n. m. Bathing and religious meditation; daily worship of the Hindūs.

ritu asnān; Hin. Wom. *mahīne kā nahān,* n. Bathing after menstruation.

Gaṅgā ashnān, n. Bathing in the Ganges.

S اشوكاشٹمي अशोकाष्टमी *ashok-āshṭmī,* n. m. from *asok, Jonesia asoca,* Wat., and *ashṭmī,* eighth of the light fortnight of *Chait,* (April-May) when a festival in honor of *Vishnu* is observed, part of the ceremonial of which consists in drinking water with the buds of *asoka* in it.

S اشومیده अश्वमेध *ash'wa-medh*; Pop. *ashwāmīdh,* n. m. S. अश्व a horse, मेध to kill.

The actual or emblematic sacrifice of a horse, an ancient religious ceremony among the Hindūs.

☞ This sacrifice is one of the highest order, and its performance a hundred times, gives a title to the dominion of *Swarga* or paradise. It appears to have been originally typical, the horse and other animals being simply bound during the performance of certain ceremonies. The actual sacrifice is an introduction of a later period. Wilson.

A أَشيا *ashyā,'* Ped. for P. *chīz,* n. f. pl. of شي

Things; effects; chattels.

ashyā-i-ʻgair-ehtimām shuda. Effects unadministered. G. G.

ashyā-i-maqrūqah. Attached property.

ashyā-i-mujib-i-nafrat-i-ʻkhalāyak. Public nuisances. G. G.

A إِصطباغ *istibāg̱,'* Pop. *bapṭazmā,* n. m. A. صبغ dipped. Dipping; baptism.

A أَصطبل *astab'al',* Pop. *tave'lā,* n. m. A stable.

Gr. أُصطرلاب *usturlāb',* n. f. An astrolabe.

A إِصطلاح *istilāh',* n. f. صلح agreed.

1. A technical term; idiom; usage.

2. The accepted signification; conventional meaning.

istilā'hī, adj. Technical; conventional.

A أَصل *asl',* Pop. *as'al,* n. f.

1. Root (*jaṛ*); origin; foundation (*neo*);

element (*tat*) ; source (*sot*) ; cause (*kāran*); principle ; rudiment ; basis ; seed (*bīj*).

2. Lineage ; genealogy ; family (*kul*) ; stock ; blood ; birth ; breed ; extraction ; race ; line ; descent ; pedigree.

3. The text ; original ; prototype ; exemplar ; the original of a document.

4. Capital ; the principal stock (*mūl*).

asal aur sūd, Principal and interest.

asal tajvīz. The judgment ; sentence ; verdict ; the judgment which follows the summing up of the case.

asal takrār. Material issue ; the actual point in dispute.

asal tanāzā. The actual dispute.

asal jamā. The land rent as originally fixed by the Emperor Akbar ; the original rent or revenue charged upon the lands of an estate, village, or district, without any *Abwāb* or extra cesses. The amount taken as the basis of a revenue settlement. [interest.

asal maë sūd' ; H. *mūl byāj*. Principal with

asal yeh hai, The fact is ; the point is ; the issue is.

dar asal, asal meṅ, adv.

1. Actually ; in fact ; in reality.

2. Absolutely ; positively ; in effect.

اصل *asl* ; Pop. *asal*, adj. [stantial.

1. Essential ; vital ; fundamental ; sub-
2. Substantive ; absolute ; positive.
3. Material ; important ; integral.
4. Principal ; chief ; capital.
5. Legitimate ; born in wedlock.
6. True ; real ; actual ; original.
7. True ; not false ; veracious.
8. Best ; fine ; exquisite ; first rate.
9. Not imaginary ; not ideal. [an alias.

asal nām. Real name as distinguished from *urf*,

asal nafā, Net profit ; clear gain.

asl o fara. Root and branch, cause and effect.

اصالتاً *asālatan'*, adv. Personally ; (appearing or pleading) in person ; himself ; *in propria persona*, in contradistinction to *vakālatan* (pleading by a *vakīl* or barrister).

aslī kharch, Real cost.

aslī kharīd, Prime cost ; real cost.

aslī zamīn, Original land, exclusive of subsequent additions, as from alluvial deposits.

aslī qīmat, Original, or real value or price.

aslī gāoṅ, The original or chief village from which others have branched out, that on which the revenue was originally assessed.

اصلیت *asli'at*, n. f. Genuineness ; originality ; reality (*asl*).

asliat-i-māāmlah. Authenticity of the case ; merits of the case ; truth of the transaction.

اصیل *asīl'*, Mah. n. f. A maid servant, who is a free woman, and therefore superior to the *launḍī* or purchased slave.

A إصلاح *islāh'* ; H. *saṅvār'*, n. f. صلح it became good or right.

1. Correction ; amendment ; revision.
2. The hair on the chin.

A إضافہ *izā'fah* ; Rus. *ijā'phā, jā'phā*, n. m.

1. Addition ; increase ; augmentation (*baṛhotrī*). [accretion.
2. Increment ; adjunct ; the thing added ;
3. Surplus (*bachat*) ; excess.

izāfah beshī, General increase in the rate of assessment. [salary.

izāfah-i-tankhuāh, Ped. n. m. Increase of

izāfah jamā.

1. Additional or extra receipts of various kinds, as from money realized by Government from the sale of presents, or from the sequestration and appropriation of revenue.

2. Money received into the treasury of one district and credited to another.

izāfah kar'nā, v. a. To increase ; enhance ; raise ; augment.

izāfah-i-lagān, Enhancement of rent.

ba-izāfah, In excess of, in addition to.

A إطاعت *itā'at*, n. f. Obedience ; submission ; subordination ; fealty ; allegiance ; loyalty ; homage.

itāat se chārā nahīṅ, albatta itāat karnī paṛegī, be-itāat guzar nahīṅ, Must obey.

itā'at kar'nā, v. a.

1. To keep to ; observe ; obey (instructions) ; comply with ; do one's bidding.

2. To pay homage to ; serve ; submit ; bend to ; bend the knee to ; knock under (*Slang*).

ba-itāat qawāid-i-mazkūr, Under such rules as aforesaid.

A أطراف *atrāf'*, n. m. pl. of *tarf* side.

Limits ; boundaries ; environs ; sides ; skirts ; confines ; districts.

atrāf-i-shahr, n. f. The environs (of a city) ; suburbs ; purlieus.

اطرافی *atrā'fī*, n. f. Trade tax.

atrāfī ravan'nā, n. m. A pass for the transit of dutiable goods beyond the limits of the custom stations. [limits.

kisī atrāf meṅ, adv. In any part ; within any

A أطفال *atfāl'*, n. m. pl. of *tifl* child, Ped. for H. *laṛke*.

Children ; offspring ; family (*aulād*).

atfāl-i-yatīm kī tālīm aur unko rozgār dilāne

ke liye, For the education and instruction of orphan children with a view to their subsequent employment.

A اِطّلاع *ittil'āā*; Rus. *it'lā,* n. f.

Information; notice; knowledge; advice; cognizance; letter of advice; intimation; intelligence; communication.
ittilāā-i-tahrīrī. Notice in writing.
ittilāā-shud likh'nā, ittilāā-yābī likhnā.
To endorse acknowledgment of notice.
ittilā kar'nā, v. a.
1. To refer; direct; acquaint; tell.
2. To apprize; notify; announce; make known; signify; advise; give notice; report; set forth; send word; write to.
ittilā-nāmah, n. m. A written declaration; a summons or citation; a written notice; a notice served on cultivators announcing an enhancement of rent, as a condition of continued occupancy. It has been ruled that this is the only legal form or purpose of an *ittilāā-namāh* under Bengal Regulation (V 1812, ch. 9, 10).
ittilāā-nāmah jārī kar'nā, v. a. To issue or serve a notice; to give notice to appear; to summon.
wāste ittilāā-i-khās o āām. For the information of all; for general information.

A اِطلاق *itlāq',* Ped. n. m.
1. Application; reference.
2. Setting at liberty; divorcing; repudiating; divorce (*talāq*).
3. Office and records of summons, and the fees thereon.
itlāq rakh'nā. To be applicable; correspond [with.
itlāq-navīs, n. m. The officer who keeps the account of the expenses and fees on the issue of summons.
itlāq ho'nā, v. n. To apply. G. G.
alal-itlāq, adv. Absolutely; universally. G. G.

A أطلس *at'las,* n. f. Satin.

A اِطمينان *itmīnān',* n. m. طمان reposing, Ped. for *dil-jamaī.*
1. Tranquillity; quiet; composure (*dhāras*); peace; content (*santokh*); satisfaction; repose; rest (*ārām*). [*nat*).
2. Guarantee; surety; security (*zamā-*
itmīnān-i-khātir ho'nā, G. G. v. n. To be satisfied or assured.
itmīnān kar'nā, v. a. To believe; credit; rely on; feel assured, satisfied.
itmīnān ke lāyaq; Ped. *qābil-i-itmīnān.* Satisfactory; reliable; trustworthy; sure.

itmīnān na kar'nā, v. a. To mistrust; doubt.
itmīnān ho'nā; dil ṭhuknā, v. n. To be satisfied.
hasb-i-itmīnān, To one's satisfaction.
hasb-i-itmīnān-i-ādālat, To the satisfaction of the court
ind-ul-husūl-i-itmīnān, On being satisfied.

A أطوار *atwār',* Ped. for H. *chalan,* n. m. pl. of *taur* way.
1. Behaviour; manners; ways (*ḍhaṅg*).
2. Habits (*bān*); course of life; conduct (*chāl chalan*).
3. Dealings; mode of business.
4. Deportment; manners; bearing; demeanour. [known.

A اِظهار *izhār'*; Rus *ijhār, jhār,* n. m. ظهر made
1. A declaration; statement; disclosure; a declaration in a court of justice or before police officers.
2. Information; communication.
3. The examination or deposition of a witness; deposition; evidence; written testimony; testimony (*gavāhī*).
izhār bābat amar-i-zurūrī mā-behin-nizā.
Statement material to the question at issue.
izhār ba-halaf de'nā, To declare upon oath; to make affidavit.
izhār-i-tahrīrī, n. m. Written testimony; a deposition in writing.
izhār-i-jāiz, A just or lawful declaration or statement.
izhār-half ī, A declaration or deposition on oath; affidavit.
izhār-i-daroġ, A false deposition; false statement or testimony.
izhār de'nā, v. n. To make a deposition; depose; certify; testify; bear testimony; give evidence; bear witness to; witness.
izhār-i-rāē, A communication; an expression of opinion.
izhār rob-rūe-i-ādālat. Judicial declaration; deposition before the court.
izhār zubānī, n. m. Oral testimony.
izhār salāmī, n. m. An illegal fee paid to the deposition writer.
izhār qānūnī, n. m. A statement conformable to law; legal declaration.
izhār kar'nā, v. a.
1. To declare; affirm; assert; protest.
2. To make known; notify.
3. To disclose; reveal; expose.
4. To describe; explain; define.
izhār-i-lā-dāwī, n. m. Denial of claim.
izhār le'nā, v. n. To take a deposition; examine a witness.
izhār-nāmah, n. m. A manifest; a notification.
izhār-nāmah-i-tahrīrī. A declaration in writing.

izhār-navīs, n.m. A deposition writer; an officer of the court who takes down depositions.

A اعانت *eā'nat*, n.f. عون helping. Ped. for مدد.
1. Assistance; help; aid (*madad*). [*bānī*].
2. Patronage; favor; countenance (*mehr*-
eānat-i-ahlkār-i-sarkār, Assistance of public officers. G. G.
eānat ba-mashvara, Abetment by conspiracy.
eānat kar'nā, v. a. To confirm; corroborate; encourage; furnish with means; second; help; aid.
eānat meṅ eānat kar'nā, Abetment of an abetment.

A اعتبار *e*ᵉ*tebār'*; Illit. *itbār*, n. m. عبر faith.
1. Confidence; trust (*partīt*); reliance; belief; faith; credence.
2. Importance; consequence; weight; credibility; credit; authority.
3. Repute; deference; respect; character.
4. Regard; view; influence; relation; consideration; reference; advertence.
etebār rakh'nā,—kar'nā, v. a.
1. To respect; give credit to; believe; trust; rely upon; confide in; make no doubt; reckon; count upon; depend upon.
Phr. To take one's word for; to take one's word.
2. To feel or rest assured, confident, secure. [*etebārā*).
etebār se khārij. Incredible; unreliable (*be*-
etebār kho'nā, v. n. To lose one's credit.
ᵉ*etebār meṅ* ᵉ*khal'al paṛā*, Confidence was shaken.
etebār na kar'nā, v. a. To mistrust; disbelieve; doubt; distrust.
etebā'rī, adj. Pop. *itbā'rū*.
1. Trustworthy; worthy of confidence; reputable; credible.
2. Trusty; confidential; responsible.
apne ōhdeh ke ᵉ*etebār se*, Under color of his office.
mahājnī etbār. Commercial or mercantile credit (*sākh*).

A اعتدال *e*ᵉ*tedāl'*, n. m. عدل being middling.
1. Evenness; temperateness; moderation; medium.
2. Sobriety; frugality; temperance; abstinence (*parhez*).

A اعتراض *e*ᵉ*tirāz'*, n. m. عرض intervening, H. *tar'ak*. Objection; criticism; strictures.
ᵉ*etirāz pizīr'*, Objectional; liable to objection; exceptional; questionable. [jection.
اعتراض ضابطہ *e*ᵉ*tirāz-i-zābita*. A technical ob-
etirāz karnā, v. a.
1. To call in question: object; dispute; make an objection; take exception to; demur to; impugn; put in a plea.
2. To protest against; find fault with; carp; cavil (*nuktā-chīnī k.*); criticise; animadvert upon; remonstrate.
ᵉ*etirāz kunin'dah*, An objector.
ᵉ*etirāz-i-qānū'nī*, A legal objection; an objection in law.
ᵉ*etirāz-i-lā-hā'sil*, Cavil; an idle objection or plea.

A اعتقاد *e*ᵉ*teqād'*; Illit. *itkād'*; H. *nish'che*; Rus. *nah'che*, n. m. عقد being very firm.
Faith; trust; dependence (*etebār*).
eteqād rakh'nā, v. n.
1. To believe in; pin one's faith upon.
2. To rely upon; depend upon; trust in.
eteqād lā'nā,—kar'nā, v. a.
1. To believe (*etebār k.*); have faith in.
2. To be converted (to a creed) (*īmān lānā*).
[straining.

A اعتکاف *e*ᵉ*tekāf'*, n. m. عکف waiting, re-
1. Continuing in the temple or mosque in prayer; retirement (especially at Mecca).
2. Curbing the passions from religious motives (as in lent). [*tyāgnā*.
etekāf meṅ baiṭh'nā, v. n. Ped. for *dunyā*
To sit in a temple or mosque, and abstain from religious motives, from worldly affairs and sensual gratifications; to retire from the world.

A اعتماد *e*ᵉ*temād'*; Illit. *itmād*, n. m. عمد leaning upon. Ped. for H. *partīt*, q. v.
Reliance; dependence (*bharosah*).
etemād rakh'nā,—kar'nā, v. n. To rely, believe; trust; confide.
etemād karā'nā, v. a. To cause to be believed.

A اعلام ᵉ*elām'*, n. m. Communication; *caveat*; a warrant; citation.
اعلام امتناع ᵉ*elām-i-imti'nā*; H. *manāī*, A ban; prohibition; inhibition; interdiction; veto; interdict; proscription.
اعلام بھیجنا ᵉ*elām bhej'nā*, To cite; summon; enjoin.
اعلام نامہ ᵉ*elām-nāmah*, n. m. Summons; injunction; proclamation (اشتہار).

A اعزاز *e*ᵉ*zāz'*; H. *ādar*, n. m. Ped. for *izzat*, q. v.

A أعصاب *ā̂ʿsāb'*; H. *paṭ'ṭhe*, n. m. Tendons; nerves; ligaments; sinews.

A أعضا *ā̂ʿ'zā*; H. *joṛ*, n. m. pl. of *azv* joint.
1. Joints; members; limbs; organs.
2. *Membrum virile.*
āzā-i-tanāsul, n. m. The organs of generation.
āzā-i-raīsa, n. The principal members; vital parts, i. e. heart, brain, and liver.

A إعلان *eʿlān'*, n. m. Ped. for *ishtehār'*, q. v.
Declaration; proclamation; publication.
ʿelān ba-murād'-i-mumā'neāt tajvīz muqaddemah. Caveat.
ʿelān-nāmah, n. m. Proclamation.

A أعلي *ā̂ʿlā*, adj.
1. Greatest; paramount; pre-eminent; highest; supreme; eminent; sublime; most high; most exalted.
2. Principal; chief; maximum.
3. Superior; upper; higher (*ūṅchā*); greater (*baṛā*); major.
ālā darje kā, Of high rank or degree.

A أعمال *ā̂ʿmāl'*; H. *kar'nī*, n. m. pl. of *ǎmal.*
Acts; actions; deeds; doings; achievements.
اعمالنامه *ǎmāl-nāmah*, n. m.
1. Register; registry of conduct.
2. The book in which the good and evil deeds of men are supposed to be recorded.

A أعمام اخيافي *ǎǎmām'-i-aʿkhyāfī.* Paternal uncles by the same mother.

T آغا *ā'ġā*; Illit. *ā'gā*, n. m. *lit.* An elder brother.
A Mugal (generally applied to Mugals coming from Kabul for traffic).

P آغاز *āġāz'*; H. *ād*, n. m. Beginning; commencement (*shurū*).
āgāz se anjām tuk; H. *ād se ant tak*, q.v.
āgāz kar'nā, v. n. To take the first step; to begin (*shurū k.*).
āgāz ho'nā, v. n. To commence; to begin to be (*shurū honā*).

A إغلام *iġ̂lām'*; Pop. H. *lauṅ'ḍe-bāzī, bachche-bāzī*, n. m. Sodomy.
اغلامي *iglā'mī*, n. m. A sodomite (*lauṅḍe-bāz*).

A أغلب *aġ̂'lab*, adv. Superlative of *ġālib.*
Very likely; more or most likely; most probably (*unnīs bisve*).
aglab hai, It is most probable.

A إغماض *iġ̂māz'*, n. m. Connivance; neglect; misprison.
iġmāz kar'nā, v. a.
1. To connive at; wink at.
2. Not to notice; disregard; overlook; forbear; pass over; pass by; make light of.
3. To refrain from; to omit.

A اغوا *iġ̂'wā*, n. m. Solicitation; seduction; instigation.

A إفاقه *ifā'qā*, n. m. Recovery from sickness, or from a swoon, etc. (*softā*).
ifāqā ho'nā, v. n. To be convalescent; to recover from sickness (*ārām honā*).

A آفت *ā̂'fat*, n. f. S. आपद्.
1. Misfortune (*musībat*); disaster; infliction; vicissitude; stroke; scourge; visitation; calamity; catastrophe; misery.
2. Difficulty; hardship; plague.
āfat-i-samā'vī, āfat-i-arzī o samāvī, qahar āsmānī. Calamity by divine permission.

P آفتاب *āftāb'*; H. *sūraj*, n. m. The sun.
āftāb-parast, n. m. A worshipper of the sun.
āftab-parastī, n. f. Worship of the sun.

P آفتابه *āftā'ba*, n. m. An ewer.

P آفتابي *āftābī'*, n. f.
1. A parasol of a particular form.
2. A target studded with gold; a shield made of tortoise-shell.
3. A kind of firework.

P أفتاده *uftā'dah*, adj. اُفتادن to fall.
1. Waste or untilled (land).
uftādah, n. f. Lands culturable but not cultivated.

P أفتان خيزان *uf'tāṅ ʿkhez'āṅ*, adv. Ped. for H. *girte paṛte*, Rising and falling alternately.

A إفترا *iftir'ā*, n. m. Calumny; false imputation; scandal; fiction; slander (*tohmat*).
iftirā kar'nā. To vilify; calumniate; slander; defame; traduce; invent lies (*tohmat lagānā*).

H أفراتفري अफरातफरी *af'rā-taf'rī* Wom.; *aphrā taphrī* Rus. n. f. Cor. of A. افراطتفريط
1. Uproar; tumult; disorder; confusion.
2. Alarm; fright; consternation; panic.
3. Flight (*bhaggī*); retreat; stampede.

A أفراد *afrād'*, n. m. pl. of *fard.*
1. Individuals; souls; persons.
2. Sheets (of paper); separate sheets.

A اِفراط *ifrāt'*, n. f. Ped. for *bauhtāt.*
Excess; superfluity; abundance; plenty.
ifrāt se ho'nā, v n. To abound; teem; to be plentiful.

P اَفزایش *afzā'ish, afzā'yash*, n. f.
Increase; addition (*baṛhotrī*).
افزود *afzūd'*; Mah. Wom. *abzūd'*, n. m. Increase; enlargement; abundance (*bauhtāt*); supernumerary.
afzūṅ' ho'nā, v. n. Ped. for *zyādah honā.*
1. To increase; enlarge (*baṛhnā*).
2. To rise in price (*bhāo chaṛhnā*).
افزوني پيد اوارى *afzū'nī-i-paidāwā'rī.* Increase of yield or produce.

P اَفسر *af'sar*, also a Cor. of E. Officer, Rus. *ap'sar, aph'sar*, n. m. [rity.
1. An officer; one who exercises authority.
2. A superior; official superior.
afsar-i-ālā; H. P. *baṛā afsar*, n. m. Chief authority; the highest officer.
afsar-i-bālā dast, n. m. Superior officer.
afsar-i-parmaṭ, n. m. A Custom's officer.

P اَفسون *af'sūn,—sāzī,—garī*, n. m.
1. Incantation; charm (*mantar*); spell; verses used in enchantment.
2. Fascination; witchery; sorcery; witchcraft; magic (*jādū*); the black art.

Gr اَفسنتين *afsantīn'*, n. f. Wormwood; *Artemisia absinthum*, or the Indian wormwood; *Artemisia Indica.* Wat.

A H اِفشا كرنا *if'shā kar'nā*; H. *kholnā*, v. a.
To divulge; expose; lay bare (*khol denā*).
ifshā-i-rāz, n. m. Disclosure of a secret; detection. [found out.
ifshā honā; H. *khulnā*, v.n. To be discovered,

P اَفشاں *af'shāṅ*, n. f. Poet.
Strips of tinsel pasted on a woman's forehead as ornaments.
afshāṅ ho'nā, v. n. To be sprinkled with (color, spangles, etc.).
afshānī kāgaz, zar afshānī kāgaz, n. m. Paper studded or spangled with gold leaf or dust, used in writing to persons of distinction.
zar-afshāṅ, n. m. Threads of *muqqaish*, or cloth woven with gold and silver thread chipped very fine, or slips of gold pasted with gum on the Koran, and on letters, etc.

A H اِفطار كرنا *iftār' kar'nā*; W. Illit. Mah. *i-khtyār k.*; H. *barat kholnā*, v. a.
To break one's fast in the evening after fasting all day, as the Musalmans do during the month of *Ramzām.*
افطاري *iftā'rī*, Mah. n.f. Things proper to be eaten in breaking a fast.

A اَفعال *afāal'*, n. m. pl. of *fel.* Ped. Actions; conduct; deeds (*karnī*).
afāl nā-munasib, Ped. Improper actions.

A اِفلاس *iflās*; H. *nahot*, n. m. Poverty; penury; want; indigence.

A اَفواج *afwāj'*, n. f. pl. of *fauj*, q. v. [navy.
afwāj-i-tarī,— -i-bahrī, n. f. Naval force;
afwāj-i-jahāzī-i-Hind, The Indian Navy.
afwāj-i-khushkī, Land force; army.

A اَفواه *af'wāh*; H. *awāī*, n. m. Report; rumour.
afwāh uṛā'nā, v. a. To raise or spread a report; blaze or noise abroad.
jhūṭā afwāh, n. m. False report; groundless rumour. [See *aphīm.*

H اَفيم अफ़ीम *afīm'*; Māṛ. *amal*, n. f. S. अहिफेन
afīm kī taīyārī kā kār-khānā. Manufacture of opium.
harkat -khilāf qānūn-i-afyūn. Breach of opium laws.

P آقا *ā'qā*; H. *swā'mī*, n. m. Master; owner; an employer; lord.

Gr اَقاقيا *aqāq'yā*, n. m. Acacia; the expressed juice of the fruit of the Acacia tree, or of the *qalqal.*

A اِقاله *iqā'lā*, n. m. A cancelling or revocation of sale, on condition of furnishing an equivalent for the original price of the article; breaking a contract or engagement.

A اِقبال *iqbāl'*, n. m. قبل admitting. [ment.
1. Admission; confession; acknowledgment.
2. Acceptance (of a bond, bill, etc.); acquiescence; assent (in law).
3. Prestige; prosperity; felicity; good fortune (*bhāg*).
iqbāl dāvā, Confession of judgment; admission of a claim; cognovit.
اقبال دعوے كرنا *iqbāl dāvā kar'nā.* To admit a claim or charge; to confess judgment.
اقبال كامل *iqbāl kāmil.* Full confession.
اقبالمند *iqbāl-mand*, adj.

1. Prosperous; happy; fortunate (*bhāgwān*); felicitous.
2. Lucky; propitious (*subh*).
iqbāl-mandī, n. f. Prosperity; good fortune.

A اِقْتِدار *iqtidār'*, n. m. قدر being powerful or able. Power; authority (*ikhtyār*); legal power; control; might; ability; dignity; rank.
اقتدار جایز *iqtidār-i- jāiz.* Lawful authority.
اقتدار خود اختیار *iqtidār-i-khud-i-khtyār.* Discretionary power.
iqtidār rakh'nā, v. n. To be able, competent, etc.

A اِقتسام *iqtisām'*, n. m. Ped. for H. *baṭāī*, q. v.
اقتسام میراث *iqtisām'-i-mīrās.* n. m. Ped. for *baṭwārā.* Division of inheritance.

A اِقْتصار *iqtisār'*, n. m. See *ikhtisār.*

A اِقْدام *iqdām'*, n. m. A قدم sending on before. Causing to go before; precedence; priority.
اقدام ارتکاب جرم *iqdām-i-irtikāb-i-jurm.* Attempt to commit an offence.
iqdām kar'nā. To attempt; aim at. G. G.
jang karne kā iqdām kar'nā. To attempt to wage war. G. G.
khud-kushī ke irtikāb kā iqdām. Attempt to commit suicide. G. G.
qatl-i-insān mustalzam-i-sazā ke irtikāb kā iqdām. Attempt to commit culpable homicide. G. G.
qatl-i-âmad kā iqdām. Attempt to murder.

A اِقْرار *iqrār'*; Pop. *qarār*, n. m. قر Establishing.
1. Promise; assurance; agreement; pledge.
2. Declaration; assertion; affirmation; confession; avowal; assent; acknowledgment; admission; consent; acceptance; acquiescence.
3. Bargain; compact; contract; settlement; covenant.
4. Receipt; acknowledgment; the notification or avowal of the right of another upon oneself.
اقرار از روی ایمان *iqrār az rūe īmān.* Solemn declaration.
اقرار بحلف *iqrār ba-halaf.* Statement on oath.
اقرار تحریری *iqrār tahrīrī.* A written engagement.
iqrār dān-patr, n. m.
1. A deed of gift.
2. A deed of gift with some reservation or declaration of right in the donor.
اقرار زبانی *iqrār-i-zabānī.* A verbal engagement or agreement.
اقرار عام *iqrār-i-âām.* A public acknowledgment, declaration, or confession; a will; a testament.
اقرار کا مرعی رہنا *iqrār kā marâī rahnā.* To adhere to one's engagement.
iqrār kar'nā, v. a.
1. To promise; engage; pledge (oneself); give a promise; to give, pass, plight one's word.
2. To declare; assert; affirm; profess; affirm solemnly; protest; allege; avouch.
3. To confess; acknowledge; admit; own; allow; grant; yield assent; accede; avow.
4. To engage; to enter on; make or form an engagement; take upon oneself: bind, tie, or pledge oneself; to contract an obligation; to undertake; bargain; agree for; subscribe; settle; stipulate; covenant.
اقرار نامہ *iqrār-nāmah*, n. m.
1. Settlement; compact; indenture; covenant; deed of covenant.
2. Written obligation; engagement; written agreement; deed of agreement; contract; bond.
اقرار نامہ ادائے زر *iqrār-nāmah adā-i-zar.* A pecuniary obligation.
اقرار نامہ اہتمام ترکہ *iqrār-nāmah ehtemām-i-tarkah.* An administration bond.
iqrār-nāmah-i-bandobast, n. m.
1. Administration paper; settlement compact.
2. The engagement entered into with Government by the Mālguzār and coparceners of a village specifying the mode of paying the revenue, how the shares are to be distributed; whether the shares are held in common or in severalty; the number, functions, privileges, etc. of the *Lambardārs*; the items of the Sayer; rights of irrigation, extent and appropriation of waste, and culturable land; and the number, duties, and pay of the village servants. This engagement is to be signed by all the *Lambardārs*, and as many *Paṭṭedārs* as possible, to be attested by the *Paṭwārī* and *Qānūngo*, and finally confirmed by the signature of the Settlement Officer, after being read out before him in open Court in the presence of the subscribing parties.
iqrār-nāmah-i-sālisī, n. m. An arbitration agreement by which the parties bind themselves to abide by the decision of the

arbitrators, to whom the matter in dispute is referred for final settlement.

اقرار نامۂ سپردگي *iqrār-namah-i-supurdgī.*
A deed of hypothecation by which property is assigned over as security for a loan.

اقرار نامۂ صلح *iqrār-nāmah sulah.* Solemn declaration.

اقرار نامۂ کي شرطيں *iqrār-nāmah kī sharteṅ.*
The terms of a contract; provisions of an engagement.

اقراري *iqrā'rī*, adj Promissory; assenting.
iqrārī, n. m. One who assents, confesses, or acknowledges.

اقراري اسامي *iqrārī āsāmī*, n. m. One who confesses judgment; a prisoner who pleads guilty.
jabran iqrār karānā. To extort a confession.

A أقربا *aq'ribā*; Pop. *aq'rubā*, n. m. pl. of *aqrab* nearer, Comp. of *qarīb* near.
Kindred; relations; relatives (*rishtedār*); kinsmen; kinsfolk (*nātī*).

A أقساط *aqsāt'*, n. f. pl. of قسط Instalments.

A أقسام *aqsām'*, n. m. pl. of *qism.* [(*bhāṅt*).
Kinds; sorts; various sorts or kinds
aqsām-i-mufassilah zail, n. m.
1. The following sorts or kinds.
2. The descriptions hereinafter enumerated. G. G.

A أقلِّ درجه *aqall-i-darjah*, n. m. Minimum; the lowest computation; the least quantity (*chhoṭe se chhoṭā*).

A إقليم *iqlīm'*, n. m.
1. Clime; climate; region; country (*des*).
2. Zone; belt of country.

H اک इक *ik*, adj. Used in Comp. for *ek* one.

اکّا इक्का *ik'kā*, n. m.
1. An ear-ring with a single pearl; an armlet or ornament containing perfume, worn on the arm. [single lamp.
2. A candlestick holding one candle; a
3. One-horse vehicle, extensively used by the natives.

اکپيچا इकपेचा *ik-pechā, ik-peṅchā*, n. m.
An ornament for the head. [dominion.
ik-chhat rāj kar'nā, v. a. To hold universal

اکسار इकसार *ik'-sār, ik'-sān, ik'-sūṅ, yak'sān*, adj.
1. Even; level; plane.
2. Equal; co-equal; co-ordinate; on a par with.
3. Similar; same; resembling.

اکلائي इकलाई *ik-lāī*, n. f. A sheet of one breadth only, generally laced. [lace.

اکلڑا इकलड़ा *ik-laṛ'ā*, adj. One-stringed neck-

اکلوتا इकलौता *ik-lau'tā*; Rus. *kalau'tā*, adj. An only son.

H آک आक *āk, ākh, āg* W.; *ak'wan, akau'ṛā.* E.; *āk'ro* Mār.; *madār*, n. m. S. अर्क.
Curled, flowered gigantic swallow-wort, celebrated among native practitioners for its many medicinal qualities; *Calotropis gigantica; Saccharum officinarum.* Wat.

H اِکادسی इकादसी *ikād'sī, ekā'dsī, ikād'shī, ikās'sī, gyā'ras*; Rus. *kād'sī, kās'sī*, n. f. S. एकादशी.
The eleventh day of the lunar fortnight on which the Hindūs generally keep fast.

H آکاربند आकारबंद *ākār'band*, n. m. A statement prepared at the time of the annual settlement, shewing the highest amount of revenue derivable from a village; the quantity of land paying rent or rent free; the sum assessed, and land cultivated during preceding years, the balances due, and instalments by which they are to be discharged; the sums payable to the village officers, and the shares in which the assessment is to be distributed among the occupants of the lands.

H آکاس आकास *ākās,' akās', ak'kās*, n. m. S. आकाश from काश to be visible.
1. The heavens; sky (*āsmān*); firmament. [dus.
2. Ether; the fifth element of the Hin-
akkās-bānī, n. f. A voice from heaven; a revelation; an oracle; Divine call or injunction (*az gaibī āwāz*).
akkās birt,—birti, ajgar birti, n. m. One who has no ostensible means or fixed source of subsistence in the world (A. *mutavakkil*).
akkās-bel, amar-bel, n. f. The air-creeper; *Cuscuta reflexa.* Wat.
akkās-dyā, akkāsī dīvā, n. m. A lamp which the Hindus hang aloft on a bamboo in the month of *Kātak*; a beacon.
akkās-mukhī, n. m. A devotee of the *Shaivā* sect, whose devotion consists in holding his face up to the sun until he is unable to turn it in any other direction.
akkās-nīm, n. m. A plant growing on the *nīm* tree; *Bignonia suberosa.* Wat.

H آکال अकाल *akāl'* E. and Rus.; *kāl*, W. n. m.

H. *a*, priv., *kāl* time, hence untimeliness, unseasonableness.
1. A bad season; a season of scarcity.
2. Drought; scarcity; a general scarcity; dearth.
akāl maut, n. m. Premature death; sudden death; unnatural death (*bin āī maut*).

P اکبری *akbar'ī*, n. f. Relating to Akbar.
A sweetmeat of rice-flour and sugar formed into balls, and after being fried in *ghī*, encrusted with clarified sugar.

E اکتوبر *aktū'bar*, n. m. October.

E اِکت *ik'aṭ*, *ai'kaṭ*, *ek'aṭ*, n. m. An act; law; enactment.

E اکٹنگ *ak'ṭang*, *ik'ṭang*, n. m. Construed by the illiterate as H. *ik* one, *ṭang* leg.
Acting; officiating; in charge.

A اکثر *ak'sar*; Rus. *askar*, adj. Comp. of کثیر [many.
1. Most; many; much; a great many; very many.
2. Frequent; common; usual; current.
aksar, n.m. The greater number, the majority.
aksar,—auqāt; Rus. *askar kar-ke*, adv. Generally; chiefly; commonly; mostly; often; many times; again and again; ever so often; time after time; for the most part; repeatedly; usually; ordinarily.
aksar huā kartā hai. Frequently is the case; it frequently occurs; it often happens.

H اکرا अकरा *ak'rā* E.; *aṛhā'yā* W. n. f. A grass or vetch which grows in the field under the spring crop, twining round the young corn and checking its growth; *Vicia sativa*. Wat. It is also termed *ankari*, and is used as fodder.

H اکرا अकरा *ak'rā*, *akrī*; Brij. *ak'ro*; *mahṅ'gā*, adj. S. अ not, क्री to buy. Dear; costly; high-priced.
ak'rī, W. Rus. n. f. Dearth; days of scarcity; bad season; dearness; high price.

H اکری अकरी *ak'rī* E.; n. m.
1. The funnel on the top of the hollow bamboo tube attached to the plough (*vair'nā*).
2. Uncleaned rice. E.

A اِکسیر *iksīr'*, *aksīr'*; *kīm'yā*, n. f. A powder or mixture pretended to be capable of converting other metals to gold or silver; the philosopher's stone; an elixir; alchemy; a medicine to cure every disease.

A اکل و شرب *akl o shurb*, n. m. Eating and drinking (*khānā pīnā*).

H اکُند अकुन्द *ak'und*, *akundar-attāhā*, n. *Calotropis gigantea*. Wat.

H اُکواں उकवां *uk'wāṅ*, adv. H. *āṅk* measure.
By guess; at a rough estimate or calculation. [Three.

H اِکوائی इकवाई *ikwā'ī*, n. (Brokers' idiom.)

H اکوتا इकौता *ikau'tā* W.; *akautā* E. n. m.
An eruption in the leg.

H اکوٹا अकोटा *akau'ṭā* E.; *dhur'ā* W. n. m.
The cross bar on which the pulley turns.

H اکول अकोल *akol'*, *ako'lā*, n. m. A plant, the oil of which is used in enchantments; *Alangium decapetatum*. Wat.

H اکولا अकोला *ako'lā*, *akol'* E.; *akhau'lā*, *kho'lā*, *agau'la*, *ago'lā*, *agol'* W.; *golā*. Sah. n. m. H. *aglā*, S. अग्र foremost.
The top shoot of the sugarcane plant.

H اِکونا इकौना *ikau'nā*; Rus. Brij. *nikau'nā*, n. m. H. *ek nā* not one. Picked; unmixed; pure. *Ikaunā gehūṅ*.

H اِکونج इकौंज *ikauṅj'*, *ikonj*, n. f. A woman who has borne but one child.

H اکّھا अक्खा *ak'khā*, *ak'kheṅ*, E.; *āṅkhā*, Māṛ. n. m. One of the pair of grain or water-bags of a horse or bullock-load.

H اکھاڑا अखाड़ा *akhā'ṛā*, *akhārā*; W.Rus. and Sah. *khāṛā*, n. m.
1. A place for exercise; any place of assembly; arena; theatre; a court; a place for wrestling or athletics; a gymnasium.
2. A band; assembly; class; party.
3. A sect of Hindu Sādhus, as *Nārāinī akhāṛā*.

H اُکھال उखाल *ukhāl'*, *uchhāl'*, n. The act of vomiting or throwing up; an emetic.
ukhāl' pukhāl',—wakhāl,' Rus. n. m.
Vomiting; cholera morbus.

H آکھت आखत *ā'khat*, n. f.
1. A portion of the crop per plough paid to the village artisans, as the smith, carpenter, etc.
2. See *achchhat*.

H اُکھلي उखली *ukh'lī, ū'khal, o'khal*, E.; *okh'lī*, W.; *okh'ari*, Brij. n. f. S. उलूखलम्, Pr. *okkhalam* A mortar. A wooden or stone mortar for pounding rice or other grain.

H اکھے بڑ अखैबड़ *akhai-bar, akhai birichh*; Bhoj. *achhai-bar*, n. m. S. अक्षय undecaying, वट A species of *Ficus indica* (?), famous in Hindu legend as being undecaying.

H اکھے تیج अखैतीज *akhe-tīj, akhā-tīj, akhai-tīj*, n. m. अक्षय तृतीया. The 18th of *Baisākh* (April-May) when the cultivators settle their accounts for the expenses of the *Rabī*, or spring crop, and the repayment of advances; a Hindu festival.
akhetīj kā bhāo, n. The rate of corn on the day of *akhetīj*, at which rate the cultivator agrees to repay in kind the advances made to him with interest.

H اکیرت अकीरत *akī'rat, ākīr'tī*; Mār. *apkī-rat*, n. f. S. अ not, कीर्ति fame.
1. Defamation; disgrace; obloquy; reproach (*bad-nāmī*).
2. Ill report; bad repute; discredit [(*apmān*).

H آگ आग *āg, ā'gī, ag'an, āg'in, ag'nī, ānch*; Mag. *ag'iyā*; Mār. *bāste*; n. f. S. अग्नि, Pr. and Sah. *ag'gi*.
Fire; flame (*lau*).
āg de'nā, v. a.
1. To set on fire; fire; consume; destroy; annihilate (used by women as a curse).
2. To fire a funeral pile; to perform the funeral rites (of a Hindū).
āg lagā'na, v. a.
To set fire to; set on fire; apply the match to; make a bonfire of.
āg lag'nā, v. n.
To be set, or be on fire; to catch fire.
آگ بوٹ आग बोट *āg-boṭ, ag'an-boṭ*; Ped. *dūd-kash*; Pop. *dhuāṅ-kash*, n. m. A steamer; a steam-boat.
اگیا अगेया *age'yā, agai'yā*, n. f. S. अग्नि H. *āg*, fire. A disease affecting plants, so that the plant seems burnt up (?).
اگیاري अग्यारी *aggyā'rī*, n. f. The sacrificial fire of a Hindu; burning incense, etc. (*hom*).
اگیانا अगयाना *agyā'nā*, v. a. To heat metallic vessels; to purify a vessel by passing it through the fire. Hin.

H اگیتي کھیتي अगेती खेती *agaitī khetī*, n. f. An early crop, in contradistinction to (*pachhaitī* late).

H اگیرا अगैरा *agai'rā*, n. m. The first sheaves of the crop presented to the zamindār.

H اگاسي अगासी *agā'sī*, n. f.
1. A turban.
2. A terrace in front of an upper room.
kaib agā'sī, n. f. *Ṭhagī*. The cry of a kite continued from midnight to early morning, which is held a bad omen.

H اگال उगाल *ugāl'*, n. m. *Ṭhagī*. Old clothes.

H اگالا उगाला *ugā'lā* W.; *lā'hī* E. n. [crops.
1. An insect which attacks standing
2. Land always saturated with moisture.

S آگامي आगामि *āgā'mi*; Bhoj. *ānihār'*, adj.
Coming; about to come; future; what is to come.
ā'gam, n. m.
1. An advance payment.
2. All future possible privileges or profits.

H اُگانا उगाना *ugā'nā*; Brij. *upchānā*, v. a.
Caus. of *ugnā*, q. v.

P آگاہ *āgāh'*, adj.
1. Apprized; advised; aware; acquainted with; knowing; privy to.
2 Informed; versed; conversant.
āgāh kar'nā, v. a. Ped. for H. *jatānā*. [nify.
1. To acquaint; inform; apprize; sig-
2. To report; send word; mention; forewarn.
3. To give notice; make known; notify.
آگاہی *āgā'hī*, n. f. Z. *āgāsī*. Information; knowledge; acquaintance.

H اُگاہنا उगाहना *ugāh'nā*, v. a. See اُگھانا

H اگڑا अगड़ा *ag'ḍā, ag'ṛā*; Tir. *akh'ṛā*, n. m.
An ear of corn or rice which has been blighted and contains no grain.

H آگر आगर *ā'gar, ag'ar, ā'gur, āih'gar*, n. m. S. आकर a mine.
A salt pit; salt work.
āg'rī, agu'rī, agar'yā, aih'grī; E. *nun'yāṅ*; Mār. *khārol*. n. f. A salt manufacturer.

H اگر अगर *ag'ar*, n. m. S. अगुरु the fragrant aloe wood.
Wood of aloes; *Aquilaria ogallochā*. Wat.
agar kī battī, n. f A candle made of aloe wood.
اگروٹا अगरौटा *agrau'ṭā, agar-dān*, n.m. A scent-bottle; a vessel for holding *agar* (perfumes).
اگري अगरै *agraī*, adj. Of the color of *agar*.

P اگر *ag'ar* ; H. *jo*, conj. If; if so be; in case; in the event of.
agar-che, Even if; although; granted; admit that; notwithstanding.

H اگرجانا उगरजाना *ug'ar jā'nā*, v. n. *Ṭhagī*.
To escape from imprisonment.

H اگروالا अगरवाला *ag'ar-wālā, ag'gar-wāl*, n.m.
1. A race of merchants of the *Vaisyā* tribe from *Agrohā*, to the westward of Dehlī.
2. The descendants of *Rājā Agar*.

H اگره उग्रह *ug'rah, ugrahn'*, n. m. Opp. of *grahn* eclipse. The illumination of the sun or moon after an eclipse.

E اگست अगस्त *ag'ast*, n. m. The month of August.

S اگستي अगस्ति *agas'ti*, n. m. [Wat.
1. A tree; *Aeschynomene grandiflora*.
2. The star Canopus; Argo Navis (A. *suhail* ; H. *nāo*).

H آگل आगल *ā'gal* Pop.; *benṭā* W. Rus. n. f. S. अर्गल, Pāli *aggalo*. A bar for fastening a door.

H اگلا अगला *ag'lā, ag'le, ag'lī* ; Rus. *ag'lo, āg'lo*, n. m.
1. The first, or foremost person or thing.
2. A second person; another party.
3. The persons now living; the present generation; contemporaries.
4. Elders; forefathers; ancestors; predecessors.
5. Descendants; posterity; successors.
6. A husband (Wom); consort; wife.
7. A member of the wife's or husband's family.
8. God; the Supreme Being.
9. One side or party in a match, or lawsuit; an opponent; adversary; antagonist.
10. A despot; tyrant; oppressor.
11. The private parts of the body.
12. Opp. of *pichhlā*. Sunset; evening; the time for breaking a fast. Mah.
agle, pro. They; those.
agle pichhle, n. m.
1. Ancestors; elders; predecessors; posterity; offspring; descendants.
2. Preceding and succeeding generations.
اگلاپردہ अगला परदा *aglā par'dā*, n. m. The foremast sail of a ship.
اگلاتهم अगलाथम *aglā tham*, n. The foremast of a ship.
اگلا جنم अगला जनम *aglā janam*, n. m. Hin.
1. Former birth or life.
2. The next world; the future.
aglī pichhlī kar'nī, n. f. The fruits of one's acts in this life, or in a former life according to the Hindu belief in the transmigration of souls.
agle waqtoṅ se, adv. From past times; long ago; from a long time; from time immemorial.
aglī, yā agāū mitī rakh'nā, v. a. To antedate.

S آگم आगम *ā'gam, ag'am* ; Māṛ. *ag'gam*, n. m. S. आ + गम् to come near.
1. Futurity; future life; the next world.
2. A *shāstra*, containing spells and incantations dictated by *Mahādeva*.
3. The East.
āgam bāṅdhnā, v. n. To determine the future; forecast; foretell; prophesy.
agam biddyā, n. f The art or science of foretelling; divination; augury; fortune-telling; prognostication.
agam gyānī, āgam jānī, agāmī, n. m.
A prognosticator; diviner; fore-knower; one who foretells fortunes; a prophet; soothsayer; one versed in the *tantras*.

H اگُن अगुन *ag'un, āg'un*, E.; *saīvrī*, W. n. f.
Grain set apart for the household god.

H اگنا उगना *ug'nā, ub'nā, upaj'nā*, v. n. S. उत् up, गम् to go.
1. To sprout; germinate; grow.
2. To spring; rise; bud; begin; dawn; set in.
اگمن उगमन *ug'man*, Rus; *pū'rab*, Pop.; *mash'raq*, Ped. n. m. The East.

S اگني अग्नि *ag'ni* ; H. *ag'in, ag'an, ā'gī, āg* ; Sah. and Pr. *ag'gī*, n. f. Fire.
agni bān, n. m. Ped. Burning arrows; a rocket; a fiery missile.
agni bāo, n. f. The farcy in horses; an eruptive disease in men and elephants; erysipelas.
agni brāhman; H. *mahā bāhman, burā bāman*, n. m. A *Brāhman* who serves as a priest at the burning of dead bodies.
agni-parikshā, Ordeal by fire as formerly practised by walking through it, or as subsequently practised by dipping the hand into boiling oil, or embracing a red hot pillar of iron.
agni dā'hā, n. f. The ceremony of burning a dead body.
agni-dik, ag'ni-kon, n. f. The south-east quarter of which *Agni* is the regent.
agni sanskār, n. m. The sacrament of fire; the burning of the dead body as an essential rite of the Hindu religion. The com-

pletion of any essential rite by worship with fire. Funeral ceremonies.

agni kiryā, n. Any ceremony with fire, but especially the burning of the dead.

agni-hotrī, n. m.

1. One who performs the ceremony of *Hom ;* a fire-worshiper.

2. A sect of Brahmans.

agni-hom, n. Performance of worship with fire ; offering oblations to fire.

H اگواسی अगवासी *agwā'sī, phālī*, n. The body of the plough-share.

H اگورنا अगोरना *agor'nā* E. ; *rakhwā'lī k.* W. v. a. S. अग्र foremost. [care of.

To watch ; guard ; to look after ; take

اگورا अगोरा *agor'ā*, *agor'yā*, E. ; *rakhwā'lā*, W. n. m. A watchman ; guard ; a man appointed to watch over crops.

H اگھات अघाट *aghāṭ', ughāṭ, aghauṭ'*, n. f.

Land held in perpetuity, and inalienable.

H اگھاڑا अघाड़ा *aghāṛ'ā*, n. m. A plant said to cure the bite of venomous reptiles.

H اُگھانا उघाना *ughā'nā, ugāh'nā*, v. a. S. उत +ग्रह to take up.

1. To gather (rent, tolls, imposts, etc) ; collect ; raise, or net (money) ; scrape together ; raise by subscription.

2. To tax : impose ; levy.

3. To beg, or ask for ; importune.

اُگھائی उघाई *ughāī, ugāī, ugāī patāī* W. ; *ugā'hī, bih'rī* E. n. f.

1. Collections ; proceeds ; produce ; collection of rent or revenue.

2. Dues ; outstandings ; money to be realized.

H اگھن अघन *agh'an, mang'sir*, n. m. S. अग्रहायन, from अग्र before, हायन् year, i. e. the beginning of the year, Old style.

The eighth month of the luni-solar year corresponding with November-December.

اگھنی अघनी *agh'nī*, E. n. f. The produce of that portion of the *Kharīf*, or cold weather crop, which is gathered in the month *Aghan* ; the harvest of the cold season.

agh'nī fasl, n. The cold weather harvest, reaped in Nov. and Dec.

H اُگھنا उघना *ugh'nā*, v. n. To be collected, gathered, raised by subscription.

H اگھورپنتھ अघोर पन्थ *aghor-panth, ghor panth, aghór-panthī*, n. m. *aghor*, a title of Shiv. from S. *a* not, *ghor* fear.

An order of Hindū mendicants who worship Siv. They eat everything, however filthy or unclean, even human carcases ; hence, a gross or filthy feeder ; a dirty-looking man.

H آگے आगे *āge*, adv. Before.

آگے ڈالنا आगे डालना *āgē ḍāl'nā* Hin. v. a.

1. To throw or place before one.

2. To supply a widow with money for her support. (This money is given her by her relations on the death of her husband).

āge se rok'nā, pahle se—, v. a. To stop beforehand ; be beforehand with ; pre-occupy ; prevent ; forestall.

اگوا अगवा *ag'vā, ag'uī, ag'uā*, n. m.

1. One who goes before ; a runner ; a village servant who acts as a guide to travellers ; a guide ; leader.

2. E. One who negotiates a marriage ; a match-maker. [man's skirt.

3. The opening or slit in a Hindū wo-

اگوار अगवार *agwār'* ; Māṛ. *ūrī*, n. m.

The portion of grain set apart for the village servants, like the customary "sharping corn" in England ; the perquisite of the ploughman in kind, rent, etc., paid in advance.

اگواڑے پچھواڑے अगवाड़े पिछवाड़े *agwā'ṛe pichhwā'ṛe, ag'aṛ bag'aṛ* ; Gaṛh. *agā pachhā* ; Māṛ. *agoṛ' pachhoṛ'*, n. m.

1. Neighbourhood (*aṛos paṛos*); vicinage.

2. Persons living in front and rear of a house ; neighbours.

اگونی अगवानी *agvā'nī, agvā'hī, āgvā'ī, agau'nī, agmā'nī*, n. f.

1. Guidance ; direction ; leadership.

2. Guide ; leader ; forerunner.

3. Reception ; welcome ; going or sending forward to meet and receive a visitor with honor (*istiqbāl*).

4. Agent ; attorney ; manager ; secretary.

agvā'nī kar'nā, v. a. To advance to meet the bridegroom, or a visitor on the road ; escort to one's home.

اگور अगौर *agaur', agau'rī*, E. adv. An advance of rent paid by the cultivator to the *Zamīndār* in the months of *Jeṭh* and *Āsāṛh*.

agaur baṭāī, n. f. A division of the crop in predeterminated proportions between landlord and tenant ; a watching and sharing, each party keeping a watch over the fields that none of the crop be fraudulently made away with. [*aggia, Buch.*

H اگیا अगिया *agiyā*, n. m. A bird ; *Alauda*

H آگیا आज्ञा *āg'gyā, aj'gyā*, n. f. S. आ + ज्ञा to command.

1. Order; command; injunction; precept.
2. Provision; direction; instruction; requisition.
3. Leave; license; warrant; permission.
4. An edict; award; decree.
5. Commission; order for goods.

āggyā pāl'nā, v. n. To obey orders (*hukm bajā lānā*).
aggyā de'nā, aggyā kar'nā, v. a.
1. To issue or pass an order; give orders.
2. To permit; allow; admit.
3. To decide; settle; conclude.
4. To instruct; direct; guide.

ag'gyā-kā'rī, adj.
1. Acting according to orders.
2. Obedient; submissive (*tābe-dār*); dutiful.

aggyā meṅ rakh'nā, v. a.
1. To keep under subjection or control.
2. To govern; rule.

āggyā meṅ rah'nā, āggyā mān'nā, v. n. To obey; submit.
aggyā meṅ lā'nā, v. a. To bring under control; subdue; master.
آگیاپتر आज्ञा पत्र *āggyā-patra*; A. P. *hukmnāmah*, n. m. A written order; a warrant or commission; an edict.

H آگیاگھاس अगया घास *ag'yā-ghās*; E.—*khar*; A. *iz̤khar*, n. f. Lemon grass; *Andropogon schœnanthus*. Wat.

H ال अल *al, alh*, n. f. Family name; patronymic.

H آل आल *āl*, n. f.
1. A plant, from the root of which a red dye is prepared; *Morinda citrifolia*. Wat.
2. A green stalk of onion.
3. A pumpkin (*ghīā*).

ālī raṅg, āl kā raṅg, n. m. A colour extracted from the *āl* tree; *Morinda tinctoria*. Wat.

H آل आल *āl*; Tir. *hāl*; Mag. *odā*; Bhoj. *odā*; P. *tarī*, n. f. S. श्रोल, Pālī *allo* wet. Moisture.
ۤلا आला *ālā, gīlā* Pop.; *tar* Ped. adj.
1. Wet; moist; saturated, especially with rain.

A آل *āl, āl aulād*, n. f.
1. Offspring; children; progeny; descendants.
2. Family; house; race; dynasty.

☛ In the original Arabic, *āl* signifies the issue born to the daughter, and *aulād*, the issue of the son.

āl bel, āl o atfāl, n. f. Offspring; children; issue.
āl-i-sultānī, n. m. Dynasty; royal dynasty; royal family.

A ال *al*, The Arabic article answering to *the*.
الامان *al-amān'*. intj. God save us! Heaven preserve me! mercy on us! God forbid!
اَلتَّوَكُّل *al-tavak'kul*, adv. A. علي التوكل resignation to the will of God. On the chance; by guess; at a rough guess; heads or tails.
al-tavaklī, Pop. adj. Conjectural; presumptive; suppositions.
الحال *al-hāl, il-hāl, fil-hāl*, Ped. adv. See *abhī*.
الحق *al-haq*, adv.
1. In truth; assuredly; verily; truly (*sach*); sooth to say.
2. Actually; indeed; no doubt (*be-shak*).

al-haq, intj. O yes! aye! exactly! surely! indeed!
الحمد *al-hamd*, n. f. The first *sūrat* in the Koran.
al-hamd parh-kar phūṅk'nā, v. a. To read the first chapter of the *Qurān* and then blow upon the face of a person to protect him from supernatural influences.
العبد *al-ābd*, n. m. A. ال the, عبد slave. *lit.* the slave, or servant. The signature or initials of a subordinate officer or servant.
القبضُ دليل الملک *al-qabzo dalīl-ul-milk, lit.* Possession is presumptive proof of ownership.
المضاعف *al-muzā'f'*, adj. Twice; double; two-fold (*dūnā*).
الوداع *al-wid'ā'*, n. m. The last Friday in the month of *Ramzān*.
[(*salām*).

A آلات *ālāt'*, n. f. pl. of آلت. Implements; tools; instruments; apparatus.
آلات حرب *ālāt-i-harb*, n. m. Ped. for *hatyār*. Arms. G. G.
آلات زراعت *ālāt-i-zarāāt*, n. m. Ped. for *khetī ke okhar*. Implements of husbandry.
آلات وزن *ālāt-i-vazan*, n. m. Ped. for *bat*. Weights.

H اُلاک उलाक *ulāk'*; Sah. *ulāṅgh'*, n.m. A kind of boat.

H آلان आलान *ālān', alān'*, n. m. S. आलान.
1. The brushwood used for creepers to run on.
2. A chain for binding an elephant to a post.

Z.H. آلاو अलाओ *alā'o, alāv*; Sah. *lāo*; W. Rus. *pūar, pūr*; E. Rus. *adāh, dhinor*, n. m.
A fire; a bonfire; a fire kindled in a pit before the village, and the villagers seated round it with their *hukkās*.

P H اِلایچي इलायची *ilā'echī, ilā'chī*; Rus. and Sah. *lāchī*; Mag. *lāṅchī, rāṅchi*, n. f. S. एला cardamoms.

Cardamoms; *Alpinia cardamomum*. War. [moms.
ilāchī bānṭ'nā, v. a. *lit.* To distribute carda-
☞ A part of the marriage ceremony among Mahomedan women, when cardamoms, betel leaf and sugar, placed in a covered dish, are sent by the hands of a female servant, attended with music, to the female relatives who are invited to the feast.
1. To invite; call; send an invitation to.
2. (Mah. Wom.) To form an attachment or intimacy.
ilāchī bun'dā, ilāchī ḍoṛā, ilāchī kā ḍoḍā, n. m. The capsule or pod of the cardamom.
ilāchī-dā'nā, n. m.
Cardamom coated with sugar; a comfit.
baṛī ilāchī, n. f. A large inferior kind of cardamoms. [cardamoms.
chhoṭī ilāchī, n. f. A small, superior kind of
الاچا इलाचा *ilā'chā*, n. m. Cloth woven of silk and thread to represent cardamoms.

P آلایش *ālā'ish*; Illit. *alāish*, n. f. P. *ālūdan* to besmear.
1. Pollution; contamination.
2. *Pus*; matter; the entrails.

Port. الپین *alpīn'* E.; *ālpīn'* W. n. m. Port. *alfinete*. A pin.

A آلت *ālat'*, *ā'la*, n. f.
1. A tool; an utensil; implement; instrument; apparatus.
2. The running or rigging of a ship.
3. The *penis*; *membrum virile* (*azv-i-tanāsul*).

H التا अलता *al'tā, artā*, E.; *ārat* Tir.; *mahā'vaṛ* W. n. m. S. अलक्त.
Cotton strongly impregnated with lac-dye ready for dyeing, used by *Hindū* women for staining their feet red.

A اِلتماس *iltimās'*, n. m. لمس Praying. A request; petition.

T آلتمغا *altamghā, tamghā*, n. m. T. ال red, تمغا a stamp or impression. [medal.
1. The royal insignia, seal, diploma; a
2. A royal grant under the seal of some of the former native princes of Hindustan, recognised by the British Government as conferring a title to rent-free land in perpetuity, hereditary and transferable.
3. A royal grant in perpetuity, descending to one's posterity.
4. A tax levied on travellers.

H الّتني अल्तनी *alta'nī*, n. f. H. *tanī* string.
The rope round the neck of an elephant, in which the driver puts his feet as in stirrups.

A اِلتوا *iltivā'*, n. m. Ped. for H. *ḍhīl*.
Delay; suspension; adjournment.
iltivā-i-chand rozah. Temporary suspension.
iltivā-i-hukm-i-phānsī, n. m. Reprieve.
iltivā kar'nā, v. a. To defer; delay; postpone; put off.
iltivā-i-nīlām, n. m. Postponement of sale by auction.
mᵉ ariz-i-iltivā meṅ rah'nā, v. n. To remain in abeyance.

H اُلتها उल्था *ul'thā, ulṭā*, n. m. Translation (*tarjumah*); version.

H اُلٹا بھاڑا उलटा भाड़ा *ulṭā bhāṛā*, n. Return hire.

H A اُلٹي سيفي *ulṭī sai'fī*, Mah, n. f. A curse or malediction which falls on the utterer.
☞ The person who pronounces the curse, places a naked sword erect before him, blowing on the sword after every word and sentence. The effect is believed to be the death or ruin of the person so cursed. But if the curse recoils on the person who pronounced it, it is called *ulṭī saifī* (the biter bit). *Saifī* is a form of imprecation against an enemy.
ulṭī taraf. The back; the other side; the reverse.

H اُلٹے کانٹے उलटे कांटे *ulṭe kānṭe*. *lit.* The power arm slightly bent.
Somewhat short weight.
ulṭī kar'nā, v. a. To vomit; cast up.

A اِلحاق *ilhāq'*, n. m. Ped. لحق Joining.
1. Annexation, addition; junction.
2. Fees formerly exacted from the parties to a suit.

A اِلحان *ilhān'*, n. m. A good voice.

T الخالق *alᵏkhā'laq, arᵏkhālaq*, n. f. A coat with sleeves; a surtout, like the *qabā*, with buttons, instead of strings at the neck, breast, and navel.

H الّڑ अल्लड़ *al'laṛ*, adj. See الھڑ.

A اِلزام *ilzām'*; Rus. *ijlām*, n. m. لزم Rendering necessary, fastening (a thing) upon one.
1. Censure; blame; imputation; crimination; recrimination; invective; denunciation; libel.
2. Accusation; charge; indictment; impeachment; arraignment; bill of indictment. [lumny.
3. Reproach; discredit; disgrace; ca-

ilzām dhar'nā, v. a. To impute a fault; find fault with.

ilzām de'nā, ilzām lagānā, v. a. [denounce.
1. To impute; taunt, or brand with;
2. To accuse; criminate; arraign; indict; to fix a charge; inform against; charge; impeach.

H السی अलसी *al'sī*, W.; *tī'sī*, E. n. f. S. अतसी.
Linseed; *Linum usitatissimum*. Wat.
alsī kā tel, n. m. Linseed oil.

H السیٹ अलसेट *alseṭ'*; Sah. *arseṭ*; Mag. *alā'sak*, n. f. S. अलम् abundance, *H. al* much, *saṭ* adhere.
1. Sham; gammon; humbug (*dhāndal*).
2. Deception; fraud; double dealing; duplicity.
3. Unlawful attachment; *liaison*.
4. Difference; discrepancy (in accounts).

A اَلفاظ *alfāz'*; H. *shabd*, n. m. pl. of لفظ. [bles.
Words; articulate sounds; terms; voca-
alfāz-i-maᶜkhsūs-i-ᶜulūm o fanūn. Ped.
1. Technical terms (*istilāh*).
2. Terms of arts. G. G.

A اَلقاب *alqāb'*, n. m. pl. of *laqab*.
1. Titles; honorary titles; patronymic.
2. Forms of address; the titles of a person of rank. Thus, the Governor General is styled *Navāb muallā alqāb* the noble, the *navāb* of lofty titles.
alqāb o ādāb, n. The address of a letter; forms of address (*ādāb o alqāb*).

H الکھ دھاری अलख धारी *alakh-dhārī*, *alakh-nāmī*, n. m. A mendicant who acknowledges no deity but *Brahma*; an *āzād*.

A اللّٰہ *al'lāh*, Mah; *Rām*, Hin. n. m. ال The, اِلٰہ God. The Being who exists necessarily, by himself, comprising all the attributes of perfection. God; the Supreme Being.

Port. الماري *almā'rī*, Port. *almario*; (Fac.) *allah-mārī*, n. f. A chest of drawers; book-case; cabinet.

P اِلماس *ilmās'*, n. m. A diamond; adamant.
ilmās-tarāsh', Ped. for H. *hīrā-kaṭ*, adj.
Cut into facets (as glass, stone, etc.).

A اَلَم نَشرَح *alam nash'rah* (Korān), adj. *lit.* have we not revealed? Well-known; self-evident; manifest; clear.

H النگ अलंग *al'ang, lang*, n. f. Side; way; direction; line; row.

is alang, adv. On this side; this side.

H آلنگ پر ہونا आलंग पर होना *āl'ang par ho'nā*, ——*ānā*, v. n. [woman).
To be in heat (a mare), lustful (a

H آلو आलू *ā'lū*, n. m. S. आलु. An esculent root; potato; *Solanum tuberosum*. Wat.

H اُلّو उल्लू *ul'lū, ulvā, ghuggū, chuᵏgat*; Bhoj. *urūā*; Mag. *urūvā*; P. *būm*. n. m. S. उलूकः. An owl; the great-eared or horned owl; the bird of night.

H اُلّو उल्लू *ul'lū, ulū*, n. m. A tree so called, the natives say, because it is a favourite perch of the owl. *Saccharum cylindricum*. Wat.

P آلوبخارا *ālū-buᵏkhārā*, n. m. [sis. Wat.
Dried plum; prune; *Prunus Bokharien*-

H الوپ अलोप *alop', lop*; Mag. *upah*, adj. S. लुप् to disappear.
1. Unseen; invisible; hidden.
2. Undiscernible; latent; occult.
alop anjan, n. m. A collyrium. When applied to the eyes it is supposed to render the man invisible.
alop' mā'yā, n. f.
1. The mysteries of nature; the imperceptible power in natural phenomena.
2. The latent power of God working in creation.

P آلوچہ *ālū'chā, alūchā*; Sah. *lūchā*. n. m.
A kind of plum; *Prunus ovalifolia*. Wat.

P آلودہ *ālū'dah*, adj. Ped. for H. *lithṛā-huā*.
Spoiled; soiled; besmeared; polluted.

A آلہ *ā'lah*, n. m. [craft.
An instrument; a tool; implement;
ālah-i-hirfat. Implements of trade. G. G.
ālah-i-muhlik. A deadly weapon. G. G.
jhūṭā ālah. A false instrument. G. G.

A اِلہام *ilhām'*, n. m. From لہم Inspiring, infusing into the mind. Divine inspiration, or revelation (*ākās-bānī*).

A اِلٰہی *ilā'hī, allāh'*, n. m. God; Lord.
ilāhī-rāt, Mah; *rat-jag'ā*, n. A night spent in religious service or in singing on any happy occasion, as a marriage, etc; a vigil.
ilāhī san, n. m. An era instituted by Akbar in the 24th year of his reign, when he embraced what he called the *Ilāhī mazhab*

or Divine Religion of *Sulah kul*, Peace with all the world, or religious toleration.

ilāhī gaz, n. m. The standard *gaz*, or yard of 41 inches instituted by Akbar, authoritatively fixed by the British Government at 36 inches.

ilāhī mohar, n. m. *lit.* Divine seal.

A debt, the payment of which is binding in the highest degree; what is owing to a hard creditor.

H اليچنا उलीचना *ulīch'nā, ulachh'nā, ulach'nā*, v. a. See *ubachhnā*.

To empty; drain; exhaust; bale out.

H آم आम *ām, āmb*; Poet. *ambā, ambvā*, n.m. S. आम्र, Pālī. *ambo*, Pr. *ambam*. A mango; fruit of the *Mangifera Indica*.

اماوٹ अमावट *amā'vaṭ, amoṭ'*, E.; *amauṭ*, Tir; *am'ras*, W. n. m. S. आम्रावर्त. The inspissated juice of the mango.

آمراي आमराई *āmrā'ī, ambrā'ī*, n. f. Revenue derived from gardens and mango groves.

آمن आमन *āman*, n. f. A large oval mango.

اموا अमौआ *amaūā*, n. m. A dark green color like that of a mango.

H اما अम्मा *am'mā, am'māṅ, mā, māṅ, māë mātā, mahtārī, maī'yā*; Poet. *māī, māyal*, n. f. S. अम्बा, Pālī. *ammā*, A. ام a mother. Mother; dear mother; mamma.

P آمادگي *āmād'gī*, n. f. *āmādah* prepared.

The state of being prepared; preparation; readiness; preparedness.

—*i-hamlah*, A show of assault; threatening.

—*shar o fisād*,—*daṅgah*, Intention to commit a breach of the peace apprehended.

آماده *āmā'dah*, adj. Prepared; ready.

āmādah kar'nā, v. a. [(*uksānā*.)

1. To incite; rouse; stir up; excite

2. To offer (to do an act); to abet. G.G.

āmādah ho'nā, v. n. To be prepared; to get ready; hold oneself in readiness; be on the alert.

laṛāī ko āmādah ho'nā. To prepare for war.

A إمارت *imā'rat*, n. f. امر He commanded him.

1. A district under the government of an *amīr*.

2. Dominion; authority; rule.

3. Dignity; nobility; stateliness; grandeur.

4. State; magnificence; display; grand living.

A ام الولد *umm ul valad*, n. A female slave who has borne a son to her master, and is therefore by the law, to be emancipated at his death.

A إمام *imām'*, n. m. Patriarch; prelate; chief; spiritual head (of the Mahomedans).

امام باڑا इमाम बाड़ा *imām-bāṛā*, n. m.

1. The place where Mahomedans deposit the *tāziah*, and where offerings are made to the dead.

2. A building in which the festival of the *Moharrum* is celebrated, and service held in commemoration of the deaths of ʿAli and his sons Hasan and Husain.

Sometimes it is used as a mausoleum for the family of the founder.

امام ضامن *imām zāmin*. The protecting *imām* or guardian.

imām zāmin kā rupayā, yā paisā. A piece of coin dedicated to *Imām Zāmin* and fastened on the arm of a person about to leave home, as a protection from evil spirits and the difficulties of the way.

امامي *imām'ī, imām'yā*, adj. Relating to an *imām*.

اماميه *imām'yā*, n. m. An epithet assumed by the followers of *Alī*; a Mahomedan sect; Shiahs, who make *Alī* the rightful *imām* immediately after Mohammad.

H إمام دستہ इमाम दस्ता *imām-das'tā*, Pop; *hamām-dastā, imām-jist'ā*, Illit. n. m. Cor. of P. *hāvan-dasta*. Pestle and mortar.

A أمان *amān', amāṅ*, n. m. امن Being safe or secure.

1. Security; safety; impregnability.

2. Protection; tutelage; refuge; asylum (*panāh*); quarter.

3. Tranquility; peace; quietude; calm.

amān māṅg'nā, v. a. To ask protection from God.

amān meṅ rakh'nā, v. a. To render, or make safe; keep in safety; defend; guard; fence; shield; shelter; secure.

A أمانت *amā'nat*; Rus. & Illit. *anā'mat, anam'mat, aman'nat*; Māṛ. *ināmat*, n. f.

1. Charge; care; trust; guardianship; surety.

2. The thing deposited; anything given in trust; a deposit; money deposited in court (*dharoṛ*).

3. Fidelity; integrity; probity; good faith.

4. Entireness; integrity; *ensemble*.

5. Security; safety; protection.

6. Safe conduct; safe-guard.

7. The office of an *Amīn*.

amānat, adj. See *joṅ kā toṅ*.

amānat bahī, n. f. Goods deposit book.

amānat jārī, Assignments of revenue.

امانت خانه *amānat-khānā*, n. Depositary; depôt; ware-house; store-house.

amānat khānī, n. f. A kind of tobacco chewed, not smoked.

امانت دار *amānat-dār*, n. m. Guardian; custodian; depositary; trustee.

amānat-dārī, n. f.
1. Charge; trust; guardianship; agency.
2. Custody; safe-keeping; deposit.

امانت دفتر *amānat daftar*, n. m. An office under the Mahomedan Government for deposit or for a register of trusts. The superintendant was invested sometimes with judicial powers in civil suits. Reg. XXII. 1795. preamble.

amānat rakhnā, v. a. To deposit; intrust; commit to the care of.

amānat ke taur bhej'nā, G. G. To consign.

amānat-guzār, n. m. A depositary with whom goods are deposited.

amānat men khyānat. Breach of trust. G. G.

امانت نامه *amānat-nāmā*. A deed of trust or deposit; a document conveying any thing.

A اماني *amā'nī*, n. f.
1. Government work in contradistinction to contract work.
2. An estate in charge of a Collector on the part of Government, as distinguished from *ijārah* or that which is farmed.
3. What is held in trust or deposit, applied especially to the collection of the revenue direct from the cultivators by the officers of Government upon the removal or suspension of an intermediate claimant or *zamīndār*, the same as the *khās* collection. It is also applied to *Ryotwārī* settlements, or settlements with each cultivator individually, where no renter or proprietor has been acknowledged; also to the lands in the possession of the Collector's officers for arrears of revenue, or which on any other account, are not held by individual tenants.

H اماوس अमावस *amā'vas, amāvasyā, māvas, māvash*, n. f. अमावास्या from अमा together, वस् to dwell. Pālī, *amāvāsī*, The conjunction of the sun and moon; the first day of the first quarter on which the moon is invisible; the last day of the dark fortnight.

A اُمّت *um'mat*, n. f. A religious sect; people of the same faith; followers; disciples.

chhoṭī ummat. Mixed race; half caste; a low caste.

اُمّتى *um'matī*, n. m. A believer in, or follower of any religious sect.

lā-ummatī, n. m. *lā* not. An unbeliever.

A اِمتحان *imtehān'*; Illit. *imtahān'*; Rus. *nīmtahān'*, n. m. محن Examining.
1. Trial (*parakh*); assay; ordeal; proof; verification; probation; experiment; inspection; review.
2. Inquest; enquiry; inquisition (*pūchh-gachh*); examination (*parīkshā*); test (*jāṅch*); criterion.

imtehān aur tahqīqāt. Examination and trial.

imtehān de'nā, v. a. To go up to an examination.

imtehān kar'nā, v. a.
1. To examine; try; prove; test; investigate; institute, pursue, conduct, carry on, prosecute, an enquiry, etc.
2. To probe; fathom; sound; scrutinize; catechise.
3. To make an experiment, or trial of; subject to trial; experiment; put, bring, or submit to the test or proof; verify.
4. To try one's power (in carnal intercourse).
5. To audit; check.

imtehān le'nā, v. a. To examine; to put through an examination.

imtehān men dar ānā, yā pūrā utar'nā, v. n. To pass an examination.

ibtidāī imtehān. n. Ped. Preliminary examination.

āzmāishī imtehān n. Ped. Trial or test examination.

sālānāh imtehān, sadrī—, Yearly examination.

shash-māhī imtehān. Half-yearly examination.

A اِمتناع *imtinā'ā*, n. m. منع Being prevented.

Ped. for A منع and H. *manāī*, q. v.

A اِمتياز *imtiyāz'*, Ped, for *tamīz*. ماز Being separated.
1. Distinction; difference; discrimination.
2. Discretion; discernment; judgment.

imtiyāz kar'nā, v. a. To discriminate; distinguish (*tamīz k.*).

H امچور अमचूर *amchūr'*, n. m. S. आम्रचूर्ण, H. *ām* mango, *chūrā* piece.
Mango-peel dried in the sun.

P آمد *ā'mad*, n. m. P. آمدن to come. See آمدني.
1. Approach; coming (*ānā*); arrival.

āmad, adj. Opp. of *āwurd* far-fetched, artificial.
1. What comes naturally; natural; spontaneous; not studied or artificial (a composition).
2. Plain; simple; not laboured; idiomatic.

āmad āmad; H. *āwan āwan*, n. f.

The news of one's coming.
āmad dūsre mahekme se, A cause received by transfer, or from another court or office.
āmad o kharch. Receipts and disbursements.
آمدو رفت *āmad o raft*, *āmad o shud*, Ped.; *āmad raft*, Pop. n. m.
1. Coming and going; ingress and egress; communication (*ār jār*).
2. Passage; way; thoroughfare.
3. Intercourse; intercommunication.
āmad o mulāhiza kāgzāt. Access to documents.
āmad-wālā, *āmadyā*, n. m. [come.
1. A rich man; one who has a large in-
2. A merchant who purchases imported goods wholesale.
bālāī-āmad, *ūpar kī āmad*, n.f. Emoluments; perquisites; illegal gratifications.
آمدني *āmda'nī*; Ped. *āmadanī*, *ā'mad*, n. f.
1. Income; incomings; receipts; returns; proceeds; produce; rents; rental; rent-roll; profits; emoluments; finances.
2. Perquisites; commission; fees.
3. Import duties; revenue; collections.
4. Importation; imports; goods imported.
5. The season in which any merchandise generally arrives; the reaping season. [assisting.

A إمداد *imdād'*, n. f. Ped. for *madad*. مد
1. The act of assisting, aiding, or abetting. [in-aid.
2. Donation; gift; endowment; grant-

H امر अमर *a-mar*, adj. S. अ not, मृ to die.
Undying; immortal; everlasting.
امر بيل अमर बेल *a-mar bel*, W; *amar lat'tar*, E; *akkās bel*, q. v. S. अमर immortal, H. *bel* creeper. An epidendron, or parasitical plant similar to the mistletoe.
امر لوک अमर लोक *amar-lok*, *surag-lok*, *baikunth'*; P. *bahisht'*, n. m. Heaven; the region of the immortals or gods; paradise.

A أمر *amr*; Pop. *amar*, n. m. [action.
1. Affair; business; proceeding; trans-
2. Event; occurrence; incident; phenomenon. [cular; thing.
3. Fact; circumstance; case; parti-
4. Point; question; issue; subject; topic; proposition; problem; matter in hand; head. [of title; a point of right.
امر إستحقاق *amr-i-istehqāq*, Ped. A question
amr bāis-i-taklīf-i-ām. A public nuisance.
امرتجويز شده *amr-i-tajvīz-shuda*. *Res judicata*.
امرتجويز طلب *amr-i-tajvīz talab*, — *tasfīyāh talab*, — *tanqīh-talab*, — *tanāza*.

A point to be determined or decided; the matter for adjudication; the point under litigation; the issue to be tried; the question or point at issue; the issue; the question; the question for decision; the matter in question; a moot point.
amr tanqīh-talab qāyam kar'nā. To frame, or lay down an issue for trial.
amr tanqīh-talab kī tajvīz. The finding on an issue; the judgment.
amr tanqīh-talab kī tajvīz kar'nā. To find on an issue.
amr tanqīh-talab maqbūla farīqain, An issue framed by the agreement of the parties.
امرتمهيدي *amr-i-tamhīdī*. Preliminary or introductory matter. [(of a suit).
امر خرچه *amr kharchah*. A question of costs
امر خطير *amr khatīr*, *amr haulnāk*. A dangerous affair.
امر ضروري *amr zurūrī*, An urgent business.
امر عمده *amr-i-ūmdah*, A material fact.
امر غير متعلقه *amr-i-gair mutālliqā*, An irrelevant point, or matter.
امر قابل لحاظ *amr qābil lihāz*, A point deserving consideration.
امر قانوني *amr qānūnī*; *amr mutālliq qānūn*, A point of law.
امر قبضه *amr qabzā*, A question of possession.
امر مابه النزاع *amr mā-bih-in-nizāā*, A disputed point, or fact; the point at issue.
amr-i-mutnāzā-fīh; *amr nizā*, A point at issue; the point. [red to.
امرمستفسره *amr-i-mustafsira*, The point refer-
امرمشتبه *amr-i-mushtabah*, Matter in question. G. G.
amr-i-mashkūk-fīh, A doubtful point.
امر نازک *amr-i-nāzuk*, A nice question; a delicate matter.
امرواقعات *amr-i-wāqeāt*, A point of fact.
امرواقعي *amr-wāqāī*, The fact; the real fact. G. G.
امروجوبي *amr-i-wajūbī*, Ped. An obligation.
امروراثت *amr-i-wirāsat*, A question of heirship.
امرو نهي *amr o nihī*, n. m. Commands and prohibitions; orders and counter orders.

A أمرا *umarā'*, Ped; Illit. *amīr' umrā'*; Rus. *umrāo*, n. m. pl. of *amīr*.
1. Nobles; noblemen; peers; grandees.
2. The nobles of an Indian Mahomedan court collectively.

H امرا अमरा *am'rā*, *amrā*, n. m.

A hog-plum ; *Spondias mangiferā.* Wat.

H امرتبان अमृतबान *amratbān', imratbān* ; Pop. *martbān* ; Tir. *mrichmān* ; Sah. *miratbān*, n. m.
1. E. A variety of the *kelā* or plantain; *Musa sapientum*, or *paradisiaca.* Wat.
2. A glazed or Chinā jar. [n. f.

H اِمرتي इमरती *im'ratī, amir'tī* ; Pop. *imar'tī*,
1. A small brass vessel for drinking out of.
2. A kind of sweetmeat made of pulse.
3. A kind of small and sweet melon. (Bundelkund).

P H امرود *amrūd,' amrūt* ; T. *murūd*, n. m. The guava ; *Pyrus communis.* Wat.

H امريان अमरैयां *amraī'yān*, n. f. आमराजि from आम, राजि a row, H. *ām* mango. Mango groves.

A اِمساك *imsāk'*, n. f. مسک Keeping back. A nostrum taken to retard the discharge of *semen.*
imsāk-i-bārān, Ped. for H. *sūkhā*, n. m. Want of rain; drought; scarcity; famine.

P اِمسال *im'sāl* ; H. *is baras*, n. m. This year.

H آملا आमला *ām'lā, āṅolā, āṅorā* ; Tir. *oṅrā*, n. m. S. आमलक See *āṅolā.*

A اِملاك *imlāk'*, n. f. A. ملک Putting in possession.
Possession ; property ; lands ; houses.
imlāk gair-manqūlā. Real or immovable property. [perty.
imlāk manqūlā. Personal or movable pro-

H أمل پاني अमल पानी *a'mal pā'nī, aml-i-jins*, n. m. Intoxicating drinks or drugs ; spirits ; strong drinks.
amal pānī kar'nā, yā jamānā, v. n. To take down, drink, or smoke any intoxicating drug; to liquor up ; have a peg.

H املتاس अमलतास *amaltās'* ; Sah. *ambaltās* ; Māṛ. *kirmālo* ; Ped. *magz-i-fulūs*, n. m. *Cathartocarpus fistula.* Wat. used as a purgative.

H اِملی इमली *im'lī, im'blī, am'blī* ; Brij. *am'rī* ; Māṛ. *ām'lī* ; P. *tam'ar hindī*, n. f. S. अम्लिका from अम्ल sour. Tamarind ; *Tamarindus Indica.* Wat.

H آمن आमन *ā'man, ā'man dhān*, n. m.
The winter rice crop, sown in July and August, and reaped in December.
آمنيا आमन्या *āman'yā, amanyā*, n. f.
1. The land on which the winter crop of rice is sown.
2. Picked or unmixed grain, etc.
āman'yā kar'nā, v. n. To pick ; sift ; clean ; clarify ; filter. [rity; safety.

A أمن *a'man*, n. m. See *amān* (2, 3.). Secu-
uman-chain, Mah. Wom. ; *zalzalā* Ped. ; *hālan-ḍolan.* Rus. n. m. Earthquake (*bhoṅchāl*).
aman meṅ rakhnā, v. n. To preserve ; keep in safety, peace, comfort, security, etc.
amn o āmān, aman-āmān, aman chain, n. m. Peace and tranquility.

A أموات *amwāt'.* n. f. pl. of *maut* death.
naqsha-i-amwāt. Register of deaths; obituary.

A أمور *umūr', amūr', umūrāt*, n. m. pl. of امر.
1. Affairs ; matters ; things.
2. Articles ; items. [lar concerns.
umūr-i-dunyavī', n. m. Worldly affairs ; secu-

P أميد *umed', umīd*, Ped. ; *ummaid', ummed*, Pop. n. f. H. *ās* q. v.
ummed par hāzir ho'nā, v. n. To be present in anticipation of.
ummed thī. It was expected.
ummed dilwā'nā, ummed dilā'nā. v. a. To give or inspire hope; raise expectations; promise ; assure ; encourage ; buoy up.
ummed rakh'nā, v. n. See *ās rakhnā.*
أميدوار *ummed-wār*, n. m.
1. An expectant ; applicant ; a candidate ; suppliant ; petitioner ; supplicant ; suitor. [tioner.
2. A dependent; hanger-on ; a proba-
ummed-wār, adj. Hopeful ; hoping ; expectant.
ummed-wār honā, v. n.
1. To apply for a post ; to be a candidate.
2. To serve as an apprentice or probationer.
أميدواري *ummed-wārī*, n. f. Expectation; expectancy ; hope ; hopefulness.
ummed o bīm, Ped. for H. *ās nirās*, Hope and fear ; suspense (*dubdhā.*)
roz-i-ummed o bīm, n. m. The day of resurrection or judgment.

A أمير *amīr'*, n. m. امر Commanded.
1. A nobleman ; peer ; lord ; chief ; prince ; ruler ; governor.
2. A person of rank or distinction.
3. A liberal, open-handed, or large-hearted person ; a gentleman. [nobles.
amīr-ul-umarā, amīr kabīr, n. m. Chief of the
amīr-ul-bahar n. m. An admiral.
amīr-zāda, n. m. *amīr-zādī*, n. f.
1. One of noble birth or family.

2. A king's son or daughter; prince or princess. [able or rich house.
potroṅ kā amīr, n. One of an ancient, honor-
امیرانہ *amīrā'nā*, adj.
1. Noble; princely; imperial. [grand.
2. August; majestic; stately; dignified;
امیري *amī'rī*; Illit. *umrā'ī*, n. f. [ship.
1. The dignity or office of an *amīr*; lord-
2. Nobility; dignity; greatness; grandeur.
amīrī kār-khānā, amīrī ṭhāṭ, n. f. A princely establishment; luxury.
amīrī kar'nā, v. n. To exercise authority; enjoy a competency; live well; live like a prince.
amīrī meṅ aish kar'nā, v. a. To live in aristocratic or luxurious ease or idleness; to neglect one's affairs; to let one's affairs go to rack and ruin.

A أمين *amīn'*, n. m. أمن Secure, safe. See *amānāt-dār*.
1. An investigator; arbitrator; umpire.
2. A law officer; an inspector; superintendent.
3. An officer appointed to make rough surveys after the native method.
4. A native officer of Government, employed either in the revenue department to take charge of an estate and collect the revenues on account of Government, or to investigate and report their amount; or, in the judicial department, as a judge and arbitrator in civil causes.
amīn-i-hisāb, n. m. An auditor of accounts.
amīn mahekmah dīvānī. An amin of the civil court.
qurq-amīn, n. m. An officer of a judicial court in charge of confiscated property.
امینی *amī'nī*, n. f.
1. Commission; deputation; delegation.
2. The office of an *amīn*.
3. Custody; guardianship; trust.

H ان अन *an*, A negative prefix equivalent to our Eng. *in* and *un*, S. अ (not), which becomes *an* before a vowel.
أنبن अनबन *an-ban*, n. m. [standing.
1. Disagreement; difference; misunder-
2. Jar; quarrel; dissension; variance.
3. Wrangling; squabbles; disputes; tiffs.
4. Dislike; hatred; enmity (*bair*).
an-biṅ'dhā motī; P. *dur-i-nā-sufta*, n.
A pearl without a hole.
ان بویا अनबोया *an-boyā, bin-boyā, rānā*; P. *khud-rau*, adj. S. वप to sow. Unsown; spontaneous; wild; uncultivated. [adj.
أنپڑھ अनपढ़ *an-paṛh, ku-paḍh*; P. *nā-khuāṅda*, Illiterate; unlettered; uneducated. [(soil).
انجاما अनजामा *an-jāmā, banjar*, adj. Barren

انجان अनजान *an-jān', a-jān'*, n. m. See اجنبي
an-jān ban'nā, jān-ke an-jān ban'nā, v. n.
To feign or affect ignorance; pretend not to know.
an-jān meṅ, an-jāne; P. H. *nādānī se*, adv. Ignorantly; unknowingly; unconsciously; unawares; unintentionally.
انرتھ अनर्थ *a'narth, an-arth'*; Mag. *anrath*, adj. S. अ not, अर्थ object.
1. Meaningless; absurd; nonsensical.
2. Vain; useless; abortive (*akārath*).
an-arth, n. m.
1. Sin; transgression; trespass; guilt.
2. Ill-treatment; oppression; tyranny.
an-arth kar'nā, v. a.
1. To hurt; injure; oppress.
2. To do wrong or evil (*burā k.* 1.)
3. To commit a sin; to sin.
انرتھي अनर्थी *an-arthī*, n. m. [oppressor.
1. A cruel, hard-hearted person; an
2. An evil-doer; a mischief maker.
3. A sinner; transgressor.
انریت अनरीत *an-rīt, ku-rīt*, adj. [practice.
1. Contrary to custom, rule, usage or
2. Contrary to good manners or etiquette; unmannerly; ill-behaved.
أنسمجھ अनसमझ *an-samajh, be-samajh*, adj. See. *abudh*.
انگنا अनगिना *an-gin'ā, angin'at, an-gan'it, be-gin'at, be-gintī*; P. *be-shumār'*, adj. S. अगणित.
1. Countless; numberless; unnumbered; without number; innumerable; untold; incalculable. [boundless.
2. Immeasurable; beyond measure;
an-ginā baras; n. m. Wom. *lit.* The unreckoned year. The eighth year of one's age.
☞ The number eight is considered an unlucky number because, they say, that an eighth month's child seldom lives. Hence the eight month or year is so called.
an-ginā mahīnā, n. m. Wom. *lit.* The unreckoned month. The eighth month of pregnancy.

اننت अनन्त *an-ant*, adj. Endless; infinite; eternal.
an-ant, n. m.
1. An epithet of Vishnu.
2. A cord with fourteen knots, which the Hindus tie on the right arm on the fourteenth day of *Bhādoṅ Sudī*, which is sacred to Vishnu and called *an-ant-chaudas*.
an-ant-chaudas, n. f. The fourteenth day of *Bhādoṅ Sudī* when a festival is held in honor of "the eternal" Vishnu, and also of the *Jain* god.

انہوت अनहोत *an-hot, na-hot, an-hotā,* n. f.
Want; indigence; poverty.

انہوني अनहोनी *an-honī, an-hotī,* n. f.
What never happens; an impossibility.

انّیاو अन्याओ *an-nyā'o, an-nyāv,* n. m. S. अ not, न्याय justice.
Wrong; injustice *(be-insāfī)*; iniquity.

انّیای अन्याई *an-nyāī,* adj.
1. Unjust *(be-insāf)*; unfair; inequitable.
2. Unfeeling; hard-hearted *(kaṭhor)*; cruel.
3. Tyrannical; oppressive.
4. Vicious; wicked; sinful; unprincipled; unrighteous; very bad.
5. Foul; gross; vile.
6. Flagrant; flagitious; villainous.
7. Felonious; nefarious; heinous.
8. Impious; profane; sacrilegious.

H ان अन *an, ann,* n. m. S. अन्न from अद् to eat.
1. Grain; corn; bread; food.
2. Sustenance; nourishment; nutriment; subsistence.

انپراسن अनप्राशन *an-prāsan,* Hin.; *khīr chaṭānā,* Mah. n. m. S. अन्नप्राशन from अन्न food, प्र before, अश to eat. The first feeding of a child with grain food.

ان پورنا अनपूरना *an-pūr'nā,* n. f.
The Ceres of the Hindūs; the goddess [of corn.

ان جل अन जल *an jal, an pān, an pānī* n. m.
Food and drink. See *āb dānā.*

an-jal pān kar'nā, v. n. To eat; dine; take one's food.

an-dā'tā, an-dā'yak, n. m.
1. Supporter; cherisher; benefactor; [employer.
2. Lord; master; patron.

an-dhan, n. m. Food and wealth; corn and cattle; competency; easy circumstances.

ان کٹ अनकुट *an-kuṭ* n. m. S. अन्न food, कूट heap.
A festival celebrated by Hindus, in commemoration of Krishna's sacrifice, on the day following the Divālī.

☞ It consists in offering up at a temple dedicated to Vishnu, a large mess composed of every variety of cooked grain, vegetables, etc. A pinch of this mess is given by the *pujārī* or temple priest to each worshipper who finds in it some one article of food from which he or she had religiously abstained for a certain period in fulfilment of a vow made for the sake of some such blessing as the removal of barrenness, etc.

H آن आन *ān,* n. f.
1. Desire; wish; craving.
2. An avowed refusal or denial; abjuration; renunciation; prohibition.

ān toṛ'nā, v. a.
1. To break one's promise, vow or oath.
2. To infringe against a lawful, or established rule or custom.

H اَن अन *an*; Bhoj. and Tir. *ān*; Old H. *ani*; Mag. *ankā*; Rus. *ankā, ankar,* pro. S. अन्य others. Another's; of another.

آنا دیس आनादेस *ānā-des,* n. m. Another country; a foreign land.

آنا دیسي आनादेसी *ānā-desī,* n. m. One of another country; a foreigner; stranger.

H آنا आना *ā'nā,* v. n. To come.

آتا आता *ā'tā,* n. m.
Dues; arrears; bills receivable; unrealized assets.

آون आवन *ā'van,* n. The field into which rice has been transplanted.

āī kar'nā, āē k. v. a.
1. To admit; accept; agree to *(mān* [*lenā).*
2. To take upon oneself; to be responsible for *(oṭnā).*

آیا گیا आया गया *āyā gayā* n. m. Plu. *āē gaē. lit.* he came, he went. One who has come and gone; a traveller who alights at a house; a chance or unexpected guest.

āē gaē honā, v. n.
1. To lose; forfeit.
2. To be got rid of, settled.

H انّا अन्ना *an'nā,* Mah.; *dhāē,* Hin. n. f. T. *anā* a mother; H. *an* food. (?). A wet nurse.

H اناتھ अनाथ *a-nāth',* adj. S. अ not, नाथ् to be master. Without a master, chief, husband.

a-nāthī banjar, n. m. Uncultivated land without an owner; unclaimed waste.

H اناج अनाज *anāj', nāj, an,* n. m. S. अन्न grain.
Grain; corn; provision; food.

H اناد अनाद *anād',* adj. S. अ not, आदि beginning.
Having no beginning; immemorial.

anād banjar. Land that has been waste from time immemorial.

P انار *anār';* Māṛ. *dāṛim;* Gaṛh. *dāṛmī,* n. m.
1. A pomegranate; *Punica granatum.* Wat.
2. A kind of firework.

انار دانہ *anār-dānā,* n. m.
1. Pomegranate seed, used in *pāchak* [(a digestive).
2. A species of millet, so called from its resemblance to the pomegranate seed.
3. A red checked cloth, worn by women.

H انت अन्त *ant,* adj. from S. अन्त् to bind.
Final; ultimate; last.

انت بھاگ अन्तभाग *ant-bhāg,* n. m. The last portion.

This term is often applied to the New Testament as distinguished from the Old (*ādi-bhāg*).

H آنت आंत *āṅt, aṅtṛī*, n. f. S. अन्त्र. [*viscera*.
Entrails; bowels; guts; intestines;
āṅt kā baṛh ānā. *Hernia*; a rapture.

A اِنتخاب *inte-khāb'*, n. m. نخب selecting.
1. Selection; choice; election.
2. Extraction; extract; compilation.
intekhāb' kar'nā; v. a. Ped. for H. *chunnā*.
1. To select; choose; elect.
2. To extract; compile. [give.

H انتر अन्तर *an'tar*, n. m. S. अन्त limit, रा to
انتر بيد अन्तर बेद *antar-bed*; P. *duāb*, n. m.
A part of the country lying between two rivers, as the Duāb, Mesopotamia.
antar-paṭ, n. m. A curtain placed between the bride and bridegroom.
انتر جامي अन्तर जामी *antar-jāmī*,—*gyānī*, n. m. *lit.* heart-searching. Pervading the inward parts; acquainted with the heart (the Deity); an epithet of *Vishnu*.

A اِنتظار *intezār'*; Illit. *intizārī*; n. نظر Seeing, looking for. [expectancy.
Looking out; prospect; expectation;
intezār karnā,—*kheṅch'nā*,—*dekhnā*, v. a.
To look out for; wait impatiently for; look forward; expect; count or build upon; anticipate; contemplate; reckon.
isdār-i-hukm kā intizār kar'nā.
To await orders.
bilā intizār-i-varūd-i-asal vasīyat-nāma. G. G.
Without waiting for the arrival of the original will.

A اِنتظام *intezām'*, n. m. نظم strung in a line.
1. Arrangement; adjustment; organization; regulation. [conduct.
2. Management; disposition; method;
3. Plan; measures; scheme; contrivance.
4. Form of government or administration; constitution; polity; policy; economy; system.
5. Order; discipline; regularity.
intizām-i-jadīd, New practice; fresh arrangement; new settlement. [rangement.
intizām-i-khāngī, A domestic or private ar-
intizām rakhnā, v. a. To keep order; maintain discipline; uphold authority.
intizām kar'nā, v. a.
1. To arrange; make arrangements; provide for or against; organize; adjust; regulate.
2. To manage; direct; conduct; carry on.
3. To plan; devise; design; contrive (*tadbīr k.*).
ba-murād durustī-i-intizām-i-faujdārī. For regulatiug Criminal Procedure.
[able.

A اِنتفاع *intifā'ā*, n.m. Ped. for نفع being profit-
Deriving advantage; profit; gain.
intifā'ā-i-hissa, Ped for H. *ans-lābh*.
Income of shares (in a bank, etc.) G. G.
intifā'ā-i-sarmāyā, Ped. for H. *mūl lābh*.
Produce of funds. G. G.
sūd yā intifāā-i-sarmāyā, H. *mūl biyāj*.
Interest or produce of funds. G. G.

A انتقاض شرط *intiqāz-i-shart*. Breach of the terms (of a contract).
intiqāz-i-muāāhadah, Breach of contract.

A اِنتقال *intiqāl'*, n. m. نقل being transported.
1. Transference; transposition; transmission; passage; transit; transport; transportation; migration.
2. Deportation; extradition. [tion.
3. Removal; translation; transmigra-
4. Passing from one to another; transfer; conveyance; assignment; alienation.
5. Death; decease; extinction (H. *antkāl*).
intiqāl arāzī maqbūzā-i-mushtaraka.
Transfor of land held in common.
intiqāl az daryāē shor, Transportation beyond seas. [property.
اِنتقال جائيداد *intiqāl-i-jāēdād*. A transfer of
اِنتقال جايز *intiqāl-i-jāiz*. A legal or valid transfer or conveyance.
intiqāl-i-chaṅd rozah. Temporary conveyance.
اِنتقال حق *intiqāl-i-haq*, Assignment of title to another; transfer of a right.
اِنتقال خانگي *intiqāl-i-khāngī*, A private transfer or conveyance. [perpetuity.
اِنتقال دايمي *intiqāl-i-dāimī*, A transfer in
اِنتقال درمياني *intiqāl-i-darmyānī*, An intermediate conveyance. [mortgage.
اِنتقال رهن *intiqāl-i-rahn*, An alienation by
intiqāl-i-sāzishī, *yā farebī*, A collusive or fraudulent transfer.
intiqāl kar'nā, v. a.
1. To transmit; transport; convey; remove; transpose (*le jānā*). [dorse.
2. To transfer; convey; assign; en-
3. To sell; vend; dispose of (*bechnā*).
4. To depart; quit; leave (*chhoṛnā*).
intiqāl k.,—v. n. To die; expire (*marnā*).
انتقال كننده *intiqāl-kunindah*. An alienor; one who conveys. [feree; alienee.
انتقال گيرنده *intiqāl-gīrindah*,—*dār*, Trans-
انتقال مقدمه *intiqāl muqadmā*. Transfer of a case to another court.

intiqāl-i-makān, Ped. for H. *jagah badal.* Change of place or house.
intiqāl mulk ġair. Transfer or removal to another or foreign country; migration.
انتقال ميعادي *intiqāl-i-mīād'dī.* A transfer for a term of years. [fer or conveyance.
انتقال ناجايز *intiqāl nā-jāiz.* An illegal trans-
انتقال نامه *intiqāl-nāmah.* Deed of transfer or conveyance. [of liabilities.
intiqāl-nāmah-i-zimmah-dārī, yā dain. Deed
تحرير انتقال *tah'rīr-i-intiqāl*; H. *sakārā.* Endorsement on a bill.
حكمي انتقال *hukmī intiqāl.* Enforced transfer.
انتقالي *intiqā'lī.* A transfer of *zamīndārī*, or other revenue property from one person to another; the property so transferred.
انتقالي بهي *intiqālī bahī.* Register of transfers of property.
intiqālī rasūm'. Fees for entering a transfer of property in the official register.

A إنتقام *intiqām'* n. m. نقم taking vengeance. Revenge; retaliation; reprisal (*badlā*).
intiqām lenā, v. a. To revenge (one's self); retaliate; make reprisals (*badlā lenā*).

A إنتها *intihā'*, n. f. نهي coming to an end.
1. The utmost point or extent; the extremity.
2. Completion; termination; end.

H انتي अन्टी *an'ṭī*, n. f.
1. The interval or junction between the fingers.
2. A reel, or frame on which thread, etc. is wound; a hank or bundle of thread.
3. Pilfering; unlawful abstraction; misappropriation.
anṭī mār'nā, yā kar'nā. v. n.
1. To hide a *kauṛī* between the fingers, chiefly in gambling.
2. To pilfer; purloin; prig (*slang*).

H آنتي आंटी *āṅ'ṭī, an'ṭī*, n. f. from H. *āṅṭ* knot.
1. E. A bundle (of grass, wood, etc.); a skein of thread (*aṭṭī*).
2. A knot or loop serving as a pocket.
3. The leg trick.

H انج अनुज *an'uj*; adj. S. अनु after, जन् to be born. A younger brother; junior.

P انجام *anjām'*, Z. *antām*; S. *antima*, n. m.
1. The end. See. آخر.
2. Result; conclusion; upshot.
anjām-i-khidmat. Performance of duties or services.
anjām-dihī. Ped. Discharge; completion; execution; performance. G. G.
anjām-dihī jāiz. Lawful discharge. G. G.
anjām de'nā,—kar'nā,—ko pauṅhchā'nā, v.a. To discharge; act up to; comply with; conduct; manage.
anjām-kār, adv. Lastly; at last; finally.
anjām-kārī. n. f. Completion; accomplishment; execution; fulfilment; performance.
anjām honā, v. n. To come or draw to an end; cease; run its course; pass away; stop; ensue.

P انجبار *anjubār'*; *anjabār'*, *injibār*, n. m. A plant from which a drink is prepared for obstinate colds, or spitting blood; *Polygonum bistorta.* Wat.

H انجلا अंजला *aṅj'lā, uṅjlā, aṅjlī, anjal, unjal, anjul, anjurī*, n. S. अञ्जलि.
1. The hollow formed by joining together the palms of both the hands so as to hold grain, water, etc.; the junction of the two hands in the shape of a boat.
2. Something given to Brahmins over the stipulated or customary payments at a wedding.

P أنجمن *anjuman'*; H. *sabhā*; E. *sosāiṭī*, n. f. An assembly; meeting; society; institution.

H انجن अञ्जन *an'jan, anjnā*, n. f. A grass which grows in the North-West Provinces abundantly and is used as fodder; *Memecylon tinctorum.* Wat. [engine.

E انجن *an'jan, in'jan*, n. m. Engine; steam-

H انجن अञ्जन *an'jan, āṅ'jan*, n. m. S. अञ्ज् to beautify or anoint.
A collyrium; a black powder or ointment applied to the eyes to make them look languid and brighter—also used for weak sight or a pain in the eye.

H انجنا अंजना *aṅj'nā, anjnā*, n. m. A coarse kind of rice.

H انجنهاري अनजनहारी *anjanhā'rī*, n. f.
1. A sty in the eye (*guṅhāṅjnī*).
2. An insect (*kumhārī*).

H آنجهنا आंझना *āṅjh'nā*, v. n. *Ṭhagī.* To pass the night in any place.

H P انجير *anjīr', injīr*, n.m. A fig; *Ficus carica.*

Gr. انجيل *injīl', anjīl'*, n. f. The New Testament; the Gospel.

E انچ इञ्च *inch*, n. m. An inch.

H آنچو आंचू *āṅ'chū, anchhu, āch'chu,* n. m.
The raspberry; *Rubus, sp?* Wat.
kālā āṅchū, The hill bramble; *Rubus vellosissimus.* Wat.

A انحراف *inhirāf',* n. m. حرف turning, turning away.
1. Deviation; deflection.
2. Breach; violation; infringement; infraction.
3. Disobedience; insubordination; contumacy.
4. Mutiny; rebellion; insurrection; revolt.
5. Recantation; recusancy; apostacy.
inhirāf-i-ahkām. Contrary to the provisions. G. G.
inhirāf-i-qā‛edah. Breach of rules. G. G.
inhirāf-i-muāāhidah.
A breach of contract. G. G.
hidāyat qānūn se inhirāf kar'nā.
To disobey a direction of law. G. G.

H اِندارا इन्दारा *indā'rā, andārā, indrā, inārā kuā,* n. m. S. अन्धु a well. A large well built of solid masonry, protected by a *koṭhī* or *nād.*

P انداز *andāz',* n. m.
Guess; conjecture; rough calculation.
انداز پتّي *andāz paṭṭī,* n. f. An estimate of the value of a standing crop (*kankūt*).

P اندازه *andāz'ah, andāz',* n. m. Guess.
Rough or approximate estimate or valuation.
andāze se, adv. By guess; approximately.
andāze se bāhar, —— ziādah, adj. Excessive; beyond measure; immeasurable.
andāzā kar'nā, v. a. To estimate roughly.

P اندر *an'dar,* prep. Within. See H. بهيتر.
andar karnā, v. a.
1. To put within (the house); hide from view.
2. To put into; insert; penetrate; effect penetration.
3. To thrust, push, force, or worm in.
andar honā, v. n.
1. To be contained or included in; belong to; fall under.
2. To go in; enter; penetrate.
qalam-rau mazkūr' ke an'dar.
Within the said Territories. G. G.

H اِندر इन्दर *in'dar,* n. m. S. इन्द्र The king of the gods; the regent of the visible heavens; the thunder; the god of rain.
indar-jāl, n. m. Deception; cheating; juggling; trick or stratagem in war.
indar-jau, n. m. Seed of the *Urightia antidysenterica,* Wat. used medicinally; sparrow's tongue.

A اِندِراج *indirāj',* n. m. درج Being rolled together.
Insertion; entry; registration.
indirāj mu‛khtalif dā̆von. Misjoinder; improper joinder or union of joinders in an action; insertion of more than one cause of action in one suit.
indirāj-i-nām, n. m. Entry of name.

H اِندراين इन्द्रायन *indrā'yan, pharpheṅdwā, mainphal;* Bhoj. *nārun,* n. f. S. इन्द्रवारुणी.
Fruit of the coloquintida plant; colocynth; a wild gourd; a fruit of beautiful appearance, but bitter taste. *Cucumis colocynthis.* Wat. used medicinally.

H اِندري इन्द्री *ind'rī,* n. f. S. इन्द्रिय an organ of sense.
The five senses, organs of perception.
اندري جلاب इन्द्री जुल्लाब *indrī jullāb.'* n. f.
A diuretic medicine.

A اِندفاع *indifā'ā,* n. m. دفع being repelled.
Warding off; repelling; overthrow; repulse; defeat.
indifāā-i-daṅgā o fasād.
Suppression of a riot. G. G.
indifāā kisī marz-i-shadīd, yā nuqs jismānī.
Curing of any grievous disease or infirmity or bodily ailment. G. G.
indifāā yā bachānā. To be prevented or avoided. G. G.
indifāā yā ‛adam waqūā. Preventing or avoiding (the commission of a crime). G. G.

H اندها अन्धा *an'dhā;* W. Rus. and Brij. *āndh'rā, andh'lā, anh'rā;* Māṛ. *āṅ'dho-āṅ'do;* Tir. *āṅ'har;* Mag. and Bhoj. *āṅdhar,* n. m. *andhī,* n. f. S. अन्ध to be blind.
A blind man; one devoid of sight.
andhā darbār, n.m. A public office notoriously ill conducted; a bad government; a corrupt court; mal-administration; misgovernment.
andher khātā, Unfairness in accounts or dealings.

P انديشه *ande'shah,* n. m. P. انديشيدن to consider.
1. Consideration (*soch*); thought; anxiety (*chinta*); concern; solicitude; anxious care.
2. Doubt (*dubdhā*); suspicion; fear; distrust; misgiving; hesitation; apprehension.
3. Risk; hazard; danger (*khatrā*); peril.
andeshah karnā, v. n. To feel anxiety, mistrust or apprehension.

معقول اندیشہ *ande'sha-i-mâqūl!* Reasonable apprehension. G. G.
andesha-nāk, jāë andeshah, adj. Dangerous; hazardous; fraught with danger.
jism ke mutazarrar hone kā andeshah. G. G. Apprehension of danger to the body.

H آنڈ **आंड** *ānḍ, āṅṛ, pel'aṛ, kapūrā*; A. *khus'-yā, fo'tah,* n. m. S. **अण्ड** A testicle.
انڈ کوش **अण्डकोश** *andkosh,* n. The scrotum.
آنڈو **आंडू** *ān'ḍū,* Rus. *aḍuā,* n.m. *lit.* Having large testicles. [(*sānḍ*).
A bull kept to serve domestic cows

A إِنزال *inzāl',* n. m. نزل Causing to descend. Emission; discharge; *emisso seminis* (*jhaṛnā*).

H انس **अन्स** *ans, ansh,* n. m. S. **अंश** a part. Pr. *anso, amso.* Portion; share; dividend; quota (*hissa*).
انسی **अन्सी** *an'sī, anshī,* n. m.
1. A sharer; shareholder; joint proprietor.
2. A deed setting forth the shares or portions of a property. A deed of partition between the members of a Hindu family. [shares.
ansī ḍālnā, v. a. To divide into portions or

A إِنسان *insān',* n. m. Man. See آدمی
insān kā badan; H. *mānkhā-deh,* n. The human body.
insān ko le bhāg'nā. Kidnapping; stealing or unlawfully conveying away a man, woman, or child; abduction.

A إِنسداد *insidād',* Ped. for H. *rok,* n. m. سَدّ he closed up. Bar; obstacle; impediment; prevention; preventive measure.
انسداد جرائم *insidād-i-jarāyam.* Prevention of crimes. G. G.
insidād-i-chand-roza. A temporary bar. [war.
insidād-i-khāna-jan'gī. Prevention of civil
Preventing a breach of the peace. G. G.
انسداد دائیمی *insidād-i-dāëmī.* A perpetual bar. G. G.
insidād o surāġ-rasānī. Prevention and detection.
insidād-i-ġaflat, yā bejā tâmīl ikhtyārāt.
Preventing abuse or neglect of duty. G. G.
insidād kar'nā. To prevent. G. G.

A إِنصاف *insāf'*; Rus. *nisāph*; n. m. A. نصف taking half.
Justice; equity; equitable adjustment; fairness; fair play; impartiality (*niyāo*).
insāf chāh'nā, v. n. To sue for or demand justice; seek redress; claim.
insāf se, ba-insāf, adv. With justice; equitably; fairly; justly; rightly; deservedly.
insāf kar'nā, v. n.
1. To administer, dispense, or do justice; to do right; to see justice done (*niyāo karnā*).
PHR. To hold the scales even; to see fair play; to see one righted; to give every one his due; *audi alteram partem.*
2. To decide (a case) equitably.
ba-nazar-i-insāf, For the purpose of justice.
muqtizāë insāf. The ends or requirements of justice.

A إِنصرام *insirām',* n. m. صرم Cut off or terminated. Performance; administration or management (of an estate).
insirām kar'nā, v. a. To manage; administer (*intizām karnā*).

A إِنضباط *inzibāt',* n. m. Rare. ضبط holding fast. The act of regulating.
inzibāt-i-auqāt, Ped. Better, H. *belā-bānṭ.* Time-table; routine.

A إِنعام *inâām',* n. m. نَعَم conferred a favor.
1. A prize; reward of merit; reward.
2. A present; gift; favor; gratuity; donation; benefaction; largess.
انعام اکرام *inâām ikrām,* Gifts and honors; rewards and dignities.
inâām pānā, v. n. To get a prize or reward.
inâām-patr, n. m. A deed of grant; a document conveying an assignment of rent-free land. [grant.
inâām-dār, n. m. The holder of a rent-free
inâām denā, v. a. To give or award a prize to; to distribute prizes; to reward merit.
inâām kā paisā. Prize allowance.

A إِنفصال *infisāl'* Ped. for H. *nimṭerā,* n. m. فصل being separated. Decision (of a case) (*faislah*).
infisāl kar'nā, v. a. To settle; decide; adjust.
tā infisāl-i-nizâ ta-tajvīz-i-âdālat. Until the question at issue is judicially determined. G. G.

A إِنفکاک *infikāk',* n. m. فكّ being put out of joint. Redemption (of a mortgage).
infikāk-i-jāëdād-i-marhūna. Redemption of mortgaged property.
infikāk-i-rahn. Redemption, release of property in pawn; redemption of mortgage.

infikāk-i-hiba. Redemption of a gift or legacy.

A إِنْقِسام *inqisām'*, n. m. Ped. for H. *baṭāī*. A. قِسم being divided.

Partition; distribution; division (*bāṅṭ*).
inqisām-i-jāēdād. Ped. for H. *baṭwāṛā*.
Division of lands, houses, or other real and personal property.

A إِنقِضاء *inqizā'*, n. m. قضا being finished.

Expiration; expiry; termination; passing away. [lapse of time.
inqizā-i-miāād. The expiration of any term;
inqizā-i-miāād-i-qaid. Expiration of the term of imprisonment. G. G.
inqizā-i-vaqt. Lapse of time.
inqizā honā, v. n. To lapse; pass away; expire (*bītnā*).

A إِنقِطاع *inqitāā*, n. m. قطع being cut off.

Discontinuance; cessation; failure.

H آنک आंक *āṅk, ank, aṅkār*, n. m. S. अङ्क a mark.
1. A spot; dot; mark; a private mark shewing the selling price of an article.
2. (*Arith.*). The product of the principal into the rate and time.
3. Figures on coins, etc. shewing the date of a raja's accession.

اُنکاری उङ्कारी *uṅkā'rī, huṅkārī*, n. f.
A curved line after a figure.
A vertical line, (I) which by itself signifies one pice, is four annas if the curved line be shewn before it, thus ا) ; eight annas if the curved line be made before two vertical lines, as اا), and so on.

آنکنا आंकना *āṅk'nā*, v. a.
1. To distinguish by some mark.
2. To measure; value; estimate; weigh.
3. To judge; think; consider.
4. To remove disease or pain by incantations (*jhāṛnā*).

انکنا अंकना *aṅk'nā*, v. n. To be appraised, priced, valued.

آنکو आंकू *āṅ'kū, aṅkvai'yā, kan-kūtā*, n. m. An officer employed to survey the standing crops and estimate their probable value; an appraiser.

انکوانا अंकवाना *aṅkvā'nā*, Caus. of *āṅknā*, q. v.

A إِنکار *inkār'*; H. *nāṅh*, n. m. A. نکر he denied.
1. Denial; negation; disavowal; retraction; refusal; protest.
2. Disallowance; contradiction; **veto.**
3. Dissent; disagreement; difference or diversity of opinion.
4. Retraction; recantation; renunciation.
5. Objection; exception; bar.
inkār-i-dāvā. Denial of claim.
inkār kar'nā; H. *nāṭnā*, v. a. [sent from.
1. To refuse; deny; disagree to; dis-
2. To disavow; unsay; contradict.
3. To refuse to admit; take exception to; disallow; dispute; impugn; question; call in question; contest; protest against.
4. To disclaim; disown; renounce.
5. To gainsay; recant; revoke; abjure; retract.
6. To repudiate; reject.
inkār karne-wālā; Ped. A. *munkir*, n. m. Recusant; objector; unbeliever.
inkār meṅ isrār karnā, v. n. To persist in refusal or denial.
barābar inkār karte āē haiṅ. Have throughout denied.
qasm khā-ke inkār karnā, v. n. To deny on oath.

H انکُر अङ्कुर *aṅk'ur, suīyāṅ*, W; *ak'urā, aṅk'urā, aṅk'rī*, E; *aṅk'uā*, Sah. and Mag. n. m. S. अङ्क any thing curved.
The first sprout from a seed; a young sprout; a shoot, germ, or blade (*phuṭāo*).

انکري अंकरी *aṅk'rī*, n. f. A kind of vetch (*vicia sativa*).

H آنکرا आंकड़ा *āṅk'ṛā*, adj. (*Ṭhagī*). One thousand.

H آنکرا आंकड़ा *āṅk'ṛā*; E. *aṅk'usī*, n. m. The barb of an arrow; a hook; a fishing-hook.

H انکس अङ्कुस *aṅk'as, aṅk'us*, n. m. S. अङ्कुश, Pr. *aṅkuso, aṅko.* The iron-hook with which elephants are driven; a goad.

H آنکھ आंख *āṅkh*; Mag. *āṅkhi*; Panj. *akkhā*; Garh. *āṅkhā*; Wom. *dīdah*, n. f. S. अक्षि from अक्ष to pervade, Pr. *achchhi*; Pāli, *akkhi*.
1. The eye; the organ of sight.
2. An estimate or appraisement of the probable amount and value of the crops in a field, salt in a pile, hay in a stack, and the like.
3. An adjustment of the rents to be paid by the individual co-parceners through the person held liable for the realization of the Government demand.
4. The sprout or shoot in the joint of a sugarcane, etc.

H انگ अङ्ग *ang, deh, de'hī, de'ī, kā'yā, pin'ḍā*; P. and H. *tan*; A. *bad'an*, n. m. S. अङ्ग to walk or go. Body; limb (*jor*).
ang bhang ho'nā, v. n. To be mutilated, cut off (a limb).
ang-jāī, n. f. A daughter (*beṭī*).
ang chhed'an kar'nā,—bhang k., v. a. To mutilate; cut off a limb. G. G.
ang sih'rī, E. n. f. The chill which precedes fever; ague (*kapkapī*).
ang god'nā, v. a. To tattoo; to puncture the skin and insert in the puncture some coloring matter, generally blue, so as to leave a permanent stain.
انگّا अङ्गा *ang'gā*, n. m. A long coat worn by men. See. *angarkhā*.

H آنگا आंगा *ān'gā*, n. m. As much grain as a man can take in between his arms (*kaulī*).

H انگارا अंगारा *angā'rā, angār'*, W.; *ingorā, ingor*, E.; Māṛ. *khiro*, n. m. *angārī*, n. f. Pr. *ingālo*; S. अङ्गार: A piece of fire; live coal; ignited matter; cinder.

H انگڈیا अंगडया *angaḍ'yā*, n. m. One who carries money concealed in his quilted coat.

H انگرکھا अंगरखा *angar'khā, ang-rakhā, angā*; Rus. *garkhā*, n. m. S. अङ्ग body, रक्ष to protect. A long tunic; a coat worn both by Hindus and Mahomedans, the former open on the right, and the latter on the left (*chapkan*).

E انگریز *angrez', farangī*; Rus. *angrej*; Fac. *rangrez* (a dyer), n. m. An Englishman; a gentleman.
angrez'an, firangan, n. f. An English woman or lady.
angre'zī,—zabān, n. f. The English language.
angrezī tumbā'kū, Cor. *isṭik bākar* a stick of tobacco, n. m. Tobacco smoked in a pipe.
angrezī amaldā'rī, n. The British Government; the English rule.

P انگشت *angusht'*; n. S. अङ्गुष्ठ H. *unglī*, Finger.
انگشتانہ *angushtā'nā*, n. m. A thimble.
angusht-i-shahādat, Ped. *Better*, H. *bat-unglī*. The fore-finger.

H اُنگل उंगल *ung'al*, W; *angul*, E; *āngal, āngul, angal*, W. Rus. n. m. S. अङ्गुल A finger's breadth; a linear measure.
ungal baṛā, ungal bīṛā, n. A whitlow; a felon.

E اِنگلس *ing'lis, inglish*, n. f. Pension; superannuation pension.
inglis'yā, n. m. Probably from the English, invalid. An invalid soldier or *sipāhī*, who receives a pension, or an allotment of land as pension; a pensioner.

H آنگن आंगन *āng'an, angnā'ī, chauk*; Poet. *ang'nā*; A. *sahn*. n. m. S. अङ्गण.

H انگوارا अंगवारा *angwā'rā*, n. m.
1. The proprietor of a small portion of a village.
2. The proceeds shared by two men who supply between them the pair of oxen necessary for a plough.

H انگوٹھی अंगूठी *angūṭhī*; W. Rus. *gūnṭhī*; Māṛ. *bīnṭī*; P. *angushtarī*, n. f. S. अङ्गुरीय. A ring worn on the finger or toe (*mundrī*).

H انگوچھا अंगोछा *ango'chhā, angauchhā*; Rus. and Sab. *gon'chhā*; E. *gamchhā, tau'liyā*; n. m. S. अङ्ग body, उछ to bind; H. *pochhnā* to wipe. A short piece of cloth which Hindūs fasten round the waist and loins. It is shorter than the *dhotī*, and is used besides as a towel.

P انگور *angūr'*, n. m.
1. The grape; *Vitis vinifera*. Wat.
2. Granulations in a healing sore.
angūr bandh'nā, angūr bhar ā'nā, — ānā, v. n. To form (the soft skin over a sore); heal.
angūr phaṭ'nā, angūr taṛakh'nā, v.n. To break (as a granulation of a sore).
angūr kā mandwā, yā ṭaṭṭī, n. f.
1. A grape-vine; vinery; vineyard.
2. Fireworks in imitation of clusters of grapes in a vine.
انگوری *angū'rī*, adj. Of or belonging to the grape.
angūrī bag̣, n. m. A grape garden; a vineyard.
angūrī sirkā, angūr kā sirkā, n. m. Grape vinegar.

H انگوریا अंगौरिया *angau'riyā*, E. n. m. The use of a plough in place of wages in kind.

H انگونگا अंगौंगा *angaun'gā, āgaun,'* E. n. m. *an* grain, *gurū* a priest. Perquisites from the threshing-floor to Brahmans, Gurūs, etc.

H انگھڑا अंघड़ा *angh'ṛā*, n. m. A ring of brass or other mixed metal worn on the large toe by women of low caste.

H انگیا अंगया *ang'yā, angiyā, āngī, cholī, chhoṭā kapṛā*; W. Rus. *anggaṭ*, Gaṛh.

āṅgṛo ; A. *mahram*, n. f. S. अङ्गिका A boddice ; a short inner jacket.

انگيٹھي अंगीठी *aṅgī'ṭhī* ; W. Rus. and Sah. *gīṭhī*, *agīṭhī* ; Mār. *sigṛī*, E. *aṅgeṭhī* ; *barosī*, *bursī*, n. f. S. अग्नि fire, स्था to place.

A chafing dish ; brasier ; hearth ; grate.

H انگيکار अंगीकार *aṅgīkār'*, n. f. S. अङ्गीकृ to agree to.

1. Assent ; consent ; acceptance ; agreement.
2. Confession ; acquiescence ; admission.
3. Choice ; option ; predilection ; adoption ; reception.

aṅgīkār karnā, v. a.
1. To agree ; accede to ; comply with ; approve of.
2. To accept ; acknowledge ; admit ; receive.
3. To undertake ; take upon ; adopt ; yield to.

H اُنمان उनमान *unmān'*, n. f. S. अनुमान from अनु after, मा to measure.

1. Measure ; appraisement ; estimation.
2. Guess ; conjecture ; approximation.
3. Inference ; hypothesis ; logical conclusion (*natījā*).
4. Duration ; period ; life ; age.
5. Dimension ; magnitude ; volume ; size ; quantity (A. *jasāmat*).

اُنماني उनमानी *unmā'nī*, adj. S. अनुमानिक Presumptive ; conjectural.

Port. اناناس *anannās'*, n. m. A pineapple ; *Ananassa sativa*. Wat.

H اَنني अन्नी *an'nī*, *ik-annī*, n. f. One-anna piece.

H آنو आंओ *āṅo*, *āṅv*, n. m. S. आम The glutinous, whitish matter or mucus voided in tenesmus or dysentry ; animal mucilage.

āṅo gir'nā, *parnā*, *yā baithnā*, v. n. To be afflicted with tenesmus ; to discharge mucus.

āṅo lahū, n. m. Dysentry.

S انو अनु *an'u*, ind. A prefix to verbs and nouns, signifying after, along, along side, near to, with, under.

انوآدھيا अनुआधया *anū-ā'dhayā*, n. f. अधेया, to be received. A class of woman's property given to her by her husband or relations after marriage.

انوپان अनुपान *anu-pān*, n. m. S. पा to drink. A. *badraqā*, A vehicle (in medicine).

Any thing in which a medicine is mixed, to facilitate the taking of it, or which is swallowed after the medicine.

انوچر अनुचर *anu-char'*, n. m. S. चर् to move. Follower ; disciple ; servant (*naukar*).

انورادھا अनुराधा *anu-rā'dhā*, n. f. The seventeenth of the lunar mansion, described by a row of oblations ; stars in Librā.

انوگمن अनुगमन *anūgam'an*, n. S. गम् to go. The burning of a widow after hearing of the death of her absent husband.

انومرن अनुमरण *anū-mar'an*, n. m. S. मृ to die. *lit.* Following in death. The burning of a Hindū widow when the husband's body is not on the spot ; burning with the husband's corpse.

انوواد अनुवाद *anu-vād*, H. *ulthā*, n. m.
1. Translation ; interpretation.
2. Answer ; reply ; rejoinder.

انوبادي अनुबादी *anū-bā'dī*, n. m. Defendant ; opponent ; respondent.

H انوا अनवा *an'wā*, n. m. The place where the men stand and throw up water from a lower to a higher level ; a water bucket.

H انوٹ अनवट *an'waṭ*, n. f.

A ring furnished with small bells, worn by women on the great toe.

H آنول आंवल *āṅ'wal*, n. m. Afterbirth ; secundines.

āṅwal-nāl, n. The navel string, etc. of a new-born infant.

āṅwal-jhāṅwal, *joṛlā*, *juṛvāṅ* W ; E. *jauṅwāṅ* ; A. *toam*, n. m. Twins.

H آنولا आंवला *āṅv'lā*, *āṅo'lā*, *ām'lā*, W. *auṅlā*, *auṅrā*, E. ; *āṅwrā*, Brij. n. m. S. आमलक, Pr. *āmalao*. A fruit used when green for making pickles ; a myrobalan ; *Phyllanthus emblica*, used in tanning and dyeing, and also as a hair-wash.

The tree is an object of worship as the *Birham birichh* (Brahm tree).

āṅwal gaṭṭā, n. m. A dried myrobalan, or one fallen from the tree.

آنولاسار आंवलासार *āṅvlāsār*,—*gandak*, n. m. S. अम्लसार Purified sulphur.

H آنہ आना *ā'nā*, n. m.
1. A copper coin, the sixteenth of a rupee.
2. One sixteenth share in any property.

انگي अनगी *an'agī*, *annī rupayā*, n. f. An allowance at the rate of one anna per rupee.

H آنہڑ आंहड़ *āṅ'haṛ*, *Ṭhagī*. n. f. H. *an* grain, *hāṅḍī* pot. Plates or vessels.

H اني अनी *an'ī*, *nok*, n. f. S. and Mār. अणी.

1. The point or sharp end (of an arrow, spear, etc).
2. The stem or prow of a boat. (?)

anī chalnā, n. A thrust (in swordmanship).

P انيسون *ane'sūn*, n. m. Aniseed; *Ptychotis involucrata.* Wat.

H آوا आवा *ā'vā, avāh*; Gaṛh. *auṛ*; Bhoj. *āvān*; Māṛ. *nyāhav*, n. m. A potter's kiln (*bhaṭṭī*).

P اوارجه *avārī'jā, avār'chā, avārijā bahī*, n.m.

1. A day book (*roz-nāmchah*); diary; journal.

2. Abstract account of collections and remittances; a book of receipts and disbursements (*jama-kharch bahī*).

A revenue account, specifying, first, the unproductive lands of a village, and next those paying revenue, field by field, arranged under the names of the occupants, with a specification in separate columns of the number of each field in the *Bhauryā* or field book, the quantity of land and kind of cultivation; the total rent payable by each occupant being also summed up.

āvārija jama-kharch. An account of receipts and disbursements.

P آواره *āvā'rah*; Z. *āvānik*, adj.

1. Roving; wandering about; separated from one's family.

2. Abandoned; lost; destitute of name or character.

āvārah phir'nā, Lurking. G. G.

To stroll about; wander up and down.

choron kā āvārah giroh, n. A wandering gang of thieves.

H اوازه توازه *avā'zah tavā'zah*, n. m. H. *bolī ṭholī*, n. f.

Taunts; jeers; inuendoes; insulting expressions.

āvāzah kas'nā,—pheknā,—mār'nā, v. n.

To speak in inuendoes; speak at; taunt or jeer at; laugh at.

H اواسي अवासी *awā'sī*, Bhoj. n. f. Unripe corn cut from time to time and brought home to be eaten without being threshed.

H آواگون आवा गवन *ā'vā-gav'an, āvā-gaman, āvā-jāī*; Gaṛh. *aūnū-jānū*, n. f. H. *ānā* to come, S. गम् to go. [(*ānā-jānā*).

1. Coming and going; ingress and egress

2. Transmigration of souls(*jīvan-maran*).

H اوال अवाल *awāl'*, E. n. f.

1. An enclosed space formed by a cluster of *rāyat's* houses.

2. A string fastened round the wheel of a distaff (*jatnī*, W). [n. f.

H اواي अवाई *awā'ī*; Illit. *havā'ī*; A. *afwāh*, Report; rumour; gossip; hearsay; false rumour or report.

A اوايل عمر *avā'yal ūmr*, n. f. pl. of اول Beginnings. Youth (*chhoṭī umar*).

——, n. m. A youth.

A اوباش *aubāsh'*, n. m. pl. of وبش the common people. A rake; debauchee; profligate; a bad character. [gate; dissolute.

aubāsh', adj. Lecherous; libidinous; profli-

اوباشي *aubā'shī*, n. f. [lewdness.

1. Rakishness; dissoluteness; debauchery;

2. Wenching; womanizing; incontinence; harlotry.

3. Depravity; profligacy.

H اوپچي ओपची *op'chī*, n. m. A man armed with weapons or clothed in mail.

H اُوپر ऊपर *ū'par*; Tir. *upar*; Gaṛh. *ubjā*, P. *abar, bar*, prep. S. उपरि, Pr. *avari* above.

On; upon; above; up; over.

اوپرا उपरा *ūp'rā, ūpara-hār, ūpār-wār*, n. Upper or high land not admitting of artificial irrigation. [Māṛ. *opro*, adj.

اُوپري ऊपरी *ūp'rī, up'rī ūpar-kā*; Sah. *oprā*,

1. Outer; outward; exterior; external.

2. Superficial; not deep; shallow.

3. Specious; artificial; affected; unreal.

4. Belonging to another (*parāyā*).

5. Strange; new; unfamiliar.

6. Foreign; of another country; alien.

7. Loose (*ḍhīlā*); not tight or strong.

8. Unbecoming; unsuitable; not matching.

اُوپري ऊपरी *ūprī*, n. m.

1. Stranger; foreigner; a new man; an outsider; one not belonging to the house, or the country.

2. One who cultivates land in a different village from his own (*pāhī*).

3. An exotic; what is not native or indigenous to the soil.

4. Surplus; surplusage; overplus (*fāltū*).

5. Perquisites; fees (*bālāī*). [goblins.

6. (*ūprī parāī*). Evil spirits; demons;

7. A cultivator not belonging originally to a village, but residing and occupying land in it, either upon a lease for a stipulated term of years, or at the pleasure of the proprietor (*pāhī*); a tenant whose ancestors have held the land for many generations, but who is not considered to have a proprietary right in the soil; an officer employed to supervise the crops when brought to the threshing floor when the Government dues are not paid in kind; an overseer; a superintendant.

H اُوت ऊत *ūt*; Hin. Wom. (*Contemptuously*) *ūt'ṛā, ūti'yā, ut'tā*; Old H. *aūt*; Gaṛh *autā*, n. m. S. अपुत्र from अ not, पुत्र a son.
One who dies unmarried; a batchelor.

H اوت ओत *ot*, n. f. [turn.
1. Gain; profit (*nafā*); advantage; re-
2 Economy; spare; frugality (*kifāyat*).
3 Overplus; surplus; saving (*bachat*).
4. Relief; convalescence; recovery.
ot kas'ar. Profit and loss.

H اَوتار ओतार *autār'*, *avtār*, n. m. S. अवतार from अवतृ to descend, Pr. *oāra*.
An incarnation of the deity.
☞ The Hindūs reckon ten incarnations of the god Vishnu:— 1st, *Machh* a fish; 2nd, *Kachh* a tortoise; 3rd, *Bārāh* a boar; 4th, *Nar-Singh* a man-lion; 5th, *Baunā* or *Bāman* a dwarf; 6th, *Paras Rām*; 7th, *Rām*; 8th, *Krishn*; 9th, *Budh*; 10th, *Kalki* or *Niskalank*, which is yet to appear on the culmination of the *kal-yug* the iron age or age of sin.

اُوتر پاتر ہونا ऊतर पातर होना *ūtar pātar honā*, *uttar pātar* —, v. n. from H. *utarnā*.
To be paid off, or discharged (a debt); to be clear, square, even with; to settle; balance, or square accounts with; to be quits.

H اوٹ ओट *oṭ*; Tir. *eroṭ*, n. f. S. अङ्कुन shield.
1. Cover. See *āṛ* (1, 2).
2. Shadow; shade; shelter. (Also *āṛ*).
3. Ambush; hiding place; concealment.
4. A veil; a covering for the face.
oṭ bandī, n. f.
1. Payment of a fixed amount for the use of each plough and pair of bullocks.
2. An estimate of the probable outturn at some future period.
اوٹا ओटा *o'ṭā*, n. m.
1. A partition or side wall.
2. A small wall against the entrance to a house; a platform of mud.
3. A heap of mud placed on the cotton machine to keep it steady. [cotton.
4. One who separates the seed from the

H اُوجڑ ऊजड़ *ū'jaṛ*; Garh. *uḍar*; Tir. *ujaṛ*, adj. Desolate. See اُجاڑ

H اوجھا ओझा *ojh'ā*, E; *syānā*, W. n. m. S. उपाध्याय teacher, Pr. *uajhhā*.
1. A diviner; soothsayer; wizard; magician (*jādū-gar*); conjuror; enchanter; sorcerer; exorcist.
2. One who pretends to cure diseases, the bite of snakes, and to cast out evil spirits by means of charms or incantations.
اوجھائی ओझाई *ojhāī*, n. f. The profession of an *ojhā*.

H اَوچھ ओछ *auchh*, n. m. A root from which an orange color is extracted; *Morinda citrifolia*. [crepancy; incongruity.

H اُوچھل ऊछल *ū'chhal*, n. f. Difference; dis-

H اُودا ऊदा *ū'dā*, adj. S. अवदात. Purple.

H اَودس ओदस *au'das*; Mag. *ajjas*; Māṛ. *ojas*, n. m. Defamation. See *ajas*.

H اُوڈ ऊड *ūḍ* n. m. A wooden roller for breaking clods in the field.

H اوڈھا ओढा *o'ḍhā*, *bojhā*, n. m. A perquisite of the village scribe, consisting of as much corn from each heap as he can enfold between both arms (*kaulī*).

H اور ओर *aur*, conj.
And; else; besides; also; likewise.
aur irādah, n. m.
A different or lurking design.
aur shai. Other thing; other commodity. G. G.
aur sūrtoṅ meṅ. Otherwise; in other cases. G. G.
aur kā. Belonging to another; not one's own.
kisī aur nīyat se. With a different intention; (G. G.) with ill will.

P آوُرد *āwurd'*, adj. *lit.* brought. Opp. of *āmad* what comes naturally. Artificial; affected; unnatural; false; far-fetched.
آوردہ *āwur'da*, n. *lit.* That which is brought over. One who is favored; a protogè.
āwurdā navīs, n. m. A writer or registrar of accounts as delivered.

S اُوردھ باہو ऊर्द्ध बाहु *ūrdh-bāhū*, n. m. S. ऊर्द्ध up, बाहु arm. An ascetic who holds up one or both arms until they become rigid and remain fixed in that position.

H اورنا ओरना *or'nā*, E.; *vairnā*, W. n. A drill plough. [*zebī*, n. m.

P اَورنگ زیبی *aur'aṅg-zebī*; Illit. *nauraṅg-*
1. A kind of cloth.
2. A boil, or eruption said to have broken out in the reign of Aurangzeb.

H اوڑھنا ओढ़ना *oṛh'nā*, *onnā*; W. Rus. *oḍh-nā*; Māṛ. *orno*, n. m.
1. A woman's mantle covering the head and upper half of the body.
2. A bed sheet; a covering.
oṛhnā utār'nā, v. a. To defame; take away one's character.

oṛhnā uṛhā'nā, v. a. *lit.* To cover with a wrapper. To marry; take one's hand in marriage. (A mode of marrying a widow among villagers).

oṛhnā bichhau'nā, n. m. Bedding and covering.

oṛhnā gale meṅ ḍāl'nā, v. a. To drag to the court for justice.

☞ In former times, the insulted woman would throw her wrapper round the offending man's neck and drag him to the king for justice, her uncovered head being a symbol of the disgrace she had suffered.

اوڑھني ओढ़नी *oṛh'nī, on'nī*; Rus. *oḍh'nī*, n. f. Diminutive of *oṛh'nā* (1). q. v.

oṛhnī piṭṭhī, n. f. A Hindu marriage ceremony.

☞ It consists in the bridegroom's presenting paint, ornaments, jewels, and a new suit of clothes for the bride, followed by a return present from the bride of money and a sweetmeat called *ṭikī*.

A أوزار *auzār*,' n. m. Pl. of وزر Tools. See آلات

H آؤس आउस *āūs*, E.; *saṭṭhī*, E. & W. n. m. S. अश् to eat. Rice sown in *Chait* or *Baisākh* (Aug.—Sep.) and growing rapidly through the rainy season.

H آوسان औसान *ausān'*; P. *hosh*, n. m. from *sān* sharpness. Sensibility; sense (*havās*); presence of mind.

ausān uṛ jānā, khatā honā, yā jāte rahnā, v. n. To be stunned, stupefied, at a loss; to stand aghast; lose one's senses.

H آوستھا अवस्था *avas'thā*; Rus. *aus'thā*, n. f. S. अव well, स्था to stand.

1. State; condition; age.
2. Period; duration; life (*ārbal*).
3. Story; narrative; history.

H اوسر ओसर *o'sar*, n. f. S. वत्स a young animal. A young cow or buffalo; heifer.

H اُوسر ऊसर *ū'sar, osar*, n. f. Barren (land). See *ussar*.

H اوسرا ओसरा *os'rā, os'rī*, n. *f.* Turn (*bārī*); time; turn (of a performer); watch; milking time (*chhāk*); the time for gathering fruits and flowers.

A اوسط *au'sat*, n.f.H. *bīch* وسط middle. Average; the mean between *āāla* highest, and *adnā* lowest.

ausat jama-bandī, n. f. Average rental.

ausat-hāzrī, n. f. Average of attendance.

ausat darje ke mizāj, aur aql kā shakhs. G. G. A person of ordinary sense and temper.

ausat raqba-i-kāsht. The average area of a cultivator's holding.

ausat sharah lagān, n. f. Ped. Average rent-rate.

ausat-i-ām nikālnā, v. a. To strike a general average.

ausat nikāsī-i-khām. Average gross proceeds or rental.

ausat nikālnā, v. a. To strike an average.

اوسط *ausat*; H. *bīch kī rās*, adj. Tolerable; middling; passable.

H اوسوال ओसवाल *os'wāl*, n. m. A tribe of *Jaiṅs*, chiefly merchants and bankers.

A أوْقات *auqāt'*, n. f. pl. of وقت Time.

1. State; condition; circumstances.
2. Means; appliances; resources; ways and means.
3. Ability; strength; power.

اوقات بسري *auqāt-bas'arī*, n. f.

1. Employment, or occupation of time.
2. Livelihood; means of living; source of income.

H آوک आवक *ā'wak, bīmā, jokhoṅ*, n. m. Insurance. In Western India, Respondentia, an advance of money to a merchant upon the goods or merchandise in a ship before sailing, on the condition that, if the voyage be profitable, the loan is to be repaid with an extra rate of interest or percentage.

āwak byājū. A transaction in which a person who has made a respondentia advance enters into an engagement with some third person, who for a bonus or stipulated interest, insures him against loss.

H اوکان ओकान *aukān'*, n. A heap of straw and grain (*lāṅk*).

H اُوکھ ऊख *ūkh*, E.; *īkh*, W.; *rūkh, ketārī*, Mag.; *sāṅṭhā*, Māṛ., n. f. S. इक्षु, Pr. *uchhchū*. Sugarcane; *Saccharum officinarum*. Wat.

اُوکھاڑي ऊखाड़ी *ū'khāṛī, ukhā'rī*, n. f. A field of sugarcane.

اُوکھراج ऊखराज *ūkh'rāj, ūkh-bhoj*, E; *nimau'nī*, W. n. m. The day on which the planting of the sugarcane commences, generally attended with some festive ceremonies at which sweet dishes only are prepared.

H اَوکھد औखद *au'khad*; Rus. *aukhadī*; *aukhat*, n. f. S. औषधि Medicine (*davā*); remedy (*ilāj*).

H اوکھر ओखर *o'khar*; Rus. *aukhar*; A. *auzār*, n. m. Tools; implements; apparatus.

H اوکھل औखल *au'khal*, n. f. S. ऊषर barren

land. Land reclaimed from waste and brought under cultivation.

H اوکھلي ओखली *okh'lī*, W; *ukhlī*, E.; *ukhri*, Mag. n. f. A mortar. See *ukhlī*.

H اَوکھي औखी *au'khī*, *boṅgī*, *burī bhalī*, n. f. from *au* bad, *kah* speak. Rude or harsh language; a crooked answer. [to rise.

H اُوگالي ऊगाली *ū'gālī*, *ugā'lī*, n. f. from اُگنا The first rays of the rising sun or moon.

H اوگ دُآس ओग दुआस *og-duās'*; (Khattrī) *bhāī-bhinnā*, n. f. A Hindu festival performed on the twelfth day of *Bhādoṅ badī*, or the dark fortnight in August.

H اوگل औगल *au'gal*, *āl*; Tir. *hāl*; Sah. *ogar*, n. f. from *gīl* moisture. Subsoil moisture.

H اوگھڑ औघड़ *au'ghar*, n. m. (*Ṭhagī*). A bad omen.

H اوگي औगी *au'gī*, n. f.

1. A whip, about seven cubits long, like a waggoner's, used in training horses.
2. An ornamental edging of superior country shoes (peculiar to Delhī).
3. A pit dug for catching elephants, wolves, etc.
4. A reel or skein (*anṭī*).

A اَوّل *av'val*; Rus. *abbal*, adj.

1. First; foremost; *primus inter pares*.
2. Highest; principal; prime; superior (*uttam*). [(*sireshṭh*).
3. Best; excellent; exquisite; tip-top
4. Preliminary; preparatory; proemial.

avval darjā, n. m. First class; first rate.
avval din se, adv. From the first; from the beginning (H. *ād se*).
avval rahnā, v. n. To stand first in order.
avval se ākhir tak, adv. Right through; one's whole generation (*ād se ant tak*). [interment.
avval manzil, n. f. Funeral rites, or obsequies;
avval manzil pauṅhchānā, *yā k.* v. a. [dead. To perform the funeral rites; bury the
اوّل *avval*, *avval to*; H. *pir'tham*, adv. Firstly; *imprimis*; in the first place; at first sight; in the first instance; *prima facie*.
av'val, n. m. Beginning; commencement (*ādh*).

H اول ओल *ol*, n. m. A pungent vegetable of which the root is boiled in acid and eaten; *Amorphophallus campanulatus*. Wat.
اول کوبي ओल कोबी *ol kobī*, n. f. Knolecole.

H اول ओल *ol*, n. f. *olā* screen. Personal bail or security; a surety; hostage (A. *yargamāl*).
ol meṅ denā, v. a. To surrender a debtor to his bail till payment of the money due; to give a hostage.

H اولا ओला *o'lā*, *ole*; *bino'lyā*, *baj'rī*, W. Rus.; *patthar*, *patthal*, E; *binaurī*, Mag. & Bhoj.; *garo*, Mār. n. m. from S. ओल wet.

1. Hail; hailstone.
2. A round lump of loaf-sugar.

A اولاد *aulād'*, n. f. ولد, Bearing children. Children; breed; issue (*āl*).
aulād-ul-halāl, n. f. Legitimate children. G. G.
اولاد اناث *aulād-i-anās*; H. *beṭyāṅ*. Female issue.
aulād rishta-i-mustaqīma.; H. A. *ek bāp kī aulād*. Lineal descendants.
aulād-i-zakūr; H. *beṭe*. Male issue.
aulād-i-sahīh-un-nasab, *aulād-i-nasabī*; H. *sachchī aulād*. Legitimate issue.
aulād-i-gair-sahih-un-nasab, *kam-asal aulād*. Illegitimate issue.
aulād kī aulād; H. *nātī pote*. Grandchildren.
aulād najīb-ut-tarafain; H. *kulvantī santān*. Legitimate issue from both sides, maternal and paternal.

H اُولو ऊलू *ū'lū*, *ul'uā*, n. f. S. उलप, Pr. *ulavo*. A kind of grass used in thatching; *Saccharum cylindricum*. Wat.

H آولي आओली *ā'olī*, E; *kaukūt*, W. n. f. A mode of estimating crops, the produce of one *bisvā* being taken as a measure of the whole.

A اوليا *au'liyā*, n. m. pl. of ولي [men. The apostles; saints; pious or holy
aulyā Allāh, n. m. In Mah. law. The next of kin, or other entitled to exact retaliation.

S اوم ओम् *om*, n. The mystic name of the triad Vishnu, Shiv, and Brahma, consisting of three letters अ, उ, म. It is used at the beginning, and, like our Amen, at the end of prayers and holy recitations, and also at the beginning of writings or respectful salutations.
oṅgkār', *oṅkār*, The mysterious word *om*, q. v.

H اُومي ऊमी *ū'mī*, n. f. W. An ear of corn half ripe; fried green Indian corn.

H آون आवन *ā'wan*, n. m. W. The iron ring round the nave.

H اُون ऊन *ūn*, n. f. S. ऊर्ण Pr. उण्ण, Panj. *unn*. Wool; coarse hair that may be woven.

H اُونا ऊना *ū'nā*; *ūn*; Mār. उणां; Brij. *unnā* adj. S. ऊन less.

1. Less ; short ; deficient.
2. Young, toothless (cattle).

H اونا ماسي ओना मासी *onā-māsī, o'nam,* n. f. Cor. of S. ओं नमः सिद्धं I prostrate myself before *om* (the Hindu triad) and all the perfect beings.
The first lesson or prayer.

H اونٹ ऊंट *ūṅṭ;* n. m. S. उष्ट्र; P. *ushtar.*
A camel.
ūṅṭ katarā, n. m. A thistle of which camels are fond; *Echinops echinatus.* Wat.
اونٹني ऊंटनी *ūṅṭnī,* n. f. A female camel.
ūṅṭ-vān ; P. *sār-bān,* n. m. A camel-driver.

H اونچا ऊंचा *ūṅ'chā, ūṅchī, ūṅche;* Sah. *unchā;* Garh. *uchā;* Panj. *uchchā;* P. *baland,* adj. S. उच्च high. Opp. of *nīchā.* [high.
Tall; lofty; elevated; exalted; raised;
ūṅchī dūkān, lit. An elevated or grand shop.
A famous, respectable, or well-known shop.
ūṅchī zāt, yā jāt, n. f. High caste.

H اوندنا औंदना *auṅd'nā,* v. a. (*Ṭhagī.*) To eat.

H اونے پونے औने पौने *aune-paune, aun-paun,* adv. S. ऊन less, H. *paun* three quarters.
From one to 25 per cent. less. At a loss.

P H آويزاں کرنا *āvez'āṅ kar'nā,* v. a. P. آويختن to hang, Ped. for H. *laṭkānā.* To suspend; affix; post (a notice).
ishtehār āvezāṅ karnā. To post a notice or proclamation.
آويزه *āvezāh;* H. *laṭkan,* n. m. An ornament for the ear; an earring.

H اہار अहार *ahār'; ā'har, āhār';* Garh., Sah. and Mag. *hār,* n. m. S. आहार from हृ to take.
1. Food; victuals; provision; sustenance.
2. Gluten (*nishāstā*); starch; paste.
ahār kar'nā, v. n. To dine; eat; make a meal.
اہارنا अहारना *ahār'nā, ahār de'nā, yā charhā'-nā,* v. a. To starch; paste.

H اُہار उहार *uhār', wahār, ujhār,* E; *parda,* W. n. A curtain or covering of a cart, litter, *pālkī,* etc. as a protection from the sun or rain, or a privacy for women.

H اُہارنا उहारना *uhār'nā,* v. a. (*Ṭhagī*).
To kill by strangulation, or hanging.

A اہالي *ahā'lī,* n. m. pl. of اہل Individuals; members; persons.
اہالي جماعت *ahālī-i-jamāāt,* n. m. Members of a force. G. G.
اہالي موالي *ahā'lī mavā'lī;* Pop. *hālī mavālī,* n. m. Courtiers; retainers; followers; servants; retinue.

A اہانت *ihā'nat,* Ped. n. f. ہون despising.
1. Contempt; affront; insult.
2. Slander; defamation; calumny. [court.
اہانت عدالت *ihānat-i-adālat.* Contempt of [for.

A اہتمام *ehtimām',* n. m. ہم Taking thought
1. Charge; care; control; superintendence; supervision; inspection.
2. Administration; guidance; direction; regulation; management.
3. Trust; responsibility.
4. Rule; sway; jurisdiction.
اہتمامدار *ehtimām-dār; mohtamim,* n. m.
The holder of a trust; the person charged with the realization of a stipulated revenue for a certain district under the Mahomedan government; a *zamīndār*; an agent or deputy of the *zamīndār,* appointed by him to realize the revenue of any portion of his *zamīndārī.*
ehtimām kar'nā, v. n. [control.
1. To superintend; overlook; supervise;
2. To administer; have, or take the direction; to conduct; direct; manage; regulate; carry on (*chalānā*).
ehtimām men rakh'nā, v. n. To put in one's charge: to entrust.
اہتمامي *ehtimāmī,* n. f. What is held in trust, as an under-tenure or part of a *taālluq,* lands, etc.
ashyāē gair ehtimām shudah. Effects unadministered. G. G.
sanad mushār atāē ikhtyār ehtimām tarka-i-mūsī. Ped. Grant of administration to the estate of the testator. G. G.
pulis kā ehtimām, n. m. Superintendence of the police. G. G.

H آہر आहर *ā'har, ah'rā,* n. m.
1. E. A reservoir for collecting rain-water for irrigation. [in a furnace. W.
2. (*ujhīnā*). A pile of cakes of cowdung

P آہستگي *āhist'agī,* Ped., *ahistgī,* Pop. n. f.
1. Slowness; delay; tardiness. [ness.
2. Gentleness; mildness (*narmī*); meek-
آہسته *ā'histah, āhistah āhistah;* Illit. *āsteh āsteh;* H. *saijh saijh, haule haule,* adv.
1. Slowly; gently; softly; mildly.
2. Gradually; step by step; inch by inch; by slow degrees; bit by bit; by degrees; by little and little. [and on.
3. At one's convenience; leisurely; off

آہستہ *āhistah*, adj.
1. Slack; slow; tardy; dilatory. [crawling.
2. Lazy; sluggish; laggard; creeping;
3. Gentle; mild; soft; easy.

A أہل *ahl*, adj. Ped. for H. *susīl*.
Meek; gentle; modest; good; clever.

اہل *ahl*, n. m. In Compos. One; an individual. One of a family, race, profession, community, or place.

اہل اختیار *ahl-i-ikhtyār*; n. m. One empowered; one vested with authority; a person in authority.

اہل الاجتہاد *ahl-ul-ijtihād*, n. m. In Mah. law. People capable of legal investigation; qualified jurists.

اہل اللہ *ahl-ullāh*, n. m. A man of God; a pious man; a dervise; faqīr.

اہل جایداد *ahl-i-jāēdād*, n. m. A man of property; owner; one possessing landed property; a land owner.

اہل حرفہ *ahl-i-hirfa*. One practising a trade or profession.

اہل حقوق *ahl-i-huqūq*, n. m. One possessing just claims, or possessed of rights. G. G.

اہل خانہ *ahl-i-khāna*, n. m. Ped. for H. *ghar ke log*.
1. People of the house; domestics. [wife.
2. Lady or master of the house; house-

اہل دفتر *ahl-i-daftar*. One employed as a clerk or *moharrir*.

ahl-i-rozgār, *naukrī-pesha*, n. m. Servants; serving men.

ahl-i-sunnat, n. m. The followers of the traditional, as well as the written law. The *Sunnīs*, as opposed to the *Shiās*.

اہل سیف *ahl-i-saif*, n. m. A military man; a soldier.

ahl-i-garaz, n. m. An interested party; one interested (*matlabyā*). [jurist.

اہل فقہ *ahl-i-fiqah*, n. m. A Mahommedan

اہل قلم *ahl-i-qalam*, n. m. A civilian; an officer in the Civil Department; a man of letters; a literary man.

اہل کار *ahl-kār*, n. m. An officer; an agent; a public or private servant. [G. G.

ahl-kār-i-pulis, n. m. A police functionary.

āhl-kār-i-sarkārī, n. m. A public officer. G.G.

ahl-kār-i-mohtamim thānā o pulis. An officer in charge of a police-station. G. G.

اہل کتاب *ahl-i-kitāb*, n. m. One who professes a revealed religion as contained in an inspired book. [of a commission.

اہل کمیشن *ahl-i-kamīshan*, n. m. A member

اہل مخاصمت *ahl-i-mukhāsmat*. All the parties concerned in a suit.

ahl-i-mad, n. m. A Persian writer, or head of a department in a court of judicature; an officer in charge.

اہل معاش *ahl-i-māāsh*, n. m. A man of property.

اہل مقدمہ *ahl-i-muqadmah*, n. m. One interested in a suit; a party in a case; an interested party; one of the two litigants.

ahl-i-virāsat, n. m. One interested in the succession; a joint heir; an heir.

اہلیہ *ahli'yā*, *qabī'lah*, n. f. A wife.

P آہن *ā'han*, n. m. Ped. for H. *lohā*. Iron.

آہنی *ā'hanī*, adj. Made of iron.

H آہن आहन *ā'han*, E. n. m. A mixture of straw and earth for building a wall.

H آہوتي आहूती *āhū'tī*, *āhut*, n. f. S. आहुति An oblation or burnt offering of *ghī*.

H اہیر अहीर *ahīr*; Sah. *hīr*; Garh. *guhīr*, n. m. S. आभीर. A caste of Hindū cowherds claiming to be descended from Krishna, called *Nand bansī*, *Jadu* or *Yadu-bansī*, and *Guāl-bansī*.

H اہیڑ अहेड़ *aheṛ*; Brij. *aher*, *ākheṭ*; Garh. *airī*, n. m. S. आखेट. [(*shikār*).
The chase; hunting; the prey or game

اہیڑي अहेड़ी *ahe'ṛī*, *aheṛiyā*, n. m. S. आखेटक A sportsman; hunter (*shikārī*); fowler.

Port. آیا *ā'yā*, n. f. A female attendant on children; a lady's maid; nurse; maid-servant (in Anglo-Indian houses); *āyah*.

A أيّام *aīyām'*, n. m. pl. of يوم a day H. *din*.
1. Time (*waqt*); space; days; season.
2. Duration; period; term; usance.
3. The menses; monthly discharge.

aīyām-i-dakhl-kārī, n. m. Period of tenancy; term of possession.

aīyām daurān-i-muqadmah, n. m. The time during which a suit is pending.

aīyām-i-daurah. During circuit, sessions.

aīyām-i-ohdeh-dārī, n. m. Incumbency; the period during which an office is held.

aīyām guzashtah, n. m. Time past.

aīyām se, *kapṛoṅ se*, *maile sir se*, *yā nahānī honā*, *phūl ānā*, v. n. Wom. To have the menses or monthly discharge.

adāē zar ba-fāsila aīyām-i-muqarrarah. Periodical payment. G. G.

A آیت *ā'yat*, n. f. ايّا He set a sign by which a person or thing might be known.

1. A sign ; mark (*nishān*).
2. A verse or paragraph of the *Qurān*. [sary.

A ایجاب *ījāb'*, n. m. وجب Rendering neces-
1. (*In logic*). Affirmation (Opp. of negation *sālib*) ; assent.
2. (*In Mah. law*). The first proposal made by one of the parties in negociating or concluding a bargain.

ایجاب و قبول *ījāb' o qubūl'*, n. m. Proposal and acceptance (in a negociation of marriage). The offer and assent must be declared before witnesses to render the marriage valid.

A ایجاد *ījād'*, *ikhtirāā*, n. f. وجد creating.
Invention ; creation ; production.

ījād karnā, v. a.
1. To create ; invent ; originate ; produce.
2. To project ; design ; devise ; strike out.

ījād honā, v. n. To be invented, etc.

A ایذا *ī'zā*, n. m. اذي He was hurt. Ped. for H. دکھ q. v. [*denā.*

īzā paunhchānā, yā de'nā, v. a. See *dukh*

īzā-dihandah, īzā-rasān, Ped. for H. *dukhdāī*. Offensive ; hurtful ; noxious ; vexatious ; injurious ; troublesome.

īzā-rasānī, n. f. Causing distress or injury ; persecution.

majma-i-mazhabī ko īzā paunhchānā.
Disturbing a religious assembly. G.G.

nālish-i-īzā rasānī bil-qasd. Charge of malicious or wilful persecution.

A ایزاد *īzād'*, n. Ped. for H. *baṛhotrī.*
Additions ; augmentation ; increase.

īzād kar'nā, Ped. for *ziyāda k.* q. v.

A ایضا *ai'zan*, Cont. (״), adv. The same ; ditto ; as above or before ; in the same manner.

A ایفا *ī'fā*, n. m. Used in Comp. وفي Paying ; keeping faith. Fulfilment ; discharge ; payment ; satisfaction.

ایفاے دگري *īfā-i-digrī*, Satisfaction of decree.

īfā-i-wādah, n. m. Fulfilment of a promise.

شرایطکاایفا *sharāyat kā īfā*, Fulfilment of conditions. G. G.

H ایک एक *ek*; (in Com.) *ik*; Gaṛh. *yek*; adj. S. एकः ; Pr. *ekkam, eam* ; P. *yak.*
1. One ; a ; an ; only ; only one ; a certain one ; each ; each one ; another.
2. Individual ; single ; sole.
3. Either ; one or the other.
4. Equal ; like ; alike ; similar.

ekā-ekī, P. *yak-bārgī, yakāyak* ; A. *'dafatan*, adv. At once ; suddenly ; simultaneously.

ایک آد एक आद *ek-ād, ek-ādh*, adj. Some ; some few ; few ; hardly, or scarcely any.

ek ek, ek ek kar-ke, ek ke bād ek, adv. One by one ; one after the other ; consecutively ; *seriatim* ; individually ; each ; every ; apiece ; severally ; singly.

ek ek ke do do, Twice as much ; double ; hundred per cent.

ek bāt, n. f. *lit.* One word. [matter.
1. The same thing ; no difference ; no
2. One price ; no variation or bargaining.

ek bāchhī, n. f. A distribution of any tax or cess levied upon all lands at an equal rate.

ek bināë muqadmah ko do shiq karnā.
To divide one cause of action into two ; splitting of claims.

ek peṭ ke, adj. Of the same mother ; own brothers or sisters.

ایک تو एक तो *ek to*, adv. Firstly ; in the first instance ; on the one hand.

ek tol, adj. Of the same weight ; equal.

ایک ٹانگ एक टांग *ek-ṭāṅg* (one leg of a quadruped), *māshā*, (Broker's idiom) ; *charannī*, n. f. A four-anna piece.

ek-jā, ek-jagah, ikhaṭṭā, ek-thān, adv. In one place ; collected together ; in a mass.

ek-jā karnā, v. a. See *ikhaṭṭā karnā.*

ek-jāt, ek-zāt ; P. *ham-qaum*, adj. Of the same caste, family, race, kind, or sort ; a co-religionist ; of the same parents.

ek-jāt, ek-mat, Prov. One caste, one mind.
A term used in agreements, contracts, and the like, by which the subscribers bind themselves jointly and severally to fulfil the terms specified.

ek dīvāl rupayā, ek thailī yā toṛā, (Broker's idiom). One thousand Rupees (*ek thailī*).

ek dūs're kī madad, Co-operation with one another ; mutual help.

ek-de'sī ; P. *ham-watan*, n. One belonging to the same place or country ; a fellow-countryman.

ایک رنگا एक रंगा *ek-raṅg'ā*, E.; *qand*, W., n. m.
A red cloth commonly worn by native women. [month.

ek rupayā saikṛā, One rupee per cent per

ایکڑا एकड़ा *ek'ṛā*, n. m. The figure one (१).

ek-tarfah, adj. One-sided ; partial ; *ex parte* ; biassed ; prejudiced.

ek-tarfah ḍigrī, n. One-sided decree.

ek-faslī, adj. Yielding but one crop annually.

ek-qalam ; P. *yak-qalam*, adv. *lit.* One pen.
At a stroke ; at once ; entirely ; altogether (*bilkul*).

ek mā bāp ke, adj. Of the same parents, the whole blood.

ایکم एकम *ek'am, paṛvā, pahlī*, n. f. The first day of the Hindu fortnight.

ekam-ek, ekam-kār, adj.
1. Mixed up; heterogenous; disordered; disarranged; unclassified; in a state of chaos.
2. Rendered unclean or impure by touch.
ek-mol, adj. Of the same value or price.
ek-muṅh, ek-zabān, adj. Agreeing; united; unanimous; of one speech; of the same mind.
ek-muṅh, ek-zabān, adv. Unanimously; with one consent; with one voice; with one accord; *una voce*; by common consent; in chorus; as one man; to a man; *nem con, or nemine contradicente*; *nemine dissentiente*; without a dissentient voice; one and all.
ek muṅh ho'nā, v. n.
1. To agree; coincide in opinion (*ek rāē honā*); to be unanimous.
2. To be of the same mind; be at one with; enter into one's views; sing in chorus; chime in.
ek-musht, ek-raqam, adv. In one payment.
ایک نام एक नाम *ek-nām*; P. *ham-nām*; adj. Cognominal; having the same name.
ek na, ek bhī nahīṅ, No one; none; not a single one; neither.
ek na ek, conj. Either; one or the other.
ایکنترا एकन्तरा *ekan'trā, ikantrā*, n. m. Hin. Fasting every other day.
ek hī ghar ke, Of the same family; from the same ancestor or stock.
ایکا एका *e'kā*, n. m.
1. Unanimity; union; concurrence; accord; concord. [bination; conspiracy.
2. Alliance; league; compact; com-
3. *Chem.* Affinity; adhesion; attraction.
ایکاسنا एकासना *ekās'nā, ikās'nā*; Mār. एकासणे, n. m. S. अश to eat. Eating once a day, reckoned as fasting. Hin.
ایکانت एकान्त *ekānt', ikānt'*, adj. S. अन्त limit. Secluded; sequestered; retired; private; lonely; *solus*; solitary; single; unaccompanied.
ایکانت एकान्त *ekānt'*, n. m. Seclusion; retirement; isolation; solitude; loneliness.
ekānt meṅ, adv. Aside; apart; alone.
ایکوترا एकोत्रा *eko'trā, ikotar*, adj. 1. A hundred and one. 2. One per cent.
H ایکھ ईख *īkh, ūkh*, n. f. Sugarcane. See اوکھ.
P ایلچی *el'chī*; H. *dūt*, n. m. T. *yalchī*, An envoy; delegate; ambassador.
ایلچی گری *elchī-gar'ī*, n. f. Embassy; the office or dignity of an ambassador.
H ایلوا एलवा *el'vā*, n. m. Aloes (*musabbar*).

A ایما *ī'mā*, n. m, وماء nod, beckon.
Hint; implication; allusion; indirect or incidental reference.
A ایمان *īmān'*; H. *dharum*, n. m. امن he was secure. [(*dīn*).
1. Belief; religion; religious faith; creed
2. Conscience; conscientiousness; truth; faithfulness; good faith; fidelity; trustworthiness; honesty (*īmāndārī*); probity; uprightness; integrity; honor.
īmān se; H. *dharam se*, adv. Fairly; honestly; conscientiously.
īmān se kahnā, yā tahrīr kar'nā, v. n. To testify or declare solemnly
īmān kā saudā, yā khel, Fair dealing.
īmān lānā, v. n.
1. To believe; have or put faith in; trust; put trust on or in; confide in.
2. To rely on; credit; give credit to.
3. To be converted to a faith.
ایماندار *īmān-dār'*, adj. P. دار keep. Opp. of *be-īmān*. q. v. Conscientious; honest; true; upright; just; trustworthy; faithful.
A ائمّه *aim'ma*, n. m. pl. of *imām* a priest.
1. Land given by the king at a very low rent; a grant of land for the support of a shrine or temple, a fief (when no rent is paid, it is called *lā-khirāj*); a grant of land, etc. to the people who attend at the tomb of a saint.
2. Land granted by the Mogul Government, either rent-free or subject to a small quit-rent, to learned or religious persons of the Mahommedan faith, or for religious and charitable uses in relation to Mahommedanism. Such tenures were recognised by the British Government as hereditary and transferable. Beng. Regulation VIII. 1793. *Wilson's Glossary.*
ائمّه باز یافت *aim'ma bāz yāft*. Lapsed *Aima* grants, subsequently assessed.
aima bāz zamīn. Land held rent-free; or at a quit-rent, under an *Aima* grant.
ائمه دار *aim'ma-dār, aima-kār*, n. m. Holder of land granted for religious or charitable uses, or to religious or learned Mahommedans; a feoffee.
ائمه موضع *aim'ma-mauzā*. A village given as a charitable endowment to learned or religious persons.
A آئین *āīn'*, n. m.
1. A body of laws; constitution; code; law; regulation; institute; statute (*qānūn*).
2. Rule; enactment; act; edict; ordinance; canon; decree.

3. The common law in contradistinction to the *shara*, or laws delivered by Mahommed (*lex scriptā*); *lex non scriptā*.

آیِنِ بحري *āīn-i-bahrī*, Maritime law.

آیِن بنانا *āīn banānā*, v. a. To legislate; enact, or make laws.

آیِنِ جنس *āīn-i-jins*. The law relating to assessments in kind.

آیِن‌دان *āīndān*, n. m. One who knows the law (*qānūn-dān*).

آئینِ دیواني *āīn-i-dīvānī*, n. m. Civil law.

آیِنِ رجستري *āīn-i-rajistarī*. Registration law.

آیِنِ شراکت *āīn-i-sharākat*, n. m. Terms or conditions of partnership. [dence.

آیِنِ شہادت *āīn-i-shahādat*, n. The law of evi-

آیِنِ طریقهٔ قرقي *āīn-i-tarīqa-i-qurqī*. The legal process of attachment. [law.

آئینِ فوجداري *āīn-i-faujdārī*, n. m. Criminal

āīn ke muāfiq kār-band honā, v. n. To conform to the requirements of the law; to obey the law, to act up to the law; to do what the law requires.

آئینِ مال *āīn-i-māl*, n. m. Revenue law.

آیِنِ معاہدہ *āīn-i-muāhidah*. Law of contract.

khilāf-i-āīn, bar khilāf-i-āīn, Contrary to law; illegal; information irregular.

H اینچنا एंचना *eṅch'nā, īṅch'nā, aiṅch'nā, kheṅch'nā*; Mag. *ghīṅch'nā*, v. a. S. कष् to draw Caus. of *iṅch'nā*, q. v.

1. To draw a line; to rule.
2. To write; scribble.
3. To draw or unsheath (one's sword).
4. To hang (on a gibbet) (*phāṅsī denā*); execute.
5. To take in; absorb; suck up.
6. To draw in the breath; inspire; inhale.
7. To extort; exact; ease of (one's money).
8. To reserve; keep or hold back.
9. To take upon oneself; engage; make oneself liable to pay for; to be responsible for.

اینچ एंच *eṅch, īṅch*, n. f.

1. Scarcity; deficiency; drought.
2. Delay; tardiness; slowness.
3. The banking system by which zamīndars pay the revenue demand.

A *banyā* is called in who pays in the amount and afterwards recovers from each *āsāmi* the amount payable by him (*iṅch-manauti*).

H ایندور ईंदूर *īṅ'dūr, īṅ'dur, iṅdūr*; Māṛ. *ūṅdro*, n. m. S. इन्दुर A rat; mouse; mole.

P آیندہ *āin'dah*, adj. Coming; future; ensuing; next.

āindah; H. *āge*, adv. In future; for the future; henceforth; hereafter. [*jātā*.

āindah-ravindah, n. m. A traveller. See *ātā*

H ایندھن ईंधन *īṅ'dhan*, n. m. S. इन्ध् to kindle, Pālī. *edho* firewood.

Firewood; fuel; wood.

H اینڈ एंड *aiṅḍ*, adj. [unprofitable.

1. Useless; worthless; unserviceable;
2. Incomplete; unfinished; imperfect.

aiṅḍ kar'nā, v. n. To render useless; to break; injure; spoil.

aiṅḍ honā, aiṅḍ rah'nā, v. n.

1. To be broken, dislocated, injured.
2. To come to a dead lock or stand-still (a machine).
3. To be locked up; remain uninvested (as money). [thing.
4. To become useless, or good for no-
5. To remain unfinished, incomplete, or *in statu quo*.

H اینڈا एंडा *aiṅ'ḍā*, n. m. A makeweight placed in the lighter scale. W.

اینڈانا ऐंडाना *aiṅḍā'nā, aiṅḍāl'nā*, v. a.

To put in the scale; to weigh roughly.

H اینڈوا ईंडवा *īṅḍ'wā, īṅḍhuā*, W.; *iṛvā*, Sah.; ईंडोणी Māṛ.; *geṅḍuvā*, Mag.; *siraiṅḍā*, Gaṛh.; *birvā*, Tir. n. m. H. *aiṅḍlī* a ring.

A roll or round fold on which a burden is carried on the head for supporting a water-jar, etc.

[(*saṅdūr*).

H اینگر ईंगुर *īṅ'gur*, n. m. Red lead; minium

H ایوارا ऐवारा *aiwā'rā*; Mag. *kūrhā*, n. A cowshed in the middle of a jungle.

ب

P با *bā*, prep. With; together with; in addition.

بااین ہمہ *bā īṅ hamah*. adv. Whereas; notwithstanding; seeing that.

bā farzand, A term inserted in a grant made to the grantee and his posterity.

bā-shauq, adv. Willingly; with all one's heart.

باضابطہ *bā-zābitah*, adj.

1. Regular; formal; according to rule or usage; in conformity with precedent.
2. Well-regulated; safe and convenient.

bā-zāb'itah, adv. According to rule, usage, or custom; with a douceur (Amlā's idiom).

باقاعدہ *bā-qāēdā*, adj. Regular, formal; according to rule.

باوجود *bā-wujūd'*, *bā-wasf*, conj. Notwithstanding; in spite of; although; withal.

بانوا *bā-nawā*, *be-navā*, n. m. A class of beggars. See *āzād*.

A باب *bāb*, n. m. A. *bāb* door.
1. Division; section; chapter; heading.
2. Particular; point; affair; case; matter; business; object; topic.
3. Tax; cess; head of accounts.

A بابت *bā'bat*, prep. Ped. for H. *maddhe*. On account of; regarding; respecting; concerning; conversant with; touching; about; as to; in the matter of; in behalf of.
bābat akhaz-i-lagān bil-jabr. On account of the illegal exaction of rent. G. G.
uske bābat, *jiske bābat*. For which; concerning which; for the sake of.
pādāsh kī bābat. For the punishment of.
بابت *bābat*, *mad*, n. f.
Account; statement; item of account.

H بابو बाबू *bā'bū*; Brij. & E. *bab'uā*, n. m. S. विप्र.
1. A title of respect, as Sir, Mr., Esq., young master, father, Sire.
2. A man of family or distinction.

P بابونہ *bābū'nā*, n. m. The camomile; wild ivy; *Anthemis nobilis*. Wat.

H باپ बाप *bāp*, *bāvā*; W. Rus. and Brij. *bāpū*; Mag. *bappā*; Gaṛh. *bubā*; E. Hin. *bābū*; Poet. *bābal*, n. m. S. विप्र, Z. *bāp*. Father.
bāp dādā, n. m.
1. Forefathers; ancestors; progenitors.
2. Ancestry; lineage; family; pedigree.
bāp māre kā bair, The blood feud caused by the murder of a father; hereditary quarrel.
bāp-hat'tyā; S. पितृ घातः; P. *pidar-kushī*, n. f. Parricide (the act).
بپوتی बपोती *bapo'tī*, *bap-ans*, n. f. Patrimony; inheritance; heritage; paternal estate; ancestral property (*virsā*).
bapo'tī, adj. Patrimonial; hereditary; ancestral; lineal; direct.
bapotī adhkār, n. m. Hereditary right; right by or of succession, or inheritance.
bapotī māl; A. *mīrās*, n. m. Ancestral property; patrimonial inheritance.

A باتّباع احکام *ba-ittebā-i-ahkām*. Subject to orders; in obedience to orders.

A باتّفاق *ba-ittifāq*, adv. Together; concurrently; unanimously; all at once.

H بات बाट *bāṭ*, *baṭ*, W.; *baṭkharā*, E.; *tolā*, Mar. n. m. S. वट् to divide. 1. A measure of weight; a weight. 2. Path; way; road.
bāṭ tarāzū, n. m. Weights and scales.
bāṭ-chhāp, n. m. Stamping weights and measures. [the weights.
bāṭ-chhapāī, n. f. A fee charged for stamping
bāṭ hārnā, *yā har'nā*, v. a. To make a weight; to test the accuracy of a weight.
bāṭ roknā, v. n. To block up or close a road; to stop one on the road.

P باج *bāj*, n. m. Old. P. *bāz*. Duty; cess; impost; tax; tribute.
باجگزار *bāj-guzār'*, n. m. A tributary; one who pays taxes, duties, etc.; a feudatory or dependant state.
باجگیر *bāj-gīr'*, n. m. A tax gatherer; a collector of tribute or revenue. [contribution.
باج و خراج *bāj o khirāj'*, n. m. Tribute and

H باجا बाजा *bā'jā*; Rus. *bājo*; Sah. *bājjā*; Poet. *bajan*, n. m. S. वाद्य from वद् to sound. A musical instrument; instrumental music; music.
bājantrī, *yā bajantrī mahāl*, n. m.
1. The quarter inhabited by musicians.
2. A tax under the Mahomedan Government imposed upon all professional singers, dancers, and musicians. [*rā*; n. m.

H باجرا बाजरा *bāj'rā*; Poet. *bajrā*; Sah. *lehaṛ*-
A species of panic or millet; *Panicum spicatum*, Wat.; a small cheap grain which furnishes the meal-cakes of the poorer classes.

P A باجرا *ba-ijrā*. In the exercise of. G. G.
ba-ijrā-i-ḍigrī. In the execution of decree.

H باچھ बाछ *bāchh*, n. f. H. *bānṭ* divide. Subscription; proportionate rate; proportion of tax; rate of distribution; assessment on a share; portion; share.

A rate or contribution from the shares in a *Bhāīchārā* estate, in discharge of their shares of the *jamʿa*, or to make up any balance in the collection. In some estates the rate is according to *Biswādārī* shares; in others, according to the quantity of land cultivated by each sharer.

The proportionate rate or division either of lands, or liabilities attached to them. The apportionment of a village or estate, or of the produce in separate portions among associated or coparcenary occupants, especially in the case of mixed *Paṭi-dārī* tenures: where part is held in common and part in severalty. The Government rent and village expenses are paid from the land held in common, and any overplus is distributed, or any deficit made good by a *bāchh*, or rate levied on the several holdings. The rate is sometimes levied according to the number of ploughs employed by the cultivators. In some parts of India the term implies a share of the village lands, which consists, in general, of as much as may be ploughed with one plough.

باچھبرار बाछबरार *bāchh-barār*, n. m. A tenure common in *Bundelkhand*, in which the shares of the revenue payable by the joint proprietors of a village are liable to occasional readjustment and alteration.

bāchh ḍālnā, v. n. To levy a tax; raise by subscription.

H باد बाद *bād*, n. m. S. बद् to speak.

1. Debate; discussion; dispute.
2. Contention; strife; rencounter; fight.
3. A law-suit; action; case; trial.
4. Alloy; mixture of a baser with a superior metal.
5. Charge; allowance; commission.
6. Remission of revenue or rent on account of deficient harvest.

bād prati bād. Altercation; discussion.

bād karnā, bād'nā, v. n.

1. To dispute; argue; discuss.
2. To contest a matter; contend for; bring an action (*muqadma laṛānā*). [with.
3. To contend, engage, cope or fight

بادي बादी *bā'dī*, Displaced by A. مدّعي n. m.

1. Plaintiff; complainant; suitor.
2. A wicked person.

prati-bādi, n. m. A. مدعاعليه q. v.

بادي پرتبادي बादी प्रतिबादी *bādī pratibādī*. Displaced by A. مدعي مدعاعليه q. v.

پرتباد प्रतिबाद *prati-bād*. Retort; rejoinder; answer; reply; defence.

P باد *bād*, n. f. Z. and Pahlavī, *vād*; H. *bāo*; S. बात Air; wind (*havā*).

بادبان *bād-bān*; H. *pāl*, n. m. A sail.

bād-i-samūm, Ped.; H. *lū*, n. f. A hot wind like the blast from a furnace; the simoom.

bād-i-muāfiq, Ped.; H. *sīdhī hawā*, n. f. Favourable winds.

bād-i-mukhālif, n. f. Ped. for H. *ulṭī hawā*. Contrary winds.

بادنما *bād-numā*, n. m. Flag; vane; a weathercock. [*penis*.

1. A eunuch born with a rudimentary
2. A species of rice.

P بادشاه *bādshāh'*; Illit. *bāshshā*; Rus. *bāchchhā*; Maṛ. *pātchhā*, n. m. Cor. of P. *pādshāh* from *pād* a throne, *shāh* an owner.

A sovereign; king; monarch. [prince.

bādshāh-zādā, shah-zāda, n. m. A king's son;

bādshāh-zādī, n. f. A princess; queen.

bādshāh-kush, n. m. A regicide (the person).

bādshāh-kushī; H. *rāj-hattyā*. n. f. Regicide (the crime).

بادشاهت *bādshāh'at*, H. *rāj*, n. f.

1. Kingdom; sovereignty; monarchy.
2. State; government; rule.
3. Realm; empire; dominion; sceptre.

bādshāhat karnā, rāj karnā, v. a. To hold the sceptre; reign; govern; rule.

بادشاهي *bādshāhī, shāhī*, adj. Kingly; royal; regal; sovereign; imperial.

bādshāhī haq, n. m. Royal prerogative.

bādshāhī hukm, n. m. Royal mandate.

bādshāhī sanad, n. f. A royal grant or charter; a written document conveying lands or titles from the ruling power; a royal tenure, or grant of land rent-free.

bādshāhī ǎdālat, n. f. His or Her majesty's court; royal court.

bādshāhī gharānā, shāhī khāndān, n. m. Royal family, dynasty (*rāj-bans*).

bādshāhī māl, n. m. State property; estates belonging to the crown.

bādshāhī imārat, n. f. Royal buildings.

bādshāhī kharch, n. m.

1. Expenditure from the privy purse.
2. Royal or princely expenditure.

H باده *bādh*, n. (*Agric.*) Pasture land when the grass has been cut for hay, and the cattle are grazed on the roots.

H بادها बाधा *bādh'a*, n. m. H. *baḍhnā* to increase. Increase; premium; progress.

In revenue, the amount added to, or deducted from, any payment according to the currency in which it is paid as compared with a fixed standard coin. Discount on uncurrent or short-weight rupees. A cess or charge imposed to make up for any probable deficiency in the value of the coin.

A بادي النظر *bādī-un-nazar*, Ped. for H. *dekhte hī*, q. v. adv. At first sight.

H بار बार *bār*, n. m. S. वार time.

1. Day; time; (Hin.) Saturday.
2. Turn; round; occasion; opportunity.

bār bār sawāl karnā, v. a. To ask repeatedly; demand urgently; importune. [happened.

bārhā aisā huā. Several times it has so

باري बारी *bārī*, n. f.

1. Time; turn.
2. A mode of keeping up the village watch in some places, the villagers keeping watch by turns; working a sugarcane mill by turns, so that there shall be no intermission night and day until the whole is ground, the villagers uniting for this purpose.

bārī bārī, adv. Turn by turn; one after the other; successively; in succession; alternately.

باريدار बारीदार *bārī-dār*, n. m. *bārī-dārnī*, n. f. Attendants who keep watch in turn.

H & P بار **बार** *bār,* n. m. S. **बार**

1. Entrance; door; gate; threshold.
2. (*bār-yābī*). Admission; admittance; access; ingress; audience (in Persian).

bār-i-khās, bār-gāh-i-khās, n. m. Private hall of audience. [the gate.

bār-rukāī, n. f. *lit.* The act of stopping at A part of the marriage ceremony in which something is paid to the sister of the bridegroom for allowing the pair to enter the bridegroom's house.

bār-i-ām, bārgāh-i-ām, n. m. Public audience.

bār-gāh, n. f. Place of audience. [or levee.

bār-yābī-i-darbār, n. f. Admission at a court

P بار *bār,* n. m. 1. Load; burden; cargo.
2. Fruit; produce; yield.

بار *bār,* adj. Burdensome; heavy; hard.

بار بٹائي *bār baṭāī, bojh baṭāī,* n. f. A division of the crop by sheaves or loads before the corn is trodden out.

بار بردار *bār-bardār,* n. m. *lit.* A burden-bearer. A porter; carrier; a beast of burden; cart.

بار برداري *bār-bardārī*; Illit. *bhāl bardārī,* n. f.
1. The means of conveyance; transport.
2. Carriage; cart or camel hire; cost of conveyance; freight; transit charges; lading; cargo.

bār-bardārī ke jānwar, n. m. Cattle. G. G. *more properly,* draught cattle.

bār-i taraddud, n. m. The burden of disproof or rebutment.

bār-i-jahāz, n. m. Ship's cargo; cargo.

bār-dār; A. *hāmila,* adj.
1. Fruitful; laden with fruit; loaded.
2. Pregnant; with child (*peṭ se*).

باردانه *bār-dānā,* n. m. [forage.
1. Supplies for an army; provisions;
2. Vessels, bags, etc. in which provisions are kept; the implements or apparatus of a trade; utensils.

بارکش *bār-kash,* n. m. A cart for carrying loads, etc. (*bhār-kas*).

H بارا **बारा** *bār'ā, bārah,* W. n. m. S. **वार्** water.
1. The act of drawing water from the well for irrigation.
2. The man who stands over the well to turn over the leathern bucket (*moṭ* or *charas*) when drawn up. [the *jantrī.*
3. The process of drawing wire through
4. Rus. A feast given on the death of some old man (*kāj*). [procession (برات)

H بارات **बारात** *bārāt',* n. f. A marriage

P بارانى *bārā'nī,* n. f. S. **वारि** water.
1. (*Pāṅḍū*) Unirrigated land dependent on rain, in contradistinction to *chāhī,* q. v.
2. A great coat or mackintosh for keeping off the rain; a waterproof (*barsātī*).

bārānī khet, n. m. A field dependent on rain.

H باراه **बाराह** *bār'āh,* n. m. S. **वराह** a hog, a boar. 1. The third incarnation of Vishnu.
2. Land next to a village, or more properly, the earth from its having been raised from the deep by Varaha.

P بارش *bār'ish,* n. f. from P. *bārīdan* to rain.
S. *varshā,* Ped. for H. *meṅh,* q. v.

P بارگیر *bār-gīr, bāl-gīr,* n. m. P. *bār* a horse, *gīr* take. A trooper who is mounted on a horse supplied by the state or the chief he serves; a cavalry man who does not find his own horse. A groom.

P بارود *bārūd;' bārūt;* H. *dārū,* n. f. T. *bārūt* saltpetre. Gunpowder.

بارود خانه *bārūd-khānā,* n. m. A powder magazine, or manufactory. [ammunition.

بارود گولا *bārūd golā,* n. m. Powder and ball; *rakhnā bārūd kā zāyid miqdār muāianā se.* Keeping excess of gunpowder. G. G.

P باره *bār'ah,* n. Point; matter; item (*mad*).

H باره پتهر **बारहपत्थर** *bārah-patthar,* n. m. A space surrounded by twelve pillars for an encampment.

H باري **बारी** *bā'rī,* E; *balhār',* W; n. f.
1. A caste of men who sew together broad leaves which serve for plates (*pattal*). [profession (Tirhut).
2. (H. *bālnā* to light) A torch-bearer by

H باڑ **बाड़** *bāṛ, bār,* n. f. S. **वाट** fence.
1. A line; margin; rim; edge.
2. Fence; paling; railings; rail.
3. Front; fore-rank; van (*āge*).
4. A line or row of soldiers.
5. Volley; a rapid discharge of shots.
6. (H. *baṛhnā* increase). Flood; inundation; swell or rise of the river; deluge.

باڑيا **बाड़या** *bāṛ'yā,* n. m. A whetter of cutting instruments.

H باڑا **बाड़ा** *bāṛ'ā.* n. m. S. **वद्** to surround.
1. An enclosure (*gherā*); circuit; area; arena (*daṅgal*).
2. Mah. A cemetry; churchyard.
3. Alms or charity dispensed at a Hin. marriage.

باڑي **बाड़ी** *bā'ṛī, bārī,* n. f. S. **वाटी**

1. Homestead; homestall; home; hearth. 2. A plantation; field; orchard; a kitchen garden. 3. A cotton field. W.

P باز *bāz*; H. *phir*, adv. Again; back.

باز آمد احکام *bāz āmad aḥkām.* A return made to the orders of the court. [on the file.

bāz ba-lambar sābiq qāyam karnā. To replace

بازپرس *bāz-purs*; H. *pūchh-gachh'*, n. f.
1. Examination; investigation; minute investigation.
2. Responsibility; accountability.

bāz-purs sarsarī karnā, v. n. To hold a summary investigation.

bāz-purs karnā, v. a. [question.
1. To examine; enquire into; call in
2. To call to account; to demand an explanation. [suit.

باز دعوی *bāz-dāwā*, n. m. Withdrawal of a

bāz-dāwā likhnā, v. n. To resign or relinquish a claim; to execute a deed of withdrawal; to withdraw an action.

bāz-dāwā-nāmah. A deed of relinquishment.

بازدهی *bāz-dihī*, n. f. Return; restitution; restoration.

باز رکهنا *bāz rakhnā*; H. *roknā*, v.a. [intercept.
1. To keep back; detain; withhold;
2. To hold back; repress; confine; constrain; restrain.
3. To keep from; stop; keep out of.
4. To suspend; intermit; stop.
5. To interdict; check; restrict; hinder; prevent; prohibit; inhibit; forbid; retrench.
6. To shut out; exclude; bar; debar; cut off; proscribe. [pel.
7. To dissuade; deter; discourage; re-

bāz rakhnā shar o fasād se. To prevent a breach of the peace; to keep the peace.

بازگیری *bāz-gīrī*, n. f. Resumption of alienated revenue of land.

بازنامه *bāz-nāmah.* Petition of withdrawal.

بازیافت *bāz-yāft*, n. f.
1. Withdrawal; drawback; deduction.
2. Readmission; resumption (either wholly or in part of alienated lands and again subjecting them to a revenue assessment); resumption of rent-free land.

P بازار *bāzār'*; Pop. *bazār*; Rus. *bajār*; H. *hāṭ*; n. m. Z. *vāzār*, P. *abā* food, and *zār* place.
1. Market; bazar; place of exchange; market place; mart.
2. Sale; demand.
3. Rate; price; charge (*bhāo*).
4. Credit; trust; tick (*sākh*).

bāzār-baṭṭā, n. m. Discount; the market rate of exchange for different coins.

bāzār banānā, v. a. To build a street of shops.

bāzār band honā; H. *haṭ-tāl honā*, v. n. To be closed (the market or shops).

bāzār-baiṭhak, tah-bāzārī, n. f. A fee or tax for setting up a shop or stall, or for trading in a bazar.

bāzār-kharch, n. m. Market expenses; daily or private disbursements.

bāzār dikhānā, v. n. To expose for sale.

bāzār kā bhāo, yā nirkh, n. m. Market rate; selling price. [the market.

bāzār kā chalan, The custom or usage of

bāzār kā roz; H. *peṅṭh*, n. m. Market day.

bāzār karnā, E. v. n. To market; go to market; go shopping.

bāzār khulnā, v. n. To be opened (the market).

bāzār kī āwāz, n. f. A street cry.

bāzār garm honā, chamaknā, yā chalnā, v. n.
1. To be lively (the market); to have a good sale; to be in great request.
2. To rage; prevail; spread; flourish.

bāzār lagānā, v. a. [shops.
1. To set up a bazar; open a number of
2. To spread or show one's wares. [ket).

bāzār mandā honā, v. n. To be dull (the mar-

بازارو *bāzā'rū, bazārū*, adj. Of ordinary make or fashion. Hence, not solid, strong, or good.

بازاری *bāzā'rī*, adj. [cantile.
1. Appertaining to the market; mer-
2. Current; prevalent; ruling.
3. Ordinary; usual; common; popular.

bāzārī ādmī; Mah. Wom. *hazārī bazārī*, n. m. Common people; the swell mob.

bāzārī bāt, gap, yā khabar, n. f. A bazar report; a bazar gup; rumour.

bazārī aurat, n. f. A market maid. [woman. A woman of the town; a common

P بازی *bā'zī*, n. f. P. *bākhtan* to play.
A stake (at play); a wager; bet; a game of chance; hazard; lottery; raffle.

bāzī badnā, budnā, yā lagānā, v. n.
1. To lay a bet or wager; to wager.
2. To toss; gamble; raffle.

bāzī-gar, n. m. A juggler; conjuror; tumbler.

P A باستثنا *ba-istisnāë*, Save and except; excepting; with the exception of; exclusive of; besides.

ba-istisnāë galatī. Errors excepted.

P باشنده *bāshin'dah*; A. *sākin*; H. *bāshī*, n. m. باشیدن to remain, H. *bās* dwelling.
An inhabitant; dweller; resident; native.

باشندگان *bāshindgān*, n. m. Pl. Inhabitants.

bāshindgān-i-sharīf n. m. Respectable inhabitants. G. G.

A باطل *bā'til ;* H. *jhūṭā,* adj. A. بطل It was or became false. [fallacious.
1. False ; not true ; fictitious ; unreal ;
2. Spurious ; unsound ; worthless.
3. Vain ; futile ; ineffectual ; nugatory ; useless (*birthā*).
4. Void ; null ; abolished.
5. Devoid of virtue ; of no effect ; of no force ; of no account ; naught.

bātil aur kal-adam. Null and void ; of no effect.
bātil samajhnā, bātil mutasavvar k. v. n. To treat as invalid ; treat as a nullity ; to set at naught.
bātil kar'nā, v. a. [lidate.
1. To vitiate ; render defective ; inva-
2. To nullify ; make void, annul ; falsify (*jhuṭlānā*). [across (*chheknā*).
3. To rescind ; revoke ; draw the pen
4. To reverse ; abolish ; quash ; cancel.
5. To supersede ; set aside ; overrule.
6. To prove false ; prove the contrary ; disprove ; refute ; defeat ; upset.
7. To thwart ; baffle ; frustrate ; foil.

bātil honā, v. n. To be annulled ; cancelled ; to become void ; to come to nought.

A باطن *bā'tin ;* H. *antar,* n. m. Opp. of *zāhir.* بطن the belly. The inward part ; the inside ; mind ; heart ; disposition.

P A باعتبار *ba-etebār,* adv. In virtue of ; in consideration of ; by reason of ; according to ; agreeably. [*ex-officio.*
ba-etebār ohdah, In virtue of one's office ;

A باعث *bāis,* n. m. بعث Sending ; causing. Cause (*kāran*) ; reason ; motive ; occasion.
bāis se, adv. In consequence of ; in pursuance of ; by reason of G. G. [induce.
bāis honā, v. n. To cause ; occasion ; produce ;
is tarkīb ke bais. In pursuance of the instigation. G. G. [quence of ; on account of.
ba-bāis, Because ; by reason of ; in conse-
ba-bāis ishtiāl-i-tabā. On provocation. G. G.
nā-lyāqatī ke bāis. On the ground of disqualification. G. G. [Z. baë.

A باغ *bāğ ;* Rus. *bāg ;* H. *bāṛī ;* n. m. S. *bāṭika,*
1. A garden ; orchard ; a small garden.
2. A cluster of trees ; plantation ; grove.

bāg-i-sair-gāh-i-awām kī taiyārī, yā khabargīrī. Formation and support of a public garden. G. G.
باغات *bāğāt',* n. m. Lands which, being well supplied with water and adapted to the cultivation of fruits and various vegetable substances, as betel, areka, hemp, sugarcane, plantains, saffron, pepper, tobacco, onions, garlic, chillies, etc., are assessed at a higher rate than other arable lands.
باغاتي *bāğā'tī,* adj. Fit for, or relating to garden land or cultivation.
1. Raised on garden ground (fruit, etc).
2. Assessed or levied on gardens (revenue tax).

A باغي *bā'ğī ;* Illit. *bağī,* adj. بغي he sought. Disloyal ; mutinous ; rebellious ; up in arms.
bāğī, n. m. An insurgent ; a rebel ; mutineer.
bāğī honā ; H. *phir jānā,* v. n. To revolt ; rebel ; mutiny ; rise against.

A باقي *bā'qī,* n. f. بقي it remained.
1. The remaining portion ; remnant ; residue ; what remains ; what is left over.
2. The balance ; dues ; arrears ; outstandings ; balance of an account ; sums receivable (*baqāyā*). [net produce.
3. Overplus ; surplus (*bachat*) ; excess ;

bāqī aīyām, bāqī ke din, n. m. The remaining period ; unexpired term ; the remainder of one's life.
باقي بهيج *bāqī bhej,* n. f. Arrears of rent.
bāqī be-bāq karnā, yā chukānā, v. a. To pay up the balance due ; liquidate a balance ; square accounts ; make good a default.
bāqī paṛnā, v. n. To fall into arrears.
bāqī paṛne kī hālat meṅ, In the event of default ; on the occurrence of default.
باقي جمع *bāqī jamā* n. f. Statement of revenue after deducting the balances of former years.
bāqī chalī ātī hai, Balance lies over ; arrears have accumulated. [rent, or taxes.
bāqī khazāna, n. m. Arrears of revenue,
باقى دادني *bāqī dādanī, bāqī dain.* Balance payable.
باقيدار *bāqī-dār,* n. m. One who is in arrears, or owes a balance ; a defaulter.
bāqī-dār-i-māl, n. m. A revenue defaulter.
bāqī-dār honā, v. n. To owe ; to be indebted ; to have a balance to pay ; fall into arrear ; to be on the wrong side of an account.
bāqī zimme falāṅ, Balance against one.
bāqī ğair mumkin-ul-wasul. G. G. An irrecoverable balance.
bāqī rahnā, yā bachnā, v. n. To remain ; to be left ; to be due ; to remain unpaid ; accrue ; have a balance.
bāqī sāqī, n. f. Overplus ; balance ; remainder.
bāqī farzī, bāqī barāë nām. A nominal balance. [a one.
bāqī falāne kī. A balance in favour of such

bāqī ke khāne meṅ nadārad likhnā. To leave a blank in the column of balances.
bāqī kī kaifīyat. A statement or account of outstanding balances; particulars of balances.
bāqī kī muāfī. Remission of a balance.
bāqī kī wajah batānā. To account for a balance or default.
bāqī lagān, n. m. Arrears of rent.
bāqī māl, yā mālguzārī. Arrears of revenue.
bāqī māl-guzārī kī illat meṅ nīlām honā. v. n. To be sold in default, or non-payment of revenue.
bāqī māṅda. Remainder; residue.
jāedād-i-bāqī māṅda. Residuary estate. G. G.
bāqī nikālnā, v. a. To strike or carry forward a balance; shew a balance sheet.
bāqī wusūl karnā, v. a. To collect arrears.
bāqī yāftanī. Receivable balance.
باقیات *bāqiyāt',* n. f. Arrears; balance; outstandings; remainders.
bāqiyāt-i-hāl. Current balances.
bāqīyāt-i-hisāb-i-rawāṅ. Balances of accounts current.
bāqiyāt-dāir-ul-wusūl. Balances in course of liquidation.
bāqiyāt-i-sinīṅ-i-māzyā. Balances of past years.
jamā wāsil bāqī, Demands, collections, and balances.
hisāb kī bāqī, n. f. Balance of an account.
zar-i-bāqī, n.m. A balance; remaining or outstanding balances.
wusūl bāqī. Recovery of a balance; a balance.
fard wāsil bāqī kā masavvida. Balance rough sheet.

A باکره *bāk'ira*; H. *kuā'rī,* n. f. بکر. A young he-camel, one in youthful vigour. A virgin; maid; *virgo intacta*; an unmarried female.

H باکهه बाख *bākh, bāk, bāg, ain,* n. m. S. बाम The udder of animals.

باکهڑی बाखड़ी *bākh'ṛī, bākh'lī,* n. f. A cow or buffalo so called when she has given milk for five months.

H باکهل बाखल *bā'khal, bak'khal*; Rus. *bākhar*; Bhoj. *bakhrī,* n. f. An enclosure, area, or court-yard comprising several houses, cattle-sheds, etc.

H باگا बागा *bāg'ā,* n. m. S. वस्त्र cloth.
1. A dress of honor; a *khilat.*
2. A wedding garment; the dress worn by the bridegroom. 3. A suit; apparel.

H باگهی बाघी *bāgh'ī,* n. f. The bubo (*bad*).

A بال *bil*; H. *se,* prep. With; by.

بالاتفاق *bil-itti'fāq*; H. *ek-muṅh,* adv. Unanimously; with one consent.

بالاجمال *bil-ijmāl*; H. *milā-julā,* adv.
1. In the gross; in the aggregate; collectively; jointly; in common.
2. As a body; as one mass; *in solido.*

بالارادہ *bil-irā'dah, bil-qasd*; H. *jān-būjh-ke,* adv. Wilfully; intentionally; designedly.
bil-irādah zarar pahuṅchāne kī sazā. Punishment for voluntarily causing hurt.
bil-ishtirāk; H. *sājhe meṅ,* adv. Collectively; in partnership.
bil-infirād; H. *alag alag,* adv. Individually; severally; separately.
bil-infirād wa bil-ishtirāk; H. *sājhe meṅ aur alag.* Jointly and severally.

بالتخصیص *bil-takhsīs,* adv. Specifically; particularly.

بالتصریح *bil-tasrīh, bil-tafsīl*; H. *khol-ke,* adv. In detail; expressly; explicitly; distinctly.

بالتفصیل *bil-tafsīl*; H. *beore-wār,* adv. Particularly; at full length; item by item.

بالجبر *bil-jabr*; P. *zabar-dastī*; H. *jorā-jorī,* adv. Forcibly; by force.

بالجملہ *bil-jumlā,* adv.
1. In all (*sāre*); altogether; in the gross; on the whole.
2. In short (*nidān*); in a word; to sum up (*hāsil kalām*).

بالضرور *bil-zarūr*; H. *neṭham,* adv. Of necessity; inevitably; unavoidably; of course; absolutely; certainly; positively.

بالعکس *bil-aks*; H. *ulṭā,* adv. On the reverse; on the contrary; *vice versa*; *per contra*; on the other hand.
bil-aks-i-hāl. The contrary; contrary to the fact. G. G.
bil-aks-manshā. A contrary intention G. G.

بالعموم *bil-umūm'*; H. *sāre,* adv. Universally; commonly.

بالفرض *bil-farz*; H. *mānā,* adv. Supposing; let it be granted; admitting for the sake of argument.

بالفعل *bil-fel*; H. *abhī,* adv. Now; at present; just now; at the present time.

بالکل *bil-kul*; H. *nirā,* adv. Entirely; completely (*nipaṭ*); fully; wholly (*sāre*); totally; altogether; without exception; universally; perfectly.

بالمقابلہ *bil-muqāb'le, bil-mushāh'dā, bil-mushāf'ā*; P. *rū-ba-rū,* H. *sāmne*; *muṅh dar muṅh,* adv. Face to face; before; in the presence of.

بالمقطع *bil-muq'ta*; H. *baṅdhī-huī,* adj. According to agreement; stipulated; fixed; consolidated.

The phrase is applied especially to a tenure by which a ryot holds his land at a fixed rate per plough or per *bighā*, or the engagement by which his rent is fixed for a given term, without liability to enhancement.

bil muqta paṭṭā. A lease for a gross aggregate rent, in which the land tax and all other cesses or *abwābs* were consolidated.

bil-muqta jamā. Stipulated assessment; consolidated revenue.

bāl denā, v. n. *lit.* To give one's hair.

1. To be shaved preparatory to performing the obsequies of the dead—a Hindu rite especially incumbent on the son.

2. E. To cause the hair of the head to fall forward and backward before the *tāziah* of the Moharrum—a Mohamedan rite performed by women who bend forwards and backwards in the act while they beat their breasts.

kān-bāl, n. m. The Hindu ceremony of shaving a child's head for the first time (*mūṅḍan*) before boring his ears (*kan-chhedan*).

H بال बाल *bāl*; W. Rus. *bāli*; E. *bār*; Garh. *bāthon*, n. f. S. बल a sprout. The ear of corn.

بالچھڑ बालछड़ *bāl-chhaṛ*, n. f. A medicine or perfume; spikenard; hyacinth.

بالرکھا बालरखा *bāl-rakhā*, n. m.

1. The wages of a person employed to watch ripe crops at night.

2. The high mat platform from which the crops are watched.

بالو बालू *bā'lū*, n. m. The beard of the Indian corn.

H بال बाल *bāl*, *bāl'ak*; Māṛ. *ṭābar*, n. m. S. बाला, Pālī. *balo*. An infant.

بالرانڈ बालरांड *bāl-rāṅḍ*, *bāl bidhvā*, n. f. A child-widow.

بالہتیا बालहत्या *bāl-hat'tyā*; P. *bachchah-kushī*, n. f. Infanticide; female infanticide.

H بالا बाला *bā'lā*, n. m.

1. A grub that eats young plants of wheat or barley when about six inches high.

2. A medicinal and fragrant plant of the roots of which lattices are made; *Andropogon muricatum*. Wat.

P بالا *bā'lā*; H. *ūpar*, prep. 1. On; upon; up.

2. Foregoing; above or before-mentioned.

bālā-bālā, adv. Ped. for H. *ūpar hī ūpar*. Apart; away from; slily; secretly.

bālā-dast, adj. Superior; higher.

bālā-gashtī, n. f. Patrolling; going one's beat or rounds; inspection (*nigrānī*).

bālā-nashīn, n. m. *lit.* Seated aloft.

1. The chief seat; the upper end of the table.

2. One who occupies the chief seat; a president; chairman.

mutazak'kira bālā, Ped. The above-mentioned or aforesaid.

A بالغ *bāl'iġ*, adj. بلغ attained. Of mature age; arrived at the age of puberty or discretion (*siyānā*).

bāliġ-bil-sin, n. 1. An adult by majority.

2. *In Mah. Law*, a woman who has attained her fortieth year without exhibiting any signs of puberty.

bālig-i-bil-alāmat, n. 1. An adult by puberty.

2. *In Mah. Law*, a girl who exhibits signs of puberty at the age of nine, ten, or any age up to fourteen.

H بالک बालक *bāl'ak*, n.m. A child.

bālak-chorī, n. f. Child stealing; kidnapping children.

bālakoṅ kī sudh na rakhnā. Neglect of children; desertion of one's family. G. G.

بالکا बालका *bāl'kā*, *che'lā*, n.m. 1. A young disciple or pupil; a young follower of a *jogī* or a *sannyāsī*. 2. (Tir.) A young girl.

P بالنگو *bāl'aṅgū*; Pop. *bālaṅg'ā*, *balaṅgā*, n.m. A kind of citron.

H بالو बालू *bā'lū*, *bālu*; E. *bālā*; Mag. *bārū*, n. f. S. बालुका Sand.

bālū-burd, H. P. n. f. 1. Arable land spoilt by a deposit of sand from inundation.

2. An item of remission of revenue on the above account.

bālū-char, n. f. Land covered by a deposit of sand; a sand-bank formed by a deposit of sand from a river.

P بالیدگی *bālid'gī*, n. f. Growth; development.

H بامن बामन *bām'an*, *bāhman*, *brāhman*; Poet. *birhaman*, *bamnā*; Dim. *bamnetā*, n. m. S. ब्राह्मण, Pr. *vamhaṇo*. The highest caste of Hindūs; the twice born.

بامنی बाम्नी *bāmnī*, *brāhmnī* n.f. S. ब्राह्मणी The wife of a Bāman.

P بان *bān*, n. m. The name of a tree; *Hyperantera morunga*, *Melia sempervirens*; that which yields benzoin (*Styrax Benzoin*); a tree the leaves and flowers of which are sweet-scented, called by the Persians *bed mushk*.

H بان बान *bān*, n. m. H. *ban* make; *bun*, S. वे weave, hence S. वर्ण quality, Pr. *vaṇṇo*.

1. A rope made of *mūṅj*, q. v.

2. The marriage rite according to which the bride and bridegroom take from 3 to 11 baths. Hin.; *māīṅyāṅ*, Mah.

bān baiṭhnā, v. n. To take the baths prescribed by the marriage rite. See *bān* (2).

بانا बाना *bā'nā*, n.m. S. वर्ण a covering, dress.
1. The woof, in contradistinction to *tānā* warp.
2. A silken thread used in weaving and sewing, etc.
3. A badge; uniform; livery (*wardī*).
4. Appearance; form; shape; colour.
5. A sect or profession (*bhek*).
6. A war instrument; a kind of weapon.
7. A kind of hemispherical bucket made of iron plates closely riveted together, used in raising water for irrigation.

bānā bāṅdhnā, v. n.
1. To be equipped, accoutred, armed, or ready.
2. To bet; wager; stake (*budnā*).

H بانٹ बांट *bāṅṭ bāṅṭā*; Brij. *baṭu, baṭotī*, n. f. S. वट् to divide.
1. The act of dividing; division; distribution.
2. Allotment; portion; part (*bhāg*); separate part; share; quota.
3. The act (or turn) of dealing the cards.
4. Food given to a cow while milking her.
5. Concern; business; lot or part; interest.

bāṅṭ-patr; P. *taqsīm-nāmā*, n. m. Record of division of property.

an bāṅṭ, n.m. Paying the revenue collectively through a representative.

بانٹا बांटा *bāṅ'ṭā*, n. m. Tying up the crops into sheaves and trusses.

بانٹنا बांटना *bāṅṭnā*, v. a. To divide; distribute; apportion; dispense; assign.

H بانجھ बांझ *bāṅjh, bāṅj*; W. Rus. *bāṅjhī*, (a woman); W. *banjar*; Brij. *bāṅjur* (land), adj. S. बंध्या. Barren; unproductive; sterile (soil or woman).

بنجھوٹی बंझौटी *bañjhau'ṭī*, n. f. A nostrum believed to cause barrenness.

H بانجھ बांझ *bāṅjh*, n. m. A hill tree. The natives usually make necklaces of the fruit for their children, as a charm against evil spirits.

H بانڈا बांदा *bāṅ'dā*, E; *bandā*, Sah; *bāṅjhī*, Tir. n. m. S. वन्दा A parasite; *Cymbidium tessalloides*. Wat.

P باندازہ *ba-andā'zā*, adv. To the amount of.

H باندھنا बांधना *bāṅdh'nā*; Tir. *bānhab*; E. *bānhnā*, v. a. S. बन्ध् to bind, P. *band*.
1. To tie; fasten; tether; gird; bind (a book).
2. To bind or join together; marry.
3. To fix; determine; settle; establish.
4. To impose; levy; assess (*lagānā*.)
5. To seize; apprehend; arrest; put on fetters; put a cordon round.

rassoṅ se bāṅdhī huī kishtī, n. f. A moored boat. G. G.

باندھنو बांधनू *bāṅdh'nū*, n. m.
1. A fabrication; invention; falsehood; fib.
2. False charge; libel; calumny; slander.

باندی बांदी *bāṅdī, ṭahalnī, dāsī, chelī*, n. f. P. *bandah*, S. वन्दो a captive slave. A female slave; a bondwoman (*lauṅḍī*).

H بانڈی बांडी *bāṅ'ḍī* n. f. A cudgel; club; stick; staff.

bāṅḍī-bāz, n. m. A clubman; one who carries a club and fights with it.

bāṅḍī chalnā, — chaṭaknā, v. n. To take place (a fight with clubs).

H بانس बांस *bāṅs*; Brij. *bāṅsū* n. m. S. वंश A bamboo; a rod or bamboo about ten feet long, used to measure fields, excavations, etc.

bāṅs-phoṛ, baṅs-phoṛ, n. f. A caste who make baskets, chicks, etc. of bamboo slips.

بانسا बांसा *bāṅs'ā*, W. n. m.
1. A drill-plough (Brij. *najaro*).
2. The bridge of the nose (E. *banāsā*; Tir. *nak-bāṅsā*,); the back-bone (*rīṛh*).
3. A plant from the leaves of which a red dye is extracted (*pīyā bāṅsā*).

بانسواڑی बांसवाड़ी *bāṅs-wāṛī, baṅs-wāṛī, bāṅsī*, n. f. A bamboo plantation; a jungle of bamboos.

بانسی बांसी *bāṅ'sī*, n. f.
1. A reed of which hookah-snakes are made. It is also used by weavers and artificial flower makers.
2. A kind of stone.

H بانک बांक *bāṅk*, n. m. S. वङ्क् to be crooked
1. Crook; curve; curvature; deflexion; bend; bow; horse-shoe; curl; winding; sweep.
2. A crook to cut bamboos or sugarcane with.
3. A dagger having a curved blade.
4. An armlet (Mah. Wom.); anklet (Hin. Wom.).

bāṅk-paṭā, n. m. Fencing with wooden dagger and cutlass.

P بانگ *bāṅg*, n. f. The crowing of a cock; the Mah. call to prayer (*azāṅ*).

bāṅg denā, v. n. To call Mahommedans to prayer; to crow (a cock).

bāṅg-i-subah, n. f. The call to morning prayer.

H بانگا बांगा *bāṅ'gā*, E.; *baṅgāh*, Tir. n. m. The cotton plant; the seed and cotton in the pod (*kapās*).

H بانگر बांगर *bāṅg'ar ;* Brij. *bāgrū ;* Māṛ. *ḍāṅg*, n. m. Opp. of *khādar*. Highland ; upland ; tableland.

H بانہ बांह *bāṅh* ; Poet. *baiyāṅ ;* Tir. *bāṅhi ;* Māṛ. *bāṅv*, n. f. S. बाहु, Pālī, *bāhā*.
1. The arm ; the sleeves.
2. Guarantee ; security, as when a person trusts himself in the power of an enemy, a third person being his *bāṅh* who engages to restore him to his house or fort in security.

A بانی *bā'nī*, n. m. بنی He built it.
1. Builder ; author ; parent ; founder ; originator ; framer ; composer ; inventor.
2. Source ; root ; spring ; main-spring.
3. Instigator ; beginner ; prime mover.
bānī-i-fasād, n. m. Ringleader ; instigator ; aggressor.

باوبرنگ बाओबिडंग *bāo-biraṅg, bāë-baraṅg, bāo-baraṅg*, W.; *bā-bhiraṅg*, E. n. m.
A medicinal seed given in cases of flatulency or rheumatism ; *Embelia ribes.*
bāo khumbā, n. m. A medicine ; *Careya arborea.* Wat.

باوٹا बाओटा *bāo'ṭā, bāvṭā*, n. m.
A flag ; banner ; standard.

H باولی बाओली *bāo'lī, bāvlī* ; W. Illit. *bābrī, bāorī, bāoṛī, bābṛī* ; Sah. *bārāṅ* n.f.S. वापी a large oblong pond. A deep well, the descent to the brink of which is by long flights of steps with landing places and covered chambers where travellers may rest and take refreshments during the heat of the day.

H باوني बाओनी *bāo'nī, bāvnī*, W. Hin. n. f. H. *bāvan* fifty-two. A community ; a company of persons who raise a fund for a *nāch* in the Holī festival ; a company of jolly fellows ; a society ; an assembly.

A باہ *bāh* ; H. *pushṭi*, n. f. باہ Coitus.
The sensual appetite ; venery ; lust.

H باہا बाहा *bāh'ā*, n. from H. *bahnā* to flow.
1. A watercourse, natural or artificial.
2. A vessel into which the juice of the sugarcane flows. [*bāre*, adv. S. बहिर.

H باہر बाहर *bā'har, bāhir* ; Gaṛh. *bhāër* ; Mār.
Externally ; outward ; outside ; without ; out ; abroad ; *ab extra.*
bāhar bhūm, n. f. Land lying beyond the village boundaries.
bāhar le jānā, v. n. To export ; take abroad.
bāhar nikalnā, v. n.
1. To come out of ; come outside ; go about in public. [hands of.
2. To withdraw from ; wash one's
bāhar nikalne ke, yā bar-āmad hone-ke waqt. While engaged in a procession. G. G.

P باہم *bā'ham* ; H. *paras'par*, adv.
1. Along with ; jointly ; conjointly ; concurrently.
2. Mutually ; each other ; one with another ; reciprocally. [or family.
3. Privately ; in private ; in the house
bāham tajwīz karnā, v. n. To concert together. [a duel.
bāham chhurī kaṭārī se laṛnā, v. n. To fight
bāham digar, adv. Together ; reciprocally (*bāham*, 1, 2). [gether ; co-operate.
bāham digar kām karnā, v. a. To work to-
bāham rafadār. Amicable adjustment.
bāham sharīk, yā bānīkār honā, v. n. To concert together. [together.
bāham salah karnā, v. a. To plan or consult
bāham karnā, v. n. To bring together ; incorporate ; join.

H باہن बाहन *bāhan* n. m. S. वह to carry.
1. Ploughed land ; land ploughed and left unsown.
2. Furrow ; wheel-marks (*līk*). E.

باہنا बाहना *bāh'nā, bānā*, v. a. To plough ; till ; cultivate.

H باہو بند बाहूबंद *bāhū-band*, Māṛ. n.m.
Association or joint interest in the property of a village, or the persons so associated, usually kinsmen of the *Patel.*
bāhū-band mīrāsī, Māṛ. Occupancy of land in coparcenership, especially by members of the same family.

H بائی बाई *bāī* ; Gaṛh. *bādin*, n. f. from Marahṭī. बायको a woman.
A lady ; mistress ; madam.

H بایب बायब *bā'yab, bāib* ; A. *shimāl-magrib*, n. m. S. वायव्य. The north-west quarter.

P باید شاید *bāyad shāyad, bāyad o shāyad*, adv. As it should be.

A بایع *bāë*, n. m. بیع exchanging. Seller (*bechā*).

H بائيسي बाईसी *bāīsī*, n. f. H. *bāīs* twenty-two.
1. The royal army, composed of the troops of the twenty-two Sūbās or provinces then constituting the Mogul empire.
2. A command of 22,000 men. [force.
bāīsī ṭūṭnā, v. a. To attack with one's whole

H ببَاد **बिबाद** *bibād'*, n. f. S. **विवाद** from **वि** against, **वद्** to speak.
1. Dispute; altercation; wordy war or strife; controversy; debate; discussion; pros and cons; plea and demurrer.
2. Law-suit (*muqadmah*); litigation.
bibād uṭhānā, yā karnā, v. a.
1. To dispute; wrangle; quarrel; litigate.
2. To raise an objection; to object.
bibād-bhog, n. m. Disturbed possession; disputed land.
ببادي **बिबादी** *bibā'dī*, adj. Litigious; quarrelsome; contentious (*jhagṛālū*). [defendant.
bibā'dī, n. m. Disputant; litigant; plaintiff or

H ببُول **बबूल** *babūl'*; E. *babūr*; Brij. *bamūr*; E. Rus. *baburī*; Sah. *bhabūl*, n. m. S. **वर्बुर**. *Acacia arabica*, the wood of which is much used in making cart wheels, agricultural implements, etc. and the bark is used in tanning leather, and in making wine (*kīkar*).

H بپريت **बिप्रीत** *biprīt'*, adj. S. **विपरीत** from **वि** against, **परि + इ** to turn. [friendly.
1. Hostile; antagonistic; inimical; un-
2. Opposite; counter; contrasted; against (*khilāf*). [wrong.
3. Informal; irregular; contrary;
biprīt, adv. In opposition; *versus*; against.
بپريت **बिप्रीत** *biprīt*, n. f.
1. Disaffection; hostility; enmity.
2. Opposition; contradiction; contrary declaration. [upset a decision.
biprīt āgyā denā, v. a. To overrule an order;
biprīt-budh, n. f. Misconception.
biprīt barnan karnā, v. a. To misrepresent; make a false statement.
biprīt samajh'nā, v. n. To misapprehend; misconceive; misunderstand; mistake.
biprīt karnā, v. a. To pervert; turn aside; go against; violate.
biprīt lekh, n. m. Misquotation; wrong citation; unfounded assertion.

P بُت *but*, n. m. S. **पुत्तल** [effigy.
1. An image; idol; statue (*mūrat*);
2. An inclined plane along which dice or cowries are rolled. (Gamblers' idiom).
بت پرست *but-parast*, n. m. An idolator; one who worships images.
but-parastī; H. *mūrti-pūjan*, n. f. Idolatry.
but-tarāsh, n. m. One who carves idols; a sculptor.
بتخانه *but-khānā*, *but-kadah*, n. m. An idol temple; a pagoda (*mandar*).
but-shikanī; H. *mūrt-khanḍan*, n. f. Image-breaking; iconoclasm. [shipping.

H بت **बत** *bat*, n. m. A worm destructive to

H بتهان **बथान** *bathān'*, *baṭhān*, E. n. m. S. **अवस्थानं** abode. Cattle fold; an open place where cattle are driven in at night (*kharak*). [warp.

H بتهري **बिथरी** *bith'rī*, E. n. f. Cleansing the

H بتهوا **बथवा** *bath'wā*, *bathuā*; Gaṛh. *bethū*, n. m. S. **वास्तूक** Wild potherb or greens; *Chenopodium album*; a weed which grows with the spring crops. [cowdung (*mānd*).

H بتهيا **बथिया** *bath'iyā*, n. f. A heap of dried

H بتيا **बतिया** *bat'iyā*, n. m. S. **वार्त्ता** Green unripe fruit or vegetables in general; the egg plant in contradistinction to the *mārū*, q. v.

H بتّيسا **बत्तीसा** *battī'sā*, *battīse ke laḍḍū*, W.; *batisā*, E. n. m. A strengthening preparation of *laḍḍū* composed of thirty-two ingredients, given to fever-patients, to women after childbirth, and to mares after foaling.

H بٹ **बट** *baṭ*, W. n. m. S. **वट्** to divide.
1. Division; lot; portion; share.
2. Twist; fold; plait; the wrinkle or fold of the abdomen. [Weight.
3. Path; way. See *bāṭ*. 4. (E. *baṭkharā*)
بٹمار **बटमार** *baṭmār'*, *baṭmā'rā*, W.; *baṭphāṛ*, Māṛ.; *baṭpāṛ*, E. n. m. A highwayman (*luṭerā*); footpad; bandit (*ḍakait*).
بٹماري **बटमारी** *baṭmā'rī*, W.; *baṭpāṛī*, E. n.f. Highway robbery; gang-robbery or *ḍakaitī*.
بٹيرا **बटेरा** *baṭai'rā*, W. n. m. Weights and scales.

H بٹّا **बट्टा** *baṭ'ṭā*, n. m. H. *baṭ* a twist.
1. Deficiency; defect; fault; flaw (*khot*).
2. Stain (*dhabbā*); stigma; blot; pollution.
3. Loss; discount; exchange.
baṭṭā denā, v. n. 1. To suffer or pay discount.
2. To make up a loss or deficiency.
baṭṭā lagānā, v. a.
1. To charge discount (*baṭṭā lenā*).
2. To vilify; slander; calumniate; stigmatize (*dhabbā lagānā*).
baṭṭā lagnā, v. n.
1. To be liable or subject to discount.
2. To suffer a stain; to lose one's good name or credit (*sākh bigaṛnā*).

3. To be tarnished; to deteriorate; fall off.
baṭṭe par kharīdnā, v. a. To buy at a certain discount or advantage.
baṭṭe-dār rupayā, n. m. Cracked, defaced, or bad coin; a rupee on which discount has to be paid.

بٹّے کھاتے बट्टे खाते *baṭṭe khāte,* n. m. Profit and loss; bad debts; irrecoverable balance; doubtful recoveries.
baṭṭe khāte likhnā, v. a. To carry to profit and loss; enter as a doubtful debt.

بٹائی बटाई *baṭā'ī;* Brij. *baṭoṭī,* n. f.
1. Partition: part; share; share of produce; apportionment in kind; division of the crop; rent of land paid in kind.
2. Division of the crop between the cultivator and zamindār or the Government as landlords.

The proportions vary: In some poor lands the share of the landholder may not exceed a sixth; in the Konkan it is one-half: but the more usual proportion was a third. *Baṭāi moasia* was a division, which in the Benares district assigned nine-sixteenths to the cultivator and seven-sixteenths to the landlord. The portion in kind was early commuted in Bengal for a money payment. Beng. Reg. ii. 1795, defines *Ba'āi* lands as those of produce of which Government or the Collector of its dues is entitled to a certain proportion, the value of which, estimated at the current market price, is paid in money by the cultivator of the land. The proportion in kind, is still receivable in some parts of the south. The word is also applied to a kind of joint interest in land, in which one party pays the Government assessment, and the other furnishes the labor. The seed and implements are provided jointly, and the net produce or profit is equally divided. *Wilson's Glossary.*

baṭāī paidāwār, n. f. Division of crops.
بٹائی پتر बटाई पत्र *baṭāī-patr;* A. P. *taqsīm-nāmā,* n. m. Deed of partition.
baṭāī-dār, n. m. A cultivator who shares the crop on the ground with the proprietor.
bhāg-baṭāī, n. f. Apportionment in kind; allotment of shares.
hisāb-baṭāī. Accounts kept by the village accountants, of the particulars of the settlement between the village and the Government.

H بٹنا बटना *baṭ'nā,* v. a. S. बट् to divide.
1. To realize. 2. To deal with.
3. To share; gain; obtain (as a profit).

بٹنا बटना *baṭnā, bañṭnā,* v. n.
To be divided, shared, distributed.

بٹوار बटवार *baṭwār',* n. m. A tax gatherer who collects in kind; a custom's or police officer stationed on the road for collecting transit duties.

بٹوارہ बटवारह *baṭwā'rah,* n. m. 1. Partition of land; division of land; allotment of shares.
2. A separation of coparceners, or the detachment of the share of an individual coparcener.
3. The deed or document under which partition of land is made (*taqsīm-nāmah*).
baṭwārah amīn, n. m. A partition measurer.
baṭwārah ba-zarye iqrār-nāmā khāngī, yā panchāyat. A partition made by private agreement or arbitration.
baṭwārah-i-hāl. Re-partition; new distribution [of land.
baṭwārah alahdah. Imperfect partition; partial division of land.
baṭwārah kā muqadmā. A case of partition; a partition suit.
baṭwārah karnā, v. a. To make a partition of [land.
baṭwārah mukammal. A complete division or partition (of land).
baṭwārah nāqis, baṭwārah nā-mukammal. Imperfect partition; incomplete division.

H بٹوری बिटौरी *biṭau'rī,* E. n. f. S. बट् to surround. A tax on village shopkeepers, etc.

بٹورا बिटोड़ा *biṭau'ṛā;* Rus. *biṭaurā,* n. m. A heap of cakes of dried cow-dung plastered on the outside to protect them from rain.

H بٹئی बटै *baṭa'ī,* n. f. H. *baṭ* twist. The art of working in silver thread, called *kalā-battū.* [*baṭaī.*

بٹیا बटैया *baṭaīyā,* n. m. One who works in

H بٹیری बटैरी *baṭai'rī, baṭairī, baṭaihrī,* n.f. H. *baṭnā* to gain. A Hindu marriage ceremony in which a wedding garment with some money is presented by the bride to the bride-groom.

P بجاآوری *bajā-āwurī,* n. f. Execution; performance; discharge; accomplishment.
bajā-āwurī-i-ahkām. Performance or discharge of a duty. [duty.
bajā-āwurī-i-hukm, yā khidmat. Execution of

بجا لانا *bajā lānā, bajānā,* v. a.
1. To discharge; execute; perform;
2. To give effect to; work out; achieve.
3. To comply with; obey; carry out.
4. To bring to pass; bring or carry through.
hukm bajā lānā, v. a. To obey an order.

P بجز *ba juz';* *ba-juz is-ke,* H. *bin,* prep. Excepting; save and except (*siwāē*); with the exception of; exclusive of; without; unless; otherwise; but.
ba-juz us sūrat ke. Except as provided. G. G.

H بجنا बजना *baj'nā,* n.m. A rupee. (Brokers')

P A بجنسه *ba-jin'sehi,* adj.

1. Identical; the very same (*wohī*).
2. Entire; whole (*kul*).

بجنسه *ba-jinsehi,* adv. 1. Intrinsically; substantially. 2. Exactly; precisely; entirely.

H بُجھوتا बुझौता *bujhau'tā, bujh'tā,* n. m.
An abstract account of a village proprietary, made out annually by the *Paṭwārī.*

H بِجيا बिजिया *biji'yā, bij'yā,* Brij. n.f.S. विजिया. The hemp plant (*bhang*); *Cannabis sativā.*

H بچ बच *buch, bachh,* n. f.
Orris-root; the root of the sweet flag; *Iris germanica,* or *Acorus calamus.* Wat.

بچناگ बचनाग *bachnāg', bachhnāg*; Mag. *bichhṛā,* n. m. S. वत्सनाभ A vegetable poison, said to be brought from Chinā; *Aconitum ferox* (?).

H بچت बचत *bach'at, bachtī,* n. f.

1. Balance; balance of an account; savings; residue; remainder; surplus (*baqīyā*).
2. Gain; profit (*ot*); interest. [pregnancy.

بچه‌کشي *bachchah-kashī,* n. f. Child-bearing; *bachchah-kushī,* P.; *bāl-hattyā,* H. n. f. Infanticide.

H بچھيا बछिया *bachhiyā, bachh'yā,* W.; *bāchhī,* E.; n. f. H. *bachchā.*

1. A female calf; an heifer.
2. A Hindu ceremony performed on the 13th or 17th day after one's death.

P A بحال *ba-hāl',* adj. 1. Established; upheld; confirmed; maintained (*bar-qarār*).
2. In a good state or condition; well; in good health (*tan-durust*).
3. Re-instated; re-established; restored (to health or office); in office. [to-do.
4. Flourishing; thriving; set up; well-

bahāl rahnā, v. n. To remain intact; to be unimpaired. [confirm; continue.

bahāl rakhnā, v. a. To maintain; uphold;

bahāl karnā, v. a. 1. To establish; confirm; affirm.
2. To re-instate; restore; restore to health; re-establish. [law).
3. To put back (in its place); revive (a

bahāl honā, v. n.
1. To be restored, re-instated.
2. To recover; to be restored to health.

بحالي *bahā'lī,* n. f.

1. The act of establishing; establishment; restoration; re-instatement. [tion.
2. Maintenance; confirmation; affirma-
3. Recovery; resuscitation.

بحالي سند *bahālī sanad,* n. f. A grant restoring to a person possessions or privileges of which he had been deprived, or confirming him in their enjoyment.

A بحث *bahs*; Pop. *bahsā bahsī,* n. f.

1. Reasoning; debate; discussion; controversy; dispute; question.
2. Argument; plea; defence.
3. Altercation; wrangling; contention; quarrel. [tion.

bahs ikhtyār-i-samāat. A question of jurisdic-
bahs tamādī-i-aiyām. A question of limitation.
bahs-i-haqīyat wa istihqāq. A question of right and title.
bahs-i-qānūnī. A question of law. [question.
bahs kī gunjāish. Room for argument; an open
bahs-i-wāqeāt. A question of facts; a discussion on points of fact.
bahs o jadāl. Dispute and altercation.

P بخره *ba-kh'rah, ba-khrā,* E; *hissā,* n. m.
Distribution; allotment; dividend (*baṭ*).

بخشش *bakh'shish*; Illit. *baksīs,* n. f. 1. Present; grant; gift; donation; a Christmas-box.
2. Reward (*inām*); honorarium; gratuity.

bakhshish-nāmā; H. *dān-patr,* n. m. A deed of gift (*hibah-nāmah*).

بخشنا *ba-khsh'nā, ba-khsh denā,* v. a. [endow.
1. To give; grant; bestow; confer;
2. To excuse; forgive; pardon.

بخشوانا *ba-khshwā'nā*; Illit. *ba-khshānā*; Rus. *baksānā,* v. a. Caus. of *ba-khshnā,* q. v.

بخشي *ba-kh'shī,* n. m. 1. Paymaster (In Mah. armies); a general or Commander-in-chief, who is also the Paymaster.
2. An officer who kept an account of all disbursements connected with military tenures, as those of *Mansab-dārs* and *Jāgīr-dārs*; paymaster of the forces; a collector of house rents. [mander-in-Chief.

bakhshī-ul-mumālik, n. m. Paymaster and Com-
bakh'shī-khānā, n. m. A military pay-office.
bakhshī-garī, n. f. The office of a general.

P بخوبي *ba-khū'bī*; H. A. *achchhī tarah,* adv.
1. Duly; properly; well. [pletely.
2. Thoroughly; fully; effectually; com-
3. Clearly; distinctly; expressly.

ba-khūbī tamām'. Completely; thoroughly.

H بد बद *bad,* n. f. A bubo; a syphilitic or pestilential swelling of the glands.

P A بدانتظامي *bad-intizā'mī, bad-amalī,* n. f.

1. Bad management; maladministration; misgovernment; misrule.
2. Disorder; anarchy.

بدچلن *bad-chalan*; Ped. *bad-atwār*, *bad-afāl*, *bad-ravaīyā*, adj. Ill-conducted.

بدچلني *bad-chal'nī*, n. f. Misdeeds; misdemeanour; unprincipled conduct; malpractices; bad conduct; misbehaviour.

بدديانت *bad-diyānat*, adj. Dishonest (*dharoṛ-mār*); fraudulent (*dagā-bāz*); false.

بدديانتي *bad-diyānatī*, n. f. Unfair dealing; fraud; dishonesty; corrupt practices.

bad-diyānatī se, adv. *Mala fide*; with fraudulent intent; dishonestly.

bad-diyānatī se jhūṭā dāwā karnā. Dishonestly making false claims. G. G.

bad-sūrat karnā, v. a. To deface; disfigure; deform; spoil. [to disfigure. G. G.

hamesha ke lÿë bad-sūrat karnā. Permanently

بدعهد *bad-ăhd*, adj. Faithless; treacherous; false.

bad-ăhdī, n. f. Breach of promise or trust.

بدمست *bad-mast*, adj. 1. Drunken; intoxicated.
2. Lustful; lewd; libidinous; lascivious.

ashkhās-i-bad-mast. Drunken persons. G. G.

بدمستي *bad-mas'tī*, n. f.
1. Drunkenness; inebriety; intoxication.
2. Lust; lewdness; lasciviousness.

بدمعاش *bad-maᶜāsh*, n. m.
1. A person of unsettled character, or bad livelihood; a notorious or bad character.
2. A vagabond; vagrant; rogue; rascal; scoundrel; knave; blackguard.

bad-māāsh ko dīdah o dānista jagah denā. Harbouring knowingly bad characters.

بدمعاشي *bad-maᶜā'shī*, n. f. Bad livelihood; vagrancy; loose conduct; villany.

بدمعاملگي *bad-muᶜāmalagī*; Pop. *bad-mām-lagī*, n. f. Unfairness in dealing; fraud; corruption.

بدنام *bad-nām*, adj. Of bad repute; disreputable; notorious.

bad-nām kar'nā, v. a. To destroy one's good name; injure one's reputation; defame; traduce.

bad-nāmī, n. f. Ill-report; defamation; disrepute; dishonor; slur; stigma (*dhabbā*).

bāis-i-bad-nāmī. Defamation; the author of a calumny.

H بداهنا बिदाहना *bidāh'nā*, v. a. To turn the plough over a field after the seed is come up; to plough immediately after sowing for the purpose of covering the seed.

badar nikālnā, v. a. To show a balance due; to debit.

بدرنويسي *bad'ar-nawī'sī*, n. f. Writing off items of an account which are objectionable or excessive; audit of an account; taxing an overcharged bill. [*anu-pān*, n. m.

P بدرقه *badra'qā*, Ped.; *badarqā*, Pop.; H.
1. A guide; guard; escort; safe-conduct.
2. A convoy, or guard on the road.
3. A charge for convoy formerly levied on merchandise at the rate of one per cent. as the expense of keeping safe the highways and rivers.

badarqa-i-hisāb. An account sent with a guard of goods or treasure under its charge; an invoice.

H بدري बदरी *bad'rī*, *bidrī*, n. f. 1. A bag.
2. A despatch of goods.

P بدستور *ba-dastūr*, adv. According to rule or practice; as usual; as before.

A بدل *bad'al*, n. m. بدل he changed.
1. Change; alteration; mutation.
2. Exchange; substitution; equivalent; *mutatis mutandis*. [tution.
3. Return; rendition; reparation; resti-

badal-ke bayān karnā, v. a. To misrepresent; pervert; twist the meaning; give a turn to.

pūrā badal, n. m. Adequate consideration. G. G.

بدلائي *badlā'ī*, *badalwāī*, n. f. Something given in exchange; barter; exchange.

بدلنا *badal'nā*, *badal jānā*, v. n.
1. To change; alter; vary; shift; chop and change; veer; turn round.
2. To be changed; to assume another form; grow or become; turn into.
3. To be removed, transplanted, transferred. [be disfigured.
4. To look worse, older, etc; lose color; to

بدلنا *badal'nā*, *badal denā*, v. a. [vert.
1. To change; alter; make different; con-
2. To barter; exchange.
3. To put one thing for another; substitute; commute. [construction upon.
4. To disguise; put a false coloring or
5. To transfer; transplant; transpose.
6. To transform; transmute. [cate.
7. To shuffle; shift; prevaricate; equivo-

بدله *bad'lah*, n. m. See *badlī*.
1. A return; requital; remuneration (*mehntānah*); consideration; compensation (*evaz*); recompense (*ujrat*); equivalent; fee; reward; honorarium. [tion; restitution.
2. Indemnification; indemnity; repara-
3. Reprisal; retaliation; revenge; retribution; atonement; redress; satisfaction; evil consequences.

badlā denā, v. a. 1. To give an equivalent;

requite; compensate; recompense; reward; pay for; make restitution. [good.
2. To indemnify; make amends; make
badlā lenā, v. a. To take revenge; revenge or avenge oneself; make reprisals; retaliate; wreak vengeance on.
badlah mushāhāra. A stipend given in money or kind to public or private servants.
بدلي *bad'lī*, n. f. 1. Change; exchange; barter; a person or thing taken in exchange for some other person or thing; *locum tenens;* relief (of a guard).
2. Substitution; stead; lieu; room; place.
badlī kar'nā, v. a. [transfer.
1. To change; make an exchange or
2. To relieve one; take one's turn.
badlī meṅ, badle meṅ, adv. In exchange; in return for; in place of; instead; in lieu of; *mutato nomine*; in the room of.
badlī meṅ honā, v. n. To take or supply the place of; to stand in the place of; officiate; act; to be put in, or to serve as a substitute; to do duty for.

A بدن *bad'an*; H. *aṅg*, n. m. [bones.
1. The body; trunk; frame; flesh and
2. The privities; *pudendum feminæ.*
insān kā badan. The human body. G. G.

H بدني बदनी *bad'nī, badan*, W; *dādanī*, E. n. f.
A contract by which the borrower gives a bond at high interest, and, as a future security to the lender, he assigns his crops valued far below the market price.

S بدھ बद्ध *baddh'*; H. *badh'*; A. *qatl*, n. m. S. वध् to kill. Slaughter; killing; murder; destruction. [punishment.
بدھدنڈ बधदंड *badh-danḍ*, n. m. Capital
بدھک बद्धक *bad'dhak*, n. m. Executioner; butcher; huntsman; fowler (*chiṛī-mār*).
بدھنا बधना *badh'nā, baddh, yā biddhuans k.* v.a. To kill (*mār ḍālnā*); murder; slaughter; butcher; destroy.

H بدھ बिध *bidh, bidhī, bid*, n.f. S. विधि from विधा to arrange.
1. Kind; sort; make; fashion.
2. A conjunction of auspicious stars for the bride and bridegroom. [an account.
3. Balance of an account; adjustment of
bidh khā'nā yā mil'nā, mī'zāṅ paṭnā v. n. 1. See *ittifāq h.* 2. To be struck (a bargain).
bidh milānā, v. a.
1. To consult the stars, especially the horoscope of the bride and bridegroom before tying them in wedlock.
2. To check, clear, or balance an account; to strike a balance.

H بدھوا बिधवा *bidh'wā*; P. *bevah*, n. f. S. विधवा from वि without, धव husband. A widow (*rāṅḍ*).

H بدھيا बधिया *badhiyā, badhyā*, n. f. S. वध् to hurt. A castrated animal (*ākhtā*).

H بدي बदी *bad'ī*, n. f. Opp. of *sudī*, S. वदि.
The fortnight of the waning moon; the dark fortnight (*aṅdherā pākh*). [puberty.
bar-jog, adj. Marriageable (a girl); arrived at
bar-dān, n. m. [trothed.
1. A wedding gift to a bride from her be-
2. The answer to a prayer addressed to a saint or God.

A بر *bar, arz*, n.m. The width (of cloth) (*panāh*).

P بر *bar*, A prefix. On (*ūpar*); at; up; out.
برآمد *bar-āmad*; H. *nikāsī*, n. f.
1. Coming or going out or forth; outgoings; drawings; expenses. [land.
2. Land thrown up (by a river); alluvial
bar-āmad honā, v. n. Opp. of *dar-āmad honā.*
1. To come out of; accrue (*nikalnā*).
2. To be recovered (stolen property).
برآمده *bar-āmdah*, n. m. 1. Outgoings. See برآمد
2. A verandah; porch; piazza (*bārjā*).
برآمد كرنا *bar-āmad karnā.* To bring forth or out; produce.
natīja bar-āmad karnā. Causing an effect. G. G.
برآمدگاه *bar-āmad-gāh.* An outlet. G. G.
daryā bar-āmad. G. G. Accrued by alluvion.
raqbe bar-āmad. G. G. Increment of land.
māl bar-āmdah, G. G. Stolen property recovered.
bar-aṅge-khtah kar'nā, v. a. To incite; excite; provoke; inflame.
برآورد *bar-āvurd*, n. m. An estimate; a calculation; budget; bill; pay abstract.
bar-āvurd karnā, v. a. To strike out (of a muster-roll); calculate; estimate; carry to account.
برآورده *bar-āvur'dah*, Brought or carried forward or over (an account). [with.
برحكم *bar-hukm.* In obedience to or accordance
برخاست *bar-khāst*, n. f. [office.
1. The breaking up or closing of a court or
2. A recalling or removal from office; dismissal (*rukhsat*).
bar-khāst karnā, v. n. To depose, or deprive of office; remove from office; dismiss; permit to depart; break up (a court).
bar-khāst ho'nā, v. n. To rise or break up (an assembly); to be dissolved, closed, dismissed.

برخاستگي *bar-khāstagī*; Pop. *bar-khāstgī*, n. f. Rising or breaking up (of a court); dissolution; dismissal; removal from office.
bar-khāstgī-i-jamāat-i tijārat. Dissolution of partnership.
bar-khāstgī-i-adālat. Adjournment of the court.
برخلاف *bar-khilāf, bar-āks,* adj.
1. Contradictory; adverse (H. *ulṭā*).
2. Inconsistent; unfounded; untrue.
bar-khilāf, adv. Against. See *ulṭā.* [informal.
bar-khilāf-i-āīn, Contrary to law; illegal;
bar-khilāf-i-sharā. Contrary to the Mah. law.
sarīhī bar-khilāf. Directly at variance; diametrically opposed.
برطبق *bar-tabaq,* adv. On; upon; agreeably to.
برطرف كرنا *bar-taraf kar'nā, mauqūf k.,* v. a. To dismiss. [dismissed, etc.
bar-taraf ho'nā, v. n. To be turned off; to be
برطرفي *bar-tarfī, mauqūfī,* n. f. Dismissal; discharge. [of dismissal.
bar-tarfī kā parvānah, n. m. A written order
برقرار *bar-qārār, ba-hāl,* adj.
1. Fixed; established; firm.
2. Standing; extant; existing; living.
bar-qarār rakhnā, v. a. [cate.
1. To maintain; uphold; affirm; vindi-
2. To establish; justify; ratify; confirm.
bar-qarār rah'nā, v. n.
1. To stand; remain; last; continue; abide; keep on; hold on; persevere; go on.
2. To live; exist; subsist; to be extant.
برملا *bar ma'lā,* adv. In open day (*din dahāṛe*); openly; in public (*khule khazāne*).
bura rāj, n. m. Mal-administration (*bad-intizāmī*).
burā samā, n. m. Bad season; a season of scarcity; dearth; drought; famine (*kāl*).
barābar kāṅṭe, adj. Of equal weight; equally balanced.
barābar ke hisse, n. m. Equal shares.

H برات बरात *barāt'*; Ped. *bārāt*; Bhoj. and Tir. *baryāt,* n. f. S. वरयात्रा, H. *bar* a bridegroom, *āt* comes. A marriage procession; the company or attendants at a marriage.

P برادر *birā'dar,* n. m. Z. *birātar*; Pahlavī. *birād*; S. भ्राता, H. *bhāī*, 1. A brother (*bīr*).
2. Relation; relative; kindred.
برادراخيافي *birā'dar-i-akhyāfī,* Ped. for H. *gailaṛ bhāī,* n. m. A step-brother; uterine brother.
برادراندر *birādar-i-andar, birādar-i-alātī,* Ped. for H. *sautelā bhāī,* n. m. A half brother.
برادرانه *birādarā'nā,* adj. Brotherly; fraternal; like a brother. [brothers.
birādar-i-toam, n. m. H. *juṛvāṅ bhāī.* Twin
برادرحقيقي *birādar-i-haqīqī,* Ped. for H. *sagā bhāī,* n. m. Full brother; own brother; brother of whole blood.
برادرخرد *birādar-i-khurd,* n. m. A younger brother (*chhotā bhāī*).
برادررضاعي *birādar-i-razāī,* Ped. for H. *dūdh bhāī,* n. m. Foster brother.
برادرزاده *birādar-zādah*; Ped. for H. *bhatījā,* n. m. Nephew; brother's son.
برادرزادي *birādar-zādī,* Ped. for H. *bhatījī,* n. f. Niece; brother's daughter. [n. f. Fratricide.
برادركشي *birādar-kushī,* Ped. for H. *bhāī-hattyā,*
برادري *birā'darī*; Pop. *birādrī*; H. *bhāī-chārā,* n. f.
1. Brotherhood; fraternity; clan; connection; relationship. [kinsman.
2. Relation; relative; kindred; kinsfolk;
3. A community; society.
4. A band of musicians called *tāshe-wāle.*
birādarī se khārij, Ped. for H. *jāt-bāhar,* adj. Outcast; one put out of caste.
birādarī se khārij kar'nā, v. a. To put out of caste; excommunicate (*jāt se nikālnā*).

H برار बरार *barār',* n. m. 1. A tax in general, as *hal barār* a tax on ploughs.
2. Land tax or rent; apportionment of revenue payments according to agreement with the village community.
براري बरारी *barā'rī,* n. m.
A shareholder; a co-parcener; one paying his portion of the assessment.

P براے *barāē*; H. *liye,* adv. For; for the sake of; on account of; in order to; because of; in respect of; by reason of; concerning; on.
براٸي إستردادناجوازي *barāē istirdād na-jawāzī.* Ped. To void as illegal.
براے خدا *barāe Khudā, Khudā ke wāste,* Mah.; *Rām jī ke līye,* Hin. adv. For God's sake; for mercy's sake.
barāē khur o posh, Ped. for H. *khāne pahnne ko. lit.* For food and clothes.
An assignment of real or personal property to a person for his maintenance for life, not conveying a right of transfer.
براٸي مطالبهٔ مال *barāē mutālibah-i-māl.* On account of the revenue demand.
براے نام *barāē nām,* adj. Ped. for H. *nām chār ko.* Nominal; fictitious; not real or essential.
barāē nām, adv. Nominally; ostensibly. [أجاز.

P برباد *bar-bād,* adj. P. بر on باد wind. See
1. Wasted; thrown away; laid waste; destroyed; lost; ruined; undone.
2. Plundered; ravaged; despoiled; sacked.
barbād kar'nā, v. a. To destroy; ruin; devastate; desolate.

barbād honā, v. n. To be ruined, destroyed.
بربادي *bar-bādī*; H. *nās*, n. f. See أجاز (1). [etc.
Destruction of crops by passing of troops,
بربادئي بالقصد *bar bādī-i-bil qasd*, Ped. for *jān būjh-ke ujārnā.* Wilful destruction. [of snake.

H بربت बरबत *bar'bat, parbat*, n. f. A species

H برت बर्त *bart, birt, barat*, Hin.; n. m. S. व्रत Fast (آپاس).

برتي बर्ती *bar'tī*, Hin.; n. m. See آپاسک (1).

H برت बिर्त *birt, brit, birat*, n. f. S. वृत्ति maintenance, from वृत् to live. [come.
1. Livelihood; stipend; pension; in-
2. Assignment; estate; property; endowment.
3. A grant or endowment for maintenance, or for religious and charitable objects.
4. A custom (*rīt*); right; privilege.
5. Supporters (*jijmān*).
6. A proprietary right, whether acquired by purchase, inheritance, or grant, heritable and transferable, subject to payment of revenue, either to Government, or to the *rajā* or *zamindār*, when not specially exempt. A right, custom, or privilege derived from the performance of offices, whether secular or religious. A right to perform certain offices claimed by different castes. Fees to the family priest.

برتاو बरताव *bartāv, bartā'o bartāvā*, n. m.
1. Conduct, etc. See اطوار
2. Usage; practice; fashion; custom.
3. Use; employment; disbursement; expenditure. [behave.
bārtāo karnā, v. a. To deal by or with; treat;
1. Story; history; account; narration; description.
2. Statement; assertion; explanation.

S برتانت پتر वृतांत पत्र *britānt-patr*, n. m. The record of a decision given by a *panchāyat.*

H برتش बरतुश *bar'tush*, n. Land sown with sugarcane after a rice crop.

H برتها वृथा *brit'hā*, n. f.
1. A dead letter; a nullity. [ing no return.
2. Land situated amidst jungle and yield-

P بُرد *burd*, n. f. بُردن to carry. See بالائي آمد
1. Gain; profit; prize.
2. Perquisites; pickings; douceur; bribes.
3. Bet (*hor*); wager.

T برده *bar'dah*; P. *bandah*; H. *dās*, n. m. A slave (*gulām*); captive; prisoner of war.
bardah-kharīd'nā, v. a. To purchase imported slaves. G. G.
برده فروش *bardah-farosh*, n. m. A slave dealer.
برده فروشي *bardah-faroshī*, n. f. Selling into slavery; sale of imported slaves; the slave trade.

H برڈا बरडा *bar'ḍā, bar'ḍī*, n. A light, sandy, or stony soil.

H برس बरस *bar'as*, E. n. f. An intoxicating drug made of opium; a specific.

H برس گانٹھ बरसगांठ *baras-gāṅṭh*; P. *sāl-girah*, n. f. S. वर्षग्रंथि *lit.* The year-knot.
The ceremony of tying a knot on the anniversary of one's birthday. Hence, the anniversary of a birthday. [n. f. S. वार्षिक.

H برسوڑي बरसौड़ी *barsau'ṛī*; Rus. *barsauḍī*,
1. An annual tax or rent. 2. An annuity.
baras'veṅ din, adv. Yearly; once a year.

H برسي बरसी *bar'sī*; Tir. *bar'khī*, n. f. A ceremony in commemoration of a deceased relation, performed at the close of the first year.

برن سنکر बर्नसङ्कर *barn-saṅkar*, Pop. *barun-shaṅkar*, n. m.
1. A man descended from a father and mother of different castes; a bastard (*doglā*).
2. A man who does not scruple to eat with one of a different caste (*sar-bhaṅgī*).
barn-hīn, n. m. An outcaste; one put out of caste (*jāt-bāhar*).

H برن बरन *bar'an*, n. f. Alluvial soil; fresh earth carried into hollows by means of water.

P برنده *barin'dah*, n. m. بُردن to carry. (*In Comp.*) A carrier; bearer.
برنده پروانه *barindah-i-parvānah*, — *hukm-nā-mah.* Warrant officer; an officer employed to serve the orders of the Court.
barin'dah-i-khuf'yah, Ped. for H. *chaukī-mār*, n. m. 1. A smuggler. 2. A secret agent.
برنده رقعه *barin'dah-i-ruqqah*, n. m. Ped. The bearer of a cheque or letter.

H برنن बर्नन *bar'nan*; A. *bayān*, n. m. S. वर्णन from वर्ण to explain.
Statement (*izhār*); account; narration (*bakhān*); recital; representation; description; specification; detail (*tafsīl*); particular mention; exposition; elucidation.
barnan kar'nā, v. a. To mention; recite; set forth; represent; exhibit; describe; propound; expound; particularize; enumerate.

H برہمن ब्रह्मन *brah'man, bāman*; Poet. *bamnā, babhnā*, n. m. S. *brāhman*, A Hindū priest; one of the sacerdotal caste.

H بري **बरी** *bar'ī* ; Mag. *bar-nautī,* n. f. H. *bar* bridegroom. A wedding garment, ornaments, gifts, etc. presented to the bride by the bridegroom on the wedding day.

H بُرّي **बुर्री** *bur'rī,* n. f. *lit.* A stream of grain or seed. Sowing seed by dropping it from the hand into the furrow, instead of sowing broadcast or by drill.

A بَري *bar'ī,* adj. بري He became clear or free of a thing. [acquitted.
1. Exempt ; free ; absolved ; exonerated;
2. Discharged ; released ; let off ; at large.
3. Innocent ; sinless ; guiltless.
4. Spotless ; stainless ; blameless.

barī kar'nā ; H. *chhoṛnā,* v. a. 1. To discharge from liability ; relieve from responsibility ; free from charge or obligation.
2. To acquit ; exculpate ; release ; let off.

barī ho'nā ; H. *chhūṭnā,* v. n. To be acquitted, etc. [responsibility.

javāb-dehī se barī karnā, v. n. To relieve from

بري الذمّة *barī-uz-zimmah,* adj. Irresponsible ; unaccountable.

برّيت *barī'yat* ; P. *rihāī* ; H. *chhuṭkārā,* n. f. Discharge ; absolution from a charge ; release ; liberation ; exemption ; relief ; immunity ; charter.

A بَرّي *bar'rī,* adj. A. *bar* land. Belonging to dry land, the opposite of *bahrī* belonging to the water.

H بڑا **बड़ा** *baṛā, baṛī* ; Rus. *baḍo,* W. Illit. and Tir. *baṛkā* ; Panj. *vaḍḍā,* adj. S. **वृद्ध** great, or **वृद्ध** increased. Great ; big ; large ; spacious ; vast ; immense ; huge ; enormous.

baṛā af'sar, n. m. Superior officer ; the head of a department.

baṛā beṭā, n. m. An elder son. [or ox ; a hog.

baṛā jānvar, n. m. *lit.* A large animal. A cow

baṛe jānvar kā gosht. Beef ; ham ; pork.

baṛā sāhib, n. m. A resident (at court) ; the chief civil functionary.

baṛā muj'rim, n. m. A notorious offender ; a desperate character.

H بڑاڑ **बड़ाड़** *baṛāṛ,'* n.f. A drove of bullocks laden with grain or merchandize.

H بڑتي بھاو *baṛhtī bhāo.* Premium ; advance ; advanced rate. [count).

baṛhtī likh'nā, v. n. To overcharge (in an ac-

khānah-i-jamā se baṛhnā, v. n. To exceed the amount at one's credit ; to overdraw.

kamtī baṛhtī. A little more or less ; about.

بڑھوتري **बढ़ोत्री** *baṛhot'rī, baṛhautrī* ; Tir. *baṛhantī* ; Mag. *baṛhantrī,* n. f.
1. Increase ; increment ; addition.
2. Surplus and balance ; overplus ; profit.
3. Advancement ; promotion ; improvement.

بڑھيا **बढ़िया** *baṛh'iyā, baṛhyal,* adj.
1. Of good quality ; superior ; prime ; first-rate ; tip-top ; superfine ; of the first water.
2. Costly ; dear ; high-priced.

بڑھني **बढ़नी** *baṛh'nī,* E. n. f.
1. An advance made for cultivation or manufacture, or for a contract.
2. A broom (*buhārī*).

H بڑھيا **बढ़िया** *baṛh'iyā,* n. m. S. **वध्** to hurt. A certain disease affecting sugarcane, Indian corn, etc. which prevents the head from shooting.

P بزور *ba-zor', zabar-dastī* ; A *bil-jabr,* adv. Perforce ; by main force ; forcibly ; on compulsion.

ba-zor hāzir kar'nā. To enforce the production of ; to compel attendance. G. G.

ba-zor le'nā, v. a. To take by force ; exact ; extort.

H بِساتي **बिसाती** *bisā'tī* ; Rus. *bisāētī, bisārtī,* n. m. from H. *bisānā* to buy. (?) A small trader in miscellaneous goods ; a pedlar.

H بِسار **बिसार** *bisār',* n. f. A loan of seed, to be repaid with increase after harvest.

H بستي **बसती** *bas'tī,* n. f. S. **वसति,** Pr. *vasahī* from **वस्** to dwell. Plantation ; settlement ; an inhabited place ; a colony ; a village ; a small town ; population ; inhabitants.

H بِسرجن **बिसर्जन** *bisar'jan,* n. m. S. **विसर्ज्जन,** from **सृज्** to throw. The finish, end, or conclusion of a religious ceremony ; throwing the image of a deity into holy water as the concluding rite of a festival.

A بِسم الله *bismil'lāh* ; Mah. Cor. of *ba-ism-i-Allāh, lit.* In the name of God.
A phrase generally used by pious Mohamedans in the beginning of all actions or lessons, and especially before eating.

H بِسوه **बिसवह** *bis'wah, biswā* ; Brij. *bisah, bisaī,* n. m. H. *bīs* twenty. The twentieth part of a *bīgah* ; a land measure ; a share of land.

biswah-barār. Assessment or collections by the *biswah.*

biswah-dār, n. m. The holder of a share or shares in a coparcenary village.

biswah-dārī, biswe-dārī, n. f. Proprietary tenure in *biswās* or shares; a share in a co-parcenary estate; the tenure of independent village communities holding under a superior *tāal-luqe-dār*.

A proportionate share of a proprietary right in a village which is conventionally taken as a *Bīgah*. It is divisible into twenty parts and distributed among the shares. Thus a holder of five *Biswās* is proprietor of one-fourth; of ten *Biswās*, of a half, etc.

bīs bisve; adv. *lit.* All the twenty *biswās* (in a *bīgah*). Certainly; surely; no doubt; necessarily. [hence a half share.

das bisweh, n. m. Ten *biswās* or half a *bīgah*,

bisār', n. Small perquisites of grain which *Chaukīdārs* receive from cultivators.

بسوانسي बिसवाँसी *biswāṅ'sī*, n. f. The twentieth part of a *Biswā*.

بسوي बिसवी *bis'wī*, n. f. Alienation of land on the payment of fines in advance. [join (?).

H بسيٹھ बसीठ *basīṭh'*, n. m. H. *sāṭhnā* to

1. The yoke attached to a plough (*jūhaṛ*).
2. An agent; a messenger; envoy (*elchī*).
3. The head manager in a village. (?)

H بسيكھ बिसेख *bisekh'*, *basekh*, *bishesh*, *bisekhā*, n. m. S. विशेष from वि and शिष् to distinguish. A special rule or distinction.

H بشن बिश्न *bishn*, *bishan*, *bishnu*, *vishnu*, n. m. S. विष्णु One of the Hindu triad.

bishn prīt, n. f. Land given for religious purposes.

bishan-devā, n. m. A sect of mendicants who beg in the name of Vishnu.

A بطن *batn*; H. *peṭ*, n. m. The womb; the interior of the belly.

batnan bād batnan; P. *pusht dar pusht*; H. *pīṛhī dar pīṛhī*. Generation after generation; hereditary.

بطن مادر *batan-i-mādar*. The mother's womb.

A بعد *bād*, Ped. for H. *pīchhe*, q.v. Afterwards.

بعد *bād*, n. m. Distance (*dūrī*); remoteness.

bʿād az wuqūë. *Ex post facto*; after the event; subsequent to the commission of.

bʿād az waqūë-i-wārdāt. Subsequent to the commission of the offence.

A بعض *bāz*; Pop. *bāzā*; P. *chand*, H. *kuchh*, adj.

1. Some; few; certain; several.
2. Sundry; diverse; miscellaneous.

بعضے باب *bāze bāb*. Various or miscellaneous items.

بعضي جمع *bāzī jamā*. Aggregate of revenue derived from other sources than the customs and excise.

بعضے خرچ *bāze kharch*. Miscellaneous expenses.

بعضي زمين *bāzī zamīn*. In official language, denotes land exempted from the payment of revenue under various denominations, as *altamg̃ā*.

[far.

A بعيد *bāīd*; P. *dūr*, adj. Distant; remote;

A بغاوت *baǧā'wat*, n. f. Opposition to and defection from; revolt; mutiny; rebellion.

A بقايا *baqā'yā*, n. m. pl. of *bāqī*.

Balances; arrears; dues; balance of revenue arrears; remainders (*bachat*).

بقاياے باقي *baqāyāë bāqī*. Arrears and balances; old balances of revenue; arrears of revenue of the preceding years as well as of the current year; arrears on arrears.

بقاياے تقاوي *baqāyā-i-taqāvī*. Balances of money advanced to tenants; *taqāvī* balances.

بقاياے توزيع *baqāyāë tauzīʿ*, n. m.

1. Account of past arrears of revenue.
2. A return showing arrears of revenue of previous years.

بقاياے لگوتا *baqāyāë lagautā*. Arrears of rent.

بقاياے مالگزاري *baqāyāë mālguzārī*, *baqāë jamā*. Arrears of revenue.

A بقرعيد *baq'ra-īd*; Pop. *bakrīd*, *bakrā-īd*, n. m. بقر a bull, and عيد q. v.

A festival observed by the Mahomedans on the 10th of the month *Zilhij*.

The feast of the cow, in commemoration of the sacrifice of Ismāil by Ibrāhim, (according to Mahomedans). Sheep, goats, oxen, and camels are sacrificed on this occasion. It is also termed *Id-uz-zuhā*.

P A بقول *ba-qaul'*, H. *wohī kahāvat hai*, adv. As it is said or written; according to.

A بقيه *baqī'yah*, n. m. Remainder. See باقي

H بكار बकार *bakār'*, n. m. S. वच् to speak. The amount or value of a crop fixed by an appraiser by word of mouth.

بكارا बकारा *bakā'rā*, n. m. 1. An answer (from one possessed by evil spirits). 2. An invoice.

A بكر *bikr*; H. *kuār-pan*, n. f. بكر a virgin. Virginity; maidenhood.

bikr ṭūṭnā, nathnī utarnā, sar-farāz honā, sir ḍhakā jānā, motī bindhnā, v. n.
To be violated (a virgin).
bikr toṛ'nā, chīrā utārnā, sir ḍhāṅknā, sar-farāz k., kuār-chhal utārnā, v. a.
To ravish, rape, or violate a virgin.

H بکري **बिकरी** *bik'rī,* n. f. S. **विक्रय** from **वि** opposite, **क्री** to purchase. 1. Sale. [disposal.
2. Selling-price; value set or paid;
bikrī-baṭṭā, n. f. Money realized by sales.
bikrī-patr, bikrī-khat, n.m. Deed or bill of sale.
bikrī-khātā, n. m. Account sales.

H بکنا **बिकना** *bik'nā;* E. *bikānā,* v. n. S. **विक्री**. Pr. *vikkei* or *vikkiṇaī* he sells. To be sold.
بکاو **बिकाऊ** *bikā'ū,* adj. For sale; saleable.

H بکھان **बखान** *bakhān',* n.m. S. **व्याख्यान,** Pr. *vakkāṇam,* from **ख्या** to speak. 1. Preaching.
2. Invocation; prayer; praise (*astutī*).
بکھانا **बखाना** *bakhān'nā,* v. a. 1. To mention.
2. To preach; pray; sing praises.
3. To give (the genealogy).
4. To abuse; call names; vilify. [go round.

H بل **बल** *bal, bali;* Bhoj. *baṛāi,* n. m. S. **वल** to Sacrifice; burnt-offering; oblation; religious offering; presentation of food to all created beings; one of the five great sacraments of the Hindu religion.
It consists in throwing a small portion of the offering, as *ghī,* rice, etc. towards eight points of the compass, the zenith, and the nadir.
بلدان **बलदान** *baldān', balidān,* Hin. n. m. The act of sacrificing a victim; an offering (*qurbānī*).
but ke liyē baldān kīyā jānā. To be sacrificed to an idol. G. G. [(*binā*).

A بلا *bil'ā,* adj. prep. (In Comp.) Without
بلاتعرض احدے *bilā taārruz-i-ahde. Nem con;* without opposition. [immediate.
بلاتوسط *bilā-tawassut.* Direct; not circuitous;
bilā tawaqquf; H. *turat,* adv. Without delay; speedily; promptly. [Exclusively.
بلاشرکت *bilā shirkat, bilā shirkat ahde yā ġaire.*
bilā shak, be-shubah, adj. Doubtless; undoubtedly; indubitably; unquestionably; of course.
bilā marzī, yā bidūn razā ke zinā karnā. To rape; make an indecent assault.
bilā nāġah; H. *nit,* adv. Duly; regularly; without fail; invariably; constantly; continually; always.
bilā wāstah, adv. 1. Direct; not circuitous.
2. Without reason.
bilā wajah, adv. Groundless; without any motive; without foundation.
bilā wajah māqūl. Without reasonable or sufficient cause; injudiciously.
bilā wasīyat faut honā. To die intestate; to die without a will. [*bol,* n. m.

H بلاوا **बुलावा** *bulā'wā, bulā'o; bulāhaṭ;* Rus. A call; summons; bidding; invitation.

H بلاہر **बलाहर** *balā'har, bulāhir,* W. n. m.
1. A caste of fishermen and basket-makers.
2. A village guide, messenger, or watchman.

H بلاہي **बलाही** *balā'hī;* Gaṛh. *balāī,* n. A low caste of *chamārs* or workers in hides and leather; a cobbler, sometimes employed to measure land. [*kaṭ* cut.

H بلکٹ **बलकट** *bal'kaṭ,* n. f. H. *bāl* an ear,
1. Cutting the ears of corn without going through the usual process of reaping.
2. Rent taken in advance. [H. *bal* power.

H بلوا **बलवा** *bal'wā;* Illit. *valbah, balbā,* n. m.
1. Disturbance; tumult; row; riot.
2. Insurrection; mutiny; rebellion. [G.
balwā karne kā jurm. The offence of rioting. G.
balva-i-ām, n. m. A general insurrection.

H بلوکي **बिलौकी** *bilau'kī,* E. n. f. A Hin. marriage ceremony which consists in the bridegroom collecting from his relations a small subscription of a farthing or half penny each for presents to the dooly bearers. (Bhāgulpore).

H بمان **बिमान** *bimān', biwān,* n. m. S. **विमान** from **विमा** to traverse. An ornamental bier on which the corpse of an old man is borne to the place of cremation. Hin.

P A بموجب *ba-mūjib,* adv. By reason of; in virtue of; on account of; in pursuance of; in conformity with; in accordance with; according to; as per; by; on.
ba-mūjib, ekaṭ hāzā. By this act. G. G.
ba-mūjib-i-farmān-i-shāhī. By royal charter; by imperial proclamation.
ba-mūjib qawāid-i-ām mutamashiah. By the general rules in force. G. G.

A بن *bin,* n. m. Cont. of ابن A son.
[**वन** a wood.

H بن **बन** *ban;* Rus. *banṛ,* n. m. *banī,* n. f. S.
1. Forest; jungle; a wood.
2. A cotton field; cotton crop (*bāngā*). W.
banobās, Pop. n.m. S. **वनवास** Banishment; exile.

ban-chārā. A tax paid by the tenant to the land owner at the rate of one load of fodder per field. Panjab.
ban-dān, n. m. Jungle or waste grants.
ban-saṭī, n. f. The wood of the cotton tree used for fuel, and in the sides of grain carts.
بنكٹا बंकटा *bankṭā,* n. m. H. *kāṭ,* cut. The crop on the field irrecoverably spoiled.
بنكٹي बनकटी *bankaṭ'ī, bankaṭāī,* n. f. The right obtained by clearing jungle and bringing it into cultivation.
بنكٹيا बनकटैया *ban-kaṭaīyā;* Bhoj. *bankaṭailā,* n. m. H. *kāṅṭā* thorn.
A prickly plant resembling a thistle, used medicinally for checking diarrhœa.
ban'kar. 1. Spontaneous produce of *jungle* or forest land as timber, brushwood, gums, wild honey, etc.
2. Revenue derived from forest lands.
بنكهرا बनखरा *bankhar'ā,* n. m. Lands on which cotton has been grown during the past season.

H بُن बुन *bun;* Tir. *banī,* n. The quantity of grain given for a day's weeding, from 2½ to 3 seers.

H بنا बना *ban'nā, banā, banṛā, banne,* + Wom; *bīnd,* Māṛ. n. m. A bridegroom (*dūlhā*).

A بنا *bin'ā,* n. f. بني he built.
1. Foundation (*neo*); basis; base.
2. Ground; footing; motive (*kāran*).
3. Root; source; origin (*asl*).
4. Beginning; commencement.
بناے دعوے *bināē dāvʿā.* Cause of action.
binā-i-dāwā paidā yā qāyam huā. Cause of action accrued or arose.
binā-i-vāhid kā mutaʿaddad dāwā qarār denā. To divide a cause of action.
ek binā ko do shiq karnā. To divide one cause of action into two. [charge G. G.
bar binā-i-illat tarmīmī. Upon an amended
taʿdād binā-i-dāwā. Multifarious cause of action.
chand binā-i-dāwā qarār denā. To divide a cause of action.
do binā-i-dāwā. Double cause of action.
nālish kī binā qāyam karnā. To furnish ground for action; shew cause of action.
binā dāl'nā, v. a.
1. To lay the foundation; found; establish.
2. To begin; commence; originate; set on foot.
بنابر *binā-bar, barāē,* Ped. adv. H. *līye,* q. v.
By reason of; for; on account of; owing to.
binābarīn, adv. Because of this; therefore; with this view or intent; on this account.
binābarāṅ, adv. Because of that; wherefore; on account of.

H بنانا बनाना *banā'nā,* v. a. Caus. of بنا q. v.
To paint; varnish; polish; gild.
banānā sikka-i-qalbī kā, yā chalānā uskā. Counterfeiting coin or uttering base coin.
jhūṭī dast-āwez banānā. To make a false document. G. G.
jhūṭe gawāh banānā. Fabricating false evidence.

A بِنت *bint,* n. f. A daughter.

H بِنتي विन्ती *bin'tī;* Rus. *mintī,* n. f. S. विनति from विनम् to bend down. A bending or bowing low; petition.
بنتي پتر विन्तीपत्र *bintī-patr.* A petition; representation; memorial.

H بنج बनज *ban'aj,* W.; *banij,* E., n. m. S. वाणिज्य. Buying and selling; traffic; trade; commerce; barter; exchange; dealings; transactions; merchandise.
بنجارا बंजारा *banjā'rā,* n. m. A grain merchant; a carrier of grain.

The term is more commonly applied to a grain and cattle merchant, who, with a more or less numerous party of the same calling, moves about to different markets, and especially accompanies bodies of troops to supply them with grain. It is especially applicable also to a numerous tribe spread along the foot of the mountains from Harduar to Gorakpur, and forming various subdivisions, many of whom are stationary and following agriculture. They comprise both Hindūs and Mahomedans, acknowledging a common origin and affinity. The most migratory are the Bahrūpā Banjāras, of whom there are five branches, four of whom assume the well-known appellations of the chief Rājpūt tribes, Rāṭhaure, Chauhān, Pawāṛ, and Tanvar. The fifth, called Barka, is said to be descended from a Gauṛ Brahman. *Wilson.*

بنجاري बंजारी *banjā'rī,* n. f. The wife, or tent of a *banjārā.* [*jārās.*
banjā'rī, adj. 1. Belonging or related to *ban-*
2. Half-boiled (grain).
بنجنا बनजना *banaj'nā,* v. a. 1. To trade (*banaj k.*).
2. To give in marriage; to marry.
ban'jī, n. f. The business of a pedlar.

H بنجر बंजर *banj'ar;* Rus. *banjaṛ, banjhaṛ,* n. f. S. बन्ध्या 1. Barren or unproductive land.
2. Land which has not been cultivated for five years and upwards.
banjar toṛnā, v. n. To break up or bring into cultivation waste land.
banjar jadīd. Land again brought into cultivation after lying fallow for some years.
banjar qadīm. Land left fallow from a remote period; land uncultivated at the settlement.

banjar khārij jama. Waste lands excluded from the rental.
banjar qābil zarāat. Culturable waste land.
banjar kamī. Abatement of revenue on account of land left uncultivated.
banjar lā-wārisī. Unclaimed waste lands.

H بنجن बनजिन *ban'jin,* n. f. [the village.
1. Lands next or close to, or surrounding
2. A weed which springs up with the *kharīf* crop to the height of about three feet.

P بند *band,* From P. بستن S. बन्ध to bind.
1. A mound raised to preserve water for irrigation; a dam; dike; embankment.
2. A list (*fard*); inventory; memorandum; note.
band baṭāī, n. f. An account of each share of the assessment paid in grain.
band bahrī. A cess levied from land proprietors towards mountain embankments.
band bardāsht. An account of the share of an instalment to be paid by each village.
band-phāṅṭā, n. m. An account of the shares of the liabilities of a village.
band jamā, n. f. Distribution of the assessed lands among the cultivators so as to allot to each an equal proportion of good and bad lands, and to make him responsible for a fixed proportion of both.
band-i-hisāb. Bill of charges; a schedule, draft, or inventory of an account; an abstract account. [peace. G. G.
fitna o fasād band karnā, v. n. To keep the

H بندا बिंदा *bin'dā;* Mag. *bundā;* Dim. *bindī,* n. m.
A sectarial round spot made on the forehead, preparatory to worship after ablution.

P بندر *band'ar, bandar-gāh,* n. m.
A port; harbour; emporium.
shāh-bandar, n. m. Chief port.

P بندوبست *band-o-bast;* Tir. *banobast;* Illit. *bandubast;* Rus. *bad-o-basat, bast-o-band,* n. m.
1. Plan; organization; administration; management.
2. Arrangement; method; order; system.
3. Settlement of the revenue; land revenue settlement.
band-o-bast-i-akhīr. Recent or last settlement.
band o bast arāzī-i-muāfī-i-muzbata. Settlement of lapsed rent free tenures.
band o bast āsāmī-wār yā raīyat-wār. Settlement with each individual cultivator.
band o bast amīn, n. m. Settlement measurer.
بندوبست سرسری *band o bast-i-sarsarī.* A summary settlement.
بندوبست شہر *band o bast-i shahar.* The government or police of a town.
band-o-bast-i-istimrārī, yā dāimī. Permanent settlement; a settlement in perpetuity.
band-o-bast-i-chand-rozā, n. m. A temporary settlement.
band-o-bast-i-hāl, yā jadīd, n. m. New settlement; new practice.
band-o-bast-i-sābiq. Former settlement.
band-o-bast k. See *intizām karnā.* [age.
1. To organize; regulate; arrange; man-
2. To farm out; fix the Government demand.
band-o-bast kī paimāish. Revenue survey.
band o bast ke kāgaz. Settlement records; administration paper.
band o bast-i-māl. Settlement of revenue.
band o bast-i-mālguzārī. Revenue settlement.
band o bast-i-mufassalah. Detailed settlement.
band o bast mukammal. Final settlement.
band o bast-i-mulk. The sum total of the revenue of a kingdom or province as settled and engaged for.
بندوبست میعادی *band o bast miādī.* A settlement for a limited time.
band o bast huā, yā ho gayā. Settled with; settlement made with; arrangement completed.
achchhā band o bast. Good arrangements or discipline, etc.
iqrār-nāmah-i-band o bast. Settlement compact.
parwāna-i-band o bast, n. m. A deed of settlement. A warrant given by the Government to the person with whom a revenue settlement had been agreed upon, empowering him to make the collections from the cultivators or land-holders.
ḍaul band-o-bast. A particular statement of the manner in which the rental of an estate or district is subdivided.
robkār-i-band o bast. Settlement proceeding.
sanad-i-band o bast. Warrant or deed of settlement. [cer.
sāhib-i-muhtamim-i-band o bast. Settlement offi-
misl-i-band o bast. Settlement record; settlement paper.
gair-band o bastī. Unsettled, as an estate of which the revenue has not been fixed.

A بندوق *bandūq',* n. f. بندق He shot a bullet. A gun; musket; blunderbuss; firelock; fowling piece; G. G. an offensive weapon.
bandūq bharnā, v. a. To load a gun. [gun.
bandūq chhatyānā, v. a. To take aim with a
bandūq'chī, n. m. A musketeer; rifleman. [v. a.
bandūq lagā'nā, chhoṛ'nā, chalānā, yā mārnā,
To discharge a gun; to fire at; shoot. [G. G.
giroh par bandūq mār'nā. Firing on the mob.

H بندھانی बंधानी *bandhā'nī,* n. m. S. बन्ध to bind. A porter; a cooly; one who carries a stone or stones over his shoulder.

بندهائي बँधाई *bañdhā'ī, bañdhvāī*, n. f.
1. Binding; fastening; tying.
2. The price paid for binding.
3. The premium paid in the exchange of money of inferior denomination.

بندهک बंधक *bandh'ak*; Bhoj. *banihak*, n. m. Pawn (*girvī*); pledge; mortgage (*rahn*); simple mortgage; mortgage deed (*rahn-nāmah*).
bandhak dātā, n. m. A mortgager (*rāhin*).
paṭ bandhak; A. *rahn-bil-qabzah*. Living pledge; mortgage with usufruct in lieu of interest; mortgage with possession.
drisht-bandhak. Mortgage without possession.

بندهن बन्धन *bandh'an*; Tir. *banhan*, n. m.
1. Binding; fastening; bandage.
2. Hindrance; check; restraint.
3. Practice; daily observance; rule.

بندهنا बँधना *bañdh'nā*, n. m. 1. A wrapper; a cloth for keeping small articles in.
2. A needle case; a housewife; a hold-all.
bañdhā-huā, bañdhī-huī, adj. Established; fixed; usual; ordinary. [expenses.
bañdhā-huā kharch, n. m. Regular or usual

بندهنوار बन्धनवार *bandhanwār'*, W.; *bandanbārī*, Farrukh.; *bandar-wār*, W. Illit.; *bannivār*, Tir.; *bannewār, ban-wār*, E. n. f. H. *bār* a door.
Festoons of leaves and flowers hung over the doors of houses on festive occasions.

بندهو बन्धु *bandh'u*, n. m. A relative; kinsman; one of the same ilk or brotherhood.
A cognate kinsman in a remote degree. Three kinds are enumerated, personal, paternal, and maternal. The first are the sons of the deceased father's sister, of his mother's sister, and of his maternal uncle. The second are the sons of his father's paternal aunt, of his father's maternal aunt, and of his father's maternal uncle. The third are the sons of his mother's paternal aunt, of his mother's maternal aunt, and of his mother's maternal uncle. *Wilson.*

بندهوا बँधवा *bañdh'wā, bandvā*; P. *qaidī*, n. m.
One who is bound; a prisoner; convict.

بندهواس बंधवास *bandhwās'*, n. m. Land embanked all around so as to retain the water.

P بندي *ban'dī*, n. f. بستن to bind. 1. Embargo.
2. Prohibition; interdiction.
bandī-khānā, bandī-ghar, n. m. Jail; prison.

H بنڈا बिंडा *bind'ā, pindā*, W. n. m. A faggot; a bundle of *mūñjh* grass (E. *pilanḍā*).

H بنس बंस *bans*, n. S. वंश. 1. Extraction; descent; genealogy; pedigree; stock.
2. Race; line; lineage; house; family.

بنساولي बन्सावली *bansā'vlī*; A *shajrā*; P. *kursī-nāmā*, n. f. S. वंशावलि A genealogical table or tree; genealogy.
bans param parā; A. *naslan bād naslan*, Hereditary; in one continuous line.
nir-bansī, adj. Childless; heirless (*be-aulādā*).

E بنک *bañk, bañk-ghar, bañghar*, n. m. A bank.

S بنوتسرگ बनोत्सर्ग *banotsarg'*, n. m. A kind of marriage ceremony performed in honor of a newly-planted orchard; without which observance it is not proper to partake of its fruit. In this ceremony, the *mauwah* and other trees, which do not bear edible fruit represent the bridegroom, and the *mango*, and other edible fruit-bearing trees, the bride. [S. वणिक,

H بنيا बनया *ban'yā*; Rus. *bāñṛyāñ*, n. m.
A grain-seller; corn-chandler; a vender of provisions. [7.).

P بُنياد *bunyād'*, n. f. Foundation. See اصل (1,5,

H بُوار बुआर *buār', buāī, bonī, buāī kī rut*, n. f. H. *bonā* to sow. Sowing; seed-time.

H بوجه बोझ *bojh, bojhā, bhār*, P. *bār*, n. m.
1. A load; weight; burden, a porter's load; a bundle of grain, grass, etc.
2. A load of grain in the straw, as much as can be carried on the head, generally about a maund.
3. Cargo; lading; freight.
4. The ballast of a boat or ship.
5. Drag; dragweight; difficulty.
6. Onus; burden; obligation.
bojh-baṭāī, n. f. A mode of distribution by stacks or bundles of cut corn.

P بُود وباش *būd o bāsh, būd-bāsh*; A. *sukūnat*, n. f. Residence. See باس
insān kī būd o bāsh. Human dwelling. G. G.

H بُور बूर *būr, bhūr*; Māṛ. *bhūrsī*, n. f. S. भूरि दक्षणा alms in plenty. [Hin.
Charity or alms given in marriages, etc.
būr bāñṭnā, v.a. To give alms at a marriage, etc.

H بورا बोरा *bo'rā*, n. f. A gunny bag.

بوري बोरी *bo'rī*, n. f. A gunny bag; a measure of three maunds. [security.

H بوڑ बोड़ *boṛ*, n. m. Redeemable mortgage;

H بوڑي बौड़ी *bau'ṛī*, E. n. f. A land measure; 1-20th part of a *kauṛī*.

P بُوزا *bū'zā*; Pop. *bozā*, n. m. A fermented liquor resembling beer.

بوزيخانه *būze-khānā*, n. m. A beer-shop; a boozing ken (probably a corruption of *būze-khāna*, introduced into Europe by the gypsies).

H بوکا बोका *bo'kā*, n. m. *lit.* the hide of a he-goat.

A basket or leather bucket for throwing water to a higher elevation.

H بُوکارا बूकारा *būkār'ā*, n. f. Land previously recovered as *būk*, but rendered useless by a deposit of sand. (?)

H بولي बोली *bo'lī*, n. f.

1. Speech; language; dialect; vernacular.
2. Usage; idiom; mode of speech.
3. A bid (at an auction).

bolī bolne-wālā, n. m. A bidder at an auction.

H بونا बोना *bo'nā*, v. a. S. वपनं Sowing.

1. To sow; plant; cultivate.
2. To cover (a buffalo).

botī zamīn. Land held by the owner of a village in his own possession to give out to the peasants for cultivation.

بوني बोनी *bo'nī*, *bāonī*; Mār. *bā*; Tir. *bāok*, *bāog ke din*; E. *ropnī*, n. f. Sowing; seed-time (*buār*).

بوجوت बोजोत *bo-jot*, P. *kāsht*; A. *zarā'at*, n. f. Tillage; agriculture; cultivation.

boyā-jotā, *bone-wālā*; Old H. *bone-hār*, P. *kāshtkār*, A. *mazār'e*, n. m. A cultivator.

بونا बूना *bū'nā*, *bū jānā*, v. n. To be covered (a buffalo).

H بونگا बोंगा *baun'gā*, *boṅgā*, n. m.

1. A stack of straw; a heap of straw in the form of a tower. W.
2. A hollow bamboo (E. *chūṅgā*); a drill.
3. The whole shell of a gourd, or (E.) a cocoanut.

H بوہرا बोहरा *bauh'rā*, *bahorā*, *behorā*; Rus. *bohrā*, n. m. H. *behwār* transaction.

A village banker or money lender.

The Bohras appear to have originated in Guzrat, where they became converts to Mahamadanism, but they are settled in many parts of Central and Western India and in the N. W. Provinces.

بوہرگت बोहरगत *bohar'gat*, *behvār*, n. f.

1. The office of a *bauhrā*.
2. Dealing; buying and selling; trade.

H بوہني बोहनी *boh'nī*, *bonī*, *bonī ṭhonī*, n. f. H. *behvār* transaction, or S. वृध to increase.

Hansel; the first money received during the day, or the first ready-money sale by shopkeepers or hucksters, no credit being given as a rule for the article first sold.

☞ The practice says Elliot, "is universal in India, and is precisely like the handsel of England," which Lemon in his Dictionary, explains to be, "the first money received at market, which many superstitious people will spit on, either to render it tenacious that it may remain with them and not vanish away like a fairy gift, or else to render it propitious and lucky that it may draw more money to it."

H بھاٹ भाट *bhāṭ*, n. m. *bhāṭan*, n. f. S. भट्ट from भट् to speak. A bard; minstrel; troubadour; a chronicler of ancient days; genealogist.

2. *Met.* A panegyrist; eulogist; flatterer.

H بھاٹا भाटा *bhā'ṭā*, *bhāṭhā*, n. m. H. *baḍhnā*, to increase. A current; tide (A. *mad*); ebb-tide.

juār bhāṭā; A *jazr o mad*, n. m. Flood tide.

بھاٹهي भाठी *bhā'ṭhī*, *bhāṭī*, n. f. Down the river; with the current.

H بھاجي भाजी *bhā'jī*, n. f. (S. भज् to divide).

1. A portion; share. 2. A present.

bhājī bāṅṭnā, v. n. To distribute; divide; share.

P بہادر *bahā'dur*; Illit. *bahādar*; H. *sūrmā*, adj. P. *bahā* value, *dur* pearl. Brave; high-spirited; courageous; bold; valiant; valorous.

بہادر *bahādur*, n. m. A hero; knight; champion.

Under the Mah. Govt. a title of honor given to the nobles of the Court, as *Khān-bahādur*. In more recent times this title is conferred on any meritorious person.

2. A game cock; a fighting cock.

bahā'durī; H. *bīrtāī*, n. f. Bravery; courage; [valour.

S بھادر پد भाद्रपद *bhādr-pad*, n. m. A name common to the 26th and 27th lunar asterisms, distinguished by the epithets prior and subsequent, or *pūrvā* and *uttar*.

H بھادوں भादों *bhād'oṅ*; Hin. *bhādwā*; Rus. *bhādauṅ*, n. m. S. भाद्र The sixth month of the luni-solar year (Aug.—Sept.). when the moon is full near the wing of Pegasus.

bhada'ī, adj. Relating to the month of Bhādoṅ, or the harvest gathered in Aug.—Sept; the autumnal crop. [بوجه

H بھار भार *bhār*, n. m. S. भृ to bear. A burden.

bhār utār'nā, v. n. See *bojh utārnā*.

To redeem; deliver from; make atonement.

بھارکس भारकस *bhār-kas*, n. m. S. कृष् to draw.

1. A cart (P. *bār-kash*).
2. The strap which binds the poles or shafts to the drawer of the weight.

S بھاريا भार्य्या *bhār'yā*; H. *bhārjā*; Rus. *buharyā*, n. f. A wife; a married woman.

2. One wedded according to the ritual of the Vedas. It sometimes denotes a second or inferior wife, as distinct from the *Patnī*, the wife first married.

H بهارا भाड़ा *bhā'ṛā* ; P. *karāyā*, n. m. Hire ; carriage ; freight ; fare ; rent (of a house).
بهڑوتي भड़ोती *bhaṛo'tī*, n. m. One who plies for hire.
بهڑيتي भड़ैती *bhaṛai'tī*, n. m. A tenant (of a house).
bhaṛaitī dar bhaṛaitī, n. m. A sub-tenant (of [a house).

H بهاگ भाग *bhāg*, n. m. S. भाग्य from भज् to share.
Partition ; apportionment ; separate portion ; a share in a partnership ; a share or portion of an inheritance ; a share in kind ; the share of the Government.
In Hindu law, partition may be regulated amongst the sons according to the number of their mothers, or the wives of the deceased, which is termed *Patni-bhāg* ; but this is allowable only where the usage has been long established as the custom of the family. The more regular distribution is according to the number of sons *(putr)*, thence denominated *Putrā-bhāg*.
bhāg-baṭāī, n. Apportionment in kind, apportionment of shares of the crop in kind between the cultivator and the Government.
bhāg-jot, n. f. Cultivation by the rayat on the terms of sharing the crop with the *zamīndār*.
bhāg'nar, n. m. Rich alluvial lands under the banks of the *Jamnā*.

H بهانمتي भान्मती *bhān'matī*, n. m. S. भानुमती from भानु light, मति wit, (?) (H. *mantr* charm). A juggler ; conjuror.

H بهانور भाँवर *bhāṅ'var, bhauṅrī, phere*, n. f. H. *bhiramnā* to wander. Circumambulation of the bride and bridegroom round the sacred fire.
bhāṅvar phirnā, yā paṛnā, v. n. To circumam- [bulate.

P بهانه *bahā'nah*, n. m.
1. Plea ; pretext ; pretence ; shame.
2. A blind ; feint ; *ruse* ; stratagem.
3. Excuse ; a false or lame excuse.
4. Evasion ; putting off ; shuffling.
5. Means ; cause.
bahā'nā-sāz, n. m. An impostor ; one who shams.

H بهاو भाव *bhāv, bhāo*, n. m. S. भू to be.
Price ; price current ; rate ; figure ; market price.
bhāo utarnā, girnā, yā ghaṭnā, v. n.
To fall (the market rate).
bhāo baṛhānā, v. a. To raise or enhance the price.
bhāo chaṛhnā, v. n. To rise in price ; to be at a premium.
bhāo hunḍī, n. f. The rate of bills ; exchange.

H بهاولي भाओली *bhā'olī*, E. n. f. Rent of land paid in kind instead of money, a field on which the rent is paid in kind ; distribution of produce between the *zamīndārs* and cultivators.
bhāolī khot, n. m. Land recently brought into [cultivation.

H بهائي بانٹ भाई बांट *bhāī bāṅṭ*, n. 1. Hereditary family share, applicable only occasionally to all the shares of a coparcenary village.
2. One connected by community of origin and joint interest in a common ancestral property.
bhāī-band ; n. m. People of the same caste ; brethren ; relations ; kindred ; kinsmen.
bhāī-bandī, n. f. Brotherhood ; fraternity ; kin.
bhāī-chārā, n. m. Relationship ; connection ; relation by blood or marriage ; fraternity.
joṛlā bhāī, n. m. Twin brother.
chacherā bhāī, n. Father's younger brother's [son ; cousin.
dūdh bhāī, n. m. A foster brother.
sagā bhāī, ek peṭ kā bhāī, haqīqī bhāī, sahodar bhāī, mā-jāyā bhāī, mādar-zād bhāī, nij bhāī, n. m. One's own brother.
sautelā bhāī, n. m. A step brother.
gur bhāī, Hin ; *pīr bhāī*, Mah. n. m. Followers of the same spiritual guide ; fellow sectarian.
mamerā bhāī, n. m. Mother's brother's son ; cousin.
muṅh-bolā bhāī, n. m. An adopted brother.
mauserā bhāī, Hin ; *khalerā bhāī*, Mah. n. m. Mother's sister's son ; cousin.

P بهبودي *beh-bū'dī* ; Pop. *bahbūdī*, n. f. P. به good, بودن to be. See بهتري
bahbūdī-i-khalāyaq, yā riāyā, n. f. The public use, benefit, or good ; public utility.

H بهتّا भत्ता *bhat'tā*, n. m. H. *bhāt* boiled rice.
1. Ploughman's wages in kind.
2. Additional allowance ; extra pay or allowances to public servants or soldiers ; subsistence money, or additional allowances to officers employed on special duties, or in distant places ; travelling allowance.
bhattā khemah, n. m. Tentage.

A بهتان *boh'tān*, n. m. A false accusation ; slander ; calumny ; scandal.
bohtān lagānā, joṛnā yā dharnā, v. a.
To charge falsely ; slander ; calumniate.
bohtān bāis kasar-i-shān. Defamation of character.
bohtān adāvatī. Malicious libel.
bohtān kī bāteṅ, n. f. Defamatory expressions.

H بهتّي भत्ती *bhat'tī*, Mah. Wom. n. f. H. *bhāt* boiled rice. A Mahomedan ceremony which consists in giving food, etc. for three days to the members of the family of the deceased by his nearest relations. [bond.

H بهتي बहती *bah'tī*, n. f. Imported goods in

bah'tī kar'nā, v. a. To permit imported goods to be exported free.

H بهتيجا भतीजा *bhatī'jā*, n. m. S. भ्रातृज

Brother's son; nephew. [daughter; niece.

بهتيجي भतीजी *bhatī'jī*, n. f. S. भ्रातृजा Brother's

H بهٹا भुट्टा *bhuṭ'ṭā*; W. Rus. *bhoṅṭā*; Mār-*makkyo*, n. m. Indian corn; maize.

H بهٹوا भटुवा *bhaṭ'uvā*, n. f. A light dry soil, yielding only an autumn crop.

H بهٹي भट्टी *bhaṭ'ṭī*, n. f. S. भ्राष्ट्र.

1. A furnace; kiln; an alembic.
2. A distillery; a distiller's fireplace.
3. A washerman's cauldron for boiling clothes.

bhaṭ'ṭī tāmīr' karnā, aur jārī karnā. G. G. To construct and work a distillery.

bhaṭṭī-dār, n. m. A distiller; one who keeps a spirit-shop; one who sells and manufactures spirituous liquors.

bhaṭṭī-i-majāz. G. G. A licensed distillery.

H بهدرا भद्रा *bhad'rā, bhaddrā, bhadr*, n. f. 1. An unlucky moment, as the second, seventh, and twelfth days of the lunar month.

bhadrā honā, v. n. To be clean or purified by shaving one's head and beard, etc. after the demise of a relative, or in a holy place.

H بهدوار भदवार *bhadwār', bhādol*, n. H. *bhādoṅ.* Land prepared for sugar-cane; land ploughed during the *kharīf* from *Asāṛh* to *Bhādoṅ* for the *rabī* sowings and allowed to lie fallow till the cotton is sown.

بهدئي भदै *bhada'ī*, n. f. Crops in season in August, the rainy weather rice-crop sown about *Baisākh* and cut in *Bhādoṅ*.

It is of inferior quality to the *Aghani*, but admits of a further crop in the cold season.

H بهرائي भराई *bharā'ī*, n. f.

1. The act of filling or stuffing.
2. Watering (a field); irrigation.
3. (*bharvāī*) The price paid for water, padding, etc. [water.

bharāī, yā bharāo karnā, v. a.; To fill; stuff;

بهرپانا भरपाना *bhar pānā*, v. n.

1. To be paid in full; to be satisfied.
2. To be discharged, or liquidated (a debt).

بهرنادار भरनादार *bharnā-dār*, n. m. A mortgagee, one who has occupation of an estate, the rent of which is retained until it liquidates the principal and interest of the debt.

H بهرت भरत *bhar'at*, n. m. H. *bharnā* to fill.

1. Room; space; place.
2. Bags; vessels; etc.
3. Goods; lading; cargo; freight; fare.
4. Conveyance; carriage; cart; cattle.
5. Transit or transport charges.
6. Payment in full; a full discharge.

bharat bharnā, v. n. 1. To stuff; fill; pad.

2. To make up the full tale or quantity; supply a deficiency. [place.

3. To export; carry merchandize to any

bhar'atyā, n. m. A trader; merchant. [God.

بهرتا भरता *bhar'tā*, n. m. 1. Providence (*dātā*);

2. Husband; support; stay.

بهرتي भरती *bhar'tī*, n. f. Cargo. See بهرت (3).

1. A store; stock; heap (*ḍher*); accumulation. [stuff.
2. Filling in or up; stuffing; padding;
3. Admission; enlistment; enrolment; recruiting.
4. Invention; fabrication; fib; falsehood.

bhartī-shudā, Ped. Enlisted; enrolled; registered.

bhartī kar'nā, v. a. 1. To fill; load; lade.

2. To store up; stack; heap; lay up; accumulate.

3. To raise, levy (soldiers, etc); engage; enlist; enroll; enter on a register; recruit; hire or employ (a servant).

4. To invent; fabricate; romance.

bhartī honā, v. n. To be enlisted, etc.

H بهركي भरकी *bhar'kī*, E. n. f. Lime.

A kind of land in Behar, superficially of a dark color but lighter when turned up by the plough. It is suited to both spring and autumn crops, but requires abundant watering.

H بهركي भुरकी *bhur'kī, bhūr*, E. n. 1. A hole.

2. A land measure. [ipāol, n. f.

H بهروتي भरौती *bharau'tī, bharpāī*; Tir. *bhar-*

A receipt in full or release; a receipt; contents received; indemnity; acknowledgment.

mūṅh bharnā, v. a. To stop one's mouth; grease the palm; give a bribe.

mūṅh-bharāī, n. f. Hush money; a bribe.

H بهري भरी *bhar'ī*, E. n. f.

1. The weight of one sicca rupī, or one *tolā*.
2. A grass used for thatching.

H بهري बेहरी *beh'rī*, n. f. P. بهره share.

1. Contribution; subscription (*chandah*); instalment; impost.
2. An extra cess or assessment.

3. An assessment on a share; distribution of an aggregate sum; the share or interest of one of the brotherhood in an estate.
behrī bāṅdhnā, v. n. To subscribe; raise money by subscription.

بهري برار बेहरी बरार *behrī-barār*, Collection on shares of the revenue in kind.

بهري بندي बेहरी बंदी *behrī-bandī*, An allowance for repairing roads, etc.

H بهڑري भड़री *bhaṛa'rī*, n. f. The corn which remains in the ear after the straw has been trodden (*gāṅṭhā*).

H بهڑوا भड़वा *bhaṛ'wā*, *bhaṛuā*, n. m. H. *bhāṛ* pimping. A pimp; procurer; pander. [ing.

بهڑوائي भड़वाई *bhaṛvā'ī*, n. f. 1. Bawdry; pimp-
2. The earnings of a pimp.

H بهس भुस *bhus*, *bhūsā*; Gaṛh. *būkhā*, n. S. बुष.
The husk of corn; the straw of grain.
bhus bharvānā, yā bhus bharā'nā, v. a.
To peel off the skin and fill it with straw and burn it. (An oriental punishment).

بهسوري भुसौरी *bhusau'rī*, *bhusaulā*, *bhusauṅdā*, *bhusaiṛā*, *bhuselā*, *bhusehrā*; Tir. *bhuskhār*; Gaṛh. *bhusṛā*, n. m. A place where straw is stacked.

H بهسمي भसमी *bhas'mī*, *bhashmī*, n. f.
1. The ashes of the corpse.
2. The place of cremation.

H بهکسي भकसी *bhak'sī*, E.; Māṛ. *bhājsī*, n. f.
A dungeon; a chamber in which revenue defaulters in native states are confined.

H بهلے برے भलेबुरे *bhale-bure*, n. m. Bad men; bad characters; rogues.
bhalā burā kahnā, bhalī burī sunānā, v. a.
To speak ill of; abuse; insult; reproach; inveigh against; rail at; vilify.

H بهلاواں भिलावाँ *bhilā'vāṅ*, *bhilāveṅ*; E. and Bhoj. *bhelā*; Tir. *bhelāo*, n. m. S. भल्लात, P. *balādur*. 1. A nut used for marking clothes, etc. commonly called Malacca bean (*Semicarpus anacardium*).
2. A medicine. It is also used for making wales on the body, shewn in a Criminal Court as evidence of having been beaten.

H بہن बहन *ba'han*, *ba'hin*; Illit. *bhain*; Wom. *bhainā*, *bhenā*, *baihnā*; (Contemp.) *ṭhainā*, *ṭhainyā*; W. Rus. *bhāṅṛ*, *bhān*; Tir. *bahīn*; Gaṛh. *bhulī*, n. f. S. भगिनी, Old H. *bhan*.
A sister; a female cousin.

بہنوئي बहनोई *bahno'ī*; Hin. *bhaneū*, *bahneū*, *bhinoī*, *bhīnā*; Rus. *bhaṅṛeū*; Mār. *bainyāī*; Contemp. *ṭhaneū*, n. f. S. भगिनीपति
Sister's husband (*jījā*); brother-in-law.

H بهنڈار भंडार *bhaṅḍār'*, *bhaṅḍārā*, n. m. S. भाण्डागार from भाण्ड a vessel.
1. The bed of a river.
2. A receptacle for water; a tank or reservoir, particularly one which supplies a fountain.
3. Storehouse; godown; warehouse.
4. The well of a native cart.
5. Head; skull (*khopṛī*).
6. Villages managed by the *Rājā* or *zamīndār* himself; his own peculiar estate, not rented or farmed to others.
7. A feast of *jogīs*, *Sanyāsīs*, etc.

بهنڈاري भंडारी *bhaṅḍā'rī*, n. m.
1. A store-keeper; warehouse-keeper.
2. A house-steward; purveyor. [A granary.

بهنڈسال भँडसाल *bhaṅḍsāl'*, *bhansāl*, *bansār*, n. f.

H بهنگيرا भँगेरा *bhaṅge'rā*, *bhaṅg-wālā*, n. m. *bhaṅgeran*, n. f. A seller of *Bhaṅg*.

بهنگيلا भँगेला *bhaṅge'lā*, n. m. Hempen cloth for wear, or for sacks; sacks made of hemp.

H بهوجائي भौजाई *bhaujā'ī*, *bhaujī*, n. f. A brother's wife (*bhāvaj*). [earth.

H بهوڑ भूड़ *bhūṛ'*; Rus. *bhūḍ*, *bhūṭ*, n. f. *bhū*
Soil of the fourth quality; sandy or porous soil.
Unproductive soil, consisting, for the most part, of seven tenths of sand and the rest of clay, with very little vegetable mould, being the third in common enumeration. Varieties of it are termed *bhūḍ khākī*, and *bhūḍ bārānī*.

H بهوم भूम *bhūm*, *bhūṅ*, *bhūīṅ*, *bhaiṅ*, *bhū*, n. f. S. भूमि. [site; estate; domain.
Land; soil; earth (*dhartī*); ground;

S بهوگوتر भूगोत्र *bhūgot'ra*, n. m. A grant of revenue for the use or enjoyment of an individual, especially a Brahman or holy man.
bhuīyāṅ thān, *bhūm'thā*, n. m. On fixing on a new village site, a shrine to *Bhuṅyāṅ* is always set up and consecrated with much ceremony.

بهوں بهائي भूँभाई *bhūṅ-bhāī*, n. m. One invited by a proprietor to reside in a village upon a portion of land assigned to him to cultivate for his own benefit, but which he may not dispose of.

بهونڈا भूँडा *bhūṅ'ḍā*, n. m. Land given rent free to the village watchman or *Chaukīdār*.

H بہي बही *ba'hī*; Māṛ. and Gaṛh. *baī*; n. f.

1. A book, not stitched at the sides but at the end. 2. A merchant's or banker's book; a register; record; journal; diary; ledger.

bahī paṭwārī, n. f. A register kept by the *paṭwārī* or village accountant.

bahī khasrā, n. m. A day-book.

bahī dākhil khārij, n. f. Register of transfers, or mutation of names.

bahī-dāṅ, n. m. An auditor; accountant; one who examines or checks the account books.

bahī roz-nāmchā, yā roznāṅvā, n. f. Daily account book.

bahī khātā; hisāb bahī, n. f. Account books; ledger; a set of books kept by merchants or bankers. [counts.

bahī murattab rakhnā, To keep books of ac-

bahī meṅ chaṛhā'nā, v. a. To bring on the books; enter in the books; place to account; debit or credit.

bahī wāz khām, khārij az siāhā, Cash account current and extra items. Panj. [book.

bahī yād-dāsht, n f. A memorandum or note

jākaṛ bahī, Suspense account book.

chiṭṭhā bahī, Bill book; trial balance book.

chiṭṭhī bahī, Letter registry book.

dūkān kī bahī, Shop-books

dharoṛ bahī, amānat bahī. Goods deposit book.

rokaṛ bahī, n. f. Cash-book.

saudā bahī, n. f. Ware-house books.

nij bahī, n. f. Private account book.

naql bahī, n. f. Day or waste book.

hunḍī bahī. Hundi or bill book.

H بهيّا भैया *bhai'yā*, n. m. Brother. See بهائي

bhaiyā-bāṅṭ, n. f. Brotherhood; fraternity.

bhaiyā chārah, n.m. 1. A community of brethren or of people from one stock. 2. A tenure in severalty; joint undivided estate.

3. A village which has not been formally divided among its proprietors, but held according to shares as divided privately.

An estate in which the land is held part in common, and part in severalty, and the profits of the common land divided according to custom. A coparcenary estate held in severalty where rights are measured by extent of possession.

taqsīm bhaiyā chārī. Division of land between co-sharers who are jointly bound for the payment of the Government revenue.

H بهيار बहियार *bahiyār'*, n. f. S. बहिर out. Lands at a distance from the village.

H بهيت भीत *bhīt, bhīnt*; Mag. *bhitī*, n. f. S. भित्ति. A wall; embankment; the vestige of an old house.

بهيتوري भीतौरी *bhītau'rī*, n. f. 1. Ground-rent paid for the site of a house by a stranger.

2. Ground either naturally or artificially raised for the site of a house, a village, etc.

3. The old or main land of a village, that which has been always cultivated, in contradistinction to that which is gained from the river, or by alluvial deposit. [water.

4. Mounds confining a tank or piece of

H بهيٹ भेट *bheṭ, bheṅṭ*, n. f. 1. Touch; contact; collision. [visit; introduction.

2. The act of meeting; an interview; a

3. Sacrifice; offerings to superiors (*bheṭ-pūjā*); a complimentary gift (*nazrānā*).

4. A bribe; douceur; an illegal gratification.

5. A present made by the cultivator to the collector or farmer on settling his assessment (*salāmī*). [present; sacrifice.

bheṭ chaṛhānā, denā, yā karnā, v. a. To offer;

bheṭ honā, v. n. [view.

1. To meet; encounter; have an inter-

2. To be sacrificed; to fall a victim.

bheṭ bakrā, n. m. 1. The sacrifice of a goat.

2. The complimentary presentation of a goat to a superior.

H بهيج भेज *bhej*; Bhoj. *bhāṅj*, n. m. S. भज् to share. 1. A proportionate share.

2. Rent of land; ground-rent.

بهيج برار भेजबरार *bhej-barār*.

A tenure frequent in Bundel-khand in which proportions of the revenue or tax (*barār*) payable by the common proprietors are subject to periodical or occasional adjustment, and balances of the revenue and of village charges arising from the dishonesty or insolvency of a sharer, are made by rateable contributions from the other shares. A village in which this tenure prevails is said to be a *bhej barār gāṅo*.

takhfīf bhej, G. G. Abatement of rent.

kāle pānī bhejnā, v. a. To transport beyond seas; banish.

zar-i-tahsīl adālat-i-dīwānī meṅ bhej denā, To pay the amount of collections into Court.

H بهيد भेद *bhed*, n. m. S. भिद् to break.

1. Difference; variance; dissimilarity; discrepancy. [intention or purpose.

2. Secrecy; secret; mystery; secret

بهيديا भेदिया *bhed'iyā*, n. f. Soil in which various kinds of crops are grown.

H بهير बहीर *bahīr'*, n. f. H. *bhīṛ* crowd. [army.

1. Camp followers; the baggage, &c. of an

2. Lines near a camp where the wives and families of the soldiers live. [tent.

bahīṛ bungā, bhīṛ bhungā, n. f. P. *bungāh* a

The rabble of camp followers; the baggage or "impedimenta" of an army on the march.

H بهيس भेस *bhes, bhek*, n. m. S. वेश dress.

bhes badalnā, bharnā, banānā, yā palaṭnā, v. a. To assume a disguise; personate a character.

H & P بے *be*, A previtive prefix, or preposition.

بے ادبي *be-adabī*, Ped.; *be-adbī*, Pop. n. f. 1. Disrespect; rudeness. [pudence; insolence.
2. Presumptuousness; impertinence; im-

بے اصل *be-asl, be-as'al*; H. *be-jaṛ*, adj.
1. Groundless; baseless; unfounded.
2. Without foundation; false; not true.

بے اعتبار *be-eᵉtibār'*; Pop. *be-etibārā*, adj.
1. Of no credit or estimation; not trustworthy; incredible.
2. Not to be trusted; unreliable; faithless.
3. Disbelieving; suspicious; incredulous; sceptical. [discredit.

بے اعتباري *be-eᵉtebā'rī*, n. f. 1. Want of credit;
2. Untrustworthiness; faithlessness.
3. Distrust; disbelief; suspiciousness.

بے انتظامي *be-intizā'mī*, n. f. Mismanagement. See بدانتظامي.

بے انتہا *be-intehā', be-andāzāh, be-had*, adj. Endless.

بے انتہا تعويق *be-intehā tāwīq*. G. G. Indefinite postponement.

بے انصاف *be-insāf'*, adj. Unjust. See انيائي (1, 3).

بے انصافي *be-insāfī*, n. f. Injustice. See انياو.

بے اولاد *be-aulād'*; H. *nis-santān*, adj. Without issue; childless.

بے ايمان *be-īmān'*; Illit. *baimān*, adj.
1. Without religion or conscience; unprincipled; corrupt. [scrupulous; crooked.
2. Dishonest; fraudulent; false; un-
3. Faithless; perfidious; slippery; treacherous (*dagā-bāz*).

بے ايماني *be-īmānī*, n. f. *lit.* Infidelity. Irreligion; dishonesty; breach of trust; unfair dealing; unfairness. [defraud.

be-īmānī kar'nā, v. n. 1. To play false; cheat;
2. To misappropriate; embezzle; peculate.

بيباق *be-bāq*; H. *chuktā*, adj. Balanced; even; quits; without arrears; paid up in full.

be-bāq kar'nā, v. a. To pay up; pay in full; adjust; liquidate; discharge an account; make good a default or balance; settle; square or balance accounts.

be-bāq honā, v. n. To be paid in full.

shai marhūneh ke munāfa se zar-i-rahan be-bāq ho chukā. The mortgage loan had been satisfied out of the profits of the mortgaged property.

matālaba be-bāq huā, All demands satisfied.

بيباقي *be-bāqī*, n. f. Full payment; discharge; liquidation; quittance; acquittance; clearance.

be-bāqī qarz, Payment or liquidation of a debt.

بے بدل *be-bad'al*, adj. 1. Without change; uniform; invariable; unalterable; immutable.
2. Positive; absolute; peremptory. [vant.

بيجا *be-jā*, 1. Out of place; misplaced; irrele-
2. Improper; unlawful; unjustifiable; illegal.
3. Unreasonable; contrary to reason; unsound; absurd.
4. Inaccurate; wrong; objectionable.

be-jā, adv. Improperly; injudiciously; wrongly.

بيجا تصرف *bejā tasarruf*, Misappropriation; embezzlement. [plea; an idle excuse.

بيجا عذر *bejā ūzr*, n. m. A weak or unsound

bejā uzr karnā, v. n. To make a vain, or idle excuse or objection.

بيجا قرقي *bejā qurqī*, n. f. Illegal distraint or attachment; a suit for replevin.

بيجا گيري لگان *bejā gīrī lugān*, G. G. Undue exaction of rent. [delay.

توقف بيجا *tawaqquf-i-bejā*, G. G. Unnecessary

بے حال *be-hāl*, adj. [used up; ruined.
1. Damaged; unserviceable; worn out;
2. Unemployed; badly off.

be-hāl, adv. On the point of death.

بے کار *be-kār'*; H. *nikammā*, adj.
1. Without work or employment; unemployed; idle; doing nothing.
2. Inoperative; ineffective; ineffectual; inefficient. [null.
3. Without force; invalid; nugatory;

be-kār karnā, v. a.
1. To thwart; balk; frustrate; disconcert; defeat; undo. [break; destroy.
2. To render useless or unserviceable;
3. To render defective; invalidate; undo.

بے کاري *be-kār'ī*, n. f. The state of being unemployed; want of employment.

H بياج ब्याज *byāj'*, Hin; *byāz*. Mah. n. m. S. ब्याज.
Interest (*sūd*); dividend.
The interest paid by the cultivators on the advances made to them by the shop-keepers for their subsistence and repair of agricultural implements, for seed, and for the Government revenue. [terest.

byāj par byāj; P. *sūd dar sūd*. Compound in-

byāj-khor, byāz-khor, n. m. An usurer.

byāj-khorī, n. f. Usury.

بياجو *byāj'ū*, P. *sūdī*, adv. At interest. [interest.

byājū denā, byāj meṅ denā, v. n. To lend at

byājū lenā, v. n. To borrow on interest.

A بيان *bayān', byān*, n. m. بين being separated. Opp. of وصل united. See برني Declaration; assertion; affirmation; allegation; dictum; exposition; report. [report.

bayān karnā, v. a. 1. To express; tell; state;
2. To declare; assert; affirm; allege; relate; depose; lay before.
3. To give an account of; describe; recount; rehearse; retail.

khilāf mānī bayān karnā. To misconstrue; misinterpret; twist or misrepresent the meaning.

lā ilmī bayān karnā, To plead ignorance; pretend not to know.

بيان امرواقعي *bayān amr wāqā̄ī.* An allegation of fact. [self; prevaricate.

بيان بدلنا *bayān badalnā.* To contradict one's

بيان تائيدي *bayān tāīdī.* A corroborative statement; statement made in support of another.

بيان تحريري *bayān tahrīrī.* A written statement.

بيان دعوي *bayān-i-dāwā.* A statement of claim.

بيان زباني *bayān zabānī.* A verbal statement; a statement made *viva voce.*

بيان ضمني *bayān-i-zimnī.* A parenthetical observation; a thing said incidentally by the way or in passing. [ment.

بيان كاذب *bayān kāzib,—˄khilāf,* A false state-

بيان مسلسل *bayān-i-musalsal,* n. m. A continuous narrative; a connective statement.

بيان واقعات *bayān wāqīāt,* A statement of facts.

bayān o subūt ba-mūjib faisla karnā. To decide *secundum allegata et probata*; to decide on the evidence. [ment.

بيان يكطرفه *bayān yak-tarfa,* An *ex parte* state-

H بيانا बियाना *biyā'nā,* v.n. S. जन to be born. To bring forth; give birth to (animals).

بيانت ब्यांत *byānt',* W.; *byān,* Bhoj. n. m. Birth; giving birth to (animals).

H بيانو ब्यानु *byān'u,* n. m. A measure equal to the length of both arms extended from end to end, including the chest.

H بياه ब्याह *byāh',* Pop; *bivāh,* Ped; *bibāh,* Rus.; *byāv,* Mār.; *biāo.* Garh. n. m. S. बिवाह from वह to marry. Marriage; wedlock.

byāh-karāī, Hin.; *nikāh parhvāī,* Mah. n. f. The marriage fees of a Brahman.

byāhne-jog, adj. Marriageable; arrived at the age of puberty. [adj. Married.

byāh'ā, byāhī, byāhyā-thāyā, byāhī thiāī, W.

بياهتا ब्याहता *byāth'tā, byāhtā,* n. f. A married woman, in contradistinction to a kept woman (Hin. *karī-huī*; Mah. *nikāhtā*).

بيارلي ब्यावली *byāv'lī, byāhlī,* n. f. A newly married woman; a bride. [v. n.

بياهنا ब्याहना *byāh'nā, byāh kar'nā, byāh lānā,*

1. To get one married; give in marriage.
2. To marry; wed; espouse; bring home.

P بي بي *bī'bī, bivī,* n. f.

1. A lady; dame; madam; matron. Mah.
2. A wife; mistress (*bīvī*). Mah.

bibyā'nā, adj. Belonging to women; female (applied to Europeans).

H بيت बेत *bet*; Illit. *bent, bait, baint,* n. f. S. वेत्र, P. bed. Reed; cane; ratan; *Calamus rotang.*

H بيت बीत *bīt,* n.f. Grazing fee charged by herdsmen; the demand on each head of cattle paid to the cowherd; a kind of agistment.

A بيت المال *bait-ul-māl,* n. m.

1. The public treasury or exchequer.
2. Escheat; confiscated property; property that falls to the crown through failure of heirs; the effects of one who dies intestate.

Payments are made on various accounts, and, according to the sources whence they are derived they are applied to the support of different classes of persons. *Bait-ul-māl* is not the property of the ruling power, but that of all Mahomedans, for whose benefit it should be administered.

H بيٹا बेटा *be'ṭā*; E. *biṭvā, biṭaunā,* n. m. S. वटु a boy. A son; boy; child; darling.

beṭā banānā, v. n. To adopt a son (*god lenā*).

beṭā beṭī, n. m. Children; offspring; issue.

beṭe pote-wālā, n. m. *beṭe pote-wālī,* n. f.

1. A grandfather or grandmother.
2. A man or woman blest with children.

beṭe-wālā, n. m. *beṭe-wālī,* n. f. The father or mother of the bridegroom. [son.

beṭā-khāū, n. m. A father who survives his

H بيٹهن बेठन *beṭh'an*; Mār. *bīṅṭno,* n. m. S. वेष्टन from वेष्ट् to surround. A pack-cloth; the envelope in which cloth, lace, etc. purchased is folded up, and to which the purchaser is entitled. [daughter.

H بيٹي बेटी *be'ṭī, biṭyā*; E. *biṭauni,* n. f. A

beṭī behvār, n. m. Intermarriage; matrimonial alliance. [marriage.

beṭī denā, v. n. To give one's daughter in

beṭī roṭī, n. f. *lit.* Abusing a man's daughter and calling him a beggar. Calling names; foul language; abuse. [insult.

beṭī roṭī karnā, v. a. To call names; abuse;

beṭī-wālā, n. m. *beṭī-wālī,* n. f. The father or mother of the bride. [बीज 1. Seed.

H بيج बीज *bīj*; E. *bīā, bī'yā, bīhan,* n. m. S.

2. Germ; source; cause; beginning; origin.
3. Advances of seed to agriculturists, in contradistinction to *khād* an advance for food.
4. *Sperma genitale*; *semen virile*; a son.

bīj bonā, ḍālnā, yā jamānā, v. a. 1. To sow seed.

2. To be the cause of; to cause; conduce.

bīj jam'nā, v. n. To germinate; sprout.

bīj-khād. Advance of seed and food to agriculturists.

bīj-rut, n. f. The sowing season.
bīj-mār dhartī, n. f. Land on which the seed has not germinated ; failure of germination.
bīj nās karnā, v. a. To destroy ; annihilate.
bīj nās honā, v. n. To be utterly destroyed ; to become extinct (a family).

بيجائي बीजाई *bījā'ī, bījwār*, n.
1. A perquisite seed-grain.
2. A portion of corn given to the village smith, carpenter, barber, and washerman by each cultivator.

بجي‌دار बजीदार *bajī-dār*, n. m. An agricultural laborer who takes corn as a recompense for his labor, in contradistinction to a *mih-dār* who receives money.

بجيلا बिजैला *bijai'lā, bijailī*; Rus. *bījar, bīyar*, adj Seedy ; abounding in seed (a soil) ; full of seeds (a fruit).

H بيجک बीजक *bīj'ak*, n. m. S. बीजक
1. Invoice ; manifest ; a bill of parcels ; a ticket attached to bags or goods to mark the price of their contents.
2. Assets ; effects ; property.

H بيجهنا बीझना *bījh'nā*, v. n. To be eaten by worms ; to be cankered. [*kaz*).

H بيچ बीच *bīch*, n. m. 1. Middle; centre (*mar-* [place.
2. Average ; mean (*ausat*).
3. Difference ; interval. 4. Room ; space ;
bīch bichāo, n. m. 1. Mediation ; intervention ; interposition ; mediatorship ; intercession.
2. Settlement ; reconciliation ; pacification.
bīch bichāo karnā, v. a. 1. To mediate; intercede; interpose. [cile ; pacify.
2. To settle ; adjust (a difference) ; recon-
bīch kī rās, adj. Middling ; passable.
bīch men̲ paṛnā, yā ānā, v. n. See *bīch men̲ ānā*, under *ānā*.
1. To negotiate in a bargain or marriage.
2. To be surety or security for.
bīch men̲ denā, v. n. To give a pledge.

بچلا बिचला *bich'lā, bichlī, manjhlā*, n. A child born after the eldest and before the youngest.

بچوليا बिचौलिया *bichaul'yā, bīch-wālā* ; Bhoj. *bichvaīyā*, n. m. [pire.
1. One who interposes ; a mediator ; um-
2. A middleman; arbitrator; agent; broker.
3. A go-between ; a matchmaker. [intruder.
4. One who interferes ; an intermeddler ;
bīchā bīch ; Illit. *bīchon̲ bīch, bīcham bīch*, adv. The very middle or centre.

H بيچنا बेचना *bech'nā, ben̲chnā, bechnā khochnā*, v. a. S. विक्री to sell.
To sell ; dispose of ; transfer ; endorse.

bechne kā adhikār, n. m. The exclusive right of selling ; a monopoly.
bechne ke lāyaq, adj. Saleable ; negotiable.
bechne-wālā, bechan-hār, adj. Seller ; vendor.
bechī karnā, bechā likhnā, v. a. To endorse.
sakāre pīchhe bechī karnā, v. a. To negotiate after acceptance.
hundī par bechī likhnā. To endorse a bill.
bech ḍālnā, v. a. To sell off.
bechā, bechū, n. m. One who offers for sale.

P بيخ *beʰkh*, n. f. Root (*jaṛ*) ; source ; origin ; extraction.
beʰkh bunyād, n. 1. Foundation ; basis.
2. Extraction ; pedigree ; lineage ; descent.

H بيد बीद *bīd, bīdh, haldāt*, n. f. The Hin. marriage ceremony in which turmeric, salt, etc. are ground on the seventh or third day before the wedding.

P بيد *bed*, n. f. Cane (بيت).
bed kī tarah kān̲pnā, v. n. To shake as an aspen leaf with fear.
bed mārnā, sazāe bed, n. Beating with a cane; flogging ; flagellation ; corporal punishment.

H بيدر बीदर *bī'dar*, n. m. S. बीज seed, दृ to tear up. A rake or harrow worked by oxen to loosen the soil and extricate weeds from among the standing crops of young rice.

H بيدڑا बेदड़ा *baid'ṛā*, n. m. P. *bad* bad.
1. A bad character (*badmaāsh*) ; a petty thief. 2. A gambler (*juārī*).

H بير बैर *bair* ; Wom. *bairā khairī*, n. f. S. वैर, Pr. *vairam*. Enmity ; hostility ; antipathy ; malice ; ill-will ; animosity.

H بيرا बीरा *bī'rā*, n. Rate of rent of lands according to the quality of the soil and value of the crops.
بيرا بيشي *bīrā beshī*, Increase of rent with increased value of produce. [A flag.

T بيرق *bair'aq* ; Illit. *bairakh', bairak*, n. m.
More especially a flag set up on taking possession of new or unoccupied land, whence it has come to signify the act of taking possession of such land, or official authority to do so.

H بيرنا बीरना *bīr'nā, bīran*, n. m. S. वीरण A tough coarse grass spreading over uncultivated lands which are inundated yearly, and removable only by digging. [n. f. S. बोटी

H بيڑا बीड़ा *bī'ṛā* ; Mag. *bīrā*, n. m. E. *bīrī*,
1. A betel leaf, folded generally in a triangular form, with spices, areca nut, and cardamum.

It is much used by the natives of all parts of India and is commonly presented by one to another in token of civility or affection. It is also given in confirmation of a pledge, promise, or betrothal, and, among the Rājpūts, is sometimes exchanged as a challenge.

2. A thong tied to the hilt of a sword by which it is retained in the scabbard; a sword-knot; the hilt of a sword.

3. A quid of tobacco; a cheroot or cigar.

bīṛā uṭhā'nā, v. a. To take up the gauntlet; take upon oneself any enterprize, or the destruction or slaughter of another.

bīṛā ḍāl'nā, v. a. To propose a premium for the performance of a task.

The phrase originates in a custom that prevailed of throwing a *bīṛā* of betel into the midst of an assembly, in token of an invitation to undertake some difficult affair. The person who took up the betel thereby bound himself to perform the business in question.

sāt pān kā bīṛā, n. m. A *bīṛā* of seven betel leaves sent by the father of the bride to the bridegroom as a sign of betrothal.

H بيڑي बेड़ी *be'ṛī, jhunjhun'yāṅ*; Mah. Wom. *thutkārī*; Fac. *sarkārī gahnā*, n. f.

1. Fetters; irons fastened to the legs of prisoners, or of a quadruped.

2. Fetters; shackles; trammels; restraint.

H بيس बीस *bīs*, adj. S. विंशति Twenty.

bīs, adj. Better; more excellent.

bīs biswe, adj. Whole; complete; total.

bīs biswe, n. m. The whole village; a full crop or amount.

بيسي बीसी *bīs'ī*; (Brokers) *sutlī*, n. f.

1. A score (*koṛī*); twenty. 2. A measure of grain. 3. A land measure of 20 *nalīs* (*biswā*).

H بيساكھ बैसाख *baisākh'*, n. m. S. बैशाख, Pr. *vaishāho*. The first month of the luni-solar year of the Hindus (April-May).

H بيسر बीसर *bīs'ar*, Tir. *loṛhan*, n. f. H. *bisarnā* to forget.

Gleanings left in the field for the poor to gather.

H بيسك बैसक *bais'ak*, n. A grazing field for cattle.

P بيشى *besh'ī*, n. f. 1. Excess; premium (برھوتري 1, 2). 2. Increased assessment, either on land or of the revenue, on the general account or on any particular items.

beshī-i-jamā. Increase of revenue or assessment upon that of the preceding year.

beshī-zamīn. Increase in lands cultivated, either by additions or by more accurate measurement.

beshī-i-lagān, n. m. Enhancement of rent.

A بيع *baī*; H. *bikrī*, n. f. بيع selling, buying. Sale; buying and selling.

بيع الدين بالدين *baī-ud-dain bid-dain, baī-us-sarf*; H. *udhār-badal*. exchange.

بيع الدين بالعين *baī-ud-dain bil ain, baī-us-sallam*. A credit transaction; advance for produce.

بيع العين بالثمن *baī-ul-ain bis saman, baī-ul-ain bid-dain*. Merchandize.

بيع العين بالعين *baī-ul-ain-bil-ain, baī muqāezah, baī mubādalah*. Barter; sale or transfer of property by a husband in satisfaction of the dower due to his wife.

بيع الفضولي *baī-ul-fazu'lī*; H. *birthā bikrī*. Unauthorized sale.

بيع المرابحه *baī-ul-murābaheh*; H. *baṛhtī bikrī*. Sale with profit.

بيع المساوته *baī-ul-masāwateh*; H. *raihtī bikṛī*. Sale in which the form of payment is stipulated.

بعع الوضيعه *baī-ul wazīāh*; H. *ghaṭtī bikrī*. Sale at a loss.

bai bāt. Foreclosure of mortgage; absolute sale; unconditional sale.

بيع بالجبر *baī bil-jabr, baī taljīh*. Nominal, fictitious, or temporary sale.

bai bil-wafā; H. *jākaṛ bikrī*, n. f.

1. Conditional sale or mortgage.

2. A contract of pawn or usufruct.

A sale depending for its completion on the consent of the seller; the nominal sale of an article, in lieu of a debt, to be returned when the debt is paid, or upon condition that the debt shall be paid within a given term, in default of which the article becomes the property of the purchaser.

بيع بالوفادار *baī-bil-wafā-dār*; H. *jākaṛ bikrīdār*. A conditional purchaser or vendee; a person having the use of an article conditionally sold to him in acquittance of a debt or having possession and usufruct of a property on its conditional sale to him.

بيع بيعانه *baī baīāna*. A contract of sale, with acknowledgment of advance on account of the purchase-money.

بيع پٹا *baī paṭṭā*; H. *paṭṭā bikrī*. A lease or sub-lease obtained by purchase.

bai jāiz yā haqīqī; A valid sale.

بيع حقيت متوسط *baī haqīyat mutawassat*. Sale of intermediate tenure.

bai-khāngī; H. *gharelū bikrī*, n. f. Private sale.

بيع دار *baī-dār*. A purchaser; a possessor or proprietor by purchase.

bai sāzishī, n. f. A collusive sale.

bai sultānī; H. *rāj-bikrī*, n. f. A Government sale.

bai fāsid; H. *jhūṭī bikrī*, n. f. A void sale.

bai farebī; H. *dhoke kī bikrī*, n. f. A fraudulent sale.

baī kā ikhtyār khās; H. *ṭhekā*. Monopoly; special license to sell.

bai kāmil yā qataī, bai shartī yā kaṭ qibālā, bai

gair mashrūt, bai mutlaq, bai lā-kalāmī, bai qataī o gair mushrūta ; H. *pakkī bikrī*, n. f.
Foreclosure of mortgage ; absolute sale ; unconditional or unrestricted sale ; an out-and-out sale. [transfer.
bai karnā ; H. *bechnā*, v. a. To sell ; alienate ;
bai muqāsāt', Property in place of marriage.
بيع مقاصه *baī-muqā'sa.* Sale of property in favor of a wife in lieu of her relinquishment of dower. In some cases it is fraudulent transfer of property to a wife as an equivalent for a dower, but which she sells. It is also laxly used for a deed of sale for settlement, and for a deed of sale to a widow by the heirs of her husband.
بيع من مزيد *baī-mim-māzīd*, Ped. for *nīlām.* An auction sale.
bai miādī. A conditional sale.
bai-nā-jāiz. An illegal sale. [sale.
bai nāqis ; H. *kachchī bikrī*, n. f. An imperfect
بيع نمايشي *baī-numāeshī* ; H. *banāvaṭī bikrī.* A coloral sale.
bai o shara ; P. *kharīd o faro-kht* ; H. *len den*, n. m. Buying and selling ; sale and purchase ; a transaction.
بيعانه *baīā'nā* ; Pop. *bayānah*, n. m. Earnest money ; advance. [bind a bargain.
bayānā denā, v. a. To give money in advance ;
بيعت *baiāt*, n. f. The initiation of one as a disciple of some saint or religious guide.
بيعنامه *bai-nāmah, bai-khat* ; H. *bikrī-patr.*
Deed of sale ; deed of conveyance ; bill of sale.
zar-i-bayānā. A deposit ; a portion of the purchase money paid before delivery.

T بيگ *beg*, n. m. A title affixed to the names of Mogals, corresponding with lord, master, etc.

P بيگار *be-gār*, n. m.
1. Impressment of workmen, carriage, etc.
2. Forced labor with or without pay.
بيگاري *be-gār'ī*, n. m. A forced labourer ; one pressed to carry burdens for individuals or the public.

P بيگانه *be-gān'ah* ; Illit. *bigānā*, adj. 1. Not related ; foreign ; strange ; alien ; unknown.
2. Not one's own ; another's (*parāyā*).

T بيگم *beg'am*, n. f. T. *beg* a lord, *am* a feminine affix. A title of Mogal ladies.

H بيگها बीघा *bīgh'ā, bīgāh*, n. m. S. विग्रह.

A measure of land. A *pakkā bīghā* is equal to ⅝ of an acre. A *kachchā bīghā* is from a third to a fourth of an acre.
bīgha paimāi'shī, yā jarībī. A survey *bīgha.*
bīgha daftrī. A record of the measurement of lands in a district.
bīgha dehī, A village *bīgha.*
bīgha-shumārī, Measurement of land.
fī bīghā, bīghā-dām, bīghā-sar, bīghe gail, bīgah-wār. Rate per *bīghā.*
Settlement of the revenue at so much per *bīgha*, especially in villages held in common, in which the lands are apportioned in *bīghas*, and the assessment proportionally rated. [measurement.
بگوتي बिगौती *bigau'tī, bagahṭī*, n. f. 1. Land
2. Rate per *bīghā* ; rent of a *bīghā.* [n. f.
بيگهاوتي बीघाओटी *bīghāo'ṭī, bighaṭī, bighauṭī*,
According to measurement by *bīghās* ; as revenue assessed at so much per *bīghā* ; also, division of lands by *bīghās* among coparceners. Settlement of the revenue per *bīgha*, with reference also to the quality and produce of the lands, generally made at a money rate, but sometimes in kind. A coparcenary village, in which the lands are distributed among the shares in *bīghās* and their fractional parts.

H بيل बेल *bel*, n. f. S. वल्लि, Pr. *bellī* from वल्ल् to move. A creeper.
bel kī had o bast, Land marks.
chaltī bel, n. f. *lit.* A climbing creeper.
At the festival of Sankrāt, q. v. Hindu women distribute five cocoanuts or other fruits among five women, each of whom is henceforth bound to distribute so many fruits among other women, and thus the process of multiplication goes on.

P بيلا *be'lā*, n. m. A bag of money carried in the hand of a person of rank for distribution among the poor.
belā kharch, n. m. 1. Alms ; charity.
2. Eleemosynary charges or account.

H بيمه *bīm'ā, bīmāṅ, bīmah*, n. f. Insurance ; rate of insurance.
bīmā uṭhāne-wālā, bīmā-wālā, bīmā-dār.
An under-writer ; insurer.
bīmā bechne-wālā, n. m. One who insures.
bīmā karnā, v. a. To insure ; effect an insurance or policy. [rance.
bīmah kī sanad, bīmāī chiṭṭhī. Policy of insu-
bīme-wāle kī koṭhī. An insurance company.
jān-bīmā, n. m. Life insurance.

H بينڈا बींडा *bīn'ḍā*, n. m. 1. A roll of paper ; a bundle.
2. A twist of grass, or fibre of any plant, a cheap substitute for a rope.
بينڈي बैंडी *bain'ḍī*, n. Throwing up water from a pond or reservoir with a basket for irrigation.

H بينگت बेंगत *beṅ'gat*, n. m. Seed, especially when lent for sowing to an indigent rayat, who is to repay the same at harvest, with such addition as may be agreed upon.

H بیوپار **ब्योपार** *byopār'* ; Pop. *baipār,* n. m. S. **व्यापार** from **पृ** to trade. Trade (بیوہار 1.).

بیوپاري **ब्योपारी** *byopā'rī, baipārī,* n.m. S. **व्यापारी**.
1. A dealer; merchant; trader; a travelling trader or pedlar. [cattle.
2. A butcher who trades in sheep and

A بیوتات *biyūtāt, būtāt,* n. m. pl. of بیت An account of household expenses.

H بیورا **ब्योरा** *byo'rā, beorā;* Pop. *baurā;* Mār. *boro,* n. m. S. **व्याहृ** to utter. See برتی
1. News; tidings; intelligence.
2. A detailed account; a day book. [timate.

byo'rā karnā, yā denā, v. a. To inform; in-
byore-wār, adj. Circumstantial; detailed (*bil tafsīl*); distinct; explicit. [(بالتفصیل).
byore-wār, adv. In detail; explicitly; distinctly

H بیوستھا **बैवस्था** *baivas'thā, bivas'thā;* A. *fatwah,* n. m. S. **व्यवस्था**.
A judgment according to Hindu law.

P بیوہ *be'wah,* n. f. Z. *veva.* A widow (بدھوا).
bewa qābiz-i-jāedād-i-shauharī. A widow in possession of her husband's estates.
bewa-i-lāwald. A childless widow.

H بیوہار **बेवहार** *bevhār', byohār, beohār, behvār;* Rus. *bivāhr,* n. m. S. **हृ** to take.
1. Dealing; traffic; trade; transaction.
2. Business; negotiation; correspondence; intercourse. [lending.
3. Calling; trade; profession; money-
4. Usage; practice; custom; procedure; manner of proceeding; course.

بیوہاري **बेवहारी** *bevhā'rī;* Pop. *behvārī, byohā'rī;* Rus. *bivāhrī,* adj. 1. Wonted; customary; usual. 2. Mercantile; commercial.
bevhārī, n. 1. The party engaged in any affair.
2. A trader; merchant; money lender.

H بیہڑ **बेहड़** *be'haṛ, bī'haṛ,* adj. Uneven; cut up; rugged; rough.
be'haṛ, bihaṛ, n. f. 1. Rugged or rough land or soil; land broken into ravines.
2. A jungle; forest; thick forest.
3. Waste or sterile land; pasturage.

H بیہن **बेहन** *be'han, bī'han;* Bhoj. *bīyaṛ,* n. f. H. *bīā* seed. 1. A nursery for rice plants.
2. Advances given for seed grain.

پ

P پابند *pā-band,* adj. Bound; restrained; fettered.
pā'band-i-hukm, n. m. Subject to rules or orders.
pā-band honā, v. n. 1. To be bound, fettered, etc.
2. To be bound or guided by; to adhere to; conform to; observe (a rule); follow; abide by. [bound.

پابندي *pā-bandī,* n. f. 1. The state of being
2. Check; restraint; restriction; control; rule; observance; practice.

پارکاب *pā-rakāb, pāē-rakāb,* n. m. Retinue; train; followers.

H پاتک **पातक** *pāt'ak, pātag,* n. m. S. **पत्** to fall.
1. That which causes to fall or sink; sin (*pāp*); wickedness.
2. Pollution from proximity to a corpse.
panch pātak, n. m. The five most heinous sins of the Brahmanical code; viz. killing a Brahman, stealing, drinking spirits, intercourse with the wife of a spiritual preceptor, and association with one who has committed these sins.

H پاٹ **पाट** *pāṭ* n. m. A promissory note.

H پاچھ **पाछ** *pāchh,* n. m. 1. Inoculation.
2. The incision made in the poppy head for the opium to ooze out.
3. Kicking out with the hind legs (a horse). [prick; inoculate.

پاچھنا **पाछना** *pāchh'nā,* v. a. 1. To puncture;
2. To make a notch with a sharp instrument on a wall, as the *dāin* (witch) is supposed to do, so that the same cuts may break out on the body of the person whose injury is contemplated.

P پاداش *pādāsh',* n. m. Satisfaction; punishment (H. *badlā*).
ba-pādāsh. By way of punishment; for.
pādāsh denā, v. a. To make good a damage; to give satisfaction.
pādāsh kī bābat. For the punishment of.
pādāsh lenā. To vindicate; avenge oneself.

Port. پادري *pād'rī,* n. m.
1. A clergyman; missionary; chaplain.
2. (*Ironic.*) One converted to Christianity.
pādriyān-i-mazhabī ke fāēde ke līē. G. G. For the benefit of ministers of religion.

H پارچا **पारचा** *pār'chā, pārchhā,* n. m. S. **पय** water **रक्ष** to protect. A trough or reservoir into which the bucket of water drawn from the well is emptied.

P پا سنگ *pā'saṅg,* n. m. A balance; a makeweight; anything placed in one scale to balance the other.
ulṭā pāsaṅg, baṛtī pāsaṅg, n. m. Overweight.
kamtī pāsaṅg, n. m. Short weight.

H پاسي पासी *pās'ī*, n. m. S. पाश a noose.

1. Any one using a noose, rope, or snare.
2. A caste of people whose occupation is to extract the juice of the *Tār* palms, so named from their climbing with the aid of a *pāsuki* or loop passed round their feet.

H پاگل पागल *pāg'al*, *paglā*, *paglī*, adj. Foolish (*bāolā*); insane; mad. [madness.

pāgal-pan, *pāgal-panā*, n. m. Foolishness;

پاگل‌خانہ पागलख़ाना *pāgal-khānā*, n. m. A mad house; a lunatic asylum; a sanitary asylum.

pāgal honā, v. n. To become mad.

H پال पाल *pāl*, n. m. S. पाल् to protect.

A dam; dyke; bank; an embankment to confine the water for irrigation.

H پان पान *pān*, n. m. S. पर्ण, Pr. *paṇṇo* leaf.

1. A betel leaf; *Piper betel.*
2. Plantations of the succulent creeper, called *pān*, (*piper chavica*) are common throughout Upper India.

pān-khilāī, n. f. A betrothal ceremony.

pān-mahāl, A tax on the cultivation of betel.

H پانس पांस *pāṅs*, E.n.m.S. पांसु dung. Manure (*khāt*); a dunghill. [become manure.

pāṅs ho jānā, v. n. To rot; become mildewed;

پانسنا पांसना *pāṅs'nā*, v. a. To manure; dung.

H پاني पानी *pā'nī*; Rus. *pāṇṛī*; Old H. *pān* (Padmāvat), n. f. S. पानीय, Pr. *pāṇiam* from पा to drink. Water (*jal*). [a field.

pānī denā, v. n. 1. To water a plant; irrigate
2. To offer a libation of water to the manes of the deceased after the corpse has been burnt.

pān'dhaṛ, n. m. Irrigated land.

pānī-devā, n. m. One entitled to offer a libation of water to the deceased; a son.

H پاہ पाह *pāh*, n. f. Land which has been three years in cultivation.

H پاہي पाही *pā'hī*; *pāhī āsāmī*; Old H. *pākhī*, n. m. S. पक्ष a side. A non-resident cultivator (*pāē-kāsht*); a temporary occupant of village land; a tenant at will.

پاہي باقي *pāhī bāqī*, In Mah. finance, the designation of such lands as were set apart for *jāgīr* grants, if required; also the revenue from lands so reserved and not yet alienated, and of lands which, having been alienated, had been resumed and which paid revenue until a fresh assignment was made.

پاہي باقي خالصہ *pāhī bāqī khālisā*. The revenue of resumed or lapsed, but suspended alienations, receivable in the public treasury.

pāhī-partī, n. f. Fallow land.

پاہي سابق *pāhī sābiq*, n. f. A non-resident cultivator who has held the lands he tills for more than a year; an item of the village rent roll shewing the rent paid by non-resident cultivators. [cultivators.

pāhī-kāsht, *pāī-kāsht*, n. m. A non-resident

pāhī kāsht zamīn. Land cultivated by peasants not residing on the spot; land held on a tenure of temporary occupancy.

پاہي نواد *pāhī-nawād*. A non-resident cultivator who engages to cultivate for the current year.

pāh'nī, n. f. Revenue survey.

H پائي पाई *pāī*, n. f. 1. One-fourth of an anna; a pice (Natives). 2. A small copper coin equal to one-twelfth of an annā; a pie.
3. A vertical line denoting one-fourth of an anna in Hindi accounts.

H پايک पायक *pā'yak*; P. *paik*, n.m. S. पादिक.

1. A messenger; courier; footman; a village watchman.
2. An armed attendant, or inferior police or revenue officer; a subordinate collector of rents.

P پايمالي *pāē-mālī*, n. f. 1. Trampling down; destruction; devastation; ruin.
2. Destruction of crops; compensation for damage done to standing crops by the passage of troops. [cast.

H پبيڑنا पबेड़ना *paber'nā*, v. n. To sow broad-

H پتا पता *pat'a* n. m. S. पद sign.

1. The address of a person; the address or place to which one is directed.
2. A book of instructions and regulations for rent collectors.

پتا موضع‌وار *patā mauze-wār*. Local index.

H پتا पिता *pit'ā*; n. m. S. पितृ, Pr. *piaram*, *piā*, *piaro*; Z. *ped*, *pīd*; P. *pidar*, *pid* Father.

pitā-khāū, n. One who survives his father.

pitā-ghāt, n. m. Parricide.

pitā-ghāt'ik, n. m. A parricide.

H پتر पित्तर *pit'tar*, *pitr*, n. m. S. पितृ Ancestors; manes of the dead.

pitr-ārpan. Gifts in honor of deceased relatives, distributed at the Sharādhs or funeral ceremonies.

pitr-asthān, n. m. The place where the manes of one's ancestors are deposited. [paternal line.

pitr-bandhū, n. m. A cognate relation in the

pitr-paksh, n. f. 1. The first or dark fortnight of *Āsauj* when the Hindūs celebrate the customary obsequies to the manes of their ancestors (*kanāgat*).
pitr-tith, n. f. The last day of the first fortnight in *Āsauj*.
pitr-tarpan, n. m. An offering of water to the [dead.
pitr-tīrath, n. m. 1. Gayā, or the city so called, where the performance of funeral rites is held to be peculiarly efficacious.
2. The part between the fore-finger and thumb, sacred to the manes.
pitr-dān, *pitr-ārpan*, n. m. Gifts in honor of one's deceased ancestors.
pitr-sharādh, *pitri-shirāddh*, n. m. The obse-[quies of a father.
pitr-karm, *pitr-kiryā*, *pitr-jag*, *pitr-kāj*, n. m. Obsequial rites; funeral ceremonies; a feast given to appease the soul of the dead.

S پتر पत्र *patr*; Pop. *pattar*, *pattrā*, n. m.
1. A letter; document; deed.
2. A grant or conveyance of land engraven on a plate of metal.
udhār-patr, n. m. A note of hand; a promissory note (*tamassuk*).
bintī-patr, n. m. A petition (*arzī*); memorial.
maut-patr, n. A will; dying testament (*vasīat-nāmah*).
nindā-patr, n. m. A defamatory writing; a [libel.
پترا पत्तरा *pat'trā*, n. m. An almanac; ephemeris; calendar (*jantrī*).

H پتلا पुतला *put'lā*, n. m. S. पुत्तल An effigy; [image; puppet.
putlā banā-ke jalānā, *putlā bidhān*, n. m. Burning in effigy; the vicarious cremation of an effigy of one who has died at a distance.

H پتوتن دینا पतोतनदेना *patotan denā*, v. a. To lend money and take over a village; to hold till the sum lent has been paid off from the village profits.

At stipulated intervals accounts are made up between the creditor and debtor, and when the profits derived from the village amount to the whole debt, the village is returned and the transaction at an end.

H پتي पती *pat'ī*, *pat*, n. m. S. पति from पा to protect. Owner; master; lord; husband.
pati-birt, n. m. Fidelity to a husband; chastity.
pati-birtā, *pati-bhartā*, n. f. S. पतिब्रता A faithful, virtuous, or devoted wife.

H پٹا पट्टा *pat'ṭā*, n. m. S. पत्र leaf, पट्ट a board.
1. A shoulder strap and badge. [or a lease.
2. A deed, commonly a title deed to land,
3. A code or book of regulations for the guidance of rent-collectors,
4. A document given to the *zemindār* by the Collector, or by some other receiver of revenue to the cultivator or tenant, specifying the conditions on which the lands are held, and the value or proportion of the produce to be paid to the authority or person from whom the lands are held.
پٹہ استمراري *paṭṭā istamrārī*. Tenure in perpetuity; a perpetual lease.
paṭṭā-pher, n. m. The conclusion of a Hindu marriage ceremony in which the bride and bridegroom change seats.
پٹہ تعلق *paṭṭa ta'alluq*. A dependent lease. G. G.
پٹہ ٹھیکہ *paṭṭa ṭheka*. A deed assigning land for farming on certain conditions; a lease of land.
paṭṭā ṭheke-dārī, n. A farming lease.
پٹہ خانگي *paṭṭa-i-khāngī*. A private lease.
پٹہ دار *paṭṭe-dār*, Ped. for H. *paṭait*. A lease holder; lessee.
پٹہ دار شکمي *paṭṭe-dār shikamī*. An under-lessee.
paṭṭā dene-wālā. The grantor of a lease; lessor.
پٹہ رهن *paṭṭā rahan*, Ped. for H. *girvī paṭṭa*. A mortgage lease.
پٹہ زرپیشگي *paṭṭa zar-i-peshgī*. A lease granted on an advance of money.
پٹہ سلامي *paṭṭa salāmī*. A fine, fee, or complimentary present of money on the grant of a lease.
پٹہ شکمي *paṭṭa-i-shikamī*. A sub-lease.
پٹہ فریبي *paṭṭa-i-farebī*, G. G. A fraudulent lease.
paṭṭā qubūlīyat, n. m The settlement paper.
پٹہوار *paṭṭe-wār*, According to shares or assessment.
حیاتي پٹہ *hayātī paṭṭā*, Ped. for H. *janam paṭṭā*.
1. Life rent; a lease terminating with one's own life. 2. Life-long slavery.
پٹ بندهک पटबन्धक *paṭ-bandhak*, n. m. A living pledge; mortgage; a pledge the usufruct of which pays both the principal and interest within a certain period, and therefore ensures its own redemption.
پٹہ کٹاي جنگل *paṭṭa kaṭāī jangal*. A forest cutting lease G. G.
پٹہ کي تنسیخ *paṭṭe kī tansīkh*. Annulment of a lease; voidance or determination of a lease.
پٹہ کي میعاد *paṭṭe kī mīād*. The term of a lease; the period for which a lease has to run.
پٹہ میعادي *paṭṭa-i-mīādī*. A lease granted for a term of years; a terminable lease.
پٹیت पटैत *paṭait'*, n. m. A lease holder. [cash.

H پٹانا पटाना *paṭā'nā*, v. a. 1. To realize;
2. To irrigate; water (a field). E.
3. To settle; conclude (a bargain).
پٹاو पटाव *paṭā'o*, n. m. 1. Irrigation.

H پتپڑ **पटपड़** *paṭ'paṛ, parpaṭ*, n. m. 1. Alluvial land; moist land caked by sunshine after rain or flood.
2. A dreary waste; a desert spot.
paṭpaṛ, adj. 1. Naturally level, even, flat, smooth (*barābar*). 2. Razed to the ground; demolished; devastated.

H پٹڑا **पटड़ा** *paṭ'ṛā*, n. m. S. पट्ट.
1. A plank; a plank to sit on (*paṭṭa*).
2. A long thick plank used as a harrow.
paṭrā phernā, v. a. To harrow; prepare the land for seed.

پٹکار **पटकार** *paṭkār', phaṭkār, paṭkārī*, n. f. See اوگي (1). A rope or whip about two yards long, used by cultivators to scare the birds.

H پٹمي **पटमै** *paṭma'ī*, n. f. Sowing fresh sugar-cane after the cutting the old.

H پٹنا **पटना** *paṭ'nā*, v. n. 1. To be paid (*paṭānā*, 1.).
2. To be irrigated.
3. To agree together; to be struck or closed (a bargain).
4. To be repaid, remitted.
paṭṭī hunḍī, n. f. A good bill.

H پٹواری **पटवारी** *paṭvā'rī*, n. m. S. पत्र a writing, वारिन doer.
A village registrar or accountant.
A land steward whose duty it is to keep and produce when required, all accounts relating to lands produce, cultivation charges, and assessments of a village.
rasūm-i-paṭwārī, n. f. The paṭwārī's fees.
پٹوارگري **पटवारगरी** *paṭwārīgarī*, n. f. The office of *paṭwārī*.

H پٹولی **पटोलो** *paṭau'lī*, n. m. An engagement between the *zamīndār* and *asāmī*. [ate.

H پٹھوال **पुठवाल** *puṭhwāl'*, n.m. A confeder-

H پٹي **पट्टी** *paṭ'ṭī*, n. f. 1. A part; portion; a division of a village; a division of land into separate portions or strips.
2. An original or separate share in a joint or coparcenary village or estate comprising many villages.
3. A smaller sub-divison of a *mahāl* or estate, the larger being termed *thoks*; the secondary share or sub-division of a principal *bhāg* or share.
paṭṭī par qābiz rahnā, v. n. To retain in severalty.
paṭṭī-dār, n. m. The holder of a paṭṭī or share in a co-parcenary village or estate; a co-sharer; co-parcener.
paṭṭī-dār be-bāq. A solvent *paṭṭidār*.
paṭṭī-dārī, n. f. An estate held in severalty.

پٹي داري **पट्टी दारी** *paṭṭī-dārī*, n. f. A tenure of a co-parcenary nature in which the lands are divided and held in severalty by the different proprietors, each person managing his own lands and paying his fixed share of the Government revenue, through an accredited representative of the whole being unable to fulfil his engagements.
paṭṭī-dārī-mutlaq. Tenure in severalty.
paṭṭī-dārī nā mukammal. Co-parcenary tenure, where part of the land is divided and part held in common. N. W. P.; tenure of an estate in partial severalty. Punjāb.
paṭṭī-wār. According to shares, assessment, etc.
sawārī-paṭṭī. A cess to defray the expense of entertaining some person of rank or in authority.
khushāl-paṭṭī. A tax levied to defray the expenses of a private or public rejoicing, as a marriage, or the birth of a son.

پٹیل **पटैल** *paṭail'*, n. m. The descendant of the founder of a village; the headman of a village.
The headman of a village, who collects the rents from the other *raiyats* therein, and has the general superintendence of its concerns. The same person in Bengal is called the *mukaddam* and *mandal*, q. v.

H پٹیت **पटैत** *paṭait'*, n. m. 1. A leaseholder.
2. A village priest.

H پجاري **पुजारी** *pujā'rī*, n. m. 1. A worshipper; an idolater. 2. A priest who officiates at a shrine and lives upon the offerings made to the idol.

H پچ **पच** *pach*, adj. In comp. Cont. of پانچ five.

پچدو **पचदो** *pach'do*, n. m. Division of grain, two-fifths to the *zamīndār*, and three-fifths to the *asāmī*.

پچوترہ **पचोतरह** *pachot'rah, pachotrā*, n. m.
Five per cent commission.

H پچار **पचार** *pachār'*, n. m. Low land.

H پچھنا **पछना** *pachh'nā*; E. *pachhnī*; Bhoj. *pachhanī*, n. m. 1. The act of scarifying; tattooing; inoculation; vaccination; cupping.
2. A scarificator. 3. The scarifying of the poppy head to procure opium.

H پچھي **पुच्छी** *puch'chhī*, n. f. H. पुच्छ a tail.
A tax on cattle. (*lit.* on tails).

P پختہ *pu**kh'ta*, adj. Ripe; strong. See پکا

P پدر *pidar, pad'ar*; H. *bāp*, n. m. Father.
پدر کشي *pidar-kushī*, n. f. Parricide (*bāp-hattyā*).
پدري *pid'arī*, adj. Paternal; patrimonial (*bapotī*).

H پراچھت **प्राछित** *prā'chhit, prāchhat, prā-*

chit, prāshchit ; E. *prāchhut*, Hin ; *kafārah*, Mah. n. m. S. प्रायश्चित्त A fine or penance imposed as the price of absolution ; atonement ; expiation.

H پران دنڈ प्रान डंड *pirān ḍanḍ*, n. m. Capital punishment.

H پرتشٹھا प्रतिष्ठा *pratish'ṭhā*, n. f. 1. Position ; rank.
2. See شہرت. 3. The consecration or endowment of a temple.
4. The marriage portion of a daughter.

H پرتلا परतला *parta'lā*, n. m. A sword-belt ; shoulder-belt.
پرتلا و توسدان *partalā o tosdān*, n. m. Shoulder-belt and cartouche ; accoutrements.

H پرجا परजा *par'jā* ; A. *raīyat*, n. f. S. प्रजा, Pālī. *pajā*. A subject ; tenant.

In Kuch Behar, a cultivator at will who has half the produce of the land for himself, but is removable at the pleasure of the proprietor to whom he is usually in debt for advances, and is more like a serf than a free agent. In Cuttack the term is applied to various low castes, as the barber, washerman, fisherman, weaver, leather worker, *tōri* gatherer, etc. who sometimes sell themselves and families into slavery until they can repay the purchase money. The children born during this period become the property of the purchaser, and with their parents, may be bought, sold, or let out for hire until redeemed. The *parjā* do not forfeit their caste or forego their occupations, living apart from their master, and retaining a title to their hereditary possessions.

پرجاپتی परजापती *parjā-patī, parjāpat*, n. m. S. प्रजापति. 1. An epithet of Brahma ; Creator.
2. A king ; a prince ; a lord ; a governor.

H پرجوت परजोत *par-jot*, n. m. Ground rent levied on houses.

A house tax levied by the *zamīndārs* upon the inhabitants of a village, other than cultivators, for the ground on which their houses stand. Also called *parja pauni*.

par-jot zamīn-i-ābādī, G. G. Ground rent of inhabited sites.

H پرچا परचा *par'chā*, n. m. S. परिचा. 1. Examination (امتحان). 2. Revelation ; miracle.

H پرچا परचा *par'chā*, n. m. Head priests of Jagan Nāth who superintend the collection and disbursement of the revenues of the temple and also see that the worship is conducted in an orderly manner.

H پرچون परचून *parchūn', paṛchūn, parchūnī*, n. m. H. *par* beyond, *chūn*, flour. Grocery. W.
پرچونیا परचूनिया *parchūn'yā, paṛchūnyā*, n. m.
A grocer ; one who sells flour, *dāl*, etc. W. ; a pedlar. E.

H پردھان पर्धान *pardhān', padhān* ; E. *purdhān*, n. m. S. प्रधान.
1. Chief ; master ; governor.
2. A head man of a village ; chief ; minister or counsellor of state ; president ; a title.
pardhān mantrī, n. m. The prime minister.

P پردہ نشین *pardah-nashīn*, *parda-dār*, *parde-wālī*, n. f.
One who always remains behind the curtain and does not appear before strange men, and who is therefore excused from appearing in person in a court of justice.

H پرسا पुरसा *pur'sā*, n. m. S. पुरुष The height of a man with his arms and fingers extended ; a fathom ; four cubits.

H پرسا परसा *par'sā*, n. A portion of grain, set aside to appease evil spirits, which the *goṛait* or watchman eventually gets.

P پرستش *parastish'*, n. f. Worship (*pūjā*).
پرستشگاہ *parastish-gāh*, A. *ma'abad*, G. G. n. f.
A place of worship (*mandir*).

H پرستو परसतो *par'sato*, n. m. Mutual assistance in tillage, allowing the use of a plough and oxen in lieu of wages in money or kind, synonymous with *harsat, dangwārā, jiterā*, and *angwārā*.

S پرش पुरुष *pur'ush* ; H. *purakh* ; Illit. *puras*, n. m. 1. Man. 2. A husband (*bhartār*).
پرش دھن पुरुषधन *purush-dhan*, n. m. Property belonging to the man or husband, in contrast to *strī-dhan* (the wife's property).

H پرکھ परख *par'akh*, n. f. S. परीक्षा = परि + ईक्ष to see. 1. Test ; proof ; trial ; examination.
2. Scrutiny ; discrimination ; judgment ; intelligence ; skill.
پرکھانا परखाना *parkhā'nā*, v. a. Caus. of پرکھنا
To give (*denā*) ; present ; pay.
پرکھائی परखाई *parkhā'ī, parakhvāī*, n. f.
Testing coin ; the fee for testing coin.
پرکھنا परखना *parakh'nā*, v. a.
1. To examine ; test ; try ; assay ; prove.
2. To get ; obtain, secure.
پرکھیا परखैया *parkhaī'yā, parakhyā* ; *pārkhī* ; *parakhne-vālā*, n. m. A money tester ; one who examines coins ; an assayer.

P & H پرگنہ *pargan'ah*, n. m. S. परगण a country.
1. A sub-division of a *zila* or district nearly equal to a barony.
2. The country ; abroad ; any distant place.
3. (Wom.) The part of the country where one's husband is employed.

پرگناتي *parganātī*, adj. Of or relating to a *parganah*.

parganātī jamā. The amount of revenue received at the head office of the pargana from the several sub-divisions composing each *pargana*, after deducting the charges of collection in each.

parganātī kharch. *Parganah* charges to be deducted from the gross revenue.

parganātī nirkh. Rates of valuation of the crops and the assessment of the revenue and other items of expense and receipt which ordinarily prevail or are established in a district.

پرگنه‌دار *parganah-dār*, n. m. The superior officer of a *parganah*; lord of the barony.

پرگنه‌وار *parganah-wār'*, n. By *parganah*, (settlement, etc). [S. मा to measure.

S پرمان प्रमाण *pramān'*; Pop. *parmān*, n. m. 1. Measure; scale; standard; magnitude; quantity; proportion. [verification.
2. Examination; trial; test; attestation;
3. Proof; demonstration; testimony; authority; authoritative or scriptural assertion.
4. (*Law.*) Proof by ordeal or oath, by evidence oral or documentary, and by possession. 5. Trust; belief; reliance.

pramān, pramānī, adj. 1. Real; substantial; authentic; authoritative.
2. Approved; admissible; credible.

E پرمٹ *par'maṭ*, n. f. Cor. of Permit. Customs; custom house.

پرمٹ‌بندر *parmaṭ bandar*. Port of entry.

H پروا पुरवा *pur'vā*, n. f. 1. A hamlet with land attached to it within the area of a *mauza*.
2. A light sandy soil, of a yellowish color and capable of irrigation.

P پروانه *parwā'nah*; Rus. *parmānā*, n. m. P. *farmūd* ordered. A written precept or command; letters patent; license; patent; warrant; writ; grant; passport; a customhouse permit or pass; an order of appointment; a vernacular letter addressed to a subordinate officer.

پروانه استقلال *parwā'na-i-istiqlāl*, n. m. An order declaratory of the right of permanent possession.

پروانه بیبات *parwānā baibāt*, n. m. An order or notice of sale, especially on the non-fulfilment of the conditions of a mortgage. [warrant.

پروانه تلاشي *parwāna-i-talāshī*, n. m. A search

parwāna-i-hifāzat zāt khās. Writ of protection of the person. [conduct; permit.

پروانه‌راه‌داري *parwāna-i-rāh-dārī*. Passport; safe

پروانه‌قایم‌مقامي *parwān-i-qāyam-muqāmī*. Instrument or writ of procuration. [arrest.

پروانه‌گرفتاري *parwāna-i giriftārī*. A warrant of

parwāna likhnā, v. n. To grant a warrant or a license; to give an order. [writer.

parwāna-navīs, n. m. A vernacular order-

پروانگي *parwān'gī*, n. f. 1. Permission. See اجازت
2. A grant, or letter under a great seal from any man in power to his dependants.

H پروٹ पुरवट *pur'waṭ*, n. Drawing water by oxen.

P پرور *par'var*, from P. *parvardan* to nourish.
Used in Comp. only. A protector; supporter; patron.

garīb-parwar, n. m. A cherisher of the poor; a title of respect applied to a superior.

پرورده *parwar'dah*, p. p. Used in Comp. only. Fed and clothed; supported; patronized; as, *namak-parwardah*. [See *pālan*.

پرورش *parwar'ish*; Rus. *parvastī*, n. f. Support.

parwarish karnā, v. a. To support (*pālnā*).

atfāl-i-maktab kī parwarish, G. G. Ped. for H. *biddyārthiyoṅ kā pālan*, n. f.
The support of scholars.

gurbā kī parwarish ke liye, G. G.
For the relief of poor people.

H پروہت पिरोहित *piroh'it*, *parohit*; *parohat*; Pop. *pirot*; Brij. *puret*, Tir., *uprohit*, *purhit*; n. m. S. पुरोहित The family priest.

kul-pirohit, n. m. The hereditary family priest.

پروہتائی पिरोहताई *pirohtā'ī*, n. f.
1. The office of a *pirohit*; priesthood.
2. The fees of the officiating priest.

H پرویش परवेश *parvesh'*; Illit. *parbes*, n. S. विश to enter. 1. Ingress; entrance; admission; access.
2. The religious ceremony observed previous to inhabiting a new house.

P پري *pur'ī*, n. f. 1. Fullness; completeness; sufficiency. 2. Also used in *Comp.* as, *khānā-purī*, filling up a column.

H پریت प्रेत *pret, paret*, n. m. S. प + इ to go forth. Pālī. *peto*. The unclean spirit of a deceased person doomed for one year to traverse the infernal regions.

paret sharādh, paret kiryā yā karm, n. m. The obsequies performed to purify the unclean spirit in the infernal regions, and speed its flight to the *pitr-lok* the abode of gods.

S پریکشا परीक्षा *parīk'shā*; H. *parichhā*; E. Rus. *parichchhā*, n. f. See امتحان

H پرجوجن प्रयोजन *prayo'jan* ; Pop. *parojan*, n. S. प्र and युज apply. 1. Occasion; necessity; cause (اوزی 7, 8). 2. The ceremony of shaving a child's head and boring his ears for the first time. Hin.

H پریہ परेह *par'eh*, n. Flooding fields before the last ploughing, when there is want of moisture.

H پڑاو पड़ाव *paṛāv'*, *paṛā'o*, n. m. H. پڑنا to lie down. [stage ; station.
1. A halting place ; halt ; encampment ;
2. A caravan ; camp ; multitude ; crowd.
paṛāo karnā, yā ḍālnā, v. n. To halt ; encamp ; pitch tents. [market price.

H پڑت पड़त *paṛ'at*, n. f. 1. Price ; rate ;
2. Cost price ; real value.
paṛat phailānā, v. a. To distribute an aggregate charge over all the individuals liable to it ; to calculate.

پڑتا पड़ता *paṛ'tā*, W ; *lagān*, E. n. m. [tion.
1. Portion; share; quota; dividend; contribu-
2. The rate at which the revenue demand falls on each *bīghā* or plough. [revenue.
paṛtā mālguzārī, n. f. Rateable amount of
paṛtā mutawassat, Ped. n. m. An average rate.

پڑتال पड़ताल *paṛtāl'*, *partāl*, n. f. H. *par* another, *tol* weighment.
1. Revision ; review ; comparison.
2. Testing the survey ; remeasurement or survey ; reweighment.
3. Remeasurement, as a test of the accuracy of a previous measurement; revision of a former land measurement or survey.
paṛtāl jarīb, n. f. Remeasurement of land with a chain.
paṛtāl karnā, v. a. To test the accuracy of a previous measurement of land by remeasuring it.

پڑتالنا पड़तालना *paṛtāl'nā*, *partāl k.* v. n. 1. To try; test; bring to the test; examine; audit ; check ; count again ; remeasure.
2. To revise ; review ; collate ; compare.
ind-ul-paṛtāl, Ped. adv. At the time of testing, or examining. [Pr. *paṛ*.

پڑتي पड़ती *paṛ'tī* ; P. *uftādah*, n. f. S. पत् to fall,
Uncultivated, fallow land ; lands culturable but not cultivated ; waste.
paṛtī jadīd, n. f. Lands recently left fallow.
paṛtī-i-qadīm, n. Land which has long been lying uncultivated.

پڑنا पड़ना *paṛ'nā*, v. n.
1. To fall ; drop ; drop down ; fall upon.
2. To cost ; to be valued at ; to come to.

H پڑوا पड़वा *paṛ'wā*, *parwā* ; Tir. *paṛīb*, n. f. S. प्रतिपद, Pr. *paḍivāā*. The first day of a lunar fortnight, the first of the moon's increase. [neighbour.

H پڑوسي पड़ोसी *paṛau'sī*, *paṛosī*, n. m. A
paṛausī kā ans, n. m. Right of vicinage ; right of pre-emption.

H پسر पसर *pas'ar*, n. f. 1. Grazing by night.
2. Letting cattle loose at night to graze, usually on forbidden pasture.
pasar charānā, v. a. To graze cattle at night.

P پسر *pis'ar*, n. m. A son ; a boy. See بیٹا
pisar-i-sulbī ; H. *sagā beṭā*, n. m. One's own son.
pisar-i-khuāndah ; H. *pos-pūt*, n. m. An adopted son.

P پشت *pusht* ; H. *pīṭh*, n. f. S. पृष्ठ.
1. Extraction; descent; generation (*pīṛhī*); ancestry.
pusht par likhnā, v. n. To endorse ; to write on the back ; to address ; write the address.
pusht dar pusht, pusht ba-pusht, adv.
Through successive generations ; generation after generation (*paramparā*).

پشته *push'tah* ; H. *meṅḍ*, n. m. An embankment; a bank ; dike ; prop. ; buttress.
pushtī-bān, n. m. 1. A backpiece used for strengthening ; a ledge ; a joint ; a tie beam.
2. A supporter ; an ally.

پشتيني *pushtai'nī*, adj. Hereditary ; ancestral.

H پکا पक्का *pak'kā* ; P. *pukhta*. The term now applied to the tenure under which a property is held under sub-settlement. (Act XXVI of 1866.)

H پکار पुकार *pukār'*, n. f. S. प्रकुश to call out.
1. Call ; calling out (*bulāo*) ; cry for help ; halloo. 2. A summons ; invitation.
3. Invocation ; address ; prayer.
4. Petition ; suit ; request (*darkhuāst*).
5. Complaint (*faryād*) ; plaint.
6. Want (*māṅg*) ; need ; necessity.
7. Scarcity ; drought ; dearth. [gain.

H پکڑ पकड़ *pak'aṛ* ; Mār. *apaṛ*, n. f. S. प्रग्रह to
1. The act of seizing ; seizure ; hold.
2. Apprehension ; capture (*giriftārī*).
3. Fighting ; wrestling (*kushtī*).

پکڑنا पकड़ना *pakaṛ'nā*, v. a. 1. To catch hold of ; clutch ; grapple ; handle.
2. To seize ; capture ; apprehend ; arrest.
3. To find out ; detect ; discover ; hit upon.
4. To press into one's service ; to press.

پکڑوانا पकड़वाना *pakaṛvā'nā*, Caus. of پکڑنا q. v.

S پکش पक्ष *paksh*, n. m. See *or* (1—4).
1. Wings (*pankh*) ; feathers.
2. The half of a lunar month, or a fortnight of fifteen days.
The half from the new moon to the full is called *Sukla-paksh*, H. *sudi*, the white or light fortnight ; that from the full to the new moon, *Krishna-paksh*, H. *badi* the black or dark fortnight.
3. Partiality *(pach)*.

H پکھالا पखाला *pakhā'lā*, n. m.
The second watering of a crop.

H پگ رس पुगरस *pug'rus*, n. A tenure by which waste land is cultivated on condition of holding it rent-free for so many years, and then paying rent at a given rate.

H پگڑی पगड़ी *pag'ṛī* ; Rus. *pāg* ; Gaṛh. *pāgṛī* ; Aug. *paggaṛ*, n. f. S. पट्ट from पट् to cover.
1. A turban.
2. Honor ; distinction ; respect ; rank.
3. Head ; poll ; individual.
pagṛī utārnā, v. a. 1. To overreach ; take in ; cheat ; rob. 2. To disgrace ; dishonor.
pagṛī utarnā, v. n. To be disgraced, dishonored.
pagṛī-bāṅt, A system of inheritance according to which a man's children succeed to property without regard to maternity.
Thus, if a man leave three children by one wife and one child by another, the property will be divided into four parts and each child will receive one portion.
It is otherwise where *chonḍā-bat*, prevails (*chonḍā* a woman's top knot). According to this system the property is divided into as many shares as there are mothers. Thus, when a man has three wives—one with one child, the second with two children, and the third with three, the property will be divided into three portions, and the one child of one wife will receive as much as the three of another wife.
These systems are found in Musalman communities only, and the village administration paper generally contains provisions on this head. N. W. P.
pagṛī bāṅdhnā, v. n. 1. To live by making turbans. 2. To put on a turban.
pagṛī baṅdhnā, v. n. To be presented with a turban as a token of honor, headship, or hereditary succession.
☞ The ceremony of the son again wearing a turban in public on the 13th or 17th day after the death of his father or mother.

H پلینا पलेना *pale'nā*, v. a. To irrigate.

پلیو पलेव *palev'*, *paleu* ; Māṛ. *pāṅṛ*, n. m. Land watered after ploughing.

palihar, n. m. Land tilled three years and then left fallow for a season.

H پن पन *pan*, Cont. of پانی water.

پنمیلا पनमेला *pan-melā*, n. m. The man who distributes water among the beds as it flows into the field from the well.

pan-mār', n. 1. Soil submerged by floods and rendered unfit for cultivation ; low lands in which water lodges.
2. A crop spoiled through excess of rain.

P پناہ *pan'āh*, n. f. Pahlavi *pāneh* ; Z. *paā* ; S. पान Refuge. See آڑ (2 to 4).
panāh-dihī, n. f. The giving shelter or protection.
panāh-dihī-mujrim, n. f. Harbouring an offender.
panāh-i-adālat se bāhar, n. An outlaw.
panāh māṅgnā, v. n. 1. To seek protection ; beg for an asylum. 2. To pray for deliverance from one. 3. To implore mercy ; to surrender at discretion.
panj'ā, n. m. Land that cannot easily be irrigated.

H پنچ पञ्च *panch*, n. m. 1. An assembly of five men ; a jury of arbitrators ; a village council ; an umpire.
2. A village head man ; the head man of a caste.
3. An arbitrator ; judge ; assessor.
panch faislah, n. m. Judgment by arbitration ; the written award of a court of arbitration.
sar-panch, n. m. A head assessor or judge ; a president ; chairman.
sultānī panch, An arbitrator appointed by the authorities, not chosen by the parties.

پنچایت पञ्चायत *panchāy'at*, *panchāt*, n. f.
1. A native court of arbitration consisting of five or more members ; a meeting ; a commission ; a committee ; a council.
2. An arbitration award.
panchā'yat-khāngī, Ped. for H. *gharelū panchāyat*, n. f. Private arbitration ; a settlement of family quarrels by relations.
panchāyat sarkārī, n. f. A court of arbitration appointed by the public authorities.
panchāyat karnā yā joṛnā, v. a. 1. To form a court of arbitration. 2. To send for the members of a *panchāyat* or private council to sit as judges.
panchāyat-nāmah, n. m. The written award of a court of arbitration.
jātī panchāyat, n. f. An arbitration by persons of the same caste as the litigant parties.
pandhar'vāṅ, *pandrvāṅ*, *pandhrvīṅ*, adj. Fifteenth.

H پنڈ पिंड *pinḍ*, n. m. S. पिण्ड to roll into a lump or ball.
1. A lump (of flour) ; a funeral cake.
A ball of rice or meat, especially that which is offered at obsequial rites or *Sharādhs* to deceased parents and progenitors, or to the manes in general.
pinḍ-adhikārī, n m. The legal presenter of the funeral cakes, usually the nearest relatives in the male line.
pinḍ-dān, n. Offering of the funeral cakes made of barley.

H پنڈا पंडा *pan'ḍā*, *pānḍā*, n. m. A Brahman.
The office is hereditary, and in some places, as at Benares, the *Panḍā* officiates only on particular occasions, the duties of the daily worship being performed by inferior priests or *Pujāris* in his employ.

E پنشن *pin'shan*; Illit. *pinsan*; H. *baiṭhī-roṭī*,
1. Pension. 2. An office in which there is little to do; a sinecure.
atāē-pinshan. G. G. Superannuation allowance.

H پنیاه पुनयाह *pun'yāh*, n. S. पुण्यअहन a day.
1. A holiday; a sacred day on which religious observances are enjoined.
2. The day on which the rent or revenue for the ensuing year is first settled, or on which the first instalment is paid.
punyāh chiṭṭhī, n. The summons from the *zamīndār* to his tenants, fixing the day for the settlement or payment of the rents.
punyāh kharch. A charge for sweetmeats given to the Rayats on settling their rent.

H پوت पोत *pot*, n. m. Assessment on cultivated fields.

H پوت पूत *pūt*, n. m. S. पुत्र, Pr. *putto*, *put*- [*pudo*. A son.

پس پوت पसपूत *pas-pūt*, *pos-put*; A. *mutabannā*, P. *pisar-i-khuāndah*, n. m. S. पोष्यपुत्र
An adopted son (*le-pālak*).

H پوتھ पोथ *pauth*, n. A tenure of land in copercenary villages under which the fields are subject to periodical re-distribution among the sharers.

H پوجا पूजा *pūj'ā*, *pūjan*, n. f. S. पूज to worship. 1. The idol worship (of Hindus); adoration; worship; heathen-worship; idolatry.
2. Offerings; oblations; libations.

H پوروا पूरवा *pūr'vā*, n. m. A small village.
A sub-division, or a dependency of a village; a cluster of houses detached from the principal village, for the convenience of agricultural operations.

H پوري पोरी *por'ī*, n. f. S. पर्व्व a joint.
A stiff strong soil.

P پوست *post*, n. m. 1. Crust; shell; rind; bark; skin.
2. Poppy head or capsule; an intoxicat- [ing drug.

P پوشیده *poshī'dah*, adj. Hidden; concealed; secret. See *chhupā-huā*.
poshīdah kharch, n. m. Secret expenditure.
poshīdah k. v. a. To conceal; hide (*chhupānā*).
poshīdah masraf. G. G. Underhand disbursement.

E پولس *polis'*, *pulis*, n. m. Police.
ahl-i-polis, n. m. One of the police; policeman; police establishment.
āmil-i-polis, n. m. Police officer or inspector.

E پون ٹوٹي *paun-ṭoṭī*, n. f. Cor. of town duty.

H پونجي पूंजी *pūṅj'ī*; A. *jama*, n. f. S. पुञ्ज a heap.
1. Stock; stock-in-trade; fund; capital; principal (*mūl*). [of a company.
pūṅjī-i-hisse dārāṅ. Joint stock; the capital
ṭaṭ-pūṅjiyā, *ṭuṭ-pūṅjiyā*, n. m. A bankrupt; a petty merchant.

H پھاٹ फाट *phāṭ*, E. n. m. The allotment or division of the revenue assessment among the shares in a joint tenancy village.
phāṭ bandī, n. f. An agreement to pay a demand in separate proportions.

H پھاٹک फाटक *phāṭ'ak*, n. m. S. कपाट.
1. A gate; door; entrance.
2. A pound (*maweshī-khāna*).
3. The bar of a court of justice, where the plaintiff and defendant take their station.
4. A bar. See اڑ (6).
phāṭak-bandī. Custody (*havālāt*); imprisonment.
phāṭak-dār. A door-keeper; a pound-keeper.
phāṭak meṅ dākhil karnā, v. a. To impound.

H پھالي फाली *phālī*, W; *phāl*, E. n. f. S, फल to cleave. A ploughshare.

H پھانت फांत *phāṅt*, n. A village register, a list of occupants and their liabilities, either as sharers or cultivators.

H پھانسي फांसी *phāṅ'sī*, n. f.
1. A snare; noose; halter.
2. Hanging; execution; strangulation; death by hanging. [or executed.
phāṅsī pānā, yā charhnā, v. n. To be hanged,
Phr.—To be hanged by the neck; to come to the gallows.
phāṅsī denā, yā chaṛhānā, v. a. To hang; strangle; suspend by the neck; punish capitally; execute.
phāṅsī kā khambā. The gallows.
phāṅsī-yar, n. m. A strangler.
A robber and murderer who strangles his victims by throwing a turban or cloth round their necks.
phāṅsī dene-wālā, n. m. A hangman.

H پهرا पहरा *pah'rā*, n. m. 1. A turn of watch; a charge. 2. A watch; a sentinel; watchman; guard; sentry; a corporal and six.
baṛhtī kā pahrā, n. m. A progressive age; prosperous times; the golden age (*sat-jug*).
bhārī pahrā. The third or heaviest watch of the night.
pichhlā pahrā, n. m. The last watch of the night.

H پهراؤ फिराऊ *phirā'ū*, adj. 1. Conditional or contingent (purchase). 2. (Opp. of *basāū*). Returning; temporary.

پهراٸي फिराई *phirā'ī*, n. f. 1. The act of returning; return. 2. Restoration (of a thing).

پهرتا फिरता *phir'tā*, *phirtī*, n. 1. Returning; turning. 2. Premium; brokerage. [cart, etc.

phirtā bhāṛā, n. m. The return hire of a boat,

phirte par bechnā, v. n. To sell at a premium.

phirtī hunḍī, n f. A dishonored bill.

phirau'tī, *phirtā*, n. 1. A charge made for receiving back a purchased article.
2. Premium.

H پهڑا फड्डा *phar'ṛā*; Rus. *phaṭerā*, *phanṭerā*; Tir. *ṭhatherā*, n. m. The stalk of maize, etc.

H پهکڑ फक्कड़ *phak'kaṛ*, n. m. S. फक्क to behave ill. [jests.
Indecent or abusive language; bawdy

H پهلکر फलकर *phal'kar*, n. Spontaneous forest collections, such as wax, honey, &c.; revenue from fruits. [burst.

H پهوٹ फूट *phūṭ*, n. f. S. स्फुट separate,
A breach; break; gap; opening; crack; cleft; fissure.

پهوٹ گانوں फूट गांओं *phūṭ gāṅoṅ*, n. m. A village of which the houses are scattered; a village assessed and managed separately.

A detached village, not included amongst those of the district in which it is situated, or the lands of an individual to whom the rest belong. Such detached portions of villages or lands are classed together as the *phūṭ gāoṅ* of the district or of an individual.

H پهوڑي फौड़ी *phauṛ'ī*, n. f.
One-twentieth of a *bauṛī*.

H پهول फूल *phūl*, n. m. S. फुल्ल a full-blown flower. [mation.
1. The bones of a corpse after partial cre-
2. (Pl.) A Mah. ceremony performed on the third day after death.

H پهيا पहिया *pah'iyā*, *paīyā*, n. An allowance of half an *ānā* on each *Rupee* of revenue, set apart for the *paṭwārī*, or village accountant.

P پياده *piyā'dah*, n. m. S. पदाति
A footman; one on foot; a foot-soldier.

پيادهمحاصل *piyāda-mahāsil*. A peon placed over defaulters at their charge to urge them to pay up arrears.

H پيٹ पेट *peṭ*, n. m. S. पिट to heap together.
The belly; stomach; bowels.

peṭ se honā, v. n. To be pregnant.

peṭ kā pardah, n. m. The omentum; caul or adipose membrane attached to the stomach.

peṭ girānā yā ḍālnā, v. a. To cause or procure abortion.

peṭ girnā, v. n. To miscarry (a female).

peṭ girnā, n. Ped. A. *isqāt-i-hamal*, Miscarriage.

peṭ-wālī, adj. Pregnant. [allowance.

پيٹيا पेटिया *peṭ'iyā*, n.m. An allowance; a daily

P پيدا *pai'dā*, part. adj. 1. Born; created.
2. Produced; discovered; manifest; exhibited.
3. Procured; acquired; gained; amassed.

paidā, n. f. 1. Gain; profit; earning; income; interest. 2. Emoluments; perquisites; bribes (*yāft*).

پيداواري *paidāvā'rī*, *paidāvār*, n.f. 1. Produce of land; harvest. 2. Profits of trade, etc.; proceeds; outturn; income; gains.

paidāwār-i-arāzī. The produce of land.

paidāwār-i-hāl. The present assets. [of land.

paidāwār-i-khud-rau. The spontaneous produce

bināe dāwā paidā huī. Cause of action arose.

takhmīna-i-paidāwārī. A rough estimate of the produce of a field. [duce of an estate.

jama paidāwār. The total amount of the pro-

dast-ras, yā dakhl kāmil paidā karnā.
To master; to make oneself master.

zarar paidā karnā, Ped. To cause harm.

H پير पैर *pair*; Brij. *pag*, n. m. S. पद 1. The foot (*pāoṅ*). 2. A foot mark; foot print.
3. The track of oxen in an oil-press, etc.
4. (*pairā*) The slope down which oxen descend in drawing water. 4. The threshing floor. 5. Corn in the straw.

پيري पैरी *pair'ī*, n. f. 1. The quantity of grain obtained after threshing.

P پير *pīr*, Mah. n. m. 1. Monday (H. *som-wār*).
2. A holy man (Mah); a saint; priest; spiritual guide; a head of a religious order.

پيران *pīr'ān*, *pīr-pāl*, *pir-ot'tar*, *piratrā*, n. m.
An assignment of land for the support of a *pīr*, or for keeping up the tomb of a reputed saint.

پيروتار पीरोतार *pīr-otār*, n. m. Allowance to Mahommadan sages. Lands held rent-free, or assignments of the Government dues from particular lands, enjoyed by such persons.

pirot'tar sādir wārid, G. G. An assignment of rent-free land to defray the contingent expenses of a mosque or Mahamedan religious establishment.

P پيرو *pai'-rau*, adj. P. پے behind, رو go. 1. A follower; attendant. 2. Followers of a religious doctrine or tenet; votary; sectarian.

pairau-kār honā, v. a. To conduct a suit; prosecute a case.

پیروی *pai'-ravī*, n. f. 1. Pursuit ; adherence. 2. Observance ; compliance. 3. Prosecution ; conduct ; investigation ; search ; quest ; research. 4. Efforts ; exertions ; endeavours.
pairavī karnā, v. n. 1. To go after ; follow ; trace ; track ; pursue. 2. To prosecute ; conduct (a suit, etc.) ; manage. 3. To continue ; persevere ; maintain. 4 To be guided, regulated, bound by ; to go by ; to observe.

پیروی حقوق *pairawī-i-huqūq*. Enforcement of rights ; prosecution of just claims.
pairavī-i-muqaddamā. Prosecution of a suit.

عدم پیروی *adam pairavī*. G. G. Default of prosecution.
peṛ lagānā, v. n. To plant trees.

H پیڑی पेड़ी *peṛ'ī, peḍī*, n. f. 1. Stubble from which a second crop is obtained (E. *doṅjī*).
2. The trunk of a tree.
3. A rate paid by cultivators to *zamīndārs* for the use of fruit trees.

Asāmis (tenants) may plant trees and are exempt from the payment of rent for the land, but if they vacate the tree is the *zamindār's*, and cultivators cannot as a rule cut it down.

H پیڑھی पीढ़ी *pīṛ'hī* ; Rus. *pīḍhī*, n. f. S. पीठिका 1. A small stool. 2. Descent ; generation ; extraction ; pedigree.
pīṛhī dar pīṛhī, adv. See *pusht dar pusht*.
pīṛhī dar pīṛhī, adj. Hereditary ; traditional.

P پیش *pesh*, adv. Before.

pesh-kharīd. Pre-emption (*shufā*).
pesh-khema, n. m. The tent or other baggage sent on before ; the camp equipage, tents, etc., sent on in advance of an army.
pesh-qadmī karnā, v. n.
1. To go before or in advance, to outstrip.
2. To commence ; take the first step.
pesh karnā, v. n. 1. To produce ; bring forward ; adduce ; urge. 2. To set before ; offer ; present.
3. To submit ; tender ; propose ; refer to ; suggest. [plead ; cite.
4. To represent ; put forth ; contend ;

پیشکار *pesh-kār'*, n. m. 1. A foreman ; agent ; manager. 2. A native officer in a Court next below the *sarishtedār*. [*pesh-kār*.

پیشکاری *pesh-kārī*, n. f. Agency ; the office of a

پیشکش *pesh-kash'*, n. f. *lit.* What is first drawn ; first fruits. 1. A present to a superior.
2. A present (*salāmī*) to the ruling power on receiving an appointment or assignment of revenue, or on the renewal of a grant, lease, etc. [vestigation.

پیشی *pesh'ī*, n. f. 1. Presence. 2. Trial ; in-

P پیشہ *pesh'ah*, n. m. Vocation ; office ; profession. See آدم (3). [n. m.

پیشہ ور *pesha-var'*, *peshā-wālā* ; A. *ahl-i-hirfa*,
1. An artisan; handycraftsman ; workman; artificer.
2. A shopkeeper (*dukāndār*) ; tradesman.
shāgird-peshā ; Illit. *sāgar-peshā*, n. m. Menial or house servants ; domestics. [dealer.

P پیکار *paikār'*, n. m. Cor. of پاے کار A retail

P پیمایش *paimā'yash*, n. f. Measurement ; survey ; land measurement ; land survey.
paimāish band o bast. Settlement measurement or *khasra* survey.
paimāyash ba-nazar band o bast. G. G. Revenue survey ; the survey necessary to a settlement of the revenue.
paimāyash-dār, Ped. A measurer ; a surveyor.
paimāyash dehī. Village measurement.
paimāyash sarsarī. A summary survey.
paimāyash sarkārī. A Government survey.
paimāyash kā kām. Survey operations ; survey work. [or cadastral survey.
paimāyash kampās. A trignometrical, revenue,
paimāyash māl. A revenue survey.
paimāyash nahar. Canal measurement. [liquor).
paimāyash o āzmāyash. Guage and proof (as of
khasrā paimāish. Field survey.

P پیوستہ *paivas'tah* ; *paivast* ; Z. *paivasto*, *paivast'ah, paivast*. Added to, or increased, as an alluvial deposit ; additional lands (properly *mulhaq*).

ت

A تاریخ *tārī'kh'*, n. f. ارخ dating a letter.
1. Date ; day of the month.
2. Epoch ; era ; chronology ; annals ; history ; chronogram.
tārīkh charhānā, v.a. To enter the date ; to date.
tārīkh zuhūr bināë-dāwa. The date on which a cause of action accrues.
tārīkh-wār, adv. According to date ; at stated periods ; in chronological order ; periodically.
tā tārīkh muaiyanah adālat. For such period as the Court may direct.
tā tārīkh wasūl. To the date of realization.
falānī tārīkh se charhtī.
Calculated from a certain date.

P تازیانہ *tāzyā'nah*, n. m. 1. A whip ; scourge.
2. Flogging ; corporal punishment.
tā ki fitna o fasād na ho. To keep the peace, to prevent a breach of the peace.

tā ki nuqsān na ho. To prevent waste or loss.

A تاکید *tākīd'*, n. f. اکد he trod wheat. 1. An injunction; order. 2. A reminder. 3. Emphasis. 4. Strictness; compulsion; force. 5. An order from a superior to an inferior officer strictly enjoining performance of any work or the execution of an order.

tākīd karnā, v. a. To enjoin strictly; insist on; urge; press; caution.

tākīd karvānā, v. a. To draw attention to; to have the attention drawn to.

bahut tākīd; Ped. *tākīd-i-mazīd.* Strict injunction.

تاکیداً *tākīd'an*, adv. Strictly; urgently; emphatically; positively; peremptorily.

تاکیدي *tākīd'ī*, adj. 1. Emphatic; positive; absolute. 2. Urgent; pressing; imperative.

tākīdī-chiṭṭhī, n. f. A letter of injunction; a written mandate or direction.

hukm-i-tākīdī, n. f. Peremptory order.

H تالا ताला *tā'lā*, n. m. S. तालक A lock.

tālā toṛnā. To break open or force a lock; break open; break into a house.

tāle-band'. A detailed account shewing each head of revenue.

P تاوان *tāvān'*; Pop. *tāvan*, n. m. *tāb* power, *ān* price. 1. Penalty; forfeit; fine; damages. 2. Retaliation; compensation; atonement; satisfaction. 3. The fine for *dīat* or bloodshed as distinguished from *qisās* retaliation.

tāvān bāṅdhnā, tāvān lenā, yā lagānā, v. a. To fine; mulct; amerce.

tāvān dilānā, v. a. To adjudge damages.

tāvān denā, v. n. To pay a penalty or damages.

A تائید *tāīd'*, n. f. اید he strengthened.

1. Aid; behalf; side.
2. Corroboration; support. [a claim.
3. A written voucher in corroboration of
4. A private assistant; an apprentice.

tāīd-i-dāvā. Support of claim.

tāīd karnā, v. a. 1. To help; assist; aid. 2. To second; take part with; support. 3. To strengthen; corroborate; bear out; justify; vindicate. [statement.

tāīd-i-kalām, Corroboration or support of a

tāīd-navīs, n. m. A private assistant; an apprentice. [claim. G. G.

wājibī dāwe kī tāīd meṅ. In support of a just

A تبدیل *tabdīl'*, *tabaddul*, n. f. بدل changing. Mutation; change; alteration; modification; transposition; transformation.

tabdīl-i-nā-jāiz karnā. To tamper (with a document); forge; falsify.

tabdīl o tahrīf k. To falsify; alter.

tabdīl-i-haiyat karnā; Ped. for H. *bhes badalnā*, v. a. To disguise; personate; to pretend to be.

تبديلي *tabdīl'ī*, n. f. 1. Relief (of a guard). 2. Transfer (of officers). See بدل [revenue.

tabdīlī-i-jamā. Alterations of Government

A تبرا *tabar'rā*, Mah. n. m. تبر Breaking, destroying. Malediction; curse.

A تبرک *tabar'ruk*, n. m.

1. Sacred relics. See پرشاد (2).

2. Commutation for an offering incumbent upon a religious mendicant holding some endowment.

A تبنی *taban'nī, tabnīyat.* Adoption of a son.

tabanniyat-i-shartī, yā mashrūt. A condition at adoption.

H تپا तपा *tapā', ṭīkā*, W. I The unit upon which the Mogal revenue system was based. 2. A collection of 10 to 20 villages feudally interconnected, and generally sprung from a common stock.

H تپڑ तप्पड़ *tap'paṛ.* Fallow land full of grass and weeds; sandy barren soil generally hard and dry.

A تتمه *tatim'ma*, n. m. تم being complete. A supplement; appendix.

tatimma-i-bayān tahrīrī. A supplemental pleading or petition.

tatimma-i-tafrīq. A supplementary record of separate interests or shares.

tatimma-i-arzī. A supplemental petition.

tatimma-i-arzī dāwā. A supplemental plaint.

tatimma-i-khat. Postscript.

tatimmā kīyā-huā, adj. Appended. [to a will.

tatimma-i-vasīyat-nāma. A codicil; a supplement

tatimma-i-yād-dāsht. A supplemental memorandum. [codicil.

mukhtalif tatimma wasīyat-nāma. A different

A تجارت *tijā'rat*, n. f. Trade. See H. بیوپار

tijārat-i-bahrī. Commerce; carrying trade.

tijārat khilāf āīn, tijārat-i-mamnūā. Illicit trade.

tijārat karnā, v. a. To deal; trade; traffic; speculate. [n. f. Emporium.

tijārat-gāh-i-ālī. G. G. Ped. for H. *baṛī manḍī*,

gulāmoṅ kī tijārat k. v. a. To traffic in slaves.

kām tijārat. A commercial concern.

تجارتي *tijā'ratī*, adj. Mercantile; commercial.

A تجاوز *tajā'vuz*, n. m. جوز passing beyond. Transgression; deviation; excess; exceeding one's authority; encroachment.

tajāvuz ikhtiyār samāāt, Excess of jurisdiction.

tajāvuz karnā. 1. To pass or go beyond bounds; overstep bounds. 2. To err; deviate; depart from. 3. To disobey; infringe; transgress; exceed one's authority. 4. To trespass; violate a rule; encroach on.
apnī had se tajāwuz karnā. To encroach; pass bounds; exceed one's powers; go beyond limits.

A تجدید *tajdīd'*, Renewal; revival, renovation.
tajdīd binā-i-dāwā. The revival of a cause of action.
tajdīd-i-nālish. Revival of a suit.
tajdīd-i-nikāh. Renewal of marriage.
tajdīdī. Renewed; revived.

H تجنا तजना *taj'nā, tiyāgnā*, v. a. S. त्यजन
1. To relinquish; quit; leave; abandon; desert; forsake (*chhoṛnā*).
2. To disclaim; renounce; abjure.
3. To repudiate; divorce (a wife).
4. To abdicate. [lawful.

A تجویز *tajvīz'*, n. m. جوز he made or held it
1. Deliberation; view; opinion; judgment.
2. Plan. 3. Estimate.
4. The early crop, on the near ripening of which a rough estimate of its value is made, and an equal portion of the revenue collected.
5. Resolution; judgment.
tajvīz-i-akhīr. A final judgment.
tajvīj amr-i-wāqa. A finding of a fact; the determination of a fact or matter of fact.
tajvīz be-tahqīq karnā, v. a. To predetermine; forejudge; prejudge; pronounce at random.
tajvīz par munhasar, G. G. Held at disposal.
tajvīz-i-sānī yā jadīd. Retrial; new trial; fresh trial; revision; review of order or judgment.
tajvīz subūt-i-jurm. Determination of guilt.
tajvīz-i-jurm karnā, G. G. To find guilty.
tajvīz hākimī. Judicial proceedings; a judicial act.
tajvīz-i-haqīat. Adjudication of a right.
tajvīz-i-khatamī. An authoritative ruling.
tajvīz-i-kharcha. Award of costs.
tajvīz dalāil muddai wa muddāilā. Consideration of pros and cons; the summing up of the judge.
tajvīz-i-ruēdād, G. G. The determination of a case on its merits; finding on the merits.
tajvīz rihāī. Acquittal; discharge. [of a point.
tajvīz zimnī, G. G. The incidental determination
tajvīz-talab. Wanting decision.
tajvīz-i-adālat-i-mā tahat. The judgment of the subordinate court.
tajvīz k. v. a. See *bichār'nā*, 3, 7, 8. & *upāē k.*
1. To determine; decide; resolve; conclude; rule; establish. 2. To pronounce or give judgment; to adjudge; award.
3. To elect; choose; nominate.
az rāh-i-tajvīz, adv. Judicially.
tajvīz ke qābil. Capable of being tried.
tajvīz-i-mukhālifānā. An adverse judgment.
tajvīz-i-muqadmā. Decision; judgment; a judicial act. [resolution.
tajvīz-nāma. A written decree; a judgment or
tajvīz wa infisāl. Trial and determination.
tajvīzī. Tried; determined; decided; adjudged.
bar sar-i-ijlās tajwīz karnā. To act judicially; hear a case or pass judgment in due form.
tā infisāl-i-niz'ā ba-tajwīz-i-adālat. Until the question at issue is judicially determined.
dāir-i-tajvīz, zer-i-tajvīz. Pending decision; pending; under investigation; under consideration.

A تجہیز و تکفین *tajhīz'o takfīn*; Pop. *kafnānā dajnānā*, Mah. n. f. جہز he fitted out a corpse. Interment; burial.

A تحالف *tahā'luf*, حلف he swore. Swearing plaintiff and defendant.

A تحت *taht*, n. m. تحت beneath.
Charge; possession; occupancy (*ikhtyār* 4, 6, 7).
taht meṅ, adv. Under control; in subjection to.
2. At foot; below. [rity.
taht meṅ ānā, v. n. To come under one's autho-
taht meṅ rakhnā, v. n. 1. To have in one's possession; to hold; have; possess. 2. To keep under; have under command; manage.
taht meṅ lānā, v. a. 1. To bring under; to bring under one's authority or control; to take possession; to occupy. [subdue.
2. To bring under subjection; subject;
taht o tasarruf. Possession and use.
apne taht o tassarruf meṅ lānā. To take charge of; to bring under one's own power.

A تحدید *tahdīd'*, Reproof. [well.

A تحریر *tahrīr'*; H. *likhat*, n. f. حر he wrote
1. A writing; a written statement or declaration; minute; composition. 2. A document; deed; a bond (*tamassuk*). 3. A fee for writing anything for another.
tahrīr-i-bain-ul-sutūr; H. *pāṅtī bīch likhat.* An interlineation. [a bond.
tahrīr tamassuk. Drawing up, or execution of
tahrīr sābit karnā. G. G. To prove the execution (writing). [the back.
tahrīr-i-zohrī, n. Endorsement; a writing on
tahrīr karnā, v. a. To write. See *likhnā.*
تحریری *tahrīrī*, adj. Written; documentary.
hukum tahrīrī. Written authority. [writing.
zabt-i-tahrīr meṅ lānā. G. G. To reduce to

A تحریص *tahrīs'*; H. *lālach.* حرص Inducement, enticement; lure; temptation; stimulation; instigation; incitement.
tahrīs denā, v. a. To induce; entice; influence.

A تحریف *tahrīf'*, n. f. حرف altering.

1. Transposition of words or letters.
2. A clerical error; an alteration.
3. Tampering; falsification.

A تحریک *tahrīk'*, n. f. حرک it moved.

1. Motion; movement. 2. Incitement; instigation; stimulation. [instigate.
tahrīk karnā, v. a. To urge; put up to;

A تحصیل *tahsīl'*, n.f. حصول became educated.

1. Acquisition; attainment; gain; profit.
2. Collection; collection of revenue.
3. The revenue jurisdiction of a *tahsīldār* or subordinate collector; a *tahsīldār's* station.

tahsīl-i-ābkārī. Abkārī collections. [ernment.
tahsīl-dār', n. m. A sub-collector of the Gov-
tahsīldār'ī, n. f. The office, duty, or jurisdiction of a sub-collector.
tahsīl-i-zar-i-bhej. Collection of the rents.
tahsīl saranjām. Charges of collection; an additional charge formerly levied to defray the expence of collection.
tahsīl-i-gair muaiyan. Contingent collections.
tahsīl karnā, tahsīlnā, v. a.

1. To gain; get; acquire; attain. [raise.
2. To collect (revenue, etc.); realize;

tahsīl-karne-wā'ā, n. m. One who collects revenue; a receiver of collections. [revenue.
tahsīl-kunanda-i-khirāj. A tax gatherer; a collector of revenue.
tahsīl kī tadbīr karnā. G. G. To proceed against a defaulter. [revenue.
tahsīl-i-mālguzārī, yā jama. Collection of the
tahsīl-i-nā-jāiz. Illegal collection of the revenue.
tahsīl-i-vāsīlāt. The amount realized by the collections of the district, whether on behalf of a zamīndār or the Government.
haq-i-tahsīl. Commission or percentage on collections.
khās tahsīl. Government collections.
zar-i-tahsīl. Collections; amount of collections.
qurq-i-tahsīl. Revenue attachment.
kachchī, yā khām tahsīl. Collections direct from the cultivators.
nisf tahsīl. Half the collections. [*hiqārat.*

A تحقیر *tahqīr'*, n. f. حقر was despicable. See

tahqīr-i-adālat. Contempt of Court.
tahqīr rutba-i-qānūnī. G. G. Contempt of lawful authority. [disgrace.
tahqīr karnā. To bring into contempt; insult;
mulāzmān-i-sarkārī ke ikhtiyār-i-jāiz kī tahqīr. G. G. Contempt of lawful authority of public servants.

A تحقیق *tahqīq'*, n. f. حق was right. [tion.

1. Careful or close investigation; verifica-
2. Exactness; certainty.

tahqīq', adj. 1. Carefully ascertained; well-established. 2. Authentic; definite.
3. Sure; correct; certain; undoubted.

tahqīq', adv. Truly; indeed; certainly.
tahqīq rāë. A carefully formed opinion.
tahqīq karnā, v. a. To ascertain; investigate; enquire into; make certain.
be-tahqīq, adj. Not established; uncertain.

تحقیقات *tahqīqāt'*, n.f. pl. of. تحقیق Investigation; enquiry; examination.
tahqīqāt-i-ibtidāī, yā māqabal. Preliminary enquiry or examination.
tahqīqāt-i-ibtidāī karnā. To hold or conduct a preliminary investigation.
tahqīqāt bar mauqā, yā sar zamīn. Local investigation; an investigation held on the spot.
tahqīqāt-i-hākimī. Authorized investigation; judicial enquiry.
tahqīqāt-i-hāl-i-maut. An enquiry into the cause of death; Coroner's inquest.
tahqīqāt-i-faujdārī. A criminal investigation.
tahqīqāt karnā, v. a. To enquire; hold an enquiry; investigate.
tahqīqāt mazīd. Further investigation.
tahqīqāt mauqā kā hukm denā. To order a local investigation.
tahqīqāt-i-nā-tamām, nā-kāmil, yā nāqis, Defective or incomplete investigation.
tahqīqāt-i-wājib. Due enquiry or investigation.
muqadme ko adālat-i-mā-taht meṅ tahqīqāt-i-mazīd ke liye vāpis bhejnā. To remand the case to the subordinate court for further enquiry or investigation. [See حکومت

A تحکم *tahak'kum*, n.f. حکم he restrained him.

A تحویل *tahvīl'*, n. f. حول altered, transfered.

1. Charge; care; trust. 2. A deposit; revenue credit. 3. Funds; capital.

tahvīl tassarruf. Misapplication of funds; embezzlement; misappropriation.

4. A treasury; the collector's treasury.

tahvīl-dār. Cashier; treasurer; cash-keeper (of a provincial treasury).
tahvīl meṅ rakhnā. To keep in deposit.
apnī tahvīl meṅ lānā. To take charge of; to bring under one's custody.
gulām ke taur par tahvīl meṅ rakhnā, G. G. To receive as a slave.

A تخارج *ta-khā'ruj.* A composition entered into by joint heirs to a property, by which some relinquish their shares for a specific payment; a partition of an estate amongst themselves by the lawful heirs. *Wilson.*

P تخت *ta-kht*, n. m. 1. A throne; a chair of state. 2. A low table or seat.

tahkt par bițhānā, v. a . To seat on the thron

takht par baiṭhnā, v. n. To ascend or sit on the throne.
takht chhoṛnā, v. a. To abdicate a throne.
takht se utār'nā, v. a. To dethrone.
takht-gāh, n. f. 1. The royal residence. 2. The capital; metropolis; seat of government.
takht-nashīnī, n. f. Accession to the throne.
تختة *takh'tah*, n. m. 1. A plank; board. 2. A bench; form. 3. A platform; deck; a gallows-board. 4. A signboard; notice board. 5. (Panj.) A bier.

A تخصيص *ta*ᵏ*khsīs'*, n. f. خص he distinguished it. Peculiarity; particularity.
takhsīs-i-jamā-bandī. A statement of the net annual settlement of rents concluded by the tenants with the zamīndārs, tâlluqdārs, etc.
takhsīsī taallluq. An undivided taâlluq held entire by an individual. [less.

A تخفيف *ta*ᵏ*khfīf'*, n. f. خف it became 1. Diminution; abatement. [economy. 2. Reduction; retrenchment; saving; 3. Remission; mitigation; relief.
takhfīf-i-jamā, Remission of the revenue; reduction of the amount assessed; abatement of revenue.
takhfīf k. v. a. 1. To lessen; abate; lower. 2. To mitigate; relax; remit; relieve. 3. To retrench; reduce; make a saving.
takhfīf-i-kasīr kīyā jānā. G. G. To be largely reduced.
takhfīf-i-lagān-i-bhej. Abatement of rent.
takhfīf meṅ lānā, v. a. To retrench; abolish; effect a saving.

A تخمينة *ta*ᵏ*khmī'nah*, n.m. خمن he surmised. Estimate. See اندازة 1.
takhmīnā karnā, v. n. To estimate.
*pakkā ta*ᵏ*khmīnah*, n. m. Precise estimate.
*kachchā ta*ᵏ*khmīnah*, n. m. Rough estimate.
*māliat-i-ta*ᵏ*khmīnah*, Estimated value.
تخميناً *ta*ᵏ*khmīn'an*, adv. 1. By appraisement; on a rough estimate; on the whole. 2. More or less; about.

A تخويف *ta*ᵏ*khvīf'*, Ped. for H. *ḍarāvā*, Intimidation.
takhvīf-i-mujrimānah, Criminal intimidation.

A تدارک *tadā'ruk*, n. m. درک overtaking, visiting with.
1. Chastisement; infliction of fines or punishment; punishment.
2. Management; provision; arrangements.
3. The instruments and measures used to procure justice (as writings, lawyers' witnesses, etc.) [pulsory process.
tadāruk bil jabr. Forcible proceedings; com-
tadāruk-i-tahsīl. Process of duress, of imprisonment; revenue process. [process.
tadāruk tahsīl karnā, To collect by coercive
tadāruk saṅgīn. Severe measures.

A تدبير *tadbīr'*; H. *jatan*, n. f. دبر forecasting. Conduct; management; prudence; economy; address; skill.
tadbīr-i-bāham. Private arrangement.
tadbīr-i-saltanat, yā mamlukat. Politics; government; administration; policy.
tadbīr se, adv. Skilfully; economically.
tadbīr-i-gizā. Regimen of diet; regimen.
tadbīr-i-fāsid. Artifice; plot; machination.
tadbīr-i-fāsid se, adv. Fraudulently.
tadbīr karnā, v. a. To contrive; devise; manage.
tadbīr karnā ki faisla kār-barāmad na ho. To contrive to make judgment of no effect, to avoid judgment.
tadbīr karnā ki māl qurq na hone pāve. To contrive to avoid sequestration or escheat, to avoid a distress.
husn-i-tadbīr. Good policy; good management.
munāsib tadbīr. A proper remedy or measure.

A تدفين *tadfīn'*, n. f. Burial; interment.
īkhrājāt-i-tadfīn. G. G. Funeral expenses.

P تراش خراش *tarāsh'* ᵏ*kharāsh'*, n. f. 1. Erasures; alterations; corrections (*chhīl chhāl*).
tarāsh kharāsh karnā, v. a. 1. To scratch out; erase; alter; amend.

A ترتيب *tartīb'*, n. f. رتب he set in order. Order; arrangement; classification.
tartīb-i-tahajjī, n. f. Alphabetical order. [tively.
tartīb se, adv. In order; regularly; consecu-
tartīb k. yā denā, tartīb se lagānā, v. a. To put in order; arrange; group; classify; regulate; put to rights.
tartīb-i-nau. Readjustment; new arrangement.
tartīb-i-nambar. Numerical order; the order of the file. [order.
tartīb-wār, adv. Regularly; methodically; in
tartīb-wār. adj. Regular; methodical.
tartīb-i-wirāsat, n. f. The order of succession.
be-tartīb, adj. Not arranged; irregular; without order; misplaced. [informal suit.
be-tartībī-i-nālish. Informality of procedure;
ترتيبي *tartīb'ī*, n. f. A preliminary proceeding.
be-tartībī, n. f. Irregularity; disarrangement.

A ترجمة *tarjam'ā, tarjumā*; H. *ulthā*, n. m. ترجمة he interpreted in another language. Translation; version.
tarjuma-i-sahīh aur motabar. G. G. n. A true and accurate translation. [tion.
tarjama k., v. a. To translate; make a transla-
lafzī tarjama. A literal translation.

A ترّدد *tarad'dud*, n. m. رد returning, causing to return.
1. Anxiety ; concern ; care (*udheṛ-bun*, 1).
2. Cultivation ; tillage.
taraddud-i-nā jāiz. Wrongful or illicit cultivation.
taraddudī, adj. Cultivated.
taraddudī-zamīn. Cultivated land, especially land that is always in cultivation, and never requiring to lie fallow.
be-taraddud, adj. Land thrown out of cultivation.
be-taraddud ho jānā, v. n. To lie fallow ; to fall out of cultivation.
تردید *tardīd'*, n. f. 1. Refutation ; rebutment ; rebutter.
2. Reversal (of a judgment).
tardīdī-dāwā karnā, v. a. To oppose a claim ; to rebut a charge.
tardīd-i-ahd, n. Impeachment of a contract.
tardīd k. v. a. 1. To rebut ; refute ; confute ; disprove ; dispose (of an argument).
2. To reverse ; set aside ; annul ; repeal.

H ترسدھ तरसिद्ध *tarsid'dha*, n. m. The under surface (of land or of a field) broken up and prepared for sowing, although the upper surface is covered with grass. Purniā.

A ترغیب *tarğīb'*, n. f. رغبت desiring greatly.
1. Exciting desire; inducement; encouragement ; incitement ; instigation ; stimulation.
2. Allurement ; lure ; sop ; bait ; decoy.
tarğīb'an, adv. By inducing.
tarğīb-i-daroğ halafī. Subornation of perjury.
tarğīb-dehinda, G. G. An abetter.
targīb denā, v. a. 1. To persuade ; induce ; encourage ; incite ; entice ; excite. 2. To allure ; lure ; tempt ; cajole ; decoy. 3. To put up to ; influence ; set on ; instigate ; abet.
tarğīb de-kar rāzī karnā. To buy off.
tarğīb-yāfta. G. G. Abetted.
shakhs-i-targīb-yāfta. G. G. The person abetted.
fāsid aur nā-jāiz wasīloṅ se tarğīb denā. To induce by corrupt and illegal means.
madadgārī kī tarğīb denī. Abetment of an abetment.

A ترقي *taraq'qī*, n. f. رقى he ascended.
1. Progress ; improvement ; advance ; increase. elevation.
2. Advancement ; promotion ; preferment ;
taraq'qī pānā, v. n. To be promoted ; to get advancement or promotion ; to rise.
taraq'qī denā yā karnā, v. a.
1. To advance ; forward ; push on.
2. To promote ; raise ; elevate.

A ترک *tark*, n. m. ترک he left it. 1. Relinquishment ; abandonment ; abdication ; renunciation. 2. Omission. 3. A catchword.
tark-i-arāzī, n. Relinquishment of land.
tark-i-mulāzāmat karnā, G. G. To withdraw from one's duties
tark-i-nā jāiz. An illegal omission.
tark karnā, v. a. To abandon. See تیاگنا
tark-i-vatan ; Ped. for H. *des chhoṛan.* Leaving one's native country; emigration.
tark honā, v. n. To be in disuse, given up or abandoned.

S ترک तर्क *tark*, n. m. 1. Objection ; plea ; argument. 2. Reasoning ; logic ; disputation ; discussion. 3. (In logic.) A proposition.
tark uṭhānā, v. a. To raise a plea or objection.

A ترکۂ *tark'ah*, n. m. ترکہ left. 1. A bequest ; a legacy. 2. Inheritance : effects of the deceased; inheritance by succession or bequest; the estate or property of a deceased person.
tarkah bilā vasīat-nāma. Intestate property.
tarkah pāne-wālā, n. A legatee.
tarkah-i-pidrī ; H. *bapautī.* Paternal estate.
tarke meṅ ānā. To inherit ; succeed to ; descend ; come into possession.
tarke meṅ chhoṛnā. To leave ; bequeath.
tarka-i-shakhs bilā wasīyat, G. G. Intestate's property.
tarka-i-shauharī kā hissa, G. G. Share of husband's estate.
tarka-i-mādarī, G. G. Maternal estate.
istehqāq-i-tarka bar bināė wasīyat-nāma. Testamentary succession.
taqsīm-i-tarka, G. G. Distribution of the property bequeathed.
mutābiq qawāid-i-wirāsat-i-tarka-i-gair wasīyatī. G. G. According to the rules of intestate succession.

A ترمیم *tarmīm'*, n. m. A رم mending.
1. Amendment; modification ; alteration ; revision ; re-adjustment.
2. Improvement ; melioration ; rectification.
tarmīm-i-bandobast. Revision of settlements records.
tarmīm-i-arzī dāwā. Amendment of plaint.
tarmīm-i-fāsid karnā. To tamper (with a document) ; interpolate ; to make a fraudulent alteration.
tarmīm ke qābil. Open to revision ; requiring amendment or modification.
bar bināė illat-i-tarmīmī, G. G. Upon an amended charge.
تري *tar'ī*, n. f. 1. Moisture ; dampness ; wet.
2. Water (opposite of *barrī* land).
3. Freshness ; juiciness ; ripeness.
4. Low lands on the banks of rivers.
5. Moist land ; swamp ; marsh.

A تزکیۂ *tazkī'ya*, n. m. 1. Purification.
2. A case in which a certain number of special witnesses bear testimony to the competency of other witnesses who are giving evidence in any cause, the former being denominated the *muzakki* or purgators.

A تزويج *tazvīj'*, n. f. Marriage (*byāh*).

A تزوير *tazvīr'*, n. f. Imposture; fraud; deceit; deception.

A تساهل *tasā'hul*, n. m. سهل became soft, easy.
1. Slowness. 2. Tardy proceedings.
tasāhul k. v. a. To defer; delay; put off; retard.

H تسو तसू *tas'ū*, n. m. (*Workmen*) $\frac{1}{24}$ of a yard. [*bisvānsī*, q. v.

H تسوانسي तिसवांसी *tisvān'sī*, n. f. $\frac{1}{20}$ of a

A تسهيل *tashīl'*, Facility.
tashīl-i-zābta-i-dīvānī adālat, Simplifying the procedure of the courts of civil jurisdiction.
mutazammin tashīl-i-īsāl zar-qarzā, For facilitating the collection of debts. [individuated.

A تشخيص *tash'khīs'*, n. f. شخص it was
1. Specification; minute description; determination; diagnosis.
2. Appraisement; valuation; estimate.
tashkhīs k. v. a. 1. To distinguish; recognize; ascertain (a disease).
2. To appraise; value; assess; adjust.
3. To fix; settle; determine; decide.
4. Assessment; corrected assessment; net standard revenue or the actual or absolute amount of realisable revenue; a particular account of such revenue, or the available funds which it constitutes.

تشخيص تعلقة *tash'khīs-i-tāluqa*. A dependent or subordinate property held of a superior upon payment of the revenue according to the current rate or the district.

تشخيص جمع *tash'khīs-i-jamā*. Allotment of revenue; assessment of land revenue.

تشخيص جمعبندي *tash'khīs-i-jamābandī,'* A statement of the net annual settlement concluded with zamīndārs, Tāluqdārs, and others.

تشخيص خام *tash'khīs-i-khām*, Rough estimate.

تشخيص مقرري *tash'khīs-i-muqarrarī*, A fixed assessment.

pakkī tashkhīs, Precise estimate.
jama tashkhīs karnā, To assess revenue.
zar-i-harjā' tashkhīs karnā, To assess damages.

A تشدد *tashad'dud*, n. m. A. شد he intensified it. 1. Aggravation; severity; hardship.
2. Coercive measures; duress of imprisonment.

A تشريح *tashrīh'*, n. f. 1. Elucidation; illustration; explanation; exposition. 2. Declaration; description; particulars; details.
3. Dissection; anatomy; a skeleton, or anatomical preparation.
tashrīh k. v. a. To particularize; enumerate; give details or particulars; illustrate; expound; explain.
tashrīh-vār, adv. In detail; with full particulars; minutely; severally. [of Anatomy.

A تشريف *tashrīf'*, n. f. A. شرف became exalted. 1. Your honor; your worship.
2. Complimentary presents made by the cultivators to the native revenue officers at the time of fixing the annual assessment.

A تشهير *tashhīr'*, n. f. شهر published abroad.
(*Mah. law*) Public exposure.
The delinquent used to be carried through the town on an ass with his face blackened—formerly the special punishment for perjury. [soundness.

A تصحيح *tashīh'*, n. f. صح was restored to
1. Correction; emendation; rectification.
2. Verification; attestation.
tashīh k. v. n. 1. To amend; correct; rectify.
2. To verify; attest.

A تصديق *tasdīq'*, n. f. from صدق truth.
Attestation; verification; authentication; confirmation; corroboration. [verify.
tasdīq k. v. n. 1. To testify; attest; certify;
2. To confirm; ratify; affirm; maintain.
tasdīq karne-vālā shakhs. G. G. The person attesting; an auditor.
ba-tasdīq. Under one's own hand or signature; in witness of. [notary.
sāhib-i-tasdīq. The attesting officer; public

A تصرف *tasar'ruf*, n. m. صرف exchanging.
1. Expenditure; expenses. 2. Use; employment; application. 3. Possession; occupancy; enjoyment. 4. Holding at one's own disposal; property. 5. Supernatural power (of holy men).
6. Any act of ownership, the rights of a proprietor over his property, as sale, lease, mortgage, etc.; usufruct.

تصرف بيجا *tasarruf-i-bejā*. 1. Waste; extravagance; dissipation. 2. Misappropriation; embezzlement. 3. Unlawful occupation.
tasarruf bejā mujrimāna. Criminal misappropriation.

تصرف تقديم *tasarruf taqdīm*, Presumptive right.

تصرف شرطي *tasarruf shartī*, Contingent use.

تصرف ضامن *tasarruf zāmīn*, Surety for possession.

تصرف ضامني *tasarruf zāminī*, Security given by the party in the possession of litigated

property that no loss shall be sustained by the opposite party or claimant in the event of its being decreed to him.
tasarruf mahāsil shaë marhūnā kā, Use of the profits of property pledged ; usufruct.
تصرف مخفی *tasarruf-i-ma‑khfī,* G. G. Underhand disbursement.
تصرف ناجایز *tasarruf-i-nā-jāiz,* Wrongful appropriation ; unlawful use.
bad-diyanatī se tasarruf meṅ lānā, To appropriate dishonesty. [of a deposit.
تحویل تصرف *tahvīl'-i-tasarruf,* Embezzlement
tasarruf k., tasarruf meṅ lānā, v. n.
1. To spend ; expend ; apply. [enjoy.
2. To occupy ; use ; take possession of ;
3. To misappropriate; misapply; embezzle.

A تصفیہ *tasfī'ya,* n. m. صفو was pure.
1. Purifying (esp. the mind from ill-will); purification ; purity. 2. Reconciliation ; settlement (of a debt). [decision.
3. Disposal (of a case) ; adjustment ;
تصفیہ حدبست *tasfiya-i-had bast,* Asettlement of boundaries.
تصفیہ حساب *tasfīya hisāb, hisāb kitāb kā tasfīya.* Adjustment or settlement of account.
تصفیہ دعوے *tasfīya dāwā,* Adjustment of claim.
tasfīyā talab, qābil tasfīya. Open to adjustment ; requiring settlement.
تصفیہ قطعی *tasfīyā qata‑ī,* Final settlement, or disposal of a case.
tasfīya k. v. n. 1. To reconcile ; effect a compromise or reconciliation ; adjust (a dispute). 2. To dispose of ; settle ; arbitrate.
تصفیہ لگان *tasfīya lagān,* Adjustment of rent.
تصفیہ نامہ *tasfīya-nāma,* A deed of compromise or composition.
amūr tasfīya, Points at issue, issues.
āpas meṅ tasfīya. Amicable adjustment ; private arbitration or arrangement.

A تصنع *tasan'nō* ; H. *bɪnāvaṭ,* n. m. صنع wrought, forged. Fabrication ; falsification ; alteration.

A تعداد *tādād',* n. f. عدد numbered.
1. Number ; amount ; sum ; a specified sum, enumeration.
2. Registry of an estate in the Collector's office ; annual calculation or registration of the produce of an estate. [*shumārī*).
tādād ādmiyoṅ kī. Population ; census (*mardum-*
tādād āsāmī. Number of persons.
tādād jama. Amount of assessment. [person.
tādād dādanī, A sum of money payable to a
tādād dāwī, Value or valuation of a suit ; amount of claim.
tādād ḍigrī shudah, The amount decreed.
tādād zar-i-mutālabah, The amount of claim.
tādād zar-i-wājib-ul-wasūl, The amount required to be realized.
tādād-i-zamīn, Quantity of land.
tādād lagān, Amount of rent.
tādād-i-masāwī, G. G. An equal amount.
tadād-i-moaiyan, A certain quantity.
تعدادی *tādādī,* adj. Amounting to ; the sum of ; valued at ; measuring ; numbering ; to the amount of ; comes to.

A تعدی *taād'dī,* n. f. عدد passed from it.
1. Force (*zabardastī*). 2. Compulsion. 3. Exaction. 4. Oppression.

A تعرض *taār'ruz,* n. m. Interruption ; objection ; obstacle ; hindrance ; impediment.
taarruz ijrāë hukm, Arrest of judgment ; resisting execution of an order.
bilā taarruz, Without opposition ; *nem con.*

A تعریف *tārīf',* n. f. عرف knew.
1. A definition (of a term) ; a description.
2. Praise ; commendation ; laudation.
3. (Eng. tariff) A table of rates of export and import duties, in which sense the word has been adopted in English and other European languages (probably through the Spanish from the Arabic).
tārīf-ul-majhūl bil-majhūl. Explaining in terms as little understood as the thing intended to be explained. [patience.

A تعزیت *tāz'iyat,* n. f. عزی he enjoined
1. Condolence. 2. Lamentation ; mourning.

A تعزیر *tāzīr,* n. f. An infliction of punishment by flagellation or otherwise, at the discretion of the judge for any offence, whether of word or deed, not subject to a specific legal penalty. Mah. law.
تعزیرات ہند *tāzīrāt-i-hind,* Indian Penal Code.
تعزیر عنیف *tāzīr-i-ānīf yā shadīd,* Severe or rigorous punishment. [office.

A تعزیل *tāzīl,* n. f. Removal or dismissal from

A تعلق *taāl'luq,* n. m. علق it hung to it.
1. Connexion ; dependance ; relation ; concern. 2. Reference ; regard.
3. Office ; function ; service ; employment.
taalluq rakhnā. To belong to ; pertain to ; to be related to ; to be concerned or connected with ; to have to do with ; relate to ; refer to ; bear upon. 2. To have an interest in.
ba-taālluq khās. With special reference to.
تعلقہ *taāl'luqa, taāl'luq,* n. m. 1. Possession ; occupancy. 2. An estate ; a manor. 3. A district ; a division of a province.

تعلقه *taål'luqa, taålluq,* A tract of proprietory land, usually smaller than a *zamīndārī*, although sometimes including several villages, and not unfrequently confounded with a *zamīndārī*.

In the N. W. P. a *taalluq* presents various peculiarities, but it is defined an estate, the profits of which are divided between different proprietors, or classes of proprietors, the one superior, the other inferior. The holder of such a *taʿalluq* exercises legally no right of interference with the proprietory and hereditary rights of the cultivators, except in some cases where, from peculiar circumstances, the inferior claimants have been absorbed in the person of a single *taʿalluq-dār*. Many modifications of rights, more or less obscure, are said to exist between the individual *taʿalluqdār* and the inferior proprietor. *Wilson.*

تعلقه‌جديد *taålluqa-i-jadīd.lit.*New dependencies.

A term applied to tracts annexed by the *zamīndārs*, being acquired by encroachments on the bordering estates.

تعلقه‌حضوري *taålluqa-i-huzūrī.* An estate of which the revenue was paid direct to the Government or it's officers.

These were called also independent *taʿalluqs*, and the holders were classed with *zamīndārs* or proprietary land-holders.

تعلقه‌دار *taålluqadār'*, n. m. The holder of a *taålluq*. In some places a Government officer; a collector of revenue from the cultivators on behalf of the estate or of the farmer of the revenue, whose undue exactions it is his duty to prevent.

taålluqa-dārī, n. f. The tenure, office, or estate of a *Taalluq-dār*.

taålluqadārī haq. The dues or allowances payable to the *taålluqdār* in addition to his stipulated proportion of the assessment.

تعلقه زبردستي *taålluqa i-zabardastī.* An estate seized by the *zamīndār* from his neighbours by violence.

تعلقه قديم *taålluqa-i-qadīm.* Old estates.

تعلقه مالضامني *taålluqa-i-māl-zāmnī.* Dependencies paying Government revenue for which the *zamīndār* is responsible.

تعلقه مذكوري *taålluqa mazkūrī.* The permanent settlement *taålluqa* of which the holders paid their revenue through the intervention of a superior, as a *zamīndār* or other proprietor.

These were termed 'dependant taʿalluqs.' They were hereditary and transferable as long as the revenue was paid, but lapsed to the superior on failure of heirs. They were also termed Mufussil or *shāmili* taʿalluqs. *Wilson.*

تعلقه‌گذرانا *taallīqa guzrānnā.* G. G. To furnish an inventory.

tāmīl-i-hukm-nāmah. Serving a warrant.

tāmīl khās. A specific performance.

tāmīl-i-qurqī. Execution of process of attachment; distress; distraint.

تعليقه *tålī'qa*, n. m. A schedule; inventory (of property); a list of articles.

A تعميل *tāmīl'*, n. f. A. عمل performed. Performance; operation; practice. 2. Execution (of an order); enforcement; putting in force (a decree); service (of a notice).

tamīl-i-ikhtiyār. Exercise of a right.

tamīl ikhtiyār-i-ohdah. Exertion of executive power; execution of official functions.

tāmīl hukm k. v. n. To execute or carry out an order.

tāmīl k. v. n. 1. See بجالانا 2. To put in execution; to serve (a writ).

tāmīl-i-munsab-i-sarkārī. G. G. Exercise of official functions.

tāmīl honā, v. n. To be executed; to come into operation.

tāmīl men. G. G. In the exercise of.

ahkām pulis kī tamīl. G. G. Administration of the police.

hukm jis kī woh tamīl kartā hai. G. G. The authority under which he acts.

kām kī tāmīl. G. G. Discharge of duty.

mansab-i-sarkārī kī tāmīl men. G. G. In the exercise of official functions.

A تعويق *tåvīq'*, G. G. Postponement.

be intahā tavīq. G. G. Indefinite postponement;

A تعهد *taå'hud.* Agreement; engagement; contract.

A تعيين *taåī'yun*, n. m. عين appointed. The act of appointing; determination; settlement; establishment; appointment.

تعين‌حصص *taåiyun-i-hisas.* Determination or apportionment; allotment.

تعين‌دعوي *taåiyun-i-dåawa.* Valuation of suit or claim.

تعين‌سزا *taåiyun-i-sazā.* G. G. Penal provision.

taaiyun k. v. n. To fix; determine; establish; institute.

تعين‌لگان *taåiyun-i-lagån.* Assessment; appraisement of revenue.

تعينات *taåīyunāt'*, Ped.; *taīnāt*, Pop. n. m. 1. Appointments. 2. A garrison.

taīnāt k. v. a. To appoint; nominate; enlist; put in possession.

taīnāt honā. To be appointed; set over or in charge of.

تعيناتي *taåīyunā'tī*; Pop. *taīnātī*, n. f. 1. Appointment; deputation; service. 2. A detachment of troops; a guard, etc. nominated for some special duty.

taåiyunātī qubūl karnā. To engage one's self to accept a post.

A تغريب *taǧrīb'*, Banishment; transportation; separation from family and friends.

A تغلب *taǧal'lub*, n. m. from غلب overpowering. Embezzlement; breach of trust; peculation (*gaban*).

tagallub rasūm-i-isṭāmp. Fraudulent evasion of stamp duty.
tagallub o tasarruf. Peculation; embezzlement; misappropriation.

A تغير *taġai'yur,* More prop. *taġaiyur o tabaddul,* n. m. غير destroying.
1. Revolutionary changes; *bouleversement.*
2. Falsification or alteration of papers.
tagaiyur o tabaddul kāgazāt bilā takmīl-i-jāl. Falsification or alteration of papers not amounting to forgery.
تغيرات *taġaiyurāt',* Alterations. [nue.
tagaiyurāt-i-jama. Alterations of *jama* or revenue.

A تفريق *tafrīq',* n. f. 1. Partition; severalty division; division of land (*baṭwāṛā*).
2. A judicial divorce, pronounced by the *Qāzī*, as distinguished from one executed by the husband himself on his own authority.
تفريق جايز *tafrīq-i-jāiz.* A legal separation or severalty.
تفريق نامه *tafrīq-nāmah.* A deed setting forth the shares claimed by different parties.

A تفصيل *tafsīl',* n. m. A. فصل cutting, defining. Details; particulars; minute particulars; specification; exposition; explanation.
tafsīl bāz adad-i-jāēdād, G. G. Enumeration of some items.
tafsīl jāēdād mudda bihā. A specification of the property claimed.
tafsīl jumlā ashyāē, G. G. Specification of all the articles.
tafsīl-i-hāl, Particulars of a case.
ba-tafsīl-i-zail, muffasilah zail, In form and manner following; as follows.
tafsīl k., yā likhnā, v. n. To exhibit in detail; enumerate; particularize; explain at full length; specify.
tafsīl-vār, tafsīlan, adv. In detail (*bil-tafsīl*); circumstantially; particularly.
tafsīl yeh hai. On this wise; to wit.
pūrī tafsīl. Full particulars or details.

A تفويض *tafvīz',* n. f. A فرض consigning. Committing to another; putting in trust or deposit.
tafvīz-i-hissa, n. m. The transfer by a defaulter of a share in a coparcenary estate to solvent shareholders. [deposit or trust.
tafvīz k. v. n. To make over (*sauṅpnā*); put in
tafvīz-i-māl. Consignment of goods.

A تقادم *taqā'dum,* Such an interval between the commission of a crime and the giving of evidence respecting it, as operates in bar of punishment. *Wilson.*

A تقاضا *taqāzā,* n. m. Pressing; dunning.
taqāzā-i-sin, yā umr, The natural tendencies of childhood, youth, or age. [pressure.
taqāzā-i-shadīd; H. *chhātī par charhnā,* Great
taqāzā k. v. n. To press; urge; press for payment; dun.
taqād-gīr, Illit. n. m. A bill-collector; a dun; one employed to look after the Indigo cultivation.
ind-ul-taqāzā, On demand.

A تقاوي *taqā'vī;* P. *peshgī;* H. *agāū,* n. f.
1. Pecuniary advance, especially to cultivators for implements or digging wells, etc.
2. Advances of money made by the Government to the cultivators for the purchase of seed grains and cattle, or the construction of wells, etc., especially in the south of India where the *Ryot-wārī* settlement prevails, to be repaid when the crop is gathered. Similar advances are made in bad seasons and the like, and sometimes to enable the cultivators to extend their cultivation.

A تقدم *taqad'dum,* n. m. قدم Priority; preeminence.
taqaddum-i-dāwa. Priority of claim.
تقدمه *taqdam'a;* Pop. *takdamā,* n. m. Final adjustment or audit of an account; an estimate (*takhmīnā*); a budget.

A تقرر *taqar'rur,* n. m. قر remaining firm, resting. See *taqarrurī,* 2. [arbitrate.
taqarrur-i-sālisī par rāzī honā. To agree to
taqarrur-i-jama. Allotment of revenue; settlement of the revenue payable.
taqsīm arāzī. Partition or division of land.
taqsīm ba hissā rasadī, taqsīm zimmawārī. A rateable distribution of a common liability.
تقرري *taqar'rurī,* n. f. 1. Settlement. 2. The act of appointing; nomination; appointment.
parvāna-i-taqar'rurī, n. f. A letter of appointment. [about.
تقريبا *taqrīb'an,* adv. Approximately; nearly;

A تقسيم *taqsīm',* n. f. from قسم dividing.
1. Division; partition; allotment (بانٹ 1).
taqsīm-i-tarka, G. G. Distribution of property.
taqsīm-i-tāalluq, taqsīmī-bandī taalluq. A *taalluq* which was separately registered in the original rent roll or *tumār jama* of the land revenue of Hindustan.
taqsīm jāēdād-i-mutawaffa bilā wasīyat. G. G. Distribution of intestate estates.
taqsīm-i-jadīd. Repartition; new division.
taqsīm-i-jama. Allotment of revenue, rental. A distribution of the assessment of the revenue upon the several sub-divisions of an estate or district.
taqsīm-i-khāngī. A private partition.
taqsīm-i-dāvā. Splitting of claims.
taqsīm dehāt-i-khālisā. Division of estates paying revenue to Government.

taqsīm-i-sarkārī. A public partition; a partition made through Government officials.
taqsīm sarmāya, G. G. A distribution of stock or capital.
taqsīm ġair-mukammal, taqsīm nā-mukammal. Imperfect partition.

This sort of partition often takes place in those co-parcenary estates in which the whole or part of the land is held and managed in common by all the community. Under it the whole of the common land is divided and allotted to the several co-parceners, and each allotment of land is assessed with its proper share of the demand upon the whole estate which still remains undivided, the joint responsibility being also maintained. Under this process the estate becomes *Paṭṭī-dārī.*

taqsīm-i-farebī; H. *chhal baṭvārah.* A fraudulent partition.
taqsīm kār-pardāzān-i-pulīs, G. G. Distribution of the police force.
taqsīm k. v. a. See *bāṅṭnā.*
taqsīm kī ujrat. G. G. Partition fees.
taqsīm-i-māl. Division or distribution of property.
tasqim-i-mukammal. A complete division.

This sort of division carries with it an entire separation of the parts of an estate from each other, and their formation into distinct estates (*māhālāt*).

taqsīm mauzawār. Divided into *mauzās.*
taqsīm-nāmah, 1. A record of division of property (*baṭvārā*).
2. An instrument or deed of partition amongst joint proprietors when ceasing to hold their estate in common.
taqsīm yak-jāī. A compact division or partition.
muqadmah-i-taqsīm. A case of partition.
taqsīm-i-virsā. A partition of inherited property.
تقسیمي *taqsīm'ī, qābil-i-taqsīm,* adj. Divisible; liable to partition; according to allotment.

A تقصير *taqsīr';* Illit *taksīr,*; H. *khoṭ,* n. f. قصر diminishing. 1. Omission; failure; neglect. 2. A mistake; error; fault. 3. Offence; misdemeanor; crime; guilt.
taqsīr-vār, taqsīr-mand, adj. 1. Blameable; faulty. 2. Guilty; culpable; criminal.
be-taqsīr; adj. Blameless; innocent.

A تقليبى *taqlīb'ī,* adj. قلب converting. Converted; changed; altered.
sikka-i-taqlībī, G.G. Counterfeit coin.

A تقليد *taqlīd',* n. f. قلد Putting a rope round the neck.
1. Imitation; copy; representation.
2. Counterfeiting.
تقليدى *taqlīd'ī,* adj. 1. Imitated; copied.
2. Forged; counterfeit; false.
mohar-i-taqlīdī; G. G. A counterfeit seal.

A تقيد *taqai'yud*; Illit. *taqaiyad,* n. f. قيد restraining; See تاكيد 1. Looking after; observation; watchfulness; vigilance.
taqaiyud k. v. n To look closely after.

A تكرار *takrār',* n. f. كر repeating.
1. Question; dispute; point at issue.
2. Objection; controversy (*bahs,* 1, 2.).
takrār āīn kī bābat. An issue of law.
takrār bābat wāqaë. An issue of fact.
khās takrār, n. f. The chief objection; the real question; the main issue; the material point.

A تكفير *takfīr',* n. f. See كفر 1. Expiating a crime; doing penance or paying a mulct as atonement. 2. Accusing one of impiety; denouncing as an infidel.

A تكاليف *taklīf,* n. f. See ايذا
amr bāis-i-taklīf-i-ām. G. G. A public nuisance.

A تكميل *takmīl',* n. f. كمل completed.
Authentication; validity; authority.
takmīl pānā, v. n. To be completed; finished.
takmīl-i-tamassuk, Execution of bond.
takmīl-i-rahn, Foreclosure of mortgage.
takmīl-i-haqīqat. Completion of title.
takmīl-i-dastāwez. The complete execution of a deed.
takmīl-i-sharāyat-i-qānūn. Fulfilment of the requirements of the law.
takmīl-i-zābita mutaalliq infikāk-i-rihn, G. G. Fulfilment of the procedure regarding the equity of the redemption of a mortgage.
takmīl k., takmīl ko pauṅhchānā, v. a.
1. To execute; complete.
2. To authenticate; to give authority to.
adam-takmīl, G. G. Non-execution.

H تكور तिक्कूर *tikūr', tihārā.* A division of the crop where the *zamiṅdar* gets one-third, and the *raiyat* two-thirds.

H تكيت *takīt'.* A monied man in a village appointed to collect the shares of the assessment from the villagers and pay them to the principal revenue payer or *mālguzār.* *Wilson.*

A تكينة *takī'na.* 1. A cess paid in lieu of fodder. 2. The rents of a number of houses collected by an agent. *Wilson.*

T تلاش *talāsh';* Illit. *tālāsh,* n. f. 1. Search; quest; scrutiny; investigation. 2. Pursuit; research; exploration.
talāsh k. v. n. 1. To seek; search; look for; look about for.
2. To explore; reconnoitre; investigate.
talāsh-i-maāsh, Search after a livelihood.
تلاشي *talāsh'ī,* n. f. Searching one's person, property, or house; searching for dutiable or smuggled goods.

talāshī le'nā, v. n. To institute a search ; search the person or house ; search for smuggled goods.
khānah-talāshī, n. f. Searching a house for stolen property, or for smuggled goods.
wārent-i-talāshī, G. G. A search warrant.

H تلاوا *talāv'ā*, n. m. Cor. of T. طلایه An advanced guard ; a patrol ; a reconnoitring party.

A تلبيس *talbīs'*, n. f. لبس 1. False personation. 2. Counterfeiting coin.
talbīs-i-sikka. Counterfeiting coin. [feiting coin.
āla-i-talbīs-i-sikka. An instrument for counter-

A تلف *tal'af*, n. m. تلف he perished. Waste ; loss ; destruction.

S تلک तिलक *til'ak* ; H. *ṭīkā*, n. m. 1. A sectarial mark or marks made with colored unguents on the forehead between the eyebrows.
2. Installation ; consecration.
rāj-tilak, n. m. Anointing a king ; coronation.

A تمادي *tamā'dī*, n. f. مدي Continuing a long time. Duration ; limitation of time length of time ; period.
tamādī-i-aīyām. Lapse or efflux of time ; limitation of time. [the hand.

A تمرد *tamar'rud*, n. m. A مرد rubbing with
tammarrud hukm-i-hākim ; *tammarrud hukm-i-adālat*. Resistance to orders or process.
tamarrud shiārī. Contumacious bearing.

A تمسک *tamas'suk*, n. m. A مسک seizing, holding fast. A promissory note or bond ; a written obligation ; note of hand ; a written acknowledgment of a debt.
tamassuk-i-aslī. A genuine bond. [perty.
tamassuk-i-jāēdādī. A bond, hypothecating pro-
tamassuk-i hāzir zāminī. A bond or recognisance as a security for personal appearance.
tamassuk rajisṭarī shudah. A registered bond.
tamassuk shartīyah, mashrūtī tamassuk. Indemnity bond.
tamassuk lā-hāsīl. Dead or bad bond.
tamassuk-masnūī. A fabricated bond.
tamassuk-i-manāt-i-dāwā. A bond on which a claim is based or founded.
tamassuk manshā-i-dāwī. A claim under bond.
kisī tamassuk kī binā par ḍigrī hāsil k. To obtain judgment on a bond.

T تمغه *tam'ğa* ; Pop. *tağma* ; Rus. *takmā* ; n. m. A medal ; royal grant or charter ; a diploma.

A تمليک *tamlīk*. Appropriation of property ; transfer of property ; an assignment of proprietory right.
tamlīk-i-nāzjāēz, Unlawful possession.
تمليک نامه *tamlīk-nāmah*. A deed of transfer or partition of property.
tamlīk o taulīat-nāmah. A deed of gift and trusteeship which assigns property in trust to a particular person, with the proceeds of which he is to defray the expenses of a religious establishment ; and, if there be any surplus, he may apply it to his private use. *Wilson*.

A تنازع *tanā'zoʻ* ; Pop. *tanāzā*, n. m. A. نزع See ان بن 1, 2, 3.
تنازع سرحد *tanāzā-i-sarhad*. A boundary dispute.

A تناسل *tanā'sul*. Uninterrupted descent through a series of generations.

A تنبيه *tambīh'*, n. f. تنبه to know. Admonition given by the judge to parties guilty of venial offences.

A تنسيخ *tansīkh'*. Cancelment ; renunciation ; revocation ; annulment ; abrogation ; quashing (a decision) ; rescission ; repeal.
tansīkh k. To cancel ; rescind ; quash ; abrogate ; repeal ; declare mill and void (*tardīd k.*).
تنسيخ تبني *tansīkh-i-tabannī*. Renunciation of adoption.
تنسيخ ٹهيکه *tansīkh-i-ṭheka*. Cancelment of a lease. [marrow.

A تنقيح *tanqīh'*, n. f. نقح extracting the
1. (*Med.*) Clearing the bowels ; physicking.
2. Verification (of accounts or revenue payments.) [issues).
3. Determination of, or laying down (the
tanqīh-i-umūr tasfīya talab. Determination of issues for trial.
tanqīh k. v. n. To fix ; determine ; lay down or draw up (the issues). [rent rate.
tanqīh-i-shareh lagān. Determination of the
umūr tanqīh-talab. Issues for trial.

A تنقيه *tanqī'ya*, n. m. Settlement ; decision.

P توده *tū'dah, todah*, n. m. 1. A mound (*ṭīlā*) ; a heap of earth ; a boundary of a field (*thūā*). 2. A butt for marksmen.
توده بندي *tūdah-bandī*, n. f. Marking off boundaries.

A توزيع *tauzʻī* ;—*i-jamā-bandī* ; Rus. *tawjīh*, n. f. وزع shaped. A statement ; account ; rent roll ; descriptive roll.

A revenue account showing, under the name of each payer of revenue, the total amount as it falls due, the portion actually paid, and the balance outstanding.

baqāyā-i-tauzī. A list of outstanding balances.

tauzī hāl. Account of current demands.

tauzīh mahāl. An estate that pays an assessed revenue.

tauzī men dākhil k. To bring on the rent roll.

tauzīh nāma. A deed of record or registry of occupation of land granted either by the Collector or by the *zamīndār* to the occupants.

tauzīh-navīs. A keeper of descriptive rolls.

A توسل *tavas'sul*, n. m. Ped. for وسیلہ q. v.

A توضیح *tauzīh'*, 1. An account of collections.

2. Construction, interpretation; note; comment.

tauzīh k. To exhibit in detail.

A توفیر *taufīr'*, n.f. وفر becoming full, complete.

1. Increase; excess; savings; overplus (بچت 1.) 2. Emoluments; perquisites.

3. A supernumerary.

4. New land liable to assessment or augmentation of the revenue, either from extended cultivation or the lapse or resumption of alienated assessments; any addition to the originally recorded lands of an estate. Land in excess of settlement. Punjab.

taufīr-i-jāgīr-dārāṅ. Increase or surplus revenue on the resumed assignments of the holders of *jāgīrs*.

taufīr zamīn. Lands in addition to, or excess of; an original grant or measurement.

taufīr kā sīgah. The department or column of mesne profits.

taufīr-i-mauza. A village not originally included in the assessment; a village in excess.

H توکا तोका *tok'ā*. The Government share of the produce; the fixed allowance for which lands are liable without reference to seasons or amount of produce. *Carnegy.*

H تول तोल *tol*; E. *taul*, n. f. S. तुल to weigh.

1. The act of weighing; weight. 2. The standard weight or measure of weight.

urṭī tol, n. f. Slightly short weight.

pakkī tol, n. f. Standard weight.

pūrī tol, n. f. Full measure; fair measure.

jhuktī tol, n. f. Slightly overweight.

kachchī tol, n. f. Under the standard weight.

kamtī tol, n. f. Short weight; false measure.

تولا तोला *to'lā*, n. m. 1. A weight of 12 *mashās*; a *tolā*. 2. A weighman (*tulvaiyā*).

A تولیت *tauli'at*. Trusteeship; superintendence; transfer by the proprietor under the original contract, at the original price, without any addition for profit. *Carnegy.*

A توہین *tauh'īn*, Ped. n. f. وہن weakening. See اہانت.

tauhīn bil qasd. G. G. Intentional insult.

tauhīn k. To defame; offer an insult.

tauhīn mujrimāna. A criminal insult.

H تھانہ थाना *thā'nā*, n. m. A subordinate police station.

تھانہدار थानेदार *thāne-dār*, n. m. A keeper of a *thānā*; a petty police officer. [a *thāne-dār*.

تھانہداري थानेदारी *thāne-dārī*, n. f. The office of

H تھانگ थांग *thāṅg*, n. f. S. स्थानगम्, H. *thān* place.

1. A den of thieves. [stolen property.

2. Trace; clue; information. 3. Trace of

thāṅg lagānā, thāṅgnā, v. n. To get a clue to hidden or stolen property; to trace; find.

تھانگي थांगी *thāṅ'gī, thāṅgiyā*, n. m. 1. An accomplice who supplies thieves with information.

2. One who traces stolen property; a detective.

3. A receiver of stolen property.

thāṅg-gīrī, n. f. Receiving stolen goods.

A تہتک *tahat'tuk*, n.m. Defamation. See ہتک

A تہدید *tahdīd'*, n. f. breaking. Threatening menace; threat (*dhamkī*).

tahdīd'an, By intimidation.

A تہذیب *tahzīb'*, n. f. ہذب Civilization; politeness; refinement.

tahzīb-i-akhlāq, Civilization; good breeding.

tahzīb ke khilāf, khilāf tahzīb, adj. Immoral.

tahzīb-yāftā, talīm-yāftā, tarbiyat-yāftah, adj. Civilized; educated; polite; refined.

A تہمت *toh'mat*, n. f. Calumny. See الزام

tohmat dharnā, lagānā, yā lenā; v. a. See *ilzām denā*.

تہمتي *toh'matī*, n. m. A slanderer; calumniator.

H تھوک थोक *thok*, n. m. S. स्तोम multitude.

1. A company; class; party; community; band (*giroh*). 2. A total amount; a sum.

3. An allotted portion; a share; lot; portion. 4. A tenure; holding; a local division of an estate.

5. A sub-division in a *bhaīyā chārī* or coparcenary estate. [lines meet.

6. A point where three or more boundary

تھوکبست थोकबस्त *thok-bast, thak-bast*, n. f.

Laying down and marking off the boundaries; fixing the limits of estates by a native survey, or preparatory to a professional survey.
thok bāndhnā, v. a. To form into parties.
تهوک بندي *thok-bandī*, n. f. A written engagement specifying the distribution of the shares of a co-parcenary village.
تهوکدار थोकदार *thok-dār*, n. m.
1. The holder of a *thok*.
2. The head of a company or society.
3. A wholesale dealer; a copyholder.

P تيار *taiyār'*; Illit. *tayār*; Rus. *tiār*, adj.
1. Ready; ready-made; prepared; willing.
2. Finished; completed; perfect. 3. Ripe; ripened (fruit). 4. Fully developed; plump; fat; arrived at puberty; robust.
muqaddamah, yā misal taiyār huā. The case is closed.

S تياگ त्याग *tyāg'*, *tiyāg*, n. m. त्यज् to leave.
1. Relinquishment; abdication; desertion.
2. Repudiation; divorce.
3. Renunciation.
tyāg-patr, n. m. A bill of abandonment or divorce.

A تيريج *terīj'*. An abstract account compiled from other detailed accounts; a register of official documents in the Collector's office.
terīj asāmī-wār. An abstract of the *Khatauni* or *Muntakhab asāmī-wār*, giving the total land held by each person in each *Thok* or *Paṭṭī*, without any enumeration of the fields.
terīj jamābandī. Particulars of the annual revenue and charges of an estate.
terīj-i-jama kharch. A summary account of the receipts and disbursements of a village, made up at the end of the year.
terīj jinswār-asāmīwār. A specification of the fields in the occupation of each person cultivating on his own account.
terīj goshwārā jinswār asāmīwār. A tabular abstract statement of each kind of produce (*jins*) of the fields of a village, with the name of the occupant.

H تيكار तीकार *tīkār'*, *tikār*; Bhoj. *tekhār*, n. m. Three ploughings.

H تيكرا तीकरा *tīk'rā*, n. m. The small stems thrown out by a young blade of wheat. (?)

H تييه तीया *tī'yā*; *tīah*; *tīā*, n. m. S. त्रि three.
A boundary mark.
tīyā-bandī, n. f. Settling a boundary.

ٹ

H ٹاٹ टाट *ṭāṭ*; Mag. *ṭappar*, n. m. 1. Canvass.
2. The mat or carpet on which a banker sits.
ṭāṭ yā ṭappar ulaṭnā, v. n. *lit.* To be turned over (the *ṭāṭ*). To be, become, or be declared a bankrupt; to be posted in the Gazette.

H ٹانڈ *ṭānḍ*. High and poor soil. (?)

H ٹپا टप्पा *ṭap'pā*, n. m. E. A small tract or division of country, smaller than a *Parganā*; comprising one or more villages.

In some parts of the N. W. P. a *Ṭappā* denotes a tract in which there is one principal town, or a large village, with lands and villages dependent upon them, or a cluster of villages acknowledging the supremacy of one amongst them and forming a sort of corporate body although not otherwise identical. *Wilson.*

H ٹكري टिकरी *ṭik'arī*, n. f. A soil which is irretentive of moisture.

H ٹكسال टकसाल *ṭaksāl'*, n. f. S. टङ्क शाला.
Assay office; mint.
ṭaksāl kā khoṭā, adj. Base-born; badly taught; ill-bred.
ṭaksālī, n. m. An officer of the mint; mint-master.

H ٹكينه टकीना *ṭakī'nā*, n. m. A petty tax levied in lieu of fodder.

H ٹوپنا टोपना *ṭop'nā*, v. a. To sow by the hand; to put down a young tree or cutting; to plant.

H ٹوٹا टोटा *ṭo'ṭā*, n. m.
1. Loss; deficit; defalcation. 2. Damages; forfeit; compensation; amends; penalty.
ṭoṭā uṭhānā, sahnā, denā, yā bharnā, v. n.
1. To suffer a loss; sustain damage.
2. To make restitution; reimburse; indemnify; make up or make good (a loss); compensate; repay; refund.
ṭoṭā bharā'ī, n. f. Indemnification; compensation; restitution.
ṭoṭā parnā yā honā, v. n. To incur or suffer a loss; to lose; fail.

H ٹهگ ठग *ṭhag*; Brij. *ṭhagyā*, n. m. S. स्थग a rogue. 1. An impostor; a cheat; rogue.
2. A swindler; sharper. 3. One of a gang who poison or strangle travellers.
banārsī ṭhag, n. m. A swell mobsman.
ٹهگائي ठगाई *ṭhagā'ī*, *ṭhag biddiyā*, n. f.
1. Cheating; fraud; deceit; imposture.
2. Swindling; sharp practice.
ٹهگنا ठगना *ṭhag'nā*, v. a. To cheat; impose upon; overreach; circumvent; delude; put upon; practise upon; dupe; trick.

ٹھگي ठगी *ṭhag'ī*, n. f. 1. The practice or profession of a *ṭhag*. 2. The Department for the suppression of *ṭhags*.

H ٹھیکر ठीकर *ṭhīk'ar*, n. The system of *chaukī-dārī* prevailing in Rohtak Berī.

The able-bodied men of the village are enrolled in the *Paṭwārī's* book, and their names written on small potsherds called *ṭhikar* (whence the name). These are thrown together into a large pot, kept in the village hall or *chaupāl*, with another empty pot by it. It is the *Paṭwārī's* duty to visit the *chaupāl* daily with the *Dhanak*, and draw at random, from the filled pot, the required number of names which he inscribes in his book. *Wilson.*

H ٹھیکا ठेका *ṭhek'ā*, W.; *ṭhīkā*, E. n. m. H. *ṭhairnā* to be settled.

1. Piece-work; work done by contract or by the job. 2. Hire; fare; contract.
3. A lease; license.
4. See *ijārah*.

ṭhekā-bandī, n. f. A farm or lease; a farm held on lease.
ṭhekā bheṭ, Extra imposts; presents or gratuities of money; personal service. Kumāūṅ.
ṭhekā paṭṭā, n. m. A document conveying a lease or farm.
ṭhekā peshgī, n. m. A lease or farm of which the rent is paid in advance.
ṭhekā hīn hayāt, A lease for the term of one's life.
ṭheke-dār, n. m. Contractor; lease-holder (*ijārah-dār* 1); one who farms a licence for the sale of spirituous liquors or the like; one who receives the rents from the cultivators and pays a stipulated amount to the proprietor.
ṭheke-dār bāqī-dār, n. m. A lessee in arrears.
ṭheke-dārī kā band-o-bast. A farming settlement
ṭheka mujraī. An usufructuary lease.
ṭheka mustājrī. A farming lease.
ṭheke-dār maurūsī, n. m. An hereditary lessee.
ṭheke-dār maurūsī kā istehqāq pesh k. To set up a title as an hereditary lessee.
ṭhekā-i-dāimī, n. m. A lease in perpetuity.
ṭhekā denā, v. a 1. See *ijārah denā*. 2. To give out in piece-work or by the job.
ṭhekā dene-vālā, Lessor; grantor.
ṭheke kī miyād. The term for which the lease has to run.
ṭhekā lenā, v. a. 1. To take or enter into a contract; to contract; lease; farm; to take out or purchase a licence.
2. To monopolize; engross.

ٹھیلنس ठेलन्स *ṭhel'ans*, n. m. H. *ans* a share.
Land acquired by force. *Carnegy.*

H ٹیبا टेबा *ṭeb'ā*, n. m. A long stitch.

H ٹیپ टीप *ṭīp*, n. f.

A *tamassuk*, q. v. on unstamped paper; a bond; cheque. 2. Security to pay a sum by a stipulated period; a note of hand.
paṭī-huī ṭīp, n. f. A cashed bill; a discharged bond.

H ٹیکا टीका *ṭīk'ā*, n. m. S. टीक to explain.

1. See *tilak*.
2. A mark of distinction, chiefship, etc.
3. A ceremony connected with betrothal.
4. Presents in money or goods, and especially cocoanuts to the intended bridegroom from the father of the bride.
5. The ceremony of installation and investiture.

ث

A ثابت *sāb'it*; Illit. *sābat, sābut*, adj. ثبت subsisted. 1. Sound; entire (*pūrā*). 2. Firm; stable; constant. 3. Proved; established; substantiated; convicted.
sābit k. v. a. To prove; support the truth of; make good (a charge).
sābit honā, v. n. To be proved; established.

A ثالث *sā'lis*, n. m. ثلث a third. A third person; referee; assessor; arbitrator; umpire (*bichaulyā*).
ثالث بالخير *sālis-bil-khair*, An impartial or unprejudiced arbitrator.
ثالثنامه *sālis-nāmah*, n. m. An award by a jury; arbitration award.
ثالثا *sā'lisan*, adv. In the third place; thirdly.
ثالثي *sālisī*, n. f. Arbitration.
ثالثي خانگي *sālisī-khāngī*, n. f. Private arbitration.
sālisī karnā, v. a. To arbitrate.
sālisī men supurd karnā, v. a. To refer to arbitration.
اقرار نامه ثالثي *iqrār nāmah-i-sālisī*. Agreement to abide by an award of arbitration; deed of assent to arbitration.
فيصلنامه ثالثي *faisal-nāmah-i-sālisī*. An award of arbitration.

A ثاني *sā'nī*, adj. ثني he doubled it. Second.
sānī-ul-hāl, adv. Secondly.
تجويز ثاني *tajvīz-i-sānī*, A second investigation or trial; review of judgment.
طرف ثاني *taraf sānī*, n. m. The opposite party; an adversary.
ملاحظه ثاني *mulāhaza-i-sānī*, n. m. *nazar-i-sānī* n. f. Second reading; revision; revisal.
نيلام ثاني *nīlām-i-sānī*, n. m. Re-sale.
ثانيا *sā'niyan*, adv. Secondly; in the second place.

A ثبت *sabt*, n. f. An impression; a seal; writing.
sabt k. v. a. To insert; enter; inscribe; subscribe or affix (one's signature).
nishānī-sabt k. v. a. To affix a mark (by way of signature).

sabt honā, v. n. To be inscribed or written.

A ثبوت *subūt'*; Pop. *sabūt,* n. m. ثبت subsisted. Proof; testimony; demonstration; determination (of guilt).

subūt-i-istehqāq, Proof of right or title.
subūt-i-badīhī, yā bādī-ul-nazr, Prima facie evidence.
subūt-i-tāīdī, Corroborative evidence.
subūt-i-tahrīrī, yā kāgzī, Documentary evidence; written testimony.
subūt-i-tardīdī, Rebutter; counter evidence.
subūt-i-tagrīrī, Oral evidence.
subūt-i-jurm, Conviction; determination of guilt.
subūt-i-jurm kā hukm sādir k. To pass sentence.
subūt-i-haqīyat, Establishment of a right; proof of claim.
subūt-i-haqīyat-i-muāfī maurūsī. Establishment of right to an hereditary rent-free estate.
subūt-i-khārijī, Extrinsic evidence.
subūt-i-darje avval, The best proof; evidence of the first degree; direct proof.
subūt-i-darje doyam, sabūt-i-adnā. Secondary proof or evidence.
subūt-i-dastkhat. Proof of signature.
subūt-i-sarīh. Clear proof; direct evidence.
subūt-i-zimnī yā muvaiyad. Collateral proof, corroborative evidence.
subūt-i-qānūnī. Legal proof.
subūt-i-qataī. Conclusive proof.
subūt-i-qayāsī. Presumptive proof.
subūt-i-lisānī, yā zabānī. Oral testimony.
subūt mabnī bar qārāyan-i-muqaddima. Circumstantial evidence; collateral testimony.
subūt men dākhil karnā. To allege as proof; adduce in evidence.
sūbūt-i-vasīyat-nāmah. Probate of will.
pāya-i-subūt ko pahuṅchānā. To establish; substantiate; bring home; prove.
rad-i-subūt, Counterproof.
indul-subūt-i-jurm. Upon conviction.
mumkin-ul-subūt. Tenable; capable of proof; what can be established.

A ثمن *sam'an,* n. m. ثمن price. Summons.

saman jārī k. v. a. To summon.
zar-i-saman, n. m. 1. Price; value. 2. The fee payable for service of summons (*talbānā*).

A ثيبه *sai'yaba,* n. f. A young woman who has consummated her marriage; *faêmina cujus periït virginitas*; (one) depucelated; one who has been robbed of her virginity.

ج

P جا *jā*; H. *jagah,* n. f. Z. *jāë.* (In comp.) A place; locality.

جانشين *jā-nashīn,* n. m. A vicegerent; viceroy; successor.
جانشيني *jā-nashīnī,* n. f. Lieutenancy; succession; vicegerency.

A جاري *jār'ī,* adj. Customary; in force; in use.

jārī rakh'nā, v. a. 1. To carry on; continue; pursue; prosecute. 2. To conduct; manage. 3. To extend. 4. To maintain.
jārī rupayā, n. m. Current rupee or coin.
jārī rahnā, v. n. To continue; subsist.
jārī-shudah, adj. Established; in force.
jārī k., v. a. 1. To issue; send out; serve. 2. To set on foot; spread; circulate; propagate; make current; promulgate. 3. To begin; introduce (a custom). 4. To carry into effect; to give legal effect to; to enforce; put in execution; put in force; enact; issue (an order). 5. To set up; establish; institute. 6. To use or exercise (a right); to administer.
jārī h., v. n. To be issued; enacted; passed into law. 2. To arise; come into operation; become operative.

H جاكڑ जाकड़ *jā'kar,* n. m. 1. Money or other pledge left with the seller for an article taken away on inspection or on commission sale. 2. Suspense account; a conditional purchase; a deposit; a memo.

jākaṛ bahī, n. f. Suspense account book.
jākaṛ bechnā, v. a. To sell on commission or subject to approval.
jākaṛ le jānā, v. a. To take goods on commission sale.
jākaṛ, adj. Lying by; old (stock).

H جاكهن जाखन *jā'khan*; Bhoj. *jamuaṭhī,* n. m. The wooden foundation of the brick work of a well.

P جاگير *jāgīr'*; Rus. *jagīr,* n. f. P. *jā* place, *gīr* take. Rent-free grant; a freehold; fief.

A grant of land made by the Government to feud an individual as a reward for some special good service.

Under the Mah. Government, it was a tenure in which the public revenue of a given tract of land was made over to a servant of the State, together with the powers requisite to enable him to collect and appropriate such revenue and administer the general government of the district. Under the British Government, such tenures (*jāgīr*) have now come to be considered as family properties, of which the holders could not be rightfully dispossessed, and to which their legal heirs succeed, as a matter of course, without the fine or *nazrāna* levied under the Mahomedan rule. With regard to the *jāgīr* in general, the special object and character of the grant was commonly specified by the designation attached to it. The term is also in use, although with some license, to designate temporary grants, allowances, or stipends, from the Government to individuals.

Under Native Governments, *jāgīrs* were of two kinds; public and private. Public *jāgīrs* were made by the Ruler for services rendered to the State.

Private *jāgirs* were lands which the owners gave rent-free generally to village servants or retainers, in lieu of money wages. Public *jāgīrs* were ordinarily made in perpetuity and they were generally respected. Pubic *jāgirs* were often hereditary, and they were contingent on the continuance of the service to be performed. The difference according to the Settlement Officer, Rāe Bareli, between it and *muāfī* is, that such a *jāgīr* was not understood, under the Native Government, to convey the proprietary right, while *sarkāri muāfī* was usually understood to do so. *Wilson.*

jāgīr-i-hīn hayāt, An estate held rent-free during one's lifetime.

جاگیر احشام *jāgīr-i-ahshām*, Lands granted for the maintenance of troops.

جاگیر خدمت *jāgīr khidmat*, Assignment of land to village servants and officers.

جاگیردار *jāgīr-dār* ; Rus. *jagīr-dār*, n. m. The holder of a fee, or *jāgīr* ; a feoffee ; grantee ; the lord of a manor ; a holder of a perpetual tenure subject to quit-rent and service.

jāgīr-i-davām, A rent-free estate descending to one's heirs.

جاگیرذات *jāgīr-zāt*. An assignment for personal support, or requiring personal service.

jāgīr gair mashrūt, yā bilā shart. An unconditional or absolute assignment.

جاگیر محال *jāgīr-i-mahāl*. A district assigned.

jāgīr mashrūt yā shartī, A *jāgīr* granted with conditions.

jāgīr-i-mansab, A grant of land attached to an office or dignity.

P جان *jān*, n. f. Life ; spirit ; soul.

jān-bakhshī, n. f. Life-giving ; pardon.

jān-bīmā. A life-insurance policy.

jān bīmā k., v. n. To insure one's life.

jān kī amān. The safety of one's life; life; pardon ; quarter.

jān mārnā, 1. To kill ; destroy a life.

A جانب *jā'nib*, n. f. جنب the side. See اور 1, 3, 4.

jānib, adv. Towards (Com. *taraf*).

jānib-dār, adj. Partial ; biassed. [partizan.

jānib-dār, n. m. A supporter ; second ; patron ;

jānib-dārī, n. f. Partiality ; bias.

jānib-dārī k., v. a. To be biassed in favor of ; to take one's part ; espouse a side.

jānib se, adv. In the name of ; in behalf of.

جانبین *jānibain'*, n. m. Dual. Both sides or parties ; the parties in a case.

īn jānib, n. m. The writer (a superior addressing a subordinate).

P جاه *jāh*, n. m. Rank (*martabah*).

جاه و جلال *jāh o jalāl*, Rank and grandeur.

jāh o hasham, n. m. Rank and dignity ; (Pop.) wealth and honors.

jāh o mansab. Rank and dignity.

P جائے *jā'e, jā* ; H. *jagah*, n. f. Place ; room.

jāë etirāz. Room for objection.

jāë andeshā. Cause for apprehension.

jāë panāh, n. f. A place of refuge ; an asylum.

jāë peshah, n. m. Place of business.

jāë se yā sir, adj. Proper ; appropriate ; right.

jāë uzr. Ground of complaint or objection.

jāë wārdāt, n. f. The place where an offence is committed, or an affray has occurred.

P جائداد *jāëdād'* ; Illit. *jadād* ; E. Rus. *jajāt*, n. f. 1. Property ; an estate ; assets ; funds ; effects. 2. E. A standing crop. 3. An assignment on land (for the maintenance of troops or an establishment, or a person).

jāëdād-i-ābāī. Ancestral property or estate.

jāëdād-i-ijmālī. Joint undivided property or estate.

jāëdād ijmālī kā muqaddama. A case of joint-ownership. [perty.

جایداد اراضي *jāëdād-i-arāzī*, n. f. Landed pro-

جایداد استمراري *jāëdād-i-istimrārī*, n. f. An assignment of revenue in perpetuity, with a reservation of a certain amount of rent, and of other Government claims.

jāëdād-i-bāqī-māndah. G. G. Residuary estate.

jāëdād-i-ʻkhās, G. G. One's own property.

جائداد زوجیت *jāëdād-i-zaujīyat*, Ped. for H. *istrī-dhan*. Wife's property ; paraphernalia.

jāëdād-i-saknī. Habitable property ; houses.

jāëdād-i-shauharī. The husband's estate or property.

جایداد صحراي *jāëdād-i-sahrāī*. Forest property.

جایداد عام *jāëdād-i-ʻām*. G. G. General assets.

jāëdād-i gair-maqbūzah, Property not in possession.

jāëdād-i-gair-manqūlah, Landed or real property ; immoveable property ; realty.

jāëdād qurq k. To take property in execution ; to attach an estate.

jāëdād kā har adad. Each article of property.

جایداد مابقي *jāëdād-i-mā-baqā*. G. G. Surplus property. [heir looms.

jāëdād-i-mutaalliqa-i-khāndān. Family property ;

jāëdād-i-mutanāziā. The property in suit or dispute ; the property under litigation ; the property which is the subject of a dispute.

jāëdād marhūnah, Mortgaged land or property.

jāëdād-i-mushtarakā, yā shirkatī, Property held in partnership or common tenancy ; an estate or property held in common.

جایداد معافي *jāëdād muāfī*. Rent-free land.

jāëdād muāfī-i-hīn hayāt. A grant of land for life.

jāëdād muāfī-i-davām. A grant for ever.

jāëdād-i-muzbitāh. Confiscated property.

jāëdād-i-maqbūzah. Property in possession.

جايدادمقروقه *jāëdād-i-maqrūqa*. Attached or sequestered property.

جايداد مكسوبه *jāëdād-i-maksūbā*. Acquired, or self-acquired property. [ed property.

jāëdād-i-makfūlah, yā mustagraqa, Hypothecat-

jāëdād-i-makfūla-i-tamassuk. The property hypothecated in a bond.

جايداد منقوله *jāëdād manqūlā*. Moveable or personal property; chattels; personalties; goods; personal effects.

جايداد موروثي *jāëdād-i-maurūsī*, Ancestral property; an inherited estate.

جايداد موصى به *jāëdād-i-mūsa-bihi*. The property which is the subject of a will.

جايداد نيلامي *jāëdād-i-nīlāmī*. Property to be sold by auction. [true; right.

A جايز *jāyaz, jāiz*, adj. جوز traversed. 1. Just; 2. Lawful; legal; constitutional; consistent with law; legitimate; authorized; warranted. 3. Competent; receivable; admissible; permissible; proper; justifiable.

jāiz-ul-etirāz. Objectionable; exceptionable.

jāiz-rakhnā, v. a. 1. To recognize; admit; receive; receive as true; allow.
2. To authorize; warrant; legalize.

jāiz qarār denā, v. a. To legalize; uphold.

jāiz hai, It is admissible; granted.

جايزه *jāiz'ah*, n. m. 1. A mark (in checking an account); examination (*paṛtāl*, 1.) 2. Muster.

jāizah denā, v. a. To give an account of one's charge.

jāizah lenā, v. a. To check the entries in an account book, etc. [lawfully.

ba-tarīq-i-jāiz. G. G. In a lawful manner;

qānūnan jāiz. G. G. Legally right or justified.

kām jāiz. G. G. A lawful act.

ناجايز *nā-jāiz*, adj. Unlawful; illegal.

nā-jāiz taur se, ba-taur-i-nā-jāiz, adv. Unlawfully; illegally; improperly.

A جبر *jabr*, n. m. جبر he set (a bone). 1. Force (زبر دستي). 2. Coercion; extortion.
3. Imposition; oppression; outrage.

jabr-i-shadīd, jabr-i-azīm. Heinous violence.

jabr-i-qahrī. Duress of imprisonment by menaces and threats; *per minas*.

jabr ko amal meṅ lānā, v. n. To employ force.

jabr-i-mujrimāna. Criminal force.

jabr-i-mujrimāna k. G. G. To commit criminal force.

jabr-i-nuqsān, n. m. Recompense of loss.

jabr o taaddī. Coercive treatment; violence and oppression. [se).

جبراً *jabr'an, bil-jabr*, adv. Forcibly (*zabardastī*

jabran iqbāl karānā, v. a. To compel to certify; to extort confession.

jabran bhartī k., v. a. To press; impress.

jabran tahsīl k., v. n. To collect by coercive process.

jabran chhuṛānā, v. a. To rescue forcibly.

jabran o qahran; H. *jaise bane taise*, adv. *Per fas et nefas*; *nolens volens*; willing or unwilling; will he nil he; willy nilly.

jabran le lenā, v. n. To take by force; usurp.

jabran nikāl lejānā mastūrāt kā. Abduction of females.

qasdan jabr k., G. G Intentionally to use force.

H جتائي जुताई *jutā'ī*, n. f. H. *jotnā* to plough. Ploughing; tillage; cultivation.

جتنا जुतना *jut'nā*, v. n.
1. To be yoked, attached to.
2. To be ploughed, tilled, cultivated.

H جتها जथा *ja'thā*; n. m. S. यूथ
1. A band; gang. [flock.
2. E. A great number; mass; heap;
3. Capital; stock.
4. A coparcenary; brotherhood; a family or corporation holding lands in common.

jathā bāṅdhnā, v. a. To form a party.

jathe-vār, adj. Corporate; joint; common; belonging to proprietary families; settled or assessed according to fraternities; possessed in common.

Hججمان जिजमान *jijmān'*, n. m. S. यजमान A client to whose custom Brahmans, barbers, washermen, and some others, have a prescriptive claim.
(The hereditary Brahman, or barber, etc. of a village must be paid his fees, whether you choose to employ him or another person).

A جد *jad*, n. m. A grandfather.

jad'dī, yak-jaddī, adj. Ancestral (property).

P جدا *jud'ā*. adj. Z. *jud*. Different. See الگ 1—15.

judā-gānā. Separately; apart.

judā h. To be separate, apart from.

A جرايم *jarā'yam*, n. m. pl. of جرم—جريمه he cut it. Crimes; offences. [crimes; felony.

jarāyam-sangīn, n. m. Serious or non-bailable

jarāyam-i-khafīfa, n. m. Petty or bailable offences; light offences. [religion.

jarāyam nisbat-i-mazhab. G.G. Offences against

jarāyam muqaddamāt bagāvat yā inhirāfi, G. G. State offences.

A جرح *jar'ah*, n. m. جرح he wounded him.
1. Inflicting a wound; an offence against the person. 2. Objection; plea; argument; denial (in law). [cross-question.

jarah k., v. a. To call in question (*eterāz k.*);

jareh ke suāl. Cross examination.

A جرم *jurm*, n. m. pl. *jarāyam*. A criminal act or offence; crime; guilt; *malum prohibitum*; positive misprision; misdemeanour.
jurm-i-aulā, n. m. G. G. Positive offence.
jurm-i-sānī, n. m. G. G. Negative offence.
jurm-i-khafīf, n. m. Minor offence; a petty offence; a bailable offence.
jurm khilāf varzī sarkār. Offence against the State. [sodomy.
jurm khilāf waza-i-fitrī, An unnatural offence;
jurm se motarif h., v. n. To plead guilty.
iqdām-i-jurm, An attempt to commit a crime.
eãnat-i-jurm. Aiding and abetting criminally.
jurm se munkir h., v. n. To plead not guilty.
jurm-i-azīm, jurm-i-shadīd, jurm qābil phāṅsī, jurm-i-kabīrah, A capital crime.
jurm qubūlnā, v. n. To plead guilty.
jurm kā murtakib h., v. n. To commit or perpetrate a crime; to do a criminal act; to be an aggressor. [an offence. G. G.
jurm ke barābar ho saktā hai. May amount to
jurm kī tārīf meṅ dākhil h., v. n. To fall under the definition of an offence.
jurm mutaãliqa-i-zāt khās. An offence against the person. [property.
jurm mutaaliqa-i-māl. An offence against
jurm mutaaliqa-i-nuqsān yā izrār khās o ām. A nuisance; an offence causing hurt or annoyance to individuals or the public.
jurm muāvan-fīh. An offence abetted.
jurm munāfī mādalat-i-āmmah An offence against public justice. [infamous offence.
jurm mansūb ba-badnāmī-i-shadīd. G. G. An
jurm vājib-ul-qatl. A capital crime.
irtekāb-i-jurm. The commission of a crime.
iqbāl-i-jurm. A confession of guilt.
subūt-i-jurm. Proof of guilt.
be-jurm, adj. Innocent; guiltless (*be-gunāh*).
be jurm ṭhairānā, v. a. To declare innocent; to acquit; exculpate. [quent offence.
har jurm mukarrar. G. G. Every such subse-
sharīk-i-jurm. *Particeps criminis*; one who aids or abets in a crime; an abettor; an accomplice or accessory. [of charge.
nāmunejāt band-i-qarār-dād-i-jurm. G. G. Forms
جرمانه *jurmā'na*; Illit. *jarimānā, jarimyānā, jaribānā*, n. m. A fine; forfeit; penalty.
jurmāna bharnā, yā denā, v. n. To pay a fine.
jurmāna k., v. a. To fine; impose, levy, or inflict a fine; mulct; amerce.
jurmāna muãf k., v. a. To remit a fine.
jurmāna vusūl k., v. a. To realize a fine.
jurmāne kā koī juzv. G. G. Proportion of fine.
kisī juzv meṅ. G. G. In any part.

A جريب *jarīb'*, n. f. جريب A certain measure.

1. A measuring chain. 20 *gaṭṭhās* or 55 Government, or 60 Native yards = 1 *jarīb*; 1 square *jarīb* = 1 standard *bīgha*.
2. A land measure, the square of one *jarīb* being equal to one *Bīghā*. [768 lbs.
3. A corn measure of 384 maunds or about
4. An iron pointed spear; a staff.

جريب بيشي *jarīb beshī*, Increase of the land on the *jamã* of the current year over the past.
جريب چٹها *jarīb-i-chiṭṭhā*, n. m. A paper or record of the measurement of land.
جريب خرچ *jarīb ᵉkharch*, n. m. The charges on *measuring* land, paid usually by the Ryot or tenant to the landholder.
jarīb ḍālnā, yā pheṅknā, v. n. *lit.* To throw the *jarīb*. To measure or survey the land.
jarīb k., v. a. To make a survey (of land).
جريب کش *jarīb-kash*, n. m. *lit.* The drawer of a measuring chain. A measurer; a surveyor; land surveyor.
جريب کشي *jarīb-kashī*, n. f. Measurement or mensuration of land; the office of a land survey; a survey; revenue survey.
جريب کمي *jarīb kamī*, n. f. Decrease in the year's measurement of the Ryot's land.
جريبي *jarīb'ī*, n. f. 1. A land measurer or surveyor; 2. Whatever relates to measurement, as the cost of it, etc.
jot jarībī kā paṭṭā. A kind of lease under which the cultivator pays rent only for the ground actually cultivated, as determined by measurement.
موقوفي جريب *mauqūfī-i-jarīb*. Relinquishment or postponement of an intended survey.

A جزوي *juz'vī*, adj. Trifling; trivial; petty.
juzv-i-qarzā. G. G. Part of a debt.
juzv-i-dāvā; Part or portion of a claim.
juzvī nuqsān, n. m. Partial injury.

A جزيه *jiz'yah, jazyah*, n. m. جزي made satisfaction. [on infidels.
A capitation tax levied by Mahommedans
In Sāgar a house-tax on the inhabitants of towns not engaged in tillage.

A جعل *jaãl*; Pop. *jāl*, n. m. جعل he made (a thing). Illicit imitation; fabrication; counterfeit; forgery.
jāl banānā, yā k., v. n. To fabricate; forge.
jāl-sāz, jāliyā, n. m. A forger; one who counterfeits. [tion.
jāl-sāzī, n. f. Forgery; counterfeiting; fabrica-
jāl se, adv. Corruptly; dishonestly.
jāl se mubarrā. 1. Not forged or fabricated.
2. Sound; without flaw; genuine; true.
جعلي *jaãlī*; Pop. *jālī*, adj. 1. Forged; fabricated; fictitious; counterfeit. 2. Spurious; not genuine; false; vicious. [child.
jālī beṭā; H. *banāoṭī beṭā*, n. m. Supposititious
jālī dastāvez banānā, v. n. To forge a document.
jālī kāgaz. A forged paper or document.

P جگہ *jag'ah*; Illit. *jaghe, jagghāṅ*, n. f.
1. Place. 2. Post; office; appointment; situation; a vacancy. 3. Occasion; time.

A جلاوطن *jalā-vatan*, adj. Banished.
jalā-vatan k., des nikālā denā, v. a. To banish from one's country.
جلاوطني *jalā-vatnī*; H. *des-nikālā*, n. f. Banishment; exile.

A جلسہ *jal'sah*; Rus. *jhalsā*, n.m. جلس he sat.
1. Meeting; assembly; sitting; committee. 2. Entertainment; feast; *nautch*; dance.
jalsa-i-umarā, n. m. Senate; House of Lords.
jalsa-i-hākim, yā adālat, The bench; a tribunal.

S جلوتسرگ जलोत्सर्ग *jalotsarg'*, n. m. S. The ceremony of marrying a pond, well, grove, etc.

A جلوس *julūs'*; Rus. *jallūs*, n. m. جلس he sat. 1. Accession to a throne.
2. Retinue; court.
جلوسي *julūs'ī*, adj. Of the year or date reckoned from a prince's accession.
sann-i-julūs, n. m. The year of the king's accession to the throne.

A جماعت *jamā'āt*, n. f. جمع he collected.
1. A party of men; a company; corporation; body; society; community.
2. A meeting; gathering; assembly; convention; congregation; band; faction.
3. Companies or crafts under hereditary chiefs who, with a *panchāyat*, settle all disputes among themselves, including those of caste. *Carnegy*. 4. Group; class; rank; order; a class in a school.
jamāāt bilā sanad, G. G. Unregistered company.
jamāat-i-sanad-yāftah, G. G. An incorporated company; a corporate body.
jamāat-i-muttafaqa, An association.
jamāat-i-mamnūa. G. G. An unlawful assembly.

A جمع *jamā*, n. f. جمع collected. 1. Total; whole; aggregate; sum; total. 2. Capital; principal; (stock; assets (*pūṅjī*); fund.
3. The total amount of rent or revenue payable by a cultivator or zamīndār, including all cesses as well as land tax.
4. Outlay; cost price.
5. Receipts; collections. 6. Credit; credits; the credit side of an account.
7. Proceeds of land; the land tax; the government demand; revenue of the state.
asl jamā, n. f. The net demand.
jamā barāë kharch-i-saṛak. Road fund.
jamā-bandī, n. f. 1. Accounts of the revenue; rental; rent roll (*jamā*, 6.)
2. Assessment of the land revenue; settlement of the revenue; assessment.
jamā bandī band-o-bast. A settlement rent roll.
jamā bande mujavvazā. An authorized rent roll.
jamā bandī muqarrarah. Fixed revenue.
jamabandī naqdī. Assessment of revenue of lands payable in money, not in produce.
jama bandī yā bastī tashkhīs. Amount of revenue assessed upon any tract agreeably to a fixed standard.
jamā-bandī k. v. a. To assess revenue.
jamā bhārī, yā saṅgīn. Excessive demand; heavy or over-assessment.
jamā bharnā, v. n. To pay the rent or *jamā*.
jamā berij. A particular statement of a revenue assessment.
jamā-i-tarmīm-shudah. A revised demand or assessment.
jamā taqsīm. The portions of the general rent or revenue roll belonging to different portions of territory.
jamā jhartī. Receipts and disbursements of a village or estate; a periodical return of either cash or grain.
jamā chandīṅ. Collections or revenue from miscellaneous sources.
jamā hāsil. The total of the revenue collected.
jamā hāl, The existing demand; the present assessment or *jamā*.
jamā hisāb. Amount; total; sum.
jamā kharch, jamā o kharch, n. m. Receipts and disbursements; revenue receipts and balances; debit and credit; cash account; account current; account of collections and charges.
jamā kharch kā muāmlah, n. m. A pecuniary transaction.
jamā kharch likhnā, yā k. v. n. To draw out an account; to book.
jamā kharch milānā, v. n. To balance or make up an account.
jamā-kharch-navīs. Book-keeper; accountant.
jamā dihandī. The net estimated amount of the revenue of the whole *ḍī* or *taraf*. *Carnegy*.
jamā dihātī. Settlement of the proportion of revenue to be paid by each village severally.
jamā raiyatī. The rent paid by a tenant cultivator.
jamā raqmī. 1. An estimate or computed total.
2. The total amount of revenue which an estate or district is estimated to yield.
jamā rakhā gayā. Kept in deposit.
jamā zamīn, n. Land, of which the assessment has been settled; land paying revenue.

As applied to an under-tenure it means one in which the revenue has been settled at a fixed rate on the land, irrespective of cultivation.

jamā sarkār. The Government *jama* or revenue; revenue of the state.
jamā sadr. The revenue assessment settled with the Government direct by the proprietors or contractors, in contradistinction to the *jama mufassal*.
jamā saṅgīn bāṅdhnā, v. a. To over assess.

jamā qadīm. The total amount of revenue as fixed from an old date. [sessment.

jamā kāmil. Complete, final, or standard as-

In Bengal the term usually denotes the settlement made by Akbar's financial minister Todar Mal.

jamā k., v. a. 1. To gather together; accumulate; heap; amass.

2. To lay by; lay up; store up.

3. To add together; add; cast up; sum up. 4. To collect; assemble; call in; raise; levy. 5. To deposit; credit; carry to credit or account. [2. A depositor.

jama karne-vālā, n. m. 1. One who collects.

jamā-kul, adv. Altogether. [sessment.

jamā kul, n. f. The total amount of revenue as-

jamā-koṭhī. Bank stock; the assets of a firm.

jamā mahāl-i-mīr-bahr. Port duties, or an account of them.

jamā murakkab, n. f. Compound addition.

jamā mushakhkhasah. Amount of assessment; estimated capital.

jamā vāsil bāqī. Payments and arrears; revenue receipts and balances.

jamā mufassal. n. f. 1. The aggregate amount of the different sources of revenue.

2. The gross revenue to be collected in all the villages of a *zamīndārī*, as rated in the accounts, and to be paid after deducting charges to the *zamīndār*.

jamā muqarrar. A fixed or permanent amount of revenue, an account formerly kept by the *Kanūṅgo* of lands permanently assessed.

jamā munāsib, A fair or reasonable amount of assessment.

jamā nāqis. The sum total of deficiencies; the amount of allowed deductions from the revenue or account of public expenses borne by the *zamīndārs* and tenants.

jamā wusūl. An abstract of collections and disbursements.

jamā wāsil bāqī-navīs. A Government clerk whose duty it is to prepare the *jamā wāsil bāqī*.

jamā-vālā, n. m. A capitalist.

jamā honā, v. n. To be collected; to assemble.

jamā hone kī jagah. A place of resort or assembly; a centre; nucleus.

āsāmī-vār jamā-bandī. An account of revenue assessments settled with each individual cultivator.

jins-vār jamā-bandī. Account of revenue assessed at certain rates, according to the produce or crops raised. [than the land tax.

sivāī jamā. Revenue raised from other sources

khet-vār jamā-bandī. An account of revenue assessed at a certain rate per field.

It shows the name of every cultivator, the fields he cultivates, and their size, with the rate, and the amount he is to pay. The primary arrangement is under *Lambardārs*, whose *sir* comes first, then the *sir* of the *Paṭṭīdārs*, then the subordinate holdings, and next the fields cultivated by tenants at 'fixed rates, and by tenants at will. It forms the basis of the *Paṭwārī's* annual papers.

qism-vār jamā-bandī. Statement of revenue assessed at certain rates, according to the quality of the soil.

جمعدار *jamādār'*, n. m. The chief or leader of any number of persons; a native subaltern officer, second to the *Sūbedār*; an officer of police, customs, or excise, second to the *Dārogā*.

جمعداري *jamā-dārī*, n. f. The office of a *jamādār*.

H جمنوتا जमनौटा *jamnau'ṭā, jamnauṭiyā*, n. m. A certain consideration given to a *zāmin* or surety, generally amounting to about five per cent.

jamnau'ṭiā, n. An allowance of about five per-cent to a security. *Carnegy.*

جموا जमोआ *jamo'ā*, n. 1. The small *jāman*, q. v.

2. Indigo planted before the rains and irrigated by artificial means.

P. & H جموگ نامه जमोग नामा *jamog-nāmā*, n. m. A deed of transfer of liabilities, as in the case of a loan contracted by a land holder, for which he transfers to the lender the rents of his tenants. [gether.

A جمهور *jamhūr'*, n. m. جمهر he collected to-

A community; a whole people or nation; a republic.

jamhūrī ryāsat, yā saltanat; H. *panchāetī rāj*, n. f. A republic; democracy.

H جنی जनी *jan'nī*; Mār. *jamaṅṛ*, n. f. S. जननी

A mother; the actual mother of a child, in contradistinction to a step mother.

A جناب *janāb'*, n. f. Your Honor.

janāb-i-man. Dear Sir. [excellency, or majesty.

جناب عالي *janāb-i-ālī.* Exalted Sir; Your or his

A جنس *jins*, n. f. 1. Articles; wares; merchandise. 2. Grain; corn; crops; products. 3. Moveables.

jins kāmil yā ʻālī. First rate crops; the best crop that a field can produce; any article of superior description.

jins-vār. adj. 1. Classified. 2. Detailed; miscellaneous. 3. Relative to crops.

jins-vār jamā-bandī. A detailed statement of the rent levied upon each kind of crop.

jins-vār khataunī. An account of the portions of an estate in which the lands are classed together according to their crops.

P جنگ *jang*, n. f. War; battle (*laṛāī*).

jang-i-zargarī, n. f. A collusive dispute between two parties to defraud a third.

malkā muazzimā ke muqabil meṅ jang, G. G. v. a. To wage war against the Queen.

H & P جنگل जङ्गल *jaṅ'gal,* n. m. S. जङ्गल.
1. A wood; forest; jungle; forest land.
2. Waste land; untilled land.
3. Pasturage; grazing ground.

jaṅgal sāf k., v. a. To clear land.
jaṅgal-burī, n. f. The act of clearing wood lands.
jangal-burī taalluqā. An estate or tract of land overrun with jangle, held on easy terms on condition of its being cleared.
jangal-tarī, n. Low forest land lying under a range of hills.
jangal-mahāl. Forest tract or estate, applied especially to the districts on the west of Bengāl between it, and Behar and Cuttack.
atīya-i-jangal o vīrān. Grant of jungle and waste lands.
mahkama-i-jaṅglāt, Forest department.

H جنم जनम *jan'am, janm;* Rus. *jaram, jalam,* n. m. S. जन्मन् birth, Pr. *jammo.*
1. Birth; nativity. 2. Life; existence; age.

janam-bāolā, janam kā pāgal, yā siṛī, n. m. A born idiot; a natural. [insanity.

A جنون *junūn',* n. m. Lunacy; madness;
junūn chaṛhnā, yā honā, v. n. To become mad.
junūn-daurī, n. m. Lunacy with lucid intervals.
junūn kī hālat, yā galbe meṅ, adv.
Under the influence of madness or a fit of temper.
جنوني *junūn'ī,* adj. Mad; insane; *non compos;* of unsound or abnormal mind; lunatic.

A جنين *janīn';* H. *kachchā,* n. m. Fœtus; embryo; an unborn child.
janīn ko zarar pahuṅchānā. G. G. To injure an unborn child.

H جنيوا जनेवा *janev'ā,* n. f. The *dūb* grass; *Agrostis linearis,* Wat.; a fragrant grass which grows with *kharīf* crops.

H جو जौ *jau,* n. m. S. यव, Pahlvī, *jov.*
1. Barley; a barley-corn.

jau-chane, n. m. *bejhaṛ,* n. f. A mixture of gram and barley.
javā'lā, javālī, adj. Mixed barley and wheat.
جونچي जौंची *jauṅ'chī,* n. A kind of smut in barley and wheat in which the ears are empty.

H جوا जूआ *jū'ā,* n. m. S. द्यूत, Pālī. *jūtam, jūto, jeu,* Gambling; gaming; playing with dice.
juā khelnā, v. n. To gamble; to play dice.
جواري जुआरी *juār'ī, jue-bāz;* P. *qimār-bāz,* n. m. A gambler.
جويخانه जुयखाना *juē-khānah;* P. *qimār-khānā,* n. m. A gambling-house.

A جواب *javāb;* Rus. *juāb, jubāb,* n. m. 1. Counterpart; correspondent part; double; pair.
2. Answer; reply; retort; rejoinder; defence.
3. Reward; compensation (*ajar*).
4. Discharge; dismissal.
5. Refusal of an offer of marriage.

javāb-ul-javāb, n. m. The rejoinder or reply.
javāb bā-savāb, n. m. A good or proper answer.
javāb-dāvā, n. m. The answer to a plaint, charge, or accusation.
javāb dugānah. A double defence. [countable.
javāb-deh, adj. Answerable; responsible; ac-
javāb-deh, n. m. A defendant; respondent.
javāb-dehī, n. f. Liability; responsibility.
javāb-dehī se barī, yā barī-ul-zimmā k., v. a. To relieve or discharge from liabilities; to exonerate. [from liabilities.
javāb-dehī se chhūṭnā, v. n. To be discharged
javāb-dehī k., javāb dehī-i-nālish k., javāb k., v. a. To contest a claim; to defend an action.
javāb denā, v. a. 1. To answer; reply.
2. To be accountable for; account for; to be amenable or responsible.
3. To discharge; dismiss; disband.
4. To desert; abandon.

javāb savāl, n. m. Question and answer; disputation (*bahs*). [(*bahsnā*).
javāb savāl k., v. a. To reason; dispute, etc.
PHR. To take one's stand upon; chop logic; try conclusions.
javāb shāfī, yā sāf. See *do ṭūk javāb.*
javāb-talab, adj. 1. Requiring an answer; called to account. 2. Questionable. [impeach.
javāb talab k., v. a. To call to account;
javāb qatai, n. m. A conclusive or definite answer.
javāb kā javāb denā, v. a. To make a rejoinder.
javāb muddāilah. A defence; an answer put in by a defendant.
javāb-i-mūjibāt yā vajūhāt. An answer to a petition of appeal, or to the arguments for an appeal to be filed by the respondent.
javāb-savālī. An agent or attorney.
javāb'ī, n. m. 1. Counterpart (*javāb,* 1). (dent.
2. A defendant (*muddāalah*); a respon-

H جوارا जुआरा *juār'ā,* n. m. 1. As much land as can be ploughed by a pair of bullocks; (*In Delhī*) the area ploughed in half a day. [a well.
2. A yoke or pair of bullocks working

A جواز *javāz',* n. m. جوز was current or lawful. Propriety; competency; lawfulness; legality; validity. [of evidence.
javāz-i-shahādat. Competency of a witness, or
javāz honā, v. n. To be lawful or allowable.
ādam-javāz, n. Invalidity.

adām-javāz, adj. Unlawful; illegal.
kisī amar ke javāz meṅ kalām k., v. n. To question the validity of something; to call the legality of a thing into question.
جوازي *javāzī*, n. Legality; validity.

H جوانسا जवांसा *jaṅvāṅ'sā*, n. m. S. यवास
A scented prickly shrub, given to camels, and sometimes used as *khas* for *ṭaṭṭīs*.

P جواني *javān'ī*, n.f. 1. Youth; manhood; adolescence; prime. 2. Puberty; the age of discretion; full age.
javānī chaṛhnā, v. n. 1. To arrive at the age of puberty. 2. To be in heat or ruttish.

H جوت जोत *jot*, n. f. S. योक्त्र, H. *jotnā* to yoke, plough. 1. Ploughing; tillage; cultivation. 2. A cultivated tract; the holding or tenure of a cultivator. 3. The rent paid by a cultivator.
4. Land held of a superior on the terms of a tenant cultivator, enjoying no proprietary rights, although sometimes holding at a fixed rate and sometimes hereditarily. *Wilson.*
jot-bot; P. *kāsht*; A. *zarāat*, Tillage; husbandry.
jot-jamā. The land cultivated, and assessment paid by the cultivator.
be-jot, A. *gair-mazrūa*, adj. Uncultivated, untilled (land).
be-jot jamā. A statement in the public account of the revenue leviable on the land left untilled.
be-jot zamīn, Land abandoned or untilled, as registered in the village accounts.
nij-jot; P. *khud-kāsht*, n. f. The lands of cultivating proprietors.
جوتا जोता *jot'ā*, *jotār*, *jotyā*, *jotan-hāṛ*, *jotū*, *jotādār*; P. *kāshtkār*, A. *mazārī*, n.m. A ploughman; a cultivator; husbandman.
jutāū, *jot jog*, *jotne lāyaq*, adj. Arable; culturable.
jutā'ī, n. f. 1. Ploughing; tillage; cultivation. 2. Cohabitation.

H جوتنا जोतना *jot'nā*, *jotnā bonā*, v. n. युज to yoke. 1. To plough; till. 2. To bring into cultivation; to reclaim land. 3. To yoke; harness. 4. To win or buy over.
jotī bhūm, A. *zamīn-i-mazrūa*, Ploughed land.

H جوٹ जोट *joṭ*, n. m. 1. One of a pair; a mate; match; fellow.
2. A pair of oxen used in ploughing, etc.

H جورو जोरू *jor'ū*; Wom. *jurvā*, n. f. S. जाया, H. *joṛā* match. A wife; consort.

H جوكهوں जोखों *jokh'oṅ*; Tir. and Mag. *jokhim*, n. f. 1. Risk; hazard; stake; venture.
2. Any valuables, as jewels, money, etc.
3. Insurance (*bīmā*).

P جولان *jaulāṅ'*, n. Irons; fetters (*beṛī*, 1).
pā ba-jaulāṅ, adv. With fetters.

H جونار जेानार *jaunār'*, *jeonār*; Māṛ. *jimnār*; Farrukh. *jyunār*, n.f. H. *jīmnā* to eat. A feast (*zyāfat*); dinner; entertainment banquet.

H جونال जौनाल *jaunāl'*, *jaunār*, n. m.
1. Land cultivated alternately for spring and autumn crops (Rohilkhund).
2. Land cropped during the past season with wheat and barley (Dehlī).

H جونڈا जौंडा *jauṅ'ḍā*, *ḍāmchā*, *machān*, n. m.
A raised platform about ten feet high whence cattle and tall crops are watched.

H جهابر झाबर *jhāb'ar*, *jhādā*, n. f. Marshy land; fen. See *Carnegy* p. 151.
jhāṛ-khanḍ, n. m. A forest; jungle.
جهاڑي झाड़ी *jhāṛ'ī*; Māṛ. *jhaṅgī*, n. f.
Forest; wood; jungle.

H جهاڑا झाड़ा *jhāṛ'ā*, n. m. 1. Sweeping; cleansing; clearing. 2. Search (of the person).

P جهازي *jahāz'ī*, adj. Naval; nautical.
jahāzī iqrār-nāmah. Charter party.
jahāzī tijārat. Carrying trade; commerce.
jahāzī ḍākū yā chor, n. m. A privateer.

H جهٹل झुट्टल *jhuṭ'ṭal*, adv. H. *jhūṭ* falsehood. For love, not for money.

A جهد *jah'ad*, *jahd*, n. m. Effort; exertion; attempt; endeavour.
jahad-i-irtikāb, G. G. Attempting to commit.

H جهرنا झुरना *jhur'nā*, v. n. S. ज्ञूर to be decayed. To have the green sickness, or *fluor albus*.

H جهوٹ झूट *jhūṭ*, *jhūṭh*, *jhūṅṭ*, n. m. S. कूट
A falsehood; a lie.
جهوٹا झूटा *jhūṭ'ā*, *jhūṭī*, adj. 1. False; untrue.
2. Unsound; not sound; invalid.
3. Not genuine; counterfeit; imitation.
4. (*jhuṭṭā*) Alloyed; base; debased; not pure; false (lace, etc.).
5. Fictitious; invented; forged; artificial.
jhūṭā baṭ yā paimānā. False weights or measure.
jhūṭā banānā yā k., v. a. To belie; falsify; disprove.
jhūṭā rupaiyā, *yā sikkā*, n. m. False or bad coin.
jhūṭā kāgaz, *yā dastāvez*, n. A forged or false document.
jhūṭā kāgaz banānā, v. a. To fabricate; forge.
jhūṭī saugand, *yā qasam*, n. f. A false oath; perjury.
jhūṭī gavāhī, *yā sākshī*, n. f. False testimony or evidence; false deposition.
jhūṭī gavāhī denā, v. a. To fabricate false evidence.

jhūṭī gavāhī kī sazā. G. G. Punishment for false evidence.
jhūṭī nālish, n. f. *jhūṭā muqadmā*, n. m. Groundless or idle suit; false charge or complaint.

H جهوتهن झूठन *jhūṭh'an, jhūṭan, jhuṭhūl*, n. f. Land yielding a double crop.

H جهورا झोरा *jhor'ā*; Bhoj. *jheṅgrā*, n. The stalks of leguminous plants, as *mūṅg* and *moṭh*, used as fodder.

جهوک چهٹي *jhok chiṭṭhī*, n. f. A fraudulent note of hand, cheque or bill.
jhok mārnā, ṭāl mārnā, v. n. To give a twist to the beam of a scale (*ḍanḍī mārnā*).

H جهونتهر झूँथर *jhūṅthar*, n. Land yielding two crops.

H جهونڈي توڑ झूँडीतोड़ *jhūṅḍī-toṛ, jhāṛ ṭārnā.*
1. Breaking tufts of grass, etc.
2. Clearing a piece of jungle for cultivation.

A جهيز *jahez'*; Illit. *dahez, dahej*; H. *dān*, n. m. جهز supplied to a bride. S. यौतुक A bride's portion; dower; dowry; *paraphernalia.*

A جيب *jeb*, n. f. 1. A pocket (*gojhā*); a fob.
2. Possession.
jeb-kharch, n. m. Pocket money; pin money.
jeb-katrā, n. m. A pick-pocket.
jeb katarnā, v. a. To pick one's pocket.

H جيتا जीता *jīt'ā.*; Tir. *jiul, ḍakosrā*, n. m. Mutual assistance in tillage; allowing the use of a plough and bullocks instead of paying wages in money or kind.
jīte jī tak kā qabzā. A life tenure.

H جيٹھ जेठ *jeṭh*, n. m. S. ज्येष्ठ 1. The husband's elder brother (*jeṭhā bhāī*).
2. The Hin. month of May—June.
jeṭh-ansī, n. The right of the eldest son; the right of primogeniture.
jeṭhī dhān. Rice sown in April along the banks of rivers, or where water is still lying, and cut in *jeṭh* (the beginning of June).
jeṭh raiyat, n. The *raiyat* who acts as *chaudharī*, in rank below the *muqaddam*. Oudh. *Carnegy.*
jeṭhī sāwan. n. m. An early *Sāwan* crop. Oudh.

جيٹها जेठा *jeṭh'ā*, adj. 1. Best; principal; highest; first-rate. 2. The first-born; eldest.
3. One born in the month of Jeṭh.

H جيچي जैची *jai'chī, jai*, n. f. A weed which grows up with the spring crops, and yields a kind of oil.

A جيد *jaiy'ad*, adj. 1. Large; spacious.
2. Good; fertile; productive.

P جيلخانه *jel-*khānah*, n. m. A jail; prison.
jel-khāna-i-dīvānī. A civil jail; debtors' prison.
jel-khāna-i-faujdārī. A criminal jail.
jel-khane kā hukm. A *mittimus.*
jel-khāne kā dārogā. A gaoler.

H جيوائي जीवाई *jīvā'ī*; Tir. *jibikā*; Mār. *jivarī*, n. f. Rent-free land; land assigned as subsistence to relations and dependants.
jīv-dhan, Wealth in flocks and herds.
jīv-ḍanḍ, n. m. Capital punishment.

جيوت जीवत *jīv'at, jīvatvān*, adj. Living; alive.

جيون जीवन *jīv'an*, n. f. 1. Life. 2. Livelihood.
jīvan birt. A stipend allowed to the family of an old servant deceased. Oudh.

H جيهن जैहन *jai'han*, n. m. Nursery rice.

چ

H چاپ चाप *chāp*, n. The refuse of the *jhaṛberī*, q. v. after the *pālā* is beaten from it.

چادر اتارنا *chādar utārnā*, v. a.
1. To take off a woman's veil.
2. To insult or disgrace (a woman).
chādar ḍālnā yā uṛhānā, Rus. v. a.
To marry a widow.

چار کاغذ *chār kāgaz, kavāgaz-i-araba*, n. m.
The proceedings in a case; viz. plaint, defence, replication, and rejoinder; the pleadings.

P چاکري *chāk'rī*, n. f. A grant for personal services in the village; service land.

P چالاک *chālāk'*; Illit. *chalāk*, adj. 1. Expert.
chālāk log. Sharpers; swindlers.

چالاکي *chālāk'ī*, n. f. 1. Expertness; dexterity; skill. 2. Cleverness; sharpness; wit; tact.
3. Stratagem; manœuvre; finesse.
4. Sharp practice; over-reaching; trickery; craft; fraud.
chālākī se, adv. By unfair means; fraudulently; dishonestly.
chālākī k., v. a. 1. To be beforehand with; to overreach. 2. To elude or avoid by artifice.

H چالان चालान *chālān'*; Illit. *chalān*, n. m. S. चल to more. 1. A list of letters sent; a certificate of despatch; invoice; way-bill; bill of lading. 2. A remittance. 3. A memorandum of money received and invested.
4. A pass; passport; clearance (of a ship).
5. A criminal case sent up to the Magistrate by the police.

chālān-dār, n. The person who accompanies a despatch or remittance and has charge of the invoice; an escort. [despatched.
chālān kīyā jānā, v. n. 1. To be forwarded or 2. To be committed for trial or prison.

چالي चाली *chāl'ī*; Tir. *chacharī*, n. f. A detachment or party of men told off for any duty.

H چالي चाली *chāl'ī*, n. f. Land that bears the highest rate of assessment, cultivated by the permanent inhabitants of the village agreeably to allotment, by which each cultivator has a fixed proportion of the lands of the highest, medium, and lowest assessment. *Wilson.*

H چانچري चांचरी *chāṅch'rī*, *bhuṛārī*, n. f. The corn which remains in the ear after treading out. *Carnegy.*

H چاندا चांदा *chāṅd'ā*, n. m. Forming the ends of the main lines from which the village boundaries are laid down.

H چانک चांक *chāṅk*, *chāṅkā*, *chāk*, *chāmp*, *chhāpā*, n. m. 1. A stamp or mark. See *thāp.* 2. The ceremony so-called. See *Carnegy*, p. 75.

H چانول चांवल *chāṅ'val*, *chāval'*; E. *chāur*; Sant. *tāben*, n. m. S. तण्डुल
1. Rice separated from the husk.
2. One eighth of a *rattī*, q. v.

chāṅval chabvānā, v. a. To cause persons suspected of theft to chew uncooked rice, a deficiency of saliva being held to indicate the thief.

P چاه *chāh*, n. m. A well (*kūāṅ*).

چاهي *chā'hī*, *chāhī zamīn*, n. f. Land irrigated from wells, etc. [n. m. S. चत्वर.

H چبوترا चबूतरा *chabūt'rā*; Pop. *chauṅtrā*,
1. A raised bank or terrace open or covered, detached from the residence; a platform.
2. A police station (*kotvālī*).

chabūtrā baṅdhnā, v. n. (*Slang*). To be big with child; to be near one's time; to be pregnant.
chabūtre chaṛhānā, v. a. To convey to the Police station.

P چپراس *chaprās'*, n. f. Cor. of *chap o rāst* right and left. A plate worn on a belt as a mark of office; the badge of a peon.

چپراسي *chaprās'ī*, n. m. A peon; orderly; beadle; messenger of a court.
chaprāsī-i-adālat. A bailiff; a process server.

H چتا चिता *chit'ā*; Sant. *sārā*, n. f. S. चि to pile, Pālī, *chitako.* A funeral pyre; a heap of wood in which a Hin. corpse is burnt.

chitā-piṇḍ, n. m. S. चितापिण्ड An offering of cakes, rice, milk, etc. to the manes during cremation.

H چٹھا चिट्ठा *chiṭ'ṭhā*, n. m. S. चिट to send out a messenger. A rough note, draft or account; a memorandum; a list; schedule; bill of charges; a list of subscriptions; a journal or day book; balance sheet; servants' pay or rations.

☞ A detailed statement of the measurement of a *zamīndar's* estate founded on actual measurement. It is also applied to an account of all the lands in a village, divided numerically into *dāghs* or shares, shewing the quantity of land in each, the sort of cultivation, and the name of the cultivator. Also a field book, more usually termed *khasra*, being an account of all the lands of a village, according to their allotment, in the order in which they have been measured.

chiṭṭhā bāṅdhnā, v. a. 1. To draw up a rough memorandum or account; to balance accounts. 2. To calculate; estimate.
chiṭṭhā bāṅṭnā, v. a. To pay; give pay to; to pay laborers. [balance.
chiṭṭhā bahī, n. f. Trial balance-sheet; trial
chiṭṭha-i-taqsīm, n. A partition list. [scription.
chiṭṭhā k., *chandā k.*, v. a. To raise a sub-

چٹھي चिट्ठी *chiṭ'ṭhī*, n. f. 1. A letter; chit; note; communication. 2. A certificate. 3. A cheque; scrip; promissory note; bill (*huṇḍī*); draft. 4. An order; a license; pass.
chiṭṭhī ittilāī. The advice of a bill. [credit.
chiṭṭhī etebārī; H. *sākhī chiṭṭhī*, n. A letter of
chiṭṭhiyāṅ chhāṅṭnā, v. a. To sort letters.
chiṭṭhī bāṅṭnā, v. a. 1. To distribute letters for delivery. 2. To deliver letters.
chiṭṭhī bahī. Letter-registry book.
chiṭṭhī pātī, *chapātī*, *yā patrī*, n. f. Epistolary correspondence; communications.
chiṭṭhī pahuṅchā'nā, v. a. To deliver a letter.
chiṭṭhī ḍāl'nā yā gernā, v. a. To make a lottery or raffle.
chiṭṭhī ḍālne ke tarīqe se. G. G. By lottery.
chiṭṭhī rāh-dārī. A passport; custom; pass; certificate of clearance. [A postman.
chiṭṭhī-rasāṅ, Ped. for *ḍākiyā*, *khat-vālā*, n. m.
chiṭṭhī kā khel, n. m. Lottery.
chiṭṭhī kī pusht par khulāsah likh'nā. To docket.
chiṭṭhī lagānā, *ḍālnā*, *yā gernā*, v. n. To post a letter.
inkārī chiṭṭhī, A refused letter.
be-pate kī chiṭṭhī. Dead letter. [dealers).
chhar chiṭṭhī, n. f. A custom's pass (to salt-
ravāngī chiṭṭhī, Port clearance.
sufārshī chiṭṭhī, n. f. A letter of introduction or recommendation.
nikāsī chiṭṭhī, A certificate of clearance.
nek-nāmī kī chiṭṭhī. A certificate; testimonial.
vāpsī chiṭṭhī, A returned letter.

hāth kī chitthī. 1. A letter under one's own hand. 2. A note of hand.

H چٹيل चटियल *chaṭ'yal, chat'tial*, n. One who collects rents from cultivators for the owner. In E. Oudh, the usual name is *zilādār*. Carnegy.

H چچر चचर *cha'char, chāchar*, n. f. Land ploughed or cultivated once in the year.

H چڑسال चडसाल *chaḍ-sāl'*, The year in which a maximum amount of revenue is derived.

P چراگاہ *charā-gāh'*; H. *charāī*, n. f. Grazing land; pasture.

H چرانا चुराना *churā'nā*; Bhoj. *chorāval*; Sant. *kombro*, v. a. S. चुर to steal; Pālī, *choretī*.
1. To steal; commit theft.
2. To embezzle; misappropriate.

H چرائي चराई *charā'ī*, n. f.
1. Sending out cattle to graze.
2. (P. *charā-gāh*). Grazing ground; grass land; pasturage; a meadow. [ing fee.
3. Rent derived from pasturage. 4. Graz-

P چرخ *char'kh*, n. m. S. चक्र The celestial globe; heavenly sphere; the sky; the heavens.

charkh-pūjā, Cor. of *chakr-pūjā*. A ceremony observed by the lower orders of Hindus in Bengal, on the day when the sun enters Aries, for the expiation of their sins.

The performer is suspended by an iron hook passed through the skin of the back to one end of the lever, which is raised on the top of a high pole and whirled round by means of a rope fixed to the other end. This penance is performed for rich people by deputy.

charkh-shumārī, Literally "counting of Persian wheels." The name given to the book in which a register is kept of wheels, or of lands cultivated each season in each *deh* or village.

H چرس चरस *har'as, charsā*, n. m. S. चर्म skin.
1. A large leathern bag or bucket used for drawing water from wells (*pur, moṭ*). 2. (n. f.) The resinous exudation of the flowers of hemp collected with the dew and prepared for use as an intoxicating drug.

چرسا चरसा *char'sā*, n. m. A buffalo or ox hide.

charsā bhar zamīn, As much land as can be irrigated by one pair of bullocks.

H چرواہا चरवाहा *charvā'hā, churvāyā, charaiyā*, n. m. S. चर to eat. वह to carry.
A grazier; a herdsman.

چرواہي चरवाही *charvā'hī, charvāī*, n. f.
1. The wages of a herdsman in grain.
2. The rent paid for pasturage.

H چڑھ चढ़ *charh*, n. f. Alluvial land; alluvion.

H چڑھانا चढ़ाना *charhā'nā*; Rus. *chaḍhānā*; Sant. *charhao*, v. a. Opp. of *utārnā*. S. उच्चर To put down; enter; enroll. [roll.

tauzī men charhānā, v. a. To bring on the rent-

charh'tī, charhāvā, charhti lagān, Settlement of revenue at a progressively increasing rate.

چڑھاوا चढ़ावा *charhā'vā*, n. m.
An offering; libation; sacrifice.

P چسپاں *chaspān'*, adj. Applicable (*ṭhīk*, 4, 6).

chaspān k., v. a. To affix (as a summon to the door of an absentee); to paste.

E چک *chik*, n. m. Cor. of cheque.
A money order. [cheque book).

chik kā miltā huā ṭukrā. The counterfoil (of a

H چک चक *chak*, n. m. S. चक्र 1. Tenure; holding; farm; cultivation; a separate estate; a sub-division of land; a patch of rent-free land. 2. A sub-division of a *Parganā*.

chak barār, n. m. 1. Collecting the rents of a *chak*. 2. Alluvion.

chak-bast. A definite portion of land.

chak-bandī, n. f. Determining the limits or boundaries of a detached piece of land, estate, or *chak*.

chakdār', n. m. The owner of a *chak*; a farmer.

chak-nāmā, n. m. A register of the extent of a piece of land.

A plan drawn up by the *Qānūngo* for each village *asli* and *dākhili*, showing its boundaries on every side. Also a deed, or statement, showing the area and boundaries of a *chak*.

chak-nāmā arāzī, A document given to a *zamīndār* from whom a portion of land has been taken by the Government for public or other purposes, defining the extent, boundaries, and quality of the land.

H چکانا चुकाना *chukā'nā, chuktā k,*; Bhoj. *chukādihal*; Rus. *chukāuṛān*; Sant. *halā*, v. a.
1. To pay off; repay; discharge (a debt); liquidate. 2. To assign; allot; give.
3. To assess; rate; value; estimate.
4. To settle (the price); fix; bargain.
5. To adjust (an account); arrange; decide; settle differences.
6. To complete; finish (*adā k.*, 1.).

chukāne ko taiyār h., v. n. To tender payment; to offer to pay.

lekhā chukā. Accounts adjusted.

چکاؤ चुकाऊ *chukā'ū*, n. m. 1. One who settles rates, bargains, etc. 2. One ready to pay.

چکائي चुकाई *chukāī*, n. f. Settlement; adjustment. [clusive. 2. Wholesale.

چکتا चुकता *chuk'tā*, adj. 1. Settled; fixed; con-

H چکت चक्कत *chak'kat*, n. m. (Opp. of *ritkat*). The loss of a whole plot of ground by diluvion. *Carnegy.*

chuk'ti, n. f. Cultivating tenancy, under which a given area is rented at a certain stated sum on the *bilmuqtā* principle. *Carnegy.*

H چکلا चकला *chak'lā*, n. m.

1. A division of a country district.

A large division of country, comprehending a number of Parganas first introduced as a recognised local division in the reign of Shah Jahan.

2. Any quarter of a town, especially the prostitutes' quarter.

chaklā-bandī, n. f. The distribution of a Zamīndāri or of a province into *chaklās*, especially for financial convenience.

chakle-dār, n. m. The governor or superintendant of a province or *chaklā*; the superintendant, proprietor, or renter of a *chaklah.*

H چکنوت चिकनौट *chiknauṭ*, n. f. 1. A clayey soil. 2. Rich, highly cultivated land.

H چکوتا चकौता *chakau'tā, chukautī, chukat*, n. m. 1. A fixed rate; a contract; bargain. 2. A settlement or composition of a debt (*adā*, 1.) 3. A deed of acquittance.

chakautā chukā'nā, v. a. To pay what is due.

chakautā chuk'nā, v. n. 1. To be fixed or settled. 2. To be paid up.

H چکوند चकवंद *chak'vand*; Bhoj. *chakaṅvaṛ*, n. f. A common weed, bearing a long legume growing from eight inches to two feet high, used by the poor as a potherb.

H چکھر चिखर *chikh'ar*; Bhoj. *chalaunsī*, n. The husk of *chanā*, good fodder for cattle.

H چکھروای चिखरवाई *chikharvā'ī*, Oudh, n. f. Wages for weeding (*nalāī*).

H چگائی चुगाई *chugā'ī*; Sant. *atin*, n. f.

1. Grazing; pasturage. 2. The fee or rent paid for pasturage.

H P چلارخرچ *chilar-kharch.* A heading in the village accounts, comprising money grants for *devasthān, teohār, dargāh, urs, masjid,* village priests, *sadar-kharch*, stationary, oil, and other petty miscellaneous items. [rupee.

H چلکی चिलकी *chil'kī*, n. m. (*Brokers*) A

H چلتا चलता *chal'tā, chaltī*, adj. 1. Now passing; current. 2. Current; in vogue.

chaltā kharch, n. m. Current expenses.

chaltā lekhā, chaltā khātā yā hisāb, n. m. Open account; account current.

chaltā hai, Is current; is in operation.

chaltī chīz, n. f. Saleable goods; goods in brisk demand (opp. of *mandā*).

چلتی चलती *chal'tī, chaltā, chaltā-huā*, n. f.

1. (Opp. of *partī.*) Lands under cultivation.
2. Potent; powerful; effective.

چلتی चलती *chaltī*, n. f. 1. Access; reach; hold; grasp; grip. 2. Competency; jurisdiction; authority; power; influence; ascendancy. 3. Active trade. [personal property.

chaltī yā uṭhāū jāēdād. Rare. Moveable or

chaltī dūkān, n. f. A thriving business.

chaltī zamīn. Land under cultivation.

chalan'tā, n. m. Duties formerly levied by *zamindars* on goods passing through their jurisdiction.

H چلوائی चिलवाई *chilvā'ī*; Sant. *ḍhula marom*, n. f. The turf or rushes on which the bucket, when drawn up from the well, rests, and which therefore becomes sloppy.

H چلی चुल्ली *chul'lī*, n. f. Supports placed beneath stacks of straw or stores of grain, called by English farmers staddles.

In some places the ground is merely cleaned and elevated and no supports raised. It is then called *ghai. Carnegy.* [*maṭ rahnā*, v. n.

H چمٹنا चिमटना *chimaṭ'nā, chipaṭ'nā, chi-*

1. To have sexual intercourse with; make an indecent assault.
2. To charge falsely.

H چمکنا चमकना *chamak'nā*, v. n. 1. To do well; thrive; prosper; flourish. 2. To be lively (the market), in good demand.

H چنچر चन्चर *chan'char*, n. m. Land left untilled for a year or two, land in the second year of tillage.

P چند *chand*, adj. Some; few; several.

chand bināē dāvā qarār denā. To divide a cause of action.

chand-roza, adj. Temporary; transitory.

qabza-i-chand rozah, n.m. Temporary possession.

چندہ *chand'ah*; H. *chiṭṭhā*, n. m. 1. Quota; subscription; contribution. 2. Assessment; in police accounts, the fund for remounts.

chandā-ugāhī, n. f. Levy of rent or revenue from the *Raiyats* according to their shares or proportions.

chandā k., v. a. To raise a subscription.

H چنگی चुंगी *chun'gī*, n. f. H. *chuṭkī* a pinch. Weighman's fees: a cess levied from grain-sellers, etc.; town duties (*puun-totī*).

☞ A handful of grain levied as a tax or fee for weighing, or as a compensation for the use or market conveniences, as bags, booths, etc. Similar contributions to religious mendicants or an allowance to *zamindars* for establishing a new market or permitting a fair to be held.

chungī-penṭh, n. A market or fair held on the tenure of giving a small portion of each saleable article to the *zamindār*.

H چنيادا चनियादा *chaniyā'dā*, Rohilkhand; *chanial*, Delhī. n. Land under a crop of *chanā* (gram).

H چو चौ *chau*; Sant. *poneyā*, n. m. H. *chār* four.
A clamp round the ploughshare.

چوباچھ चौबाछ *chau-bāchh*, n. m. Four taxes formerly levied under Native rule, viz. *pāg*, *tāg*, *kūṛī*, and *puchchhī*: i. e. *pāg* a turban (an adult), *tāg* a thread worn by a child round its waist, *kūṛī* a hearth, and *puchchhī* the tails of cattle.

The first two correspond with the poll tax, the third with hearth-money (the fumage of Domesday Book). *Carnegy.*

chau-haddā, *chau-gaḍḍā*, *chau-khanḍī*, *chau-sīmāṅ*, *chau-sivānā*, *chomṭā*, n. m. A raised mound indicating where the boundaries of four villages meet.

chau-haddī, *chau-sīmā*; A. *hudūd arbā*, n. f. 1. The four boundaries; environs; the surrounding country. 2. Neighbourhood; vicinage.

chau-lāvā, n. m. A large well with water enough for four *lāos*, q. v.

چوماسا चौमासा *chau-māsā*, *chatur-māsā*, *chau-mās*, n. m. S. चातुर्मास, Pālī, *chatumasam*. [(*barkhā*).
1. The four months of the rainy season
2. Lands ploughed and left fallow during the *chau-māsā* and prepared for the *rabī* sowing. [rainy season.

chau-māsiyā, n. m. A ploughman hired for the

chau-mekhā, n. m. 1. The act of tying the four legs of a horse. 2. A punishment which consists in tying a man's arms and legs.

chau'pā, n. m. S. चतुष्पाद; P. *chau-payā*. A quadruped; cattle; beast of burden.

chau-haṭṭā, n. m. A square surrounded by shops.

H چوانا चिवाना *chivā'nā*, *chihāṅ*, *chihānī*, *marghat*, *bhoi-dagdhā*, *samsān*, n. m.
A place for cremation; a burning *ghāṭ*.

H چوبدار *chob-dār*, n. m.
A mace-bearer; herald.

H چوبيسا चौबीसा *chau-bīs'ā*, n. m. A tract of country containing 24 villages in the occupation of a particular tribe.

H چوپاڑ चौपाड़ *chau-pāṛ'*, *chau-pāl*, n. f. S. चतुष्पाटिका A place of public meeting of the village; a shed or court in which the village community assemble for public business or where boys from adjoining villages assemble to be taught by a *gurū*.

H چوپنا चोपना *chop'nā*; Bhoj. *ubichhal*; Sant. *arej*, v. n. To throw water from a *daurī*, q. v. See *ulīchnā*.

H چوتھ चौथ *chauth*; Tir. *chauṭh*, n. f. S. चतुर्थी, Pr. *chotthī*, or *chauththī* fourth. 1. The fourth part. 2. A blackmail of one-fourth, levied by the *Marhaṭṭās* from the neighbouring princes, Hindū and Mahomedan.
3. The fourth day of the lunar month.

چوتھيا चौथैया *chauthai'yā*, n. m. The landlord's share of the produce where rents are paid in kind.

H چوٹا चोट्टा *choṭ'ṭā*; Rus. *chorṭā*, n. m. *choṭṭī*, n. f. H. *chor* a thief. [pocket.
A petty thief; a pilferer; shoplifter; pick-

H چودش चौदश *chau-dash*, *chaudas*, n. f. S. चतुर्दशी The 14th day of the lunar fortnight.

H چودنا चोदना *chod'nā*; Gaṛh. *chīknā*; Sant. *depeṛ*, v. a. S. चुद to drive in. To copulate; to have sexual intercourse with.

H چودھر चौधर *chaudh'ar*, *chaudhrāyat*, *chaudhrāī*, n. f. The office, jurisdiction, dignity or privileges of a *Chaudhrī*.

چودھري चौधरी *chaudh'rī*, n. m. 1. The head man of a caste, guild, profession, or trade.
2. A title; an honorific form of address.

H چور चोर *chor*, n. m. S. चौर, Pālī, *choro*.
A thief; pilferer. [or unauthorisedly.

chor-inām. Land enjoyed free of rent by stealth

chor-thāṅg. A receiver of stolen goods.

chor ḍhor, *chor moṭh*; P. *māl mujrim*.
A thief taken with the property.

chor-saudāgar, *chaukī-mār*, n. m. A smuggler; a dealer in contraband or stolen goods.

choroṅ kī dhāṛ, *āvārah choroṅ kā giroh*.
A gang of wandering thieves; bandits.

bālak-chor, n. m. One who kidnaps children.

چوري चोरी *chor'ī*, n. f. S. चौर्य, Pr. *choriam*; Pālī. *chorikā*. Stealing; theft; embezzlement.

chorī jārī, *chorī chhinalā*, n. f.
Theft and adultery.

chorī khafīf. Small or petty theft.

chorī kā māl, n. m. Stolen property.

chorī k., v. n. To steal (*churānā*). [theft.

chorī lagānā, v. a. To charge or accuse of

chorī maë wārdāt-i-saṅgīn. Aggravated theft.

ḍhor chorī, Cattle lifting or stealing.

H چورا चौरा *chaur'ā*, n. m. The funeral pile on which *Sattī* is performed.

H چوراسي चौरासी *chaurās'ī*, adj. S. चतुरशीति Pālī, *chullāsīti*. Eighty-four; a mystic number.

Formerly a sub-division of a *parganā* or district comprising 84 villages. See *Elliot's* Supplemental Glossary, pp. 178—206.

H چوڑا चौड़ा *chauṛā*, n. m. An open field or plain far from human habitation.
chauṛe meṅ luṭ jānā, v. n. To be robbed on the highway in broad daylight.
chūṛā bhanḍār, n. m. An allowance for the maintenance of the junior members of a zamindar's family. [(a row of shops).

H چوک لگنا *chauk lagnā*, v. n. To be opened
chauk-nikās, A tax on goods sold in the market.

چوکی चौकी *chau'kī*; Illit. *chauṅkī*, n. f. S. चतुष्क a hall resting on four columns.
1. A police, customs, toll, or railway station.
2. A guard's post; a watch; an outpost.
chaukī badalnā, v. n. To be relieved (a guard).
chaukī-pahrā, n.m. One's turn of watch or guard.
chaukī denā, v. a.
To watch; guard; mount guard.
chaukī-mār, n. m. A smuggler (*chor-saudāgar*).
chaukī mārnā, v. a. To smuggle. [market tax.
chaukī-mārī, n. f. Smuggling; evading the
chaukī meṅ rakhnā, v. n. To detain a suspected person; to keep in the guard house; to keep in custody. [man; sentinel; guard.

چوکیدار चौकीदार *chaukī-dār*, n. m. A watch-
chaukī-dār-i-dehātī, A village watchman.
chaukī-dār ke bhed meṅ, With the privity of the watchman. [the *chaukīdārī*, q. v.
chaukī-dāroṅ kā bakhshī, One who collects

چوکیداری चौकीदारी *chaukī-dārī*, E.; *chaukī-dārā*, W. n. f. 1. The office of a watchman.
2. The tax on account of watch and ward. 3. The fees or wages paid to the town or village watchman.

H چونی चवन्नी *chavan'nī*; Illit. *chuannī*; *chau-annī*; Tir. *char-annī*; Sant. & E. *sukī*, n. f.
1. The fourth part of a rupee (*pāolā*); a four-anna piece. 2. A four-anna share.

H چھکر छकुर *chha'kur*, n. A division of crops in which the *zamīndār* gets one-sixth.

H چھاپ छाप *chhāp*; P. *chāp*, n. f.
1. A stamp; impression; print, copy. 2. A seal; signet; an office seal. 3. A mark on weights and measures to shew their accuracy. 4. The village seal used to impress grain heaps with. 5. Sectarial marks representing a lotus, trident, etc. delineated on the body by the worshippers of *Vishnu*.
6. The custom house stamp on goods which have paid duty (*chhāṅṭā*). [print.
chhāp k., yā lagānā, v. a. To stamp; seal;

چھاپنا छापना *chhāp'nā*, v. a. To print; bring out an impression; publish.

چھاپہ छापा *chhāp'ā*, n. m. 1. An impression. See *chhāp*.
2. The press; printing. 3. An edition.
4. A stamp for making sectarial marks on the body. 5. A night-attack (P. *shab-khūn*).
chhāpā lagānā, v. a. 1. To stamp.
2. See *chhāpā mārnā*.
chhāpā mārnā, v. a. To make a night attack; to surprize.
chhāpe kī āzādī, The freedom of the press.
chhāpe meṅ chhapnā, v. n. 1. To be published.
2. To be defamed or exposed in print.

چھاپہ حاصل छापा हासिल *chhāpa hāsil*,
A tax on stamping cloth.

چھاپہ خانہ छापे ख़ाना *chhāpe-khāna*, *chhāpā*, n.m.
A press; printing office. [press.
chhāpe-khāne-wālā, n. m. The proprietor of a
chhāpne-vālā, *chhapaiyā*, A printer; a pressman.

H چھانٹا छांटा *chhāṅ'tā*, n. m.
Throwing additional seed in a growing crop of rice (Delhi); land in which seed has been sown after a single ploughing, especially at the extremities of a village, to secure possession.

H چھاونی छावनी *chhāo'nī*, *chhāunī*; Bhoj. *chhājnā*, n. f. H. *chhānā* to cover.
1. Thatching; the art of thatching. [diers.
2. A cantonment; barracks or huts for sol-

H چھپنا छुपना *chhup'nā*, Mah.; *chhipnā*, Hin. v. n. 1. To hide; to lurk; lie hid; to be concealed. 2. To elude or escape observation. 3. To veil or put on a mask; to keep *pardah*, q. v.
chhup chhup-ke, adv. Secretly.
chhupā rakhnā, v. a. 1. To hide; conceal; secrete; keep secret. 2. To abstract.
chhupte phir'nā, v. n. To be in hiding.
chhupne kī jagah, *chhupāo*, n. f.
Hiding place; concealment.

H چھٹنا छुटना *chhuṭ'nā*; Sant. *chhaḍāo pos-kāo*; v. n. S. छुट to cut. 1. To be liberated, set free, dismissed, discharged, acquitted.
2. To be redeemed (a mortgage).

چھٹوتی छुटोती *chhuṭau'tī*, n. f.
Remission of revenue.

چہرہ بندی *chehrah-bandī*, *chehrah-navīsī*, n. f.
A descriptive roll.
chehreh-shāhī rupayā yā sikkā, Current money or coin, so called from the Queen's head.
chehrah likhnā, v. a. 1. To make a descriptive roll; to enter a description (of a person).
2. To register; enroll.
chehrah honā, v. n. To be registered or enlisted.

H چھری مارنا *chhurī mārnā*, v. a. To stab.

H چہل चहल *cha'hal*, n. m. A strong soil, ranking between *rauslī* sandy and *ḍakura* clayey. W. [wane.

H چھیج छीज *chhīj*, n. f. S. चय from चि to
1. Decrease; diminution; wane; ebb; decay.
2. Waste; wear and tear; loss; damage.

chhīj baṭṭā, chīj chhapaṭ, n. m. Tare and tret.

H چھیر छीर *chhīr*, *sīr*, n. f.
The lessee's own cultivation.

H چیپا चेपा *chep'ā*, n. m.
A disease which affects standing crops.

H چیتی चैती *chait'ī*, *chait kī fasl*, n. f. The principal or vernal harvest; the spring crop which is cut in March. [head.

H چیرا चीर्रा *chīr'ā*, n. f. Virginity; maiden-

chīrā toṛnā, yā utārnā, (Slang) v. a. To deflour a virgin; to take a maidenhead.

chīre-band, n. f. A virgin (*kuārī*).

ح

A حاجب *hā'jib*, n. m. حجب he debarred it.
A legatee who bars the right of the next heir. [needed.

A حاجت *hā'jat*, *hājit*; Sant. *hajot*, n. f. حوج
A lock-up for prisoners pending trial.

hājat meṅ rakhnā, v.a. To detain in the lock-up.

A حارج *hār'ij*, n.m. حرج he became straitened.
An obstacle; obstruction.

hārij, mānaʿ, yā mukhil-i-dāwī. Bar of claim.

A حاشیہ *hāsh'yah*, n. m. حشي excluded.
Margin; border.

hāshye kā gavāh, gavāh-i-hāshiyā. A witness to the execution of a deed, so called because the signature of the witness is written on the *hāshyā* (margin). [margin.

hāshye meṅ mundarij k. To note in the *gavāh hāshiā*. An attesting witness.

A حاصل *hā'sil*, n. m. حصل was extracted.
1. Proceeds (*paidāvārī*, 2); outturn.
2. Produce (*prāpt*); return; gain (S. लब्धि, H. *hāth lage*).
3. The amount derived from the produce of the soil (*paidāvārī*), or other impost or duty; revenue. 4. Effect (*phal*, 5).

hāsil-bāzārī, n. m. Market dues; revenue from duties on markets (*tah-bāzārī*).

hāsil bād mujrā-i-akhrājāt. What remains after deducting all expenses; net receipts.

hāsil-tafrīq; S. शेष n. f. The net difference; remainder; balance. [ing revenue.

hāsil-zamīn. Land under cultivation and pay-

haqīyat pahuṅchī yā hāsil huī. The right accrued.

حاصلہ *hā'sila*, n. Cultivated or cropped land.

A حاضر *hā'zir*, adj. حضر was present.
Present; in attendance.

hāzir-bāsh, n. m. *lit.* be ready. A constant or regular attendant; follower; retainer.

hāzir-bāshī, n. f. The act of waiting; constant attendance.

hāzir-bāshī-i-kachahrī, n. Attendance at a court.

hāzir-bāshī kī zerbārī, n. Irksome attendance.

hāzir rahnā, v. n. To be in attendance; to attend; wait on.

hāzir-zāmin, n. m. A surety for another's personal appearance; one bound with the personal surety; a bail.

hāzir-zāmnī, n. f. Security for personal appearance; personal bail; bail-bond.

hāzir-zāmnī lenā, v. a. To bind over; to take security for the appearance of a person.

hāzir-karānā, Caus. To cause to appear.

hāzir k., v. a. 1. To bring forward; exhibit; introduce; present; deliver up (a person).
2. To lay before; to place in front.

hāzir o nāzir, Present and seeing (an epithet of God) used in formal oaths; omnipresent; omniscient.

hāzir h. yā ānā, v. n. 1. To be present; to be in attendance; to attend. 2. To make or enter an appearance; to be at hand.
3. To witness (a writing, event).
4. To be ready for; to consent to.

gair-hāzir, adj. Not present; absent; *non est inventus; non est;* away; gone from home; nowhere; absquatuated; vanished.

hāzrī asālatan, Personal attendance.

hāzrī-i-asālatan se muāf.
Exempted from personal appearance.

hāzrī kā muchalkā likhvānā, v. To bind over a person to be in attendance (at a court) at some fixed time.

hāzrī-nau ābād. A resident cultivator who takes up new land for the first year.

hāzrī bahī, hāzrī kā rajisṭar,
A muster-roll; a register of attendance.

hāzrī lenā, v n. To call over the names; to muster; to take the attendance. [attendance.

hāzrī meṅ khaṛā rahnā, v. n. To be in constant

hāzrīn', n. m. The persons present; company; assembly; audience.

naqsha-i-hāzrī o gair hāzrī,
A muster-roll; register of attendance.

A حاکم *hā'kim*, n. m. حکم he restrained him.
One who exercises, or is intrusted with authority; one empowered; a ruler; govern-

or ; chief ; master ; a magistrate ; judge ; an officer ; the administrative authority in a district.

E. Landlord ; zamīndār. [decree.

hākim ijrāē ḍigrī. The court enforcing a

hākim-i-āmir-i-qurqī yā nīlām. An officer directing the attachment or sale of property.

hākim-i-bā-ikhtiyār, yā zī-ikhtiyār, yā majāz, G. G. A competent authority.

hākim-i-bālā, A superior officer.

hākim-i-dīvānī. An officer of the civil court ; the civil power. [officer.

hākim-i-zer-dast. An inferior or subordinate

hākim-i-adālat, A judge ; an administrator of justice. [authority.

hākim-i-ālā, The paramount power ; highest

hākim-i-faujdārī, A judge who presides over a criminal court.

hākim ke kutte, More com. *kachahrī ke kutte. lit.* The dogs of men in authority, i. e. ministerial officers ; jacks in office ; myrmidons of the police.

hākim mujavvaz. A judge ; administrator of justice ; the adjudicating officer.

hākim-i-mustafsir. Ped. The officer making a reference ; the referring Officer.

hākim-i-vaqt. The present ruler or rulers; the government of the day.

حاكمانه *hākimā'nah,* adj. *lit.* as one having authority. Judicial ; official. [magisterially.

hākimā'nah, adv. With authority ; judicially ;

حاكمي *hā'kimī, hukū'mat,* n. f. 1. Sway; governance ; government ; dominion. 2. Power ; authority ; legal or judicial authority. 3. The office or functions of a ruler ; magistracy.

hā'kimī, adj. Belonging to the government ; governmental.

khud-hākimī, n. f. Arrogation of authority.

A حال *hāl,* n. m. حال condition. State ; condition ; present or actual state.

hāl-ābādī. 1. Waste land under present cultivation.

2. Assessment on newly cultivated land.

hālāṅ-ki, adv. Though (*bā-wujūd*) ; even ; however ; whereas ; on the contrary.

hāl-bāqī, Current or present balance.

hāl tauzī. A statement of revenue demands and collections of the current year.

hāl sābiq, Former or past state or condition.

hāl kī nikāsī, The existing assets (of an estate); the actual produce or proceeds.

hāl yā āindah. Now or hereafter.

hāl jama. The present *jama* ; the actual revenue payable to Government.

hāl hāsil, n. The actual produce (of land).

hal-i-dakhl. Actual possession. [at.

hāl-sākin, At present living at ; now residing

hāl muqadmāt dāërah. The state of the file shewing what cases are pending.

ba-nazar hālāt-i-muqadmah. Considering the circumstances of the case.

haqīqat hāl, The actual circumstances ; the facts of the case ; the acts ; the truth.

حالات *hālāt',* n. f. pl. of حالت q. v. Circumstances ; facts ; particulars ; details.

hālat-tavaqqā, yā muattal. Expectancy in law.

adālat kī kār-ravāī kī hālat.

Stage of a judicial proceeding.

hālāt-i-khās, Special circumstances.

hālāt-i-muqadmah, n. The circumstances, facts, or merits of the case ; the case.

hālat meṅ, adv. In the event of. [digence.

hālat-i-nādārī. Inability to pay ; poverty ; in-

ba-hālat, adv. In the state of ; under. [ness.

ba-hālat-i-junūn. Under the influence of mad-

ba-hālat-i-lā-ilmī. G. G. In ignorance of.

ba-hālat-i-mulāzemat. In service ; during service.

A حامل *hā'mil,* n. m. حمل bore.

(*In Comp.*) A carrier.

hāmil-ul-matan, The body of the writing.

hāmil-i-khat, yā ruqqāh. The bearer of a letter or cheque.

A حايل *hā'il;* Pop. *hāyal,* adj. حول intervening.

1. Intervening ; interposing.

2. Restraining ; hindering ; preventing.

A حبس *habs,* n. m. حبس he confined it.

1. Imprisonment ; confinement ; a prison.

2. Suffocation ; stifling ; choking.

habs-i-bejā, G. G. Wrongful confinement ; unlawful imprisonment.

habs-i-davām ba-abūr-i-daryā-i-shor. G. G. Transportation for life beyond seas.

A حبوب *habūb,* 1. Pills. 2. Grain, etc. but applied to cesses or imposts extra to the regular assessment.

☞ The terms seem to have been used indiscriminately with *Abvāb* (Harrington's Analysis, III. 236 note) ; but they more correctly define exactions in kind, for the use of the *zamīndār* or of persons in authority, as milk, eggs, sheep, oil, ghi, blankets, skins, etc. which were sometimes commuted for money. [Exclusion.

A حاجب *hajb,* n. m. حجت he debarred him.

☞ In Mah. law, exclusion from inheritance is either *entire* or *partial. Entire* exclusion is the total privation of right to inherit ; whereas *partial* exclusion means diminution of the portion to which the heir would otherwise be entitled.

hajb-i-hirmān, n. Entire exclusion.

hajb-i-nuqsān, n. Partial exclusion.

A حجت *huj'jat,* n. f. حج argued.

1. See *takrār,* 1, 2, and بحث

2. Altercation ; disputation.

hujjat tāidī-o-tardīdī. n. *Pros* and *cons* ; the arguments for and against a party.

hujjat k., yā lānā, v. a. To call in question; challenge; demur; contest (*takrār k.*); argue; plead; take exception to.
hujjat-i-lā-tāil, n. f. A useless objection; cavil.
hujjat-i-muqadmah qāyam k. To join issue; to fix the issues on a case. [objection.
hujjat nikāl'nā, v. a. To take exception; make
bilā hujjat. Undisputed; unchallenged.

A حد *hadd*, n. f. حد was conterminous with.

1. Boundary; limit; term. 2. A landmark; bar (of a harbour). 3. The utmost point or degree; the maximum (*ant*, 1).

☞In Mah. penal law, statutory punishment for certain crimes, distinguished from *kisās* or retaliation, as not being claimable by the aggrieved parties, and from *Tāzīr*, as not being inflicted at the discretion of the judge, but defined by law.

had bāṅdhnā, had bandī k., had bast k., had muqarrar k., v. a. To fix, determine, or mark off the limits or boundaries; to define.
had-bast, n. f. The adjustment, settlement, or demarcation of boundaries.
had-bast arāzī, n. A landmark.
hadd-i-bulūġ, n. f. Majority; full age.
hadd-i-bulūġ ko pahauṅchnā, v. n. To attain puberty or majority. [boundary case.
had-bandī kī takrār, Disputed boundaries; a
had-pār, had-bāhar, An outlaw. [to encroach.
had toṛnā, v. a. To pass or transgress bounds;
had-javāb, Rejoinder; surrejoinder.
hadd-i-samāāt, n. Limitation statute. [limitation.
hadd-i-samāat se bāhar, Barred by the statute of
hadd-i-siyāsat meṅ. Within jurisdiction.
had se bāhar, had se ziyādah, adv. 1. Beyond limits. 2. Extremely; excessively.
had se baṛhnā, v.n. To overstep bounds; go beyond limits; encroach on; transgress; exceed one's power. [gal punishment (Mah. law).
had-i-sharā, n. The extremity of the law; le-
had-shiknī, Encroachment; violation of a neighbour's landmark; trespass.

had ke andar. Within limits.
had-mahdūd, n. A term in leases or farming contracts which recognises the power of the farmer over all the land and crops within the defined limits. [ment.
had miād-i-qaid. Limit of term of imprison-
se-haddā, n. m. The point where three village boundaries meet.
حدود *hudūd'*, n. f. pl. of حد Boundaries. [aries.
hudūd arbah; H. *chau-sīmā*, n. The four bound-
hudūd-i-arzī n. Local limits.

A حراست *hirā'sat*, n. f. حرس guarding. 1. Custody; guard; escort. 2. Charge; care.
hirāsat-i-jāiz, n. Lawful custody.
hirāsat se bhāg'nā, v. n. To escape from custody.
hirāsat meṅ rakhnā, v. a. To keep or detain in custody; to detain a suspected person.
hirāsāt meṅ rawānah k. To forward in custody.
hirāsat meṅ supurd k. To commit to custody.
hirāsat meṅ lānā, v. a.
To take into custody; to secure.

A حرام *harām'*, adj. حرم was unlawful.

1. Illegitimate; adulterous.
2. Unlawful; forbidden; unclean; impure.

jimā-i-harām, n. Illicit intercourse. [intercourse.
حرام *harām'*, n. m. Adultery (Sant. *lāṭ*); illicit
حرامي *harām'ī*, n. m. A bastard.

A حرفة *hir'fa*, n. m. A craft; handicraft.

ahl-i-hirfa, n. m. Workmen; operatives; artizans; artists.
nishān-i-hirfa. G. G. Trade-mark.

A P حركات بيجا *harkāt-i-bejā*, n. A wrongful or improper act.
harkāt-i-khilāf qānūn, n. An offence by law.
harkāt khilāf qānūn afyūn.
Breach of opium laws.
harkāt khilāf qānūn sarishta-i-ḍāk sarkārī.
Breach of Post office laws.
harkāt khilāf qānūn mashār mumāneat chiṭṭhī-andāzī. Breach of laws prohibiting lotteries.
harkāt khilāf qānūn nisbat ravāngī-i-asbāb-o-ālāt-i-jang ġair mulkoṅ meṅ. Breach of laws relating to export of military stores, etc.
harkāt khilāf qavāid-i-jel-khānā.
Breach of jail discipline. [laws.
harkāt khilāf qavānīn isṭāmp. Breach of stamp
harkāt khilāf qavānīn ba māddah kanīz o gulām.
Breach of laws relating to slavery.
harkāt khilāf qavānīn dār-ul-zarb.
Breach of mint laws.
harkāt khilāf qavānīn mutalliqa riyāyā-i-mulk, ġair, Breach of laws relating to aliens.
harkāt khilāf qavānīn mutalliqā nahr.
Breach of canal laws.
harkāt khilāf qavānīn matba yā chhāpa-khānā.
Breach of laws relating to printing presses.
harkāt khilāf qavānīn namak aur parmaṭ.
Breach of salt and custom's laws.
harkāt dahshat-aṅgez. Menacing gestures; a threatening movement.
insidād harkāt bejā, G. G. Prevention of the commission of offences. [See آبرو

A حرمت *hur'mat*, n. f. حرم being inviolable.
hurmat-bahā kī nālish, Action for defamation of character; an action brought to recover damages for loss of reputation or character.
hurmat musāharat, The prohibition of marriage with different women on account of their mutual affinity.

A حساب *hisāb'*, n. m. حسب computing.

1. Accounts (آچاپت 1). 2. Computation; calculation; cyphering; arithmetic. [charges.
3. Rate; price; cost; charges; bill of

4. Measure; measurement; rule; standard; proportion. 5. Estimation; opinion; judgment; view. 6. Condition (*hāl*, 1.). 7. Method; way; manner. 8. Economy.
sāb barābar k., v. a.
1. To square accounts; pay one's score.
2. To do one's business; to finish a task.
hisāb bahī, n. Account books.
hisāb be-bāq k., yā chukānā, v. a. To settle or liquidate a balance; adjust an account.
hisāb be-bāq huā. The account was settled.
hisāb pāk-sāf. Settlement of a debt.
hisāb par charhānā, yā darj, yā syāhā k., v. a. To post (an account); to book; carry to an account; charge; debit.
hisāb taqsīm. Rate of distribution.
hisāb jāṅchnā, imtehān k., yā dekhnā; partāl k., v. a. To examine or audit accounts.
hisāb jamā. Account of receipts and balances.
hisāb joṛnā, v. a. To calculate; total.
hisāb-chor, n. A defaulter (in accounts).
hisāb khatm yā band k., v. a. To close accounts.
hisāb kharch, n. Account of disbursements; a particular revenue account.
hisāb-dāṅ, n. m. An arithmetician.
hisāb denā yā batānā, v. a. To render an account.
hisāb-deh, adj. Answerable; accountable; responsible.
hisāb-dehī, n. Village accounts.
hisāb rakhnā, v. a. To keep accounts; keep account of; to register.
hisāb-i-rahan. Mortgage accounts.
hisāb samjhānā, v. a. To render an account; account for.
hisāb se bāhar, adv. Beyond calculation; beyond measure; extraordinary.
hisāb se khārij huā. Written or struck off the account.
hisāb-kitāb, n. m. 1. Accounts. 2. Book-keeping.
hisāb-kitāb durust k., To make up accounts.
hisāb kitāb dekhnā, v. a. To look over or check an account.
hisāb-kitāb rakhne-vālā, hisāb-navīs, n. A book-ing clerk; a book-keeper.
hisāb-kitāb kā tasfīyā, Adjustment of accounts; winding up or settlement of an account.
hisāb k., v. a. To make up or settle an account.
hisāb kī bāqī, Balance of account.
hisāb kī rū se, az rūe hisāb, As per account.
hisāb laṛnā yā lagnā, v. n. To be formed (an attachment).
hisāb lagānā, v. a. To reckon; calculate.
hisāb lenā, v. n. To take accounts.
hisāb meṅ jamā k., To credit to an account; to credit.
hisāb meṅ ziyādah charhā'nā, To overcharge (in an account).
hisāb meṅ farq. Defalcation; deficit.
hisāb meṅ lagānā. To appropriate in account.
hisāb meṅ lenā, To take into account; consider.
alal-hisāb, Suspense account.
amīn-i-hisāb. An auditor of accounts.
ba-hisāb rasadī. Pro rata; rateably; in proportion.
bikrī kā hisāb, Bill of sales; account sales.
band yā parchah-i-hisāb. Account sales.
pakkā hisāb, Exact measurements, or accounts.
tasfīah hisāb, Adjustment of account.
chaltā hisāb, Account current; demand account.
khāngī yā nij kā hisāb, Private accounts; house accounts.
khulāsah band-i-hisāb. Abstract of accounts.
roz-marrah hisāb. Accounts running from day to day; a daily account.
fard-i-hisāb. A bill or schedule of charges.
kachchā hisāb. A rough account.
naqdī hisāb. Cash account.
حسابي *hisāb'ī*, adj. Belonging to accounts.
hisābī sāl, n. m. The official year.

A حسب *hasb*, adv. Agreeably to; conformably to (*ba-mūjib*).
hasb-i-ittifāq, ittifāqan, By chance (*ittifāq se*, 2).
hasb-itmīnān. To the satisfaction of; satisfactory.
hasb-ikhtiyār ekaṭ hāzā. G. G. Under the authority of this act.
hasb-ul-irshād, hasb-ul-hukm, hasb-ul-amr. Agreeably to orders; as ordered; by order of; according to order; in obedience to.
hasb-ul-irs. According to the Mah. law of inheritance.
hasb-ul-hāsil, hasb-ul-hāsilī. According to the produce; according to the kind and value of the crops.
hasb-ul-vasūl, According to the collections or receipts.
A term formerly used in revenue accounts to designate items of an uncertain value, of which no estimate can be computed, and which are entered only after their actual receipts. *Wilson.*
hasb-i-hāl, hasb-i-wāqe. Agreeably to circumstances; as the urgency, or the conditions may require.
hasb-i-zail. As follows; as under; as below-mentioned; as proceeding.
hasb-i-sarishtā. As provided or regulated; as before.
hasb zābitā, hasb qānūn, Legal; lawful; constitutional; regular; according to rule; as usual; duly; according to practice; formally; in due form of law or practice; as before.
hasb sarishta tajvīz k., hasb zābite amal k. To deal according to law.
hasb-i-zābitah wa qānūn. In a formal and legal manner; in due form of law and practice.
hasb-i-qāeda, hasb-i-zābta yā māmūl. Duly; according to rule or practice; formally.
hasb-i-qānūn, According to law; legally.
hasb qānūn nāfiz. Agreeably to the laws in force.
hasb-qīmat. Ad valorem; according to the value of.
hasb mahkūmā ḍigrī. According to the terms of the decree.
hasb-i-maqdūr. As far as possible.
hasb-i marqūma-i-bālā muqarrar ho. G. G. As appointed.
hasb-i-māmūl, hasb-i-dastūr, adv. According to custom; as usual.
hasb-i-manshā, In the sense of; agreeably to the import or intent of.
hasb-i-mauqa. According to circumstances.

A حسب *has'ab, hasab o nasab,* n.m. Pedigree; lineage. [provement of land.

A حسن زراعت *husan-i-ziräat,* G. G. Im-

husn-i-siyāsat meṅ fatūr lānā. To commit a breach of the peace or a political offence.

husn-i-intizām. Good discipline, management, or administration.

A حصص *his'as,* n. pl. حصه To cut off. Shares; portions; lots.

hisas-bil-infarād. Distinct shares.

hisas-i-sharaī. Legal shares.

ba hasas musāvī. In equal shares.

A حصول *husūl',* n. m. Issue (حاصل 1, 2.)

husūl bil-jabr, istehsāl biljabr, Extortion; forcible; appropriation; exaction.

husūl bejā. Wrongful acquisition; illicit gains; misappropriation; peculation.

husūl rihāī az rue āīn madyūn muflis. G. G. To take the benefit of the insolvent act.

bād husūl manzūrī. With the sanction of.

bilā husūl wāraṅṭ. Without a warrant.

dar-bāb husūl-i-arāzī. For taking up land.

A حصه *his'sah,* n. m. Pl. *hisas* حص to divide.

1. A share; share in a partnership; a share of revenue or rent; dividend.
2. Class; compartment; department.
3. A part or division of a book.

hissa-i-ausat. An average share.

hissa-i-bank yā kāgaz-i-sarkārī kharīdnā. To take a loan or a share in a stock by investing money.

hissah-i-tarka. Portion of an inheritance.

hissah-i-taqsīmī. Distributive share.

hissah-i-hākimī. The Government share of the produce of the land.

A fourth or a sixth is the proportion agreeably to the institutes of the Hindus. A third was nominally taken by the Mah. Governments, but the proportion was very variable. A third was the prevailing rate adopted by the British Government, but in practice this is greatly modified, and the proportion is the subject of special determination, according to previous practice and the circumstances of the land. *Wilson.*

hissa-i-khurd. The lesser part.

hisse-dār, One of a community of sharers; a copartner; coparcener; a partner in a business or firm; a sharer; shareholder; one who pays his share of the revenue either to a zamīndār or to the State.

hisse-dārāṅ, Sharers; shareholders.

hisse-dāroṅ kī jamāat. A joint-stock company.

hisse-dāroṅ kī sanad, Bank scrip.

hissā-dārī, n. Coparcenership, applied especially to a village in which a number of sharers have a joint proprietary right in the land.

hissah dārī-i-be-bāq. A solvent share.

hissah rasad. Composition (of a debt).

hissah-rasadī, A proportional share, part, or contribution; a fractional share of land; a dividend on a share; a rate; cess.

hissah-i-rasadī lagānā, v. a. To fix in due proportion; to assess. [assigned to the ryot.

hissah-raiyatī. The proportion of the produce

hīszah-raqam-dārī. A fractional portion.

hissah k., v. a. To divide (*bhāg k.*).

hissa-kashī, n. f. Distribution of shares; drawing lots; a lottery.

hīssah-kashī, Distribution and apportionment of shares agreeably to hereditary succession.

hissa-i-kalāṅ; H. *baṛā bāṅṭ,* The greater part.

hissa-i-mahsūl, Proportion of tax.

hissa-i-masāvī, An equal share.

hissa-i-muaiyan, yā raqam-dārī, G. G. A fixed or specific portion or share.

hissah-i-mukassar, yā raqamdārī, G. G. A fractional share or portion. [vidends.

hīssah munāfā gair-mudāwah. Unclaimed di-

hīssa-i-muntaqila. A transferred share or portion.

hīssah-i-mauzah. A share in a *mauzah.*

A حضور *huzūr';* Illit. *hazūr;* Rus. *jūr,* n.m. حضر

1. The presence; the royal presence; the presence of a superior authority, as of a judge or collector of revenue; hence also, the person of the prince or any high functionary.
2. The presence chamber; the hall of audience; the court. 3. Your honor; your highness. 4. Government estate.

huzūr, yā sadar tahsīl. Collection of revenue by the chief fiscal officer of the Government, without the intervention of a third party.

hazūr tahsīl, n. 1. Revenue paid into the chief office of the district. 2. Land on which the revenue is paid into the Sadar Treasury.

The term was formerly applied to land paying revenue to the chief authority in a province, as distinguished from those paying it to the head of a *zillā,* or sub-division of a province or Collectorate, thence termed *tahsil zillᵃa.*

huzūr-mahāl, Estates paying revenue direct to Government.

huzūr meṅ, In presence of; before.

huzūr-navīs, Secretary of State, one who registers all royal or viceregal grants and orders.

huzūr-i-vālā, The high or exalted presence.

حضوري *huzūr'ī*; Illit. *hazūrī,* n. f.

1. Presence; attendance; audience.
2. (n. m.) An attendant; a courtier.
3. Collections made by the Government direct. [royal.

huzūrī, adj. Of or belonging to the court;

huzūrī-mālguzārī, n. f. A land holder or tenant paying revenue direct to Government.

huzūrī nālish, A complaint preferred direct to Government. [*i-fitrī,* G. G. Unnatural lust.

A حظ خلاف وضع فطاري *hazz-i-khilāf-i-vaza-*

A حفاظت *hifā'zat*, n. f.

1. (*hifz*) Protection; security; safety.

2. Custody; care; charge (*bachāo* 1, 2).

hifāzat-i-khud-ikhtiyārī. Private defence.

hifāzat khud-ikhtiyārī kā istehqāq. Right of private defence.

hifāzat-i-khud. yā zātī, Self-defence.

hifāzat k., hifāzat men rakhna, v. a. To keep; preserve; guard; keep in one's custody; secure.

hifāzat-i-nafsī; H. *āpā bachāo*, n. Self-preservation.

hifzān-i-sehat, n. f. Sanitary precaution.

A حق *haqq*, adj. حق was right.

Just; right; true (*ṭhīk*, 15).

حق *haq*, pl. *huqūq*, n. m. 1. Right; equity; justice; merits. 2. A right; privilege. 3. Right of action; charter; franchise; title.

4. Duty; obligation. 5. Dues; claims; a legal fee or perquisite. 6. Interest; advantage; concern; behalf.

haqq-i-ājirī. A proprietor's right to the hire or rent of property let by him on lease. *Behar*.

haqq-i-adnā, Subordinate right.

haqq-i-iāda-i-virāsat az-rūë qāida-i-virāsat. Reversionary right or title by virtue of the inheritance.

haqq-ut-tahsīl, 1. The right or due of collection; the payment made to a *mālguzār* for collecting revenue cesses on smaller proprietary holdings. 2. Expenses of collections.

haq-i-ālā, Superior right.

haq-ul-saī, haq-ul-mehnat. The wages of labour; remuneration.

haqq-ul-khidmat. Wages due for services performed.

haqq-i-ilhāqī. A contingent right.

haqq-ul-nās, 1. A public right; the rights of man.

2. The punishment of crimes against society.

haqq-ul-abd, lit. the right of the slave (of God). The right of an injured individual to demand redress and justice.

haqq-ul-vāqeā, A statement or record of facts.

haqq-i-amānat, 1. The custodian's fee.

2. The profits of the priest.

haqq-i-intifā. Revenue profits on payment of the Government demand.

haqq-i-infikāk-i-rahn. Equity of redemption.

haqq-un-nāzirīn, The right of servants or spectators to the leavings of a banquet.

haq ba-zarya-i-qabzah o tassarruf-i-qadīm. The right acquired by continuity of possession; prescriptive right; prescription.

haq-bhet. Presents formerly made half-yearly, generally by the land-holder or payer of revenue, to Government officers.

haqq-i-paṭvārī, The fees payable to the *paṭvārī* or village Accountant.

haq par laṛnā, v. a. To fight for one's rights.

haq-i-tahrīr, n. m. 1. A letter-writer's fee.

2. A quit-rent taken by the Oudh Native Govt. from those who were found in possession of villages formerly in the *Bahū Begam's jāgīr* in E. Oudh when that revenue assignment was resumed by Saādat Alī.

haq-i-tahsīl. 1. The right of collection.

2. The rate, or fee of the officer employed to collect the rents.

haq-i-tahsīl-i-lagān. The right to levy rent.

haq-i-tasnīf, Copyright.

haq-talfī, n. f. Violation of right; injury; detriment; perversion of justice (*annyāo*).

haq-talfī k., v. a. To deprive of a right; to wrong; injure; defraud; affect injuriously.

haq ṭhairā'nā, v. a. To determine or adjudge a right.

haq sābit k., To make good a claim; establish a right.

haq jān'nā, To hold to be right or just; to approve.

haq chāhnā, v. a. To assert or claim a right; demand as due; to claim; sue.

haqq-i-chahārum, One-fourth share.

haq huqūq. Rights and interests.

haqq-i-havālah-dār. A portion of grain given to the officer of the *zamīndār* employed to collect the revenue, usually at the rate of a seer and a half per maund of forty seers.

haqq-i-haiy-ul-qāim. The right of survivorship.

haqq-i-hīn hayāt. A life interest.

haqq-i-khidmat. A right earned by service.

haq-dār, adj. Having a just claim or right; entitled; rightful.

haq-dār, n. m. One possessing a right or title; the rightful nominee; the holder of a right.

A person vested with any property, perquisite, or privilege; the holder of a share (of the revenue, crops, etc.); a Government or village officer who claims prescriptive rights or fees.

haq-dār aur gair haq-dār. Those who had or had not the right.

haq-dār k., G. G. To give a claim to; to entitle to.

haq-dār h., yā haq rakhnā, v. a. To have a title to; to be entitled to; to own.

haq-dārī, n. f. The holding any right or privilege; the right of claim, privilege, or property; ownership.

haq dabānā, v. a. To usurp a right; dispossess wrongfully; deprive of a right.

haqq-i-dakhīl-kārī. G. G. Right of occupancy.

haq dilānā, v. a. To award a right; enforce a claim.

haq-i-dosotrā. An allowance equal to ten per cent on the amount payable to Government by lessees in lieu of waste lands.

haq denā, v. a. To concede a right; administer justice.

haq-rasī, n. f. Justice; redress; relief; remedy; deliverance from wrong; the ends of justice.

haq-rasī chāhnā, v. n. To seek redress; claim a right.

haq-i-riāyā, 1. The right of the subject.

2. Tenant right.

3. Tenant right. The right of a cultivator to retain possession while paying the demand of the Government or *zamindār*.

haqq-i-rahan. Right of mortgage.

haqq-i-zamīndārī. The rights and interests of land owners; proprietary right.

haq Zamīndārī yā taalluq-dārī. An allowance drawn by the superior land owner.

The rights or dues of a *zamindār* agreeably to the *sanad* under which he holds his lands or his engagement with the Government.

haqq-i-sar-barāh, n.m. The right of management, as of the head of a village to conduct its affairs.

haqq-i-sarkār. The right of Government to a share of the crops, or a money commutation.

haqq-i-saī. Brokerage; counsel's fees.

haq se, adv. Deservedly; fairly; justly.

haq-i-shufa. Right of pre-emption.

haqq-i-shufā bar bīnā-i-jār-i-malāsiq. Right of pre-emption, on the ground of vicinage.

haqq-i-shufā-i-shara-i.

The Mah. right of preemption.

haqq-i-ʿusūbat. Residuary right.

haqq-i-qāim-maqāmī. The right of being represented by another.

haqq-i-qānūnī, qānūnī haq, A legal right.

haqq-i-qadāmat. The right of usage, of long established, or immemorial usage or custom; a right acquired by prescription; a prescriptive right. [or obtained his rights.

haq ko pahaunchā. He recovered his property,

haqq-i-lambar-dārī. The village headman's fees.

haq lenā yā mārnā, v. a. To deprive of a right; defraud; injure; wrong.

haqq-i-māl yā milkiyat. A right to a property.

haqq-i-mālikānā. 1. A proprietary right.

2. The right to a percentage on the net revenue, or when dispossessed of the *zamindārī*, to an allowance for his support.

haqq-i-mālguzār. An allowance drawn by a superior proprietor.

haqq-i-murajjah. A preferential right.

haqq-i-muravvaja. A customary due.

haqq-i-mustājirānā. Farming right.

haqq-i-mustaqil qāim bil wajūd. An indefeasible inchoate right. [or allowances.

haqq-i-mushāharā. The right of receiving pay

haqq-i-muqābazat. Right of occupancy.

haqq-i-muqābazat ba-vajah-i-shud-āmad-i-qadīm.

Right of occupancy by prescription.

haq men. In re; with respect to (*bābat*).

haqq-i-nān nafqā. Right of maintenance.

haqq-i-nā-tamām. An imperfect title.

haq nā-haq, adv. *Per fas et nefas*; right or wrong; *nolens volens*; wrongfully; unjustly; arbitrarily; for nothing; without reason.

haqq-i-vājib. A just right; a good title.

haqq-i-virāsat. Right of inheritance; heirship; right by succession.

haq-i-yāft-i-bankar. Forest rights.

haq-i-yāft-i-charāgah. Rights of pasturage.

haqq o murāfiq. Rights and interests.

haq h., v. n. 1. To belong of right; to belong or appertain. 2. To die.

apne haq men. In his right, behoof, or favour.

dūdh kā haq, n. m. The rights of a mother.

A حقارت *hiqā'rat*, n. f. حقر was contemptible.

Contempt; scorn.

hiqārat āyad huī. Exposed to contempt.

A حقوق *huqūq'*, n. m. pl. of حق Rights; claims; privileges; fees; dues; duties.

huqūq-i-āsāmīyān-i-be-dakhl.

Rights of ousted tenants.

huqūq jāiz kā istihsāl bataur na-jāiz. Illegal pursuit of legal rights. [terests.

huqūq-i-chand-rozah, Temporary or limited in-

huqūq-i-zaujīyat. Conjugal rights.

huqūq-i-shartī yā mashruta.

Contingent or partial interests.

huqūq i-shauharī. Marital rights.

huqūq-i-shauharī kā nifāz.

Enforcement of marital rights.

huqūq-i-kāshtkārī. Cultivating rights.

huqūq-i-mundarija-i-fehrist-i-band-o-bast.

The rights entered in the settlement record of rights.

huqūq wa dayūn. Rights and liabilities.

huqūq wa muttaalliqat.

Rights and appurtenances.

حقه پاني *huqqā pānī*, *lit.* smoking and drinking. Social intercourse. [from one's caste.

huqqā pānī band k., v. a. To excommunicate

A حقيت *haqī'yat*, n.f. حق right. 1. Property; ownership; right; claim; interest; title.

2. A holding; tenancy; share. [of a right.

haqīyat izhārī, n. The manifestation or proof

haqīyat-i-istiqbālī. A prospective right. [terest.

haqīyat-i-bilā shirkat-i-gair. An exclusive in-

haqīyat pahunchī yā hāsil huī. Right accrued.

haqīyat-i-theka-dārī.

The right or tenure of a lessee.

haqīyat jo vaqū men ānā chāhiye, yā jiske binā dūsre kā haq guzar jāne se shurū ho. An estate in expectancy; a reversionary title; a right which begins as soon as the right of another party has ceased.

haqīyat-i-dakhl. Occupancy right.

haqīyat-dār, n. m. A proprietor; owner; partner; shareholder.

haqīyat-dār ʿāla. G. G. A superior tenant.

haqīyat zamīn. Property in the soil.

haqīyat-i-shikmī. An under-tenure.

haqīyat-i-gair-munqasam. An undivided holding.

haqīyat-i-qābil nīlām. A saleable tenure.

haqīyat-i-kāsht. A cultivating title.

haqīyat kī dastāvez. Title deeds.

haqiyat kī qism, yā qism-i-haqīyat. The nature of a tenure.
haqīyat lā-khirāji. Rent-free tenure.
haqīyat-i-muhtamil-ūl wuqū. A contingent right.
haqiyat-i-muāfī. See *haqīyat lākhirā-j-i-haqīyat muattal.* Reversion of an estate; an estate in expectancy.
haqīyat maqbūzah. A right in possession; the thing possessed.
haqīyat nāqis. A defective title.
haqīyat-i-virsā. Right of inheritance.

A حقيقت *haqī'qat*, pl. *haqāyaq*, n. f.
1. The fact; the merits.
2. Circumstances; case (*hāl.* 1).
haqīqat-tahsīl, n. A statement or account of collections; the actual state of the revenue collections.
haqīqat-i-jamā. A particular account of the public revenue in all its branches; the account prepared of the revenues of Bengal and Behār to the period of their assignment to the Company.
haqīqat-i-jama-tūmārī. A particular account of the public revenue agreeably to the recorded rates.
haqīqat-i-hāl; Pop. *haqīqat-hāl*, n. f. The facts, circumstances, or merits of a case; statement.
haqīqat hāl amar mutanāzā. The general merits of the question at issue.
haqīqat rozīna-dār, n. An account of payments made to daily pensioners, formerly kept by the *Qanūngo.*
haqīqat-zamīndārī, n. The condition or statement of a *zāmīndār's* estate and engagements.
haqīqat likh'nā, v. a. To set down the facts; make a statement; certify or testify to.
haqīqat-i-muāmilah. The merits of a case; particulars of a transaction.
haqīqat meṅ, fil haqīqat, dar haqīqat, adv. In fact; in truth; in deed; *bona-fide*; essentially; virtually; in practice.
haqīqat-nāmā. A written statement of particulars.

حقيقي *haqīq'ī*, adj. 1. Genuine; real; true; *bona-fide* (اصلي 2, 6, 7, 9).
2. Own (*apnā*); whole blood.
haqīqī bhāī; E. *ek lād ke bhāī*, Own brother; brother of the full blood; a full brother.
haqīqī mālik. The real owner.
rishta-i-haqīqī. A relation of the full blood.
vārisān-i-haqīqī. Rightful heirs.

A حكام *hukkām'*, n. m. pl. of حاكم Rulers; governors; commanders; authorities; officers; magistrates.
hukkām-i-bālā-dast. Superior officers or authorities.
hukkām-i-zila. District officers; local authorities.
hukkām-i-faujdārī. Magisterial authorities; criminal officers.
hukkām-i-mātahat yā tābe, Subordinate officers.
hukkām-i-māl. Revenue authorities.

A حكم *hak'am*, n. m. حكم commanded. An umpire; arbitrator; a mediator.

حكم *hukm*, n. m. pl. *ahkām.* 1. Order; injunction; sentence.
2. Provision; stipulation; enactment.
3. Jurisdiction; authority; legal or executive authority.
4. Direction; control; management.
5. Leave; sanction; permission; license.
6. Decision; judgment; finding; decree; award; verdict; sentence. 7. (*hukm-nāmā*) A warrant. 8. A rule; law; precept.
9. A call; demand; requisition.
hukm uṭhā'nā, v. a. To countermand or cancel an order.
hukm-i-akhīr, A final order.
hukm akhīr denā, v. a. 1. To issue final orders; to pass a final judgment. 2. To settle finally.
hukm ulaṭ'nā, v. a. To upset an order; countermand.
hukm-i-imtināī, A prohibitory order; an injunction.
hukm-i-imtināī ijlās se sādir k., To forbid judicially; to issue an injunction.
hukm-i-imtin āī bābat āne jāne jahāz ke. Embargo.
hukm imtināī jārī k., To issue an injunction.
hukm-i-imtināi kī tāmīl k., To enforce an injunction.
hukm-i-infisākh-ī-bandobast, G. G. Order of cancelment of a settlement.
hukm bāz-āmad Return of process.
hukm ba imtināi-infisāl muqadmah. A caveat; a formal notice or caution to a judge or other officer to stay proceedings.
hukmi intiqāl. An enforced transfer.
hukm bajā lānā, yā uṭhānā, hukm par chalnā v. a. To execute; carry out, or obey an order; to act in obedience to orders.
hukm-bardār, adj. Obeying an order; obedient.
hukm-bardārī, n. f. Obedience.
hukm bhej'nā, v. a. To send or give an order; to order; enjoin; give notice.
hukm-i-be-dakhlī. Order of ejectment, or dispossession; ouster.
hukm-i-baibāt. Order of foreclosure.
hukm par mauqūf, hukm par multavī. Held at disposal; pending orders.
hukm-i-tākīdī, A peremptory order; an order strictly enjoining the execution of some previous order.
hukm-i-tatimma. A supplemental order.
hukm-i-tahrīrī. A written order.
hukm tartībī, yā darmiyānī. An intermediate or interlocutory order; interlocutory proceedings; an order passed *pro forma.*
hukm toṛ'nā, v. n. To disobey; to violate an order.
hukm sānī. A second writ.
hukm jārī yā sādir k., v. n. To give, issue, or circulate an order.
hukm-jārī-kunindah, Ped. An executive officer; minister.
hukm chalā'nā yā k. To exercise authority.
hukm-i-khās. A special order.

hukm-i-kharchā. Order of costs. [an order.
hukm khilāf denā. To countermand or overrule
hukm denā, v. a. 1. To give or pass an order; to order; give a verdict; pass sentence. 2. To instruct; direct; enjoin; issue an injunction. 3. To authorize; empower. 4. To decide; adjudge; sentence. 5. To let; permit; sanction; allow; grant. [(of a case).
hukm-i-dismisī yā khāriji, Order of dismissal
hukm-rānī, n. f. Rule; sovereignty; government; administration.
hukm-rānī k., v. a. To administer; rule; govern.
hukm-i-sakht, sakht hukm, n. m.
A strict or positive order.
hukm-i-sazā. Award of punishment; sentence; verdict. [sentence.
hukm-i-sazā-i-maut, Sentence of death; capital
hukm se bulānā, v. a. To cite; summon.
hukm-i-shadīd yā qahrī. Coercive process.
hukm-i-zabtī. Order of resumption.
hukm-i-talbī. Summons for the appearance of any person or persons.
hukm-i-zohrī. An order written on the back of a writing; an endorsement. [warrant.
hukm zohri parwāna par likhnā. To back a
hukm-i-ām. A general order.
hukm-i-adālat. A judicial award; judgment.
hukm fakk-i-rahn, yā infikāh-i-rahn.
Order of redemption of a mortgage.
hukm falāne ke nām jārī k.
To give an order on one.
hukm-i-qānūn. The authority or force of law.
hukm qataī hai. It is imperative.
hukm i-qaid. A mittimus; a warrant by which a judge commits an offender to prison; sentence of imprisonment.
hukm k., v. a. 1. To order; command; bid; direct; enjoin; charge.
2. To rule; govern; administer; manage.
hukm kīyā. Ordered; laid down; prescribed.
hukm-i-gashtī, n. m. A circular order.
hukm lagā'nā, v. a. 1. To affirm or assert positively. 2. To foretell; predict.
hukm mānnā, v. n. To obey.
hukm-i-mutafarriqā. Ped. A miscellaneous order.
hukm-i-mutlaq. Absolute power. [son).
hukm-i-mauqūfī. Order of dismissal (of a per-
hukm-nā-jāiz rakhnā. To overrule an order.
hukm-i-nātiq, yā qataī. A peremptory or final order. [imperative.
hukm-nātiq hai. The order is absolute; it is
hukm-i-nā-manzūrī. An order of rejection.
hukm-nāmah, n. 1. A written order; writ; a judicial writ; a written award or judgment; decree. 2. A precept; rescript; injunction; process. 3. A deed conveying certain authority; a license.
hukm-nāmah-i-ijrāë-i-dīgrī. A process of execution; an execution writ.
hukm-nāmah dar-āmal. Return of process.
hukm-nāmah-i-adālat. Legal or judicial process or proceeding.
hukm-namāh qanūnī. Legal process.
hukm-nāmah-i-qurqī. *Fieri facias*; a writ of execution; attachment of personal or real property; order of sequestration or confiscation.
hukm-nāmah-i-giriftārī. Warrant of arrest.
hukm-i-vāpasī, An order of remand. [into law.
hukm hotā hai. It is hereby enacted or passed
hukm huā yā hai. It is enacted or provided.
hukmī vazā. Authorised deductions.
ahlkār barīnda-i-hukm-nāmah. The officer entrusted with the execution of the process.
ind-ul-ijrā-e-hukm-nāmah. G. G. Under the warrant.
ba-mūjib-hukm-nāmah-i-giriftārī.
Under the warrant of arrest.
bilā hukm. Without order.
حکومت *hukū'mat*; Pop. *hakūmat,* n. f.
1. Power; sway; rule; administration; government; sovereignty (*hukm,* 4). [tion.
2. Province; dominion; domain; jurisdic-
hukūmat-i-arzī. Local jurisdiction.
hukūmat-i-angrezī. British rule. [government.
hukūmat-i-sha'khsī, n. f. Monarchy; despotic
hukūmat k., v. a. To exercise authority; rule; govern; administer; dispense justice.
hukūmat ke zor se zabar-dastī k. Oppressive exercise of authority; undue exertion of executive power. [mocracy.
hukūmat yā riyāsat jamhūrī. A republic; de-
A حلالہ *hallāl'āh,* n. f. A woman married again with her first divorcer after she had been divorced by her second husband.
A حلف *hal'af*; H. *dharam,* n. m. حلف he swore. Swearing by what is sacred; an oath.
halaf uṭhāne se inkār k., G. G. Refusing oath.
half'an, ba-halaf, adj. On one's oath. [sworn.
halfan tasdīq huī. Attested or deposed on oath;
halaf uṭhānā, v. a. To make oath; to swear.
halaf-darogī, n. f. Perjury; false-swearing.
halaf denā yā uṭhvānā, v. a.
To administer an oath.
halaf se izhār denā, v. a. To depose on oath.
halaf lenā, yā uṭhānā. Making oath; swearing.
halaf-nāma, n. m. A declaration upon oath; a written solemn declaration by a person exempt by the Regulations from being sworn in the ordinary manner; an affidavit.
ba-halaf jhūṭ bayān k., To make a false statement on oath; perjure one's self. [form
hasb-i-zābitah halaf diyā gayā. Sworn in due
A حلقہ *hal'qa,* n. m. حلق he drew a circle.
1. A circle; circuit.

2. A boundary line which includes all the lands and dwellings of a village or hamlet.
halqa-bandī, n. f. 1. A concentric division of villages, etc. 2. Arrangement of villages in circles or groups for village accountants, schools, etc.

A حليه *hul'yah*, n. m. 1. Countenance; features; personal appearance.
2. A description of a person.
hulyah-nāmah; *hulyā*, A descriptive roll.

A حمله *ham'lah*; H. *hillā*, n. m. Assault; attack; onset; aggression; invasion; assault and battery.
hamlah-āvar, n. m. An assailant.
hamlah khafīf. A petty assault.
hamlah k., v. a. To assault; attack; offer violence. [assault.
hamle kī dhamkī denā, v. a. To threaten an
hamle kī numāish. G. G. Show of assault.

A حوالات *havālāt'*; W. Rus. *halvāt*, n. f. A lock-up (E. *hājat*).
havālāt k., *havālāt meṅ denā*, v. a. To put in custody. [ed person.
havālāt meṅ rakhnā, v. a. To detain a suspect-
حواله *havā'lah*, n. m. 1. Reference; allusion; citation. 2. Commitment; charge; care; trust; disposal; consignment of any property, duty, or liability in trust; assignment for payments.
havālah-dār; Pop. *haval-dār*, n. m. 1. One employed to protect the grain before it is stored; a steward or agent employed for the management of a village. *Elliot.*
2. A head constable; a tipstaff.
havālah denā, v. a. To make a reference; to cite; quote an authority.
havāle k., v. a. To make over; give in charge or possession; consign; commit; deliver in trust; intrust; surrender; deposit; transfer; delegate. [of a city; suburbs.
حوالي شهر *havālī-i-shahar*, n. m. Ped. Environs

A حيثيت *haisī'yat*, n. f. 1. Capacity; ability; capability (of soil); means; resources.
2. Condition of life; *status*.
haisīyat rakhnā, v. a. 1. To possess means; to have property. 2. To constitute; contain; hold; have capacity.
haisiyat se, adv. According to; as. [or means.
haisīyat se baṛh-kar, adv. Beyond one's power
haisīyat-i-urfī, n. f.
Repute; reputation; character; name.
haisīyat-i-farīqain ba-lihāz-i-yak-digar. G. G. The relative position of the parties. [enabled.
haisīyat-yāftah. Ped. Supplied with means;
jāedād kī haisīyat, Nature of the property.
fel kī haisiyat, Nature of the act.
har ek kī haisīyat. Respective means.
حين دوران مقدمه *hīn daurān muqaddamah*. *Pendente lite*; during the pendency of a suit, while a suit is pending.

خ

A خارج *khā'rij*, adj. خرج extracted. Excluded; separated from; extraneous to; out of; except; exempt; rejected; ousted; nonsuit.
khārij az bahs, Out of the question.
khārij az samāat. Inadmissible; (a suit) which cannot be heard or entertained.
khārij az zābitah. Ultra-judicial.
khārij az aql, adj. n. m. Senseless; foolish.
khārij az muqadmah. Irrelevant to the case; not concerning the matter in hand.
khārij az miād, *kharij az miād-i-samāat*, *khārij az hadd-i-samāat*. Barred by efflux of time or the law of limitation; beyond statutory limits.
khārij paṭṭā. A lease of a detached or separate portion of an estate.
khārij jamā. Separated or detached from the rental of the estate, as lands exempt from rent, or of which the revenue has been assigned to individuals or institutions.
khārij kar-ke. Exclusive of; except.
khārij k., *yā rakhnā*, v. a. 1. To throw out; cast off; renounce; reject; bar; condemn (*bāhar k.*).
2. To except; enclude.
khārij karnā ba bāis bad-muāmlagī yā ğair-hāzirī. To deprive of or put out a thing by the judgment of a court for malpractice or non-appearance.
khārij-nāma. A deed of transfer; a deed for the partition of a joint estate, or for the separation of an individual share, or for making a dependent *taālluq* separate and independent.
khārij h., v. n. 1. To be excluded; exempted; dismissed. 2. To fail; to be exhausted; to cease; become extinct. [outlawry.
khārij honā panāh-i-adālat se. Civil death;
khārijah, n. m. What is excluded or excepted.
khārījah-taālluq. Separation of a portion or dependency of an estate, or of a *Pargana* from the general assessment, and the payment of the revenue due from it direct to the Government.

A خاص *khās*; H. *nij*, adj. خص particularized, appropriated. 1. Private; personal; individual.
2. Specific; special; appertaining to; own; proper; appropriate; peculiar; particular; distinct; definite.

khās apīl. A special appeal.
khās paṭṭī-i-char.
An alluvial accession to an estate taken possession of by the Government.
khās patit. Government land left uncultivated.
khās tahsīl. Government collections without the intervention of a *zamīndār* or farmer of the revenue.
khās taällluq. A *taällluq*, or particular district under the immediate management of the state.
The *Nawabs* of Bengal formerly selected such tracts and occupied them for their own benefit; but the term is now applied to estates which, in consequence of the default of the occupant, or his death without heirs, are kept in the hands of the State and managed by the Government officers.
khās takrār. Material point or issue; particular issue.
khās haq. 1. Prerogative; special privilege.
2. A rent-free tenure.
khās khās log. People of rank and consideration; persons who have access to the private council; chiefs; nobles; ministers.
khās khās waqton men, adv. At certain times.
khās khavās, n. A great man's domestics. [kindred.
khās darje kā rishtā. Particular degree of
khās zamīn. Land of which the collection is made by the Government officers immediately from the cultivators. [property.
khās sarmāyā yā jāëdād. Specific fund or
khās shart. An express provision; a particular condition; the basis of a treaty or agreement.
khās qānūn. A special law; the law itself.
khās kām, n. m. Special business or work.
khās-kar, adv. Especially; particularly; in particular; expressly; emphatically.
khās-kar, is lihāz se. With special reference to.
khās k., v. a. To specify; particularize. [ment.
khās-mahāl. An estate managed by the Govern-
khās-navīs. A private clerk or secretary.
khās o ām. The public; the community; noble and vulgar; great and small (*chhoṭe-baṛe*).
jāëdād-i-khās. Own property; private property.

A خالصه *khāl'isah*; Pop. *khālsā*, n. m.

1. Lands under the management of Government; Crown or Government land.
2. Revenue paying lands (opp. of *muāfī*, q.v.) 3. A respectful Punjāb term for Sikhs who profess a pure Hinduism.
4. The exchequer. Under the Mah. administration, the officer under whom the business of the revenue department was transacted, and which was continued during the early period of British rule. As applied to lands, it means those of which the revenue remains the property of Government, not being made over in *jāgīr* or *jama* to any other parties. It is termed in some official papers the rent-roll of the Government, meaning the revenue receivable from Government or *khālisa* land.
khālse lagnā, v. n. To be confiscated, seized.

P خام *khām*; H. *kachchā*, adj. Opp. of *pukhtah*.
1. Raw; green; unripe; immature.
2. Defective; unsound; imperfect; bad.
khām āmdanī. Gross receipts or collections.
khām amānī. Lands under the management of Government.
khām tahsīl, n. Lands under the management of Government; collections direct from the cultivators; collections on an estate not settled; gross produce or revenue; sequestration of revenue or of profits for a period of years in consequence of default in the payment of revenue. [tion.
khām tadāruk. A general or cursory investiga-
khām-tashkhīs. Ped. A rough estimate of the produce of a field.
khām jama-bandī, n. f. Gross assessment before making deductions for charges; assessment or settlement with the cultivators direct. [account.
khām-chiṭṭhā, n. m. A rough statement or
khām-ilāqah, n. m. An estate under direct management in lieu of leasing it.
khām nikāsī, khām vasūl. 1. Gross rental or revenue; total collections; the gross revenue of a village or an estate before the allowed charges are deducted. 2. A record or account of the gross revenue.
hujjat-i-khām. Specious reasoning; cavil.

P خاندانی *khāndān'ī*, adj. 1. Relating to the family. 2. Descended from father to son; ancestral; hereditary. [rank.
khāndānī aurat; H. *kulīn istrī*, A woman of
khāndānī nām, Family name.
khāngī jhagṛā, n. m. A family quarrel or feud; internal factions.
mutālibā-i-khāngī. G. G. A private demand.

P خانه *khān'ah*, n. m.

A column (of a tabular statement); a heading; a head in an account or statement
khānah-badosh, adj. Nomadic; wandering from place to place.
khānah-badosh, n. m. *lit.* bearing one's house on his shoulders. 1. A nomadic tribe.
2. A man who has no fixed residence; a vagrant; vagabond.
khānah-badoshī, n. f. Vagrancy. [or form.
khānah-purī, n. f. Filling up of a column
khānah-purī-kun'nda. The person who fills up a tabular statement; the returning officer.
khānah-talāshī; H. *ṭohī*, n. f. The act of searching a house. [amount at credit.
khāna-i-jam'a se baṛh jānā, To exceed the
khānah-jangī, n. f. 1. Domestic or family quarrels; intestine broils; civil war.
2. Disturbance; riot; affray.
khānah-jangī bil zarb. Affray with wounding.

khānah-jangī haqīqī yā vāqaī. Actual affray.
khānah-jangī khafīf. Simple affray.
khānah-jangī sāth shar aur fasad-i-azīm. Riot with violent breach of the peace.
khānah-jangī sāth qatl shubah-āmad. Affray with homicide.
khānah khālī. A term given to an estate which has been settled with farmers in consequence of the absence of any proprietary right. The name arises from the column in the settlement papers devoted to "proprietor" remaining blank.
khānah-i-siyāsat. House of correction.
خانہ شماري *khānah-shumārī,* n. f. A census.
khānah-muaiyan. The appointed or appropriate column. [particular column.
khāne meṅ paṛnā, v. n. To come under a
khānah-nashīn, goshah-nashīn, 1. One who has no employment. 2. A retired officer; a pensioner.

P خبرداري *khabar-dārī,* n. f.
1. Taking care (احتياط); charge.
2. Custody; guardianship; guard.
khabar-dārī-i-munāsib. Ped. Proper precaution.
khabar-gīrāṅ, n. m.
A guardian; protector; patron.
khabar-gīr, n. m. 1. An informer; a spy (*jāsūs*).
2. A guardian; protector; patron.
khabar-gīrī, n. f. 1. See *khabar-dārī.*
2. Protection; support; maintenance.

A خدمت *khid'mat,* n. f. Service.
khidmat-i-mulk. The public service.
khidmat-i-mansabī. The duties of a post.
خدمات *khidmāt',* pl. of خدمت Services.

A خراج *kharāj';* Pop. *khirāj';* H. *kar,* n.m. خرج passed out. 1. Tribute. 2. Impost; tax; duty; revenue. collector.
khirāj tahsīl karne-vālā. Tax-gatherer; rent-
khirāj-i-zamīn, Revenue from land; land tax.
khirāj-guzār, n. m. A tributary (*bāj-guzār*); one who pays revenue to Government.
khirāj lagānā, v. a. 1. To assess; tax.
2. To levy tribute or contribution. [tary.
خراجي *khirāj'ī,* adj. Revenue-paying; tribu-

P خرچ *kharch;* Pop. *kharach;* E. *kharchī,* n. m. A. *kharj.* 1. Expenses; expenditure; consumption; disbursement; outlay; outgoings.
2. Cost; charge; debit; the debit side of an account.
kharch uṭhānā, yā k., v. a. 1. To spend; disburse; invest or lay out money. 2. To bear the cost, expenses, or charges.
3. To act as a disbursing officer.
kharch akhrājāt, n. Disbursements.
kharch bardār, n. m. A servant whose office is to supply the household requirements.
kharch be-āmad, Expense without return.
kharch-i be-jā, kharch-i-fuzūl. Needless expense.
kharch-i-khāngī, Private expenses.
kharch-i-khānah-dārī; H. *gharelū uṭhāo,* Household expenses.
kharch-i-khairāt, n. m. A charge or allowance for charitable gifts or endowments.
kharch-i-daftar. Office charges.
kharch-i-dehī. Ped. for *kharch gāon.* Village charges or expenses.
kharch denā, v. a. To advance money for expenses (*kharch k.* 2).
kharch-i-rozmarrah. Current expenses.
kharch-i-sadr. Charges on account of the establishments of the principal local authorities.
kharch-i-gair māmūlī, 1. Unusual or extraordinary expenses. 2. Contingencies.
kharch līyā jāvegā. Shall be charged the cost.
kharch-i-mutafarreqāt, n. m. Contingencies.
kharch-i-muttafarriqā; H. *phuṭkal kharch,* Extra or miscellaneous expenses.
kharch-i-māmūlī, Ordinary or usual charges.
kharch-i mufassal. 1. Details of expenditure.
2. Provincial charges.
The expenses of collection and other authorised items of expenditure deducted from the gross revenue of a province.
kharch-i-mulk. Imperial expenditure.
kharch meṅ likhnā, v. a. To charge; charge against; debit; set down as a debt; enter as costs; enter in the column of disbursements.
kharch nānkār. Allowance or deduction from the revenue of an estate, as the subsistence money of the *zamīndār.*
kharch h., v. n. 1. To be spent or consumed.
2. To be exhausted; to fail.
خرچہ *kharch'a,* n. m. 1. Costs; expenses; charges. 2. Costs of a law suit.
kharchah ba-hisāb rasadī. Rateable costs; proportionate costs.
kharcha dilānā, v. a. To adjudge or award costs.
kharcha-i-adālat, yā muqaddamā, Costs of suit, or of court. [recoverable.
kharchah qābil-i-vusūl, yā yāftanī, Costs
kharchah zimmah āyad huā. Ped. Charged or saddled with costs. [one set of costs.
ek kharchah āyad k. To charge a party with
bilā-vasūl kharchah. Free of costs. [costs.
dāvā maē kharcha-i-ḍigrī. Claim decreed with

A خريج *kharīj',* adj. Sundry; miscellaneous.
kharīj-jamā, Extra collections; miscellaneous items of revenue.

P خريد *kharīd',* n. f. P. خريدن to buy.
1. Purchase; the thing bought. 2. The cost price. 3. Demand; want; requisition.
kharīd-khat, kharīd-nāma, Deed of purchase.
kharīd-o-farokht, kharīd farokht. 1. Buying and selling. 2. Dealings; trade.

kharīd-o-farokht k., v. a. To buy and sell; negotiate; transact business.
kharīd ke mol. Prime cost; cost price.
khush-kharīd, n. 1. Free purchase with ready money; hence, a bargain.
2. Private sale.
zar-kharīd. 1. A purchased estate. 2. A slave.
zar-i-kharīd, The purchase money, the price paid (commonly used in deeds of sale).
gulām ke taur par kharīdnā, G. G. To buy as a slave.
hundī kī kharīd o farokht kā chauk. The exchange.
خريدار *kharīdār*; H. *kharīdne-vālā*, n. m. Purchaser; buyer; holder by purchase.
kharīdār zar-i-ḍigrī. The purchaser of a decree or judgment-debt.
kharīdār-i-farzī. The ostensible purchaser.
kharīdār muqaddam. A prior purchaser.
kharīdār-i-nīlām. One who purchases at an auction.
kharīdar-i-nīlām ijrāë ḍigrī. A purchaser at an auction sale in execution of a decree.

A خريف *kharīf*; W. H. *sāonī*; E. *bhadaī*, n. f. خرف plucked (fruit). Autumn; the autumnal or lesser harvest; autumnal crops.
خريفي *kharīfī*; H. *sāonī*, adj. Grown in or relating to the autumnal harvest.

A خزانه *khazā'nah*, n. m. خزن laying up.
1. (*khazāna-i-āmirā, yā sarkārī*) A treasury; Government treasury; exchequer; the public revenue; finances. 2. A store; magazine. 3. A repository; reservoir.

A خساره *khisār'ah*, n. m. خسر he lost.
Injury (H. *ṭoṭā*, 6, 7).
khisārah uṭhānā, v. a. See *ṭoṭā uṭhānā*, 1.
khisārah-i-zātī. Personal damages.
khisārah muqarrar k. To assess damages.
khisārah-i-munāfā, Loss of profit.
khisārah-i-naqdī, A pecuniary loss.

A خسره *khas'rah, khasrā*; H. *khet bahī*, n. m. [S. खेत field.
1. A list of the fields in a village; a field book or index compiled at the time of a village survey. 2. A day or waste book; a rough draught.
khasrah ābādī. A list of the houses in a village with their occupants.
khasrah taqsīm, n. A register of shares in a field.
khasra kishtvār. A list of fields showing the number of occupants, etc.

H خشكي *khush'kī*, n. f. 1. Dryness.
2. High land not flooded with water, and upon which millet and other grains not requiring much moisture are cultivated.

A خط *khat*, n. m. 1. A letter. 2. A note of hand.
khatt-i-sarrāf. G. G. A bank-bill; a cheque.
khatt-i-lā-dāvā. 1. An unclaimed letter. 2. Quittance; acquittance; written release; no-claim certificate; relinquishment of claim.
khat meṅ khat milānā, v.a. To forge a hand writing.

A خطره *khat'rah*, n. m. خطر was in peril.
Danger (*andeshā*, 3.).
khatrah-i-khisārah. Risk of loss.
khatrah rafā k., To ward off danger.
khatra-i-zarar. Risk of harm.
khatra-i-ām. A common danger.
khatre meṅ ḍāl'nā, v. a. To endanger; risk; imperil; expose to danger; hazard.
khatar-nāk, adj. Dangerous; perilous; hazardous.

A خفيف *khafīf*, adj. خفت
Small; slight; petty; trivial; unimportant; of no weight or consequence.
khafīf jarāim. Petty offences.
khafīf duzdī, n. f. Petty theft; petty larceny.
khafīf sā, adj. Very little.
khafīf fasād. A petty disturbance.
khafīf muqaddama. A trivial suit or action; a small cause.
jurm ko khafīf k. To mitigate the offence.
jamā khafīf. Light assessment.
uzr-i-khafīf. A petty objection; cavil.
خفيفه *khafīf'ah, adālat-i-khafīfah*, n. f.
A small cause court.

A خفيه *khuf'iyah*, adj. خفا hiding. Hidden; concealed; secret; covert.
khufiyah khabar, n. f. Private or secret intelligence.
khufiyah kār-ravāī k., v.a. To investigate secretly or privately; make a private inquiry.
khufiyah-navīs, n. m. A secret correspondent, or informer; a secret emissary.
khufiyah-navīsī, n. f. Secret intelligence; the office of a secret intelligencer.
خفيه *khufi'yah*, adv. Privately. Opp. of *alāniyā*.
Khufiya wa alāniyā daryāft huā. (Police reports)
khufiyah-faroshī, n. f. Contraband traffic.

A خلاص *khalās*; Com. *khalāsī*, n. m. خلص he freed himself.
Emancipation; manumission (*āzādī*).
khalās, adj. Free; liberated (*āzād*, 1, 2.).
khalās-patr, n. A deed of release; an order of discharge; deed of dissolution.
khalās k., *khalāsī denā*, v. a. To discharge; acquit (*āzād k.*).
khalās h., v. n. To be freed or set at liberty [(*āzād h.*).
خلاصه *khulā'sah*; Rus. *khullāsā*, n. m. 1. Substance (*tat* 2, 3). 2. An abstract (*ijmāl*, 2.).
khulāsah izhār. The substance of a deposition or examination.
khulāsah dāvā. The substance of a claim or plaint.
khulāsah k., v. a. 1. See *ikhtisār k.*, (2.) 2. (*Pop.*) To resolve; unriddle; explain; make clear.
khulāsah muqadmah. Merits of a case.
khulāsah nikālnā, v. a. To sum up; summarize; make an abstract.

A خلاف *khilāf*; H. *ulṭā*; adj. خلف came after.
Against; *versus*; in opposition; contradictory.
khilāf, n. m. Opposition; contrariety.
khilāf-ikhtiyār. Unwarranted; not authorized.
khilāf-ismī. A misnomer. [founded on fact.
khilāf amr-i-wāqaī. Contrary to the fact; not
khilāf bayānī, n. f. A contradictory statement; contradiction; prevarication; misrepresentation. [sentation.
khilāf bayānī bil-ạmad. A wilful misrepre-
khilāf hukm. Contrary to orders; unauthorized; unwarranted; not allowed.
khilāf hukm ke amal k., v. a. To act against an order; contravene orders.
khilāf-i-dastūr, Contrary to custom; irregular; informal. [course.
khilāf-i-dastūr-i-muạiyana. Out of the ordinary
khilāf dāvā. Contrary to the claim. [case).
khilāf rū-dād. Opposed to the merits (of the
khilaf-i-sarishta yā zābitah, adj.
Against or opposed to the rules of practice; irregular; informal.
khilāf-i-shara. Contrary to the Mah. law.
khilāf-i-zābitah, Contrary to precedent or procedure. [tice.
khilāf zābtah-i-sahīh. Contrary to sound prac-
khilaf zābita-i-adālat. Contrary to judicial usage. [course.
khilāf zābta-muqarrarah. Out of the ordinary
khilāf-i-tabạ. Unnatural; against one's will or disposition.
khilāf-i-aql, Contrary to reason (*lạid-ul-aql*).
khilāf-i-qāidah. Irregular; against rule.
khilāf-i-qānūn. Contrary to law; illegal.
khilāf-i-qayās, adj. Inconceivable; improbable; absurd; incredible.
khilāf k., v. a.
To act contrary to; go against; oppose; contravene; infringe; break; violate.
khilāf kahnā, v. n. To make a contradictory or false statement; to contradict; prevaricate; misrepresent; tell a falsehood.
khilāf-goī, n. f. Lying (*jhūṭ*); misstatement.
khamar mahāl, See *ālkārī mahāl*.
khilāf-i-marzī. Against one's will.
khilāf mạnī kahnā, yā bayān k., v. a. 1. To pervert or twist the meaning; misconstrue.
2. To misrepresent; misinform. [charge.
khilāf-nālish. A cross suit or action; counter-
khilāf natījā. An opposite effect.
khilāf-i-wāqiā. Contrary to the fact.
khilāf vajah subūt. Contrary to the evidence.
khilāf-varzī. 1. Misconduct; misdemeanor; offence; crime. 2. Infraction; violation.
khilāf-varzī az qavānīn-i-sarkār.
Infringement of the law of India.
khilāf-varzī bā sarkār. G. G. Against the State.
khilāf-varzī k., 1. To oppose; infringe; contravene.
2. To misbehave; commit an offence.

khilāf-i-vazạ. Unnatural; contrary to good manners or custom.
khilāf-i-vazạ-i-fitrī. Unnatural gratification (sensual). [ment.
khilāf-i-wāda. Contrary to promise or agree-
khilāf h., v. n. To be on the opposite side; to make against; to oppose.
ba-khilāf, adj. 1. Against (الٹا 1, 4). 2. Adverse; in opposition; inimical. [the contrary.
par ba-khilāf iske. But on the other hand; on

A خلعت بہا *khilat-bahā*, n. A cess, or *abwāb* levied by the Mahommedan Government to defray the cost of honorary dresses presented at court. [of the peace.

A خلل انداز *khalal-andāz*, n. m. A disturber
khalal-andāz h., v. n. 1. To interfere; meddle; interrupt. 2. To disturb; molest; impede.

A خمس *khums*, n. m. The fifth part.
A double tithe, or twenty per cent. levied on the owners of land in which there are mines of metal; the fifth of booty taken in war with infidels, and set apart for orphans, the poor, and travellers.

P خود *khud*, adj. Self (*āp*); private (*khāngī*) own; personal; in person.
khud apnī zāt se, adv.
Of one's own self; independently of.
khud-intizāmī. Self-government.
khud-ba-khud; H. *apne āp*, adv.
1. Spontaneously; of itself; naturally.
2. Voluntarily; of one's own accord.
khud-rukhsatī, n. f. One who quits a service of his own accord.
khud-kāsht, 1. One's own cultivation; land which the proprietor, or the payer of the Govt. revenue, cultivates himself. 2. A cultivating proprietor; resident cultivator.
khud-kushī; H. *ātam-ghāt*, n. f.
Self-murder; suicide; *felo de se*.
khud-kushī k., v. a. To commit suicide.
khud-mukhtār, n. m. A free agent.
khud-mukhtār, adj. Independent; free; able; competent; not subject; unrestrained; uncontrolled. [of action.
khud-mukhtārī, n. f. Independence; freedom

P خورد برد *khurd-burd*, *lit*. he ate and took away. 1. Fraudulent or dishonest gains; fraud. 2. Peculations; embezzlement; misappropriation; bribes.
khurd-burd k., v. a. 1. To spend; use; enjoy; consume. 2. To embezzle.

P خوش باش *khush bāsh*, n. A cultivator holding land at an easy or quit-rent.
khush-bāshī jamạ, Quit-rent; light assessment; low-rent.

A خوف *ᵏkhauf*; Rus. *khaup*, n.m. Fear (H. ڈر).
khauf dikhā-kar bāz rakhnā. To deter.
khauf-nāk, adj. Frightful (ڈیانک).
fauran jān se halāk karne kā khauf denā. To threaten instant death. [threaten; alarm.
kisī shakhs ko khauf men ḍālnā. To intimidate;

P خون *ᵏkhūn*; H. *lahū*, n. m. 1. Blood; gore.
2. Slaughter; murder; homicide.
khūn-ālūlah. Stained with blood; bloody; reeking with blood. [money.
khūn-bahā, n. m. The price of blood; blood
khūn ᵏkharābā, ᵏkhūn ᵏkhachchar, n. m. Bloodshed; bloody work. [massacre.
khūn-rezī, n. f. Bloodshed; slaughter; carnage;
خوني *ᵏkhūn'ī*, n. m. *ᵏkhūnan*, n. f. A shedder of blood; murderer; assassin.
khūnī, adj. Bloody.

P خويد *ᵏkhavīd*; Pop. *khūd*, n. f. Unripe wheat or barley crop used as fodder.

A خيانت *ᵏkhayā'nat, khiyānat*, n. f. خون was unfaithful. A breach of trust; dishonesty (*khurd burd*, 2.).
khayānat k., v. a. To embezzle; misappropriate.
khayānat-i-mujrimāna, Criminal breach of trust.
khairātī zamīn, n. G. G. Land given for charitable endowments.
khairātī mad, n. f. Charitable or relief fund.
khairātī shafā-khānā, n. m.
A charitable dispensary.

د

A داخل *dāᵏkhil*, adj. دخل entered.
1. Entering; penetrating; arriving.
2. Included or comprehended in.
3. Inserted; entered; registered. 4. Filed.
dāᵏkhil, n. m. 1. Inclusion of a minor in a larger piece of land. 2. An entry in a book or account. 3. Taking possession (of land).
داخل خارج *dāᵏkhil ᵏkhārij*, n. m. *lit.* including and excluding. A transfer of land under one name to another name in the Govt. register of landed proprietors; mutation of names.

This process consists in the entry, in the register of the proprietor, of the name of the person to whom the Collector is to look as responsible for payment of the Government revenue, and whom he is to recognize as authorized to collect the rents of the estate and manage its affairs.

dākhil khārij kā muqaddama, A mutation case.
dākhil khārij k., v. a To register a transfer of property by taking out the name of the former proprietor from a deed or register, and inserting instead that of the new proprietor.
dākhil khārij men kuchh tajwīz haq kī nahīn hai. The register of mutations has no judicial character.
dākhil daftar. Placed on record; filed with the record; pigeon-holed or postponed indefinitely; struck off the file (of a judicial officer).
dākhil daftar k., v. a. To file with the record.
dākhil k., v. a. 1. To incorporate; comprise; include. 2. To admit; lodge. 3. To insert; enter; set down; write; register. 4. To enrol; enlist. 5. To file. 6. To deposit; carry to credit. 7. To pay; give; hand in (as money into the treasury). 8. To effect penetration (*dakhūl k.*). [depositor.
dākhil-kunindah, dākhil karne-wālā, Payer;
dākhil h., v. n. 1. To enter; come or go in; arrive. 2. To take possession; occupy; enter upon. 3. To fall or come under or be included in; to belong to. 4. To be entered, enlisted, etc. 5. To be filed.
6. To be paid, deposited, etc.
داخلا *dāᵏkhilā*; *dāᵏkhlā*; H. *bharat paiṭh*, n. m. See *dāᵏkhil*, (2.). 1. Delivery or payment of money, etc. 2. Admittance; admission; insertion. 3. Entrance; entrance fee. 4. A receipt, esp. a receipt for revenue payments.
dākhilā-navīs, A clerk who gives receipts for revenue instalments paid into Government treasuries.
داخلي *dākhlī*, n.

The phrase is applied also to villages which have become included in the revenue list of villages paying revenue, having branched off from and being dependent upon those on which the assessment was originally levied and which are therefore termed *aslī* original, in opposition to *dākhilī* the subordinate or included.

dākhilī mauzā, A newly formed village attached to or included in the older (*aslī*) village.
umūr-i-dākhlī o khārajī,
Domestic and foreign affairs.
aslī maē dākhilī. The original village and its dependencies or additions.
dakhīl-kār, n. m. An occupant, either in his own right or as a manager or trustee; the person in possession.

P داد *dād*, n. f. P. *dādan*, S. दा to give.
Justice; equity. [or redress.
dād chāhnā, v. n. To demand or sue for justice
dād-khuāh, n. m. 1. A petitioner for justice; a suitor; applicant; claimant.
2. (*dādī faryādī*) A complainant; plaintiff; prosecutor. [redress.
dād-khuāhī, n. f. Application for justice or
dād-dihī, n. f. Administering justice (داد 3.).
dād-rasī, n. f. Redress; redress of grievances; deliverance from wrong.
dād sitad; H. *len den*, n. *lit.* giving and taking. See بيوپار, 1, and *kharīd farokht.*

Money dealings. [the relief sought.
dād-i-mutada'wya, G. G. The thing claimed;

دادني *dā'danī, dād'nī*, n. f. 1. Advances for purchase of produce; advancing pay to laborers and manufacturers 2. Debts.
dādnī-dār, Ped. n. m. One who has taken advances on a contract. [vation of indigo.
nīl-dādnī, n. f. An advance made for the culti-

H دادا दादा *dā'dā*, n. m. S. तात तात
1. (Sant. *tātāt*) Paternal grandfather.
2. (Sant. *dada*) An elder brother.
3. An appellation of Brahmins, used by *Jāṭs* and *Gūjars*.

دادس दादस *dād'as*, Hin.; *dad-sus*, W. Rus; *dadiyā sās*, Mah.; *dadisasu*, Mār; *ajiā sāsu*, Bhoj. n. f. The mother-in-law of the wife's or husband's mother-in-law.

دادسرا दादसरा *dā'dasrā*, Hin; *dādsusrā*, W. Rus.; *dadiyā susar*, Mah. n. m. *dādā* grand father, *susrā* father-in-law. The father-in-law of the wife's or husband's father-in-law.

دادي दादी *dād'ī, ājī*, n. f. Paternal grandmother.
dadhiyāl', *dadyāl*; W. Rus. *dādkā*, n. m.
1. Paternal grandmother's house.
2. Forefathers on the paternal grandfather's side; lineage. [Oudh. *Carnegy*.

A دار *dār*, n. m. A subordinate tenure in E.

P داروغه *dāroğ'ah*; Pop. *ḍarojā*, n. m. 1. An overseer; inspector; superintendent; keeper.
2. An inspector of police; the prefect of a town or village.

داروغائي *dāroğāī*; Pop. *daroğāī*, n. f. The office or duty of a *dāroga*; superintendence.

داروغۀ جيلخانه *dāroğa-i-jel-khānah*, n. m. Jailer.
dārogah-i-rāh-dārī, n. m.
Toll-gatherer; toll-collector.

A داعيۀ *dāiā*, Wom. n. m. دعا See *dāvā*.
1. A claim; a plaint; complaint.
2. Claim; pretention.

P داغ بيل *dāğ-bel*, n. f. Marking off the lines for a road; a line of road; mark.

H دام दाम *dām*, n.m. S. द्रम्म 1. (*dām damṛe*) money. 2. Price; value; rate (*qīmat*).
dām-ans, n. m. A purchased share of an estate or village. *Carnegy*.
dām bharnā, v. n. 1. To take the price or value of; to charge for. 2. To pay the price.
dām dām, habbā habbā, Every *kaurī*; to a farthing.
dām denā, v. a. To pay the price. [slave.
bin dāmoṅ kā gulām, n. m. An unpurchased

H داماساهي दामासाही *dāmāsā'hī*, n. f.
An equitable partition of the effects of an insolvent amongst his creditors; hence, any fair proportionate distribution.

H دامي दामी *dām'ī*, n. An assessment.
dāmī-bīghā, n. m. The assessment of the lands of a village per *bīghā*.
dāmī paṭwārī. Fees of a *paṭwārī*.
dāmī lagānā, v. n. To assess.
dāmī vāsīlāt. The gross assets of a village.

H دان दान *dān*, n. m. S. दा to give.
1. A gift; grant; alms (*dān pun*); charity.
2. (Sant. *gonang*) A dowry (*jahez*).
dān-patr, n. m. One to whom a grant may be made or to whom by law property may be conveyed. [Brahmans.
dān-patr, dān-paṭṭī, n. m. A deed of gift to
dān denā, dān k., v. n.
To make a gift or grant; bestow alms.

H دانڈي दांडी *dānḍ'ī*, n. f.
A dry hard soil that does not retain moisture, and dries quickly when irrigated; a gravelly soil on high ground.

H دانوري दांवरी *dānv'rī*, n. f.
The rope by which the bullocks are tied together when treading out the corn.

P دانه‌دار *dāna-dār*, n. m. The act of fixing the *jamā* according to the actual produce.
dāna-bandī, n. f. A rough survey; (*dānā bandī k inkūtī*) an assessment of the revenue upon a valuation of the standing crops.

P داي *dāī*, n. f. A female commissioner employed to interrogate and swear native women of quality who are exempted from appearing in the law courts.

H دايجا दायजा *dāē'jā*; P. *jahez, dahez*, Wom. n. m. S. दाय. A dowry; portion.

A داير *dāy'ar*, adj. دور going round. Pending; in process of adjudication; in process.
dāyar tajwīz. Under consideration or trial; pending decision; pending.
dāyar k., v. n. To file or institute (a suit).
az rūe qānūn dāyar k'yā gayā.
Instituted conformably to law.

A دايم *dāim*, adv. دوم endured.
Always; perpetually; continually.
dāim-ul-habs, Imprisonment for life.

دايمي *dā'ēmī*, adj. 1. Perpetual; lasting. 2. Imprisoned for life (Opp. of *miyādī* for a term).
bandobast dāēmī, The permanent settlement of the revenue.

A داين *dā'yan*, n. m. دين became indebted.
A creditor; an obliger.

H دائیں दायें *dāeṅ, dāneṅ*, W; *daṅvarī*, Bhoj.; *eṅ*, Sant.; *davāṅhī*, E. n. f. S. दा to part.
1. Threshing the corn by bullocks.
2. The unthreshed corn in the ear.

H دبانا दबाना *dabā'nā, dābnā*, v. a. S. दम
See دبنا v. n. 1. To sow; to make a layer.
2. To keep possession by force or fraud; to usurp.
dabā baiṭhnā, v. a. 1. To keep possession by force or fraud; to usurp. 2. To cohabit.
dabā-kar, adv. By force or compulsion.
دباو दबाओ *dabā'o, dabāī*, n. m. 1. Pressure. 2. Constraint; influence (داب).
dabāo mānnā, v. n. To submit; to be influenced (*dābnā*).

H دبسی दुबसी *dubs'ī* n. f. H. *do* two, *bīs* twenty. The percentage allowed to government farmers on the revenue paid to government, formerly ten per cent.

H دبيهرا दबेहरा *dabeh'rā*; Sant. *ṭoḍā*, n. m.
A large wooden plough-share attached behind the iron share.

H داوي दलोई *dato'ī*, n. f. Land which has been lately cropped with *makkā*, or *juār*.

A دخل *da^khl*; Pop. *dakhal*, n. m. 1. See *an-danī* 1, and *ikhtiyār*, 6, 7.
2. Occupancy; occupation; possession.
dakhl bil-jabr, n. m. Forcible or violent entry or possession. [trespass.
dakhl-i-bejā, dakhl-i-nā-jāiz, Unlawful entry;
dakhl be-sabab, yā be-ijāzat, n. m. Entering a place without leave; intrusion. [admitted.
dakhl pānā, v. n. 1. To have access; to be
2. To obtain or be put in possession.
dakhl-dihānī, Ped. n. f. Delivery of possession.
دخل دينا *da^khl dena*, v. n. 1. To interpose (*bīch meṅ ānā*, 2.). 2. To interrupt; disturb.
3. To admit or allow one to enter.
dakhl fil hāl, Present or actual possession.
dakhl k., v. a. 1. (*dakhīl h.*) To take possession; occupy; keep; possess. 2. To encroach upon; enter on the rights of another.
dakhl karne-wālā, n. m. An occupant; intruder.
dakhl meṅ rakhnā, v. n. To keep; retain.
دخلنامه *dakhl-nāmah*, n. m. A document giving the right of occupancy; a writ or warrant of entrance or possession (of lands, etc.).
dakhl o qabzā, qabz o dakhl, Entry and possession.
دخليابي *dakhl-yābī*, n. f. Obtaining entrance or admission; taking possession.
دخول *du^khūl, dakhūl*, Slang. n. m. Penetration in sexual intercourse. [and egress.
du^khūl o khurūj: Ped. for *ānā jānā*. Ingress

دخيل *da^khīl*, adj. Occupying; possessing.
dakhīl-kār, 1. An occupant; a hereditary occupant. 2. One who has authority to interfere. [occupancy.
dakhīl-kārī, 1. Possession. 2. Hereditary
da^khīl-hāl. The party in possession; present possessor. [ed party.
dakhīl-sābiq. The former possessor; the oust-
بيدخل *be-da^khl*; Pop. *be-da^khal*, adj. Excluded; ejected; ousted; dispossessed.
be-dakhl k., v. a. To dislodge; disturb one's possession; oust; dispossess.
kāsht se be-dakhl k., To oust from a holding.
be-da^khlī, n. f. Dispossession; ouster; ejectment; disseizin.
be-dakhlī bil-jabr. Forcible dispossession.
be-dakhlī nā-jāiz. Wrongful dispossession.
haq-i-dakhīl-kārī, Right of occupancy.

H ددری ददरी *dad'rī*; Sant. *tovā pereh*, n. f.
H. *dūdh*, milk. Unripe corn, chiefly barley which is cut occasionally and brought home to be eaten without being taken to the threshing-floor.

S ددهيشو दिधिषु *did'hishu*, n. m.
The husband of a widow.
didhishū, n. f. 1. A child-widow remarried.
2. An elder unmarried sister whose junior is a bride. 3. The childess widow of a brother whom, under the old law, a surviving brother was required to marry.

H در दर *dar*, n. f. S. दृ to honour.
1. Value; esteem (*ādar*).
2. Rate; price; market or current rate; standard charge. 3. Per; each; at.
4. An account of fees paid for serving a process. 5. A return of process.
dar-bandī, Rent rates used for assessments.

P در *dar*, prep. P. *dar* a door. In (Sant. *re*); at; on; into. [a sublease.
دراجاره *dar-ijārah*, An under-tenure or farm;
درآمد *dar-āmad*, n. f. 1. Coming in; ingress.
2. Import.
darāmad barāmad, Receipts and disbursements.
درپيش *dar-pesh*, adj. 1. On the table (آگے, 1).
2. *Sub judice* (*dāyar*); under trial or consideration.
dar-pesh k., v. a. To lay before; introduce (*pesh k.*); submit; bring to notice.
dar-pesh h., v. n. 1. To be in front or before (*āge ānā*, 1). 2. To be on the carpet or anvil. 3. To be in hand, on foot, pending.
4. To happen (*āge h.* 5).
درصورت *dar-sūrat*, adv. In case; suppose that; provided; should; since; in the event of.

P درباب *dar-bāb, dar-bārah,* prep. Respecting; in *re*; relating to; for (*bābat*); anent.
dar-bāb-i-intizām. Relative to the organization or administration of.
dar-bāb husūl arāzī. For taking up land.
dar-bāb hifāzat qirār vāqaī. In relation to the due preservation of.

P دربار *darbār',* n. m. P. در within, بار a court-yard. 1. Court; audience; royal audience; hall of audience.
2. The executive Govt. of a Native State.
3. A Native levee held by a Native Prince or high English officer.
darbār bāndhnā, v. a. To bribe; give bribes.
دربارخاص *darbār-i-khās,* n. m. Private audience.
دربارخرچ *darbār-kharch,* Political or diplomatic expenditure; court charges; charge for presents and gratuities made to princes and public functionaries, bribes, etc.
☛ Under the old *regime,* an addition made to the assessment by Government officers or the zamindars on the plea of providing for gratuities exacted by their superiors or the State on their payment of the revenue.
دربار داري *darbār-dārī,* n. f. Presence at court.
darbārdārī k., 1. To be assiduous at court. 2. To dance attendance on; to be obsequious.
دربارعام *darbār-i-ām,* n. m. Public audience; public hall of audience.
darbār k, v. a. To hold a *darbār,* q. v.
درباري *darbār'ī,* adj. Of or belonging to the court; attending court.
darbārī, n. m. 1. A courtier. 2. The elegant, polished language of the court.
darbārī zabān, n. f. Court language.

H درپتني दरपटनी *dar-patnī,* n. m. A subordinate or sub-lease or tenure.
darpatnī-taaluq. An estate held under a sub-lease.
darpatnī-dār, n. m. The holder of a lease from a lease-holder; a sub-lessee.

A درج *darj,* n. m. See اندراج
darj-i-rajistar, Written on the register or roll; registered.
darj k., v. a. 1. To include (*dākhil k.*); record.
2. To book; carry to account.
darj h., v. n. To be inserted, booked, etc.

A درجه *dar'jah,* n. m.
1. Degree; grade; division (جماعت 5.).
2. Honorable or high place; dignity.
darjah ghatānā, v. a. To degrade.
darje-vār, adv. According to one's rank or degree.
us darje tak, adv. To this degree; so far.
har darje ke mahkamejāt fauj-dārī. Criminal courts of the several grades.

P درخواست *dar-khuāst,* n. f. 1. A petition.
2. A tender; offer; proposal.
3. In judicial proceedings, an application which is required to be made for the admission of each exhibit in a suit, and for the summoning of each witness. In revenue matters, the representation of the proprietor of an estate as to the amount of revenue he is able to pay, or a proposal for renting or farming an estate or any branch of the public revenue, or the engagement entered into by the *Lambardār* to be responsible for a stipulated amount of revenue-payment for a given time.
dar-khuāst-i-sarsarī. A summary application.
dar-khuāst-i-apīl. A petition of appeal.
dar-khuāst ijrāë digrī. An application for authority to enforce or execute a decree.
dar-khuāst-i-baībat.
An application for foreclosure.
dar-khuāst-i-khās, A special application.
dar-khuāst dākhil khārij. A petition to the Collector for the exclusion of the name of a proprietor whose interest has lapsed by death or sale, and the insertion of that of another in the public books.
dar-khuāst-i-ravannah jo parmat men dākhil kī jātī hai. Bill of entry.
dar-khuāst-i-uzr-dārī. A petition of objection.
dar-khuāst qabūliyat. Agreement; settlement; compact.
hasb-i-qānūn dar-khuāst k., To make a legal application.
dar-khuāst k., yā guzrānnā. v. a. 1. To apply; present, submit, or tender an application.
2. To beg; seek; entreat (*ardās k.*).
darkhuāst-kunindah, ahl-i-dar-khuāst, Ped. n. m. An applicant; a petitioner.
dar-khuāst-i-muhāfizat k., v. a. To apply for protection.

P دردزه *dard-i-zeh*; H. *dard lagnā,* n. m.
The pains or throes of labour.

P درست *dur'ust*; Illit. *durast,* adj. Right.
durust samajhnā, v. n. 1. To apprehend rightly; to have a correct apprehension of.
2. To admit; allow; receive.
durust lagānā, v. a. To set in order (*tartīb k.*).
durust vaza, Propriety of demeanor (*bhalā chalan*); good manners.
durust-havās, yā aql, adj. Of sound sense or mind; sensible.
درستي *durust'ī*; Illit. *durastī,* n. f. 1. Soundness; propriety; fitness. 2. Justness; exactness.
3. Accuracy; correctness. 4. Arrangement (*tartīb*); adjustment.
5. Amendment (*tarmīm*). 6. Correction; reformation.

H درشت द्रष्ट *drisht, drisht, dith,* n. f. S. दृष्ट, Pr. *ditthī.* Sight (*ānkh,* 2, 3.).
drisht-bandhak. Mortgage or pledge without possession; deed of hypothecation.
درشني هندي दर्शनी हुण्डी *darshanī hundī,* n. f. A bill of exchange payable at sight.

H دركهي दुखी *dur'khī*, n. f.
An insect whose ravages are very destructive to indigo when the plant is young.

P درميان *dar-miyān'*, prep. About; concerning; in the midst (*bīch.*)
darmiyān tajvīz, During the proceedings.
darmiyān denā, v. n. 1. To propose as a judge, umpire, or security. 2. To give as a hostage.
darmiyān lānā, v. n. To include; bring under or within; introduce.
qurān darmiyān denā, v. n. To swear by or appeal to the Kurān (let the Kuran decide between us). [interim.
is darmiyān meṅ, adv. In the interval or
درمياني *darmiyān'ī*, adj. 1. Interior; inner. 2. Middling; fair.
darmiyān'ī, n. m. 1. A middleman; go-between (*bichauliyā* 1, 2, 3.).
2. An interpreter (*mutarjim*).

P درو بست *dar o bast*, adj. Entire; whole.
dar o bast āimmā. A grant of the whole of the lands constituting a rent-free estate.
درو بست حقوق *dar o bast huqūq*,
All right and title whatsoever.

P دروغ *darog̈'*, n. m. A lie.
darog-halafī, n. f. Perjury; false swearing.
darog̈-halfī fāsh, n. Deliberate perjury.
darog̈-halfī k., v. a. To commit perjury.
darog̈-halfī karvānā dūsre se. Subornation of perjury; causing another to perjure himself.
darog̈-halfī kī illat meṅ, On a charge of perjury.
دروغگو *darog̈-go*, n. m. A liar (*jhūṭā*).
دروغگوي *darog-goī*, n. m. Lying (*jhūṭ*).
ba-rāh-i-darog-goī, adv. Falsely.

P دريا برآمد *daryā-bar-āmad, daryā-barār*, n. m. Alluvial land; alluvion; lands reclaimed from a river; increment of land.
daryā-burd, n. Land carried away by the encroachments of a river; land cut away; diluvion. [a river.
daryā-burd ho jānā, v. n. To be cut away by
daryā-burdī, n. f. Diluvion.

P دريافت *daryāft'*; Illit. *daryāfat*; Rus. *daryāphat*, n. f. Reference enquiry; finding out.
daryāft k., v. a. 1. To enquire into; find out; ascertain; perceive; infer; discover; detect. 2. To make a reference. [tained, etc.
daryāft h., v. n. To be investigated, ascer-

H دساور दिसावर *disā'var*, n. m. S. देशापर from देश country, अपर other.
1. A foreign country. 2. A place of importation to or exportation from. 3. Imports.
disāvar ānā, v. n To be imported (the commodities of foreign countries).
disāvar charhnā, disāvar kī māṅg h., v. n.
1. To be required for exportation; to be in demand abroad. 2. To be high or dear.
disāvar ko bharnā, v. a. To export.
دساوري दिसावरी *disāv'arī*, adj. Of or belonging to a foreign country. [products.
disāvarī māl, n. m. Imported goods; foreign

P دست *dast*, n. m. Hand.
دست اندازي *dast-andāzi*, n. f.
Interference; encroachment; trespass; illegal exercise of authority.
dast-andāzī k., v. a. 1. (*dast-andāz h.*) To lay one's hands on; meddle; intermeddle; interfere. 2. To exercise illegal authority.
دستاويز *dast-āvez*, n. f. *lit.* what one takes into his hand. A deed; document; bond (*tamassuk*); voucher; an instrument.
dast-āvez-i-jālī, n. f. A forged document.
dast-āvez-i-shikastgī-i-shirākat; H. *sīrtoṛ likhtam.*
Deed of dissolution of partnership.
dast-āvez-i-zamānat. A bail bond; a security bond. [ment.
dast-āvez qābil-i-baī o shira. A negotiable instru-
dast-āvez-i-lā-dāvī, A deed of renunciation.
dast-āvez-i-mahr, kābīn-nāmah. A deed of dower.
dast-āvez-i-intiqālī. A negotiable security; a deed of transfer or conveyance.
dast-āvez tabdīl k., To alter a document.
dast-āvez-i-taqsīm yā hissa. Deed of partition.
dast āvez ṭheka-i-mujraī.
A deed of usufructuary lease.
dastāvez jālī ba-taur dast-āvez sahīh kām meṅ lānā. To use a forged document as genuine.
dast-āvez chhupānā yā talaf k., To secrete or destroy a document. [ment.
dast-āvez rajisṭarī-shudah. A registered docu-
dast-āvez-i-g̈air rajisṭarī-shudah.
An unregistered document.
dast-āvez qist-bandī. A deed of instalment.
dast-āvez qabūliat,
A deed of acceptance or agreement.
dast-āvez-i-mushtabah, A suspicious document.
dast-āvez-i-mussaddaqā. An attested document.
dast-āvez nīlāmī, An auction-sale deed.
dast āvez-i-hiba, A deed of gift or bequest.
dast-ba-dast muāmlā; H. *hāthoṅ hāth len den.*
A ready-money purchase or transaction.
dast-burd, gaban, n. f. Encroachment; embezzlement; plunder; rapine.
dast-burd k., v. a. To embezzle; plunder.
dast-bardār h., v. n. To give up; wash one's hands of (*tajnā*, 1, 2.).
dast-bardārī, *lit.* drawing back the hand. Withdrawal; relinquishment; renunciation.

dast bardārī az istehqāq-i-mā-bād. To waive a reversionary title. [of preemption.
dast-bardārī az haqq-i-shafā. To waive a right
dast-bandhak, n. f. A pledge; deposit. [cument.
jhūṭī dast-āvez banānā, v. a. To make a false do-
دست خط *dast-khat*; Pop. *das-khat*; Rus. *das-kat*, n. f. *lit.* hand writing.
1. Signature; initials.
2. An endorsement or acceptance (*sakārā*).
dast-khat ba-mohar sāde kāgaz par. A blank endorsement; *carte blanche*.
dast-khat kiyā huā ba-nām-i-fulāṅ. Endorsed to one; endorsed in favor of a person.
dast-khat k., v. n. 1. To sign; to affix one's signature. 2. To endorse; endorse in blank.
دستخطي *dast-khatī*; Pop. *das-khatī*; Rus. *das-katī*, adj. Signed; bearing signature; endorsed; under one's own hand and signature.
dast-khatī zohrī, An endorsement; a writing on the back of a paper.
dast-darāz; H. *hāth lapak yā chālāk*, adj. Having long arms; oppressive; extortionate.
دست درازي *dast-darāzī*, n. f.
Exaction; imposition; encroachment; excess; outrage; violence; oppression.
dast-darāzī k., v. a. 1. To molest; plunder; pillage. 2. To oppress; beat; ill-treat.
3. To commit rape or an indecent assault.
dast-gardān, 1. A short-term loan on a verbal promise to pay (*hath-udhār*). 2. Any article hawked about for sale (*biktī-huī*).

P دستک *dast'ak, dastak chiṭṭhī*, n. f. *lit.* knocking at the door. 1. Summons; judicial writ; process; legal process; warrant; revenue process, esp. a notice to pay land revenue which has fallen due. 2. A fee for serving summons, a writ, or passport.
3. Commission; tax (*kar*).
4. A passport; permit.
Formerly, a document authorizing the free transit of certain goods and their exemption from custom dues in favor of English traders.
dastak talab-i-zar, A revenue process.
A warrant issued against defaulters of revenue, demanding payment and subjecting them to the expense of maintaining the officer who serves it until the amount is paid.
dastak lagānā, v. n. To impose or levy a tax.

P دستور *dastūr'*, n. m. Z. *dastobar*; P. *dast* hand, *bar* take. 1. A common practice (*rivāj*).
2. Settled or established order.
3. A customary fee or perquisite; a commission or percentage on the collections.
dastūr-i-tijārat, yā mahājanī, Mercantile or commercial usage. [rule or practice).
dastūr jārī h., v. n. To be established (a
dastūr-i-khāndān, n. m. Family usage.
dastūr-i-mustamara. An invariable practice.
dastūr-i-mulk. Local usage; the usage of the country.
dastūr muāfiq, adv. According to custom; as before; ordinarily; customarily.
ba-dastūr, adv. According to rule (*hasb-i-dastūr*); as heretofore; as before; *in statu quo*.
be-dastūr, adj. 1. Unprecedented; novel; anomalous (انوكها, 1.).
2. Irregular; informal; unlawful.
دستور العمل *dastūr-ul-amal*, n. m. 1. Rules of practice; manual of regulations; a code of laws; procedure; a hand-book.
2. Constitution; form of government.
dastūr-ul-amal-i-ahalkārān-i-māl, G. G. Body of instructions for revenue officers.
dastūr-ul-amal paṭvāriyāṅ, The paṭvārī's handbook or manual.
دستوري *dastūr'ī*, n. f. 1. Perquisites; commission of a broker; perquisites paid to servants by one who sells to their master.
2. Emoluments; allowances.
dastūr'iyā, n. m. A broker.

H دسوترا दसोत्रा *dasot'rā, dasotarā*; Tir. *dasāṅk*; Bhoj. *diotrā*, adj. S. दशोत्तर Ten per cent.

A & H دسهرا خرچ *dasahrā kharch*, 1. The expenses attending the Dasehra festival.
2. A cess levied by a Zamindar on his tenants. It consists of rice, milk, *ghee*, etc.

H دشٹ بندهک दिष्ट बंधक *dishṭ-bandhak*, n. f. S. दृष्टि बंध A simple mortgage of real property; hypothecation; mortgage without occupancy.

A دعوى *dā'va, dāvā*; Wom. *dāiyā*, n. m.
1. Claim; title. 2. Requisition; demand application; plaint.
3. A suit; action cause; lawsuit.
4. Charge; accusation; impeachment; indictment; count of an indictment.
dāvā ijrāē digrī, Claim for execution of decree.
dāvā az-ruē tamassuk.
A claim or charge under a bond.
dāva istaqrār-i-istehqāq va haqīyat. A claim for recognition of right and title.
dāva istaqrār-i-haq-i-milkīyat. Claim to establish a suit to obtain judicial ownership; declaration of the right of ownership.
dāva istaqrār-i-haq-i-muqābazat va bahālī qabzā.
A suit to establish the right of occupancy and confirmation of possession.
dāva istiqrār-i-haq-i-muqābazat-i-kāsht-kārānā va mahfūzī-i-be dakhlī-i-na-jāiz min-jānib-i-zamīndār. G. G. Claim to obtain a declaration of a right of occupancy as a cultivator, and to be protected from illegal or wrongful ouster by the *zamīndār*.

dāvā izāfa-i-lagān.
A claim for enhancement of rent.
dāva-i-īzā-rasānī, Charge of persecution.
dāva-i-bilā-dalīl, An unsupported claim; a groundless charge.
dāva-i-bejā, dāva-i-be-asl. 1. An unfounded claim; false pretension. 2. Arrogation of authority. [ouster, or ejectment.
dāva-i-be-daᵏkhlī, An action for dispossession,
dāva-i-baibāt, A foreclosure claim.
dāva-i-husūl-i-huqūq-i zaujīyat; dāva-i-husūl-i-istehqāq izdavāj,. G. G. Claim for restitution of conjugal rights.
dāva-i-husūl-i-dakhl mālikānā. A claim to recover proprietary possession.
dāva-i-husūl-i-qabza-i-mālikānā va mansūkhī-i-tashkhīs-i-lagān ek qita arāzī gang-barār. Claim to recover the proprietary possession of, and to set aside the assessment of rent made upon an alluvial tract of land.
dāva-i-haqq-i-shufā, Claim for preemption.
dāva-i-haq-i-shufa se dast-bardār h. To renounce a claim to preemption. [preemption.
dāve-dār haq-i-shufa. A claimant to a right of
dāvedār h., dāvā k., v. n. 1. To hold; maintain; contend for. 2. To claim; to demand or maintain as due; set up, advance, urge, or prefer a claim or title; lay claim to.
3. To charge; accuse; indict; arraign.
4. To affect; pretend to.
dāva ḍigrī kīyā. Claim decreed.
dāva rakhnā, v. a. To have a claim.
dāva galat. Plea of error.
dāva-i-qabz o daᵏkhl. A claim for occupancy and possession; possessory action.
dāve kā javāb denā, yā muqāblā k., v. a. 1. To make answer in a suit. 2. To contest a claim. 3. To oppose a demand.[counter-suit.
dāve ke muqābale meṅ dāvā. Cross-demand;
dāve ke nifāz kī nālish k. To institute a suit for the enforcement of a claim.
dāvā khārij k., v. a. To dismiss a suit or claim.

دعویدار *dāve-dār, dāve-gīr*; Wom. *dāīye-dār,* n. m. Plaintiff; suitor; claimant.
dāva-i-daᵏkl-yābī, Possessory action; a suit for occupancy or possession. [claim.
dāvā karnā, v. a. To claim; sue; institute a
dāva-i-mubham. G. G. A vague claim.
dāva-i-muᵏkhtalif. A conflicting claim.
dāva-i-mukhta'ifa nālish-i-vāhid meṅ, ek nālish meṅ kaī dāve. Misjoinder.
dāva-i-muddāilah. 1. The defendant's claim.
2. A cross suit; a set-off.
dāva-i-masdūd. Claim barred.
dāva-i-mahr, A claim to dower.
kisī istehqāq kā dāvā k.
To claim a certain right or interest.
dāva-i-mansūkhī-i-ḍigrī farebī. Claim to set aside a decree obtained by fraud.

dāva-i-nīlām-i-haqūq-i-zamīndārī vāqa-i-mavāza-i-chand. G. G. Claim to enforce the sale by auction of the zamīndārī right in certain villages.
dāva-i-vāguzāsht-i-qurqī. Action of replevin.
taaiyun-i-dāva. Valuation of suit. [a suit.
taaiyun dāva kam iqrār denā. To undervalue
khulāsah-i-dāva. Substance of the claim.
do bināē dāva, Double cause of action.
shaē dāva. Subject of action.
sūrat-i-dāva. Form of suit.
dāva-i-muāvazā. A claim for compensation.
dāva-i-vājib, vājibī dāvā, A just claim.
dāva-i-virāsat, A claim to inheritance. [claim.
binā-i-dāva, Cause of action; ground of
lā-dāve, be-dāve, adj. Unclaimed; relinquished (a suit).
lā-dāve dastāvez, be-dāve-patr, Deed of release or acquittal; a deed acknowledging the abandonment of a claim or suit.
lā-dāve yā be-dāve h., v. n. To withdraw a claim.

P دغا *daǧ'ā,* n. f. 1. Deception; imposition; treachery (*buttā*); cheat; artifice; delusion.
dagā denā yā k., v. a. To impose upon; circumvent; defraud; act deceitfully or treacherously; play false; betray.
dūsrā shaᵏkhs ban-kar dagā k.; H. *bhes badal-kar ṭhagnā,* Cheating by personation.
دغاباز *daga-bāz,* adj. Deceitful; fraudulent.
dagā-bāz, n. m. 1. A cheat; swindler; rogue; sharper. 2. A traitor; a knave.
دغابازي *dağā-bāzī,* n. f. Cheating; trickery; imposture (*dagā*); *mala fides*; villainy.

A دفتر *daf'tar,* n. m. 1. Register; roll; archives; an official statement or report, especially of the public revenue.
2. An office; office of records; place of business; counting house; agency.
3. An establishment.
daftar-ᵉkharch. Office charges.
daftar-i-kalaktarī meṅ nām dākhil k. Registration; entry in the Collector's books.
daftar meṅ dākhil kīyā. Registered; filed. [clerk.
sar-i-daftar, The head of an office; a head

A دفعه *dafā,* n.f. Section; paragraph; article.

H دکهائي दिखाई *dikhā'ī,* n. f. 1. Show; appearance; exhibition.
2. The inspection of registered women under the Contagious Disease Act. [poverty.
nā-dārī dikhlā'nā, v. n. To appear poor; sham

A دلال *dallāl',* n. m. دل guiding. A broker.
دلالت *dalāl'at,* n. f. 1. An indication; a sign; token. 2. Proof; evidence.
dalālat k., v. a. To point; indicate; show; betoken; denote; argue.

دلالہ *dallāl'ah, mashshāṭā*, n. f. A go-between; an old procuress (*kuṭnī*).

دلالي *dallāl'ī*, n. f. 1. The business of a broker. 2. Brokerage; the commission of a broker.

H دلانا दिलाना *dilā'nā*; Tir. *diyāeb*; Bhoj. *diāval*, v. a. Caus. of دينا q. v. To cause to be given; to put in possession.

dilā pānā, v. n. To recover; get back.

dilāne-vālā, n. m. One who causes to be given.

vāpis dilānā, v. a. To order a refund.

A دليل *dalīl'*, n. f. Pl. *dulāil*, دل guiding. Argument; reason; proof.

دليلاً *dalīl'an*, adv. By way of proof or argument.

dalīl peshk., v a. To adduce argument or proof.

dalīl-i-khām. A weak or untenable argument.

dalīl k., v. a. 1. To argue; reason. 2. To dispute; raise objections. [argue; plead.

dalīl lānā, yā nikālnā, v. a. To adduce proofs;

dalīl-i-nāqis. A bad plea.

H دمڑي दमड़ी *dam'ṛī*, n. f. 1. A pie; one-fourth or ⅛ of a pice. 2. A nominal coin. 3. A subdivision of land, one *damṛī* = 25 *kachā bīghās*.

H دنگا दंगा *daṅg'ā*; Rus. *diṅgā*, n. m. A row; riot; disturbance; affray; breach of the peace; breach of the public peace.

H دو दो *do*, adj. Two.

دوبسوي दोबिसवी *do-bisvī*, n. An allowance or deduction of one tenth or two *bisvās* out of a *bīghā*.

The right of the *zamīndārs* in land, as the *Mālikānā* is in money. A concession sometimes made by holders of rent-free land to the *zamīndār*, in acknowledgment of his superior or proprietary right, especially, according to Mr. Elliot, when they are not confident of the validity of their tenure. Ten per cent. allowed to farmers of the Government revenue. *Wilson*.

du-chāh, The second reservoir to which water is raised for the purpose of irrigation.

du-chand sazā. (*Law*) Double punishment.

do-ras, n. m. Clay and sandy soil.

This word is used in the Eastern District, as Domat in the North-West, to signify a mixture of two soils (*Matiār* and *Bālua*); and, like Domaṭ is in some places, as in Azamgarh, considered the best quality; in others, as in Gorakhpur, the second quality of soil, except in Tilpūr and the Forest Parganās, in which the *Maṭiār* is considered too adhesive.

du-sālā, n. m. Lands that have been two years under cultivation.

du-faslī, du-sākhī, du-har, du-phalī, du-tanābī, (opp. of *ek-faslī*, or rice lands). n. f. Land yielding two crops in a year.

du-gānā, n. m. A woman who engages with another woman in sexual intercourse with the aid of a dildo.

du-lāvah, n. m. A well with two *lāos*, or well buckets and ropes.

band o bast-i-du-sālā. Biennial settlement.

āmezish kī-huī davā. G. G. Adulterated drug.

H دوالا दिवाला *divā'lā*, n. m. H. *dīvā* a lamp, *ālā* a niche. Bankruptcy; insolvency.

Lighting a lamp in a shop in broad day light is a declaration of bankruptcy.

divālā nikālnā yā piṭnā, v. a. To declare bankruptcy; to become a bankrupt.

دواليا दिवालिया *divāl'iyā*, n. m. A bankrupt; an insolvent.

H دوت दूत *dūt*, n. m. S. दूत from दु to go, Pālī. *dūtako, duto*.

1. An ambassador; envoy; a delegate.
2. A secret messenger; an emissary.

dūt-pan, n. m. 1. See *jāsūsī*. 2. Mischief-making.

dūtā'ī, n. f. Embassy.

دوتي दूती *dūt'ī, dūtnī*, n. f. 1. A female messenger, or spy. 2. A go-between; a procuress (*kuṭnī*). 3. A backbiter. 4. An incendiary; a firebrand.

H دودهبهائي दूध भाई *dūdh-bhāī*, n. m. A foster-brother (*birādar-i-rizāī*).

H دور दोर *dor*, n. m. *do* two, *era* earth. Land ploughed twice.

A دوران مقدمه *daurān-i-muqaddama*. Pendency or duration of a case or suit.

daurān-i-muqadmeh men. During the pendency of a case or suit; *pendente lite*.

دوره *daur'ah*, n. m. 1. Circuit; tour; sessions.

daure supurd, Commitment for trial before the Sessions.

daure supurd k., v. a. To commit to the Sessions.

daurah k., daure ko uṭhnā, v. n. 1. To go on tour or circuit. 2. To hold Sessions.

H دوري दौरी *daur'ī*; Sant. *ḍopkā*, n. f. A sling basket used in irrigation; a basket.

H دوڑا दौड़ा *dauṛ'ā*, n. m. A mounted highwayman.

dauṛ'ā'hā, dauṛā, n. m. A village runner, messenger, or guide. [one; to assault one.

kisī ke ūpar dauṛnā, v. a. To run at or against

H دوسائي दोसाई *dosā'ī, do-sāhī, du-sākhī*; Bhoj. *do-saliā*, adj. H. *do* two, *sākh* crop. See *du-faslī*.

dusā'ī, n. f. Any spring crop sown after an autumn crop, most commonly gram and linseed sown after rice.

H دوسرا दूसरा *dūs'rā*, adj. Second. [cument.

dūsrī sanad yā kāgaz, n. f. A duplicate of a do-

dūsre ke nām se. In another's name.

دوسري दोसरी *dos'arī*, 1. The ploughing of land twice. 2. Land twice ploughed.

S دوشت दूषित *dūsh'it*, adj. 1. Calumniated; falsely accused (esp. of adultery).
2. Contaminated; violated; corrupted.
dūsh'itā, n. f. A girl who has been violated.

P دوشيزگي *doshīz'gi*, n. f. Virginity.

دوشيزه *doshīzah*; H. *kuārī*, n. f. A virgin; maid; an unmarried daughter.

H دوكهي दोखी *dokh'ī*, *tokhā*, n. f.
A raised mound, indicating the junction of two boundaries (*had-bast*).

H دوگلا दूगला *dūg'lā*, n. A large sling-basket used for irrigation.

H دومت दूमट *dū'maṭ*, n. f. H. *do* two, *maṭṭī* soil. A mixture of clay and sand; land of the second quality.
dūmaṭ-i-arāzī, n. f. G. G. Rich highly cultivated land.

H دوهاجو दूहाजू *dūhā'jū*, Mah.; *duhejū*, *dhejū*, Hin.; *duj-bar*, Mīr. n. m. H. *do* two, *jorū* wife. A widower who marries again.

H دوهائي दूहाई *dūhā'ī*, intj. Mercy!
duhāī pher'nā, v. a. To make a proclamation.
duhāī tihāī k., yā machānā, v. a. To cry aloud for justice; to make reiterated complaints.
duhāī denā, v. a. To cry for justice, mercy, quarter, or help.

H دوهر दोहुर *do'hur*, n. A loose sandy subsoil which is apt to give way in sinking a well without masonry, while the water from it is oily and brackish.

H دوهلي दोहली *doh'lī*, *dohrī*, *dohilā*, *bishunprīt*, n. f. Rent-free lands granted to religious mendicants or *brahmans* for a public or charitable object, as the sinking of a well, the erection of a *chaupāl*, the building and maintenance of a temple, etc.

P ده *deh*; H. *gāṅo*, n. m. A village.
deh-bandī, n. f. A detailed statement of villages and their assessment.
دهدار *deh-dār*, n. m.
The village overseer or superintendant on the part of the landholder or the state, whose duty it is to exercise a superintendence over the village cultivation, so that the *zamīndār* or Government may not suffer loss through negligence or fraud. He is also to see that the lands are properly distributed, the village boundaries preserved, and to assist in making the collections. Also, one holding a prescriptive right of occupancy at a fixed rate.

دهداري *deh-dārī*, n. f. 1. The office.
2. The assignment in perpetuity of a portion of the purchased property for the support of the original proprietor.
deh-dārī salāmī. A tax of one rupee annually collected from every village of a district to defray the expenses of a *deh-dār*.
دهكشت *deh-kāsht*, n. m. A resident villager.
deh-kāsht zamīn, Land cultivated by a resident cultivator.
deh-sanī, n. f. A record of the collections, accounts, etc. of ten years.
دهات *dehāt'*, *dihat*, n. m. pl. of ده. 1. Villages.
2. The country.
dehāt puṭṭīdārī yā zamīndārī, *Paṭṭīdārī* or *zamīndarī* estates or villages.
dehāt khālisah. Estates paying revenue directly to Government.
dehāt'ī, n. m. A villager; countryman.
dehātī jamā. Village assessment.
The revenue assessment upon any number of villages forming a local division.
dehāt-i-istamrārī, Villages held at a fixed rent.
dehāt nahar, Canal distributary.
deh-jamā, n. f. The revenue assessment of a village.
dehī kharch; H. *malbā*, n.m. Village expenses; an assessment on a village for its quota of charges of settlement and collections.
dehī āsāmī, n. f. A resident cultivator holding the right of cultivation at a fixed rent.
dehī rīt, n. f. The village custom or rate.
dah-sālā, adj. Decennial.

P ده *dah*, adj. Ten.
dah-nīmī, n. f. *lit.* half of ten. Five per cent.
dah-yak, n. m. The tenth part; one in ten; a tithe.

H دهارا *dhār'ā*, n. m. A fixed assessment or customary rate; a proportionate share or charge (*dhār bāchh*).
دهارباچه धारबाछ *dhār bāchh*, n.
Any even or general distribution of a charge or rate, etc., especially that which is levied from the individual holders of a coparcenary estate to make good any deficiency in the produce of land held in common, or let to cultivators. In the central part of the N.-W. P. the term denotes an imperfect *Paṭṭi-dārī* tenure in which part of the village land is held in common, and part in severalty. The profits of the former are first applied to the payment of the Government assessment and the village charges, and any deficit is made good by the proprietors in proportion to their holdings.

H دهاڙ धाड़ *dhār*, *dhāṛā*, n. f. S. धारा a multitude. 1. A band; banditti; an overwhelming multitude or crowd of robbers, locusts, etc. 2. An onset.
dhāṛ parnā, v. n. To be attacked by a band of robbers, etc.
dhāṛ mārnā, v. a. 1. To plunder in bands; commit; dacoity. 2. To plunder a crowd.
dhāṛ'ī, n. m. One of a band of robbers.

دهاڑي *dhāṛ'i*, n. m. 1. One of a band of robbers. 2. A ringleader.

H دهالا धाला *dhāl'ā*, n. m.

Collections from the individual villagers to cover village expenses in Rohilkhand, usually at the rate of one *anna* in a rupee, or one seer of grain per maund. In the Central and Lower Doab it is generally used with *jamā* as *jamā dhālā*, and signifies a particular tenure.

H دهاے धाय *dhāē*, *dhā*; P. *dāyā*, n. f. S. धात्री A wet nurse (*dāī-pilāī*).

dhāē ke denā, v. a. To put out to nurse.

dhāē-bhāī, *dūdh-bhāī*, Hin.; *kokā*; Mah. n. m. Foster-brother (*birādar-i-razāī*).

H دهتورا धतूरा *dhatū'rā*, *dhathūrā*; Sant. *datrā*, n. m. S. धत्तूर

A narcotic plant poison, the seeds of which are often given with sweetmeats to cause stupefaction or death.

dhatūrīyā, n. m. One who poisons with *dhatūrā*.

dhatūrā denā, v. n. To poison. [Wat.

sādā yā safaid dhatūrā, n. m. *Dhatūrā albā*.

kālā dhatūrā, n. m. *Dhatūrā fastuosā*, Wat.

H دهرا جانا धरा जान *dharā jāna*; E., *dharāuā*, v. n. To be apprehended; imprisoned.

H دهراوٹ धरावट *dharāv'aṭ*, n. Land ascertained by estimate, not measured. *Carnegy*.

H دهرتا धरता *dhar'tā*, n. m.

Discount; commission.

H دهرتي धरती *dhar'tī*, n.f.S. धरित्री, Pālī.1, 2.

dhartī bāhnā, *jotnā*, *yā chīrnā*, v. n.
To plough; break up land.

dhartī-patī, n. m. Landlord (*zamīndār*).

H دهرکٹ धुरकट *dhur-kaṭ*, n. An advance of rent paid by *asāmīs* to *zamīndārs* in the months of *Jeṭh* and *Asāṛh*.

H دهرم धर्म *dharm*, n. Religious forth.

dharm-ārth, n. m. A charitable grant; religious endowment. [one's caste.

dharm bigāṛnā, *yā bhishṭ k.*, v. a. To destroy

dharm-patr, n. m. A deed of gift or endowment for a religious purpose.

dharm-patnī, n. f. A wife who is of the same caste as her husband, or who has been married to him in due form. [on one's faith.

dharm se, adv. In good faith; honestly sworn

dharm se kahnā, v. n. To declare solemnly.

dharm khānā, *yā uṭhānā*, v. n.
To swear by one's faith; take an oath; call Heaven to witness.

دهرماڈري धर्मश्राद्री *dharmāḍ'rī*, n. f.

Land held by *Brāhmans* for religious purposes. *Carnegy*.

H دهرنا دينا धरना देना *dharnā yā dhannā denā*, Compelling payment of a debt or compliance with any demand by sitting at one's door, or causing annoyance by obstructing the conveyance of water to the house, etc, etc.; dunning.

H دهروانا धरवाना *dharvā'nā*, *dharānā*, v. a.

To bring an action against; bring to trial; bring to the bar.

دهروڑ धरोड़ *dharoṛ'*; Rus. *dharohaṛ*, *dharot*; Bhoj. *dharohari*; Tir. *dharārī*, n. f.
A deposit (*amānat*, 2).

dharoṛ rakhnā, v. a. To place in one's charge, trust, or custody; to deposit.

H دهروکي धरौकी *dharau'kī*, n. f.

A rough estimate of the quantity of cultivated land to be assessed.

H دهرونا धरोना *dharo'nā*, n.m. H. *droh* fraud.

A second marriage of a girl brought about by her father.

If the father of a girl has betrothed his daughter to a person and received the *tikā* or wedding or betrothal gifts, and afterwards treacherously betroths and marries the girl to another person, the father is said to have committed *dharonā*. [low ground).

H دهري दहरी *dah'rī*, n. f. Stiff clay soil (in

H دهريچا धरीचा *dharī'chā*; Bhoj. *ardhuā*, n. m. H. *dharnā* to keep. The second husband of a Hin. widow among the lower classes.

H دهريل धरेल *dharel'*, n. f.

A kept mistress; a concubine.

H دهس धुस *dhus*, n. 1. A sterile sandy eminence; a glacis. 2. Red sterile soil.

A دهشت *dah'shat*, n. f. Fear.

dahshat-aṅgez, adj. Threatening; menacing.

dahshat khānā, v. n. To be intimidated.

H دهکا दहका *dah'kā*, n. m.

A reservoir for irrigating high lands.

H دهمکي धमकी *dham'kī*, n. f.

Threat; menace.

nuqsān pahauṅchāne kī dhamkī denā, G. G.
To hold out a threat of injury.

H دهنکر धनकर *dhan'kar*, *dhankaṛ*, n. f. H. *dhān* rice. A stiff soil on which rice is grown; a field cropped with rice in the previous season.

H دهني جوگ धनी जोग *dhanī-jog,* n. m.
The holder of a bill.
dhanī-jog hundī. A bill payable only to the owner; a crossed cheque.
aṭal dhan, A *jāedād-i-gair-manqūlā,* Immoveable property. [property.
uṭhāū dhan, A. *jāedād-i-manqūlā,* Moveable

H & P دهوکا دهي *dhokā-dihī, dhoke-bāzī,* n. f. Fraud; imposture.
dhokā denā, v. a. To cheat (*buttā denā,* 1),

H دهونٹي धोंटी *dhon'ṭī,* n. f.
A shepherd's crook; an instrument for digging or cutting with. (?).

H دهونڈال धोंडाल *dhonḍāl',* Mār. adj. Stony; abounding with stones (soil).

H دهونس धौंस *dhauns,* n. f. S. ध्वंस
1. (*dhauns paṭṭī*) Trick; cheat. [ment.
2. Exaction; extortion; compulsory pay-
3. A threat; menace.

H دهيانگي धियानगी *dhiyān'gī,* n. f. S. दैनिकी, day's hire. 1. Daily work. 2. Daily wages.

A دهيز *dahez'*; Hin. *dahej,* n. m. Dowry (جهيز),

H دهيلا धेला *dhel'ā,* n. m.
1. Half a share. 2. (*Brokers*) Fifty Rupees.

H دهيلي धेली *dhel'ī,* W., n. f. See ادهيلي

H ديارا दियारा *diā'rā, devārā,* Cont. of *daryā-barār,* n. m. A tract of alluvial land (*char,* 2.).

A ديانت *dyā'nat, dyānat-dārī,* n. f. Honesty.
dyānat-dār, adj. Honest (ايماندار),
dyānat se, adv. Honestly; conscientiously.
bad-dyānat, adj. Dishonest.
bad-dyānatī, n. f. Dishonesty; fraud.

H ديپ انتر ک दीप अनतर क *dīp antar k.,* v. n. To transport beyond seas.

A ديت *di'yat,* n. f. Blood-money (*khūn-bahā*).

P ديده و دانسته *dīdah. o dānista,* adv. *lit.* having seen and known.
Wittingly (*jān būjh-kar*).

H ديس देس *des,* n. m. Country.
des-āchār, des byohār, des-chalan, n. m.
1. Local usage or observance. 2. Public policy; custom or fashion of the country.
des-adhkārī, n. m. The chief governor or superintendant of a province or country.
des-ānt, deshānt, n. f. The boundaries of a country or district.
des-tiyāg; A. *hijrat,* n. m. 1. Abandoning one's country; expatriation. 2. Emigration.
des chhoṛ'nā, hijrat k., v. n. To leave one's country or home; to emigrate.
des ko jānā, v. n. To go home; to go on furlough.
des-nikālā, n. m. Exile (*jalāvatnī*).
des-nikālā denā, jalā-vatan k., v. a.
To banish from the country. [district.
desvār', n. A statement of the villages in a

A دين *dain*; Pop. *den,* n. m. A debt; liability.
دينداد *dain-dār*; Pop. *den-dār,* n. m. A debtor.
dain tamassukī, G. G. n. f. The certificate given to a bankrupt who has given up his effects.
dain hākimī. The share of the produce due to the Government.
dain muājjal, n. 1. A debt payable on demand.
dain muwajjal, n.
A debt of which payment is deferred.
dain mahr, n. m. Debt of dower; wife's portion.
dain mahr muajjil, n.
A dower paid at the time of marriage.
dain wājib, n. m. A just debt.
دينا देना *den'ā,* n. m. Debt; liability.
denā pānā, n. m. Assets and liabilities; debits and credits.
den len, More properly, *len den,* Dealings.
divāl', part. adj. Solvent.
de marnā, v. n.
To leave at one's death; bequeath.

P ديوان *dīvān',* n. m. 1. A royal court; a court of audience. 2. A minister; a chief officer of state; a financial minister; the head officer of the revenue or financial department. [a *vazīr.*
ديوان اعلا *dīvān-i-ālā,* n. m. A prime minister;
ديوان خاص *dīvān-i-khās,* n. m. The cabinet; privy council. [chequer.
dīvān-i-khālisa, n. m. Chancellor of the ex-
ديوان خانه *dīvān-khānah,* n. m. A hall of audience; a chamber; court; a public room detached from the house. [audience.
ديوان عام *dīvān-i-ām,* n. m. Public hall of
ديواني *dīvān'ī,* n. f. 1. The office of a *dīvān*; ministry. 2. A civil court.
qānūn-i-dīvānī, n. Civil law.
majmūa-i-qānūn-i-dīvānī mutaalliqa-i-hind.
The Indian Civil Code.

ڈ

H ڈابر डाबर *ḍāb'ar, ḍabrā*; n. m. H. *ḍūbnā* to be drowned. [marsh; lowlands.
1. Low ground where water lies; swamp;

H ڈابی **डाबी** *ḍāb'ī*, E.; *dasāvan*, W. n. f. One-tenth of the harvest given to the reaper.

H ڈاک **डाक** *ḍāk*, n. f. A post.

ḍāk-bahṅgī, n. f. Parcel post. [relay is posted.
ḍāk-chaukī, n. f. A stage or station where a
ḍāk-khānā, ḍāk-ghar, n. m. A post office.
ḍāk kā kharch, ḍāk kā mahsūl, n. m.
Postal charges; postage.

H ڈاکا **डाका** *ḍāk'ā, ḍāṅkā*, n. m.
An attack by a gang of robbers or bandits.
ḍākā paṛnā, v. n. To be attacked by Dacoits.
ḍākā paṛne-vālā, G. G.
Dacoity about to be committed. [dacoity.
ḍākā ḍālnā; Rus. *ḍākā ghālnā*, v. a. To commit
ḍākā-zanī, n. f. Dacoity; highway robbery.

H ڈاک بولنا **डाक बोलना** *ḍāk bolnā*, v. n.
To bid at an auction.

H ڈاکر **डाकर** *ḍāk'ar, ḍākrā*, n. f.
A strong, rich, clayey soil, breaking up into large clods, containing minute micaceous particles, and requiring abundant rain to saturate it sufficiently for sowing.

H ڈاکو **डाकू** *ḍāk'ū, ḍakait*, n. m. One of a gang of *ḍakaits* or robbers; a bandit.
ḍākuoṅ kā bhāī, sāthī, yā hamrāhī, n. m. One who belongs to a gang of dacoits. [bough.

H ڈال **डाल** *ḍāl, ḍālī, ḍār*, n. f. 1. A branch;
2. A basket, used to throw up water from a pond, etc. for irrigation.
3. Irrigation of land by throwing up water from a lower level.
khalal yā futūr ḍālnā, To affect injuriously; to cause mischief or disturbance.

H ڈانٹ **डांट** *ḍāṅṭ, ḍāṅṭ ḍapaṭ*, n. f. S. **दान्ति** subjection. Threat; menacing gesture.
ڈانٹنا **डांटना** *ḍāṅṭ'nā*, v. a.
To threaten; menace; browbeat.

H ڈانڈ **डांड** *ḍāṅḍ, ḍāṅṛ*; Tir. *tāṅṛ*; Mār. *ḍāṅg*. n. m. S. **दण्ड** a stick.
High land, not culturable for lack of water; upland fields, opp. of *khādar*. [boundary.
ḍāṅḍ dhurrā, dhar dhurrā, n. m. Village
ڈانڈا **डांडा** *ḍāṅḍ'ā*; Bhoj. *ḍaṅḍār*, n. 1. A landmark; field boundary; boundary line. 2. Raised ground or ridge; a path for cattle.
ḍāṅḍā meṅḍā, n. 1. A boundary road between two estates; bar (of a harbour). [n. f.
ḍāṅḍe meṅḍe kī takrār; Ped. *sarhaddī tanāzo*, Boundary cases or disputes.

H ڈبری **डबरी** *ḍab'rī*, n. f. A division of profits among a village community according to their respective shares.

H ڈبیا **डिबिया** *ḍib'iā*, n. f.
A small portion of grain given at harvest to some of the inferior village servants.

H ڈر **डर** *ḍar*, n. m. S. **दर** Fear.
ḍar dikhā-ke. By intimidation. [overawe.
ḍar dikhā-ke roknā, v. a. To deter; scare;
ḍar dikhānā, v. n. 1. To intimidate; frighten; put in fear; bully. 2. To deter.
ḍarā'vā, n. m. Threat; intimidation.
ڈرانا **डराना** *ḍarā'nā*; Rus. *ḍarāvnā*, v. a. Caus. of ڈرنا to fear. To intimidate.
jabr nā-jāyaz ke zarye yā numāyash se ḍarānā yā ḍar dikhlānā. To overawe by means of criminal force or the show of criminal force.
ڈراونا **डरावना** *ḍarā'onā, ḍarāonī, ḍarāū, ḍarānī*; Rus. *ḍarpāonī*, adj. Threatening; fearful (*bhyānak*); menacing. [a menace.
ḍarāonī harkat, n. f. A threatening gesture;

H ڈکیت **डकैत** *ḍakait'*, n. m. See *ḍākū*.
ڈکیتی **डकैती** *ḍakai'tī*, n. f.
Gang-robbery; dacoity.
ḍakaitī qatal-i-amad ke sāth, G.G. Dacoity with murder. [a dacoity.
ḍakaitī ka murtakab h., G. G. v. n. To commit
ḍakaiton ke garoh ke sharīk hone kī sazā. G. G.
Punishment for belonging to a gang of dacoits.

E ڈگری *ḍigrī'*, n. f. Cor. of decree (حکم 6.).

ḍigrī apīl-shuda yā zer apīl.
The decree under appeal.
ḍigrī isbat-i-baē. A decree declaratory of sale.
ḍigrī ijmālī. A joint decree.
ḍigrī akhīr yā qataī, Final decree.
ḍigrī iqbālī, n. A decree passed on confession of judgment; a judgment by cognovit.
ḍigrī pānā, yā hāsil k., v. a. To obtain a decree. [execution.
ḍigrī jārī k. To enforce a decree; to take out
ḍigrī jārī karānā, v. a. To sue out execution.
ḍigrī jārī karne-vālā, n. The party praying for execution of decree; the party who enforces a decree.
ḍigrī-dār, n. Decree-holder; judgment creditor; the person in whose favour judgment has been given.
ḍigrī dakhl-yābī ba-vajah be-dakhlī nā-jāiz.
A decree for recovery of possession on the ground of illegal ejectment.
ḍigrī zar-i-naqd. A decree for money.
ḍigrī sarsarī, n. f. A summary decree. [judgment.
ḍigrī se bachne kā upāē k. To elude or avoid

ḍigrī shufā, yā haq-i-shufa. A decree.
ḍigrī gair-vasūlī. An unsatisfied decree.
ḍigrī-i-farebī, A fraudulent decree.
ḍigrī qataī. A final decree. [award.
ḍigrī k., yā denā, v. a. To adjudge; decree;
ḍigrī ke ijrā meṅ, In the execution of decree.
ḍigrī kī illat meṅ,
On account of execution of decree.
ḍigrī nāfiz k. To enforce a decree.
ḍigrī yak-tarfah par muqadmah chhoṛnā, To suffer a default; let judgment go by default.
fareb yā aur tarīq nā-jāiz se ḍigrī hāsil k.
To obtain a decree by fraud or other improper means. [*ḍālnā.*
kisi ḍigrī ke ijra meṅ hārij honā yā tākhīr
To obstruct or delay the execution of a decree.

H ڈنڈ डंड *ḍaṅḍ,* n. m. S. दण्ड.
1. Punishment; compensation for injury; mulct; damages; ransom; fine. [payable.
2. A tax. 3. *Rus.* The rent or revenue
ḍaṅḍ bharnā, yā denā, v. n. To pay damages; make good; pay a fine.
ḍaṅḍ ḍālnā, v. a. To levy or impose a tax.
ḍaṅḍ se chhūṭnā, v. n. To be let off the payment of a fine or tax.
ḍaṅḍ lenā, v. n. To amerce; to levy a fine.
ḍaṅḍ-yog, adj. Punishable; penal.
ḍaṅḍī āgyā. Penal provision.
ḍaṅḍā-zanī, n. f. A mode of torture.
It consists in fastening a man's arms behind his back with a cord which is twisted round by means of a stick so as to increase the tension until the pain inflicted becomes intolerable. *Elliot.*

ڈنڈنا डंडना *ḍaṅḍ'nā, ḍāṅḍnā,* v. a.
To inflict a fine or penalty.
ḍaṅḍ'nā, v. n. To be fined, taxed.

H ڈنگوارا डंगवारा *ḍangvār'ā;* Bhoj. *agvārī,* n. m. Mutual accommodation, consisting in the loan of ploughs and oxen without charge.

ڈنگواری डंगवारी *ḍaṅgvār'ī,* n. f.
Partnership in cattle.

H ڈوبنا डूबना *ḍūb'nā,* v. n. To be drowned.

ڈوبا डूबा *ḍūb'ā, ḍūbī zamīn;* Bhoj. *ḍubaṅt,* n. f. Low land covered with water.
ḍūbā-chār, ḍūbārā, n. A bank or island in a river; low alluvial lands liable to be flooded, but cultivable in the cold weather for spring crops.
ḍūbā-mār, dobā-mār, n.
Lowlands which lose their moisture from sand being too near the surface.

ڈوبان डोबान *ḍobān',* n. Land situated around and in the beds of dry ponds.

ڈوبای डूबाइ *ḍūbā'ī,* n. f. 1. Drowning.
2. A bribe which is given absolutely, whether the briber gain or lose his suit, in contradistinction to *Tirānī,* a crossing over, i. e. a bribe which is to be returned if the suit is lost.

H ڈول डौल *ḍaul, ḍol,* n. f. Rich black soil.

ḍaul, An estimate of assets for the purpose of assessment.
ḍaul vāsil-bāqī, n. Statement of collections and balances. [or return.
ḍaul-patr. Exemplar of a form; a blank form

H ڈونڈی डोंडी *ḍoṅ'ḍī, ḍauṅṛī, ḍhaṅḍorā;* E. *ḍhiṅḍhorā;* Bhoj. *ḍiṅgirī;* Mag. *ḍigrī,* n. f. S. डिण्डिम 1. A small drum beaten by a public crier. 2. Proclamation by beat of drum. [*pīṭnā.*
ḍauṅḍī phernā, yā pīṭnā, v. a. See *ḍugḍugī*

H ڈھال باچھ ढालबाछ *ḍhāl bāchh,* W.
1. Calculating the incidence of the *bāchh* (rate) upon each individual.
2. Preparation of the *ḍhāl bāchh,* a paper distributing the amount to be realised from the village for any crop among the *asāmīs.*

H ڈھیا ढैया *ḍhai'yā, ḍhahiyā, ḍuhiyā,* n. P. *deh* a village, or H. *ḍhig* near.
Land near a village.

H ڈھیری ढेरी *ḍher'ī,* n. f. 1. A sub-division of a *Paṭṭī.* 2. A sharer in a joint estate.
ḍherī, n. f. 1. A sub-division of a *Paṭṭī.*
2. A share in a joint-tenancy village.

H ڈھینکلی ढेंकली *ḍheṅk'lī, ḍhekolī;* Sant. *ṭena,* n. f. A long beam working on an upright post as a pivot, having at one end a weight which suffices to raise the bucket at the other. [(*Brokers*).

H ڈیک آنے डेकआने *ḍek āne,* n. m. Six annas

H ڈیک اوبن डेकओबन *ḍek oban,* n. m.
Six rupees. (*Brokers*).

H ڈیوڑھا डेवढ़ा *ḍeoṛ'hā, ḍevṛhā, ḍevaṛ,* adv.
One and a half times.
ḍeoṛhā, n. m. Interest in kind, at 50 per cent esp. in seed grain, a maund of seed repaid by a maund and a half of grain at harvest.
ḍeoṛhā k., v. a. To balance the books; close an account.
hisāb ḍeoṛhā, An old system of account during Native rule, under which interest was not decreed when it had run beyond 50 per cent of the principal. *Carnegy.*
lekhā ḍeoṛhā barābar huā, Accounts adjusted.

ذ

A ذات *zāt*, n. f. Caste.

zāt se girā-huā, An outcaste.
zāt se nikālnā, v. a. To put out of caste.
zātī taällug yā fāëdā.
Personal interest or advantage.
zātī muāmelāt, Personal affairs or circumstances.
rusūkh-i-zātī, Personal influence.
qaid-i-zātī. Personal restraint.
بذاته *bi-zātihī, ba-zāt-i-khud, ba-zāt-i-khās*, adv.
Of himself; of itself; in person (*asālatan*); absolutely; *ex necessitate rei.*
bi-zātihī zimmeh-dār. At his personal debit; personally liable or responsible.

A ذريعه *zaria*, n. m.
1. Medium; means; instrument; instrumentality; agency. 2. Influence; interest; favor.
zariye se, ba-zariye, adv. In or by virtue of; through the intervention or instrumentality of; under cover; thereby; hereby.
is zariye se, G. G. By these presents.
ba-zariye isdār kisī qāëdah ām. G. G. By any general rule to be made. [true allegation.
ba-zariye izhār-i-darogh, By means of an un-
ba-zariye tahrīr wasīqa-i-mohrī. G. G.
By an instrument under seal.
ba-zariye rahn zamīn. On the security of land.
ba-zariye zarb-i-duhal. G. G. By beat of drum.
ba-zariye qurqi-o-nīlām. G. G.
By distress and sale.
ba-zariye khilānā zahr yā ashyāë hosh-rubā. G.G.
By administering poisonous or stupefying drugs.
ba-zariye nālish. G. G. By a suit. [one's office.
ba-zariye ohdeh-dārī, Ex-officio; in virtue of

A ذكاوت *zakā'vat*, n. f. ذكو was sharp.
Acuteness; penetration; acumen.

A ذمه *zim'mah*, n. m. ذم a compact. Charge; trust; responsibility. [proof.
zimma-i-subūt, Onus probandi; burden of
zimme k., v. a. To entrust; deliver in trust; deposit with; give in one's charge.
zimmah k. yā lenā, zimme-vār h., v. a. To undertake a charge; take on oneself; to bail.
zimmeh-nāmah, n. m. A deed of trust; authority to have charge of and make the collections of an estate.
zimmeh-vār, zimmeh-dār, adj. Responsible; answerable; liable. [trustee; assignee.
zimmeh-vār, zimmeh-dār, n. m. Guarantor;
zimmeh-vār, n. m. A person placed by the Government in charge of an estate in arrears of revenue, pending its sale.
zimmeh-vārī mahdūd. Limited liability.
zimmeh-vārī mushtarak. Joint liability.
qānūnan zimmeh-vār h., To be legally liable; to lie under a legal liability.
zimmeh-vārī, zimmeh-dārī, n. f. 1. Trust; charge; custody. 2. Engagement; guarantee; obligation. 3. Responsibility; liability. [liability.
zimmeh-vārī se barī k. To discharge from
zimmeh-vārī qānūnī. Legal liability.

A ذمي *zim'mī*, n. f. One living under protection, as a Christian, Jew, etc. who is allowed to live under a Mah. Government without molestation on paying tribute.

A ذي *zī*, n. m. Lord; master.
ذي اختيار *zī-ikhtiyār, zī-iqtidār*, n. m.
One empowered or in authority; a competent authority; a functionary; one having competent jurisdiction. [titled.
zī-haq, adj. Rightful; having the right; en-

A & H ذيل ميں *zail men, mundarje zail*, adv. ذيل had a long tail or pendant.
As follows; as undermentioned; as proceeding; as below.
hasb-i-mufassila zail. As detailed below.

ر

H راب राब *rāb*, n. f.
Ground prepared by the burning of leaves, grass, sticks, etc. for sowing. 3. The crops raised on the ground so prepared.

H راپڑ रापड़ *rāp'ar*, n. m. Barren soil (*banjar*).

A راتب *ra'tib*; Pop. *rātab*; Wom. *ratebā*, n. m. Daily allowance of food; rations.
راتبخور *rātab-khor*, n. m. 1. A stipendiary.
2. A pensioner. [bricklayer.

H راج राज *rāj*, n. m. S. राज्य. 1. A mason;
2. Government; rule; administration; jurisdiction. 3. Kingdom; monarchy; principality; state; realm; dominion; reign.
4. The ruling power; supreme authority; royalty; sovereignty. [power.
rāj-adhikār, n.m. Royal prerogative; paramount
rāj-adhikārī, n. m. A regent.
rāj-asthān, rāj-bhavan, rāj-ghar, n. m.
A king's palace; royal residence; court.
rāj-āggyā, n. f. The king's order; the royal edict or command; edict; rescript.
rāj-ishuar, mahārāj-adhirāj, n. m.
A king of kings; a paramount king.
rāj-ans, n. m. Government share or property.

rāj-basīṭ, rāj-dūt, n. m. An ambassador; envoy; a plenipotentiary. [matic.
rāj-bishe, adj. Governmental; political; diplo-
rāj-bans, n. m. Royal Family or dynasty.
rāj-bansāolī, rājāolī, n. f.
A line of kings; royal genealogy.
rāj-bansī, n. m. 1. A descendant of a *rājā.*
rāj-bahā, raj-bahā, The main distributory.
rāj-bhanḍār, n. m. 1. Royal exchequer; public treasury. 2. A public warehouse.
rāj bhang h., v. n. To be subverted (a kingdom).
rāj-bhog, n. m. Endowment of a temple.
rāj-bheṭ, n. f. A present made by an inferior on his admission to the presence of a great man; a fee paid to a public functionary for permission to reap the harvest.
rāj-baivasthā yā prabandh, n. m.
The government of a state; public policy; public administration.
rāj-pratinidh, n. m. Viceroy; regent.
rāj-tilak, rāj-abhishek, n. m. *rāj-gaddī,* n. f.
1. A royal mark on the forehead. 2. Accession to the throne; installation; coronation.
rāj-tilak yā rāj-gaddī denā, v. a.
To instal a king; to put on the throne.
rāj-darbār, n. m. Court; royal audience. [king.
rāj-darshan, n. m. A royal levee; an audience of the
rāj-darshan-sālā, n. m. The presence chamber.
rāj-drohī, adj. Rebellious; disloyal.
rāj-drohī, n. m. A rebel; traitor.
rāj-dulār, rāj-kumār, rāj-kuānr, rāj-kanvar, n. m. A prince (*shahzādah*).
rāj-dulārī, rāj-kunārī, rāj-kumārī, rāj-kanniyā, n. f. A princess (*shahzādī*).
rāj-dhānī, n. f. See *dār-ul-khilāfat.* The metropolis; capital; seat of Government.
rāj-dharam, n. m. Pālī, *rāja-dhammo.* Royal duty; the duties of the military caste.
rāj-dhan, n. m. Public property; royal revenue.
rāj-ḍanḍ, n. m. A tax; a punishment ordered by the king.
rāj-rānī, n. f. 1. A queen; royal consort.
2. An epithet of the goddess *Kālī.*
rāj-sabhā, rāj-darbār, n. f. See *darbār.*
rāj-kā, adj. Royal; national; public. [tion.
rāj-kāj, n. m. State affairs; public administra-
rāj-kar, n. m. Tax or toll imposed by the king.
rāj k., v. a. To govern; rule; reign. [nasty.
rāj-kul, n. m. Pr. *raaūlam.* Royal family or dy-
rāj-gaddī, yā singāsan; Royal throne.
rāj-gurū, n. m. The spiritual adviser of a prince or chief.
rāj-ghāt, n. m. Regicide.
rāj-ghātī, n. m. A regicide.
rāj-mudrā, n. f. Privy seal; the royal signet.
rāchchhas byāh, n. m. A marriage in which the appointed rites have not been observed; violent seizure and rape of a girl after the repulse or destruction of her relatives.

P راز *rāz,* n. m. A secret (*bhed,* 2.).
rāz fāsh k., v. a. To betray a secret; expose one.
rāz-i-maʼkhfī, A hidden secret; a private matter.
رازدار *rāz-dār,* n. m. 1. A confidant; one who is entrusted with a secret. 2. One cognizant of, or privy to a criminal transaction; a confidant; an accessory to a fact.
رازداری *rāz-dārī,* n. f. 1. Keeping a secret.
2. Having the knowledge of a crime and not giving information.
rāz dārī-i-bad mājrā, Cognizance of a crime after its perpetration; being accessory after the fact.
raz-dār qabal-i-mājrā. One cognizant of an intended crime; an accessory before the fact.
rāz-dārī-i-mājrā. Cognizance of a criminal transaction; being accessory to a crime.

H راس रास *rās,* n. f. S. राशि a heap.
A heap of husked grain in the field.
rās uṭhāna, v. a. To gather the harvest.

A راس المال *rās-ul-māl;* H. *mūl,* n. m.
Principal; capital; stock. [ness in dealing.

P راست معاملگی *rast muāmlagī.* n. f. Fair-
rāstmuāmlā, n. A fair transaction. [takes bribes.

A راشی *rāsh'ī, murtashī,* n. m. One who

A راضی *rāz'ī,* adj. رضو was content. [ready.
1. Contented; satisfied; agreed. 2. Willing;
rāzī k., v. a. 1. To content; satisfy. 2. To please; gratify. 3. To reconcile; conciliate.
4. To prevail upon; persuade, win, or get over. [satisfied, willing.
rāzī h., razāmand h, v. n. 1. To be content,
راضی نامہ *rāzī-nāma, rafa-nāma,* n. m. A deed of agreement or compromise by which the plaintiff or prosecutor acknowledges that he has been satisfied by the defendant.
rāzī-nāma likh denā, v. a.
To execute a deed of compromise.

A راغب *rāg'ib,* part. act. رغب Inclined to; prone to; leaning towards.
rāgib k., v. a. 1. To incline; dispose.
2. To encourage; incite to.
rā'gib h., v. n. To be inclined or disposed to.

A راقم *rā'qim, al rāqim,* n. m. رقم impressed.
A writer; correspondent.
rāqim-ul-hurūf, The writer of these letters, of this epistle, book, etc.; the undersigned.

H راکڑ राकड़ *rāk'aṛ,* n. Stony sandy soil.

H راکھي राखी *rākh'ī*; Panj. *rakhrī*, n. f. S. रक्षा

1. A fee paid for protection. 2. The black mail formerly levied by the Sikhs in the parganas on the Jamnā. *Bāghpat.*

3. In Purnya, the portion of village lands assigned as the watch or charge of each *rakhvālā.*

4. (*rākhā*) One who watches a field when the crop is ripening.

H رام جني राम जनी *rām-janī*, n. f. A *fille de joie*; a Hin. dancing-girl; a prostitute.

rām raule kā gāṅo. A village constantly changing hands, as new free-booters came and possessed themselves of it.

H رانڈ रांड *rāṅḍ*; Wom. *raṅḍiyā*; (*In comp.*) *raṅḍ*, n. f. S. रण्डा A widow (*bidhvā*).

H رانوا रांवा *rāṅ'vā*, *rāhvā*, n. m. 1. Wooded or waste land, esp. near a town or village.

2. A tax on cattle grazing on waste land.

P راه *rāh*, n. f. Way; road.

راهدار *rāh-dār*, n. m. 1. A collector of tolls or transit duties. 2. A road patrol. [duties.

راهداري *rāh-dārī*, n. f. Tolls; duties; transit

rāh-dārī zakūt. Black mail; a fee paid to escape plunder. [clearance certificate.

rāh-dārī kā parvāna hāsil k. To get a port

rāh rīt, *rāh o rasm.* Usage; custom.

راهزن *rāh-zan*; Pop. *rah-zan*, n. m.

A highwayman (*baṭmār*).

راهزني *rāh-zanī*; Pop. *rah-zanī*, n. f. See *baṭmārī.*

rāh-zanī bā-khūn.

Highway robbery with murder.

rāh-zanī ba-zakhm. Highway robbery with wounding; robbery on the road with personal injury. [highway.

rāh mārnā, v. a. To rob or plunder on the

A راهن *rāh'in* H. *girhvīn rakhne-wālā*, n. m. رهن placed as a pledge. A mortgager.

A رائے *rāë*, n. f. رائي seeing with the eye or mind. 1. An opinion; a judgment.

2. Counsel; advice. 3. Minute; vote.

rāë pūchhnā, v. a. To consult; take advice.

rāë taslīm k., *yā mānnā*, v. a.

To accept an opinion as correct.

rāë denā, v. a. To give an opinion; to vote.

rāë lagānā, v. a. To pronounce judgment.

rāë lenā, v. n. To ask one's opinion or vote.

rāë milānā, v. a. To concur or comply with.

izhār-i-rāë. An expression of opinion; a communication.

mutasāvī-ul-rāë. Equally divided in opinion.

A رائج *rā'ij*, adj. روج had a ready sale.

1. Generally received (*chaltā*, 1, 2, 3.); common. 2. Fashionable.

rāij-ul-waqt, n. m. Current (coin). [to; to pass.

rāij k., v. a. To make current; give currency

rāij h., v. n. To be in force; to prevail.

A ربا *rib'ā*, adj. Usuary.

A رب السلام *rabb-ul-sallam.* A purchaser who pays for an article in advance or anticipation.

رب المال *rabb-ul-māl*, An owner or possessor of property or capital.

A ربيب *rabīb'*, n. m. A step-son.

A ربيع *rabīā*, *rabī*; H. *āsāṛhī*, Bund. *unhārī*, n. f. ربع a fourth part. The spring; hence, the vernal or principal harvest.

Grain sown in Oct. & Nov. and cut in the spring months, March & May, comprising wheat, barley, peas, gram, oilseed, *arhar*, etc.

H رتن रतुन *rat'un*, n. A second crop of sugar-cane from the same roots, yielding almost as much as the first. *Carnegy.*

H رتوا रतवा *rat'vā*, n. m S. रक्त red.

A red insect which destroys a wheat crop.

E رجسٹر *raj'isṭar*, n. m. A register.

rajisṭar par chaṛhānā, *rajisṭar meṅ darj k.*,

To enter in the register; to register. [fers.

rajisṭar-i-tabdīlī, *yā inteqālī.* Register of trans-

rajisṭar rakhnā, *rajisṭar murattab karnā*,

To prepare, maintain, or keep a register.

rajisṭar-i-ʻām. A general register.

رجسٹري *rajisṭar'ī*, *rajisṭar par nām chaṛhānā*, n. f. Registry; registration.

rajisṭrī-shuda, adj. Registered.

ragisṭrī-shuda jamāat. A registered company.

rajisṭarī karānā, v. a. To cause to be registered.

rajisṭarī k., v. a. To register. [ing.

A رجعت *rajaāt'*; Illit. *rijat*, n. f. رجع return-

1. (Mah. law.) Receiving back a divorced wife. 2. A return of a fit of lunacy.

A رجوع *ru'jū*, n. f. رجع returning. Turning towards; inclination; bent; leaning.

rujū-min-al shahādat. Retraction of evidence, which is allowed by Mah. Law under certain restrictions, as before sentence; or, if after, the witnesses are liable to make good any injury done to the party against whom a cause has been decided.

nālish rujū k., v. n. To file a suit.

P رخت *raʻkht*, n. m. Clothes. See اسباب 6, 7, رخت و متاع *rakht o matā.*

Personal property, exclusive of cash, bullion, or negotiable stock.

A رخصت *ruᵘkh'sat,* n. f. رخص gave permission. See چهٹی 1, 3.
rukhsat-i-ittifāqī, Casual leave.
rukhsat-i-riāyatī, Privilege leave.
rukhsat-i-bilā vaza tankhuāh, Leave on full pay.
rukhsat denā, v. a. See *chhuṭṭī denā.*
rukhsat ba-vaza tankhuāh. Leave without pay.
rukhsat k., v. a. 1. To permit to depart; give leave to go (*bidā k.*). 2. To dismiss.
rukhsat milnā, v. n. See *chhuṭṭī milnā,* 1.
rukhsat h., v. n. 1. To take leave; depart. 2. To depart this life.
رخصتانہ, *ruᵘkhsatā'nā,* n. m. A present made on one's departure (*bidāegī,* 2.).
رخصتي *ruᵘkhsatī,* adj. On leave.

A رد *radd, rad,* n. m. رد returned. (*Mah. law*) The return of the surplus to the shares, after a distribution of the shares owing to the absence of the residuaries.
radd-i-subūt, n. m. Counter-proof; disproof; overthrow of the evidence; rebutment.
radd-i-javāb, n. m. Rejoinder; refutation of a defence; reply; replication.
radd-i-javāb k., v. a. To rejoin; refute.
radd-i-qarz, n. m. G. G. Discharge or liquidation of a debt.
radd k., v. a. 1. See *tardīd k.* 2. To reject; pronounce unfit for service.
radd-i-kalām. Counter-statement; contrary declaration; contradiction; refutation.
radd h., v. n. To be refuted, abrogated, etc.
ردنامہ *radd-nāmā,* n. m. G. G. A deed of rescission; an instrument abrogating a former engagement.

A رذالہ *rizāl'ā, rezīl,* n. m. A vagabond; villain; an impudent or shameless person.
rizālī bāt, Obscene language.

P رسد *ras'ad;* Illit. *rast,* n. f.
1. Imports, esp. of grain.
2. A store of grain, etc; commissariat supplies for an army, etc. 3. Allowance of food; rations. 4. Share; contribution.
Fees; duties; perquisites.
rasad-beshī, n. f. Increase of assessment.
rasadī jama, n. f. Progressively increasing rent or Government demand.
rasad pahuṅchānā, v. n. To furnish supplies for an army, etc.
rasad-rasān, n. m. One who provides supplies.
ras'adī, adj. Rateable; proportionate; progressively increasing or decreasing.
hissa-i-rasadī, n. m. A proportionate share.

A رسم *rasm,* n. f. رسم marking. 1. Usage; custom; practice. 2. Settled mode; order. [practice.
rasm ahl-i-tijārat; H. *byohār rīt,* Mercantile law; commercial usage.
rasm par chalnā yā jānā, v. n. To act according to custom. [custom.
rasm-i-khāndān; H. *kulā beohār,* n. f. Family
rasm-i-zamānah, The fashion of the day; conventional usage.
rasm-i-mulk; H. *desā chāl,* n. f. The custom of the country.
rasm o rivāj. Custom and usage; established
bāp dādā yā baroṅ kī rasm, purānī yā qadīm rasm. An old custom.
mazhabī rasm; H. *dharm-rīt.* Religious ceremony.

رسوم *rusūm';* Illit. *rasum,* n. f. Pl. of رسم
rusūm-i-paṭvārī, n. f. Patvari's fees.
rusūm-i-tihāī, n. f. A fine or quit rent levied formerly on rent-free lands in Bundelkhand, supposed to be a third of the usual assessment.
rusūm-i-chaudhrī, n. f. Fees and perquisites of the head man of a trade or of a village.
rusūm-i-khazana. Fees on receipts and payment of the public treasury.
rusūm-i-khazānchī. Fees paid to a treasurer.
rusūm-dār, G. G. n. m. The holder of certain fees or perquisites.
rusūm-i-zamīndārī, n. f. The fees or perquisites allowed to *zamīndārs* by the Mah. Government, or by a commission, generally of five per cent on the gross collections. Fees levied by a *zamīndār* on his tenants, either on particular occasions or as a fine or quit rent.
rusūm-i-sarkār. Stamp duties.
rusūm-i-adālat. Court fees.
rusūm-i-gair-mahkūmā. Arbitrary cesses.
rusūm-i-qānūṅ-go. A small fee to the *qānūṅgo* levied on the revenue collections.
rusūm-i-nazārat. The fees payable to the Nāzir of a court on serving a process. [q. v.
rusūm-i-karāo; H. *karāo-rīt.* The custom of *karāo,* The marriage of a widow with the brother of a deceased husband, which especially obtains among the Jāts, Gūjars, Ahirs, and other inferior tribes in the N. W. P.
rusūm-i-gaṭhṛī, G. G.; H. *gaṭhṛī-kar,* n. f. Fees on bales and packages.
rusūm-i-mohtarafa, G. G. Taxes levied on trades and professions. [monies.
rasmiyāt-i-byāh; H. *byāh-rīt,* Marriage cere-
rasmiyāt-i-maiyat; H. *kiryā karam.* Funeral ceremonies; obsequies.

H رسوائی रसवाई *rasvā'ī, rasyāval,* n. f. The ceremony of distributing the first juice of the sugarcane; hence, the season.

A رسوخ *rusūᵘkh', rasūkhīyat,* n. m. رسخ was firm. Firmness; constancy; stability.

rusūkh-i-zātī kisī mulāzim-i-sarkārī ke sāth amal meṅ lānā. To exercise personal influence over a public servant.

P رسید *rasīd'*, n. f. P. *rasīdan* to arrive.
1. Acknowledgment; a receipt.
rasīd-bahī, n. f. A receipt-book. [ledgment.
rasīd denā, v. n. To give a receipt or acknow-
rasīd kā ṭikaṭ, A receipt stamp.

H رشاو, रसाव *rashāv', rashāo, mairā*; Bhoj. *heṅ gāv*, n. Dressing a field; pulverising and smoothing the soil, and leaving it exposed to the air some days before sowing.

P رشتہ *rish'ta*, n. m. Kin; relation; connection; relation by blood or marriage.
rishta-i-haqīqī, n. m. Relation by the full blood.
رشتہدار *rishte-dār*, n. m. Relation; relative.
rishta k., v. a. To form an alliance or connexion with. [relation.
rishte-dār-i-baīd; H. *dūr kā nātā*, A distant
rishte-dār-i-qarīb; H. *pās kā nātā*, A near relation. [alliance; affinity.
رشتہداري *rishte-dārī*; H. *nātā*, n.f. Relationship;
rishta-i-sababī, *yā nasabī*, G. G. Connection by marriage or by consanguinity.

A رشوت *rish'vat*; H. *ghūs*, n. f. رشو he bribed him. A bribe; an illegal gratification; hush-money (*mūṅh-bharāī*).
rishvat-khor; Pop. *rishvat-khorā*, n. m.
One who takes bribes.
rishvat-dihī, n. f. G. G. Giving a bribe.
rishvat denā, v. a. To offer or give a bribe; to bribe. [bribery.
rishvat-sitānī, n. f. The act of taking bribes;
rishvat sitānī ba-jabr. Exaction of a bribe.
rishvat se milānā. To buy off (a person). [bribe.
rishvat-i-shartī; H. *tirāī*, n. f. A contingent
rishvat-i-gair mashrūt, n. An absolute or unconditional bribe (H. *ḍubāī*, 2.).
rishvat khānā, yā lenā, v. n. To swallow or take a bribe; to be bribed.
rishvat o bad-kirdārī, n. Bribery and corruption.

A رضا *raz'ā*, n. f. رضو was content.
1. (*razā-mandī*) Consent; assent; acquiescence; will; pleasure.
2. Leave; esp. furlough. [pleasure.
razā o rağbat, n. f. Free consent; free-will and
razā o rağbat se, adv. Of one's own free will (*āp se*). [(راضي 1, 2.).
رضامند *razā-mand*, adj. Willing; consenting
razāmandī bilā ikrāh, razāmandī khātir-khuāh.
Free consent; willing consent.
razā-mandī ba-shaūr, razā-mandī bā-samajh, razā mandī āaqilāna. G. G.
Intelligent consent.

razā-mandī tahrīrī, Written consent. [ties.
razāmandī-i-tarfain. The consent of both par-
razā-mandī mutlaq. Unconditional assent.
bilā razā-mandī ausiyāë nām-zada vasīyatnāma,
Without the consent of the executors named in the will. [Fosterage.

A رضاع *razāā*, n. m. رضع sucking, as an infant.
In Mah. law, a bond of affinity between persons nursed by the same female, analogous to consanguinity.
razāī-bhāī; H. *dūdh bhāī*, n.m. A foster-brother

A رعايا *riāā'yā*, n. f. pl. of رعيت q. v. رعي pastured. 1. Tenants; subjects; the peasantry.
2. (*riāyā barāyā.*) The community; the masses; the people; the public.
riāyā-i-Inglistān. British subjects.
riāyā kī nālisheṅ yā dāve, Private claims.
riāyā-i-mulk-i-gair,
Subjects of another power; aliens.
رعايت *riāy'at*, n. f. Favour; consideration.
رعايتي *riāā'yatī, riāetī*, n. m. One to whom remission or abatement has been granted.
riāyātī chhuṭṭī yā rukhsat, Privilege leave.
riāāyat ba-taur hākimāna k.
To take judicial notice.
riāāyat sāzindagān-i-shorah. G. G. Protection to saltpetre manufacturers.
riāāyat-i-qānūn. The authority of law.
ba-riaāyat qayūd-mundarja. Under the restrictions mentioned. [cultivator.
riāāyatī beshī. Surplusages remitted to the
riaāyat-i-paṭṭā. A lease granted to a cultivator at a favorable rate.

A رعيت *raāī'yat*; Pop. *raiyat*, n. f. رعى
1. A subject of a state.
2. Tenant; cultivator; peasant.
3. A dependant; follower; servant.
raiyat-i-kāsht-kār. A cultivating tenant.
raiyat-nāma, n. m. An engagement given by the cultivators to the landlord or proprietor.
raiyat-wār jamā-bandī. Settlement with each individual cultivator.
raiyat-wārī, n.f. According to or with *Raiyats.* A revenue settlement made by the Government with the actual cultivators of the soil for a given term.
raiyat-vārī faisla. Settlement of land-rents, made with the cultivators themselves, without the intervention of any *zamīndar* or landlord, commonly known as the 'Ryotwarī system.' [to a *raiyat.*
رعيتي *rai'yatī*, n. f. *lit.* relating or belonging
Lands of which the revenue is paid in money, in contradistinction to the *Khamār* lands, of which the revenue is paid in kind.
Also, a settlement direct with the cultivator.
raiyatī paṭṭā. A lease given to a cultivator.

A رعي *rai* Rate; the local rate of assessment.

The standard rate at which the lands of a village or district are assessed, according to their several qualities.

rāī-bandī, A statement or table of rates.

A document shewing the rates at which different descriptions of land are usually assessed in any particular district.

rāī-kankūtī. Lands of which the assessment was rated according to the value, or a fixed or customary rate of produce per *bīghā*.

A رفع *raf'ā*, *rafa-dād*, *rafu-dafa*, *rafa-i-shar*, n. m. رفع put away. Settlement (*tasfīyā*, 3).

rafa k., *rafa dafa k.*, v.a. To settle or dispose of.

رفع نامه *rafā-nāmah*. A deed of compromise.

رفع نقصان *rafa-i-nuqsān*. A remedy.

rafa h., v. n. To be settled or disposed of.

rafadād-i-hisāb.

Winding up or settlement of an account.

A رفيق *rafīq'*, n. m. رفق tying together a camel's forelegs. 1. A companion; associate; ally; comrade; friend; co-adjutor. 2. A follower; dependent; adherent; partisan. 3. A confederate.

رفيق جرم *rafīq-i-jurm*. An accessory to a crime; an accessory.

A رقبة *raq'ba*; H. *bistār*, n. m. 1. An area; extent of land. 2. The lands comprised within the boundaries of a village measurement.

raqba-i-āb-pashī, An irrigated area.

raqba-i-arāzī. The area of the land.

raqba-i-arāzi-i-muzbitā. The area of resumed [lands.

raqba-barāmad. Increase of land.

raqba-i-bandobastī. An assessed area.

raqba-bandī, n. f. A statement shewing the area of an estate, village, or township, the total quantity of land belonging to the community, the portions that pay or are exempt from revenue, and those which are cultivated or uncultivated or incapable of cultivation.

raqba-i-gair-mazrūa. An uncultivated area.

raqba qābil-uz-zarāat. A culturable area.

raqba qābil tashkhīs-i-jama. An assessable area.

raqba lagānī az rūe bīghā-dihī. A rent-paying area by village *bīgha*.

raqba-i-mazrūa. A cultivated area.

A رقعة *ruq'qā*, n. m. رقع he patched it.

1. See *chiṭṭhī*. 2. A receipt.

ruqqa likhne-wālā; H. *hunḍī-bhejā*. The drawer of a cheque.

hāmil-i-ruqqa, n. m. The bearer of a cheque or [note.

رقعات *ruqqā'āt*, *ruqqājāt*. n. Pl. of رقعه [book.

1. Notes. 2. A collection of letters; a letter

A رقم *raq'am*, n. f. رقم marked, impressed; pl. رقوم 1. See *ṭūm* (1—3). 2. A mark; figure; initial. 3. A mode of arithmetical notation taken chiefly from the initials of the Arabic terms for numbers. 4. Entry; item. 5. Amount; sum; total sum.

6. A fractional share of an undivided estate (*paṭṭī*, 1.) 7. Rate of assessment.

8. Kind; sort (*bhāṅt*).

raqam-i-jamā. An item of credit.

raqam-i-kharch. An item of disbursement.

raqam-sivāī. 1. What is over or in excess of the stipulated sum. 2. Cases. 3. Perquisites.

raqam k., v. a. To mark; note; write.

raqam-i-mutanāzia. A disputed item.

raqam-ï-mushtabah-ul-vusūl. A sum of money the recovery of which is doubtful.

raqam-wār, adv, In detail; item by item.

raqam-wār likhnā.

To particularize; to exhibit in detail.

H رکهنا रखना *rakh'nā*, *rakh lenā*; Rus. *rākhnā*, v. a. S. रक्षण

1. To stake; bet (*aṛnā*, 13).

2. To mortgage; pawn; pledge.

bahī murattab rakhnā. To keep account books.

رکهوالا रखवाला *rakhvā'lā*; Rus. *rakhvaīyā*, *rakhvār*; E. *agoreā*, n. m. 1. (*rakhī*) A guardian; guard; protector; custodian; curator.

2. A watchman; warden; gate-keeper.

3. A cowherd; shepherd; goatherd.

4. (*Agric.*) The man who looks after the standing crop and scares away birds, etc.

رکهوالي रखवाली *rakhvā'lī*; Rus. *rakhvārī*, n. f.

1. Guard; watch; protection; charge; custody; keep; care; trust. 2. The wages of a guard or watch. 3. (*rakhī*) Tribute; black mail. 4. A grazier (*pālī*, 4).

رکهي रखी *rakh'ī*, n. f. (*Rus.*) A stack of hay.

H رکهي रिखी *rikh'ī*, n.f. (*Brokers*) Six rupees.

rikhī aṣīr. (*Brokers*) Sixteen rupees.

rikhī mainā. (*Brokers*) Twenty-six rupees.

H رن रिन *rin*, E. n.m.S. ऋण 1. A debt (*qarz*).

P A رنج عام *ranj-i-ām*, G.G. Common annoyance; a public grievance.

H رنڈاپا रंडापा *ranḍā'pā*, n. m. Widowhood.

رنڈسالا रंडसाला *ranḍ-sālā*, n. f.

A widow's dress; widow's weeds.

رنڈک रंडक *ranḍ'ak*, n. m. A barren tree.

رنڈوا रंडवा *ranḍ'vā*, n.m.1. A widower. [wench.

رنڈي रंडी *ranḍ'ī*, n. f. 1. (*Mah. Wom.*) A woman;

2. (*ranḍī munḍī*) A woman of the town; a prostitute; strumpet; whore.

randī-bāz, n. m. A rake ; a gay Lothario ; a fornicator ; whoremonger. [tery ; whoredom.
randī-bāzī, n. f. Wenching ; fornication ; adul-
رنڈیا रंडिया *rand'iyā*, n. f. 1. A widow.
2. A low woman (an abuse) ; a prostitute.

H رنواس रनवास *ranvās'*, *ranbās* ; A. *mahl*, n. m. S. राज्ञीवास ; H. *rānī* a queen, *bās* abode. A royal seraglio ; a queen's apartments ; a palace.

H رنيا रिनया *rin'yā* ; Tir. *rīnyā* ; A. *qaraz-dār*, n. f. S. ऋणी A debtor.
rinyā h., v. n. To owe ; to be in debt.

P رو *rū*, n. m. 1. Face ; surface.
2. Mode ; manner. 3. Cause ; reason.
روپوش *rū-posh*, adj. In hiding ; absconded.
rū-posh h., v. n. To abscond ; run away ; conceal one's self ; evade service of summons.
روپوشي *rū-pos'hī*, n. f. Absconding ; hiding.
rū-poshī kī sūrat men. G. G.
In the event of non-appearance.
rū riāyat, n. f. Partiality ; countenance ; favor.
rū riāyat k. v. a. To countenance ; favor.
is rū se, adv. So. See *az-rūë*.
hukm-i-sazā kī rū se. G. G. Under the sentence.

P روا *rav'ā*, adj. 1. Right. See جائز
2. Allowable ; current. 3. Approved ; worthy of reception or attention.
ravā jān'nā, yā samajhnā, v. n. To think fit or proper ; to approve. [to be right.
ravā-dār, adj. Approving ; judging or holding
ravā rakh'nā, v. a. 1. To receive ; acquiesce in ; countenance. 2. To uphold ; maintain ; justify.
3. To warrant ; make legal (*jāiz rakhnā*).

A رواج *rivāj'*, n. m. روج was easily saleable.
1. Usage ; practice. 2. Prevalence ; currency.
3. See *rasm*. [force of law.
rivāj ba-manzila-i-qānūn. Usage having the
rivāj pānā yā pakar'nā v. n.
1. To become prevalent. 2. To have effect.
rivāj parnā, v. n. To prevail or become current.
rivāj haq-i-shufā. The custom of pre-emption.
rivāj-khās ; H. *nij-rīt*, n. f.
A special usage or custom.
rivāj-i-khāndān ; H. *kul kī rīt*. Family usage or custom. [local usage.
rivāj-i-deh ; H. *gāon kī rīt*, n. Village custom ;
rivāj denā, v. a. 1. To make current ; give currency to. 2. To introduce ; issue.
3. To extend ; spread abroad ; propagate.
rivāj-i-shud-āmad. Prescriptive usage. [custom.
rivāj-i-muqām ; H. *des beohār*. Local usage or
rivāj-i-mulk, n. 1. Public policy ; custom of the country. 2. Usage which, when clearly established, is held to be of force in the decision of law suits although contrary to the written law. [vance.
rivāj mulkī yā dehātī, n. Local usage or obser-
rivāj hai. Is usual.
رواجي *rivāj'ī*, adj. 1. Current ; current in the market. 2. Ordinary ; usual.

P روان *ravān'*, adj. رو go. See جاری 1.
sāl-i-ravān, n. m. The current year.
روانگي *ravān'gī*, n. f. 1. Setting out ; departure ; embarkation. 2. Despatch (of a letter, etc). 3. The purport of a permit, pass, or authority to proceed.
ravāngī chitthī, n. 1. A pass ; passport.
2. Port clearance.
ravāngī-i-māl. Despatch of goods ; consignment.
روانه ک *ravānah k.*, v. a. To send ; despatch (a letter, messenger, etc.). [depart.
ravānah h., v. n. 1. To proceed ; set out ;
2. To be sent or despatched.

A روايت *rivā'yat*, *ravāyat*, n. f. روی related.
A written legal opinion by a Mah. law officer.

P روبرو *rū-ba-rū'* ; Pop. *robrū*, adv. Before one's face ; face to face (آگے 1, 2.).
robrū k. yā lānā, v. n. To bring in the presence of ; to confront. [order.

P روبکار *rūbakār'* ; Pop. *robkār*, n. m. An
روبکاري *rūbakār'ī* ; *robakārī* ; Pop. *robkārī*, n. f. See *peshī* (2). 1. A judicial act or proceeding ; a record in a cause. 2. A Persian or Urdu communication addressed to an equal.
rubakārī asnāë tajvīz.
Mesne process ; an inter-pellation.
rūbakārī akhir, n. Final process.
rūbakārī bandobast. Settlement proceeding.
rūbakārī-i-tanqīh. Preliminary proceedings.
rūbakārī tanqīh-talab, yā subūt-talab.
A proceeding laying down the issues.
rūbakārī-i-adālat. Judicial proceedings.
rūbakārī nīlām. A sale proceeding. [session.
rūbakārī yā parvāna-i-dakhl. Warrant of pos-
rūbakārī navīs. Proceeding writer.
robkārī h., v. n. To be tried or heard (a case).

H روپر रोपर *rop'ar* ; Sant. *rohoi horo*, n. m.
1. Transplanted rice.. 2. A rate in a lease for crops of rice raised by transplanting.

H روپنا रोपना *ropnā*, v. a. S. रुह Sant. *er*.
To sow ; plant ; transplant.
ropnā, n. f. Betrothal.

H روپيه रुपया *rupay'ā* ; Rus. *rupaiyā*, *rapaiyā* ; Sant. *takā*, n. m. S. रूप्य Pr. *ruppam*.

1. A rupee, the general denomination of the silver currency of India, and the standard measure of value. 2. Coin; specie; cash.
rupayā bhejnā, yā irsāl k., v. a. To remit money.
rupaë kā len den, rupaë kā muāmlah, Money dealings; a pecuniary transactions.
rupaë ke bishe. Pecuniary; relating to money.
rupaë-vālā; Sant. *kisānṛ*, n. m. A wealthy person; a rich man.

H روٹي کپڑا रोटी कपड़ा *roṭī kapṛā*, n. m. Food and raiment.
roṭī kapṛe, yā nān nafqe kā dāvā. A claim for maintenance on the part of a deserted wife.
roṭī kapṛe kī khabar lenā, roṭī kapṛā d., v. a. To feed and clothe; to maintain or support one.
روٹيا रोटिया *roṭ'iyā*, n. m. A domestic servant who gets food in lieu of wages.

P روز *roz*, n. m. 1. Day. 2. Daily wages.
roz baṭnā, v. n. To be distributed (daily wages).
roz-ba-roz, roz-marrah, adv. 1. Day after day. 2. Constantly.
roz-marrah, adj. 1. Everyday; ordinary; customary; usual. 2. Conventional; idiomatic.
roz-marrah hisāb. Daily account; account current.
roz-nāmchah, roz-nāmah, n. m. A diary; day book; journal; daily account.
roz-nāmchah khās. A special diary.
roz-nāmchah-i-ām. A general diary.
روزانه *rozā'nah*, adv. Daily.
روزگار *rozgār'*, n. m. 1. The world; age; time. 2. The means of subsistence; service; employment; business; livelihood.
rozgār-peshā, n. m. Serving man; servant.
روزه *roz'ah*, n. m. A deduction formerly allowed in Bengal to the *zamīndārs* to cover the expenses of daily charitable allowance; pensions assigned by Government in 1718 to various persons in the province of Benares.
روزي *roz'ī*, n. f. Daily food or allowance; maintenance.
روزينه *rozī'nah*, n. m. Daily pay or wages; daily allowance; a stipend; pension.
rozīnah-dār, n. A stipendiary; pensioner.

H روسلي रौसली *raus'lī, rosalī, rosal, raustī*, n. f. S. कषित A light loamy soil.
It is sometimes considered little inferior to the first quality or *ḍākar*, and assessed at the same rate.

H روک रोक *rok*, n. f. S. रोध 1. Limitation; restriction. 2. Hindrance.
rok-ṭok, n. f. 1. Obstruction. [challenge. 2. Opposition; resistance; a sentry's
rok ṭok k., v. a. 1. To challenge (as a sentry). 2. To take exception to.
rok rakh'nā, v. a. 1. See *bāz rakhnā*, 1 to 6. 2. To impound; pound (cattle).
rok rok-ke, adv. By little and little; sparingly.
be-rok-ṭok, adv. Without let or hindrance.

H روک रोक *rok, rokṛā*, adj. S. रोक buying with ready money. Ready money or cash.
روکڑ रोकड़ *rok'aṛ*, n. m. 1. Cash; ready money. 2. Specie, jewels, or valuables readily convertible into coin. 3. Stock; capital.
rokaṛ bikrī, n. f. Ready-money sale; cash transaction.
rokaṛ-bahī, n.f. Cash-book. [surer; cash-keeper.
روکڑيا रोकड़िया *rokaṛ'yā*, n. m. A cashier; trea-

H روکن रूकन *rūk'an, rūkhan, rūkan jhūkan, rūṅgan*; Sant. *unkā*; E. *maṅgnī*, n. f. Given in the bargain; over and above.

E رول *rol*, n. m. 1. Roll; register; catalogue. 2. Rotation; turn. 3. The Govt. revenue.
rol-dār, n. One who is entered on the Collector's roll or record.

H رولي रोली *rol'ī, rorī*; Tir. *rorī*, n. f. 1. A mixture of rice, turmeric, and alum, with acid, used to paint the forehead. 2. A red insect which attacks standing wheat crops.

H رونا रौना *raun'ā, raun*, n. m. S. रमण Bringing home a wife to consummate a marriage.
It is an intermediate ceremony between the marriage and the *gaunā*, q. v. In some places the two meanings are inverted.

H رونپي रोंपी *roṅp'ī*; Bhoj. *ropni hārī*, n.f. One who transplants rice, etc.
The head woman of the party is called *siraitīn* (arranger). She leads the line of transplanters, and receives a double share of *chabenī* parched grain.

E روند *rauṅd*; Tir. *roun*, n. f. Cor. of Eng. Round. The round of guards, etc.; patrolling.
rauṅd-gashtī, n. Going the rounds; patrolling.

H روندن रौंदन *rauṅd'an, rauṅdh'an*, n.f. S. मद to tread on. Trampling, treading under foot.
rauṅdan meṅ ānā, v. n. To be trampled or crushed under foot.
روندنا रौंदना *rauṅd'nā, rauṅdhnā, khūṅdnā*; Tir. *khūnab*, v. a. 1. To tread or walk on. 2. To tread out (corn). [der foot. 3. To trample on; ride over; crush un-

A رويت *ro'yat*; Pop. *rūyat*, n. f. راى seeing. 1. Aspect; view. 2. Countenance.
gavāh-i-rūyat, H. *āṅkh-dekhā*, An eye witness.

P رُوئیداد *rüedād'*; Pop. *rūdād*, n. f. A statement; proceeding; record in a case.
The report of a subordinate officer deputed to inquire into any affair; the return to an official inquiry.
rüedād-i-adālat. A judicial proceeding.
rüë-dād-i-tajvīz, n. A statement of the investigation of a suit at law.
rüēdād-i-arzī. The statement in a plaint.
rüēdād-i-misl. The facts shewn in the records of a case.
rüēdād-i-muqaddama. The narrative or whole course of proceedings in a cause; the merits of a case. [facts of the case.
khilāf ruë-dād-i-muqaddama. Opposed to the
P رہا *rihā'*, adj. Freed; liberated; set at liberty (*barī*, 1, 2). [(*barī k.*).
rihā k., *rihāī denā*, v. a. To discharge; relieve
rah-zanī ba-zakhm.
Highway robbery with wounding.
P رہائي *rihā'ī*, n. f. رستن to be free.
1. Escape; freedom. 2. Exemption; relief.
rihāī ba-zamānat k. To discharge on bail; to accept bail. [ing money.
H رہٹي रहटी *rah'ṭī*, n. f. A system of lend-
So called from *rahaṭ*, because the original debt, at compound interest, rolls on like a ball.
rahṭī chalā'nā, v.a. To lend money according to the *rahṭī* system. [saline soil.
H رہڑي रहड़ी *reh'ṛī*, *ṛehar*, n. f. Sandy or
A رہن *rahn*; Pop. *rahan*, n. m.
Giving in pawn; a mortgage (*bandhak*).
Property given as security for a loan, but of which the usufruct is not enjoyed by the lender, nor it can be transferred or sold.
rahn ijmālī, A joint mortgage.
rahn intifāī, n. A usufructuary mortgage.
. It is a mortgage "where a man borrows money and gives up his land to the lender who, unless his debt is paid off by the mortgager, may retain possession until he has, from the rents and profits of the land, repaid himself the interest, or, according as the terms of the agreement in each case may be the principal and the interest of the sum advanced by him." It may be said to resemble usufructuary mortgage (بھوگ بندھک). [tuary mortgage.
rahn intifāī shartī, n. A conditional usufruc-
It is where a mortgagee by conditional sale has the usufruct of the property, either by being merely put in possession and allowed to receive the rents and profits, or by having a lease given to him by the mortgager. [mortgage.
rahn intifāī mufrad. A simple usufructuary
It is, a mortgage in which, though the property is only collaterally pledged, as in the case of a pure simple mortgage, the mortgagee is permitted to have the usufruct of it.
rahn-bil-kafālat, *rahn bilā-daᵏkhl*. Hypothecation (*drishṭ bandhak*, *rahn mutlaq*).
rahn tamassuk, n. A mortgage bond.
rahn khālis. A real mortgage. [gage-deed.
rahn-nāmah bai bil-vafa. A conditional mort-
rahn-bil-qabz, n. Mortgage with possession.
rahān-dār, n. The holder of a mortgage; a mortgagee (*murtahin*). [gage right.
rahn-dārī, n. f. Holding a mortgage; a mort-
rahn dar rahn. A sub-mortgage.
rahan rakh'nā, v. n. To pledge; mortgage.
rahan se chhuṛā'nā, v. a. To redeem.
rahan shartī, *rahan mashrūt*,
A conditional mortgage.
rahn-sahīh, n. A valid mortgage. [(دشت بندھک).
rahn mutlaq. An unconditional mortgage.
rahn miādī. A mortgage for a limited period.
rahn-nāmah. A mortgage deed.
dar-rahn-dār, n. A sub-mortgagee. [vant; slave.
H رہوا रहवा *rah'vā*, *rahitvā*, n. m. 1. A ser-
2. A destitute person taken into a family.
رہوائي रहवाई *rahvā'ī*, n. f.
1. House-rent (*kirāyah*). 2. *Rus.* The wages due for watching the crops.
H رہواري रहवारी *rahvā'rī*, *rahbārī*, n. m.
A class of Hindus who trade in camels.
A ریاست *riyā'sat*, n. f. راس became chief.
1. Nobility; nobleness; high-mindedness.
2. See *rāj*, 2, 3.
riyāsat-i-jamhūrī, n. f. A republic; democracy.
riyāsat se khārij. G. G. An outlaw.
H ریت रीत *rīt*; Sant. *ari* n. f. S. रीति See *rasm*. Rite; ceremony; observance (*rasm*,).
rīt dikhānā, v. a. To point out a course of proceeding; to direct.
rīt rasm, *rīt rakam*, n. f. Manners and customs.
rīt se, adv. According to custom.
rīt se bāhar. Out of the ordinary course.
is rīt se, adv. Accordingly.
burī rīt se, adv. Badly.
be-rīt, *an-rīt*, adj. 1. Contrary to custom; irregular; unlawful. 2. Bad; disagreeable; unpleasant; offensive.
kaī rīt se, adv. In many respects. [old custom.
naī rīt k., v. a. To innovate; depart from an
ریتلي रेतली *ret'lī*, *retlā*, adj. Sandy; barren.
ریتي रेती *retī*, *retlī*, n.f.1. Sandy soil (4th quality).
2. A tract of alluvial land. [piece.
P ریزگي *rez'gī*, *rezgārī*, n. f. 1. A scarp; bit;
2. Small change; a two-anna, four-anna, or eight-anna bit. 3. Small pieces of gold or silver wire. 4. (*rezā*) Children employed in masonry work, etc., who receive half, one-third, etc., of a man's pay.
A رئیس *rais'*, n. m. pl *roasā*, راس head.
1. A prince; a chief.

2. A nobleman; one of the gentry; a gentleman; a respectable person.

3. A citizen; townsman; burgess. [power.

raīs-i-bā-ikhtiyār, n. m. A chief invested with

raīs-i-be-ikhtiyār, A chief having no power.

raīs-i-khud-mukhtār,

An independent prince or ruler.

رؤسا *roasā'*; Pop. *raūsā*, n. f. pl. of *raīs*.

Gentry; the respectable residents of a place; big wigs.

raī'sah, n. f. A princess; a lady of rank.

A ريع *raī*; H. *dar*, n. m. Rate; the local rate of assessment.

The standard rate at which the lands of a village are assessed according to their several qualities.

raī-bandī, n. A table of rates.

A document showing the rates at which different descriptions of land in a district are usually assessed.

raī kankūṭī, n. An assessment of rates of lands made according to the customary or fixed rate or value of the produce per *bīghā*.

H ريكان रेकान *rekān'*, *rekhān*, n. f. Land beyond the reach of river-water. (?)

H ريه रेह *reh*, *miṭṭī-khār*, n. f. An alkali; impure nitrate of soda; fuller's earth.

It abounds in some soils as an efflorescence, rendering them unproductive even for grass.

ز

A زايد *zā'id*, *zāyad*; Pop. *zyāda*, adj. زيد increased. 1. Overplus; over; over and above; supplemental; surplus; superfluous.

2. Useless; worthless; waste; vain.

parcha-i-zāid, An extra, or extraordinary.

javānān-i-pulis zāid, *ahālī-i-pulis zāid*. G. G. Extra police force; police force in excess.

P زبان *zabān'*, *zubān*, *zabāñ*; Rus. *jubān*, *jabān*, n. f. Z. *husvān*, *hazvān*; Pahlvī, *zafān*; S. *jihvā*; H. *jībh*. 1. The tongue. 2. Language.

zabān-bandī, n. f. A deposition; a written testimony; an affidavit (in a court of law).

zabān-bandī k., v. a. To take down a deposition.

zabān bandī-i-gavāh.

The deposition of a witness.

zabān palaṭnā, *phernā*, *yā badalnā*, v. a.

To equivocate; prevaricate; shuffle.

ba-zabān-i-muravvaja-i-zila, G. G. H. *des-bhākā*,

In the language of the district. [lingsgate.

fohsh zabān. Indecent or obscene language; Bil-

khoṭī zabān bolnā, *gandī zabān k.*, v. a. To use foul language.

زبانى *zabān'ī*, adj. 1. By word of mouth; verbal; oral; *viva voce*.

2. Unwritten; traditional.

zabānī imtehān, Oral examination. [force.

P زبردستى *zabar-dastī*, n. f. Forcibly; per-

zabar-dastī, *zabar-dastī se*, adv.

1. By force or violence; forcibly.

2. Wrongfully; unjustly; *per fas et nefas*; arbitrarily. 3. Wantonly.

zabar-dastī bhagā le jānā. Forcible abduction.

zabar-dastī pakaṛ bulānā, v. a. To bring one by force. [indecent assault; to rape.

zabar-dastī chaṛh baiṭhnā, v. a. To commit an

zabar-dastī chhīn lenā, *yā le lenā*, v. a. To take by force, or snatch from; to extort.

zabar-dastī hāzir k. To enforce the production of; to compel one's attendance.

zabar-dastī rok rakhnā, v. n. To keep back by force; withhold wrongfully. [cent assault.

zabar-dastī izzat lenā, v. a. To make an inde-

zabar-dastī qabūl karvānā, *yā qubulvānā*, v. a. To extort confession.

zabar-dastī k., v. a. 1. To use force; to force; compel; oblige. 2. To press or bear hard upon; to oppress.

P زخم *zakhm*, n. m. Wound.

zakhm-i-kārī, A fatal or mortal wound.

زخمى *zaᵃkhm'ī*; H. *ghāil*, adj. Wounded; hurt.

zakhmī k., v. a. To wound; hurt.

zakhmī h., *zakhm khānā*, v. n. To be wounded.

زخمى *zakhm'ī*, n. A wounded man or woman.

P زد و كوب *zad o kob*; H. *mār pīṭ*, n. f.

Assault and battery.

P زر *zar*, n. m. 1. Gold. 2. Riches.

zar-i-asl, n. m. A principal sum bearing interest. [fund.

zar-i-amānat, n. m. Deposit money; trust

zar-i-āmdanī, n. m. Proceeds; receipts; income; profits; dividend; revenue.

zar-i-bāqī, *bāqī*, n. m. Outstanding balance.

zar-i-bhej, n. m. Revenue (from land); rent.

zar-i-byā'na; H. *sāī*, n. m. Earnest money.

zar-parast, adj. 1. Venal; mercenary.

2. Selfish; sordid.

zar-i-peshgī, n. m. 1. Payment in advance.

2. A bonus or premium on a lease; an advance of money upon the farm of the revenue; money lent upon a usufructuary mortgage.

zar-i-peshgīdār. One who has advanced money.

zar-i-peshgī-ṭhekā, n. m. A lease granted on a sum of money being advanced.

It is on the same footing as pure usufructuary mortgages, and is dealt with as such; but this is only when there is a power of redemption reserved to the lessor, either expressly or impliedly.

zar-i-tāvān; H. ḍanḍ, n. m. Penalty; fine.
zar-i-tahsīl, n. m. Collections; revenue.
zar-i-tahsīl adālat divānī meṅ bhej denā. To pay the amount of collections into Court.
zar-i-taufīr, n. m. Mesne profits; surplus; excess amount.
zar-i-taufīr-i-tahsīl. Surplus collections.
zar-i-taufīr nīlām, n. m. Surplus of sale proceeds; balance realized over the amount of defalcation for which the lands are sold, payable to the defaulters.
zar-i-jurmānā. A fine. [realization.
zar-i-hāsil, n. m. Proceeds; sums realized;
zar-i-kharchā. Costs of suit.
zar-i-kharīd, Purchase money. [money.
zar-kharīd, adj. Purchased with one's own
zar-i-khisārā, n. m. Damages.
(Bengal) A taālluq, bought of a zamīṅdār.

It implies generally a dependent taālluq held hereditarily under a zamīṅdār and reverting to him on failure of heirs. [money (peṭiyā).

zar-i-khurāk, n. m. Diet money; subsistence
zar-khez, zar-rez, adj. lit. producing gold. Fertile (soil); rich (land).
zar-khez k., v. a. To enrich; fertilize.
zar-khezī, n. f. Fertility; productiveness.
zar-dār, adj. 1. Wealthy; rich (amīr).
2. Solvent; able to pay.
zar-doz, n. m. One who works in embroidery.
zar dozī, n. f. Embroidery.
zar-dost, adj. Fond of money; covetous.
zar-i-ḍigrī. The amount decreed.
zar-i-rahn. Money lent on a mortgage.
zar-i-surkh, n. m. lit. red gold. Pure gold; gold coin; gold (sonā). [ment money.
zar-i- sarkārī, n. m. Public money; Govern-
zar-i- safaid, n. m. Silver.
zar-i-saman, n. m. Purchase money; purchase money of same property bought at public auction; consideration money or proceeds.
zar-i-saman-i-nīlām, n. m. Proceeds of sale of property sold by auction; sale proceeds.
zar-i-zāmnī, A deposit security.
zar-i- fāzil, n. m. Surplus money; excess.
zar-i- fāzil sālāna, n. m. The annual surplus.
zar-i- fāzil munāfa, n. m. Excess profits.
zar-i- qarz, n.m. Debts; the amount of a debt.
zar kā jūtā, lit. gold shoes.
A bribe; an illegal gratification.
zar-i-mutālbah, zar-i-yāftanī, n. m. Claims; demands; calls; debts due; balance receivable; balance in favor of one; outstandings.
zar-i-muaāfī, n. m. Remission; discharge.
zar-i-moāvza, Compensation.
zar-i-munāfa, n. m. Income; profits; revenue.
zar-i-naqd, n. m. Ready money; cash.
zar-i-nīlāmī, n. m. Sale proceeds.
zar-i-vāsilāt, n. m. Usufruct; mesne profits.
zar-i-harja, n. m. Damage; demurrage. [done.
zar-i-harja bābat nuqsān. Damages for an injury
zar-i-harja bil-evaz. Alternative damages.
zar-i-yāftanī dilvānā, v. a. To enforce a claim or payment of a debt.

A زراعت zarā'āt, zirā'āt; H. khetī, n. f. زرع he sowed. 1. Tillage (bo-jot). 2. A cultivated farm or field; sown land; the standing crop.
3. Indigo factories, the lands cultivated by the factory in contradistinction to asāmīwār, the crop grown by cultivators.
zirāat-pesha; H. kisān, An agriculturist.
zirāāt k.; H. khetī k., v. a. To cultivate; grow crops; to reclaim (land).
zirāat ke kāmoṅ ke līye, G. G. For agricultural purposes. [agriculture.
zirāat ke mutāalliq. Agricultural; relating to
gair mumkin-ul-zirā'at, n. Unproductive, or unculturable land (banjar).

زراعتي zarāāt, zirāati, Arable land; lands subject to assessment.
zirāatī arāzī, n. f. Land fit for cultivation; arable land.

A زكوة zakāt', n.f. زكو blessed by God. 1. Alms.
2. A portion of a Mussalman's property given in charity agreeably to the Qurān.

P زمين zamīn'; Rus. jamīn, n. f. Z. zamīk.
Vedic S. jam. 1. See بهوم
zamīn uftādah, n. m. Waste or fallow land; land left uncultivated (parti).
zamīn khālisah. Royal rent-free land.
zamīn khirājī. Lands paying tribute.

زميندار zamīṅ-dār', zim'īṅ-dār, n. m.
A landholder; landlord; landed proprietor; landowner; lord of a manor.
zamīndār huzūr-tahsīl. A zamīṅdār in the ceded provinces formerly paying his revenue instalments to the Collector of the zilā, and charged with the superintendence of the police in his zamīndāri. Ben. Reg. xxv. 1803.
zamīṅ-dārah, n. 1. The allowance to a zamīn-dār who is set aside. 2. Country (dihāt).
zamīṅ-dār aur jotā. Landlord and tenant.
zamīṅ-dār'nī, zamīn-dāran, n. f.
The wife of a zamīn-dār.

زميندارى zamīṅ-dār'ī, zimīṅ-dārī, n. f.
1. Real or landed estate; landed property; estate; tenure in severalty; fee farm; freehold; manor; fief.
2. The office or tenure of a zamīn-dār; the land or estates held by him.
zamīṅ-dārī paṭṭā, n. m. A document granted by Government in recognition of the possessions of a zamīn-dār.
zamīṅ-dārī jama, n. f. The amount of revenue which the holder of a zamīn-dārī has engaged to pay to the Government.

zamīṅdārī chaukī, n. f. A post at which the Officers of the *zamīṅdār* formerly collected tolls and customs on goods passing through his estate. [in shares.

zamīṅdārī hisse-dārī, n. m. A *zamīṅdārī* held

A village or estate in which the sharers cultivate separately, and raise the Government revenue by a *bāchh*. The lands are not divided amongst the sharers in proportion to their shares and interests of the village, and no sharer can have his share separated except by decree in a civil suit. The term is regarded, however, as somewhat ambiguous.

zamīṅdārī rusūm, n. f. Cesses or fees levied by a *zamīndār*. [ing a *zamīṅdārī*.

zamīṅdārī sanad, n. f. A deed or patent grant-

zamīṅdārī muchalkā. An obligation entered into by a *zamīṅdār* on receiving the grant of a *zamīṅdārī*, binding himself to the observance of certain conditions.

zamīṅdārī mutlaq, n. f. *Zamīṅdārī* tenure in which the revenue is paid jointly.

zamīṅ-daryā barāmad, zamīn gang bar-āmad. Increment of land ; alluvion. [Government.

zamīṅ atāë sarkār, n. f. A grant of land from

zamīṅ qābil zarāat. Culturable or arable land.

zamīn ki hālat-i-milkīyat.

The state of the property.

zamīn-i-gair-mazrūā, n. f. Uncultivated land.

zamīn kā karāyā yā mahsūl.

Revenue from land ; land rent.

zamīn kā mālik, n. m. A landowner.

zamīn kī bhej. Ground rent.

zamīn-i-lā-khirājī. Rent-free land.

zamīn-i-lā-vāris. Unclaimed land.

zamīn-i-mazrūah, Cultivated land.

sakht zamīn, n. f. Hard soil ; hard ground.

P زن *zan*, n. f. A woman ; a wife (استري).

zan-i-mankūhah. A married woman (Opp. of *mad-khūlā*, a concubine).

be-zan o farzand. Without wife and children.

A زنا *zin'ā*, n. f. Adultery (حرام).

zinā bij-jabr, n. m. An indecent assault ; rape.

زناكار *zinā-kār*, n.m. An adulterer; a fornicator.

زناكاري *zinā-kārī*, n.f. Adultery; illicit intercourse ; criminal conversation.

zinā-kārī bā-kheshāṅ, n. f.

Incest ; sexual intercourse between persons who by reason of consanguinity or affinity cannot lawfully be united.

ba-nazar insidād ehtimāl-i-zinā.

To guard against the possibility of adulterous intercourse.

P زنانه *zanā'na* ; Illit. *janānā*, adj. 1. Female ; feminine. 2. Womanish ; effeminate.

3. Weak ; imbecile ; impotent. [ments.

zanāna-makān, zanān-khānah. The female apart-

zanān'a, n. m. 1. A woman ; a female.

2. A family ; a wife.

3. The female apartments.

4. A eunuch who is also a catamite (*hījrā*).

zanāne, n. m. A class of eunuchs whose occupation is singing and dancing, with sodomy.

zanjīr-i-zāmnī, n. f. Chain or joint security ; mutual or collateral surety or assurance.

P زنخه *zan-kha*, n. m. 1. A eunuch.

2. A dancing boy.

P زندان *zindān'*, n. m. A prison (*jel-khāna*).

A زوال امان *zavāl-i-amāṅ*.

Forfeiture of bail, security, etc.

A زوايد *zavā'id, zavāyad*, n. pl. of زايد more. Additions ; augmentations ; superfluities.

A زوجه *zauj'a*, n. f. A wife (*jorū*).

zauja-i-mutalliqa, n. f. A divorced wife.

zauja mankūhā, n. f.

A married woman ; a woman who has been married according to Mah. law.

زوجيت *zaujī'yat*, n. f. The married state ; the state of coverture. [woman.

haqq-i-zaujīyat. The rights of a Mah. married

zorā-zorī, jorā-jorī, adv. By force (*zabar-dastī*).

P زهر *zahr* ; Illit. *jahar*, n. m. 1. Poison.

zahr-khurānī, n. f. Administering poison.

zahr-dār, adj. Poisonous.

zahr denā, v. a. To administer poison.

zahr-i-qātil, zahr-i-halāhal, A deadly poison.

zahr khānā, v. n. To take poison.

zahr khānā kisī par. To take poison on account of one (through love, jealousy, shame, etc.) ; to perform the happy despatch.

zahrīlā mādda, n. m. G. G.

A poisonous substance.

A زياده *ziyā'dah*, adv. and adj. More.

ziādah-sitānī, n. f. Extortion ; exaction.

ziyādah istehqāq, G. G. n. m. A stronger claim ; a higher right ; better title. [fine.

ziyādah tāvān, n. m. Higher penalty ; larger

ziyādah jamā, n. m.

Larger revenue ; enhanced rate.

زيادتي *ziyād'tī* ; Pop. *ziāttī* ; Illit. *jāstī*, n. f.

1. See برهوتري 1, 2, under برهنا

2. Force ; oppression ; tyranny.

P زيان *ziyāṅ'* ; Rus. *jiān* ; H. *ṭoṭā*, n. m.

1. Loss ; damage. 2. Hurt ; harm ; injury.

ziyāṅ uṭhānā, v. n. To suffer a loss. [loss.

sūd o ziyāṅ, Ped. for *nafa o nuqsān*, Profit and

A زيد *zaid*, prop. n. A hypothetical name (often used with *Amar*, as John Nokes with Thomas Stiles, in English).

P H زیربار کرنا *zer-bār k.*, v. a.
To put one to expense, or into debt.
zer-bār h., *zer-bārī uṭhānā*, v.n. To incur great expense; to be thrown into debt.
zer-bārī, n. f. Expenses; liabilities; burdens.
zer-i-tajvīz; Pop. *zer-i-tajvīz*, Under consideration; on the *tapis*; *sub judice*; pending.
zer-i-tahqīqāt. Under investigation.
zer hirāsat. Under custody.
zer-i-hukūmat. Under one's authority; subject to one's jurisdiction.

س

H سابر साबर *sāb'ar*, n. m. S. शम्बर. A burglar's instrument for breaking into houses.

A سابق *sāb'iq*, adj سبق he preceded him.
Former; prior; past; foregoing; preceding.
sābiq, n. An old established rate of assessment.
sābiq-ul-zikr. Before-mentioned.
sābiq dastūr, As before; as usual.
sābiq men, adv. Of yore; heretofore; in times past.
سابقا *sāb'iqan*, adv. As formerly; as before.

H سات پھیرے सातफेरे *sāt phere*; E. *sāt bhaunrī*, n. f.
Seven turns round the sacrificial fire, temple, pole of the nuptial bower, etc.

H ساتھ رہنا साथ रहना *sāth rahnā*, v. n.
1. To live with; dwell together.
2. To cohabit with; live together as man and wife.
sāth misl-i-muqadmah. Filed with the case.
ساتھي साथी *sāth'ī*, n. m. A colleague; retainer; follower; accomplice; second; supporter.

H ساٹھي साठी *sāṭhī*, *sānṭhī*; Pop. *saṭṭhī*, n.f.
A coarse rice ripening in the rains about sixty days after sowing.

H ساجھا साझा *sājh'ā*, n. m. S. साहाय्य. 1. An association; a company; joint concern; community of sharers; partnership. 2. A share.
sājhā ṭūṭ gayā. The partnership was dissolved; the connection was severed.
sājhā chhūṭnā. Dissolution of partnership.
ساجھي साझी *sājh'ī*, n. m. A partner (in business); co-partner; co-parcener; shareholder.
sājhiyon kā iqrār-nāmah, *sājhe kā kāgaz*.
A deed of partnership.
sājhī h., *sājhā k.*, v. n. To enter into partnership; to form a company.
sājhe, *sājhe men*, adv. Jointly; in partnership.
nafe o nuqsān kā sājhī, A partner in gain and loss.

T ساچق *sāch'aq*, Mah. n. f.
The customary presents from the husband to the bride on the day before marriage.

P ساختہ *sā'kht'ah*, part. adj. 1. Artificial; not natural (جعلی). 2. Surreptitious.
sākhtah pardākhtah, n. m. *lit.* done and executed. Deed; act.
sākhtah pardākhtah ek kā misl sākhtah pardākhtah dūsre ke hai. The act of one shall be held as the act of the other.
sākht yā farokht āla-i-talbīs sikhā, G. G. Making or selling any instrument for counterfeiting coin.
sādahkāgaz, n. m. 1. Blank paper. 2. Unstamped paper.

H سادھ साध *sādh*; E. *sadhor*, n. m. S. सिध to be accomplished. A present of sweetmeats, etc. to a woman in the 7th month of pregnancy.
sādhāran adhikār, A common right.

H سارا सारा *sār'ā*, *sal*, n.m. The pile on which Hindūs burn their dead.

E سارٹیفکٹ *sārṭifikaṭ'*, n. m. 1. A certificate or testimonial. 2. A document.
sarṭīfikaṭ valāyat, n. m. A certificate authorizing one to act for a minor.
bīmārī, yā ḍāktar kā sārṭifikaṭ. A medical certificate.
nek-chalnī kā sārṭifikaṭ, A certificate of good conduct.

H ساڑھو साढ़ू *sāṛ'hū*, *sāḍhū*; Sant. *sāḍge*, n. m. S. स्यालीवोढा Wife's sister's husband.

H ساڑھی साढ़ी *sāṛ'hī*; Rus. *sāḍhī*, n. f. S. आषाढी. See *āsāṛhī*. The spring harvest.

P سازش *sāz'ish*; Sant. *mis*, n. f. Confederacy; unlawful combination; conspiracy; collusion.
sāzish k., v. a. To plot together; conspire; tamper (with a witness).
ba-sāzish-i-yak digar. In collusion with each other.
سازشي *sāz'ishī*, adj. Collusive; fraudulent.

A ساقط *sā'qit*, part. act. سقط fell. Dropped; lost.
sāqit k., v. a. To throw out; cast; reject.
sāqit huā. Abated; destroyed.
sāqit h., v. n. To abate; lapse; to be lost.

S ساکشي साक्षी *sāk'shī*; H. *sākhī*, n. f. See اظہار (3). 1. Attestation; sign manual.
2. Testimony. 3. An eye-witness; a witness.
sākshī aur chhāp-i-ādālat.
The attestation of the court.
sākshī denā yā k. To give evidence.
sākshī likh'nā, v. n. To attest; witness.
pramān sākshī. A subscribing witness.

A ساكن sā'kin, n. m. سكن was at rest.
An inhabitant; a resident.

H ساكھ साख sākh, n. f. S. शाखा sub-division.
1. Season. 2. Harvest; crop.

H ساكھ साख sākh, sāh, n. f. S. साक्ष्य 1. The evidence of a witness. 2. Weight or credibility; authority. 2. Trust (etebār, 1); mercantile or commercial credit.
4. Name; reputation; good report; credit.

P سال sāl; Sant. sermā, n. m. Z. saredha, S. वर्ष
A year.
sāl-i-āindah, n. m. The next or ensuing year.
sāl-i-bāqīdārī. A year of default; a year in which default occurs.
sāl ba-sāl, adv. Year by year (sālāna).
sāl bhar, adv. All the year round.
sāl-i-paivastah; H. tevras, The year before last.
sāl tamām, sāl tamāmi, An annual report.
sāl tamām par, At the end of the year.
sāl jhaṛtī jama kharch.
A yearly account of receipts and disbursements; a debit and credit account.
sāl hāsil, Yearly produce.
sāl-i-hāl, sāl-i-ravāṅ. The present or current [year.
sāl-i-hisābī, hisābī sāl. The official or financial year.
sāl-khurdā, adj. 1. Old; used up; worn out. 2. [Experienced.
sāl-i-zirāat, Ped. The agricultural year.
sāl-i-faslī. The faslī year.
سال كبيسه sāl-i-kabīsah; H. laund kā baras, n. m.
The year of 13 months, which comes round every three years.
sāl-girah; H. baras-gāṅṭh, n. m. Birthday; the anniversary of a person's nativity when a knot is tied on a string or thread, kept as a record of his age. Hin.
sāl-i-guzashtā; Sant. dinkalom, The past year; [last year.
sāl-i-mālī, n. m. The revenue year.
sāl-i-mahājnī. The mercantile year, concurrent with the Samvat year, but commencing two months later.
sāl mohlat. Year of remission or grace.
sāl-vār. By, or according to the year or years.
sālvār vasūl-bāqī. Accounts of the annual collections and balances for a series of years.
sālhā sāl, adv. For years; year after year.
ab-ke sāl, is sāl, n. The present or current year.
سالانه sālā'nah; Illit. sālyānā, adj.
Annual; yearly.
sālānah, n. m. 1. Land taken up for the whole year. 2. Annual pension; an annuity.
sālānah āmdanī, n. f. Annual income or revenue.
sālānah hāsil, yā tahsīl. Yearly collections from a district or estate.
sālānah hīn hayāt, n. A life-annuity.
sālānah-dār, An annuitant; a pensioner.
naqshajāt-i-sālānah. Annual returns.

H سالا साला sā'lā; W. Rus. sāṛā; Bhoj. sār, n. m. S. श्याल 1. A wife's brother. 2. A common term of abuse implying the disgrace attaching to a man whose sister has been had by another; hence, a pander; pimp.

A سالم sā'lim, adj. سلم was safe. 1. Safe.
2. Whole (ثابت 1.)
baē-sālim, See baē kāmil, under بيع

H سالي साली sāl'ī, n. f. S. श्याली Wife's sister.

H سامك सामक sām'ak, W.; sāṅvak, sāṅvā, sāṅvāṅ, W. Rus; sāmā, E. n. m. S. श्यामक P. shāmāᵏkh, 1. A grain-bearing grass, found wild in khādar lands. 2. A very small grain; Panicum frumentaceum, Wat.

H سامي सामी sām'ī, n. f. Rich arable land.

H سانگ آنے सांग आने sāṅg āne, n. m.
(Brokers.) One anna.

H سانگھر सांघर sāṅg'har; Sant. dever poṭom, n. m. H. sāth with. A wife's son by a former husband (gailaṛ).

H ساني सानी sā'nī, n. f. H. sānnā to mix.
1. Chopped straw mixed with oil-cake, given to cattle. 2. A caste of cultivators.

H ساور सावर sāv'ar, sārval, kassā; Panj. sābal, n. 1. An implement for picking out bricks or house breaking; a crowbar.
2. A centre bit.

H ساوڑي सावड़ी sāv'ṛī; W. Rus. asāvrī, siyā, baḍī; E. bishun pirīt, muṭhiā, n. f. (Agric.)
The share of grain given from the threshing floor to Brahmans, faqīrs, jogīs, &c.

H ساون सावन sāv'an; Sant. sān, n. m. S. श्रावण
The 4th Hin. month, the full moon of which is near श्रवण or Aquila; July—August.
ساوني सावनी sāv'anī; Māṛ. sāvnū, n. f.
1. The kharīf or autumn harvest.
2. The full moon in the month of Sāvan
3. Sweetmeats and fruits, etc. presented by the bridegroom to the bride in Sāvan.

H ساه साह sāh, sāhū; Sant. saū, n. m. S. साधु Pr. sāhū. 1. A merchant; banker.
2. (sāh jī) A title of respect, applied to merchants, bankers, etc.
3. An innocent person.
sāh yā sāhū-pan, n. m. Mercantile or commercial credit.

sāh-jog; Tir. *sarāhak jog*, adj. Creditable; reputable.
sāh-jog hunḍī, n. f. A bill payable to the bearer.

H ساہا साहा *sāh'ā, sāyā*; Saut. *baplā*: *din*; Mār. *sāwo, sahārag*, n. m. S. साहित्य union.
1. The day on which the Hin. nuptial knot is tied. 2. Season; weather.
3. Crop; harvest (*sākh*).

H ساہوکار साहूकार *sāhū'kār, sāh, sāhū*; Rus. *sāhū-kāl*, n. m. S. साधु merchant, कार doer.
A banker; money lender.
sāhūkār, sāhū, adj. Honest; respectable.
sāhūkārī ṭīp, n. f. A banker's bill of exchange.
sāhūkāroṅ kī sabhā, n. f.
Exchange; change; bourse.
sāhūkāre meṅ baṭṭā lagnā, v. n. To be bankrupt; to be destroyed (one's credit). [exchange.
ساہوکارہ साहूकारा *sāhūkār'ā*, n.m. Money market;
ساہوکاري साहूकारी *sāhūkārī*, n. f.
Banking; banking business.
sāhūkārī gaddī, n. f. The mattrass or carpet on which a banker sits. [Earnest-money.

H سائي साई *sā'ī*; A. *baiānā*, n. f. S. सत्यन्कार
sāī denā, v. a. To give earnest-money.

A ساير *sāir*, n. m. 1. Octroi.
2. Market dues; taxes on goods sold in the *bāzār*; land customs; transit duties; miscellaneous imposts. 3. Collections on account of spontaneous products, as the piscatory of tanks, the gums of trees, the fruits of the forest, wax, lac, &c., commonly called *jalkar, phalkar*, and *bankar*.
sā'ir pachotrā, Five per cent levied on the transit of goods.
sā'ir jamā, n. The total amount of revenue in addition to the land tax.
sāir jahāz. A tax on boats; an inland toll.
sāir-chalantā,—chaltā,—chaltāo, n. Transit duties formerly levied by the *zamīndārs* on goods passing through their estates; octroi.
sāir kharch. Extra or miscellaneous expenses.
sāir mahāl, n. An extra head or impost, especially one still allowed in some places, such as rents of stalls or standings in a *bāzār*, imposed by the owner of the ground.
sāir yā tahsīl sivāē, sāir or *sivāē* collections.
These are the items which, besides the *products of the cultivated land* forming the main assets to be taken into account in making assessments, are also much prized by the proprietors, and which, in some cases, constitute a valuable property. In so far as these items consist of petty dues or services from the inhabitants, in the shape of small periodical collections or presents, they are never taken into account in fixing the Government assessment. When, however, they come to be of considerable value, such as the piscary of large tanks, the produce of trees, like *Mahuā* trees or forest produce, as wax, lac, etc., all of which come under the denomination of *jalkar, phalkar*, and *bankar*, they may be considered in estimating the assets.

A سايل *sā'yal, sāil*, n. m. سال he asked him.
A petitioner; suitor; prosecutor; an applicant.

A سبب *sab'ab*; Rus. *sabag*, n. m. 1. Cause; ground (باعث 1). 2. Means; instrument.
sabab-i-nālish, Cause of complaint; ground of action.
ba-sabab; H. *kāran se*, adv. By reason of; because of; in consequence of; on account of; in pursuance of (*zariye se*).
be-sabab, adj. 1. Groundless; without foundation.
2. Causeless; wanton. [2. Wantonly.
be-sabab, adv. 1. Causelessly; for nothing.

H سبها सभा *sabh'ā*, n. f. S. सभा from सह with, भू to be. 1. A meeting; assembly; convention; council. 2. A court.
sabhā-patī; P. *mīr-majlis*; *sadar-nashīn*, n. m.
A president; chairman.
sabhā-sad, n. m. 1. A member of an assembly or council. 2. An arbitrator; assessor.
sabhā sammat. Award of a council.
sabhā k., v. a. To convene or hold a meeting.
rāj-sabhā; P. *darbār*, n. m. 1. A royal court.
2. The chief court of justice, at which the king or his representative presided.
grām-sabhā; Saut. *kulhī durup*, (*lit.* to sit in the street) n. m. A village court composed of the principal inhabitants with the head man presiding.

A سبيل *sabīl'*, n. f. سبل See *tarkīb*. 1. Course; way; process; manner of proceeding. 2. Instrument; means. 3. Mode; manner.
sabīl zar-i-adāē bāqī, n. f. Source of payment.
sabīl karnā, v. a. To obtain money by borrowing or begging; raise the wind; fly a kite.

P سپاس نامه *sipās-nāmah*, n. m. An address presented to one. [livery (حواله)

P سپرد *supurd'*; Illit. *sapurd, suprad*, n. De-
supurd-i-havālāt k., v. a. To commit to close custody; to give in charge.
supurd-dār. An assignee, a trustee. [(*havāle k.*).
supurd k. 1. To entrust; delegate; charge
2. To resign; recommend to one's care.
3. To make over for trial to the sessions.
supurd-kunindah, n. m. The committing officer.
supurd-nāmah, n. m. Assignment; delivery, trust or hypothecation.
supurd-vārī, n. The thing deposited; a deposit.
supurd h. v. n. To be consigned or entrusted to.
سپردگي *supurd'agī, supurdgī*, n. f.
1. Delivery; charge; surrender (حواله 2).
2. Commitment (by a magistrate).

supurdgī-i-jelkhānā,
Commitment; sending to prison.
supurdgī-i-daurah, n. m.
Commitment for trial before the sessions.
supurdgī kā vārant. A warrant of commitment.
supurdgī-i-māl. Consignment of goods.
supurdgī meṅ lānā, v. n. To take charge of.

H ستانا **सताना** *satā'nā;* Sant. *santāo,* v. a. S. **सन्तापन** executing. 1. To molest; harass; trouble; annoy. 2. To persecute; oppress; afflict; give pain to.
3. To exact; take by force.

A ستر *satr;* Pop. *satar;* Sant. *bebhorom,* n. m.
The privities; private parts.
be-satar h., v. n. To be naked; to expose one's person.
بےستري *be-satrī,* n. f. 1. Unveiling; exposure. 2. Immodesty; boldness. 3. Dishonor; disgrace.
be-satrī be-hūdah, G. G. Public nuisance or indecent exposure of the person.

H سترورين **सत्तवीं** *sattar'vīn,* n. f.
An obsequial rite performed on the seventeenth day after decease.

H ستري **सतरी** *sat'rī,* n.f. (*Brokers*) Two Rupees.

H ستكار **सत्कार** *sat-kār, karm, yā kiryā,* n.
1. Funeral or obsequial rites.
2. Respect; reverence.
ستكاري **सत्कारी** *sat-kārī,* n. f. 1. Truth; fidelity; honesty.
2. One who burns the dead.

H ستلي **सुतली** *sut'lī,* n. f. (*Brokers*) A score.

H ستوانسا **सतवांसा** *satvāṅ'sā;* Tir. *satmāsā,* n. m. 1. A child born in the seventh month of pregnancy. 2. Mah. An entertainment given to a pregnant woman by her parents in the seventh month of her pregnancy (*sādh*).

H ستهاور **स्थावर** *sthāvar yā sthir drab; aṭal dhan,* n. m. Real or immoveable property.

H ستي **सती** *sat'ī, sattī,* n. f. S. **सती**
1. A faithful wife.
Especially one who consummates a life of duty by burning herself on the funeral pile of her husband, either with the body, or separately if her husband has died at a distance. 2. The burning of a widow on her deceased husband's funeral pile.
satī-maṭh; Bhoj. *sativāṛ,* n. m. A place where a Sati's bones are deposited.
satī h., v. n. To burn alive on the funeral pile of one's deceased husband.

H ستيا **सतिया** *sat'iyā, sathiyā;* Tir. *sattā,* n. m. 1. An oculist.
2. (S. **स्वस्तिक**) A mystical mark made on persons or things to denote good luck.
Its shape is a Greek cross, with the extremities of the four arms bent round in the same direction. It is made with vermilion by Hindus at the beginning of their account-books at the commencement of a new year. It is a symbol of the goddess Kāli and it signifies the obligation to make true and faithful entries. The same figure is formed on the ground with flour at marriages and other ceremonies.

H ستا **सट्टा** *saṭ'ṭā, saṭṭhā,* n. S. **षट्ट**
An engagement to supply grain, etc. for which advances have been made.
saṭṭā-bahī, n. f. A deed of transfer. [n. m.

P سجادہ نشين *sajādah-nashīn;* H. *mahant,*
1. The spiritual superior of a mosque or religious endowment, as distinguished from the *Mutavvalli,* or secular manager. The two offices are not unfrequently united in the same person.
2. Any religious ascetic of the Mah. faith.

H سجل استهل **सजल ग्रस्थल** *sajal asthal,* n.m. A term used in deeds of transfer or sale of landed property to denote the absolute alienation of the whole.

P سخت *sakht,* adj. Severe; serious; great.
sakht be-insāfī, Great injustice.
sakht be-īmānī, Gross breach of trust.
sakht zamīn, n. f. Hard soil or ground.
sakhtī se, adv. Harshly; severely, etc.
sakhtī se pesh ānā, v. a. 1. To treat harshly.
2. To be strict or rigorous.
sakhtī k., v. a. To use force or violence, etc.

H سدامت **सदामत** *sadā'mat, sudāmat, shudāmad,* n. Time immemorial.
sadāmat se, adv. From time immemorial.

A P سدراہ *sadd-i-rāh,* n. f.
An obstacle; obstruction.
sadd-i-rāh h., v.a. To stop one's way; obstruct.

H سدي **सुदी** *sud'ī,* n. f. Opp. of *badī;* S. **सुदि**
The bright half of the lunar month.

H سر **सिर** *sir;* Sant. *boho:,* P. *sar,* n. m.
S. **शिर** 1. The head; *caput;* skull; pate.
sir uṭhā'nā, v. n. 1. To rebel; mutiny; revolt; make head against. 2. To be disaffected, contumacious, refractory.
sir kāṭnā yā utārnā, v. a. To behead; cut off one's head.
sir h., v.n. 1. To stick to.
2. To be ready, eager for, all agog.
3. To accuse falsely (*bohtān lagānā*).
sar-i-ijlās, In court; in the presence of.

P سرانجام *sar-anjām,* n. m. 1. Materials (*asbāb,*2,4). 2. Preparations; arrangements.
sar-anjām k., v. a. To make preparations; provide; arrange; manage.

sar-i-bāzār, adv. In the open market; in public; on the public road.
sar-ba-rāh, *sar-ba-rāh-kār*, n. m. 1. A manager; an agent; administrator; steward; major domo. 2. A man sent ahead to lay a *ḍāk*.
sar-ba-rāhī, *sar-ba-rāh-kārī*, n. f. 1. Management; direction. 2. Management of property; stewardship; administration (of an estate).
sar-ba-rāhī k., v. a. To manage; administer, etc.
sar-ba-mohar, adj. Sealed.
sar-parast, n. m. A guardian; patron.
sar-parastī, n. f. Patronage.
sar-panch, n. m. Chief umpire or referee; president; chairman; foreman of a jury.
sar-tābī, n. f. 1. Disobedience; insubordination; contumacy. 2. Contempt (in law).
sar-had, n. f. A boundary; border; confines; land-mark; the boundary line; limits of jurisdiction; frontier.
sarhad-bandī, n. f. Fixing the boundaries.
sar-had hāsil. Frontier duties. [dispute.
sar-had, yā sīmā kā jhagṛā. 1. A boundary- 2. The frontier question.
sar-khail, n. m. The head of a clan or sect.
sar-i-daftar, n. m.
A head clerk; the head of an office.
sar-i-dehī. One or two rupees at each harvest, a right conceded to the local chieftain in each village in his *parganā* or *rāj*. *Carnegy*.
sar-i-rāh, adv. On the road, or high road.
sar-zanish, n. f. Reproof; rebuke.
sar-zor, adj. Refractory; rebellious.
sar-zorī, n. f. 1. Force; violence. 2. Refractoriness; insubordination. 3. Revolt; rebellion.
sar-shikan. Charitable grants by *zamīndārs*.
Lands held rent-free by vitue of *sanads* conferred by *āmils*, *chaudharīs* and other revenue officers under the Mah. Govt. *Carnegy*.
sar-gasht, n. m. Patroling.
sar-gasht phirnā, v. n. To patrol; go the rounds.
sar-kash, adj. 1. Refractory; factious; mutinous. 2. Revolted; disloyal.
sar-kashī, n. f. Insurrection (بغاوت).
sar-kashī k., v. n. 1. To be refractory.
2. To revolt; rebel.
sar-kashī meṅ sharīk h. To join an insurrection.
sar-kobī, n. f. *lit.* beating one's head.
Punishment.
sar-giroh, n. m. 1. See *sar-khail*.
2. A ringleader. 3. A commander.
qānūnan sar parast. G. G. Lawful guardian.

H سرا सिरा *sir'ā*; Sant. *sir*, n. f. S. शिरा
1. An artery or other tubular vessel of the body. [field.
2. Channel for irrigation. 3. Flooding a
sarā-sar, adj. Cursory; rough (measurement).
سراسري *sarā'sarī*, *sarsarī*, adj. 1. Easy; facile.
2. Cursory; summary.
sarāsarī ikhtiyār, n. m. Summary powers.
sarāsarī tajvīz, n. f. Summary process.
sarāsarī nālish, n. f. A summary suit.
سراسري *sarāsarī*, *sarsarī*, n. f.
1. A rough estimate; a summary.
2. Summary or rent suits formerly so called.
sarsarī apīl, n. f. A summary appeal.
ba-nazar-i-sarāsarī, adv. Cursorily. [clue.

T سراغ *surāġ'*; H. *khoj*, n. m. Trace; track;
surāg-rasānī, Ped. n. f. 1. Tracing; tracking.
2. Detection; discovery.
surāg lagānā, v. a. To trace or find out.
سراغي *surāġ'ī*; H. *khojī*, n. m.
One employed to track a criminal; an emissary; a secret agent; a detective.

P سرائے *sarā'e*, *sarā*; Illit. *sarāṅ*, n. f.
An inn; a caravansary.
sarāë-vaqfī, n. f. A *sarāë* maintained by an endowment, and affording gratuitious accommodation to travellers.

A سرايت *sarā'yat*, n. f. سير went.
An incidental or additional result, as when a person designing to wound one man unintentionally wounds another.

H سرتال सरताल *sartāl'*, A third measurement, after *partal*, 2. q. v.

P سرخط *sar'khat*, n. m. 1. A lease of a house.
2. A receipt given to an *asāmī*; an agreement with a servant or householder.
sarkhat miādī chand sāl. A lease for a term of years. [ceipt.
mahājanī sarkhat. A *mahājan* or merchant's re-

P سردار *sar-dār*, n. m. Z. *sandār*. 1. A representative of a community; a president.
2. A head man; chief; commander; laird; the head of a clan. 3. A nobleman; grandee.
4. A ringleader (*sar-giroh*, 2).
سردارني *sardār'nī*, *sardāran*, n. f. 1. The wife of a *sardār*. 2. The mistress of a house.
3. The female head of an establishment or a community. 4. A proprietress of a bawdy house. 5. The bearer's wife. [lordship.
سرداري *sar-dārī*, n. f. Headship; chiefship;

P سرشته *sarish'ta*, *sar-rishta*, n. m. 1. Course; usage; form (*chāl* 4—7). 2. Judicial usage.
3. Ceremonies; rites. 4. Office; office of record; establishment; department.
sarishte-dār, n. m. The superintendent of a vernacular office; chief record-keeper and court-reader. [*dār*, q. v.
sarishte-dārī, n. f. The office of a *sarishtah-sarishtā-i-adālat kī rāh se*. Judicially.
sarishta yā mahkama-i-ḍāk, n. m.
Post office department.

sarishta-i-māl. Revenue court. [official record.
sarishte meṅ dākhil karnā, v. a. To place on
ba-sarishtah, adv. In due form; regularly.
be-sarishtah, gair-sarishta, adj.
1. Extra-judicial (*be-dastūr*, 2).2. Unusual; anomalous. 3. Incoherent; unconnected.
be-sarishta, adv. Contrary to rule or practice.
be-sarishtagī, n. f. Irregularity; defect of form; informality. [1, 2, 4).

P سرغنة *sarğan'ah*, n. m. A chief (*sardārī*

A سرقة *sariq'ā*; Pop. *sarqā*; H. *chorī*, n. m. سرق stole. 1. Robbery; larceny. 2. Plagiarism.
3. The taking away secretly the property of another at the time when it is, or is supposed to be, in security or under charge.
sarqa-bil-jabr; H. *ḍākā*, n. m. Robbery.
sarqa-bil-jabr ke irtikāb kā iqdām, G. G.; H. *ḍākā ḍālne ko*, Attempt to commit robbery.
سرقة خفيف |*sarqa-i-khafīf, sarqa-i-sağīr, halkī chorī*, Petty larceny.
sarqā-i-kabīr. Robbery with violence.

P سركار *sarkār'*, n. f. 1. Master; chief; lord.
2. Government; ruling authority.
3. (*sarkār darbār*) The king's court.
4. A sub-division of a *sūba* in Bengal.
5. A bill collector in Bengal.
sarkār darbār k., yā charhnā, v. a.
To sue or complain in a law court.
سركاري *sarkār'ī*, adj. 1. Official; relating or belonging to the government or to any superior authority. 2. Public; pertaining to the nation. 3. Pertaining to the person of rank addressed. [ment post.
sarkārī āsāmī, n. f. A public office; govern-
sarkārī āmdanī, n. f. Government collections.
sarkārī ahlkār, yā mulāzim, n. m. A government officer or servant; a public servant.
sarkārī patit, n. f. Land left uncultivated for more than two years, and then claimable by the landlord or the government; all lands lying waste and not included in the assessment.
sarkārī kharch, n. m. Public expenses.
sarkārī khazānah, n. m. Government treasury.
sarkārī sākh, n. f. Public credit.
sarkārī amal-dārī, n. f. British rule.
sarkārī kāgaz, n. m. Government paper; promissory note. [work.
sarkārī kām, n. m. Official business; office
sarkārī māl, n. m. Public property.
sarkārī mahkma, n. m. A public court or office.
sarkārī makān, n. m. A public building.
sarkārī mohar, n. f. Government seal or stamp.
sarkārī naukar, n. m. A Government servant.
sarkārī naukrī, n. f. Government service.
sarkārī vazīfa, n. m. Allowances, assignments, or pensions from Government.

P سرماية *sarmā'yah*, n. m. Materials (پونجي).
sarmāya-i-judāgānā. G. G.
Separate or distinct funds.
sarmāya-i-zātī, n. m. Personal or private funds.
sarmāya-i-ām pulis. G. G. General Police Fund.
sarmāya-i-mushtarak, n. m. A joint fund or stock. [patrimony.
sarmāya-i-maurūsī, n. m. Inherited property;
sarmāya-i-naqdī, n. Funded property; realized assets; capital.

H سرنگ सुरङ्ग *sur'aṅg*, n. f. S. सुरङ्गा
A mine; gallery; tunnel; subterraneous passage; an adit.
suraṅg uṛānā, v. n. To explode; blow up. [mine.
suraṅg ke tale suraṅg lagānā, v. a. To under-
suraṅg lagānā, v. a. 1. To mine.
2. To plot against.

P سروكار *sarokār'*, n. m. 1. Business; concern; interest; share. 2. Intercourse.
sarokār rakhnā, v. a. To have to do with; to be concerned in.

H سرهي सुरही *sur'hī*; Sant. *saoṛī*, n. f. A grass growing on neglected or uncultivated land.

H سرير सरीर *sarīr'*; Sant. *hoṛmo*, n. m.
S. शरीर Body. See بدن
sarīr-bandhak, n. m. A hostage (*ol*).
sarīr-ḍand, n. m. Corporal punishment.
sarīr-sambandh. Relation by blood. [lence.
sarīr kī choṭ, n. f. Bodily hurt; personal vio-
سريري सरीरी *sarīr'ī*, adj. Bodily; corporeal.

H سريها सरेहा *sareh'ā*, n. m.
A long narrow field.

P سزا *saz'ā*, n. f. *sāz* fit. 1. Punishment; chastisement; correction.
2. Requital; penalty (*badlā*, 3).
sazā pānā, yā milnā, v. n. To be punished.
sazā par sazā, sazā-i-mutaddad.
Cumulative punishment.
sazā denā, v. a. To award or inflict punishment.
sazā se bachne ke vāste. To avoid punishment.
sazā taē k., yā bhugatnā, v. a. To complete one's term of punishment. [be punished.
sazā karānā, yā dilānā, v. a. 1. To cause to
2. To bring to punishment.
sazā-i-badanī, yā jismānī, G. G.; H. *deh ḍanḍ*, n. f.
Corporal punishment; flogging; flagellation.
sazā-i-phāṅsī, yā maut, n. f. Hanging.
sazā-i-phāṅsī kā sazā-vār. G. G.
Subject to the punishment of death.
sazā-i-tāziyāna, n. f. Caning; whipping.
sazā-i-jāyaz. Legal or lawful punishment.
sazā-i-saṅgīn; H. *kaṭhin shāsan*, n. f.
Severe punishment.

sazā-i-qatl yā maut, n. f. The punishment of death; capital punishment.
sazā-i-maut kā hukm denā. To sentence to death. [punishable.
sazā-yāb, sazā ke lāyaq, Liable to punishment; *sazā-yāftah*, G. G., n. m. An old offender.
qābil-i-sazā; H. *shāsan-jog*, adj. Punishable.
سزاوار *sazāvār'*, adj. 1. Liable; proper, suitable. 2. Worthy; deserving; meritorious.
sazāvār h., v. n. To deserve; merit.

T سزاول *sazā'vul, sazāval*, n. m. 1. A rent-collector. 2. A land steward; tax-gatherer; bailiff. 3. A superintendent; supervisor.

P سست *sust*; Sant. *kuṛhia*, adj. Dull (market); depressed. [market).
سستي *sust'ī*, n. f. 1. Depression; dullness (of the

H سسرا सुसरा *sus'rā, susar*; Panj. *saurā*; E. *sasur*; Sant. *hoiṅghār*; P. *khusar*, n. m. S. श्वशुर 1. A father-in-law. 2. An abuse; a pest; devil. [Tir. *sāsur*, n. f.
سسرال सुसराल *susrāl', susrār*; Farrukh. *sasurāri*; The father-in-law's house or family.
susrāl kā rishta. A marriage connexion.
susrāl'yā, adj. Of the father-in-law's family.
سسري *sus'rī*, n. f. Mother-in-law. (An abuse).

A سعي *saī*, n. f. 1. Attempt; endeavour; essay. 2. Exertion; effort.
saī k., v. a. To try; strive; exert one's self.
be-saī, adv. Without effort or exertion.

A سفارت *sifār'at*, n. f. Embassy (*elchī-garī*).

P سفارش *sufār'ish, sifār'ish*; W. Rus. *sipāras*; H. *sāhit*, n. f. Recommendation; intercession; influence; interest. [for.
sifārish k., v. a. To recommend; intercede
sifārish-nāma, sifārshī khat, n. m. A letter of introduction or recommendation.
sifārshī, adj. Recommendatory.
sifārshī chiṭṭhī, n. f. A letter of recommendation, or of credit.

A سفير *safīr'*, n. m. سفر An envoy (ايلچي).

A سفينه *safīn'a*, n. m. 1. Cor. of *subpœna*. 2. Summons of a law court.

H سكار सकार *sakār'*, n. S. स्वीकारक Acceptance or endorsement of a bill.
سكارا सकारा *sakār'ā, saukārā, sakrāī*, n. m. The fee charged for acceptance of a bill of exchange. [accept, or honor a bill.
سكارنا सकारना *sakār'nā*, v. a. To endorse,
sakāre pīchhe bechnā, v. a. To negotiate a bill after acceptance. [endorser.
sakārne-wālā, n. m. The acceptor of a bill;

A سكونت *sukūn'at*; Illit. *sikūnat*, n. f. 1. Habitation (*bās*). 2. *Illit.* Contentment.
sukūnat-i-mustaqil ibtidāī. Domicile of origin.
sukūnat-i-mustaqīl jadīd. A new domicile.
sukūnat-mustaqilah. A domicile.

A سكه *sik'kah*, n. 1. A stamp; seal; signet; royal signet. 2. An impression on money. 3. Sterling; current coin.
sikka-i-aslī, G. G. Sterling coin.
sikka-banānā, v. a. To coin money.
sikka parne kā ghar; H. *ṭaksāl*, n. m. A mint.
sikka-i-chehre-shāhī, n. m. The English Rupee.
sikka-i-rāyaj-ul-waqt, n. m. Current coin; legal tender.
sikka-zan; H. *ṭāksālyā*, n. m. A coiner.
sikka-zanī, n. f. Coining.
sikka-sanad, A paper bearing the royal signet; a grant from the crown under sign-manual, or bearing the Ruler's seal.
sikka-i-qadīm; H. *purānā rupayā*, Old coin.
sikka-i-qalab yā jālī. Counterfeit coin.
sikka-i-qalabī banānā yā chalānā. Counterfeiting coin, or uttering base coin.
sikke kī haisīyat se chalānā. To pass for the coin of the realm.
kisi aur sikke kī haisīyat se chalānā. To pass for coin of a different description.
kisī sikke kī tarkīb yā sūrat badalnā. To alter the composition or appearance of a coin.
kisī sikke kā vazan kam k. To lessen the weight of a coin.
ghisā sikka, yā rupayā, Rubbed coin.

H سگا सगा *sag'ā, sagī*, adj. S. स्वकीय Own; full; whole blood. *Sagā bhāī.* Own brother.
sagā, n. m. *sagī*, n. f. 1. A blood relation.
sagā'rat, n. f. Blood relationship; kin.
sagā-sodrā, Wom.; Sant. *mit lāi: ren (lit.* of one womb); n. m. *sagī-sodrī*, n. f. S. सह with उदर womb. 1. One's own brother. 2. Of the same family.
sage sambandhī. Relations.
سگائي सगाई *sagā'ī*, n. f. 1. Betrothal. 2. E. A second marriage among the lower classes. 3. Relationship; kin.
sagāī k.; Sant. *horo: chikhnā*, v. a. To betroth; contract a marriage; to affiance.

H سگها सघा *sagh'ā*; Sant. *dāṅg*, n. m. A stack of grain.

H سلا सला *sal'ā*, adj. (*Brokers*) Ten.
salā ohan, n. (*Brokers*) Ten rupees.

H سلا सिल्ला *sil'lā, silā*; Sant. *tumal*, n. m. S. शिल to glean. Gleanings.
sillā bīnnā, yā chugnā, v. a. To glean.

sillā-hār, siliyārā, n. A gleaner.

A سلاح *sil'āh, salāh*, n. 1. Weapons; arms.
2. (*In law*) Any sharp-edged weapon capable of mutilating or causing death.
silāh-bar-dār, salāh-dār, 1. An armour-bearer. 2. An officer who has charge of the armoury. 3. An esquire.
silāh-band, adj. Armed; accoutred.
silāh-khānah; H. *hathyār-ghar*, n. m. An armoury; arsenal; a magazine.
silāh-sāz, n. An armourer.
silāh-i-mohlik. G. G. A deadly weapon.

A سلامي *salām'ī*, n. f. 1. A salute of guns; salvo of artillery. 2. A present to a superior, or to a bridegroom.
It is given by the tenant to a landlord for granting him a lease of land, etc. or by one receiving an appointment, or paying a visit to a great man.
salāmī khānah-bārī, n. A compulsory present or tax exacted by the *zamīndār* from his tenant on his erecting a new hut.

H سلائي सिलाई *silā'ī*, n. f.
A grub that injures *makaī* and *īkh*, q. v.

A سلسلة *silsil'ah*, n. m. سل running down in a stream. A chain; series; line; succession. 2. Pedigree; genealogy.
silsilah-i-khāndān, yā qarābat, Genealogy; genealogical tree.
silsila-i-mustaqīma-i-mutsāida. Upwards in the direct ascending line.
silsila-i-mustaqima-i-mutanazzilā. Downwards in the direct descending line.

A P سلک بندي *silk-bandī*, n. An account of the daily receipts of revenue made out at the end of the month, when the whole is added together, and formed into one total.

A سلم *sil'am*. A contract of sale for immediate delivery and payment. *Carnegy.*

H سلي सिली *sil'ī*, n. f. The grain and chaff on the threshing floor before winnowing.

H سليج सलैज *salaij', salhaj, salaj, salej*, W.; *sarhaj*, E.; *salaēlī*, Mār. n. f. S. श्याल जाया Brother-in-law's wife.

H سما समा *sam'ā, samāṅ, samai, samaiṅ*, n. m. S. समय 1. Time; season.
2. A good harvest, or season.

S سماچار समाचार *sam-āchār'*, n. m. The advice of a bill.

A سماعت *samā'ằt*, n. f. (H. *sunvāī*) Hearing or trial (of a suit); [cognizance.
samāằt-i-nālish, Jurisdiction.
samāằt k., v. a. To hear or try (a suit); to entertain or take cognizance of (a complaint, etc.). [cognizable (a suit).
samāằt ke qābil, qābil-i-samāằt, adj. Admissible;
samāằt-i-muqaddamah. The hearing of a case or suit. [jurisdiction.
ikhtiyār-i-samāằt, The power of trying a case;
hadd-i-samāằt. Statute of limitation. [limitation.
hadd-i-samāằt se bāhar. Out of the statute of

H سمان اودهک समान ओदका *samān'odakā*, n. m. A kinsman who is connected by oblations of water only to the names of common ancestors. *Carnegy.*

H سمبندهي समबन्धी *sambandh'ī*, n. m.
A relation by marriage.
sambandhī-patr; A *shajrah*. Kindred roll; genealogical tree.

H سمجهه آنا समझ आना *samajh āna*, v. n.
To grow to years of discretion.
samjhotī-patr. An amicable adjustment; a deed of compromise.

H سمدهن समधन *sam'dhan*; Bhoj. and Tir. *samdhini*, n. f. S. सम्बन्धिनी relation. The mothers of the bride and bridegroom respectively who become *samdhans* to one another.

سمدهي समधी *sam'dhī*; Sant. *sumdhī*, n. m. S. सम्बन्धि The fathers of the wedded pair who become *samdhīs* to one another.

سمدهيانا समधियाना *samdhiyā'nā*, n. m. 1. The mutual relationship between two parties whose children are married to each other. 2. The respective parental homes of the wedded pair.

E سمن *sam'an*, n. m. Cor. of Eng. summons.
saman pahuṅchānā, To serve a summons.
saman jārī k., To issue a summons. [summons.
saman kī tāmīl, yā tāmīl-i-saman. Service of a
kisī saman ki qarār-vāqaī tamīl. The due service of a summons.

A سن *sinn*, n. m. Year; age (*ārbal*).
sinn-i-bulūġ, sinn-i-bulūgat, sinn-i-tamīz, sinn-i-shaūr, Years of discretion (*bulūgat*).
sin-rasīdah, adj. Advanced in years; old.
kam-sinn, adj. Young; of tender age.

S سنتان सन्तान *santān'*; Sant. *hopon*, n. m. Offspring (اولاد).

A H سنت ک *sun'nat, k.*, v. a. To circumcise.
sunnat-i-rakat, Ceremonial observances enjoined upon the authority of tradition, distinguished as *mavakkad* absolute, and *gair-mavakkad* not absolute.
be-sunnat, adj. Uncircumcised.

H سنجهلا संझला *sañjh'lā, sanhdlā*; adj.

Of the third rank or degree; the third of four brothers.

A سند *san'ad*, n. f. 1. A patent, grant, or charter from a man in authority; a commission; warrant; charter; patent. 2. A document; deed; credential; diploma; testimonial; certificate. 3. A precedent; an example; authority. 4. Reliance; trust. 5. Authority. 6. The title-deed of the estate of a *taāl-luq-dār* given to him by the British Government. 7. A title-deed conveying to an individual emoluments, titles, privileges, offices, or the Govt. rights to revenue from land, etc. under the seal of the ruling authority.
sanad-i-khūn-bahā, n. A grant or deed conveying property from a person or family implicated in a murder, as a retaliatory fine to the heirs of the murdered person.
sanad-i-divānī, n. A grant or assignment of land or rather of the Government revenue assessed upon it.
sanad-i-zamīndār. A *zamīndār* appointed under a royal patent, on default of heirs, or supercession to succeed another *zamīndār*.
sanad-i-shāhī. A royal grant or charter.
sanad-i-kārguzārī. A certificate of one's services.
sanad k., *yā gardānnā*, v. a. To trust, believe in, or rely on. [ities.
sanad lānā, v. a. To quote precedents or author-
sanad-i-liyāqat, *yā fazīlat*.
A certificate; testimonial.
sanad-i-muāfī. A rent-free grant.
sanad milkīyat-i-istimrār. A deed or document by which the British Government recognised the absolute ownership of the *zamīndārs* of Bengal and in some parts of the South, at a fixed assessment. The term is current chiefly in the Northern *Sarkārs*.
sanad-i-virāsat. Certificate of heirship.
sanad-yāftah, adj. Holding a certificate. [reliable.
سند *san'ad, san'adī*, adj. Authentic; trustworthy;
be-sanad, adj. Unaccredited.
kampnī-i-sanad-yāftah, A chartered company.

H سنکلا آنے संकला आने *sank'lā-āne*, n. m. (*Brokers*) One rupee and two annas.

S سنکلپ सङ्कल्प *san'kalp*, n. 1. A solemn purpose; a vow. 2. A bequest made by word of mouth. 3. A charitable donation. 4. Land given often rent free to a Brahman (generally without consideration given). 5. The declared wish or will of a person deceased, made known before his decease, with regard to the disposal of property, adoption of a son, or the like, made before the witnesses. This is considered in some degree equivalent to a will or testament, an act which, strictly speaking, is not recognised by Hindu law. Also lands held under a grant or bequest.
sankalp-brit. A grant to a Brahman.
sankalp k., *sankalp'nā*, v. a. 1. To make a vow. 2. To make a grant; to dedicate. 3. To give alms in fulfilment of a religious vow. 4. To bequeath.
sankalp-nāma. A deed of gift or assignment according to a previous vow.

P سنگین *sangīn'*, adj. Grave; aggravated; serious; heinous.
sangīn jamā-bandī, n. A heavy assessment.
sangīnī-i-jamā, G. G. Over-assessment.

H سنگار सिंगार *singār'*, n. m. S. शृङ्गार 1. Dress. 2. Sexual union; coition.

H سنگھاڑا सिंघाड़ा *singhāṛ'ā*; Tir. *singhār*, n. m. H. *sīngh*, horn. (*Brokers*) Three rupees.

H سنوت सनौत *sanaut'*, n. m. The pine tree.

H سنوڑھیا सनोढ़िया *sanoṛ'hiyā*, n. m. 1. A subdivision of Brahmans, called also *snādh*. 2. A pilferer; a thief; robber.

A سنہ *sanh*; Sant. *sermā*, n. m. Year; era.
sann-i-julūs, The year of accession to the throne.
sann-i-ravān, The current year.
sann-i-īsvī, The Christian era.
sann-i-faslī, The *faslī* or harvest year.
sann-i-hijrī, The Mahomedan era.

H سو सौ *sau*, adj. Hundred.
sau par sau. A hundred per cent.
sau ke savāë. Twenty-five per cent.

A سوال *suāl*; Pop. *savāl*, Pl. *savālāt*, n. m. سال asked. 1. Query (استفسار 1). 2. Application; petition; request.
savāl-i-ishārī, *yā hidāyatī*, A leading question.
savāl-i-tardīd, *yā jirah*,
A cross-question; cross-examination.
savāl javāb. Question and answer; debate.
savāl javāb aur pairavī k.,
To prosecute or conduct (a case).
savāl javāb k., v. a. 1. To argue; cross-examine. 2. To plead; advocate. 3. To transact or negotiate.
savāl-khuānī, n. f. Hearing or entertaining an application or suit.
savāl-dar-savāl. Cross-examination.
savāl dar-savāl k. To cross-examine.
savāl-i-daqīq. *Vexata questio*; a nice question.
savāl denā, v. a. To present a petition; to petition; make an application.
savāl-i-zurūrī, A material question.
savāl k., v. a. 1. To question; ask; interrogate. 2. To examine (a witness). [petition.
savāl guzrānnā, v. a. To move the court by
savāl mutamman qīmat.
A petition put in to make up the value of an insufficiently stamped plaint.

savāl marammat. A petition intended to amend another petition previously filed.
savāl-i-muqarrar, n. A petition or representation to the ruling authority of the proceedings in respect to a grant of revenue.
savāl-i-vakīl. Cross-examination by counsel.
fard-i-savāl, n. An application; a petition.

H سوان स्वान *suān, suhān*, adj. (*Brokers*) Two.
savāneh-nigār, vaqāë-nigār, n. m. A newswriter.
An officer stationed by the Mogul Government in distant provinces to transmit weekly to the court an account of all public transactions, such as the collection of revenue, the management of lands, and the state of the country.

H سوانسا सुआंसा *suāṅ'sā*, E.; *sūbṛā*, W. n. m. An alloy of gold and copper.

H سوانہ सिवाना *sivān'ā*; Rus. *simānā, sīm, sīmā*; Tir. *simān*; Sant. *simā*; A. *sarhad*, n. m. S. सीमा A boundary of a field or village.
sivānā-adhkār, n. Limits of jurisdiction or authority.
sivānā-bibād; A. *tanāzo-i-sarhadī*, n. A boundary dispute.
sivānā-bandī k., To fix the boundaries.
sivānā pūjā, sīmā pūjā, n. Honors paid at the village boundary to a bridegroom, etc.

A سوائے *sivā'ē*, n. 1. Cesses; additional items of income from an estate over and above the ordinary rents.
2. Any addition to the standard or customary revenue, whether as an increase of the amount or in the shape of a new or additional cess or impost; profits from land other than those of cultivation, as the rent of fisheries, forest produce, etc. some of which are included in fixing the assessment; dues claimed by the proprietors of a village from non-proprietary residents for houses, shops, and temples, in some cases recognised and recorded officially.
سوائي *sivā'ī*, n. f. A rate of interest on seed grain advanced, a maund and a quarter to be repaid at harvest for every maund lent at sowing time.
sivā-i-jamā. Extra revenue; extra or miscellaneous collections.
In the South the term denotes the revenue derived from all taxes except those raised from land, and exclusive of customs and transit dues, comprising, under the native governments, a vast number of petty and vexatious imposts.

H سوائي सिवाई *sivā'ī, sevāī*, n. f. A mixture of clay and sandy soil suited to any grain except rice.

H سوبڑا सूबड़ा *sūb'ṛā*; Farrukh. *subro*, n. m. Alloyed gold or silver.

H سوتيلا सौतेला *saute'lā*, adj. *lit.* belonging to relating to *saut.* Half blood; sprung from a different wife.
sautelā bāp, n. m. A stepfather.
sautelā bhāī, n. m. A stepbrother.
sautelī-bahan, n. f. A stepsister.
sautelī-beṭī, n. f. A stepdaughter.
sautelī-mā, n. f. A stepmother.

S سوتنتر स्वतंत्र *swatantar, sutantr*, n. m. 1. One who is independent, or acts for himself. 2. One who is legally entitled to act without control or guardianship.

P سود *sūd*; H. *byāj*; Sant. *sud*, n. m. 1. Profit; gain. 2. Interest; simple interest.
sūd aur munāfa. Interest and dividends or profits.
sūd baṭṭā; H. *byāj baṭṭā.* Profit and loss.
sūd par denā, sūdī chalānā, v. a. To lend at interest.
sūd par lenā, v. n. To borrow at interest.
sūd-khorī, sūd-i-nājāiz, n. f. Usury.
sūd dar-sūd; H. *byāj par byāj*; S. चक्रवृद्धि n. m. Compound interest.
sūd kā qānūn. Law regulating to the rate of interest; usury law.
sūd khānā, v. n. To take or receive interest.
sūd lagānā, v. a. To charge interest.
sūd mābād ḍigrī, sūd-i-āindah, sūd tārīkh ḍigrī se. Interest subsequent to decree.
sūd masāvī-ul-asal. Interest equal to the principal.
sūd muzāf. The accumulation of interest so as to double the original debt.
سودي *sūd'ī*; H. *byājū*; adj. Lent or borrowed at interest.

P سودا *sau'dā*, n. m. 1. (*saudā sulaf*) Goods; wares (اسباب 3, 4).
saudā banānā, yā k., v. a. To strike or settle a bargain.
saudā bannā, yā ho jānā, v. n. To be settled (a bargain).
sudā-patr, n. A written agreement to deliver goods to a purchaser on specified terms; a bill of sale.
saudā paṭnā, v. n. To be struck (a bargain).
saudā kharīdnā, yā mol lenā, v. a. To make purchases.
saudāg'rī, adj. Mercantile; commercial.
سوداگري *saudāg'rī*, n. f. 1. Trade; commerce. 2. The business of a merchant.
saudāgrī māl yā asbāb, n. m. Merchandise.
saudāgrī k., v. a. To trade.
saudāgaroṅ kā godām. A public warehouse.

H سورني सोरनी *sor'nī, sohenī*; Tir. *trirātrī*, n. f. An obsequial rite performed on the 3rd day of one's demise when the ashes are thrown into the river.

H سوکا सोका *sok'ā*, W.; *pal-maruā*, E. Frost-bitten crops.

P & H سوگند *saug'and*; Wom. and Rus. *soṅ, sūṅ*, n. f. Oath (*kiryā*); solemn asseveration.

saugand, yā sūṅ denā, dilvānā, yā khilānā, v. a. To administer an oath; to swear one.
saugand se kaknā, v. n. To declare upon oath.
saugand khā-ke inkār k., v. a. To deny on oath.
saugand khānā, v. a. To make oath; to swear.
saugand yā qasam khānā, yā dilānā, Swearing.

H سولي सूली *sūl'ī,* n. f. S. शूल 1. A stake for impaling criminals; a gibbet; gallows.
sūlī pe chaṛhānā, sūlī chaṛhānā yā denā, v. a. 1. To impale a criminal.

H سونڈي सूंडी *sūṅ'ḍī, sūṅṛī;* Sant. *huti,* n.f. 1. A small brown insect which destroys gram crops.
2. The navel (*tūṅḍī*). 3. The manufacture of spirituous liquors. 4. A distiller and vender of spirituous liquors.
5. A grocer; a dealer in rice.
sūṅṛī-mushakhkhasī, n. m. G. G. A tax on the venders of spirituous liquors.

H سوہائي सोहाई *sohā'ī, nalāī,* n. f. Weeding.

H سونيا सोनिया *son'iyā, niyāriā,* n. m. One who separates gold from ashes.

P سہ *sih, si, seh;* Sant. *pea,* H. *tīn,* adj. Three.
si-bandī, n. f. 1. Quarterly payment.
2. A tribute; a contingent.
3. A militia soldier employed in collecting revenue or in police duties, etc.
4. Charges in the revenue accounts for the maintenance of such troops.
si-bandī ughānā, v. n. To levy or collect quarterly payments.
si-māhī, seh-māhī, adj. Quarterly; every three [months.

H سہاگن सुहागन *suhāg'an,* W.; *suhāgin,* E. n. f. S. सौभागिनी 1. A married woman whose husband is alive; a *feme covert.*

A سہام *sihām',* n. m. pl. of *sahem* share. Portions or shares of an estate or inheritance.

A سہل *sah'al;* Illit. *sahaj,* adj. Easy.
kisī fel yā jurm ke irtikāb ko sahl k. To facilitate the commission of an act or offence.

A سہم *sah'am,* n.m. Pl. *sihām,* A lot; portion; share.
saham baṭvārah, n. m. Division of an estate amongst the coparceners according to their several shares.
saham-i-muaīyan. Allotted shares.

A سہو *sahv,* n. f. Oversight; fault; mistake.
sahv-ul-qalam, A slip of the pen; inadvertence; oversight.
sahv-i-zābitah, sahv-i-tartībī. A technical error; faulty arrangement.
sahv-i-kātib. A clerical error.
سہواً *sahv'an, sahv se;* H. *bhūle se, bhūl-kar,* adv. Erroneously; by mistake; through inadvertence; inadvertently.

A سياست *siyā'sat,* n. f. سوس managed, ruled.
1. Jurisdiction; legal authority; government; administration; management. 2. Correction (*ḍaṅḍ,* 4). 3. Severity; rigour.
siyāsat-khānā, A solitary cell.
siyāsat k., v. a. 1. To administer. 2. To chastise.
siyāsat ke tābe. Amenable to jurisdiction.

H سياوڑي सियावड़ी *siyāv'aṛī, siyāvaḍhī, sāvarī, asāvrī,* n. f. A particular allotment of a portion of the grain heap.
Three handfuls are taken out, one for the *Pirohit* or *Brahman* priest; the second for *Devī,* given to Jogīs; the third for *Bhagwān.* God, given to a *faqīr.*

P سياہا *siyāh'ā,* n. m.
1. An account-book or written account.
2. A daily ledger or account-book of the receipts and disbursements of a village or estate, in which are entered all sums received whether regular or miscellaneous, and all items of customary or contingent disbursement.
siyāhā āmdanī, n. A treasury account of daily collections received from the cultivators.
siyāhā-bahī, n. f. 1. The ledger or day-book in which daily receipts and disbursements are entered. 2. A journal in which the orders of a court of justice are recorded.
siyāhā-khazānā, n. The day-book of the collector, or any public treasury.
siyāhā k., v. a. To enter; register; record.
siyāhā-i-maujūdāt. An account of the daily receipts, remittances, and disbursements.
siyāhā-navīs, n. m. An accountant; one who keeps the rough day-book or accounts.

H سيچنا सीचना *sīch'nā, sīṅchnā;* Tir. *sichab,* v. a. S. सिञ्च, to water.
To irrigate (*pānī denā*).
sichāī, siṅchāī, n. f. 1. Irrigation.
2. The cost of irrigation.

H سيدھا सीधा *sīdh'ā,* n. m. S. असिद्ध unripe.
1. Provisions; uncooked victuals.
2 A settled allowance. 3. A charge made for supplies to travellers.
ser-hāsil, adj. Rich; fertile.

H سير सेर *ser,* n. m. S. सेटक A seer.
The Govt. seer, as fixed by law = 1 Kilogramme = 2·2055 Lbs. avoirdupois. See act XIV of 1877.

H سير सीर *sīr;* Sant. *si, nāhel,* n. f. S. सीर a plough. Land under the immediate cultivation of the proprietor.

These lands were sometimes allowed to be held at a favourable assessment, or were unassessed so as to provide Nānkār or subsistence for the proprietor. The term is also sometimes applied to lands cultivated on account of the state, or to those in which the revenue is paid by cultivators without any intermediate agent. *Wilson.*

sīr-jotā, ghar-jotā, Home farm. [vation.

sīr-i-zamīndār, n. The *zamīndār's* own culti-

sīr sājhī, n. m. The *zamīndār's* own land, cultivated by tenants at will for a share of the produce.

sīr-rār, adv. According to the proprietory or privileged land, cultivated after the same manner, or on the same terms as the *zamīndār's nij jot.*

sīr, adv Together; in partnership. [A sharer.

سیری सीरी *sīr'ī, sājhe-dār, baṭāī-dār, sajāī,* n. f.

Technically the members of a *lānā* or confederation of cultivators under which they cultivate in common and divide the proceeds according to the number of ploughs, bullocks, or men contributed by each.

H سیگون सेगौन *segaun', segoṭā,* n. f. A mixture of sand and clay. It holds a middle place between *maṭyār* and *bhūṛ,* q. v.

H سیندھ सेंध *sendh, sendhī, sen* E.; Bhoj. *senhi*; Mār. *sainto*; W. *kūn'bhal*; P. *naqab,* n. f. S. सन्धि

1. A hole made in a wall by burglars.

2. (*sendh-chorī*) House-breaking; burglary.

sendh-chor, sendh-mār, n. m.

A house-breaker; burglar.

sendh lagānā, v. a. To break into a house or wall; commit a burglary.

sendh-kātī, n. f. A burglar's tool. [Per cent.

H سینکڑا सैंकड़ा *sainkṛā*; P. A. *fī sadī,* adv.

H سینگنا सींगना *sing'nā,* v.a.

To identify stolen cattle. [of cattle.

سینگوتی सिंगौटी *singauṭ'ī,* n.f. A tax on the sale

H سیوکپتر सेवकपत्र *sevak-patr,* n. m. A deed or bond by which a person binds himself to servitude either for a term or for life.

ش

H شاشن پتر शाशनपत्र *shāsan-patr,* n. m.

A copper plate, stone, paper, etc., on which an edict or grant is inscribed.

A شامل *shām'il, shumūl,* adj. شمل included.

1. Comprising; including; included; comprehending; extending to; blended; mingled; united; joint (*sāth*). 2. Associated; confederated. 3. Annexed; appended; attached. 4. Concerned; connected with; having one's finger in. 5. Living together; having a common bed and board.

shāmil, shāmil-hāl, adv. Together; jointly.

shāmil, prep. With; along with.

shāmil-i-birādarī, yā panchāyat,

A member of a fraternity or society.

shāmil-i-hāl. Similarly circumstanced.

shāmil hāl h., v. a. To have a part in; to be similarly circumstanced.

shāmil rakhnā, shāmil-i-kāgzāt rakhnā. To file with other papers; to place among the records.

shāmil k., v. a. 1. To affix; annex; append.

2. To mix; incorporate; comprehend; include.

3. To insert; set down; enter (*bhartī k.*).

shāmil kīyā huā. 1. Annexed; appended. [rated.

2. Brought under; included; incorpo-

shāmil-i-misl, adj. Filed with the record or papers of a case.

shāmil-i-misl k., v. a. To record; file; put in a bundle; put up with the case.

shāmil h., v. n. 1. To be included, comprised; to consist of. 2. To fall under; come under. 3. To belong to; to be connected with; to be a member of. 4. To have part in; to partake or participate in. [together.

ek ahd o paimān men shāmil k., v. a. To bind

sab men shāmil. Common to all. [territory.

qalam-rau men shāmil k., v. a. To annex

شاملات *shāmilāt', shāmlāt,* n. 1. See شامل. 2. A coparcenary estate; undivided property; land held in common or in partnership by the whole proprietary body of a village.

shāmilāt banjar.

Portions of common land; portions of a field within its area left uncultivated, chiefly where the field is very large.

shāmilāt berij. The entire assessment; the original assessment with all additions.

shāmilāt-i-deh. Lands included in the village lands. [ship.

shāmilāt ke muqaddame. Cases of joint owner-

shāmilāt men, adv. In common. [common.

شاملاتی *shāmilāt'ī,* adj. Coparcenary; joint;

shāmlātī, n. Tenure in severalty.

shamlātī taalluq. An estate comprehended within a *zamīndārī* and paying revenue through the *zamīndār*, but held to be hereditary and independent property, inalienable as long as the dues to the superior holder and government are paid. [coparcenary village.

shamilātī mauza. A village held in common; a

qabza-i-shāmlātī. Common tenancy.

A شاہد *shā'hid*; P. *gavāh*; H. *sākshī,* n. m. شہد testified. A witness; deponent. [to a fact.

shāhid-i-hāl, n. m. An eye-witness; a witness

شاهدي *shā'hidī, gavāhī, shahādat*, n. f.
Attestation ; testimony (اظهار 1, 3).
be-shāhidī, adj. Without witnesses, or evidence.

A شبه *shub'ah*, n. m. شبه likened. 1. Demur; suspense; question; scruple. 2. Uncertainty. 3. A legal defect; a flaw.
shubah-i-ibāhat. Doubt as to justification in the commission of a crime sufficient to prevent the infliction of the full measure of punishment.
shubah-i-khafīf. Light presumption; slight suspicion.
shubah-i-shadīd yā qavī, n. m.
Strong presumption (of guilt).
shubah-i-zaīf, Uncertainty as to the truth or falsehood of a charge.
shubah-i-aqd. An error or informality of marriage.
shubah-i-qatl, n. m. Homicide.
shubah-i-qatl-i-amad va zakhm-i-kārī.
Homicide and severe wounding.
shubah k., v. a. To distrust; doubt; suspect.
shubah-i-māqūl, n. m. Reasonable doubt.
shubah miṭānā, yā nikālnā, v. a. To remove a doubt.
shubah-i-milk.
Erroneous appropriation of property.
shubah hai. Is doubtful.
be-shubah, be-shak, adv. Undoubtedly; indisputably (*bilā-shak*).

A شجره *shaj'rah, shijrah*, n. m. 1. A genealogical tree (H. *bansāolī*). 2. A field map.
shajra nasab. A tabular statement uniting the ordinary pedigree table of a community of proprietors with the *khevaṭ* or register of coparcenary responsibility. *Carnegy.*

A شخص *sha^khs*; H. *pursh*, n. m.
A person; individual (*ādmī*, 2).
shakhs-i-be-jurm, yā nā-kardah gunāh; H. *nirdosh pursh*, n. m. An innocent person.
shakhs-i-be-dakhl, n. m. The party ousted.
shakhs hai-ul-qāyam, H. *bachā pursh*. A survivor.
shakhs-i-sālis, tīsrā shakhs. A third person.
shakhs-i-gair; H. *an pursh*, n. m. Another party.
shakhs-i-farzī; H. *mānā pursh*, n. m. A hypothetical person.
shakhs-i-qābiz, n. m. The party in possession; the possessor.
shakhs maslūb-ul-havās; H. *pāgal pursh*. An insane person.
shakhs-muān; H. *sahāyak pursh*, n. m. The person abetted.
shakhs-i-mādūm-ul-vujūd, n. m. No such person (non-existent).
shakhs-i-mafqūd-ul-khabar; H. *be-byorā pursh*. One who is missing.
shakhs-i-mākhūz; H. *doshit pursh*, n. m.
An accused person; the prisoner; one under arrest.
shakhs-i-mulk-i-gair hāl sākin mumālik-i-sarkār, G. G.; H. *pardesī*, n. m. An alien.
shakhs-i-nā-dār; H. *nirdhan pursh*, n. m. An insolvent.
shakhs-i-nā-karda-i-gunāh, G. G.
An innocent person.
shakhs-i-vāhid; H. *ek pursh*, n. m. 1. One unassisted. 2. One person; an individual.
شخصيت *shakhsī'yat'*, n. f. Identity.

P شدكار *shudkār'*, n. m. A rough estimate made on the spot of the rental value of the standing crop on a field or estate. *Carnegy.*

P شديد *shadīd'*, adj. 1. Heavy; grave; heinous (*sakht,*). 2. Vehement; intense.
sazā-i-shadīd, Severe punishment.

A شر *shar*, n. m. شر was corrupt. Vice; depravity.
shar uṭhānā, yā k., v. a. To raise a quarrel; to make a riot.
shar o fasād, shor o shar, A breach of the peace; a riot.
shar'rī, adj. 1. Vicious. 2. Quarrelsome; litigous.

A شرا *shir'ā*; Pop. *sharā*, n. m. Purchase; sale.

A شراب *sharāb'*, n. f. شرب drank. Spirits.
sharāb-i-mukhmir, n. f. A fermented liquor.
sharāb-i-muqattar, n. f. A distilled or spirituous liquor.

S شراده श्राद्ध *shrāddh*; H. *sarādh, kanāgat*, n. m. Funeral obsequies.
It consists chiefly in offering cakes (*pinda*), water, etc. to deceased ancestors before a sacrificial fire.

A شرارت *sharā'rat*, n. f. Mischief; wickedness.
sharārat-i-nā-dihandagī,
Contumacious refusal to pay what is due.

P شرافت پناه *sharāfat-panāh*, lit. refuge of nobility. An epithet employed in addressing a subordinate officer.

A شراكت *shirāk'at, shirkat*, n. f. شرك shared
1. A combination; alliance; league; confederacy; amalgamation. 2. A corporation; coparcenary; joint-stock company (*sājhā* 1).
3. Land held in common (*shāmlāt*).
4. Community of interests.
shirākat-i-birādrī, n. f. An association of brothers, or members of one family living together on a common property.
shirākat k., v. a. To enter into partnership.
shirākat-nāmah, n. m. Deed of partnership.
kār o bār-i-shirākatī, G. G. n. m.
The affairs of a partnership.

A شرايط *sharā'yat*, n. f. Pl. of شرط q. v.
Stipulations; requirements.
sharāyat-i-iqrār-nāmah, n. f. The terms of a contract.
sharāyat-i-tamhīdī, n. f. Preliminary conditions.
sharāyat-i-sulah-nāmah, n. f. The terms of a treaty or of a compromise.
sharāyat kā asar, G. G. The effect of (certain) provisions.
sharāyat-i-mashrūtah, The stipulated conditions.
sharāyat-i-nikāh, n. f.
The terms of a marriage contract.

sharāyat-i-wājib-ul-arz, Terms or stipulations of the village administration.
ekaṭ kī sharāyat. G. G. The provisions of an act.

HP شربت پلانا *sharbat pilānā*, W. v. a. To give the barber a sherbet to drink and so seal the betrothal which he has arranged.
sharbat-pilāī, W. n. f. The present made to the barber by the bride and bridegroom.

A شرح *sharh*; Pop. *shar'ah*, n.f. شرح laid open.
1. Explanation. 2. Commentary).
3. Rate of assessment; proportion; charge (H. *dar*, 2.).
sharah-i-āb-pāshī, n. f. Irrigation rate.
sharah-bandī, n. f. A table of rates.
sharah pānī, n. f. Water rate.
sharah-i-paṭṭa, n. f. The rent rate fixed by lease.
sharah-i-parganā, n. f. The rate of assessment in the *pargana*.
sharah-i-paunṭoṭī, n. f. Rate of town duty.
sharah charhānā, v. a.
To annotate; write a commentary.
sharah khūrāk-i-gavāhān,
Rate of allowances to witnesses.
sharah-i-riāyatī, n. f. A favorable rate.
sharah-i-sūd, n. f. Rate of interest.
sharah farzī lagān, n. f. An assumed rent rate.
sharah k., v. a. 1. To define; determine with precision. 2. To detail (*tafsīl k.*).
3. To assess; fix the rate.
sharah lagān, Rent rate.
sharah māl yā mālguzārī. Revenue rate.
sharah mālguzārī vasūlī, n. f. The rate at which revenue has been collected.
sharah māmūlī, n. f. The customary or usual rate.
sharah-i-muqarrarah, n. f. A fixed rate.
sharah-i-mauzā, n. f.
The rate of assessment on village lands.
sharah-nāmah, n. m. A statement of rates at which the cultivators agree to hold their lands.
sharah naqdī, n. f. A money rate.
sharah nahr, n. f. Canal rates.
sharah-vār, adv. As detailed; explicitly; at length; in full.
ujrat kī sharah, n. f. Rate of fees, or wages.
ba-sharah-i-zail, adv. On the terms herein after set forth; as hereinafter shewn; shewn below; in form and manner following; to wit.
lagān kī sharah vāhid. A uniform rate of rent.

A شرط *shart*; Illit. *sharat*; Pl. *sharāyat*, n. f.
1. Condition; stipulation; engagement; term; provision; proviso.
2. A bet; wager.
shart bāndhnā, badnā, budnā, k., yā lagānā, v. a.
1. To make terms; stipulate; provide; bargain. 2. To bind by contract; contract an obligation. 3. To bet (*bāzī badnā*).
shart-i-tamhīdī, n. f. A preliminary condition.
shart-i-khās, n. f. A specific condition.
shart-i-khārijī, n. f. An extraneous condition.
shart-i-zurūrī, n. f. An indispensable condition; a *sine qua non*.
shart-i-mashrūt, Cartel; indenture; covenant.
shart-i-muzhirā, An express condition.
shart-nāma, n. m. A treaty; contract; covenant.
shart yeh hai. Provided; provided that.
shartā shartī k., v. a. 1. To enter into mutual obligations. 2. To wager.
ba-shart-i-manzūrī. Subject to the sanction or approval of.
ba-shart-subūt-i-jurm; H. *aprādh pāë jāne par*.
On conviction.
ba-shumūl is shart ke. G. G. With the proviso that.
bilā-shart. Unconditional; absolute.
ba-sharte ki., On condition that; provided that; if.
zar-i-shart. Money lost or won at bets.
kisī shart se mashrūt h., v. n.
To be subject to a proviso.
شرطي *shart'ī, shartīyah*, adj. Contingent; conditional; provisionary; provisional.
istehqāq-i-shartīyah. A contingent interest.

A شرع *shar'a, sharīyat*; Wom. *shara torā*, n. f. The law, or precepts of Mahomedanism as derived from the *Qurān*.
shara mahammadī, n. f. Mahomedan law.
be-shara, adj. Contrary to the Mah. law; unlawful.
شرعاً *shar'ān*, adv. According to the Mah. law; legally.
sharan jāiz h., v. n. To be good in (Mah.) law.
شرعي *shar'āī, bā-shara*, adj. Conformable or according to the *shara*; lawful; constitutional.
sharāī qasam, Mah. A solemn oath.

A شركت *shirk'at*, n. f. See *shirākat*.

In Mah. law partnership is of two kinds, *shirkat-i-imlāk*, partnership by right of property, where the absolute right of property belongs equally to all associated, and *shirkat-i-uqūd*, partnership by contract effected by mutual consent, and in which one partner may act for the rest. Partnerships of this kind are also classed under four heads, 1. *mufaviaza*, when the contracting parties agree that all their property shall be in common, a partnership not admitted by the *Shia* law-giver. 2. *inān*, when the contracting parties contribute a stipulated amount either of money or goods to a common capital, to be employed for their common benefit. This is also designated by the simple term *shirkat*, and may again be distinguished as *shirkat al amvāl* partnership in property, and *shirkat-us-tijāraṭ* partnership in trade or commerce. 3. *shirkat-us-sanāia*, *shirkat-ul-abdān* association or partnership in mechanical arts or bodily labor. 4. *shirkat-ul-vujūh* ostensible partnership, when persons not having any property conjointly obtain goods for sale upon their personal credit. *Wilson.*

bilā shirkat-i-gaire, yā shakhse, Sole ownership.

P شرمگاه *sharm-gāh, sharm kī jagah*.
The privities.

A شريف *sharīf*, n. m. 1. A title given to the rulers of Mecca; a prince.

2. Cor. of Eng. sheriff.
sharīf khāndān kā, khāndān kā sharīf, qaum kā sharīf, adj. Of high birth; of a good family or stock. [2, 4).

A شريک *sharīk'*, adj. Joint; united (*shāmil*,
sharīk, n. m. 1. A member of a community.
2. A co-sharer; co-partner (*hissedār*).
3. An accessory. 4. A confederate (*rafīq*).
sharīk-ul-rāē. Of the same opinion. [in a crime.
sharīk ba-vaqt-i-jurm. G. G. An accomplice
sharīk tadbīr huā.
Concerted; become aparty to.
sharīk-i-jurm, G.G. *Particeps criminis.* [crime.
sharīk-i-jurm k. To implicate or include in a
sharīk-i-hāl. See *shāmil-i-hāl*.
sharīk rahnā, shāmil rahnā, v.n.To live together.
sharīk-i-shikmī, n. m. A co-parcener whose revenue payments pass through an intermediate representative; a partner who does not take an active share in the conduct of a joint concern; a co-sharer.
sharīk fī nafs-ul-mubaiyat. A partner in the matter of buying and selling.
sharīk k., v. a. 1. To include (*shāmil k.* 3).
2. To make one a partner in.
sharīk mā qabl-i-vaqu, G. G.
An accessory before the fact.
sharīk-i-majma. A member of an assembly.
sharīk-i-majma-i-khilāf-i-qānūn.
A member of an unlawful assembly.
sharīk h., v. n. See *shāmil h.*, 1. To join in; cooperate with (*shāmil h.*, 4).
2. To have a share in; to be a partner (*sājhī h.*); to have or possess in common; go halves; go snacks. [cessory.
jurm meṅ sharīk h., To abet; to be an ac-
sharīk ho-kar, adv. Conjointly.
sar-kashī meṅ sharīk h. To join an insurrection.
mashvare meṅ sharīk h. To join in a consultation or conspiracy.

P ششماہي *shash-māhī*, adj. Half-yearly.

H ششوہتیا शिशु हत्या *shishu-hattyā*, n. f.
Child murder; procuring abortion.

A شفع *shuf'a*, n. m. شفع joined. Preemption.
shufa rivājī, n. m. Pre-emption based on well established local custom and usage.
shufa-vājib-ul-arz. In co-parcenary estates, the right of pre-emption, as stipulated in the administration paper at the time of settlement. [preemption.

A شفيع *shufī'*, n. m. One who has a right of
shufi-i-jār, An occupant of ground in the neighbourhood of another estate.
shufī-i-khalīt,
An occupant of ground in actual contact, or intermixed with another estate.

A P شقدار An officer appointed to collect the revenue from a certain division of land.

A شكايت *shikā'yat*, n. f. شكي complained.
1. (*shikvā*) A complaint. [complaint.
shikāyat rafa k., v. a. To remove a cause of
shikāyat k., v. a. To complain.
shikāyatī', adj. Complaining; plaintive.
shikāyat pesh k. v. a. To sue or lay an information against; to bring an action; charge.
shikāyat rafā karnā, v. a.
To remove a cause of complaint.
shikāyat-i-marjūā. G. G. Charges preferred.
bināē-shikāyāt. G. G.
The subject matter of accusation.

A P شكرانه *shukrān'a, shukriyah*, n. m.
1. Thanksgiving. 2. A present or fee paid to a pleader, etc. by a successful litigant over and above the legal fees.

P شكست و پيوست *shikast' o paivast'.* lit. broken and joined. Alluvial land.
shikast o rekht; H. *ṭūṭ phūṭ, lit.* breaking and falling. Injuries; damage.
shikast o rekht zimma-i-mālik-i-makān.
The landlord to be liable for all injuries.

P شكمي *shik'amī, shikmī*, adj. 1. Included.
2. Private; secret.
shik'mī, n. m. 1. A subordinate tenure in which the holder pays the Government revenue, or his share of it, not direct, but through some other person. 2. The person who cultivates land on such terms.
shikmī ijārah-dār.
A subordinate cultivator holding lands in farm; a sub-lessee; an under-farmer.
shikmī asāmī raiyat yā kāshtkār, n. m. A subordinate cultivator; an under cultivator; a holder of part of the village lands as a subordinate or dependent occupant, occupying his own share, and paying his own quota of the Government revenue through the representative of the community.
shikmī-paṭṭīdār, n. m.
A coparcener in a joint tenancy village who cultivates his own lands, and pays his proportion of the Government revenue through one or more of the community whose names are recorded in the Government books as responsible for the whole.
shikmī taalluqa. An estate comprised within a *zamīndārī*, and paying the revenue through the *zamīndār* or other revenue contractor or *mālguzār*.
shikmī divāna; H. *janam pāgal*, n. m.
A born idiot; a natural.
shikmī taraf. A subordinate portion of the division of land called a *taraf*.

talluqāt-i-shikmī. Dependent *taällugs,* the rent of which is paid to *zamīndārs,* and not to Government.
dar-shikmī. Subordinate, as a tenure or sharer under a *shikmī* holding or holder.
qābiz-shikmī. G. G. An under-tenant.
muqarrarī dar-shikmī. G. G. One holding a tenure at a fixed rent under a *zamīndār.*
kāshtkār-i-shikmī, A subtenant.

H شگن शुगन *shug'an, sagun, sugan, saun;* Sant. *sārsagun,* n. m. S. शकुन, P. *shugūn.*
1. An augury; omen. 2. A present of money.

P شماري *shumār'ī,* n. f.
A revenue account, shewing the daily receipts of every kind, and a rough statement of the day's transactions; a numbering with a view to the imposition of a tax.
shumār-navīs, n. m. An accountant; a registrar.

A P شمسي سال *shamsī sāl;* H. *sūraj baras,*
The solar year.
shamsī qamarī, adj. *lit.* solar and lunar.
A perquisite taken by the officers of Government, being the difference between the pay for a lunar and solar month.
shamsī mahīna. Solar month.

A شمول *shumūl', shumūliyat,* n. f.
The whole; gross; aggregate.
ba-shumūliyat, G.G. With the aid of.

P شناخت *shanā'kht', shinākht,* n. f.
Recognition; cognizance.
shanākht k., v. a. To know again; recognize.
shanākht karvānā, Caus. of *shanākht k.,* q. v.
shanākht ke gavāh. A witness who identifies one.

A شنيعة *shanī'ă, fel-i-shanīă;* G.G. *burā kām,* H. n.m. 1. Adultery. 2. Prostitution. 3. Sodomy.
fel-i-shanīa kī garaz se ujrat par chalānā. Ped. for *kharchī kamvānā.* Letting to hire for the purpose of prostitution. [rent or tenure.

H شوٹرم शोतरम *shot'ram,* n. m. A kind of

P شور *shor,* n. m. Cry; outcry; din; clamour.
shor k., yā machānā, v. a.
To make a noise, uproar, row.
شوره پشت *shorah-pusht,* adj Unruly.
shorah-pushtī, n. f. Refractoriness; turbulence.
شورش *shor'ish,* n. f. Disturbance, etc. (*balvā*).
shorish barpā k., v. a. To excite an insurrection.
shor zamīn; H. *kallar,* E. *ūsarl,* n. f. Land impregnated with saltpetre; saline soil.

P شوہر *shau'har;* H. *pati,* n. m. Husband.
shauhar kī zindgī tak. During coverture.
شوہري *shau'harī,* adj.
Of, or belonging to the husband.

P شہبالہ *shah-bāla,* Mah.; *shivālā,* Hin. n. m.
The companion of a bridegroom; the best man. [witnessing.

A شہادت *shahād'at,* n. f. شہد being present,
Written or oral testimony (اظہار 3).
shahādat-i-aslī, Primary evidence.
shahādat-i-tāīdī, shahādat-i-muāidah, n. f. G.G. Corroborative evidence.
shahādat-i-huzūrī, n. f. Ocular evidence; evidence of the first order. [evidence.
shahādat-i-dastāvezī, yā tahrīrī, n.f. Documentary
shahādat denā, v. a. To give evidence (*izhār d.*).
shahādat-i-samāī, yā manqūlah, n. f.
Hearsay; secondary evidence.
shahādat-i-zannī, n. f. Presumptive evidence.
shahādat gair-mumkin-ul-tardīd.
Incontestible evidence.
shahādat qalam band huī. Evidence taken.
shahādat-i-qayāsī. Conjectural evidence.
shahādat lenā, v. a. To take evidence.
shahādat lene kā majāz h.
To be competent to take evidence.
shahādat-i-mazīd, Further evidence. [in writing.
shahādat-nāmah; H. *sākshī-patr,* A testimony
jhūṭī shahādat, shahādat-i-kāzib. False evidence.

P شہربدر *shahr-badar,* G. G. n. 1. Banishment (جلاوطني). 2. An outlaw. [banish.
shahr badar k., v. a. To expel from the town;
shahr-panāh, n. f. The city walls (*chār dīvārī*).

A شي *shaë,* n.f.Pl.*ashyā.*A thing (اسباب3—5,7).
shaë dāva, shaë mudaābihā. The thing claimed the matter, or subject matter of a suit.
shaë mubīa, The subject matter of a sale; the thing sold.
shaë mutanāzea. The thing or property in dispute or under litigation.
shaë marhūna. The subject of a mortgage; the thing or property mortgaged.
shaë marhūnā kā zabt yā qurq k. Foreclosure of a mortgage; foreclosure (*baᵉe bāt*).
shaë makfūlā. Hypothecated property.
shaë mauhūba. 1. The thing given; a dotation; present; gift; benefaction; contribution; donation; gratuity; bonus; grant; subscription; largess; endowment. [legacy.
2. The property bequeathed; a bequest;
shaë nā-gavār. Anything noxious, offensive, or unpleasant; a nuisance.

ص

A صاحب *sāḥ'ib;* Pop. *sāhab, sāb,* n. m. *sāhibah,* n. f. Pl. *as'hāb.* صحب kept company.

1. (*In comp.*) Owner; possessor, as *sāhib-i-takht.*
2. A gentleman; a European gentleman.
sāhib-i-ikhtiyār. One invested with authority or power.
sāhib-i-band o bast, n. m. A settlement officer.
sāhib-i-tasdīq, n. m.
An attesting officer; a public notary.
sāhib-i-haisīyat, n. m.
A man of property or substance.
sāhib-i-zila, barā-sāhab, n. m.
An officer in charge of a district; a collector or magistrate or deputy commissioner.
sāhib-ālam. A title of a prince, including the Delhi shahzādas.
sāhib-i-adālat. An administrator of justice; [the court.

A صادر *sād'ir, sudūr*, p. p. صدر issued.
1. Proceeding; going forth; issuing.
2. Issued; passed.
sādir-kunindah. One who issues (an order).
sādir yā sudūr k., v. a. To issue; pass (an order); enact.
sādir yā sudūr h., v.n. 1. To be issued or enacted.
2. To happen; befal.
3. To be committed or perpetrated.
sudūr-i-hukm. Passing of an order or verdict.
ba-taur-i-māqūl sādiq ānā, G. G.
To reasonably answer.

A صاف *sāf, safā*; Rus. *suāph*, adj.
صفو was clear. 1. Clear; fair; clean.
2. Cleaned out; swept.
3. Unsoiled; unspotted. 4. Unadulterated.
sāf inkār k., sāf mukarnā, v. a.
To deny or decline outright.
sāf bayān k., sāf kahnā, v. a. 1. To make a clear statement. 2. To speak out; let out.
sāf muāmlagī, G. G. Plain or honest dealing.
sāf na kahnā, v. a. 1. Not to speak out plainly; to hum and haw. 2. To prevaricate.
صاف *sāf*, adv. 1. Distinctly; clearly; plainly; expressly; in plain terms. 2. Frankly; openly. 3. Without reserve or guile.
4. Outright; entirely; thoroughly.
sāfī-nāmā, See *rāzī-nāmā.*

A صحیح *sah'īh*; H. *shudh*, adj. 1. Correct. 2. Perfect; whole; integral. 3. Sound; healthy.
sahīh, n. f. 1. Signature; sign or mark; attestation. 2. Sanction (*tasdīq*).
sahīh-ul-aql. Sane; of sound mind.
sahīh-ul-mizāj. In perfect health.
sahīh-un-nasab, adj. Legitimate.
sahīh-un nasab betā. A legitimate son.
sahīh aur pukhtah. Good and valid.
sahīh aur durust aql, thīk samajh, Sanity.
sahīh dāvā, n. m. A just claim.
sahīh sālim, yā salāmat, adj. Safe and sound.
sahīh sālim, yā salāmat rahnā, v. n.
To keep safe and sound.
sahīh sālim k., v. a. To restore to health; heal.
sahīh farz k., v. a To assume or accept as true.
sahīh qarār denā yā tajvīz k., v. a. To determine or receive as genuine or valid.
sahīh k., v. a. 1. To sign (*dastkhat k.*). [register.
2. To enter in one's account; to book;
3. To strike; hit. [tion of the court.
sahīh o mohar-i-adālat. The seal and attesta-
sahīh h., v. n. 1. To be signed, witnessed.
2. To be confirmed. 3. To be corrected.
sahīh hai, All right, quite correct; exactly.
sihat pānā, yā h., v. n. To recover; get well.
sihat-i-āmmā men̐ khalal dālnā, v. a. G. G.
To cause a public nuisance.
sihat-nāma, n. m. 1. A health certificate.
tajvīz kī sihat par etirāz k. To question the correctness of a judgment.

A صد داخلا *sad dā-khlā*, n.m. Interest formerly paid on bonds given to the treasurer for revenue paid in arrears. *Carnegy.*
fī sadī; H. *sain̐krā.* Per cent.

A صدر *sad'r, sadar*, adj. صدر facing, upper.
Principal; capital
sadar amīn, n. m. 1. A head *amīn*, q. v.
2. A subordinate judge lower than *sadr-āla*, q. v. The office has been abolished.
sadar-us-sudūr, sadar āāla, n. m.
The chief judge or chancellor under the Mah. Government.
He was especially charged with the investigation of the cases of all those who applied to the sovereign for grants of revenue. He had also charge of *vaqf* property or religious endowments, and the appointment of *Qāzīs* and other law officers.
sadar bord, n. m. The highest revenue court; the Board of Revenue.
sadar panchāyat. A supreme *panchāyat*, q. v.
sadar jama yā māl-guzārī, n. f. The sum total of revenue payable to Government direct, exclusive of cesses, etc.
sadar dīvān, dīvān-i-ālā, n. m. A chancellor.
sadar dīvānī adālat, n. f. The highest Civil Court, now the High Court.
sadar sarishta, n. m. 1. The chief revenue office in a district; the Collector's office.
2. The head of an office; higher authority.
sadar adālat. The Supreme Court of Justice.
sadar fauj-dārī, adālat, ya nizāmat adālat, n. f.
The Chief Criminal Court.
sadar qist-bandī. An engagement for revenue instalments payable to Government by the principal revenue payer as distinguished from those entered into with him by his under-payers.
sadar māl-guzār, n. m. The head man or representative of a joint-tenancy village who engages for and pays the revenue due from the community to the Government.

sadar majistreṭ. Chief magistrate.
sadar-maqām, n. m. Head quarters.
sadar-nashīn, n. m. A president; chairman.
mufassiala-sadar. Before-detailed.
qānūnan sudūr pānā. To lawfully issue.
صدراعلي *sadar āāla, sadar-us-sudūr, sadar sadūr*, Principal *Sadar amīn*, now called a subordinate Judge.

A صدمه *sad'ma, sadmā*, n. m. صدم knocked. against. A blow.
sadmā pahoṅchānā, v. a. To give a blow; to hurt; injure.
sadmā pahoṅchānā gusse meṅ. An assault in hot blood.
sadma-i-jismānī. Personal violence; bodily hurt.

A صراف *sarrāf'*; (Contemp.) *sonṭhiyā sarrāf*; Rus. *sarāph*, n. m. صرف dealing.
A money-changer (*sāhūkār*).
صرافه *sarrāf'ah*, n.m. 1. Banking; money-changing. 2. The money-market; exchange.
sarrāfah kholnā, sārrāfī k., v. a.
To open a banking firm.
sarrāfe kī koṭhī. A banking firm.
صرافي *sarrāf'ī*, n. f. 1. Banking (*sarrāfā*).
2. The discount on exchange of coins.
3. (*munḍe*) The commercial (*mahājnī*) character used by *sarrafs* and shopkeepers.
sarrāfī chiṭṭhī, hunḍī, yā parchā, n. f. A bank bill; a cheque; draft.
صرف n. m. 1. Cost.
sarf-i-makhfī, G.G. Secret expenditure.
sarf-i-sikkā. 1. A charge or discount on the different currencies receivable at the public treasury. 2. An impost or cess established at one time in Bengal to cover the loss accruing on exchange of coin.
sarkār ke sarf meṅ, G. G. At the disposal of Government.

A صرف دستخط *sirf dastkhat*. A blank endorsement; *carte blanche*.
sirf sahīh yā daskhat k., To endorse in blank.
sarf-i-ābādī. Outlays for improvements of land.

A صريح *sarīh*,' adj. صرح was clear.
Gross; great; palpable.
sarīh mukarnā, v. n. To deny absolutely.
zurūrat-i-sarīh. Manifest necessity.
صريحا *sarīh'an, sarīhī*; Illit. *sarīyan*; Hin. Wom. *saryan*, adv. 1. Expressly; palpably (*sāf* 1,2). 2. Manifestly; evidently.
az rūe alfāz-i-sarīhī. In express terms.
sharāyat-i-sarīh. Express provisions or terms.

A صغيرسن *sağīr-sin*, n.m. A minor; a youth.
sagīr-sinī, n. f. Minority; tender age; youth.

A صفائي *safā'ī*, n.f.1. Cleanliness; clearness.
2. Conservancy.
safāī-i-hisāb, Settlement of an account.
safāī-i-muāmilah. Plain or fair dealing.
safāī-nāmah, n. m.
1. A settlement; discharge; acquittance.
2. A deed of release or of acquiescence in the terms of a *Rāzī-nāmah* of which it is the counterpart, the latter or deed of consent being executed by the plaintiff, the *Safāī-nāmah* or deed of acquiescence by the defendant.
gawāhān-i-safāī. Witnesses for the defence.
qānūn-i-safāī. Conservancy laws.
mahkama-safāī. The conservancy department.

A صلاحيت *salāh'iyat*, n. f.
1. A deposition (*izhār*, 3).
2. A report or return made by the police.
salāhiyāt-bahī, n. f.
A diary kept in police and revenue offices.
salāhiyat likhnā, v.n. To keep a register of travellers in a road-side inn.

A صلب *sulb*, n. m. 1. The loins. 2. Offspring.
صلبي *sulb'ī*, adj. 1. Descended or sprung from.
2. Legitimate.

A صلح *sul'ah*; Illit. *sullā*; H. *milāp*, n. f.
صلح was good. Peace; truce; reconciliation.
sulah-ikhtyārī, n. f.
A voluntary act of composition.
sulah-i-chand-rozah. An armistice.
sulah-shiknī, n.f. A breach of the peace.
sulah-kāmil, Perfect reconciliation; a lasting peace.
sulah qahrī. Compulsory composition, made by order of the judge or other authority.
sulah-nāmah kī khilāf-varzī.
A breach of compromise.
sulah-nāmah, n. m. 1. A treaty of peace.
2. A deed of compromise.
sharāyat-i-sulah, Terms of peace.

A صوبه *sūb'ah*; H. *khanḍ*, n. m. Pl. صوبجات
A province.
sūbeh-dār, n. m. 1. A governor of a province.
2. A native military officer holding a rank equivalent to that of Captain.
sūbeh-dārī, n. f. 1. A lieutenancy of a province; viceroyalty. 2. The rank of *sūbehdār*.
sūbeh-dārī-abvāb. Taxes imposed by the *sūbeh-dārī* in addition to the fixed rates.
sūbeh-dārī parvāna.
An order issued by a *sūbeh-dār*.

A صورت *sūr'at*, n. f. See *bhes*.
sūrat badalnā, v. a. To transform; change.
sūrat bigāṛnā, v. a. To deform; disfigure.
sūrat banānā, v. a. 1. (*sūrat denā*) To form; figure; give shape to. 2. To personate (*bhes badalnā*). 3. To sham; feign.
4. To put a false coloring or construction upon; pass off for.
sūrat-i-hāl; Pop. *sūrat hāl*. 1. (*sūrat-i-muāmlah*)

The facts or complexion of a case.
2. A statement of the facts or circumstances of a case; a written declaration; a manifesto; report; return.
sūrat qayām kī hai. Is likely to remain.
sūrat mahāl. A list or register of estates.
sūrat mufīd-i-matlab. Favorable circumstances or state. [the case.
sūrat-i-muqaddamah. The presumptions of
sūrat-nāmah, n. m. A written detailed account of an estate or a transaction. [possession.
qabze ke sūrat yā qabīl. The character of the
sūrat yeh hai. The fact is. [event of.
is sūrat meṅ, adv. In this case; but in the
par jis sūrat meṅ. If on the other hand.
dar sūrat, dar sūrate ki. In case; provided that.
dar sūrat adā na hone. In case of non-payment.
zāhirā surat-i-maāsh. G. G.
Ostensible means of subsistence.
har sūrat meṅ. In all cases.
صورتاً *sūratan',* adv. 1. As to form; in form.
2. In appearance; apparently.

A صيانت *siyān'at,* n. f. صون preserving.
The privilege of being under the protection of the law, restricted to the faithful and withheld from aliens and infidels.

A صيغه *sīg'ah,* n. m. صوغ formed.
Section; department; office.
sīgah-i-āb-pāshī, yā nahr,
Canal or irrigation department.
sīgah-i-ābkārī, Distillery department.
sīgah-i-parmaṭ. Customs department. [knot.
sīgah paṛhānā, Mah. v. a. To tie the nuptial
sīgah-i-tāmīrāt-i-sarkārī,
Public works department.
sīgah-i-dīvā'nī. Civil department. [appellate).
sīgah-i-adālat. Side of the Court (original or
sīgah-i-fauj-dārī. Criminal department.
sīgah-i-māl. Revenue or Financial department.
sīgah-i-mutafarriqāt. Miscellaneous department.
sīgah-i-muflisī. Forma pauperis. [per.
ba-sīgah-i-muflisī. In forma pauperis, as a pau-

ض

A ضابطه *zāb'itah;* Rus. *jāb'ā,* n. m. Pl. *zavābit,* ضبط maintained.
Judicial usage; manner of proceeding; ordinance; regulation.
zābtah baratnā, v. n. To act according to law; take legal measures.
zābitah-dāṅ, n. m. One acquainted with the procedure of the Court.
zābitah-i-dīvānī. Civil procedure.
zābitah-i-zamānat-nāmah. Form of bond.
zābitah-i-adālat. Legal procedure; judicial usage.
zābitah-i-adālat ke khilāf. Opposed to judicial usage; contrary to judicial practice.
zābitah-i-fauj-dārī. Criminal procedure.
zābite kī rū se, hasb-i-zābitah, adv. In due course; through the regular channel; according to rule or established practice.
zābitah-i-māl.
Body of instructions for revenue officers.
bā-zābitah ānā, (Amlah idiom) v. n.
To come into Court with the usual bribe.
bā-zābitah mashhūr k. To duly promulgate.
be-zābitah, adj. Irregular; contrary to rule; unusual; informal.
khilāf-i-zābitah. A deviation; irregularity; an anomaly. [or law.
ضابطگی *zāb'tagī, zābtgī,* n. f. Conformity to rule
be zābtagī, n. f. Informality; irregularity.
be zābtagī kī sūrat. Want of form.
be-zābtagī-i-nālish. Informality of procedure.

A ضامن *zā'min;* Pop. *zāman;* Rus *jāman,* n. m. ضمن was responsible. A surety.
zāmin dar zāmin. A collateral security.
zāmin kī bariat. Discharge of a surety.
zāmin h., n. m. To be surety for another; to give or stand bail; guarantee; engage for another.
zāmin denā, v. a. To give a surety.
fel-zāmin. A surety or security for good conduct or for a person's refraining from any proscribed offence or misdemeanor.
māl-zāmin. A security for the discharge of a debt; recognizance; bail.
ضامني *zā'minī;* Pop. *zāmnī;* Rus. *jāmnī,* n. f. Security; bail; pledge; guarantee.
zāmnī par chhoṛnā, zāmnī manzūr k., v. a. To admit to, or accept bail.
zar-i zāminī, n. m. Money paid as a security.
zanjīr-zāminī, n. f. Chain security.
A number of persons binding themselves severally or jointly for each other; the joint responsibility of the cultivators of a village or district for the whole revenue or for money borrowed of a banker.
fel-zāminī, n. f. Security to keep the peace or for good conduct. [pecuniary obligation.
māl-zāminī, n. f. Surety for the payment of any

A ضبط *zabt;* Rus. *japat,* n. m *zabtī,* n. f. ضبط held fast. 1. Control; restraint. 2. The act of confiscating. 3. Seizure; confiscation; resumption; sequestration.
zabt k., v. a. To seize or attach property; confiscate; resume (an estate). [fiscated.
zabt h., zabtī meṅ ānā, v. n. To be seized, con-
māl-i-zabtī. Property confiscated.
zabtī arāzī-i-lā-khirāj yā muāfī.
Resumption of rent-free lands.
zabtī-i-jāēdād, yā māl. Forfeiture of property.

zabtī kā hukm, n. m. An order to confiscate.
zabtī ke lāyaq, qābil-i-zabtī, adj.
Liable to seizure; contraband.
zabtī-nāmā, n. m. A deed of confiscation.

A P ضرب شدید *zarb-i-shadīd*, Grievous hurt.
jisse zabtī niklī, Involving forfeiture.
zarb-i-shadīd, Grievous hurt.
zarab-i-khafīf. G. G. A slight wound or blow.
zarab-i-shamshīr, n. f. A sword-wound or cut.
zarab-i-mohlik, n. f. A mortal wound.
āla-i-zarab-i-sikka. A coining instrument.
dār-ul-zarab; H. *ṭaksāl*, n. m. The mint.

A ضرر *zar'ar*, n. m. ضر hurt 1. Injury; detriment; wrong (*choṭ*, 1). 2. Damage (*zyān*).
zarar pahuṅchānā, v. a. To injure; hurt.
zarar-i-jismānī, G. G. n. m. Bodily hurt or injury.
zarar-i-khafīf, n. m. Slight harm.
zarar-rasānī, n. f. Causing injury, annoyance.
zarar-i-shadīd, G. G. n. m. Grievous injury.
zarar kā khatrah, n. m. Risk of harm.
bil-irādah zarar pahuṅchānā, G. G.
Voluntarily causing hurt.

A ضرور *zurūr'*, *par-zurūr*; Pop. *zurūr'ī*, adj. ضر necessitated. 1. Necessary; urgent; important. 2. Essential; indispensable.
3. Incumbent; obligatory; imperative.
zurūr, zarūr; Rus. *jarūr*, adv. 1. Urgently.
2. Certainly; of course; without fail; absolutely; peremptorily.
zurūr zurūr, zurūr hī, bil-zurūr, zurūratan, adv.
1. Urgently; indispensably.
2. *Ex necessitate rei*; necessarily; of or by necessity; perforce.
zurūr hai. It is imperative; he is bound to.
zurūrat-i-ashadd.
Extreme or urgent necessity; emergency.
zurūrat parṇā yā h., v. n.
To have need of or occasion for.
ba-qadr i-zurūrat. As needed.
zurūrī chiṭṭhī, n. f. An urgent letter or despatch.
zurūrī kām. Urgent work.
maṣārif-i-zurūrī. Necessary expenses.
ضروريات *zurūriyāt'* n. f. pl. of ضروري Necessaries.

A ضلع *zil'ā*, n. m. Pl. *azlā*. 1. A division of a province; a district; a tract of country constituting the jurisdiction of a judge and collector, or, in Non-Regulation Provinces of a Deputy Commissioner.
2. A column (of a page).
zila-bandī, n. f. The division of a province into *zillas* or districts.
zila jis men band o bast ho gayā ho. A settled district.
ضلعدار *zile-dār*, n. m. 1. A district superintendent.
2. An officer who makes advances to cultivators and collects rents, etc; a Canal Officer.
3. An officer in the Canal Department who supervises measurements and the distribution of water.
ضلعداري *zile-dārī*, n. f. The office of a *zile dār*.

A ضمار *zimār'*, Anything uncertain, as disputed debts, treasure-trove, fugitive slaves, and the like; any property of which the possession or recovery is doubtful.

A ضمان *zamān'*, *zaman*, n. f.
According to the *Shias*, security for property, whilst *kafālat* is personal bail.
zamān bil-dark. Bail for accidents or contingencies, or any undefined amount.
zamān ba-ohdat-ul-samanī'.
Security for the fulfilment of a bargain of sales on the part of the vendor.
zamān tamlīk. Compensation for appropriation of property.
The indemnification which a man who possesses only a share in a slave pays to his partners on setting the slave at liberty.
zamān-i-fasād Damages for personal injuries.

A ضمانت *zamān'at*, n. f. Security (ضامني).
zamānat jadīd dākhil k. To give fresh security.
zamānat-i-hifz-i-aman, yā adam-fasād, Security to keep the peace.
zamānat dākhil k., yā denā. To furnish security; give bail.
zamānat-i-kāfī. Sufficient security.
zamānat kāfi dākhil k. To furnish sufficient security.
zamānat ke qābil. Bailable.
zamānat le-kar chhoṛnā, zamānat pe rihā k., v. a.
To discharge on bail; to hold to bail.
zamānat-nāmah, n. m. Bail bond; security bond; a deed of suretyship.
zamānat na dākhil karne kī hālat men, ba-sūrat adam idkhāl-i-zamānat. In default of security; in the event of security not being furnished; failing to furnish security.
zamānat-i-nek-chalanī, n. f.
Security for good behaviour.
gair-qābil-ul-zamānat. Not bailable.
ضمانتا *zamānatan,'* adv. By way of security.
zamān'atī, zāmin, zamānat dene-vālā, n. m.
One who gives bail or security.

A ضمن *zimn*, n. m. 1. A clause; section; article.
2. Contents; body.
zimn k. Ped. v a. To include; take in; comprise.
zimn men, adv. 1. In the course of; by the way.
zimn navīsindah. A form of words, 'let them write the abstract', formerly inscribed upon a *sanad* granting an assignment of revenue or *zamīndārī*, which served as the authority for the subordinate officers to make out the particulars of the assignment or grant.
ضمنا *zim'nan, ishāratan*, adv. By implication; by the way; indirectly. 2. By way of security.

ضمنوت *zimnaut'*, n. m. A consideration usually received by a surety. [*mā*).

A ضميمه *zamīm'ah*, n.m. An appendix (*tatim-*

ط

A طايفه *tāë'fah*, n. m. طوف going round.
A corps; gang.
tāëfah-i-ṭhagoṅ kā sharīk h. G. G.
Belonging to a gang of thieves.

A طرز *tarz*, n. f. Way.
tarz-i-tahqīqāt. The mode of conducting an investigation or enquiry.
tarz-i-taqsīm-i-robkārī. A proceeding laying down the conditions and provisions of the partition, and showing the mode in which it is to be effected.
tarz-i-zirāāt, Ped. Mode of cultivation.
tarz-i-zirāāt kī khūbī. Improved husbandry.

A طرف *tar'af*, n. f. Pl. *atrāf*, طرف looked towards. 1. See اور 1—3.
2. A division of a *pargana* or estate.
taraf bāṅṭ, n.m. A modification of the *bhaiyā-chārā* tenure.
The area is divided into two or more *thoks*, held in commonality by two or more branches of the proprietary community. *Carnegy.*
taraf sānī, n.m. The opposite or adverse party; the defendant.
taraf-dār, n. A party-man.
taraf-dār, adj. Partial (*jānibdār*).
taraf-dārī, n. f. Leaning; party-spirit; partizanship (*pās*, 3).
taraf-dārī k., v. a. To side with (*jānib-dārī k.*).
taraf se. On the part of (*jānib se*).
bar-tarf, Dispensed with; dismissed; discarded.
jiskī taraf se. On whose behalf.
yak taraf, adv. Apart; separate.
yak-tarfah. One-sided; *ex-parte*.
yak-tarfah ḍigrī, n. f. An *ex-parte* decree.
طرفين *tarfain'*, n. m. Both parties; the parties concerned (*jānibain*).

A طريق *tarīq'*, *tarīqa*, n. f. طرق made away.
1. Way; road. 2. Manner.
tarīqa batānā, v. a. 1. To show the way; to direct. 2. To point out the proper course.
tarīqa-i-baṭvārā. Mode of partition.
tarīqa baratnā, G. G. To work a system.
tarīqā tahsīl.
A statement of arrangements for the collection of the revenue in a village or estate, and its general financial result.
tarīqa-i-hisāb. System of account.
tarīqa-i-darbār. Forms and ceremonies proper to a *darbār* or levee; forms of state.
tarīqa-i-amal-dar-āmad. Procedure.
tarīqa-i-muqarrara-i-qānūn.
The mode prescribed by law.
tarīqa-i-milkīyat.
Land tenure; mode of tenure of land.
tarīqa-i-munāsib. The proper mode.
ba-tarīq, *ba-taur*, adv.
In the way of; by way of; as though.
ba-tarīq-i-amānat. By way of deposit.
ba-tarīq-i-mujavvazah-i-qānūn. As by law enacted. [pauper.
ba-tarīq-i-muflisī. *In forma pauperis*; as a
adālat meṅ talab karne kā tarīq. How brought before a court. [to be brought.
muqaddama pesh karne kā tarīq. How a suit is

A طعن *tān*, *tān*, *tāna*; Wom. *tāna tishnā*, *tānā menā*, n. m. Taunts.
tānā denā jaise 'tum se kyā ho saktā hai.' G. G.
To defy; manifest contempt of opposition.

A طفل *tifl*; H. *bachchā*; Sant. *gidrā*, n. m. pl. *atfāl*. A child (*bachchā*, 1). [foundling.
tifl-i-uftādah, Ped. for; H. *pāyā bālak*. A
tifl-i-shīr-khuār; H. *dūdh pītā bālak*, n. m.
A sucking child.
tifl-i-sahīh-un-nasab; H. *kulvantī bachchā*.
A legitimate child.
tifl-i-gair-sahīh-un-nasab. G. G. A bastard child.
tifl-i-gair-sahīh-un-nasab kisī kī aulad nahīṅ hai. A bastard child, *filius nullius*.

A طفيل *tufail'*, n. m. Intervention; mediation (ذريعه). [agency of.
tufail, *tufail se*, adv. Through the merits or

A طلاق *talāq'*; Illit. *tallāq*; Sant. *sakām* (leaf) *orej* (rend), n. f. طلق loosed, separated. 1. A divorce; repudiation. 2. Oath (*qasam*).
talāq-i-bidat, (*bidat* innovation, heresy.).
Heterodox divorce, in which the husband makes the usual declaration three times in one month. This is deemed irreversible.
talāq ba-nān o nafqa. *A mensā et toro*; from bed and board.
talāq jo qarīb-ul-marg hone kī hālat meṅ dī jāve.
A death-bed divorce. [away (a wife).
talāq denā, v. a. To divorce; repudiate; put
talāq-i-sunnat. Mah. A divorce according to the traditional law.
talāq kināyat. A divorce in which the terms used, although not expressly declaring a divorce, are legally sufficient.
talāq-nāma. A deed of divorce.
talāq'ī, *talāqan*. A divorce; one divorced.

A طلب *tal'ab*, n. f. (*In compos.*) Seeking.

talab-i-ishhād,
A declaration made before witnesses.
One of the legal forms to be observed in asserting the right of preemption. Its observance consists in the preemptor calling persons to witness either on the premises or in the presence of the party in possession (whether seller or purchaser) and saying.—"such a one has purchased this property and I have a right of preemption, to which I have laid claim and which I still claim. Bear witness, therefore, to the fact." This form has to be gone through after the immediate claim (*talab mavāsbat*) has been made. Mah. Law.
talab-bāqī. An account showing the sums realized and balance due.
talab-chiṭṭhi, talab-dastak; talab-nāmā,
A warrant; summons; writ; a written demand for arrears of revenue.
talab khusūmat.
The claim by litigation, or the formal institution of a suit at law by a preemptor. This is preceded by the *immediate claim* and affirmation by witnesses (*talab nawāsabat* and *talab ishhād*). Mah. Law.
talab mavāsabat.
An immediate claim or demand as applied to the right of preemption.
It is made as soon as the fact of the sale of the property claimed is known to the claimant by preemption. Mah. Law.
talab k., v. a. 1. To call for; summon.
2. To demand; claim. 3. To exact.
talab-gār, n. m. A seeker; claimant.
talab-nāma, n. m. A summons (*safīnah*).
طلبانه *talbā'nah*, n. m. 1. Fees to peons for serving process. 2. The fee payable to a witness. 3. Daily pay to constables, etc.
talbānah dākhil k., v. a. To pay witness's fees.
طلبي *tal'abī*; Pop. *talbī*, n. f. Summons (*bulāvā*).
talbī h., v. n. To be called or summoned.

A طاور *taur*, n. m. Way; conduct.
ba-taur-i-rasadī, adv. Rateably; in proportion; share and share alike.
ba-taur-i-māmūl. Regularly; as usual; as established by custom. [way of comparison.
ba-taur-i-muqābilah, adj. Comparative; by
ba-taur-i-muqaddamah. As a preamble; introductory; prefatory. [a slave.
gulām ke taur par kharīdnā. G. G. Buying as

A طوعاً وكرهاً *tauan o karhan*, adv.
Nolens volens; by force.

A طومار *tūmār'*, n. m. طمر heaped. A heap.
tūmār-jamā. The sum total of the land revenue according to the register.
The recorded standard assessment of the land revenue of the provinces of the Mogal empire in the reign of Akbar, as settled by his minister, Todar Mal, and subsequently revised at different periods down to the time of the grant of the *Divānī* to the East India Company.

ظ

A ظالم *zālim zulm'ī*; Rus. *julmī*, adj.
Oppressive; tyrannical.

A ظاهر *zāhir*, adj. Apparent. [ing that.
zāhir ho ki. Be it known that; whereas; see-
iflās zāhir k., v. a. To sham poverty.
razā-mandī zāhir k., v. a. To signify consent.
lā-ilmī zāhir k., v. a. To affect ignorance; to pretend not to know.
ظاهرا *zāh'irā, zahiran, zāhir meṅ*, adv.
Apparently; so far as appearances go; ostensibly. [sistence.
zāhirā sūrat-i-maāsh. Ostensible means of sub-
zāhirī hālat. External state or condition.

A ظلم *zulm*; Rus. *julam*, n. m. 1. Oppression; extortion; tyranny. 2. Violence; force; outrage. 3. Grievance; duress; hardship.
4. A heavy assessment.
zulm bar zāt-i-khās. Private injury or wrong.
zulm se, adv. Unjustly; tyrannically.
zulm-i-sarīh. Flagrant injury; gross injustice.
zulm-i-ām. A public wrong.
zulm k., v. a. 1. To oppress; tyrannize.
2. To wrong; injure; extort.
zulm o bidat se, adv. Vexatiously.
zulm o sitam, yā tāaddī, n. f. Maltreatment.

A ظن *zann, zan*, n.m. ظن opined. 1. Impression; notion. 2. Conjecture.
zann-i-gālib. Strong or violent presumption; great probability.

A ظهر *zohr*, n. m. The back; the upper or outer portion, as the outer fold of a letter.
zohr-i-saman par. On the back of a summons.

A ظهور *zuhūr'*; Pop. *zahūrā*, n. m. Accruing or arising (as a cause of action).
zuhūr binaë dāvā. Cause of action.
zuhūr meṅ ānā, v. n. To arise.
bar vaqt zuhūr-i-binaë dāvā. At the time when the cause of action arose.

ع

A عادتاً *ādatan'*, Ped. adv. From habit; habitually. [ing in slaves.
ādatan gulāmoṅ kā kār o bār k. Habitual deal-

A عادل الرهن *ādil-ul-rahn.*
In Mah. law, a third party to whose keeping a pledge or security given by a borrower to a lender is entrusted.

A H عارض ہونا *āriz h.*, v.n. عرض happened.
1. To befall.
2. (*Law*) To bar; debar; interdict.
āriz-i-qatāī. A perpetual bar.

A عارضة *ār'iza, ārzah,* n. m. An incident; [event.
āri'za-i-jismānī. Infirmity of body.
āriza-i-dimāgī. Infirmity of mind.
ārizā had-i-samāat kā lāhaq h. To be barred by lapse or efflux of time; to be barred by the law of Limitation or statutory limits.
ārza-i-qānūnī. G. G. A legal defect.
عارضي *ār'zī,* adj. Not real, essential, or inherent.

A P عاریت نامة *āriyat-nāmā.* An engagement to return any article or property which has been given on loan or in trust.

A عافیت ذاتي *āfiyat-i-zātī.* Personal safety.
āfiyat-i-khalāyaq.
Public tranquility; the public good.

A عاق *āq,* adj. Disinherited; cut off from hereditary right.
āq karnā, irs se khārij k., v. a.
To disinherit; cut off from hereditary [right.
عاقنامة *āq-nāma.* Deed of disinheritance.

A عام *ʿā'm,* adj. عم was common. pl. *avām.*
1. (*āmmā*) {Common; general generic.
2. Ordinary (*sādhāran*). [in which.
ām is se ki, G. G. Whether; including the case
ām-fahm, adj. Intelligible to all; popular.
ām-kī, adj. Public; pertaining to the nation.
ām log, avām, avām-ul-nās,
The common people; the mass.
ām māl. Common property.
ām meṅ, adv. In public.
ām vajah istihqāq. A general ground of right.
ām vajah mukhāsamat yā nālish.
A general cause of enmity; a general ground of action.
ikhtiyār-i-ām, G. G. Ordinary jurisdiction; general powers. [ing.
jalsa-i-ām. A general assembly; a public meet-

A عامل *ʿā'mil,* n. m. 1. Doer; agent. 2. An authority; an executive or ministerial officer.
3. Revenue collector. 4. Conjuror (اوجها).
āmil-i-pulis, G. G. A police officer.
āmil-i-qurqī. An officer executing distress.
āmil-nāmā. A warrant of power from Government, authorizing a person to take possession of anything; a power of attorney.
āmil-i-nīlām. An officer holding or conducting a sale.
fel kā āmil. The person doing the act.

A عاید *ā'yad,* adj. عود returning.
1. Alighting; resting.
2. Liable; subject to; amenable; open to; incident; obnoxious to; exposed to.
āyad huā. Subjected to; laid on; charged.
āyad h., v. n. 1. To alight or rest upon.
2. To be amenable, liable, or subjected to.
hiqārat āyad huī. G. G. Exposed to contempt.
sazā āyad kī jāvegī, G. G. Shall be punished.
vohī tāvānāt āyad ho sakeṅge.
Amenable to the same penalties.

A عبارت *ibā'rat,* n. f. Style.
ibārat-i-tasdīq. Verification; attestation.
ibārat-i-zohrī. A blank endorsement.
ibārat-i-zohri-i-khās. A special; endorsement.
ibārat-i-zohri likhnā. To endorse; to write on the back of a paper or writing.
ibārat zohrī kā na likhā rahnā. Bearing a blank endorsement. [tence).
ibārat kī kotāhī, G. G. Deficiency (in a sen-

A & P عبور دریاے شور *ubūr-i-daryā-i-shor,* H. *kālā pānī,* Transportation beyond seas.
ubūr-i-daryā-i-shor k.; H. *kāle pānī bhejnā,* v. a. To transport beyond seas.

A عدالت *ādāl'at, adālat-i-mujavviza,* n. f.
A court of law, judicature, or justice; a tribunal; bench.
adālat-i-ib'idāī ikhtiyārāt-i-dīvānī.
A court of original Civil jurisdiction.
adālat-i-ibtidāī ikhtiyārāt-i-faujdārī.
A court of original Criminal jurisdiction.
adālat-i-apīl. G. G. A court of appeal.
adālat-i-apīl-i-akhīr vāqe Hind. Court of the last resort in India; the High Court.
adālāt-i-asgar, mātaht, yā adnā.
A subordinate, inferior, or lower court.
adālat āmir-i-nīlām. The Court issuing an order for sale by public auction.
adālat bādshāhī, yā shāhī. The king's court.
adālat-panāh. Asylum of justice.
adālat-i-chhāonī, A military court.
adālat khafīfa, yā khurd. A small cause court.
adālat-i-dīvānī, n. f.
Civil court; a court of Civil jurisdiction.
adālat-i-sishan. Sessions court.
adālat-i-zila. A District court.
adālat-i-āliyah, The High Court.
adālat āmil-i-hukūmat-i-munsifānā. A court exercising an equitable jurisdiction.
adālat-i-firistinda-i-kamīshan. The Court from which a Commission issues. [diction.
adālat-i-faujdārī. A court of criminal juris-
adālat kā muhāfiz, muhāfiz-daftar. A record-keeper; prothonatory.
adālat k., v. a. 1. To administer, or dispense justice. 2. To exercise judicial powers; to try suits at law.

adālat ke hukm se. By a reference from the Court; by order of the Court.
adālat ke hukm kā tāmīl karne-vālā. A bailiff; an officer of the Court who serves writs, etc.
adālat ek zarye se.
Judicially; by a power of the court.
adālat-i-māl. A revenue court.
adālat-i-majāz. A competent court or tribunal; a court of competent jurisdiction. [decree.
adālat-i-mujavviza digrī. The court passing a
adālat-i-murāfa-i-ūlā. A court of first instance; the court in which a suit is first brought; court of original jurisdiction.
adālat-i-murāfa-i-sānī. A court of second instance; a lower Appellate court.
adālat men āne kā mansab rakhnā.
To have a *locus standi* in Court.
adālat men mākhūz k. To bring to justice.
ba-kār-i-adālat. Acting judicially.
khārij az adālat honā. To be out of court; to have no *locus standi* in court.
dastūr-i-adālat. Judicial usage.
nizāmat-adālat. The Supreme court of criminal justice, nominally presided over by the *Nāzim*, or viceroy of the province.
naubat tā ba-adālat pahunchnā. To resort to legal proceedings; to have recourse to law; to go to law; institute legal proceedings; to resort to a court of law.
عدالتی *ădā'latī*, adj. 1. Just; true.
2. Judicial. 3. Actionable.
عدالتین *ădālatain'.* Two courts of justice, i. e. the civil and the criminal.

A عداوت *ădāv'at*; Rus. *kadāvaṭ*; P. *dushmanī*; H. *bair*, n f. عدو returning.
Hatred; spleen. [malice.
adāvat bil-qasd. Malice prepense; deliberate
adāvat-i-jibillī, as'ī, yā zātī,
Natural antipathy; animosity.
adāvat-i-dilī, yā qalabī. Secret malice or enmity.
adāvat rakhnā, v. n. To bear malice.
adāvat se, adv. Maliciously; feloniously.
adāvat nikālnā, v. a. To resent; avenge oneself.
عداوتی *adāv'atī*, adj. Malicious; felonious.
adāvatī nālish. A malicious prosecution.

A عدت *id'dat*, Mah. n. f. The time of legal probation which a divorced woman or a widow must wait before she marries again, in order to determine whether she is pregnant.
iddat men baiṭhnā, v. a. To pass the time of *iddat* in seclusion from strange men.

A عدل *ădl*; Pop. *adal*, n. m. Justice (انصاف).
adl k., v. a. 1. To do justice; to decide according to equity and good conscience.
2. To judge; decide.
adl-gustarī, n. f. The administration of justice.

A عدم *ăd'am*, n. m. عدم lacked.
Non-existence; nonentity.
adam-ehzār yā hāzirī. Default of appearance; non-appearance.
adam-ikhtiyār-i-samāat. Want of jurisdiction.
adam-i-adā. Non-payment; default of payment.
adam-adāē-jurmānā. Default of payment of fine.
adam-idkhāl-i-zamānat. Default of security.
adam istetāat. 1. Insufficient or no assets; insolvency. 2. Inability to pay; want of means; disability; impecuniosity.
adam-itāāt. Non-compliance; non-observance, disobedience; insubordination; contumacy.
adam iqrār. Non assumpsit.
adam-indirāj. Non-entry.
adam-pairavī yā khabargīrī. Default of prosecution; default; failure; neglect.
adam-tasrīh. Want of specification. [ance.
adam-tāmīl. Non-execution; non-service; abey-
adam-tāmīl shart-i-muchalka.
Forfeiture of recognizance.
adam-takmīl. Non-execution.
adam-tan-dihī. 1. Absence of effort; remissness.
2. Negligence; habitual neglect.
adam-tavajjahī. 1. Inattention; inadvertence; non-observance. 2. Disregard; neglect; carelessness. [dence.
adam-subūt. Absence of proof; defective evi-
adam-javāb. Nihil dicit.
adam-javāz, adam-javāzī. Illegality; invalidity.
adam-havāla. Non-delivery.
adam-dākhilā. Non-entry.
adam-darpeshī. Non-production.
adam-dastiyāb. Non est inventus; *non est.*
adam-i-ilāqagī.
Want of connexion or relationship.
adam-qābiliyat. Incapacity; disqualification.
adam-qābiliyat-i-zātī. Personal disqualification.
adam-qābiliyat sharāī. Legal incapacity.
adam liyāqat. Disability; inability.
adam-fursatī. Want of leisure.
adam-mutābiqat. Want of correspondence; anomaly (*ikhtilāf*, 1, 2.).
adam maujūdgī men, In one's absence.
adam-vāqfiyat, n. f. Ignorance; unconsciousness.
kal-adam, adj. Non-existent; null and void.
kal-adam k., v. a. To rescind; quash; make void.
kal-adam jānnā, v. n. To set at nought; treat as null. [nought.
kal-adam h., v. n. To become extinct; come to

A عدول حکمی *udūl-hukmī*, n.f. Disobedience of orders; evasion of process; insubordination.
udūl-hukmī k., v. a. To disobey; to refuse to obey; to be refractory.

A عذر *ŭzr*; Illit. *uzar*; Rus. *ujar, vajar*, n. m.
1. Objection (*bahs*). 2. Pretext.
3. Apology.

uzr ikhtiyār-i-samāat. Pleain bar of jurisdiction.
uzr bāqī rakhnā, v. a.
To reserve a right of objection.
uzr bāqī na rakhnā, v. n. To leave no objection unanswered; to leave no ground for objection.
uzr-i-barīat. Plea of exemption.
uzr i-be-bāqī. Plea of payment in full.
uzr-i-bejā, lagv, yā be-fāëda, 1. A frivolous excuse. 2. A weak, vain, or bad plea; an improper objection.
uzr-i-be zābtagī yā khilāf sarishtagī. A technical objection; an objection as to the irregularity, or informality of a proceeding.
uzr-pizīr, adj. 1. Excusable.
2. Admissible (plea). [ception to.
uzr pesh k., v. a. To plead; object; take ex-
uzr-i-tabnīyat. A plea against adoption.
uzr taslīm k., yā manzūr k., v. a. To admit, recognize, or allow a plea or objection.
uzr-i-tamhīdī. A preliminary objection.
uzr-i-kharchā. Plea of costs.
uzr-dār. Objector; claimant.
uzr-dārī, n. f. 1. A statement of objections. 2. A cross-demand; a caveat.
uzr-dārī k., v. a. To put in a petition of intervener; to bring forward an objection.
uzr raqūm mujrāë. A plea of set-off.
uzr-i-rivāj. A plea of custom or usage.
uzr-i-zabānī. A verbal plea.
uzr-i-ām, A general plea. [jurisdiction.
uzr-adam-ikhtiyār-i-samāat. Plea of want of
uzr-i-galatī. Plea of error.
uzr-i-fareb. Plea of fraud. [apologize.
uzr k., yā lānā, v. a. 1. To offer an excuse;
2. To take objection; contest (*etirāz k.* 1).
uzr qābil-i-pizīrāī, uzr-i-māqūl, An admissible, reasonable, or valid plea or objection.
uzr-i-qānūnī. A plea in law; a legal objection.
uzr-i-qavī. A valid objection. [jectionable.
uzr ke qābil, qābil-i-uzr, 1. Excusable. 2. Ob-
uzr-i-Gang-barār. Plea of alluvion.
uzr-i-Gang-shikast. Plea of diluvion.
uzr nā-qābil-i-samāat. An inadmissible plea.
uzr-i-muddaā-alaih. A plea urged for the defence.
uzr manzūr, yā qubūl na k., v. a. To overrule an objection; to reject a plea.
uzr-i-nābāligī. Plea of minority.
uzr nahīn, No objection.
uzr-i-virāsat. Plea of inheritance or heirship.
be-uzr, Without an excuse.

A عرصة *ārs'ah*, n. m. عرص space. Space.
arsa-i-mumtad tak hāzir rakhnā. G. G.
Prolonged detention.
arsa-i-vāhid yā mutaaddad. Ped. Portion or portions of time. [of money.

A عرض *ārz*, n. m. Personal property exclusive
arz-i-irsāl. A report; return; invoice.
arz-begī, (In Eastern Govts.) An officer who presents letters and representations; the chief petitioner. [presentation.
arz-i-hāl, n. m. A statement; complaint; re-
arz k., v. a. 1. To request; beg; apply; make application. 2. To submit; state humbly.
3. To propose; suggest; move.
4. To report; represent; memorialize.
arz-kunindah, arzī dihandah. n. m. Petitioner.
arz mārūz. Petition; request; case.
عرضي *ārz'ī, arz-dāsht*; Rus. *arjī, ardās*, n. f. pl. *arāiz* A written statement, petition, or representation.
arzī purzā k., v. n. To bring an action; sue.
arzī marammat, marammat savāl. A petition to amend or add something to a petition already filed; a petition of amendment.
arzī-i-mūjibāt. A representation of reasons or pleas; a petition or plaint setting forth the grounds thereof.
rue arzī-dāve par. Upon the face of the plaint.
marātib mundarja-i-arzī-dāvā.
The subject matter of plaint.
marātib mundarija-i-arzī-dāve hāzā se vajah nahīn paidā hotī.
The subject matter of this plaint does not constitute a cause of action.
arzī-dāvā, n. m. A petition of plaint; the first pleading in a suit.
arzī guzrānnā, lagānā, tānnā, ṭhoknā, yā denā, v. a. To present a petition; file a plaint.
arzī lenā, v. n. 1. To receive a petition.
2. To entertain a case.
arzī musanna. A duplicate plaint.
arzī-navīs, n. m. A scrivener; one who writes out petitions for suitors; a notary. [pondence.
ārāiz aur ahkām, Petitions and orders; corres-

A عرف *ūrf*; H. *boltā nām*, n. m.
Otherwise called; *alias*; or.

A عزت *īz'zat*; Rus. *ijjat*, n. f. عز was high.
Honor (آبرو).
izzat bigārnā, utārnā, khonā, yā lenā, be-izzat k., v. a. 1. See *ābrū utārnā*.
2. To insult; deflour; ravish; outrage.
izzat-vālā. A respectable man; a man of rank,
be-izzat, adj. Disgraced (*rusvā*). [defamation.
be-izzatī, n. f. Loss of reputation; dishonor;

A عشر التجارت *ashar-ul-tijārat.*
A duty on merchandise amounting to a tenth of it's value.

A عصبيت *asbī'yat'.* Affinity entitling to a share of inheritance—according to some authorities, to a sixth.

A عصمت *āsm'at, ismat*, n. f. عصم preserved.
1. Chastity. 2. The *pardah* (screen) or seclusion in which women are required to live.

3. The care and defence of property by the owner, and the protection of person and property by the state or the law.

A عضو *ăzv*; H. *joṛ*, n. m. pl. اعضا q. v.
Member; limb.
azv-i-tanāsul, n. m. *Membrum virile*.
azv-shikanī. Mutilation; maiming.
azv kā kātnā yā bekār k., v. a.
1. To cut off a limb. 2. To mutilate.

A عطا *ăt'ā*, n. f. عطو giving. 1. Bounty; benefaction (انعام). [sideration.
2. An endowment. 3. A concession; con-
atā k., v. a. To assign (*bakhshnā*); concede; accord; vest in.
atā-nāma. A grant (*bakhshish-nāma*).
sanad mashar-i-atā ikhtiyār ihtimām tarka-i-maurūsī. Grant of administration to the estate of the testator. [(عطا).

A عطيه *ătī'yah*, n. m. A grant; an assignment
atiya-i-arāzī. A grant of land.
atīyah-i-imdādī, A grant-in-aid. [grants.
atiya-i-jangal va vīrān. Jungle and waste
atīyah-i-dār, G. G. A grantee; an assignee; a graut-holder.
atīyah-i-sarkār, n. m. A Government grant.
atīya-i-shāhī, yā sultānī. A royal grant.
atīya-i-mazhabī, A religious grant. [(عصمت).

A عفت *ĭf'fat*, n. f. عف abstained. Modesty
iffat meṅ khalal ḍālnā, G. G., v. a.
To outrage modesty.

A عفو *ăfv*; Pop. *afū*, n. m. عفو erased.
Pardon; forgiveness; remission of sins.
afv k., v. a. To pardon (*bakhshnā*, 2).
afv-i-mashrūt. Conditional pardon.
afv h., v. n. To be pardoned.

A عقد *ăqd*, n. m. عقد tied. 1. A contract; compact. 2. (*aqd-i-nikāh*) The marriage knot or covenant.
aqd-i-kitābat. A contract of *kitābat* or conditional ransom granted by a master to his slave. [(*nikāh-paṛhvāī*).
aqdā'nah; H. *biyāh-karāī*, n. m. Marriage fees
aqd-bandī, n. f. Concluding a contract, more esp. the tying of the marriage-knot. [chase.
aqd-i-baē o shira, A contract of sale and pur-
aqd-i-tahrīrī. A contract (*ṭhekah*).
aqd-i-rahn. A mortgage contract.
aqd-i-zabānī. A verbal contract.
aqd k., v. a. To take or give in marriage; to marry; wed. [contract.
aqd-nāmah, nikāh-nāmah, Marriage deed or
aqd, yā aqd-bandī h., v. n. To be married.

A عقل *ăql*; Illit. *aqal*; Rus. *akal, akkal*; H. *samajh*, n. f. عقل restraining. Sense.
aql meṅ futūr. Unsound mind.
durust aql, Sound mind.

A عقوبت *ŭqūb'at*, n.f. عقب came after. Punishment inflicted by the Magistrate at his discretion (?). [of (اخيافي)

A P علاتي *allāt'ī*, adj. Of half-blood. (Opp

A علاقه *ălāq'ah*; Pop. *ilāqā*, n. m. علق clung to. See تعلق 1, 3. [affinity.
1. Dependency; affiliation; correlation;
2. Part (*sarokār*). 3. Bearing; relevancy; allusion. 4. Tenure; holding.
5. An estate; manor. 6. Province; division; district; circle; parish.
7. Jurisdiction; beat. 8. Office; post.
ilāqah uṭh gayā. The connection was severed.
ilāqah rakhnā, v. n. To be allied, or associated with; have affinity with; to be correlated, or dependent on (*tāalluq rakhnā*).
ilāqeh se bāhar. Beyond the limits. [ponsible.
ilāqah se mavākhizā thā. The estate was re-
ilāqa-i-adālat. The jurisdiction of a court.
ilāqe meṅ. Within the limits, or jurisdiction of.
ilāqa-dār. One who engages as agent or representative for the payment of the assessed revenue.

A علامت *ălām'at*, n. f. علم knew. 1. A sign.
alāmat-i-dastkhat.
A mark in place of a signature.
alāmat-i-mardī. *Membrum virile*.

A علانيه *ălānī'yah*, adv. Openly; in public; before everybody. [publicly.
alānīyah kahnā, v. n. To speak openly or
khufyah o alāniyah tahqīqāt k., v. a. To make enquiry both secretly and openly; to make a thorough investigation. [tion.
alāniya rishvat-sitānī. G. G. Notorious corrup-

A علت *ĭl'lat*, n. f. عل befel. 1. Cause (باعث 1).
2. A charge (*ilzām*, 2); count (of an indictment).
illat-i-dāvā. An indictment.
ba-illat, adv. Through; for; in a charge of (*ba-sabab*). [charge.
bar bināē illat-i-tarmīmī. Upon an amended
ba-illat-i ibhām, G. G. Through dubiousness or uncertainty. [of decree.
ba-illat-i-jrāē ḍigrī. In satisfaction or execution
ba-illat bāqī. On account of arrears.
ba-illat-adam adāē baqāyā-i-lagān. On account of the non-payment of arrears of rent.
fard-i-qarār-dād-i-jurm meṅ ek yā ziyādah illateṅ shāmil ho saktī hain. A charge may contain one or more heads.
jurm kī illat meṅ. For any offence. [knowledge.

A علم مجرمانه *ilm-i-mujrimāna*. G. G. Criminal

A علوفة *ālūf'ah*, n. m. علف feeding.

A pension; stipend; salary; subsistence money (خوراک 1, 2). [upon.

A علی *ālā*; (In comp.) *al*; H. *par*, prep. On;
al-al-ittisāl, adv. In a series; in succession; consecutively; *seriatim*. [severally.
al-al-ijmāl o al-al-infirād, adv. Jointly and
al-al-itlāq, adv. Absolutely; solely.
al-al-infirād, adv. Severally. [successively.
al-at-tavātur, adv. In succession; repeatedly;
al-al-hisāb, adv. Suspense account.
al-ul-hisāb denā, v. a.
To make advances to be adjusted afterwards; make payments on account.
al-al-khusūs, adv. Particularly; especially.
al-ad-davām, adv. Permanently; in perpetuity; for ever.
al-as-sabāh, adv. In the morning. [(*sādhāran*, 1.).
al-al-umūm, *umūman*, adv. In general; generally
ala-qadr-i-marātib According to rank, or degree.
علی ہذا القیاس *ala-hāz-al-qayās*,
In like manner; similarly; likewise; *mutatis mutandis*; ditto; on this measure.

A P علیحدگی *ʿalaihd'agī*; Pop. *alahdgī*, n.f.
Severalty; separation.
alāh'dagi-i-hisas. Separation of shares.
علیحدہ *ālaih'dah*, *a'ahdah*, adj. and adv. Separate.
alahdah rakhnā, v. a. To appropriate; set apart; segregate. [apiece.
alahdah alahdah, adv. Separately; one by one;
alahdah k., v. a. To separate.
alahdah h., v. n. To be separated (*alag h.*).
māl alahdā k., To part with a property.

A عمارت *īmār'at*, n. f. عمر lived, inhabited.
Any large building; an edifice.
mahakma-i-imārat-i-sarkārī, G. G. n. m.
Public works department.

A عمداً *ʿamadan'*; P. *dīdah o dānistah*; H. *jān būjh-ke*, adv. Wilfully; in cold blood.
amadan ikhfāē i-jarāyam-i-sangīn. G. G. Wilful concealment of heinous offences.
amadan zarar shadīd pahuṅchānā, v. a.
Voluntarily causing grievous hurt.

A عمر *ūmr*; Pop. *umar*; H. *ārbal*, n. f. Age.
umr bhar, adv. For life; during the term of natural life. [land.
umr bhar kī muāfī. A life tenure of rent-free
umr-paṭṭā, A lease for life. [ment for life.
umr-qaid, n. f. *dāim-ul-habs*, n. m. Imprison-
umr-qaidī, n. A prisoner for life.

A عمرو زید *āmr o zaid*; H. *kalvā malvā*, n. m.
John Doe and Richard Roe (زید).

A عمل *ām'al*, n. m. عمل worked.
1. Practice; work; business; employment; operation (*ikhtyār*, 8). 2. Act; deed; work; action; agency. 3. A charm; spell; a mystic word or incantation.
4. Measure; process; procedure.
5. Execution (*sādhan*). 6. Effect (*asar*).
7. Administration (*amaldārī*).
8. Intoxicating drinks.
9. The management of any land or business on behalf of another.
amal paṭṭā, *amal dastak*, *amal sanad*.
A deed appointing an agent or manager; a warrant authorizing a person to collect the rents of an estate. [charm.
aml paṛhnā, v. n. To mutter a spell or
amal'dār'. A manager; an agent; a collector of revenue; an officer appointed to collect the revenue of an estate which has been attached by Government.
amal-tamarrud. Contumacy; contempt; recusancy; defiance.
amal-i-hākimī. A judicial act.
amal-dārī, n.f. 1. Limits of jurisdiction (حکومت).
2. Government; reign; lordship. 3. The district governed; a collectorship. [cess.
عمل درآمد *ʿamal dar-āmad*. A proceeding; pro-
amal-dar-āmad k., v. a. To act upon; observe.
amal-dar-āmad h., v. n. To be acted upon.
amal-dastak. Warrant; writ; a deed of conveyance; a certificate of title.
2. A document giving possession of property; a written order from the proper authority to enable the purchaser of an estate to obtain possession of it.
amal k., *yā amal meṅ lānā*, v. a.
1. To put in execution; carry into effect; bring into operation (*bajā lānā*).
2. To act; set to work; transact (business).
3. To use (*istemāl k.*).
4. To dispense; administer.
5. To effectuate.
amal-guzār, Obs. n. m. A collector.
عملہ *ʿam'lah*, n. m. Establishment; office.
amlah-pulis yā faujdārī. Police establishment.
amlah-khurd. An inferior native clerk. [sion.
amlah dakhlah k., v. a. To bring under posses-
عملہ فعلہ *āmlah fʿelā*, n. m. Ministerial officers; clerks; officials; executive authority.
amal-i-qānūnī Process or operation of law; due course of law.
amal-i-mansabī. An official act; an act done in virtue of any office held by the doer.
amal-nāmah. Authority to manage or administer property.

A warrant from a competent public functionary to an individual, authorising his taking possession and management of landed other or property.

qānūnan amal meṅ lānā. To exercise lawfully.

A عمو *ām'mū* ; H. *chachā*, n. m.

Father's brother ; paternal uncle.

ammū-zādah ; H. *chacherā bhāī*, n.m. Father's brother's son ; cousin.

A عند *ind*, adv. At ; near ; nigh ; before ; with ; by ; about ; in ; on ; according to, etc.

ind-ul-ijrāë, ind-ul-tahrīk. At the instance of.

ind-ul-ijrāë vārant. By warrant.

ind-ul-istifsār, yā tahqīqāt. During interrogation, inquiry, or investigation.

ind-ul-partāl, A. H. On examination or inquiry.

ind-ul-tajvīz. Under consideration ; pending trial or investigation ; before the court.

ind-ul-talab, adv. On demand.

ind-ul-subūt. On proof ; on conviction.

ind-ul-zurūrat. When required or demanded.

ind-ul mulāqāt. During the interview.

ind-ul-nizāa. In question ; in dispute ; litigated.

ind-ul-vusūl. On receipt.

ind-ul-vuqū. When it happens ; in such an event.

A عوام *avām*, n. m. pl. of عامه

The common people, the public.

avām-un-nās ; H. *sab log*, The people ; the community ; the population ; the public.

avām kī ittilā ke liye mushtahar hotā hai. Is hereby promulgated for general information.

avām ke fāëde ke liye.

For the public good or welfare.

avām ke liye. For the public ; common.

A P عود ناجايز *aud-i-nā-jāiz.*

An unlawful return.

A عورت *āur'at*, n.f. *lit.* naked. A female (استري).

aurat kī zāt ; Hin. *aurat-bānī* ; Rus. *baiyar-bānī* ; Mah. *mastūrāt*, n. f. The female sex ; womankind.

aurat-i-hāmila ; H. *garabhvantī istrī*, A pregnant woman.

aurat-i-zī-rutbah. G. G. A woman of rank.

aurat kā bhagā le jānā. G. G. Abduction.

kisī aurat ko le uṛnā yā phuslā le jānā.

To take or entice away a woman.

kisī aurat ke khilvat-khāne meṅ ghus jānā.

To intrude upon the privacy of a woman.

kisī aurat kī nisbat be-iffatī kā ittehām āyad k.

To impute unchastity to a woman.

A عوض *ev'az, evzah, evzānah*, n. m. See بدله

1. A substitute; *succedaneum.* 2. An amends. 3. Penalty ; forfeit.

evaz irsāl. Return of a writ.

evaz denā, v. a. To make compensation ; to reimburse ; repay (*badlā denā*).

عوض معاوض *evaz maāvaz, yā maāvaza.*

A return ; commutation.

evaz māvaz k., v. a. To interchange.

evaz meṅ h., v. n. To represent ; replace ; supersede ; supplant (*badlī meṅ h.*).

evaz meṅ, ba-evaz, 1. As compensation or indemnity ; in satisfaction.

2. *Mutatis mutandis*; in supercession of.

evaz-i-nuqsān, tāvān ; H. *ṭoṭe kī bharautī, ḍanḍ*, Indemnity ; indemnification.

ba-evaz qīmāt-i-muaiyan. G. G. At a certain price.

ba-evaz hatak-i-izzat, G. G. For defamation.

ahd-nāmah ba-murād mubādilā-i-asīrān.

Cartel ; an agreement between hostile states relating to exchange of prisoners.

evazānā kāfī. Sufficient amends. [representative.

عوضي *ev'azī* ; Pop. *evzī*, n. f. 1. A substitute ; 2. The person officiating ; a *locum tenens.*

evazī, adj. Officiating ; acting ; in charge.

evzī denā, v. a. To supply a substitute (as a servant).

evzī rakhnā, v. a. To take or accept a substitute.

evzī k., v. a. To officiate ; to act in the place of.

A عهد *ahd*, n. m. 1. Engagement ; stipulation (اقرار 1, 3). 2. Reign (*rāj* 2, 4).

ahd toṛnā, v. a. To break one's promise or engagement.

ahd ṭūṭnā, v. n. To be broken (a contract).

ahd-i-hukūmat. In the reign of.

ahd-shikan, adj. Faithless to one's word or engagement.

ahd-shiknī, n. f. Breach of faith, contract, or engagement ; infraction of a treaty.

ahd k., v. a. 1. See *iqrār k.* 1, 4.

2. To abjure. 3. To make a vow.

ahd karvānā, v. a. To bind ; make conditions.

ahd meṅ, adv. In the reign of.

ahd-nāmah, n. m. A convention ; charter ; treaty (*iqrār-nāma*).

ahd-nāma-i-tijārat. A commercial treaty.

ahd-nāmah likhvānā. To bind ; oblige by contract.

ahd o paimān, n. m. Articles of agreement ; treaty of alliance.

ahd o paimān k., v. a. To enter into, or make a convention ; make a treaty ; make terms or conditions (*iqrār k.*, 4).

ahd o paimān karne-vāle. The contracting parties.

عهده *oh'dah*, n. m. Office ; duty ; occupation ; charge (*jagah*, 3).

ohdah-barā h., v.n. To discharge a duty ; fulfil an engagement.

ohdah-barāī, n. f. 1. Discharge of duty ; completion of an engagement. 2. See *barīyat.*

ohdah-barāī k., v. a.

1. To acquit one's self of an obligation.

2. To discharge the duties of an office.

ohdah pānā, v. n. To be appointed to an office, entrusted with a commission.

ohde par māmūr, yā muqarrar k., ohdah denā, v. a. To appoint to, or instal in an office.

ohda-i-jajī, G. G. The office of a judge.

ohdah-i-jalīl. An honorable or high place, office, or dignity.

ohdeh-dār. An office-holder; officer; functionary; civil or military authority. [officer.
ohdeh-dār-i-kharch-kunindah. The disbursing
ohdeh-dār-i-sarkārī, n.
A government official; a public officer.
ohdeh-dār-i-mātahat. A subordinate officer.
ohdeh-dār-i-māfauq, yā ālā. A superior officer.
ohdeh-dārī. Holding an office; incumbency.
ohdah rakhnā. To hold or fill an office.
ohde se bartaraf, yā māzūl h., v. n.
To be dismissed from an office.
ohdeh se dast-bar-dār h., v. n. See *istefā denā.*
ohda-i-āmil. An executive authority. [ment.
ohda-i-qāyam-muqāmī. An officiating appoint-
ohde ke etabār se, ba-etabār-i-ohdah. By virtue of one's office; *ex officio.* [office.
kisī ohde ke hīle se. G. G. Under color of any
masrūf ba-kār-i-ohdah; G. G. H. *kām par.*
On duty.

A عيار ***āiyār'***, n. m. A knave; an impostor.
aīyār, adj. Crafty (*chālāk*).
عياري ***āiyār'ī***, n. f. Imposture; deception; circumvention (*chālākī*, 4). [era; A. D.

A عيسوي ***īs'vī***, *san-ī-īsvī*, adj. The Christian

A عين ***ain***, adj. 1. Exact. 2. Very.
ain-ul-māl. 1. Principal (*rās-ul-māl*).
2. Net profit; land revenue.
ain vaqt par, adv. 1. In the very nick of time.
2. Punctually; at the proper time. [act.
ain vaqt-i-jurm. Flagrante delicto; in the very

غ

A غالب ***ğālib***, Overcoming.
gālib ānā fan yā fareb se.
To circumvent; overreach; cheat; trick.
gālib thā. It was likely or expected.
gālib hai, adv. It is probable.
غالباً ***ğā'liban***, adv. Most likely; in all probability; very likely; like enough; ten to one.

A غبن ***ğab'an***, n. m. 1. Misappropriation of money; unlawful abstraction (*khurd burd*).
2. (*Mah. Law*) The sale of property for a price grossly unadequate to its value.
gaban-i-fāsh. A gross fraud.
gaban k., v. a. To misappropriate (*khayānat k.*).

A غدر ***ğadr***; Pop. ***ğadar***; Rus. *gadar*, n. m. غدر was perfidious. See بلوا Confusion; disorder.
gadar machānā, yā k., v. a. 1. To raise a riot or disturbance. 2. To rebel; riot; revolt.

A غرقي ***ğarq'ī***, n. f. 1. Flood; inundation.
2. Depression; low ground.
garqī meṅ ānā, v. n. 1. To be flooded.
2. To be lowered or depressed (ground).
غرقيدگي *garqī'dagī.* Drowning (a barbarism of the Police *munshīs*, i. e. *jāë gārqīdagī* the place where a man was drowned).

A غصب ***ğas'ab***, n. m.
Embezzlement; misappropriation.

A غفلت ***ğaf'lat***, n. f. 1. Inattention; remissness; carelessness 2. A faint; swoon.
gaflat bil-amad, yā bil-qasd, G. G.
Wilful neglect.
gaflat-i-zamīndārān ba-tāmīl-i-marātib-i-māmūrah. Neglect of duties in zamindārs.
gaflat se, adv. Negligently.
gaflat-i-kār. Neglect of one's duty.
gaflat k., v. a. To neglect; disregard.
gaflat-i-māmūlī. Habitual neglect.
gaflat-i-mujrimānāh jis se kisī kī zāt-khās yā jāëdād ko nuqsān pahuṅche.
Culpable neglect by which injury is caused to person or property.
gaf'latī, adj. Neglectful; careless; negligent.

A غلام ***ğulām'***; H. *sevak*, n. m. 1. A slave; bondsman; helot; serf. 2. Among Mahomedans, a household servant who receives food and clothing but no wages.
3. A youth concealed from his birth till the age of puberty.
gulām-i-zar-kharīd, A purchased slave.
gulām azādah-shuda. An enfranchised or emancipated slave.
gulām kā tilām. A slave of a slave. [to slavery.
gulām k., yā banānā, v. a. To enslave; reduce
gulām mol lenā, v. a. To purchase a slave.
gulāmoṅ kī kharīd farokht, yā kār o bār, Sale or purchase of imported slaves; slave-dealing.
غلامي ***ğulām'ī***, n. f. Slavery; bondage; thraldom; serfdom; vassalage; enslavement; involuntary servitude.
gulāmī ikhtiyār k., v. a. To serve one as a slave.
gulāmī-khat. A certificate of slavery.
gulāmī kā khat likhnā,
To bind oneself to slavery by a bond.

A غلبه ***ğalb'ah***, n. m.
1. Ascendancy; influence; mastery; predominance. 2. Excess.
galbah pānā, v. n. To get the upper hand; to be victorious. [majority; a majority.
galba-i-rāë, galba-i-ārā. The opinion of the
galba k., v. a. To overcome; predominate; override; gain the ascendancy; get the upperhand; expose (*tardīd k.*).

A غلط *ġal'at*, adj. Wrong.
galat khabar denā, v. a.
To misinform; give false intelligence.
galat rāē. A wrong or erroneous opinion.
galat samajhnā, v. a. To misapprehend; misconceive; misunderstand; misjudge.
galat-fahmī, n. f. A misconception; misunderstanding; misapprehension. [of law or facts.
galat-fahmī qānūn yā vāqeāt A misconception
galat k., v. a To annul; set at naught.
kisī galat-fahmī ke sabab amal k. To act under a misconception. [*rata.*
غلطنامه *ġalat-nāmah*; H *ashudh-patr*, n.m. *Er-*
غلطي *ġal'atī*; Illit. *ġaltī*, n. f.
1. Inaccuracy; miscalculation; *erratum*; 2. A misstatement. 3. An oversight; a slip; miss. 4. A fallacy. 5. See *galat-fahmī.*
galatī parnā, v. n. To occur (a mistake).
galatī se, adv. Erroneously.
galtī-i-qānūnī. A mistake of law.
galatī k., yā khānā, v. n.
2. To labour under a mistake.
galtī meṅ parnā, v. n. To fall into a mistake.
galtiyoṅ kā insidād. A check in account.

A غله *ġal'lah*; Illit *gallā*, n. m.
1. Grain; corn (*anāj*). 2. Sale proceeds of the day. 3. The box in which they are kept.
gallai, Rents paid in kind. *Carnegy.*
2. Close attention or care.

A غور *ġaur*, n. f. Deep thought.
gaur pardākht. Bringing up; maintenance.
gaur se dekhnā. To observe minutely; consider attentively.
gaur-talab, Worth consideration. [beration.
gaur-i-kāmil. Full consideration; mature deli-
gaur-kardah, adj. Deliberate; prepense.
gaur kar-ke, bare gaur se, gaur o tāammul se, adv. Deliberately; advisedly.
gaur k., v. a. To incline towards; countenance.

A غير *ġair*, Other; another; foreign.
gair-ābād, adj. Uncultivated; uninhabited.
gair-ikhtiyārī, Involuntary.
gair-band o bast. Not settled, applied to lands not included in the revenue assessment.
gair-pukhtagī. Immaturity; unripeness.
gair-tajvīz. Undetermined; not decided.
gair-tahqīq, adj. 1. Vague; indefinite.
2. Undetermined; doubtful; not certain.
gair-hāzirī, n. f. 1. Non-attendance; absence.
2. Non-appearance; default.
gair kharch. Extra or miscellaneous expenses.
gair-rāij, adj. Not current.
gair-sākin. Non-resident. [stranger.
gair samajhnā, v. a. 1. To regard one as a
2. (*Rare*) To misconceive; misunderstand.
gair-shāfī, adj. Inconclusive.
gair-shakhs; H. *an-purush.* 1. A third person; any other person. 2. A stranger.
gair-ilāqah, 1. Territory beyond the limits of one's jurisdiction.
2. Foreign rule or administration.
gair ke hāth intteqāl k. To alienate.
gair-mālik, adj. Without an owner; unappropriated; unclaimed.
gair-mutaassir, adj. Ineffectual; ineffective.
gair-mutahid, adj. Uncovenanted.
gair-mutaiyan, gair-muaiyan, gair-muqarrar, adj. 1. Undetermined; unsettled, not posted.
2. Undefined; indefinite; uncertain.
3. Wavering; fluctuating.
4. Contingent; accidental.
gair-mahdūd. adj. Unlimited; unbounded.
gair-mazrūā, adj. Uncultivated; not cultivated.
gair-mustāmal, adj. 1. Not in use; obsolete.
2. Unusual; extraordinary; rare.
*gair-musha*kh*khas*, adj. 1. Undetermined; undefined; indefinite. 2. Not appropriated; unappropriated. 3. Indiscriminate.
gair-mashrūt, adj. Unconditional; absolute.
Applied to grants of land, etc. without any stipulations of service or the like being attached to them.
gair-maslahat, adj. Unadvisable; inexpedient.
gair-matlūb, adj. Undesirable; not desired.
gair-motabar, adj. 1. Incredible; unreliable.
2. Invalid; null.
gair-māmūl, adj. Unusual; informal [imperfect.
gair-mukammal, adj. Incomplete; defective;
gair mukammal paṭṭi-dārī. Imperfect pattidārī tenure. [not feasible.
gair-mumkin, adj. Impossible; impracticable;
gair-mumkin-ul-tardīd, 1. Not to be refuted; unanswerable; irrefragable.
2. Irrevocable; irreversible.
gair-mumkin-ul-taqsīm. Indivisible; not liable to partition; impartible.
gair-mumkin-ul-zarāat. Unproductive, barren, or unculturable (land).
gair-mumkin-ul-vusūl; H. *gāl khātā*, n. m. Irrecoverable balance; bad debts. [proper.
gair-munāsib. Unsuitable; unbecoming; im-
gair-munqasam. gair-munqassamah. adj.
Undivided held in joint tenancy.
gair-manqūla; H. *aṭal*, adj. Immovable; fixed; real. [mate.
gair-mankūha, adj. 1. Unmarried. 2. Illegiti-
gair-maurūsī; H. *an-bipautī*, adj. Not holding by hereditary descent; not inherited.
gair-nāfiz. Inoperative; of no effect.
gair, yā farzī nām se. In another name; under an assumed title.
gair-vājib; gair-vājbī, adj. 1. Contrary to reason or law; not due; bad.
2. Wrong; unreasonable; unjust.
gair-vājibī, adv. 1. Improperly; unjustly; wrongly. 2. Fraudulently.

gair-vusūl, adj. Outstanding; not realized.

ف

A فاجر *fāj'ir*; P. *zinā-kār*; H. *istrī-gāmī,* n.m. فجر transgressing. 1. A sinner. 2. A whoremonger; fornicator.

فاجره *fāj'irah,* n. f. A loose woman.

A فاحشة *fā'hisha,* n. f. A harlot.

A فارغخطي *fārig-khatī;* Pop. *fār-khatī;* Rus. *phārkhatī;* H. *bhar-pāī,* n. f. A deed of release or discharge; written acquittance; acquittance; deed of dissolution of partnership.

fārig-khatī, yā fārkhatī likh denā, v. a. To give a written acquittance.

A فاسد *fā'sid, fāsidah,* adj. فسد was corrupt. See *jhūṭā,* (1,3,6.) 1. Corrupt; malignant. 2. Bad; wicked; unprincipled. 3. Wrong; sinister; guilty; culpable; criminal; felonious. 4. Unlawful (*nā-jāiz*).

fāsid, n.m. One who,according to some authorities, may be deprived of the management of his own affairs, as unfit to be trusted with them.

fāsid taur se, adv. Corruptly.

fāsid k., v. a. 1. To pervert; corrupt; vitiate; debase. 2. To invalidate.

nīyat yā ilm-i-fāsid. Criminal intention or knowledge.

A فاضل *fā'zil,* adj. فضل exceeded. 1. Superfluous; supernumerary; over and above; more than enough; running over; *satis superque.*

fāzil, n. m. pl. *fāzilāt.* 1. Surplus; excess; remainder; balance. 2. Receipt in excess of revenue, etc.

fāzil-bāqī, n. f. Balance in favour.

fāzil bāqī nikālnā, v. a. To strike the balance.

fāzil-badar, badar fāzil. Vulg. *badal fāzil.* Exclusion and addition; an interchange of fields between two estates to secure a uniform boundary.

fāzil nikalnā yā h., v. n. To exceed amount at credit.

fāzil vāsilāt, fāzil vusūl. Surplus receipt; extra or additional collections.

A H فاعل و مفعول ہونا *fāil o mafūl h.,* v.n. To commit sodomy on each other.

A فايده *fāëd'ah;* Rus. *phāëdā,* n.m. pl. *favāid,* فيد gain. 1. Advantage; benefit; interest (*paidā*). 2. Outturn; yield.

fāëdah-i-zātī. Self-interest.

fāëdah-i-zimnī. An incidental advantage.

A فتور عقل *futūr-i-aql.* Unsound mind.

A فتوى *fat'vā;* H. *baivastah,* n. m. The written verdict of the Mah.Law officer of a court, according to the *Shara.*

fatvā denā, v. a. To give a verdict. [*Sharā.*

fātva-i-sharaī. An injunction according to the

fātva-i-adālat. See *hukm-i-adālat.*

fatva-i-qāzī. The sentence or verdict of a Qāzī

fatvā lenā, Mah., v. a. To take a legal opinion of the lawfulness of an act.

A فحش *fohsh,* adj. Obscene; bawdy; indecent.

fohsh, n. m. Obscenity; bawdry.

fohsh bāten, yā zabān. Obscene language.

fohsh bāten baknā, fohsh baknā, v. n. To talk smut or bawdy.

fohsh sher. Obscene ballad or verse.

fohsh kitāb. An obscene book.

fohsh kitābon kā bechnā. Sale of obscene books.

fohsh gāliyān, n. f. Indecent abuse.

fohsh gīt. A bawdy song.

A فديه *fid'iyah,* n. m. Ransom.

A H فرار ہونا *farār' h.,* v. n. To run away.

farār honā ashkhās-i-mujrim yā mākhūz kā. G. G. Running away of criminal or accused persons.

فراري *farār'ī,* adj. Absconded; fled; escaped.

farārī mafrūr, n. m. 1. A runaway; fugitive; deserter. 2. A cultivator who has absconded from or thrown up his land.

farārī mujrim. An escaped convict.

farārī naukar. A servant who has absconded or run away.

A فرايض *farā'yaz,* n. m. Pl. of فرض q. v. 1. The obligatory or divine precepts, or statutes of the Mah. religion. 2. The law of inheritance or partition of property.

farāyaz lāzim malzūm. Reciprocal or correlative duties; mutual obligations.

A فربهٔ اندام *farbah andām,* G.G. A stout person.

A فرد *fard,* n. f. Pl. *afrād.* 1. A draft of an account. 2. Register; record; statement; account. 3. List; roll; catalogue; muster-roll (*tālīqā*).

fard-i-ahkām-i-musalsal, The register of consecutive orders in a judicial case.

fard-i-bātil. A useless thing.

fard bāqiyāt. A balance sheet.

fard-i-bāqiyāt-i-mālguzārī, A revenue balance sheet.

fard-i-pattī-dārī. n. f. A list or schedule of the shares of a joint estate.

fard-i-tashkhīs, n. f. Settlement record.

fard-i-taālīqā, fard-i-hisāb, n. f. A schedule of property; inventory of distrained property.
fard-i-tafrīq. A paper or deed of partition.
fard-i-taqsīm. Statement of distribution of land.
fard-i-huqūq, n. f. A record of rights.
fard-i-haqīqat, n. f. A memorial; a statement of the circumstances of a case; a return made to a requisition for information; a report.
fard sazā The sentence sheet.
fard qarār-dād-i-jurm. A charge.
fard-i-kāsht, n. f. Statement of a *raiyat's* cultivation.
fard-i-taqsīm-i-khidmat, n. f. Roster duties.
fard-i-jurm, n. f. Calendar of crime.
fard-i-jama-bandī, n. f. Rental.
fard-i-huliyah. A descriptive roll.
fard-i-sharāyat-i-shirākat. Articles of association of partnership.
fard-i-illat, A charge framed under the Indian Penal Code.
fard fard, fardan fardan, furādā furādā, adv. Severally; each one.
fard-i-qarābat. Kindred roll.
fard-i-qarār-dād-i-jurm, The formal charge of an offence.
fard-i-mukammal, G. G. A complete record.
fard men nām charhānā, v. a.
To register; enlist; enroll.
fard-i-nā-mukammal. An incomplete record.
fard-i-vāsil-bāqī kā masvadah.
A rough balance sheet.
du-fardī. A double account, shewing the amount of land held and rent paid by each *Raiyat*.

P فرزندي *farzandī*, n. f.
(*Mah. Law.*) Lineal descendants in the male line. Females and their posterity are excluded from the order of descent, one's own daughter excepted.
farzandī men lenā, farzand banānā, yā k., 1. To adopt as a son. 2. To make one his son-in-law.

A فرض *farz*, n. m. فرض made lawful.
1. Divine command; a duty, the omission of which is considered a mortal sin.
2. Duty; moral obligation; bounden duty.
3. *Onus*; responsibility; liability.
farz, n. m. A definite portion of the inheritance due to an heir, a widow's jointure, or her share of her husband's property. *Carnegy*.
farz-i-khidmat ke khilāf k. To violate a duty; to fail in one's duty.
فرضاً *farz'an*, adv. Specially; definitely, as applied to the Mah. law of inheritance.
farzan o raddan. Conformably to a direct or special claim, and also to an indirect or reversionary claim, as coming back from failure of nearer heirs.
farzī muddaī, n. m. A fictitious plaintiff or prosecutor; a person put forward in the place of the real plaintiff.
فرضي *farz'ī*, n. m. A suit instituted by others than those really interested.

فرضي *farz'ī*, adj. 1. Incumbent; obligatory; bound; obliged; indispensable; imperative.
2. Supposititious; fictitious; not real or essential; nominal.
3. Assumed; hypothetical.
farzī muqaddama, yā muāmala. A fictitious suit.
ism-i-farzī, n. m. A fictitious or assumed name.

A فرقة *fir'qah*, n. m.
A tribe; sect; class (جماعت 1).
firqe ke ashkhās. G. G. A class of persons.
firqa-i-mukhālif az sarkār, G. G. A faction; a cabal.

P فرمان *farmān', farmān-i-shāhī*, n. m. A mandate; edict; patent; charter (*āgyā*, 1).

P فروخت *faro'kht*; H. *bikrī*, n. f.
Sale; disposal.
farokht k., v. a. To sell (*bechnā*).

P فرود *farod'*, n. m. 1. (*In comp.*) Alighting.
2. Arrival and deposit of goods within certain limits.
farod-gāh, n. f. A halting or landing place; a camping ground.
farod mal, Goods in bond.

P فروشنده *faroshin'dah*, n. m. A vendor.
faroshindah-i-majāzī, n. m. A licensed vendor.

P فرياد *faryād'*, n. f. 1. A complaint; suit; charge. 2. A cry for help, succour, etc.
faryād-ras, n. m. A redresser of grievances; a just judge; an administrator of justice.
faryād-rasī, n. f. Redress of grievances.
faryād k., v. a. 1. To complain; lay a suit against one. 2. See *duhāī denā*.
faryād ko pahunchnā, v. a. To hear one's suit or complaint.
فريادي *faryād'ī*, n. m. A complainant (*dāvedār*).

P فريب *fareb', fan fareb, land phand*, n. m.
Fraud (*dhokā-dihī*).
fareb-āmez vasīqā. G. G. A fraudulent act.
fareban ḍigri hāsil k.
To obtain a decree fraudulently.
fareb-dihī, n. f. Cheating; swindling.
fareb denā, yā k., v. a. To cheat (*dagā denā*).
fareb se, fareban, adv. Fraudulently; dishonestly; *malā fide*; unfairly.
fareb khānā, fareb men ānā, yā phansnā.
فريبي *fareb'ī, fareban*, adj. Dishonest; collusive.
farebī, farebiyā, n. m. *fareban*, n. f. A cheat.

A فريق *farīq'*, n. m. 1. Order (*firqā*).
2. Division; section; department.
3. A party in a suit.
farīq-i-avval, n. m. The principal party in a suit.
farīq-i-ḍigrīdār, n. m. The party in whose favor decree has been given.

farīq-i-maglūb, n m. The defeated party.
farīq-i-muqaddamah qāyam k., yā gardānnā. To make a party in a suit.
farīq-i-sānī, farīq-i-mukhālif, n. m.
The opposite or adverse party; the other party; the defendant.
farīq-i-muāmila, n. m. A party to a transaction; one interested in a suit.
فريقين *farīqain'*, n. m. Pl. of فريق
The parties in a suit; the parties concerned; plaintiff and defendant.
farīqain se, adv. From both sides or parties.
farīqain-i-muqaddamah. The litigant parties.

A فساد *fasād'*; Illit. *fisād*, n. m. فسد was corrupt. 1. Brawl; outbreak (دنگا).
2. Dissension; ferment. 3. Intrigue.
4. Any species of mental depravity not arising from defect of understanding.
fasād barpā k., uṭhānā, machānā, yā k., v. a. To instigate riot.
fasād-i-azīm. Violent breach of the peace.
fasād kī jar, n. f. 1. Matter or cause of dispute.
2. A fomentor of disturbances.
fasād kī nīyat se, adv.
Corruptly; maliciously; with evil intent.
fasād i-mulk. Political disturbance.
فسادي *fasād ī*, adj. 1. Mischievous; vicious.
2. Factious.

A فسخ *fas*ᵉ*kh*; Illit. *fis*ᵉ*kh*; n. m. 1. Breach; infraction; infringement; violation. 2. Breaking or dissolution of a contract; annulment.
faskh i-izdivāj, faskh-i-nikāh.
Annulment of a marriage.
faskh k., v. a. 1. To infringe.
2. To break a contract, etc. 3. To cancel; make void (*tardīd k.* 2). [annulled.
faskh h., v. n. To be rendered invalid; to be

A فسق *fisq, fisq o fujūr*, n. m. فسق transgressing. Sin; adultery.

A فصل *fasl*; Illit. *fasal*, n.f. فصل cut, separated. See *sākh*. 1. Section. 2. Season; the reaping season. 3. Crops.
fasl-i-istādah; H. *kharī khetī.* The standing crop.
fasl-i-tukhm-rezī; H. *buār-belā.* The sowing season; seed time. [harvest.
fasl-i-kharāb; H. *burī sākh*, n. f. A deficient
fasl-i-kharīf; H. *sāonī*, n. f. The autumnal harvest of rice, millet, etc., requiring irrigation.
The seed is sown at the commencement of the rainy season, and the crop is usually reaped after its close, or about Oct—Nov. The sub-divisions are *Bhadai, Kuārī, Aghanī.*
fasl-i-rabī; H. *āsāṛhī*, n. f. See *rabī*. This crop does not require irrigation or much water.
The *rabī* includes the following crops—wheat, barley, pease, gram, poppy, *masūr, sarsoṅ*, linseed, tobacco, *marvā, radhiā*, cotton, *arhar, jeṭhī dhān, kusum*, mustard, *birrā, schuāṅ*, and sugarcane.
fasl kaṭne aur khaliyān se uṭhne ke bād. After the crops have been cut and carried away.
فصلي *faslī*, adj.
Belonging to the harvest, or season when cultivated or culturable lands are assessed according to the value of the crops, or frequency and abundance of the harvests.
faslī raiyat, n. f. A cultivator paying revenue according to the crops he raises.
faslī sāl, n. m. The revenue or harvest year.
The *faslī* year began on the 10th of the lunar month *Asin*, corresponding to the 10th Sept. 1555.

A فضولي *fazūl'ī*, n.f. (*Mah. Law.*) An unaccredited agent; one who acts for another without authority, and whose transactions are invalid unless confirmed by the principal.
fazūlī bae. A sale of another's property without his authority, which sale may be confirmed or annulled at pleasure by the owner.

A فعل *f*ᵉ*el*, n. m. 1. Act; action; deed; work; operation. 2. (Pop. *fail*) Feigning; pretence; pretext; sham. 3. An unnatural act; adultery. 4. Carnal intercourse.
fel-i-jāiz, n. m. A lawful act.
fel-i-shaniā, n. m. Evil deeds; prostitution; adultery; unnatural offence.
fel-zāminī, n. f. Security for good conduct.
fel-i-farebī. G. G. A fraudulent act.
fel karānā. To submit to improper sexual intercourse, sodomy, etc.
fel k., v. a. 1. To do an act. 2. To have sexual intercourse with. 3. To be exacting.
4. (*fail bharnā, yā k.*) To pretend.
fel-i-nā-jāyaz. An unlawful act.
fel-i nā-shāistah. An improper act. [offence.
koī fel jo jurm hai, G. G. Any thing which is an
koī fel nahīṅ, No act; nothing. [indeed.
فعلاً *f*ᵉ*el'an*, adv. 1. Practically. 2. In fact;
felan o qaulan, In word and deed.

A فقه *fiq'ah*, n. f. The Mah. ecclesiastical law.

A فك الرهان *fak-ul-rahan*; H. *bandhak-chhūt*, n. m. The liquidation of a debt for which property had been pledged; redemption of a mortgage.

A فلان *ful'āṅ, falāṅ*; Pop. *falānā, falānī.*
A certain person or thing; such a one.
falān', n. m. The organs of generation.
falān-maranī, n. f. A woman who prostitutes herself for pleasure, in contradistinction to *peṭ-maranī*, q. v.

A فوت *faut*, n. f. *Rare.* Death (انتقال 5).
faut bilā-vasīyat. Intestacy.
faut h., v. n. 1. To die; depart this life.

fautī, n. f. The property of one who dies intestate and without legal heirs, which therefore reverts to the sovereign.

فوتي *faut'ī*, adj. Deceased; dead.

fautī farārī. 1. Dead or absconded (persons). 2. A list of cultivators who have died, or have deserted their cultivations or homesteads.

fautī-nāma, n. m. 1. A document reporting the death of the incumbent and the name of the heir; a certificate of death.
2. A list of the killed.

naqsha-i-fautī, n. An obituary.

A P فوجدار *fauj-dār*; Rus. *phaud-dār*, n. m.
Under the Mah. Government, a criminal judge or magistrate; a superintendent of the military force in a district.

فوجداري *fauj-dārī*, n. f. 1. The office of a magistrate; the criminal court.
2. A criminal case.

fauj-dārī adālat, adalat-i-fauj-dārī, n. f.
The subordinate criminal court, formerly the *Nizāmat adālat*.

faujdārī supurd k. To send a case to the criminal court.

fauj-dārī k., v. a. To commit an assault or criminal offence.

faujdārī karne ko mustaid h., v. n. To threaten, or be about to commit a breach of the peace.

faujdārī kī bāz-purs ke lāyaq. Liable to criminal proceeding.

fauj-dārī meṅ mākhūz k., v. a.
To prosecute criminally; to accuse or charge with a crime or misdemeanor.

fauj-i sehbandī, n. f. The troops of the *Fauj-dār*; provincial troops or militia employed in garrisoning forts and escorting treasure, and in revenue and police duties.

فوجي *fauj'i*, adj. Military.

faujī hukkām. Military officers.

P فوطة *fot'ah*; Rus. *potā*, n. m. 1. The scrotum; testicles. 2. Taxes; revenue; collections.

fota bharnā; Rus. *potā bharnā*, v. a.
To pay tax or revenue.

fote-khāna, n. m. A treasury (*khazāna*, 1).

fote-dār, n. m. Cashier; treasurer.

fote-dārī The office of collecting tenant dues.

P فهرست *feh'rist*, n. f. A table; index (*fard*).

ferist-i-bāqyāt se khārij h. To strike a case off the file.

ferisht-i-mālikānā. A proprietary list; list of [proprietors.

ferisht murattaba-i-mahkma-i-band-o-bast. A list drawn up in the settlement Department.

ferisht-i-muqadmāt-i-bāqiyāt. A list of pending cases; a list of cases remaining undisposed of on the file of a judicial officer.

fehrist-i-dehāt, n. f. A list of the villages of an estate or district.

fehrist-i-rishteh-dārī. Kindred roll.

fehrist-i-ām. A general list; file of suits.

fehrist-i-fautī farārī, A list of dead and deserted.

fehrist-i-kāgzāt. A list of papers.

fehrist-i-mardum-shumārī, n. f. A census; poll.

fehrist-i-mazāmīn; H. *sūchīpatr*, Table of contents.

fehrist meṅ nām charhānā, dākhil karnā, yā likhnā, v. a. To insert in a register, etc. enroll; register; enlist.

P فهمايش *fahmā'yash, fahmāish*, n. f.
1. Instructions; directions; injunction.
2. Expostulation; warning; caution.

fahmāyash k.; v. a.
1. To enjoin; direct; instruct; warn.
2. To exhort; impress upon.

A في *fī*, 1. In (*bīch*) 2. Per; each.

fī, n. f. 1. Flaw. 2. Intrigue (*sāzish*).

fil-jumla, adv. 1. Upon the whole; putting all things together. 2. In brief; in effect.

fil-hāl, adv. Now; presently; anon.

fil-wāqe, adv. In fact; really.

fī dukān. Each shop.

fī rupayā. Per rupee.

fī roz, fī yaum, Per day; per *diem*.

fī zamāna, fī zamānānā, adv. At this day; for the present; up to the present time.

fī-sāl, Per annum; per year.

fī sabīl-allah k., v. a. 1. To give alms in the name of God. 2. To make free to all.

fī sadī, Per cent.; per hundred; percentage.

fī qata. Per sheet; one by one.

fī kas, ādmī, yā nafar, Per head.

fī ghar. Each house.

fī-mābain. Between; reciprocal. [two parties.

fī-mābain-i-farīqain. Inter partes; between the

A فيصلة *fais'lah, faisal*, n. m. فصل divided.
1. See *chukāī*, and *hukm*, 6.
2. Adjudication; arbitration; judicial determination; disposal of a case; decision.

faislah-i-akhīr. Final decision or judgment.

faislah az sar-i-nau. Judgment *de novo*.

faislah jamāat-i-shūrā. Award of a council.

faislah zer-i-apīl. A judgment under appeal.

faislah-i-adālat. A judicial decision. [decision.

faislā ke murāfah k., v. a. To appeal from a

faislah murāfah-i-ūlā, Judgment of the court of first instance.

faislah yā faisal k., v. a. 1. See *tasfiyā k.* and *chukānā*, 1, 5. [(*tajvīz k.* 2.)
2. To decide; determine judicially; judge

faislah yā faisal h., v. n.
To be decided, settled, adjudicated.

فيصلنامه *faisal-nāma*, n. m. A decree, or award.

faisal-nāma-i-sālisī An arbitration award.

ق

A قابض *qāb'iz*, n. قبض taking. 1. Possessor; holder. 2. Occupant; occupier; the party in possession. 3. A sequestrator.
qābiz o dakhīl, n. An occupant in possession.
qābiz o mutsarrif. Possessor and occupant.
qābiz o dakhīl, In possession and enjoyment (of an estate). [prietory possessor.
qābiz aur mālik. 1. Owner and occupant. 2. Pro-
qābiz barāë nām. The ostensible possessor; nominal holder. [actual possession.
qābiz-i-hāl. The present possessor; the party in
qābiz-i-hīn-hayātī. A life-tenant.
qābiz-i-shikmī. An under-tenant; a sub-lessee.
qābiz ho baiṭhnā, v. n. To take possession; settle on another's lands. [one's nose.
A قابل *qāb'il*, adj. قبل looking to the tip of
Worthy; qualified; competent.
qābil-i-apīl. Appealable; open to appeal.
qābil-i-adā; H. *dene jog*. Payable (a bill, etc.) due; owing; liable for.
qābil-i-adā, n. Solvent.
qābil izāfa lagān. Liable to enhancement of rent.
qābil-i-itlāq; H. *lagtā*, Applicable.
qābil-i-etibār; H. *partīt-jog*, Credible; worthy of credit; reliable. [to objection.
qāibl-i-etirāz; H. *tarak-jog*; Objectionable; open
qābil-i-iltifāt; H. *dhiyān-jog*,
Worthy of reception or attention.
qābil-i-intiqāl; H. *palaṭne-jog*, Transferrible; capable of being transferred.
qābil-i-bāz-purs; H. *uttar-jog*, Answerable; accountable; responsible. [tiable.
qābil-i-bai o sharā; H. *bisāhne bechne-jog*, Nego-
qābil-i-pizīrāī; H. *mānne-jog*, Receivable; admissible; that may be accepted.
qābil-i-pizīrāī ke nahīṅ, Inadmissible.
qābil-i-tabdīl, Variable; liable to change or modification. [be refuted.
qābil-i-tardīd, Liable to be contested; that may
qābil-i-taslīm. Presumable; probable; that which may be taken for granted; worthy of acceptation. [ment.
qābil-i-tasfīyah; H. *chuktāne-jog*, Open to adjust-
qābil-i-tādād; H. *ginne jog*, Computable.
qābil-i-taqsīm, yā inqisām; H. *bāṭne-jog*, Divisible.
qābil-i-tavajjoh. Worthy of attention or consideration. [heritable.
qābil-i-taurīs; H. *bapautī-jog*, Descendible;
qābil-i-ṭaiks. Leviable; liable to tax; assessable.
qābil-i-javāb. Answerable; accountable.
qābil-i-javāz. G. G. Admissible; allowable.
qābil dāir hone-ke, yā rujū karne-ke.
May be instituted; actionable.
qābil-i-zirāāt, yā taraddud; H. *bone-jog*,
Culturable but not cultivated; arable; fit for cultivation.
qābil-i-zirāāt k., To fertilize; to clear (waste land); to make culturable. [(*daṅd-yog*).
qābil-i-sazā, Culpable; liable to be punished
qābil-i-samāāt yā sunvāī; H. *sunne-jog*.
Capable of being heard; that may be admitted or entertained.
qābil-i-zabtī. Liable to forfeiture or confiscation.
qābil-i-talab; H. *māṅgne-jog*, Leviable; what may be demanded. [ance to.
qābil-i-gaur samajhnā, v. a. To attach import-
qābil gaur ke; H. *bichār-jog*, Considerable; worthy of consideration; important.
qābil-i-farokht; H. *bechne-jog*. Saleable.
qābil qurqī ke murtakib h.,
To commit an act of forfeiture.
qābil-i-mākhūzī. Chargeable; indictable; penal.
qābil-i-mākhūzī-i-faujdārī. Liable to criminal proceedings. [tion; leviable.
qābil-i-mahsūl; H. *lagān-jog*. Subject to taxa-
qābil-i-muāfī, Pardonable (H. *chhimā-jog*).
qābil-i-māzūrī. Veniable; justifiable; pardonable.
qabil-i-manzūrī. Sanctionable; fit to be chosen.
qābil manzūrī-i-zamānat. Bailable. [ceedings.
qābil nālish-i-faujdārī. Liable to criminal pro-
qābil-i-nikāh; H. *bar-jog, byāhan-jog*.
Marriageable. [able.
qābil-i-vusūl; H. *pāne-jog*, Receivable; recover-
qābil-i-vaqūā. Incidental; apt to happen; likely to occur. [skilled.
qābil h., v. n. To be competent, proficient,
T قابو *qāb'ū*, n. m. 1. Grip; hold; reach.
2. Command (اختیار 4, 6).
3. Favorable opportunity.
qābū pānā, v. n. To get an opportunity; have the whip hand; get the upper hand.
qābū chalnā, v. n. To be able to do.
qābū se bāhar h., v. n.
To lie beyond one's power or control.
qābū meṅ, adv. Within one's control.
qābū meṅ rakhnā, v. a. To keep within one's control.
qābū meṅ k., yā lānā, 1. See *taht meṅ lānā*. 2. To secure. 3. To acquire an ascendancy over.
A قاتل *qā'til*; H. *māran-hār*, n. قتل
A murderer; cut-throat; assassin.
A قارق *qā'riq*, n. قرق A distrainer; an officer who makes an attachment.
A قاسم A public officer deputed by the *Qāzī* to make a legal distribution of joint property.
A قاضي *qāz'ī*; Rus. *kājī*, n. m. قضا a mandate.
1. A Mah. magistrate or law officer.

2. An officer formerly appointed by the government to administer both civil and criminal law chiefly in towns, according to the *sharah* or precepts of the *Qurān*. Under the British administration the judicial functions of *Qāzīs* in that capacity ceased; and, except as the legal advisers of the Courts in cases of Mahomedan law, the duties of those stationed in the cities or districts were confined to the preparation and attestation of deeds of conveyance and other legal instruments, and the general superintendence and legalization of the ceremonies of marriage, funerals, and other domestic occurrences among the Mahomedans.

qāzī-ul-quzzāt. The Head *qāzī* under the British government, an office since abolished.

A قاعدة *qā'e'dah*, n.m. قعد sat. pl. *qavāid*, A rule.

qāëdah-i-batvārah. Principle of partition.

qāëdaeh jārī k , yā chalānā, v.a. To bring a rule into operation; to enforce a rule.

qāëdah-i-qānūnī. A rule of law.

qāëde kā pā-band rahnā, v. n. 1. To observe or conform to a rule; to obey; comply with.
2. To be wont or accustomed to.

qāëdah-i-kār-ravāī. Rule of procedure.

A قانون *qānūn'*; Rus. *kanūn*, Pl. *qavānīn*, n.m.
Canon; law; legislative act (آئین). [law.

qānūn'an, adv. According to law; legally; by

qānūnan nā-durast. Erroneous in law.

qānūnan va insāfan. By law and justice.

qānūn banānā, yā tajvīz k.
To make laws; to legislate.

qānūn banāne-vālon kī jamāat. A parliament; senate; congress; diet; legislative council.

qānūn banāne-vāle, muqannin, The legislature.

qānūn par tamīl k. To administer the law.

qānūn par chalnā, v. a.
To act according to law.

qānūn tamādī-i-aiyām. Limitation statute.

qānūn jo kisī jamāat kī taraf se muqarrar ho.
A bye law.

qānūn hadd-i-samāat, yā miādī.
The law of limitation.

qānūn-i-haqq-ul-shufā. The law of pre-emption.

qānūn-i-khās. An express law.

qānūn-dān; Pop. *qānūniyā*. One versed or learned in the law; a lawyer; jurist.

qānūn-dānī. Jurisprudence.

qānūn sādir k., v. a. To enact or pass a law.

qānūn-i-ām izdivāj. A general law of marriage.

qānūn-i-faujdārī. Criminal law.

qānūn-i-qatai. A positive law. [law.

qānūn kā hukam rakhnā. To have the force of

qānūn ke khilāf k., v. a. To break a law.

قانون گو *qānūngo'* n. m. Registrar of the Purganah; superintendent of village accountants; hereditary registrar of landed property in a *pargana*.

qānūn-i-māl. Revenue law.

qānūn hī. The law itself.

qānūngo'. A village and district revenue officer.

Under the Native Government the *Qānūngo* recorded all circumstances within his sphere which concerned landed property and the realization of the revenue, keeping registers of the value, tenure, extent, and transfers of lands, assisting in the measurements and survey of the lands, reporting deaths and successions of revenue payers, and explaining, when required, local practices and public regulations. He was paid by rent free lands, and various allowances and perquisites.

qānūn-goī. The office of a *qānūngo*.

qānūn i-majrīyah yā nāfizā. The laws in force.

qānūn-i-mujavvazah, Legislative acts.

qanūn-i-mukhtas-ul-amr. A special law.

qanūn-i-mukhtas-ul-muqām. A local law.

qānūn yā zābte kī rū se.
By or according to law or practice.

قانوني *qānūn'ī*, adj. 1. Legislative.
2. Legal; according to law; constitutional; having the sanction or authority of law.
3. (*qānūniyā*) Controversial; litigious.

amr-i-qānūnī ki mughālita. A mistake of law.

manshāë qānūn nāfiz k. To administer the law.

woh qānūn jiske rū se barā betā vāris kul māl-i-ġair manqūlah kā hotā hai.
The law of primogeniture.

A قايم *qā'yam*, adj Standing.

qāyam rakhnā, v. a. 1. To keep up; preserve.
2. To make good; stand up for; support.

qāyam k., v. a. See *binā dālnā, had bāndhnā*.
1. To set up; institute; constitute (*bāndhnā*, 3—4).
2. To post; instal. 3. To uphold (*istehkām denā*, 1, 2). 4. To create (a right).

qāyam-muaqām. 1. One acting in the place of another; *locum tenens*. 2. A procurator; vicegerent; surrogate; proctor.

qāyam-muaqām, adj. Officiating. [sentative.

qāyam-muaqām-i-jāiz yā qānūnī. A legal repre-

qāyam-muaqām h., v. n. To stand in the place of; to officiate; act for; represent.

qāyam-muaqāmī. Deputation; representation; succession; vicegerency. [instrument).

qāyam-muaqāmī kī sanad. Procuration (the

qāyam h., v. n. 1. To arise; spring up.
2. To take place; happen; occur; reveal or manifest itself.

dāva qāyam k., v. a. To establish a right.

A قبالة *qabāl'ah*; W. Illit. and E. *qibālā*, n. m. A title deed; bill of sale (of a house).

qabāla-i-bai sultānī. Certificate of sale of crown land. 2. One entitled to any right in consequence of forfeiture of a bond, or the like.

qabāla-navīs. A scrivener; scribe.

qabāla-i-nīlām. Deed of sale.

qabāla-i-nīlāmī. Certificate of auction sale.

qabāle-dār. 1. The holder of a bond.

kat-qabāla be-miādī. A conditional agreement as to terms, but not as to time.

kaṭ-qabālah. A conditional engagement; a deed of conditional sale, stipulating that if the purchase price be not returned within a given period the sale is absolute; a mortgage-deed with liability of sale if not redeemed by a stipulated time (*baʿe-bil-wafā*).

A قبر سلامي *qabr-salāmī.* A fee to the proprietor for permission to dig a grave on ground belonging to him.

A قبض *qabz,* n. m. Possession.

qabz-ul-vusūl. A receipt; an aquittance roll; acknowledgment.
qabz bil-jabr. Forcible possession.
qabz o dakhl, Complete or full possession.
qabz-vār. In the way of seizure or distraint.
qabz-vār paimāish. Measurement of an estate to determine the extent of sequestration.
qabz o dakhl, n. Tenure and possession.
haq-i-qabza-dārī. The right of occupancy.

قبضه *qabz'ah, qabzā,* n. m. قبض seizing. [2).
Holding; tenure; tenancy; tenement (*dakhl,*
qabzah uṭhānā, v. a.
To disturb one's possession; to oust.
qabzah bilā-muzāhemat. Undisturbed possession.
qabzah bahāl rakhnā, v. a. To leave in possession; uphold the right of possession.
qabzah bahāl k., v. a. To reinstate. [*pānā,* 2).
qabzah pānā, v.n. To enter on possession (*dakhl*
qabzah paṭṭī-dārī. Land held in severalty.
qabzah tāvīlī. Constructive possession.
qabza-i-judāgānā bilā shirkat-i-gaire.
Exclusive separate possession.
qabzah-i-judāgānah, yā alahdah. Separate possession; land held in severalty; an independent holding. [session.
qabzah-i-chand-rozah. Temporary tenure or pos-
qabzah-i-hīn hayātī. A life tenure.
qabza-dārī, n. f. Occupancy.
qabzah dilānā, v. a. To put in possession.
qabzah denā, v. a.
To make over charge; to give delivery.
qabzah rakhnā, v. a. 1. To keep; retain; hold; to be in possession of; enjoy; to have in hand; own. 2. To hold fast; clutch; grasp; detain. [tenancy.
qabzah-i-shāmilātī. Joint-tenancy; common
qabza-i-alahda. Independent holding.
qabzah alahda alahda. Land held in severalty.
qabzah k., qabze meṅ lānā, v. a. See *dakhal k.*
1. To acquire; get hold of; step into.
2. To seize; usurp; possess oneself of.
qabzah-i-mutasarrifānā. Beneficial or serviceable possession. [session.
qabzah-i-mutanāza. Disturbed or contested pos-
qabzah-i-mukhālifānā. An adverse possession.
qabzah-i-murtahinānah, Possession by mortgage.
qabzah-i-mustājirānā. A farming tenure.
qabzah-i-maurūsī. Hereditary possession.
qabza-i-nā-jāiz k., v. a. To acquire wrongfully.
qabza-i-nāhaq k., v. a. To take unlawful possession.
qabza i-vāqaī va nafs-ul-amrī.
Actual and tangible possession.
qabze se bāhar h., To be out of one's possession.
qabze meṅ khalal k, qabze meṅ dast-andāzī k.
To disturb possession.
fauran qabza pāne kā mustahaq. Entitled to immediate possession. [session.
kisī ke qabze meṅ ānā. To come into one's pos-

A قبل *qabl, qabal,* adj. 1. Previous; anterior (سابق). 2. Preliminary; preparatory.
qabl-i-ikhtitām-i-nīlām.
Prior to the lot being knocked down.
qabl az āṅ-ki. Before that; *ante quam;* previously; prior to; beforehand. [before now.
qabl az īṅ, is se pahle. Before this; heretofore;
qabl do pahar ke. Before noon (*do pahar pahle*).

A قبول *qubūl';* Illit. *qabūl,* n. m. See انگیکار
1. Acknowledgment; avowal. 2. Accord; concurrence. 3. Favorable reception.
4. Recognition; sanction; confirmation; ratification; approbation. [firm.
qubūl aur manzūr k., v. a. To approve and con-
qubūl jama. The stipulated rent or revenue.
qubūl-i-javāb. An answer filed in a suit acknowledging the justice of the demand.
qubūl-khat. A written assent or agreement.
qubūl k, v. a. See انگیکار ک and *iqrār k.,* 3, 4.
1. To assent; nod assent; say yes.
2. To acquiesce, concur, or coincide with; concede. 3. To receive or entertain (a petition).
4. To recognize; sanction; grant; allow.
qubūl na k., v. a. See *inkār k.*
qubūl h., v. n. To be accepted, agreed to, etc.
rishvat qubūl k., v. a. To accept or take a bribe.

قبولنا *qubūl'nā,* v. a. 1. To accept; receive; approve. 2. To make a confession (*iqrār k.* 3).

قبولیت *qubūl'iyat,* n. f. 1. An acceptance.
2. The counterpart of a lease; an agreement (to pay rent). 3. A document in which a payer of revenue, whether to the government, the *zāmīndār,* or the farmer, expresses his consent to pay the amount assessed upon his land.

A قبیل *qabīl',* n. m. 1. Class; genus.
2. (Mah. Law) Surety; bail; bail-bond.
qabīl-i-anās, Ped. G. G. The female sex.
az qabīl. Of the nature of.
min qabīl unnās. Of the female sex. [family.

قبیله *qabīl'ah,* n. m. 1. A tribe; clan. 2. Wife;

A قتل *qatl;* Illit. *qatal, katal,* n. m.
1. Slaughter; execution. 2. Homicide; manslaughter. 3. Murder; assassination. 4. Bloodshed; carnage; butchery; massacre.

qatl-i-insān, G. G. Homicide.

qatl-i-insān mustalzim-i-sazā. Culpable homicide.

qatl-i-insān mustalzim-i-sazā jo qatl-i-amad kī had tak na pahunchtā ho. G. G. Culpable homicide not amounting to murder.

qatl-i-bā-sabab. Accidental homicide by an intervenient cause.

As where a person has dug a well and not guarded it against accidents, and some one falls into it and perishes.

qatl ba-jehat-i-hifāzat-i-khud. Homicide in self-defence.

qatl ba-khatā, yā qatl-i-khatā.
Manslaughter; accidental homicide.

qatl ba-shubah. Manslaughter.

qatl-i-padar. Parricide (*pitā ghāt*).

qatl-i-shubah-amad. Felonious or culpable homicide; manslaughter.

qatl-i-ām. A general massacre.

qatl-i-amad. Wilful murder; wilful homicide by an adult and sane person; homicide with premeditated malice.

qatl qābil-i-sazā, yā mustalzim-i-sazā.
Voluntary culpable homicide.

qatl qābil-i-uzr. Excusable homicide.

qatl qāyam-muqām-i-khatā. Involuntary homicide by an involuntary act; killing a person by injuring him unintentionally or through misadventure.

qatl k., v. a. 1. To take away or deprive of life; to kill. 2. To execute; punish capitally; put to death. 3. To murder; assassinate.
4. To slay; massacre; slaughter.

qatl-gāh. The place of execution; gallows.

qatl-i-mubāh, qatl mumkin-ul vajūb.
Justifiable homicide.

iqdām-i-qatl, G. G. Attempt to murder.

sazā-i-qatl-i-amad. Punishment for murder.

A قحبة *qah'ba*, n. f. قحب to cough.

A whore who notifies her profession by a cough; a light skirt.

A قحط *qaht*; H. *kāl*, n. m. 1. See اكال

2. Want; lack; need; scantiness. 3. (*qaht-sālī*) Failure of the crops or harvest; famine.

qaht parnā, v. n. To occur (a famine).

qaht-zadah; H. *kāl kā mārā*, adj. 1. Starving; famine-stricken. 2. Died of want of food.

A قدامت *qadām'at*, n. f. قدم going before.

1. Age; antiquity. 2. Prescription.
3. Length of service.

A قدر *qadr*, n. f. Quantity; value.

ba-qadr, adv. 1. *Ad valorem*; valued at; at the rate of; at. 2. According to; as; corresponding with; in proportion to; to the extent of: to the amount of (*jitnā*).

ba-qadr jurmānah adā k.
To pay the amount of fine or forfeit.

ba-qadr-i-hājat, ehtiyāj, yā zarūrat. *Quantum sufficit*; as occasion may require.

ba-qadr-i-haisīyat, ba-qadr-i-māliyat. 1. *Quantum valeat*; according to value. 2. According to one's circumstances or means.

A قديم *qadīm'*; Pop. *qadīmī*, adj. قدم going before.
1. Old; ancient; immemorial. 2. Antiquated; archaic. 3. Ancestral; hereditary.

qadīm, qadīm-ul-aiyām se, adv. Of old; from ancient times; long ago; a long time ago; in the olden time; in days of yore; from time immemorial.

qadīm raiyat. An occupant of land by old hereditary descent.

qadīm naukar, yā namak-khuār. An old servant.

qadīm'ī, qadīm, n. 1. An old inhabitant of a village. 2. One holding by hereditary descent.

qadīmī gāoṅ. The original or old established village.

A قرابت *qarāb'at*, n. f.

Propinquity; relationship; consanguinity; family connexion or tie (*rishtā*).

qarābat-dār, qarābtī. A relation by blood or marriage; a kinsman; family connexion.

qarābat-dārī, n. f. See *rishtedārī*.

qarābat-i-tarfi. Collateral consanguinity.

qarābat-i-mustaqīmah. G. G. Lineal consanguinity; of the same blood.

qarābat-i-nasabī. Consanguinity.

قرابتي *qarāb'atī*; Pop. *qarābtī*, adj. Related to; connected; of kin; consanguineous.

A قرار *qarār'*, n. m. قر to rest. Rest.

qarār pānā, v. n. To be settled.

qarār pāyā. 1. Arose; based. 2. Decided; determined. 3. Provided; ruled; established; prescribed; laid down.

qarār-dād. 1. Establishment; settlement.
2. Engagement; agreement; contract.

qarār-dād-bāham. A private bargain.

qarārdād-i-jurm, The formal charge of a crime read out to a prisoner on his trial.

qarār dīyā gayā. Laid down; determined.

qarār denā, v. a. 1. To determine (the issues in a case). 2. To adjudge (*tajvīz k.* 1, 2).

qarār k., qarār dād k., v. a. See *iqrār k.* 4.
1. To take one's stand. 2. To make terms; conclude (an agreement.)

qarār-vāqaī, adv. 1. Definitively; positively.
2. Effectively; effectually.

qarār o madār. See عهد 1—3, and *ahd-o-paimān*.

be-vajah, yā yoṅhī qarār denā.
To assume arbitrarily.

dar-bāb hifāzat-i-qarār vāqaī. In relation to the due preservation of.

sahīh qarār denā. To receive as true; to admit.

fāil qarār denā durust hai. G. G. Shall be deemed to have committed such act.

mustalzim-i-sazā qarār dīyā gayā yā mustaujib-i-sazā qarār-pāyā. H. *ḍand jog ṭhairāyā.* Made punishable. [ceive.
nutfah yā hamal qarār pānā, Ped. v.a. To con-
قراري *qarār'ī*, adj. 1. Fixed; established. 2. Agreed; ratified.

A قراض *qirāz'*, n. قرض cutting (a rope).
A partnership in which one party advances the capital, and the other the labor or skill, the profits being divided in stipulated proportions.
qirāzī kachahrī. An office for the collection of out standing revenue balances.

A قرائن *qarā'yan*, n. m. pl. of قرينة 1. Conditions; circumstances. 2. The context.
qarāin-i-āīn. Legal presumptions. [of the case.
qarāin-i-muāmlah yā muqadma. Presumptions

A قرباني *qurbān'ī*, n. f. A sacrifice; a victim.
qurbānī k., v. a. To sacrifice according to Mah. law.

A قربت *qurb'at*, n. f. Nearness; adjacency.
قرب و جوار *qurb o javār*, n. m. Environs; suburbs; purlieus; borderland.

A قرض *qarz*; Illit. *qaraz*; Rus. *karaj*; Sant. *rīn*; H. *rinh*, n. m. Loan; debt; a pecuniary obligation or liability.
qarz adā k., yā utārnā, v. a. To pay one's debt.
qarz uṭhānā, lenā, kāṛhnā, yā nikālnā, qarzdār h., v. n. To contract a debt; to owe; run up an account, a bill, or score.
qarz-i-be-mīyād. A loan for an indefinite term;
qarz-i-jadīd. A new loan; fresh obligation.
qarz chukānā, v.a. To discharge or liquidate debt.
qarza-i-hisābī. A debt on account.
qarz-i-hasnah, Mah., n. m.
A loan bearing no interest, and repaid at the pleasure of the borrower.
qarz-khat, khat, n. m. An I. O. U; a debenture; endorsement; acceptance, (*tamassuk*).
qarz-khuāh, qarz-dihandah, n. m.
1. See *udhār dene-vālā*. 2. A dun.
qarz-dār, qarz-gīrindah; H. *udhār lene-vālā*, adj. Indebted; owing; involved.
qarz-dār; H. *udhār lene-vālā*, n. m. A debtor.
qarz-dār-i-be-zar. An insolvent debtor (*divālyā*).
qarz-dārī, n. f. Indebtedness; pecuniary embarrassment. [at interest (*udhār denā*).
qarz denā, v. a. To supply on credit; to lend
qarz zimma-ī-jāëdād. A loan made on the security of certain property.
qarz se barī. Free from debt. [from debt.
qarz se chhuṛānā, v. a. To redeem; to free
qarz-i-gair-mumkīn-ul-vusūl; H. *ḍūbī-udhār.*
A bad debt (*ḍūbant yā burī ṭip*).
qarz lenā ba kafālat jihāz (*Com. Law*) A contract by which money is lent upon a ship's bottom, or by pledging the ship as security, the risk of the voyage being borne by the lender; bottomry. [ed debt.
qarz-i-mutanāzea; H. *jhagṛe kī udhār*, A disput-
qarz-i-mumkin-ul-vusūl; H. *paṭṭī udhār.*
A good debt.
qarz meṅ garq rahnā. To be plunged in debt; to be over head and ears in debt.
qarz-i-maurūsī; H. *bapautī udhār*, An ancestral debt. [bills receivable.
qarz-i-yāftanī; H. *pānā.* An outstanding debt;
قرضه *qarz'ā*; H. *udhār*, n. m. A loan. See قرض.
qarza-iqbālī. An admitted debt.
qarza-i-tamassukī. A bond debt; a debt secured by the execution of a bond in favor of the creditor.
qarz'a chukānā, v. a. To liquidate a debt.
juzv-i-zar-i-qarza. Part of a debt.
qarza mutaalliq-i-jāëdād. Legal claims on an estate; encumbrances.
qarzah vusūl h., v. n. To realize one's dues.

A قرق *qurq*; Rus. *kuṛak*, adj. Forfeited; distrained; attached; sequestered.
qurq-amīn, qurq-sazāval. An officer of the court employed to attach a property and realize the proceeds; a bailiff; sheriff's officer.
qurq-pizīr. Contraband; liable to seizure.
qurq tahsīl. Collection by sequestration; revenue attachment; collection of the revenue of an estate which has fallen into arrears and from which the proprietors are nominally set aside by the native officers of the revenue.
qurq tahsīl-i-chand-rozā. Temporary attachment.
qurq k., v. a. To distrain; sequester; attach; take in execution.
qurq-kunandah, āmil-ī-qurqī. Distrainer.
qurq-mahāl. An estate under attachment. [cution.
qurq-nāmah, parvānah-i-qurqī. A writ of exe-
qurq-huā, adj. Attached; sequestered.
qurq hone-vālā. About to be taken in execution.
قرقي *qurq'ī, qurqī-i-māl*; Rus. *kuṛkī*, n. f. Distraint; distress; attachment; sequestration.
qurqī uṭhā lenā yā bar-khuāst k., qurqī se chhuṛānā, vā-guzasht, yā khalās k., v. a. To withdraw or remove an attachment or distraint.
qurqī biṭhānā, v. a. 1. To set a guard over distrained property. 2. To prevent egress from a house. [an attachment.
qurqī bhejnā, v. a. To send an officer to execute
qurqī-i-ām. A general attachment. [judgment.
qurqī qabal faislah. An attachment before
qurqī kā parvānā. v.a. A warrant of attachment.
qurqī karne-vālā, āmil-i-qurqī, n. m. The officer executing a distress; distrainer.
qurqī meṅ dakhal andāzī. Breach of attachment.

kharcha-i-qurqī. Costs of distress.
māl kāfī qābil-i-qurqī. Sufficient distress.
māl-i-maqrūqa. Property distrained.
maqrūq minho, The person whose property is distrained.

A قريب *qarīb',* adv. قرب drawing near.
Adjacent; neighbouring (*pās* 1).
qarīb-ul-ikhtitām. Near the end or close.
qarīb-i-marg. On the point of death; dying.
qarīb, yā qarīn-ul-vuqu. Imminent; impending.
qarīb-kar, A. H. adv. Approximately (*pās pās*).
qarīb kī rishte-dārī, n. f. Near relationship.

A قرين *qarīn',* adj. See *qarīb.*
qarīn-i-insāf. Just; equitable.
qarīn-i-aql thā, yā qarīn-i-qayās thā.
It is expected.
qarīn-i-maslahat, yā salāh. Advisable; expedient.
قرينه *qarīn'ah,* n.m. 1. Way; mode (*ḍhang,*1).
2. Arrangement; system; order. [analogy.
3. Context; correspondence; connexion;
qarīne se, adv. 1. In order (*tartīb se*). 2. From the context; from the general tenor.
3. By analogy.
kisī qarīne se yaqīn h., v. n.
To have reason to believe; to know or conclude from certain circumstances.

T قزاق *qazzāq',* n. m. See *baṭ-mār.*
A robber; freebooter; brigand; Cossack; one who robs in a gang and who sometimes plunders on horseback.
قزاقي *qazzāq'ī,* n. f. The profession of a *qazzāq,* q. v.; brigandage (*baṭmārī*).
قزاقي *qazzāqī,* adj. Predatory.

A قسطا *qist;* Rus. *kist, kisht,* n. f.
Instalment; partition; dividend (*bāṅt,*2).
There are generally four *qists* in the year, the *rabi* paid in May and June, and the *kharif* in November and December.
qist bāṅdhnā, v. a. To pay by instalments.
qist-bandī, n. f. Paying the revenue by instalments; the revenue demand roll paid in instalments.
qist khilāfī, n. f. Failure in the payment of an instalment.
qist-kār, n. m. A payer of a debt or tax by instalments.
qist munqazī, G. G. An instalment in arrear.
qist-vār, adv. By instalments.
The portion of the annual assessment or Government revenue to be paid at specified periods in the course of the year; a revenue demand; a demand-roll, relating to fixed periodical payments of the revenue or of a debt. [*gand*).

A قسم *qas'am;* Rus. *kasam;* n. f. Oath (*saugand*).
qasam dilānā, denā, yā khilānā, To give an oath.
qasam khā-ke inkār k., v. a. To deny on oath.
qasam khānā, v. a. To take an oath.
qasmā-qasmī, n. f. Swearing both parties.
qasmī'yah, adv. On oath; sworn. [upon oath.
qasmīyah bayān k., v. a. To testify or declare

A قسم *qism;* Illit. *qisam,* n. f.
Description; species; nature; rank.
qism-i-avval. The first or prime quality.
qism haqīqat. 1. Tenure; description of tenure.
2. The nature of a right.
qism-i-zamīn. Quality, description, or denomination of land.
qism seh-gānah. Three kinds of tenure.
qism-i-muqaddama. Nature of the suit.
qism-vār, Classed; according to its sort or kind, or according to shares.
qism-vār jamā-bandī. A statement of the assessment on the lands of a village or collectorate according to their quality.
qismvār goshvārā. An abstract statement of lands classed according to their quality.
قسمت *qism'at,* n. f. 1. Section; head; category (*hissah,* 2). 2. A division of a province.
3. A share (*bhāg,* 1). 4. Equal partition of a husband's property amongst his wives.

A قصاص *qisās',* n. m. Opp. of *diat.* قص cut.
Blood for blood; capital punishment.
qisās ke lāyaq. Liable to sentence of death.
qisās lenā, v. a. To take blood for blood.

A قصبه *qasb'ah, qasbā;* Rus. *kasbā,* n. m. pl. *qasbāt.* A town or large village.

A قصد *qasd,* n. m. Attempt; project. [cide.
qasd-i-halākat-i-khud. Attempt to commit sui-
qasd'an, adv. 1. Wilfully. 2. In cold blood.
qasd'an iānat k. G. G. To intentionally aid.
qasd k. v. a. To attempt; essay; strive; make an attempt; venture.

A قصور *qusūr';* Illit. *qasūr;* H. *khoṭ,* n. m.
قصر being short. See *taqsīr.*
1. Deficiency; defect; shortcoming.
2. Incorrectness; inexactness; misconstruction; cross-purpose (*galatī,* 5).
qusūr-i-khidmat. Breach of duty.
qusūr-i-aql. Defect of understanding.
qusūr k. v. a. 1. To fail; miss.
2. To commit a fault.
qusūr karvānā, v. a. Caus. of *qusūr k.* q. v.
To mislead; lead astray; lead into error.
qusūr-vār, qusūr-mand, adv. Blameworthy; reprehensible (*taqsīrvār*). [*taqsīr*).
be-qusūr, adj. Without fault; guiltless (*be-*
be-qusūr ṭhairānā, v. a. To pronounce innocent; to free; discharge (*barī k.*).

A قضيه *qaz'yah, qazyā,* n. m. pl. *qazāyā.*
1. Dispute; debate; disputation.
2. (*qazyā qazāyā*) Quarrel.
3. A law-suit; suit at law; cause; action.

A قطامه *quttām'ah*; Pop. *khuttāmā*, n.f. قطم *Appetens coitus vel edendæ carnis fuit homo vel brutum*. 1. An unchaste, bad woman, (An abuse). 2. A strumpet; an adulteress.

A قطاعه *qat'āh, qitā*, n. m. 1. A detached portion; scrap; fragment; piece.
2. A patch or plot of ground; a tract.
qatā-bandī, n. f. 1. A mode of assessment formed upon an equal distribution among the cultivators of the good and bad soils of a village in like proportion, each cultivator being held responsible for his share of both.
2. The assessment of the cultivators according to the shares of each, without reference to the soil or the cultivator.
qata jarīb-bandī. Specification of the dimensions of each field in a *Paṭṭā* or lease.
qata-vārī baṭvārā. Partition of a joint estate in small sub-divisions.
qatā-i-zamīn yā arāzī. A piece or patch of land.
qata-i-girānṭ, A. Eng. A grant of land.
qata-huā. Adjusted; settled.
قطعي *qat'āī*, adj. Final; absolute; imperative; peremptory (*akhīr*, 3).
qataī, qatan, adv. Completely; finally; absolutely; positively; peremptorily; once for all.
hiba qataī, An absolute bequest.

A قفل *qufl*; Pop. *qufal*; Illit. *qulaf*, n. m. A lock (*tālā*).
qufl tornā, v. a. To break open a lock.
qufl kunjī, A lock and key.
qufal men band k., To lock up or in.
qufal lagānā, bhernā, yā denā, v. a.
To lock; put on a lock.
makān kā qufal tornā, v.a. To force the door of a house.

A P قلب‌ساز *qalb-sāz*, n. m.
A counterfeit coiner.
qalb-sāzī, n. f. Making counterfeit coin.

A P قلبه‌راني *qulbah-rānī*; H. *halāī*, n. f. *qullah* a plough. 1. Ploughing; driving the plough; tillage. 2. Assessment according to the number of ploughs.
qulbah-rānī k; H. *hal chalānā*, v. a. To plough; till the soil.

A قلبي *qalb'ī, qalb*, adj. Counterfeit; false.

P قلمبند *qalam-band*, adj. 1. Written; penned; written out. 2. Taken into account.
3. Inserted; entered.
qalam-band k., v. a.
To set or take down in writing; commit to writing; book; make an entry of; note; take a note of (*dākhil k.* 3, and *darj k.*).
qalam-band h., v. n. To be written, noted down, inscribed, engrossed (*darj h.*).
qalam phernā, yā kheṅchnā, v. a. To strike out.
qalam davāt, 1. Pen and ink (inkstand).
2. (*Slang*) *Rem in re.*
قلمرو *qalam-rau*, n. f. Territories; domain (*rāj*).
qalam-rau-i-angrez vāqe Hind. G. G. British India.
yak-qalam, adv.
With a stroke of the pen; at once.
قلمي *qal'amī*, Ped.; *qalmī*, Pop. adj.
1. Written; not verbal. 2. Manuscript.

A قليل *qalīl'*, adj. Deficient; scant.
miād-i-qalīl. Short term or limitation.

A P قمارباز *qimār-bāz*, n. m. A gambler (*juārī*).
qimār-bāzī, n. f. Gambling (*juā*).
qimār-bāzī k., v. a. To gamble (*juā khelnā*).
qimār-bāzī majma-i-ām. G. G. Public gambling.
قمارخانه *qimār-khāna, qimār-bāzoṅ kā ghar.*
A gambling house; a hell (*jue-khāna*).

A قواعد *qavā'īd*; Illit. *qavād, kavād*, n. m. pl. of قاعده 1. Rules of procedure, as distinguished from substantive law. 2. Principles.
qavāid-i-āmma-i-virāsat. The ordinary rules of devolution of property.
qavāid-i-ibtidāī. Preliminary rules.
qavāid-i-taqsīm. G. G. Rules or principles of distribution or partition.
qavāid-i-zannī. Rules of presumption.

A قوانين *qavānīn'*, n. m. pl of قانون See *qavāid*, 1.
qavānīn-i-faujdārī, Criminal laws.
qavānīn-i-māl, Financial laws.
qavānīn-i-lagān. Revenue laws.

A قول صالح *qaul-i-sālah*. Solemn affirmation.
qaul se phirnā, v. n. To break one's word or promise; go back from one's word.
qaul qarār, n. m. Mutual agreement; convention; treaty; league (*iqrār*, 3).
qaul qarār k., qaul k., v. a. To make terms; bargain; bind by contract (*iqrār k.*, 1, 4).
qaul-nāmah. More commonly *paṭṭa*. See اقرار نامه
The written voucher granted to the revenue payers, specifying the terms of their payments and the amount payable; written rules on the subject of rent.
qaul o fel, n. m. Word and deed.

A قوم *qaum*, n. f. 1. Tribe; race. 2. Breed.
qaum'ī, adj. National; belonging to race.
qaumī bhalāī. The interest of the nation.
قوميت *qaumī'yat*, n. f. Race; nationality.

A قياس *qayās'*, n. m. قيس measuring, comparing.
1. Thought; judgment; opinion. 2. Conjecture.
qayās-i-qavī ba manzilā subūt.
Violent presumption.
قياساً *qayās'an*, adv. By guess.
qayās se bāhar, Beyond conception or calculation.
qayās k., yā lagānā, v. a. To guess (*aṭkalnā*, 1).

qayās men ānā, v. n. To be conceivable.
قياسي *qayās'ī*, adj. 1. Imaginary; theoretical. 2. Hypothetical (*atkalī*).
amar-i-qayāsī. An assumption; hypothesis.
subūt-i-qayāsī. Presumptive proof.

A قيد *qaid*, n. f. 1. Imprisonment; confinement. 2. Control.
qaid-i-intihāī, n. The longest term of imprisonment.
qaid-i-bā-mashaqqat. Imprisonment with labour; rigorous imprisonment.
qaid bā-mashaqqat yā ba-jaulān. Imprisonment with irons and hard labour.
qaid bilā-mashaqqat. Imprisonment without labour.
qaid bilā-mashaqqat va jaulān. G. G. Imprisonment without irons and labour.
qaid bharnā. bhugatnā, yā kāṭnā, v. n. To undergo the full term of imprisonment.
qaid-i-be-jā. Illegal duress or confinement.
qaid-i-tanhāī. Solitary confinement.
qaid-khānah. Prison; jail; gaol (*jel-khānah*).
qaid rakhnā, v. a. To detain; hold in custody.
qaid rahnā, v. n. To remain in bonds, in prison, etc.
qaid-i-sakht. Rigorous imprisonment.
qaid se chhūṭnā. Gaol delivery.
qaid-i-farang. Imprisonment from which there is no escape.
qaid k., v. a. See *band k.*, 1, 2.
qaid kī āgyā, yā hukm, A mittimus.
qaid lagānā, v. a. 1. To limit; circumscribe. 2. To regulate; subject to rule. 3. To make conditions (*shart bāndhnā*, 1, 2).
qaid-i-mahaz. G. G. Simple imprisonment.
qaid men. Under restraint or control.
qaid-i-nā-jāiz. False imprisonment; wrongful restraint.
qaid h., v. n. 1. To be limited. 2. To be imprisoned, bound, or fettered, etc.
be-qaid, bilā-qaid, adj. 1. Unrestrained; uncontrolled; free; unchecked. 2. Unconditional; unlimited; indefinite (*be-hadd*, 1). 3. Without due regard to or for; irregular; lawless.
be-qaid, adv. Without restraint, opposition, or reservation; openly.
2. At large; at random; irregularly.
قيدي *qaid'ī*, n. f. A convict; prisoner (of a prison).

A قيمت *qīm'at*; Illit. *kīmat*; Rus. *kimmat*; H. *mol*, n. f. قوم being brisk (the market). Price (*dām*, 2).
qīmat takhmīnī. Estimated value.
qīmat chukānā, v. a. To settle the price.
qīmat rasadī. Proportionate or rateable value.
qīmat ravannā. A customs pass, specifying the value of the goods that have paid duty.
qīmat kam k., yā ghaṭānā, v. a. To beat down the price.
qīmat lagānā, v. a. To value; make an offer; bid.
qīmat-i-māl mubīa. Value of goods sold.
qīmat muqarrar k. To fix the price; appraise.
karāyah-nāma-i-besh-qīmat. A valuable lease.
kāmil-ul-qīmat, Ped. for *pūra mol*, Adequate value.
قيمتي *qīm'atī, qīmtī*, adj. 1. Of the value of; valued at. 2. High-priced; costly. 3. Valuable; precious.

ك

P كابين *kābīn'*; A. *mahr*, n. m. A marriage portion; settlement on a wife; a jointure.
kābīn-nāma, mahr-nāma, n. f. A deed of dower; a marriage settlement.

H كاتها काथा *kāth'ā, phal-pārī*, n. m. A circular piece of iron placed on a ploughshare to prevent its going too deep into the ground.

H كاٹھ काठ *kāṭh*, n. m. The stocks (for delinquents).
kāṭh men pāon ṭhoknā yā denā, v. a. To put in the stocks.

P كار *kār*; H. *kām*, n. m. P. *kardan*, S. कृ to do. 1. Act (فعل 1). 2. Work; mission. 3. Function; duty (*farz*).
كارآزموده *kār-āzmūdah, kār-kardah*; H. *bhugtā-huā*, adj. Experienced; practised.
كارآمد *kār-āmad*, adj. *lit.* what comes into use. Applicable; conducive.
kār-bārī, n. m. 1. A man of business. 2. A manager.
kār-barārī, n. f. Performance; execution.
kār-band. Acting up to or upon.
kār-band h., v. n. To act up to; to perform or discharge a duty; fulfil; comply with.
كارپرداز *kār pardāz, kārindah*, n. m. One who manages a business; a negotiator; factor (*sarbarāh*).
kār-pardāzān-i-pulis. Police establishment.
kār-pardāzī, kārindgī, n. f. Management; agency.
kār-pardāzī men gaflat. Negligence of one's duties.
kār-i-jangī. Military affairs.
kār-o-bār; Pop. *kār-bār*, n. m. 1. Business; affairs. 2. Dealings; transactions.
kār hākim-i-adālat. Judicial functions.
kār-i-khās. A special, particular, or peculiar duty.
kār-i-khāngī, Private or domestic affairs.
كارخانه *kār-khānā*, n. m. 1. A factory; manufactory; workshop; dockyard.
kār-khāne-dār; n. m. A proprietor of a factory, etc.
kār-khānah-dārī, n. f. The business of a factory or workshop.

kār-khānā k., v. a.
To open a workshop or business.
kār-dān, n. m. An adept; a connoiseur.
کارروائی *kār-ravāī*, n.f. 1. Working; operation; carrying on a business. 2. Process; proceeding; procedure. 3. Execution; management; conduct; administration.
4. Discharge or performance of work.
kār-ravāī baĉbāt. Foreclosure proceedings.
kār-ravāī sarsarī. Summary procedure.
kār-ravāī-i-adālat. Judicial proceedings.
kār-ravāī k., v. a. 1. To execute or discharge a function or duty.
2. To hold proceedings.
kār-ravāī multavī rakhnā. To stay proceedings.
kār-ravāī mahkūma-i-qānūn.
A legal proceeding.
kār-ravāī-i-nīlām. Sale proceedings.
kār-i-roz-marrah, n. m. Daily duty.
kār-i-sarishtā, n. m. Official business.
kār-i-sarkārī, n. m. Public or Government service; official functions. [Majesty's Service.
ba-kār-i-sarkār yā malikah muazzamah On Her
kār-i-zurūrī, n. f. Urgent business or affairs.
kār-i-farz, n. m. Imperative or bounden duty.
kār-farmāī, n. f. Execution; administration.
کارکن *kār-kun*, n. m. A director; manager; assignee; a manager of a minor's estate; a representative; an attorney.
کارگر *kār-gar*, adj. 1. Operative; active (a medicine). 2. Effective; effectual (*fāēdemand*, 3).
3. Serviceable; useful. [& *h.*, 1).
kār-gar h., v. n. 1. To be operative (*asar k.*,
2. To be productive or useful.
کارگزار *kār-guzār*, n. m. 1. Expert; expeditious.
2. Dutiful; attentive.
kār-guzārī, n. f. 1. Despatch of business; discharge of duty. 2. Employment; service; good service. [duties.
kār-i-mufavvazah, n. m. Charge; business;
kār-i-mulkī, n. m. 1. Public functions.
2. Revenue affairs; finance. [duct.
kār-i-nā-jāyaz. A wrongful act; unlawful con-
adālat ki kārravāī kī hālat.
Stage of judicial proceedings.
کاری *kār'ī*, adj. Mortal; fatal.
kārī-zakhm, zakhm-i-kārī. A mortal wound.

P کاشت *kāsht*, n. f. 1. (*kāshtkārī*) Cultivation (*bo-jot*). 2. Cultivated land or tract; field; farm. 3. Holding; tenure (of land).
4. A tenure by which the revenue is assessed according to the value of the crop.
kāsht se dakhal uṭhānā, kāsht yā qabze se be-dakhal k. To oust from a holding.
kāsht karānā, v. a. To farm out land.
kāsht k., v. a. To cultivate (*bonā*, 1).
kāsht meṅ lānā, v. a. To bring into cultivation; reclaim land.
be-kāsht, Ped. for H. *be-jot*; Tir. *aphāṛ*, adj.
Uncultivated; fallow; waste.
کاشتکار *kāsht-kār, kisht-kār*; H. *kisān*, n. m.
A cultivator; farmer (*jotā*).
kāsht-kār-i-jadīd. A cultivator newly settled in a village. [vator.
kāsht-kār-i-gair-mālik. A non-proprietory culti-
kāsht-kār g̃air-maurūsī yā pāhī. A non-hereditary cultivator. [ed in a village.
kāsht-kār-i-qadīm. A cultivator long establish-
kāsht-kār-i-mālik. A proprietory cultivator.
kāsht-kār-i-maurūsī. A hereditary cultivator.
kāsht-kārī; H. *kisānī*, n. f. Culture; tillage.

P کاغذ *kāğ'az*; Rus. *kaggaj, kāgaj, kāgad*; *kājak*; Tir. *kāgat*, n. m. pl. *kāgzāt, kavāgzāt*.
1. Paper.
2. A writing; deed; document; charter.
3. An account-book. 4. A printed or written sheet; a newspaper. 5. A note of hand; bond.
kāgaz-i-arba, Obs. The four written documents on which the proceedings in a suit are grounded; i. e. the written complaint; the answer; the rejoinder; and the reply. [ings.
kāgaz-i-arba kā tatimma, Supplemental plead-
kāgaz-i-baṭvāra. Partition paper.
kāgaz-i-khām, H. *kachchā chiṭṭhā*,
Rough draft of a document, or account; account of gross produce.
kāgaz-i-sarkārī, n. 1. Registered or stamped paper. 2. (*sarkārī kāgaz*) A currency note; Government promissory note.
kāğaz kāmil-ul-qīmat.
A document duly stamped. [accounts.
kāgaz k., v. a. To adjust, make up, or balance
kāgaz likhnā, likh denā, yā k., v. a.
To give a bond or note of hand.
kāgaz likhvā lenā. To take a bond.
kāgaz milānā, v.a. To examine or check accounts.
kāgaz meṅ dākhil k., v. a. To register.
kāgaz-i-nikāh. See *kābīn-nāmah.* [paper.
pakkā kāgaz, n. 1. Thick, stiff paper. 2. Stamped
chiṭṭhī kā kāgaz, n. m. Note paper.
kachchā kāgaz. 1. Inferior country paper.
2. Unstamped paper.
korā yā be-likhā-kāgaz. Blank paper.
kāgzāt-i-bando-bast, n. m. Settlement records.
kāgzāt-i-dehī, n. m. Village accounts or administration papers. [ings or records in a case.
kāgzāt-i-muqaddama yā adālat, n. m. Proceed-
kāgzat-i-kalaktarī, n. m. Revenue records.
kāgzāt-i-muqaddam e meṅ shāmil.
Filed with the case. [papers.
kāgzāt munsalakah yā manthūthā. The annexed
kāgzāt-i-maujūdah. The records as they stood.
kāgzī subūt, n. m. Documentary proofs.

A کافی *kā'fī*, adj. Sufficing; enough; competent; satisfactory.

kāfī tasavvur k., G.G. v. a. To hold or consider sufficient. [2. Effectually.
kāfī taur se, adv. 1. Adequately; sufficiently.
kāfī na h., v. n. To be deficient, or wanting.
kāfī h., v. n. To be adequate, equivalent to; to cover; do; answer.
kāfī hai. Is sufficient. [the interest.
sūd kā juzv-i-kāfī. G. G. A competent part of

H کال **काल** *kāl*, n. m. 1. Season. 2. Famine.
kāl-upkār, kāl meṅ kaṅglā pālan kā rupayā. Famine relief fund. [derable time.
kāl banjar, n. f. Land left fallow for a consi-
kāl-koṭhrī, n. f. 1. A black-hole.
2. Solitary imprisonment.
kālā bāl, n. m. 1. The *pubes*. 2. The groin.

H کالاپاني **काला पानी** *kālā pānī*, n. m. *lit.* black waters. Beyond the sea; transportation beyond India; the Andaman islands.

H کام **काम** *kām*; Rus. *kār*, n.m. S. **कर्म्म**, Pālī, *kammam*; Pr. *kammo.*
1. Work; handiwork; job. 2. Office; department; function; task; duty; part.
kām bigaṛnā, v.n. 1. To be spoilt, marred (one's work, plan, plot, etc.). 2. To be bankrupt.
jhūṭe nishān-i-hirfe kā kām meṅ lānā, G. G. Using a false trade-mark.
کامدار **कामदार** *kām-dār*, H. P., n. m. Manager; agent (*kārkun*).
jhūṭ nishān-i-milkīyat kā kām meṅ lānā. G. G. Using a false property mark.

A کامل *kām'il*, adj. See *pūrā*, 3, 5.
1. Whole; full.
2. Positive; decisive; absolute.
kāmil-ul-qīmat. Of full or adequate value.
kāmil-ul-ayār. Of perfect standard or assay (a coin).
kāmil jamā yā kāmil berīj, The highest assessment leviable.
kāmil h., v. n. 1. To be completed, finished.
2. To master; make oneself master.
ijrāë kāmil, G. G. Complete execution.
ikhtiyārāt-i-kāmil. G. G. Full powers.
shaë kāmil. G. G. The entire thing.

H A کانجي حوض *kāñjī-hauz*, n. m. 1. A lock-up; congee-house. 2. A pound for cattle.

H کپال کریا **कपालक्रिया** *kapāl-kiryā*, n. f. A Hin. funeral ceremony.
When the burning corpse is nearly reduced to ashes, the son or the nearest relation breaks the skull with a stroke of a bamboo and pours melted butter into the cavity. [book

A کتاب *kitāb'*, n. m. pl. *kutab*, کتب wrote. A
kitāb-intiqāl, n. f. A book or record of transfers and other changes of property.
kitāb hukmī. A letter from one *Qāzī* to another, containing an authenticated transcript of evidence taken in a case, the decision on which has been removed to the jurisdiction of the latter; any authoritative writing.

H کتکنه **कटकनह** *kaṭkan'ah*, n. m.
Farm; sub-lease (اجارہ).
kaṭkanā denā, v. a. To sublet (*ijārah denā*).
kaṭkane-dār, n. m. Under-lessee; tenant; farmer; a sub-tenant.
kaṭkane meṅ thā. Leased in *kaṭ-kanah.*

H کتنا **कुटना** *kuṭ'nā, kuṭṭan, bichauliyā, miyāṅjī*, n. m. *kuṭnī*, n. f. S. **कुट्टन**
A go-between; bawd (*bhaṛvā*).
کتناپا **कुटनापा** *kuṭnāp'ā, kuṭṭan-panā*, n. m. Pimping; cuckoldom (*bhaṛvāī*).
kuṭnāpā k., v. a. To pimp; pander.
کتنانا **कुटनाना** *kuṭnā'nā*; Bhoj. *kuṭnāval*, v. a.
1. To wheedle; coax (as a go-between).
2. To entice; seduce. [*conciliatrix.*
کتني **कुटनी** *kuṭ'nī*, n. f. S. **कुट्टनी** A procuress;
kuṭnī kā ghar; Panj. *chhallā-koṭhī*, n. m.
1. The house of a procuress where clandestine prostitution is carried on. [of call.
2. A bawdyhouse; a bagnio; brothel; a house

H کتوان بیاج *kaṭvān byāj.* Simple interest.

کتوتي **कटौती** *kaṭaut'ī*, n. f. Discount.

H کتها **कट्ठा** *kaṭ'ṭhā*, E.; *gaṭṭhā*, W. n. m.
1. The 20th part of the Bengal Bigha of 1600 sq. yards, or 720 sq. feet.
2. A corn measure of five seers. (?)

H کتھ باپ **कठ बाप** *kaṭh-bāp*; Sant. *kākāt āpāt*, n.m. A step-father.
☞ Women of the lower classes often leave, or are given up by their husbands, and on re-marrying (*karão* or *dharão*) they take with them the younger children to whom the new husband is *kaṭh-bāp*, while the children are called his *ḍagarvā laṛke* (picked up on the road or *ḍagar*).

H کتھڑي **कठड़ी** *kaṭh'ṛī, kaṭṭari*, n. f.
1. The horizontal beam to which the bullocks are attached in a sugarmill. [rivers.
2. Land recovered from, or left by large

A کثیرالازواج *kasīr-ul-azvāj*, Ped. G. G. A polygamist.

H کچا **कच्चा** *kach'chā, kachchī*; Tir. & Bhoj. *kāñch, kañchkharā*; Mār. *kācho*, adj. Opp. of *pakkā*, See خام (1, 2, 3). 1. Raw. 2. Below a certain standard of weight or measure.
(2½ of all *kachchā* weights and measures make one *pakkā* weight or measure).

kachchā takhmīnā. A rough estimate.
kachchā dakhl. A precarious tenure.
kachchā ser, n. m. A *seer* which is below the standard of eighty rupees weight.
kachchī āsāmī. A temporary cultivator; one having no permanent or hereditary right of occupation.
kachchī peshī, n. f. Primary hearing of a case.
kachchī tahsīl, n. Collection of the revenue from the cultivators direct.
kachchī jamā-bandī. The gross rent roll of a village before setting off the charges and expenses, whether the balance be payable to a *zamīndār* or the government. [run.
kachchī mitī, Opp. of *pakkī mitī* n. f. Date to
Interest from the day preceding the loan to the day after, according to the practice of Native bankers.
kachchī nāp, n. f. Rough measurement.

H کچوانسي कचवांसी *kachvāṅ'sī*; Old H.
karvāmsī, n. f. A minute division of land measure, 1-20th of a *bisvāṅsī*, q. v.

H کچهار कछार *kachhār'*, *kachh*, n.m. S. कंच्छ
Moist low land by a river; alluvial formation.

H کچهري कचहरी *kachah'rī*; Rus. *kachairī*;
Sah. *kichhrī*, n. f. S. कुत्सितहरी from कुत्सित bad, हरी to take away. A court house or office; a court of justice; tribunal; cutchery.
kachahrī barkhāst, The rising of a court.
kachahrī barkhāst k., v. a.
To close or adjourn a court. [into court.
kachahrī charhnā, v.n. To bring an action; to go
kachahrī ām. A public office.
kachahrī ām maftūhā. An open public court.
kachahrī-kā, adj, Official.
kachahrī k., v. a. To hear cases in court.
bharī kachahrī meṅ. In open court. [office.
sarkārī kachahrī, n. f. A public or Government

H کچهوا कछुआ *kachh'uā*, W. n. m.
One side of a yoke.
kachhuā kā sājhā. A partner who provides half the team of cattle needed for ploughing; the owner of one *kachhuā*.
کچهوا ڈابر कछवा डाबर *kachhvā-ḍābar*, E.; *kachro dabro*, Bhoj. n. f, An uneven tract of land or bed of a river partially submerged in places.

P کدخدائي *kad-khudāī*, *kat-khudāī*, n. f.
Marriage.
kad-khudāī k., v. a. To marry.
aurat-i-kadkhudā. A married woman.

H کدهيلڑ कढेलड़ *kaḍhel'aṛ*, *kaḍhelṛā*, *gailaṛ*;
Tir. *kaṭh pūt*, n. A step son or daughter.
kaḍhelaṛ, adj. 1. Banished; exiled. 2. Outcasted.

H کر कर *kar*, n.m.S. कर from कृ to do. [(خراج).
1. Revenue from taxes. 2. A settled allowance to village officers and servants.
kar ughānā, v. n. To collect taxes.
kar-ughāū, n. Tax gatherer; toll collector.
kar bāṅdhnā, *yā lagānā*, v. a. To impose a tax.
kar-lagān, n. Imposing a cess or tax; taxation.

H کراو कराव *karāv'*, *karā'o*, n. m.
1. The marriage of a widow with the brother (generally with the younger brother) of the deceased husband.
The custom prevails among the *Jāṭs*, *Gūjars*, *Ahīrs*, and other inferior tribes, etc. as it did amongst the Jews.
2. Concubinage.
karāo k., v. a. 1. To marry a widow. 2. To keep a mistress.
3. To keep a man (to live with).

A کراهيت *karāh'iyat*, n. f. کره hating.
1. Aversion; disgust; abhorrence.
2. (*In law*) Abominable acts; abominations; any infraction of moral or religious obligation, as eating or drinking impure or prohibited food, wearing obnoxious attire, committing acts of indecency, etc.

A کرايه *karā'yah*, *kirā'yah*, n.m. Hire (*bhāṛā*).
kirāyā ughānā, v. a. To collect the rents, etc.
kirāē chalānā, *yā denā*, v. a. To let; hire out.
کرايه‌دار *kirāye-dār*, n. A tenant (*bharaitī*).
kirāē-dār utarnā, v. n.
To occupy a house (the tenant).
kirāya-zamīn. Ground-rent.
kirāyā lenā, v. a. To realise the rent or fare.
kirāya-nāmah, n. m. A lease of a house (*sarkhat*, 1).
kirāya-i-vāpisī; H. *phirtā bhāṛā*, *phirāū*, n. m. Return fare or hire.

H کردا करदा *kard'ā*, n. m. 1. Exchange; barter. 2. Tare and tret; abatement; allowance or customary deduction.
3. Balance of value to make up a deficiency in goods or coin, or the difference between the price of new things and old given in exchange.

H کرماگت कर्मागत S. *karmāgat*, adj. 1. Descended or inherited in regular succession.
2. Traditional.
karamāgat dās. An inherited slave.
karmāgat drab. Hereditary property.
karm-an'uyāī. Succeeding or following in a line.
karmjuṛ'ia, n. Assignments from *khālsa* lands to the junior branches of a Rājpūt family.

H کرمي कुरमी *kurm'ī*, E. n. m.
A cast of agriculturists in Eastern and Central *Hindustān*, the same as the *Kunbīs* of the West and South.

H كريا क्रिया *kri'yā, kiryā,* n. f. S. क्रिया, Pr. *kiriā.* 1. Act (فعل). 2. Obsequial rites; a religious ceremony, esp. such as are purificatory and essential.
3. An act of law or judicial investigation, either by witnesses, documents, or ordeal; the last of the two acts of a process which is upheld, as when a loan and repayment are both proved, the latter is called *kriyā,* the decisive act. 4. E. An oath (*saugand*).
kriyā pād. The evidence; the third division of a suit at law, the counter-evidence or re-joinder of the plaintiff.
kriyā karm, n. 1. Religious service; daily observances, such as oblations, prayer, etc.
2. Funeral ceremonies; obsequies.
kriyā k., v. a. To perform one's obsequies.
kriyā khānā, v. a. To take an oath.
karī dhartī, n. f. Hard soil.
kaṛāhī meṅ hāth ḍālnā, An ordeal.
The accused is required to take out a piece of gold which has been dropped into a vessel of boiling oil. If he can do this without being scalded he is held innocent.

H كڑها कढा *kaṛ'hā.* n. A division of crops in equal proportions. *Carnegy.*

H كڑها कढा *kaṛh'ā, kaṛhuā,* n. 1. A loan.
2. A deduction from the sum lent.

H كسا कस्सा *kas'sā;* Rus. *kas,* n. m. S. कषाय
1. The bark of the *kīkar* or *babūl* (acacia), used in tanning. 2. A spirit extracted from the bark of the *kīkar.* [less than; underweight.

H كسا कसा *kas'ā,* adj. *lit.* tight. Less; barely

H كسان किसान *kisān';* Rus. *kisānṛ,* n. m. S. कृषिमान् See *kāsht-kār.* A farmer; peasant (*jotā*).
kisān qadīm, n. A long-established cultivator.
In some places the same as *maurūsī*, or hereditary cultivator, and having the right of sale and mortgage of their lands, and many of the privileges of proprietorship except those of electing the *lambardār.*

A كسب *kasb;* Pop. *kasab,* n.m. 1. Profession; occupation (*peshā*). 2. Art; skill.
3. Prostitution; whoredom. [prostitute.
kasab k., yā kamānā, v. a. To lead the life of a
كسبي *kasb'ī, kasban,* n. f.
A woman of the town (*besvā,* 1).

A كسر *kas'ar,* n. f. pl. كسور & كسرات from كسر breaking. 1. Damage; loss.
2. Want (*ṭoṭā* 5). 3. Defect; flaw.
kasar bharnā, v. n. To indemnify (*ṭoṭā uṭhānā,* 2); to make up a deficiency.
kasar beshī. A fraction more.
kasar paṛnā, v. a. To come short; fail.
kasar denā, v. a. To make one suffer a loss.

H كسوتي कसौती *kasau'tī,* n. An account of the revenue due by each cultivator (?).

H كسي خود كشي ميں ترغيب دينا
kisī khud-kushī meṅ targīb denā, Assisting in a suicide.
kisī āmil se bachnā, v. n. To evade a law officer.
kisī anuvān se, kisī na kisī tarah se. Somehow; in some way or other; any how.
kisī kāl tak, kisī muddat tak, kisī miād tak.
For a term. [out money.
kisī kām meṅ kharch k., v. a. To invest or lay
kisī kampnī kā mukhtār, A representative of a company.
kisī kī taraf se, On one's behalf. [suit.
kisī kī taraf se nālish k. To represent one in a

H كشاورتي कुशावृत्ती *kushā-vrit'tī,* Maintenance by or through *kusha* grass; but in the west of Bengal, an under tenure of land granted at a quit rent, or rent free, for the support of a Brahman or devotee. Also the absolute gift of land to a Brahmin at an eclipse, or on some solemn occasion.

P كشت *kisht,* n. f. A field. [tion.
kishtvār', By fields; according to the cultiva-
kistvār, n. m. A list showing the fields.

A كفالت *kafāl'at,* n.f. كفل Surety; lien (ضامني).
Security in general, according to the *Shiās,* but limited to personal bail by the *Sunnīs.*
kafālat arāzī, n. An assignment on land.
kafālat-ul-māl A valuable security.
kafālat bil māl, kafālat ul māl, Pecuniary bail.
kafālat-bin-nafs, Personal bail.
kafālat jahāz, Bottomry.
kafālat jahāz par rupayā qarz denā.
To lend money on bottomry.
kafālat-dār nek nīyat. A *bonā fide* incumbrance.
kafālat denā. To indemnify; secure against.
kafālat-rahn. A mortgage lien or security.
kafālat k., v. n. To cover; secure.
kafālat-nāmah, n. A bail bond, or written engagement or security.
kafālat nāmjāt sarkārī. Government securities.
kafālat nāmjāt naqd-i-Inglistān. Consols.
kafālat yakjāī. A consolidating security.

A كفايت *kifā'yat,* n. f. كفي sufficed.
Profit or increase in the amount of revenue received by the government, whether by raising the rate of assessment or imposing additional taxes.

H كفے اسپينا *kafe-aspīnā,* (*Horsedealers*) Five.
kafe deṅgā (*Horsedealers*) Fifty.
kafe lāṅg, (*Horsedealers*) Five hundred.

A كفيل *kafīl'*, n. m. كفل. 1. Surety or bail (the person). 2. A hostage.
kafīl-kār, n. A responsible agent.
kafīl h., v. n. To give or stand bail. [n. f. S. कच.

H ككهيالي कखियाली *kakhiyāl'ī*, E.; *kaulī*, W.
Bundles of sheaves of corn given as perquisites to reapers and village servants.

A كل *kul*, adj. All; aggregate (*tamām*).
kul jurmānā yā koī jaz uskā.
The fine, or any part thereof.
kul jama, n. The sum total; full amount.
kul-jama-bandī, n. f. The gross rental.
kul dāvā. The entire claim.
kul raqbah, n. m. The whole area or contents of a village and its lands. [of a case.
kul ruedād-i-muqadmah. The full particulars
kul kāgzāt-i-muqadmah. The whole course of proceedings in a cause. [prietor.
kulkulāṅ mālik, n. m. 1. Sole and entire pro-
2. One entrusted with the whole economy of a house; a major-domo; *factotum.*
3. A plenipotentiary armed with full powers.
kul-mukhtārī, n. f. Full authority.
kul mīzān, Grand total.
kul-vusūl pānā, v. n. To receive in full.
kul'lan, adv. Wholly; all.
kullan yā juzan ikhtiyārāt, With all or any of the powers. [tally.
كلهم *kullohum'*, adv. Altogether; wholly; to-

H كل कुल *kul*, n. m. Family (اصل 5).
kul achār'iyā, The family priest who conducts the religious ceremonies, etc.

H كلال कलाल *kalāl'*, *kalār*, n. m. *kalāran*, n. f. S. कलाद 1. A sect of Hindus whose profession originally was distilling spirits.
2. A distiller. 3. (*kalālī*) A seller of spirituous liquors; a publican; tavern-keeper.
kalāl jama. Revenue from the excise, or duty on spirits.
كلال‌خانه कलालख़ाना *kalāl-khānā*, n.m. 1. A distillery. 2. A liquor-shop; public house; tavern.

H كلر कल्लर *kal'lar*, *kallaṛh*, adj.
Sterile; barren; unproductive.
kallar, n. f. 1. A soapy soil; fuller's earth. 2. Land likely to produce saltpetre or *reh*. 3. (*Tir.*) A class of men of no caste, or men who have lost their castes during a famine.
kallar-khāī dhartī, A barren soil.
kallar lagnā, v. n. 1. To be impregnated with alkali or *reh*. 2. To become barren (soil).

E كلكتر *kalak'ṭar*, *kalaṭṭar*, n. m. The collector or chief revenue officer of a district.
كلكتري *kalak'ṭarī*, *kalaṭṭarī*, n.f. A collectorate.

E كلندره *kalan'drah*, n. Calender of crimes.

H كلنك कलंक *kal'aṅk*, n.S. कलङ्क, Pālī, *kalanko*, Calumny; scandal; aspersion (*dāg*, 3).
kalaṅk kā ṭīkā lagnā, *kalaṅkī h.*, v. n.
To be branded, traduced. [(*dāg lagānā*).
kalaṅk lagānā, v. a. To calumniate; traduce

H كلهاڑي कुल्हाड़ी *kulhāṛ'ī*, *kuhāṛī*; Māṛ. *kaṅvāryo*; Tir. *kurhāṛī*; Gaṛh. *kurāṛo*; Old H. *kuṛāṛī*, n. f. *kulhāṛā*, n. m. S. कुठारी
Payment of rent at a rate per hatchet for the land which may be cleared by it in a given time; a tenure by which land is held in the Northern *Sirkārs.*

P كم *kam*, *kamtī*, adj. Old P. and Z. *kamā*.
Little; few.
kam-vazan, adj. Short weight.
be-kam o kāst, adj. Ped. for H. *joṅ kā toṅ*.
Without increase or diminution.
kamtī-bāt, n. m. Light weight.
كمي *kam'ī*, n. f. 1. Deficiency; scantiness.
2. Dearth; paucity; scarcity; want; lack.
3. Loss; decrease; waste. 4 Reduction; diminution; abatement. 5. Defalcation; deficit. 6. Remission; relaxation.
kamī beshī, n. f. 1. Excess and deficiency; inequality. 2. Fluctuation; profit and loss.
kamī beshī barābar huī. Inequality made up.
kami-jāēdād. Deficiency of assets.
kamī qīmat-i-istām. Undervaluation of a suit.
kamī k., v. a. To fall short (*kam k*).
kamī māliyat-i-muqaddama.
Defective valuation of suit.

A كماحقه *kamā-haqqa-hū*, adj. As it ought to be; properly; duly; effectually.

A كمال فتور *kamāl futūr*, n. m. An aggravated breach of the peace (politically). [get.

H كمانا कमाना *kamā'nā*, v.a.S. कर्म 1. To earn;
2. To prepare the land; to enrich; fertilize. 3. To live by prostitution.
كمائي कमाई *kamā'ī*, n. f. 1. Earnings; income.
2. Profits; gains; perquisites.
jorū kī kamāī khānā, *bīvī kā dānā khānā*, v. n.
1. To live on one's wife earnings.
2. To wear horns; to be a cuckold.
dūsroṅ kī kamāī khānā, v. a. To live on others.

A كماينبغى *kamā-yan-baġī*, adj. See. كماحقه.

P كمر كشائي *kamar-kushāī*, n. f.
1. Undoing or opening the waistband.
2. (*Mil.*) The order to take off accoutrements.
3. An illegal fee levied by a Govt. peon from a person over whom he is placed in charge for permission to perform the common functions of life

P H کمند پھینکنا *kamand pheṅknā yā ḍāl-nā*, v. a. To throw up a scaling ladder.
kamand lagānā, G. G. Scaling.

H کمیرا **कमेरा** *kamer'ā*; Sant. *kamīyā*; Bhoj. *kaminihār*, n. m. *kameran*, n. f. S. **कर्मकर** Pālī, *kamakāro*. A workman; laborer, esp. a hired agricultural laborer.

E کمیشن *kamīsh'an*, n. f. Cor. of Commission.
kamīshan baiṭhnā, v. n. To sit (a commission).
kamīshan jārī k., v. a. To issue a commission.
kamīshan denā, v. a. To allow commission or discount.
kamīshan kī tāmīl k., v.a. To execute a commission.
kamīshan ke bamūjib izhār lenā. To examine under a commission.
kamīshan lenā, v.a. To charge commission.
ahl-i-kamīshan. One to whom a commission is issued.
kisī kamīshan kī tāmīl kī kaifīyat. The return to a commission.

A کمین *kamīn'*, n. m.

In the N.-W. P. the artificers and servants of a village who, besides allowances in grain, receive small allotments in land, and are therefore minor or inferior cultivators; also, all the residents of a village, except religious mendicants, who are not cultivators.

kamīnī bāchh, n. m. A tax levied by the proprietors of a village on every resident who is not engaged in agriculture; a ground rent for non-cultivators' dwellings.

H کن **कन** *kan*, n. m. S. **कण** A minute particle.
kan-baṭāī, n. f. Collections by estimate and division of crops; apportionment of the crops amongst the coparceners of a village.
kan karnā, v. a. To appraise; value.
kan-kūt, kanhāī, n. f. 1. Appraisement of a standing crop. 2. (*kanyā*) An appraiser of a crop. [Side.

P کناره *kanār'ah*; Pop. *kinārā*, n. m. Z. *karānā*.
kinārā-kashī az ijrāë hukm-nāmah, kinārā kashī hukm se. Evasion of process.

H کنال **कनाल** *kanāl'*, Panj. $\frac{1}{8}$th of a *ghumāo*.

A کنایه *kinā'ya*, n. m. See اشاره 6, 7. [inuendo.
کنایتاً *kināyatan'*, adv. Indirectly, as an
kināyatan manā k., v. a. To forbid by winks.

H کنجر **कंजर** *kanj'ar*; Tir. *kāyar*, n. m.
1. A low caste, who live by making and selling strings of hemp, cotton, and leather, and who catch and eat snakes.
2. A class of gipsies. 3. (Panj.) The husband of a prostitute; a cuckold.

H کنچن **कंचन** *kan'chan*, n. m. S. **काञ्चन**, Pālī, *kanchanam*. 1. Gold (*sonā*).
2. The prostitute class. 3. A whoreson.
kanchan-bachchah, n. m. The son of a dancing girl.
کنچنی **कंचनी** *kanch'nī, kanchinī*, n. f.
1. A dancing girl by caste and profession.
2. A woman of the town.

H کنڈا **कुण्डा** *kun'ḍā*; Tir. *kaṭh-pūt*, n. m. S. **कुण्ड** The child of a woman by another man than her husband.

H کنرمنڈلا **कुनरमण्डला** *kunarmanḍ'lā, kunarbojī*; Bhoj. *kurmunḍanī*, n. m. The last day of the sowings in Benares and the Duab.

It is observed as a holiday, and the residue of the seed-corn is made into a cake, which is partaken of in the field, and in part distributed to Brahmins and beggars. Mr. Elliot adverts to a similar practice once observed in England.

H کنکوت **कनकूत** *kankūt'*; Rus. *kanyaṅ, kanahā*; Tir. *kuṭanyā*, n. m. One who appraises the standing crops.
kankūt', kanhāī, n. f. Valuation of the standing crop.

H کنگلا **कङ्गला** *kaṅg'lā*, n. m. A beggar.
kaṅglā-pālan rupayā. A relief or poor fund.

H کنیا **कन्या** *kan'nyā*; E. *kaniyā*; Sant. *ḍangva kuṛī*, n. f. S. **कन्या** Pr. *kanjā*; Pālī, *kannā*.
An unmarried girl under ten.
kannyā-pānī grahn. The taking of the bride's hand by the bridegroom.
kannyā putr, yā sut. The son of an unmarried girl; an illegitimate son.
kannyā-dān, n. m. 1. Giving a girl in marriage. 2. A dowry.

P کنیز *kanīz', kanīzak*; H. *launḍī*, n. f.
A slave girl.
kanīzak-zādah; H. *launḍī-bachchā*, n. m.
The son of a bondswoman.

H کوارا **कुआरा** *kuār'ā, kuṅārā*; Wom. *kuārā bālā*; Tir. *kumār*; Sant. *dangvā koṛā*, n. m. S. **कुमार** A bachelor.
kuārā nātā; Brij. *kuāre manḍhve*, n.m. Relationship after betrothal and before marriage.
kuār-pat, kuār-chhal, n. f. A maidenhead.
kuār-pat, yā kuār chhal utārnā, v. a.
To take a maidenhead; to deflour.
kuār-pan, n. m. Bachelorship.
kuār-pan utārnā, v. a. To get one married; to have a poor marriage.
کواری **कुआरी** *kuār'ī*, n. f. A virgin; maid; spinster.

H کواری **कुआरी** *kuār'ī*. A sub-division of *kharīf* which includes *dhān, kodo, til, paṭuā, sanī*, Indian corn, and cotton.

P کوتاه *kot'āh, kotā*, adj. 1. Short.
2. Settled (*chuktā*, 1).
kotāh-qad, adj. Of short stature.

kotāh k., To settle (chukānā, 4, 5). [ahrī).

E كوت koṭ, koraṭ n. m. Cor. of Court (kach-koṭ-māsūl, Cor. of Court-martial. [Court. hāī-koṭ, yā koraṭ; Rus. harī koṭ, Cor. of High

H كوٹلا कोटला koṭ'lā, n. m. Dim. of koṭ.

A place where the property of a temple is kept, and its affairs are managed; a chapter.

H كوٹهي कोठी koṭ'hī, n. f. Pālī, koṭṭham.

1. A factory.
2. A banking house; a bank.
3. (Panj. chhallā koṭhī) A house of call; a bawdy house. 4. The womb.

H كوري कोरी kor'ī, n. f.

Assesment upon four heads—plough, head-money, hearth-money, and cattle.

korī-bandī, n. f. 1. A new arrangement.
2. A list of villages or fields to be registered according to an allotment.

H كوڑا कूड़ा kūṛ'ā, kūhṛā, kūṛā karkaṭ; Tir. kūṛh, n. m. 1. Sweepings; rubbish.
2. Share; lot.

H كوڑنا कोड़ना koṛ'nā, E.; koṛab, Tir.; kholau, Sant. v.a. To dig; scoop; bore; hollow; excavate; turn up (the soil).

H كوڑهي कूढ़ी kūṛh'ī, kūḍhī, n. f.

1. A heap of corn. 2. A household; family.
3. A house tax. 4. A share.

H كوڑي कौड़ी kauṛ'ī, n. f. Cowrie.

kauṛī kauṛī adā k., chukānā, yā denā, v. a. To pay every penny.

kauṛī kauṛī bhar pānā, v. n. To receive in full.

kauṛī kauṛī lenā, v. a. 1. To exact every farthing. 2. To be paid in full.

H كوڑے لگانا कोड़े लगाना koṛe lagānā, yā mārnā, v. a. To lash; whip. [sugar mill.

H كولهو कोल्हू kol'hū, n. m. An oil press; a

kolhū meṅ pilvā denā, v. a. To crush in a mill.

zan bachcha kolhū meṅ pilvānā. A native punishment of crushing a whole family in a mill.

H كوليت कौलियत kaulī'yat, n. m.

The taking of lands on lease from one Ryot by another, or the cultivation of them by other than the party who rents them.

H كومار कोमार komār', n. Lands cultivated by contract, having no tenant. *Carnegy.*

E كونسل kauṅ'sal, n. f. Cor. of Counsel.

kauṅsal k., v. a. 1. To consult; advise with; take counsel. 2. To plot; intrigue.

kauṅs'lī, kauslī, n. m. A counsellor; barrister.

H كويري कोयरी ko'ērī, E.; koer, kabāri, Tir. A Hin. caste of cultivators. [ledger.

H كهاتا खाता khāt'ā, n. m. 1. An account; a
2. A merchant's or banker's book (bahī, 2).

khātā ḍālnā, v. a. To open accounts with.

khātā k., v. a. To post an account; adjust accounts. [ful recoveries.

gāl khātā, n. m. Irrecoverable balance; doubt-

khāte bāqī. Balance of account.

khāte parnā, v. n. To be entered in an account.

H كهاد खाद khād, n. f. S. खाद to eat. An advance made to cultivators for food.

khād bīj, n. m. Advances to cultivators for food and seed.

كهادر खादर khād'ar; Tir. khādī; Panj. bet, n. f. Opp. of bāṅgar.

Low alluvial land habitually saturated by the drainage from higher levels.

H كهار لگنا खार लगना khār lagnā, v. n. To be impregnated with alkaline salts (land).

khārī-pan, n. f. Brackishness. [with alkali.

khārī miṭṭī, n. f. Saline soil; soil impregnated

khārī non, yā namak. Alkaline salt; a kind of sulphate of soda, used in medicine and for the adulteration of common salt.

H كهالا खाला khāl'ā, khāl, n. m. S. खल्ल
1. Low land full of ravines. 2. A rivulet; creek; inlet; watercourse; a gully.

H كهانا खाना khā'nā, khā jānā; Tir. khāib; Sant. jom, v. a. S. खाद, Pr. khāi. To embezzle; misappropriate; (Sant. ghus jom) take a bribe.

khāū, adj. One who takes bribes.

H كهتيانا खतियाना khatiyā'nā; Tir. khatiyāib, v. a. To enter in the ledger.

khatau'nī; Bhoj. khatiavnī, n. f.

An account of the total village lands, with particulars of their distribution.

H كهدني खुदनी khud'nī, n. f. 1. Digging.
2. Mining. 3. Search for treasure.

khudnī k., v. a. To search by digging.

H كهرا खर्रा khar'rā; n. m. A schedule; memorandum of transactions; rough account.

H كهرا खरा khar'ā, kharī, adj. 1. Unalloyed.
2. Sound; sterling; standard.
3. Unadulterated; pure.
4. Good; valid.

kharā khoṭā. Good and bad.

khare khure, adj. Without commission; nett.

H کھرپلٹا खुरपलटा *khur-palṭā*, n. m. An Indian gipsy tribe who trade in cattle by turning feeble old oxen into young looking and strong ones which find a ready sale.

H کھریل खुरैल *khurail'*, n. Soil broken up for sowings. *Carnegy.*

H کھڑک खड़क *kha'ṛak, khiṛak*, n. m. 1. A cowshed; sheepfold. 2. A pound for cattle.

کھڑے رکھنا *khaṛī-rakhnā*, v. a. To strike a balance. [crop.

H کھڑي کھيتي *khaṛī khetī*, n. f. A standing

dām khaṛe k., v. a. To sell off; realize.

H کھليت खलैत *khalait'*, n. m. 1. (*khilāṛī*) A gambler. 2. A petty thief; a pickpocket.

zahr khilānā, v. a. To administer poison.

H کھنٹيتي खुंटैती *khunṭai'tī*, n. f.

Payment of revenue according to the ancestral shares, without reference to the actual condition or produce of the shares.

H کھوٹ खोट *khoṭ*, n. m. कूट 1. An alloy. 2. Vice. 3. Immorality.

khoṭ milānā, v. a. To mix with a base metal.

کھوٹا खोटा *khoṭ'ā, khoṭī*, adj.

1. Defective; faulty. 2. False; spurious; base. 3. Vicious; corrupt; malignant. 4. Dishonest; unfair; fraudulent. 5. Perfidious; treacherous. 6. Malicious; revengeful.

khoṭā irādah. A sinister design.

khoṭā rāj, n. m. Mal-administration.

khoṭā sikkā. False coin.

khoṭā kharā dekhnā, v. a. To distinguish good from bad. [transaction.

khoṭā muāmilah. Unfair dealing; a dishonest

khoṭī tadbīr. Machination; crooked policy.

khoṭī kharī, n. f. Abusive language.

khoṭī hunḍī, n. f. A fraudulent note or bill.

H کھوج खोज *khoj*, n. m.

Trace. See سراغ, پتا 1, and تلاش.

khoj lagānā, v. n. 1. To trace; track; follow up a clue. 2. To search; search about.

khoj miṭānā, yā malyā meṭ k., v. a. To destroy the foot prints; leave no trace.

khoj nikālnā, v. a. To trace stolen property.

کھوجي खोजी *khoj'ī*, n. m. See سراغي. A tracker; detective.

H کھود खूद *khūd*, n. f. See خويد [stocks. (?)

H کھوڑا खोड़ा *khoṛ'ā*, n. Handcuffs; manacles;

H کھوکھا खोखा *kho'khā, thothā*, n. m. S. कोटर A paid bill of exchange kept as a voucher.

H کھو کھي खूखी *khūkh'ī*; Māṛ. *khaparyo*, n. Small insects appearing in wheat and barley after heavy rains and producing a red blight.

H کھونٹ खूंट *khūṅṭ*, n. f. S. कोण

1. A share in the lands of a village by hereditary descent, with all the rights and privileges which it comprehends.

2. A tax leviable on timber. *Carnegy.*

3. Each division pays the same amount of revenue without reference to the state of cultivation, number of sharers, or other circumstances. *Carnegy.*

khūṅṭ khat. A deed of mortgage under which the mortgager parts not only with his share of the *khūṅṭ bāṭ* land, but also with all the rights and privileges attached to them.

khūṅṭ-baṭ Tenancy in common by ancestral shares.

H کھوندنا खूंदना *khūṅd'nā, khundalnā*, v.a. खुद trample upon. To work with the feet (روندنا).

H کھوندر खोंदर *khoṅd'ar, khobṛā*, n. m.

Gleanings or leavings on the threshing floor.

H کھوئي खोई *khoī, khoiyā*, n.f. 1. Husks; refuse. 2. The refuse of sugarcane, used as fuel.

H کھيپ खेप *khep*, n. f. S. क्षेप

1. A load; cargo; shipment; an assortment. 2. A piece of base metal inserted in a coin; cracked coin. (?)

khep bharnā, yā lādnā, v. a. To load.

khep hārnā, v. n. To sustain a loss.

kauṛī khep, yā pherā, Earth work paid at the rate of one *kauṛī* per basket-full.

H کھيت खेत *khet*; Old. H. *chhetr*, n. m. S. क्षेत्र Pr. *chhettam*; Pālī, *khettam*. 1. A field. 2. Ground; land. 3. Breed; caste.

khet bāṅṭ. A disposition of fields where the lands of two villages are completely intermixed with each other. *Carnegy.*

khet patr, yā khat, n. m. A mortgage of a field.

khet chiṭṭhā, n. m. A rough field-book.

khet-dār, n. m. The occupant or owner of a field.

khet kāṭnā, v. a. To reap a field.

khet k., v. To cultivate; till (land).

khet kamānā, v. n. To manure land.

khet nikālnā, v. n. To clear land. [field.

khet nalānā, narānā, yā nikānā, v. a. To weed a

khet-vār, adv. By fields.

The assessment is made upon each separate field according to its quality and the description of crop grown in it.

khetvār jama bandī, n. f. The amount of revenue assessed upon each field.

bīt khet, n. m. Land cultivated by forced labor.

کھيتي खेती *khet'ī*, n. f. Sown lands; corn-fields; crops.

khetī bāṛī, khetī kyārī, khetī, n. f. *khet kyār, khet karm,* n. m. Husbandry (*bo-jot*).
khetī bāṛī, khetī, khet, yā khet kyār k. To till; cultivate.
khetī-jog, adj. Arable; culturable.
khetī-yār, n. m. A cultivator; husbandman; peasant.
agaitī khetī. Early crops.
pichhaitī khetī. Latter crops.
harī khetī, n. f. Unripe crops.
kharī khetī; A. *fasl-i-estādah.* Standing crops.

H کهیڑا खेड़ा *kheṛ'ā;* Sant. *ḍih,* n. m. S. खेट A small village; a hamlet.
kheṛā basānā, 1. To people a village. 2. A mound indicating the site of a deserted village.
kheṛā-patī, n. m. 1. A Brahman entitled to perform certain religious ceremonies and to receive the fees appertaining thereto.
2. The head man of a village.

H کهینٹنا खेंटना *kheṅṭ'nā,* v. a. To turn over (grain).

H کهیوا खेवा *khe'vā,* n. m. S. क्षेप्य. 1. Crossing a river. 2. Ferry-money; boat fare; passage money.

H کهیوت खेवट *khev'aṭ,* n. f. H. *khet* field.
1. Assigned quotas of revenue.
2. Record of village shares; a record or register of shares in which a coparcenary village is divided; register of mutations; administration paper.
khevaṭ-dār, n. m. The holder of a share in a co-parcenary village.
khevaṭ khatauni, n. f. An account of the village management; the distribution of lands and rights of the occupants.

H کیت केत *ket, kait,* n. f. A strap or thong used in the courts for flagellation.

H کیت कैत *kait;* Farrukh. *kaithā;* Bhoj. *kaṅiti,* n. m. S. कपित्थ.
An intoxicating drink made from the fruit.

A کیف *kaif,* n. m. An intoxicating drug.

A کیفیت *kaifi'yat, kaifyat,* n. f. کیف to be.
1. Condition. 2. A statement; return.
3. Remarks.
kaifīyat-i-akhrājāt. Bill of charges.
kaifīyat banānā, v. a. To draw out a schedule, etc.
kaifīyat-i-band o bast, v. a. A particular statement of revenue assessments, or any other settlement.
kaifīyat bahī. Account books; note book.
kaifīyat talab k., v. a. To call for information, explanation, or report.
kaifīyat kā khānā, n. m. The column of Remarks.
kaifīyat kāmil. Full particulars.
kaifīyat likhnā, v. a. To make a report or record.
kaifīyat-i-muāmilah, yā muqaddamah, The facts, circumstances, or merits of a case.
kaifīyat-i-nāzir. The nāzir's return.
kaifīyat-i-vāqah. A statement; an account.
kaifīyat hast o būd. A comparative statement.
amar-i-mushtabah ki kaifīyat. G. G. A statement of the matter in question.
ta roz guzarne kaifīyat tāmīl-i-hukm-nāmah-i-qurqī. G. G. Until the return can be made to such warrant of distress.

H کیلیا कीलिया *kīl'iyā,* n. m. The man who drives the oxen at a well.

H کینڈا कैंडा *kaiṅ'ḍā,* n. m. 1. A rough plan.
2. Pattern; model.
kaiṅḍā k., v. a. To make a rough measurement.

گ

H گابها गाभा *gābh'ā, gābh,* n. m.
Unripe crop; half-ripe ears of corn.

H گاٹا गाटा *gāṭ'ā, gāṭah,* n. m.
1. A piece of land; a plot. 2. Yoking bullocks together to tread out grain. 3. A sect of Baniyās, or inferior Brahmans.
gāṭā-bandī, n. f. Division of a village by *Gāṭās.*
It is a peculiar kind of tenure under which the fields of individual proprietors are not found in juxtaposition, but scattered through many villages.

H گاجا गाजा *gāj'ā,* n. The first sowing of rice at the foot of the hills, which takes place in the month *Baisākh.*

H گالی गाली *gāl'ī;* Brij and Poet. *gārī;* Rus. *gal,* n. f. S. गालि Abusive language; abuse.
gālī denā, v. a. To abuse; call names.
gālī galauj, yā gālam galauj k., gālī galauj se pesh ānā, v. n. To abuse one.

H گانٹھ गांठ *gāṅṭh';* Bhoj. *gāṅṭhī;* Sant. *ghent,* n. f. S. ग्रन्थि Pālī, *gantho.* A knot; tie.
gāṅṭh-dār, gāṅṭhi-dār, n.
An occupant of lands under a landlord at a fixed rent and by heritable tenure.

گانٹھا गांठा *gāṅṭh'ā,* n. m.
The knotted parts of the stalk and the ear-ends of straw separately piled on the threshing floor; the colder of English agriculture; grain mixed with straw.

H گانجها गांझा *gāṅjh'ā, gāṅjā,* n. m. S. गञ्जिका or गञ्जाविका The hemp plant; *Cannabis sativa.* The leaves, called *bhaṅg* and *sabzī,* are intoxicating.

H گانڑ गांड़ *gāṅṛ,* n. f. The anus.

gāṅṛ mārnā, v. a. Slang. To commit sodomy.
gāṅṛ marānā, Slang, v. n.
To suffer sodomy, as a catamite.
gāṅṛ-marānī, A strumpet. (An abuse).
gāṅṛ-maravval, Slang, n. f. Reciprocal sodomy; unnatural gratification.

H گانو गांव *gāṅv, gāṅo, gāṅoṅ, gāoṅ, gāoṅ goṭ, gāoṅ gavīṅ*; Rus. *gām*; Sant. *āto*, n. m. S. ग्राम Pālī, *gām'ako*. A village.

In some parts of India villages are primarily divided into a certain number of nominal integral parts, usually twenty, which are called *bisvās*, and then again into fractions of twentieths, termed *bisvāṅsis* and *karvāṅsis*. The portions are distributed among the representatives of the original proprietor or proprietors, constituting the proprietary shares, termed *paṭṭīs*. The *paṭṭī* is divisible according to the number of the heirs of a *paṭṭī-dār* into smaller portions, called *thoks, tholas*, or *ḍheris*, and these may again be subdivided into smaller shares, termed *behris*. *Thok* is sometimes convertible into *paṭṭī*.

gāṅo asthān, n.m. The site of a village, whether in ruins or still standing.
gāṅo bāṅṭ, n. f. Division of villages.

The division of an estate into separate villages, or of the several additional or subordinate (*dākhilī*) villages attached to the one originally assessed. Also, the division of a village by parcels or plots of land, some of which may be scattered among the fields of several other villages.

gāṅo-jan, n. m. The village community.
gāṅo-kharch. Municipal or village charges or expenses.
gāṅo kā uṭhāo, gāṅo kharch, malbā, gauṅṭā, The municipal expenses of a village; village charges. [lage expenses.
gāṅv kā kharchā muqarrarah. Authorized vil-
gāṅo kī ābādī.
The cultivation or population of a village.
gāṅo kī nikāsī. Assets from land.
gāṅo ke kāgazāt. Village papers or accounts.
gāṅo gāṅo ke baste. The records of each village.
gāṅo-gannā. By villages; distributively, as village assessments.
gāṅo-vālā, A villager. [head man of a village.
گونٹیا गोंटिया *goṅṭ'iyā*; Bhoj. *gauṅāṅ*, n. m. The

P H گاوچرای *gāo-charāī*, n. f. 1. Grazing.
2. Grazing or pasture ground. 3. A tax levied on pasture land; a charge for grazing.

P گاوشماري *gāo-shumārī*, 1. An enumeration of cattle. 2. A tax upon cattle.

P گاوكشي *gāo-kushī*, n. f.
Killing kine; slaughter of cows.

H گاوگهپ *gāo-ghap, gāū-ghap, ghāū ghap*; Bhoj. *ghauā ghap*, n.m. 1. Embezzlement (غبن).
2. One who embezzles.

gāo ghap k., v.a. To embezzle (*gaban k.*). [corn.

H گاہٹا गाहटा *gāh'ṭā, gāh*, n. Treading out

H گاہک गाहक *gāh'ak*; Bhoj.; *gaṅhkī*; Sant. *ki rin ko*, n. m. S. ग्राहक from ग्रह to take.
A purchaser (خریدار). [action.

گاہکي गाहकी *gāh'akī, gāhikī*, n. f. Sale; trans-
gāhikī paṭnā, v. n. To be concluded (a sale).

H گاہن गाहन *gāh'an*, n.m. S. ग्रह to take.
A harrow with teeth for eradicating grass from ploughed land. [to move.

H گاہنا गाहना *gāh'nā*; Tir. *dingāib*, v.a. S. गाह
To thrash or tread out corn.

H گاہي गाही *gāh'ī*, E. n. f. A total of five.
Counting by *gāhīs* is counting by fives.

H گبھوني गभूनी *gabhūn'ī, garat bhūmī, goind, gauhānī*, n. f. Land round the village. *Carnegy*.

H گپت गुप्त *gupt*, Hidden.
gupt-āmdanī, n. f. Income from a hidden source, as bribes, etc.
gupt māl, n. m. Hidden wealth or treasure.
گپتي गुप्ती *gupt'ī*, n. f. A sword-stick.
guptī chalānā, v. a. To stab secretly.

H گپسا गपसा *gap'sā*, n. m. Hard whitish soil.

H گٹھ गठ *gaṭh*, n. Cont. of *gāṅṭh*, q. v.
gaṭh-bandh chorī, n. Gang robbery.
gaṭh-joṛā, gaṭh-bandhan; Tir. *geṭh-jorvā*, n. m.
Tying the knot.
A Hin. marriage ceremony, at which the mantles of the bride and bridegroom are fastened together.
gaṭh-kaṭā; Tir. *geṭh-kaṭṭā*, n. m.
1. A pick-pocket; a cutpurse.
2. One who cuts open parcels.
gaṭh-kaṭī, n. f. Pick-pocketing.
گٹھا गट्ठा *gaṭ'ṭhā*; Gaṛh. *gaḍaro*, n.m.
1. A package; load.
2. The 20th part of a *jarīb*, each *gaṭhā* containing three *ilāhī gaz*, q. v.
gaṭhrī mārnā, v.a. To rob; plunder.
گٹھوانسي गठवांसी *ghaṭhvāṅ'sī*, n. f.
1-20th of a *gatthā*, q. v.

گٹھونڈ गठौंद *gaṭhauṅd'*, n. m.
A pledge or deposit tied up in a bag.

H گٹھاني गठानी *gaṭhān'ī*, n. f. A tax levied by *zamīṅdārs* on cultivators.

H گجھا गझा *gaj'jhā*, n. m.
P. *ganj*. 1. A heap; store. 2. Wealth.
gajjhā dabā baiṭhnā, gajjhā mārnā, v. n.
To obtain fraudulently.

H گدھوئی गदघोई *gaddho'ī*; W. *ḍhūlā*; Sant. *ḍhui*, n. f. A boundary mark.

H گدھے پر چڑھانا *gadhe par chaṛhānā yā savār k.*, a. v. To put one on an ass.

A punishment in native states. The culprit had to sit with his face blackened, and turned towards the tail; hence, to disgrace a person.

H *guddī se zabān nikālnā*, v.a. To extract one's tongue. (A punishment in the East).

H *grām-adhikārī*, n.m. The headman of a village.

H گراوا गरावा *garāv'ā*, n. A light poor soil.

H گربھ गर्भ *garbh, garabh, garb, garab*, n. m. S. ग्रह to conceive, Pāli, *gabbo*.

(Sant. *asiaṛ hoṛmo*) Pregnancy.

garabh-ādhān, n. m. A ceremony performed on the first indications of pregnancy, one of the *sanskāras* or essential rites of Hinduism.

garbh-pāt, garbh-pātan, Miscarriage; abortion.

garbh-pāt k., garabh girānā; Sant. *dasāo giḍi*, v. a. To cause or procure abortion.

garbh-pāt h., yā girnā, v. n. To miscarry.

garbh rahnā, garabh se h., v. n. To be pregnant.

garbh men paṛnā, v. n. To conceive.

garbh-vantī, garbhanī; Sant. *gorobīā hor*, adj. Pregnant; with child.

P گرد آور *gird-āv'ar*, n. m.

A customs' patrol; a watch; a superintendent or inspector of police or customs.

گرد آوري *gird-āv'arī*, n. f. 1. Collecting; bringing together. 2. Watching; guarding.

3. Looking after smugglers or contraband goods. 4. Division; beat.

gird-āvarī k., v. a. To patrol; go one's rounds.

P H گرد اڑائي *gard-uṛāī*, n. f.

A tax formerly levied on travellers.

P H گرز مار *gurz-mār*, n. m. A Mah. Faqir who carries a club armed with spikes with which he wounds himself to extort alms.

P گرفتار *giraftār'*; Rus. *giraphdār*, adj.

Arrested; seized.

giraftār-kar saknā, G .G. v. n.

To be authorized to apprehend.

giraftār k., v. a. To apprehend; seize; capture.

giraftār h., v. n. 1. To become a prisoner.

ashkhās-i-giraftār-shudā. G. G.

The persons arrested.

گرفتاري *giraftār'ī*; Rus. *giraphdārī*, n. f.

1. Seizure; arrest.

2. Captivity; imprisonment; bondage.

giriftārī jāiz. G. G. Lawful apprehension.

girftārī qabl faisala. Arrest before judgment.

giriftārī kā parvānah, hukm, yā v ārant.

The order or warrant for arrest.

giraftārī kā hukm jārī h.

To be issued (a warrant of arrest).

giraftārī kī darkhuāst k. G.G. To apply for arrest.

giraftārī māl-i-mahsūlī, n. f.

Seizure of smuggled goods.

giraftārī-i-mufsidāṅ. Apprehension of rioters.

H گرکھئي गुरखै *gurkha'ī*, n. f. A mortgage where the mortgager has to pay ¾th of the revenue of the mortgaged land. *Carnegy*.

P گروه *gir'oh*, n. m. See جماعت (1, 2, 3).

1. A collection or party of men; a gang.

2. A class; order.

giroh-i-shurakā, n. m. A community of sharers.

ādmiyoṅ kā giroh. G. G. A mob.

ḍākuoṅ kā giroh. G. G. A gang of dacoits.

sāriqon yā ḍākuoṅ kā avārah giroh.

A wandering gang of thieves.

H گروئي गिरुई *girūi'*, n. f. A red fungus which robs the grain of the sap as it ascends (*rolī*).

P گروي *gir'vī, girvīṅ, girvīṅ gānṭhā*; Cor. of P. *girau*, T. *garob, garov*.

The thing pledged or pawned (*bandhak*,2).

girvī-patr, girvī-nāmah, A mortgage deed.

girvī-dār, n. m. The holder of a pledge or mortgage.

girvī rakhnā, gahne rakhnā, v. a. To pawn or [pledge.

girvī rakhne-vālā, n. m. 1. A mortgager.

2. A mortgagee; pawn-broker.

girvī se chhuṛānā, Redemption (*fak-ur-rahn*).

girvī zabtī, n. Foreclosure of a mortgage.

H گرہستن ग्रहस्तन *grahast'an, girastan*, n. f.

A married woman; a housewife.

گرہستي ग्रहस्तो *grahast'ī*; Pop. *girhastī, girastī*, n. m. ग्रहस्थ; Pālī, *gahaṭṭho*. See *dunyā-dār*.

1. One who lives and marries; a householder. 2. A husbandman.

H گرينيا गरेनिया *garen'iyā, gahnīā*, n. m.

Land mortgaged for a time or until the loan is repaid by the rents.

H گڑابٹائي गड़ाबटाई *gaṛābaṭā'ī*, n. f.

A division of a crop by stacking the sheaves in shares.

H گڑھي بند गढ़ी बन्द *gaṛhī-band*. A *muāfī* tenure by which lands are held at a fixed yearly tribute much under their value.

H گڑھے بيٹھنا *gaṛhe baiṭhnā, yā gāṛhe baiṭhnā, Ṭhags*, v. n. To be concealed; to lie in ambush.

P A گزرعام *guzar-ām, guzargāh-i-ām, guzargāh*, n. A public road; highway; thoroughfare.
haq-i-guzar, n. m. Right of way.

P گزري *guz'arī*; Pop. *gudṛī*, n. f. A market held in the afternoon by the road side.

P گشت *gasht*, n.m. گشتن to roam. See پهيري 1. The beat or round of a patrol, or watch.
gasht phirnā, lagānā, mārnā, yā k., v. a. To patrol; go the rounds.
gasht-salāmī, gashtī, n. f. A tax or fee levied on their tours by public officers under native governments.
gasht mahāl, n. A toll or transit duty formerly levied on boats.
gashtī parvānah, yā hukm. A circular order.

H گلا गुला *gul'ā*, (Butchers) One anna.

H گلاكاٹنا *galā kāṭnā*, v.a. To cut one's throat.

H گلتنس गलतंस *galtaṅs'*; Bhoj. *galitavaṅs*, n. m. Dying without issue. *Carnegy.*

H گلٹوا دينا *galṭuā denā*, v. a. To throttle; strangle; suffocate.

H گلدب كرنا *gal-ḍab k.*, Slang. v. a. To embezzle; bag.

H گل لگنا *gal lagnā*, v. n. To be hanged (*phāṅsī pānā*).

H گلنس गलंस *gal'aṅs*, n. m. H. *galnā* to melt. A lapsed share escheating to the community in default of heirs of the original shareholder. *Carnegy.*

P گما شتہ *gumāsh'tah*, n. m. گماشتن to appoint. A deputy; representative; agent; correspondent (*kār-pardāz*).
gumāshtah-i-qānūṅgo, n. m. The agent or deputy of the *qānūngo*, or village registrar and accountant.
gumāshtah k. To appoint a manager.
gumāshtah-garī, n. f. 1. Agency; office of an agent. 2. Commission.

P A گمان غالب *gumān-i-gālib, yā qavī*, n. m. Strong probability.
گمان ہے *gumān hai.* It is expected or likely.

H گميني गमीनी *gamīn'ī, būṭī*, W.; *kamīnī*, E. n.f. The duties of barbers and *pirohits*, or the fees paid to them for taking messages or presents to distant friends.

P گنا ہگاري *gunāh-gārī*, n. f. 1. Sinfulness; criminality; guiltiness. 2. Forfeit; mulct (*tāvān*). 3. Loss; deficit. 4. Revenue derived from judicial fines.
gunāh-gārī denā, v. a. To pay a fine, etc.
be-gunāh ṭhairānā, v. a. To exculpate; acquit.

H گنٹھ गुंठ *guṅṭh*, n. Rent-free lands given for religious purposes, as the endowment of a temple. *Carnegy.*

P گنجايش *gunjā'yash*, n. f. 1. Room.
2. Profit (اوت, 1.).
3. The revenue capabilities of a village.
adāē jama kī gunjāish rakhnā. To be able to bear assessment.

P گندم رنگ *gandum-raṅg, gandum-gūṅ, gandumī*; Tir. *gahūmī-raṅg*, adj. Brownish yellow; tawny.

S گندهرب بواہ *gandharb bivāh.* A marriage contracted without the usual ceremonies; a kind of Scotch marriage.

H گنگا جلي اٹهانا *gaṅgā-jalī uṭhānā, gaṅgā kī qasam khānā, gangā kī mānī paiṅḍ bharnā*; Bhoj. *gangā-pial*, v. n. To swear on the water of the Ganges.
gaṅgā-jamnā, n. m. A mode of adjusting the interest of a loan, the debtor being credited with the interest of the instalments paid by him, while he is debited *per contra* with the interest on the full amount of the original loan.

گنگالہ गङ्गाला *gaṅgā'lā*; Bhoj. *gangolh*, n. m. Lands subject to inundations of the Ganges.
gang barāmad jadīd. Newly recovered lands; fresh increments of land.

گنگ برار *gaṅṛ-barār, gaṅg-bar-āmad*, n. m. Alluvial land recovered from a river, especially from the Ganges; alluvion; land reclaimed from a river; newly-formed land.
gaṅg-shikāst, gaṅg-shiknī. Diluvion; lands cut away by the encroachment of a river; encroachment of the Ganges or any other river.

H گو गौ *gau*, n. f. A cow.
گوڑهي *gauṛ'hī*, n. m. Pasturage.
gaū-kos, n. m. A land measure, being the distance at which the lowing of a cow can be heard.

H گوادري गवादरी *gawādar'ī*, n. f. A subordinate heritable and transferable tenure acquired from the superior proprietor by Brahmans in E. Gāzīpur. *Carnegy.*

H گواند गोइन्द *goind*; Bhoj. *goĕṅḍ*, n. f. The manured land round the village.

P گواه *gav'āh, gavāh-shāhid*; Rus. *guāh, ugāh*; Sant. *gohā*, n.m.pl. گوا ہان A witness.
gavāh banānā, yā ṭhairānā, v. a. To name a person as a witness.
gavāh-i-tālīmī, sikhāyā yā paṛhāyā gavāh, A tutored witness.
gavāh-i-hāshiyah, yā mundarjā dastāvez, A marginal witness; an attesting witness.
gavāh denā, v. a. To produce a witness.
gavāh-i-rūyat, gavāh-i-chashm-dīd, ainī, yā mashāhdā, An eye-witness (*sākshī*, 3).
gavāh-i-samāī, n. m. A hearsay witness.
gavāh-i-aqd-i-nikāh, n. A witness to a marriage contract.
gavāh k., v. a. To make one a witness.
gavāh ko paṛhānā, yā sikhānā. To instruct a witness.
gavāh muddaī, A witness for the prosecution.
gavāh-i-muddāilah, n.m. A witness for the defence.
gavāhoṅ kī ism-navīsī. A list of witnesses.
گواہی *gavāh'ī, gavāhī shāhidī*; Rus. *guāhī, ugāhī*, n. f. Deposition; written testimony; testimony; evidence.
gavāhī denā, v. a. To depose; give evidence; testify; bear witness to; witness; bear testimony.
gavāhī likhnā, yā k., To witness a document; to attest.
gavāhī-likhī huī. Evidence taken.
gavāhī mārfat dūsre ke. Second-hand evidence.
jhūṭe gavāh banānā, v. a. To produce false witnesses.

H A گوپ محال *gop-mahāl*, n. 1. The cowherds' quarter. 2. Pasture ground.

H گوپیا **गोपिया** *gop'iyā*, W.; *guphnā*, Farrukh.; *ḍhelvāṅs*, E.; *genḍwaṛ*, Sant. n. m. S. **गोफणा** A sling, esp. one used in a field of corn to drive away cattle, birds, etc.

H گوت **गोत** *got, gotrā*; Bhoj. *gotar*, n.m.S. **गोत्र**
1. Lineage (اصل 5). 2. A family; a tribe.

H گوتارا **गोतारा** *gotār'ā*, n. m. Rich lands immediately adjacent to the village.

H گوتھ **गोथ** *goth*, n. m. A yoke.

H گوٹ بستي **गोट बस्ती** *goṭ bastī*, n. f. A village site.

H گوجر **गूजर** *gūj'ar*, n. m. *gūjrī*, n. f. S. **गोचारक** 1. A cowherd; a milkman. 2. An inferior Hin. caste chiefly engaged in agriculture, and notorious for cattle-stealing.

H گوجرا **गोजरा** *goj'rā*; Bhoj. *gojaī*; Mār. *gojyūṅ*, n. m. Cont. of *gehūṅ jau-vālā*.
1. A mixture of wheat and barley. 2. A crop of wheat and barley grown together.

S گوچر **गोचर** *go-char*, n. m.
1. Extent of pasture ground. 2. Range of vision or mind. 3. (Rus.) Broken and bad ground where cattle mostly graze.

H گوچني **गोचनी** *goch'nī*; Mār. *gulchaṅṛī*, n. f. S. **गोधूम चणक** Cont. of *gehūṅ chanā*.
1. A field of wheat and *chanā* sown together.
2. A mixture of wheat and gram.

H گود **गोद** *god, godī*; Tir. and Bhoj. *korā*; Farrukh. Rus. *kaniyāṅ*; Sant. *koram*, n. f. S. **क्रोड** Adoption of a child.
god denā, v. a. To give one's child to another to adopt.
god lenā, v. a. To adopt one (*mutabannā k.*).

H گوڈنا **गोडना** *goḍ'nā*, Rus.
To have sexual intercourse with.

H گوڈھر **गोढर** *goḍh'ar*, n. m.
Weeds or grasses collected from a ploughed field by the *ḍhīṅkhar*, q. v. (?)

P گور کفن *gor kafan*, Mah. Funeral ceremonies.
gor-kan, n. m. A grave-digger.
gor gaṛhā k., v. a. To perform the funeral obsequies.

H گورائي **गोराई** *gorā'ī, gorāī zamīn*, n. f.
A mixed soil of sand and earth. *Carnegy.*

H گورب **गूरब** *gūr'ab, gurab*, n. m.
1. Turning up the soil. 2. Deep weeding.

H گورٹ **गोरट** *gor'aṭ*, n. m. Sandy soil.

H گوڑنا **गूड़ना** *gūṛ'nā*; Tir. *hūrab*, v. a.
To thrash; beat corn, etc.

H گوڑھا **गोढ़ा** *goṛ'hā, goṛad*, n.m. The homestead; fields near the village.

H گوڑھل **गूढ़ल** *gūṛ'hal*, Well-beaten or threshed.

H گوڑي **गोड़ी** *goṛ'ī*, n. f. S. **यद्द** take.
Profit; gain.
goṛī k., v. a. 1. To earn; gain; make. 2. To bag; pocket.
goṛī hāth se jānā, v. n. To lose one's prey.

H گوڑيت **गोड़ैत** *goṛait'*, *chaukī-dār, bisarvar, balāhar*; Sant. *goḍet*, n. m.
A village watchman or informer.

P گوش وارہ *gosh-wārah*, n. m.
The abstract of an account.
gosh-wārah-i-qubūliat. Counterpart or acceptance of an abstract account.
gosh-wārah kul. A complete abstract or summary of the whole.

H گول गूल *gūl, gol*; Bhoj. *karhā*, n.m. A channel by which water is conveyed to a field (*barhā*).

H گولک गोलक *gol'ak*, n. m. See غولک 1. A till.
2. A bastard son or daughter by illegitimate connection with a widow.

H گونا गौना *gaun'ā*; Poet. *gavanvāṅ*; Rus. *gauno*; Bhoj. *gavan*; Tir. *dusra gaman*, n. m. S. गमन Bringing home the betrothed wife to her husband's from her father's house when she arrives at the age of puberty; consummation of the marriage (*raunā*).
gaunhār', n. m. The company who attend the husband to bring his child-wife home.
gaunehā'i, gaunāolī, n.f. The child-wife brought to her husband's home.

H گونٹھ गूंठ *gūṅṭh*, n. f. Land assigned rent-free for religious purposes.

H گونجي गौंजी *gauṅj'ī*, E.; *donjī*, Bhoj. n. गोंजी
Fresh shoots of rice put forth after the crop has been cut and cleared. (?)

H گونڑا गोंड़ा *goṅ'ṛā, goṅḍrā*, n.
A reservoir into which water is thrown up from a pond or pool below. (?)

H گوہان गोहान *gauhān'*, n. m.
A village made over by its proprietors to any person on a permanent *jama* with all the privileges of a *zamīndār*.

H گوہاني गोहानी *gauhān'ī, guhānī*, n. m.
1. The entire lands of a village.
2. Lands situated close round a village; (*guhārī*) pasture land.

H گوہائي गोहाई *gohā'ī*, n. f.
Treading out grain by bullocks.

H گوہن गोहन *goh'an, paiṛā*; Mār. *gūṅṛī*, n.
A ramp along which bullocks draw water from a well.

P گویندہ *goin'dah*, p. act of گفتن 1. A speaker.
2. An approver; Queen's evidence. 3. A spy.
goinde kā izhār. The deposition of an approver.

H گھات کرنا *ghāt k.*, v. a. To kill; destroy.
ghāt meṅ baiṭhnā yā rahnā, v. n.
To lie in ambush; lurk; waylay.
گھاتي घाती *ghāt'ī*, adj.
Lurking; intent on taking one's life.

H گھاٹا घाटा *ghāṭ'ā*, n. m. See توٹا
ghāṭā uṭhānā, v. n. See *ṭoṭā uṭhānā*.
ghāṭā bharnā, v. n. To make good a loss or damage.
ghāṭā paṛnā, ānā, yā h. See *ṭoṭā paṛnā*.

H گھاٹ مارا *ghāṭ-mārā, ghāṭ-mār*, n.m. 1. One who evades payment of a toll or duty.
2. A smuggler (*chaukī-mār*).
ghāṭ mārnā, To smuggle dutiable goods (*chaukī mārnā*).

H گھار घार *ghār*, n. Clay soil in low situations, where rainwater lies for a time.

H گہار गुहार *guhār'*, n. f. An unruly mob; rioters.

H گھاس گرینیا घास गिरेनिया *ghās greniā*, n. f. A mortgage redeemable on payment of the principal, the produce going to liquidate the interest. *Carnegy.*

H گھام घाम *ghām, ghāmo*, n. f. S. घर्म्म
1. Sunshine.
2. The operation of causing the green ears of corn to ferment slightly so as to make the seeds separate easily from the husk when threshed. This is done by heaping up the ears as soon as cut, and covering them with straw.

H گھائي घाई *ghā'ī*, n. f. An aggregate of five.

H گھٹاو घटाव *ghaṭā'o*, n. m. See *kamī*.
1. Decrease. 2. Deduction. 3. Falling (of a river, price).
ghaṭāo baṛhāo. Increase and decrease; excess and deficiency.
گھٹتي घटती *ghaṭ'tī, ghaṭī*, n. f. 1. Decrease.
2. Decline; declination.

H گہرا गहरा *gah'rā, gairā*, n. m.
1. A large bundle of sheaves, containing about ten seers of grain. [in harvest time.
2. The daily wages in kind of a labourer
gahre chalo, (*Ṭhags*) Murder the traveller!

H گھربار घरबार *ghar bār*, n. m. 1. A house and premises. 2. Dwelling place. 3. Family; household. 4. Household goods.
ghar phoṛnā, v. a. To break into a house.
ghar jot, n. f. The homestead; the proprietor's own cultivation.
ghar-duārī, n. f. A tax formerly levied on shop-keepers.
ghar kā bāman, n. m. The family priest.
ghar kā bhāṛā, n. m. House-rent.
ghar kā hisāb, n. m. Private accounts.
ghar kā kharch. Household expenditure.
ghar ke log yā ādmī, ghar meṅ se, n. m.
1. The family. 2. The wife.
ghar meṅ paṛnā, v. n. To be lodged or kept in a man's house (as a mistress); to become a kept-mistress.
ghar meṅ ḍālnā, v. a. To keep a woman (as a mistress).

H گھرت घुरत *ghur'at*, E. W. *kharak*, n. m.
Cattle pens.

ghirā'ī, n. f. A fee for feeding cattle.

H گهڑوا घड़वा *ghaṛ'vā, ghaṛuā*, n. m.

(Sant. *baḍhā*) Gleanings from the threshing floor fallen amidst rubbish and dirt, the perquisite of the lowest castes. (?) [forage.

H گهسکر घसकर *ghas-kar*. A tax on grass or

H گهماو घुमावं *ghumā'o*, Panj. n. m.

As much land as can be ploughed by one pair of bullocks in a day.

H گهوٹی घूटी *ghū'ṭī*, n. f. Land which has been under a rice crop. (?)

H P گهوربرار *ghūr barār*, n. Duties levied on every sharer and under-tenant in proportion to the whole expenses incurred during the year (*Bundelkand*). *Elliot.*

H گهوزری घूज़री *ghūz'rī*, n. f. Payments in kind by tenants at will. *Carnegy.*

H گهیروا घेरवा *gher'vā*, n. m.

A mortgage in which land is held as security, and in payment of the interest.

H گیاری ग्यारी *gyār'ī, gyāl*, n. The land of deceased *Bisvedārs* lying unclaimed; land coming under the management of the *mālguzārs* after an *asāmī* deserts his village.

H گیلاڑ गैलड़ *gail'aṛ*; Sant. *dever poṭom*, n. m. *lit.* gone with. A child by a former husband.

ل

A لا *lā*, Hin. *nā*, A neg. particle.

lā-bud, adj. See *zurūr*. 1. Unavoidable; inevitable; certain. 2. Positive (*qataī*).

lā-bud, adv. Infallibly; assuredly (*bilā-shak*).

lā-bud mālūm h., G. G. To consider essential.

lā-hāsil, adj. 1. See *be-kār* (3, 4). 2. Barren; unprofitable; unproductive; abortive; fruitless; bootless. 3. Needless; unavailing.

lā-khirāj, n. f. Rent-free land.

lā-khirāj abvāb jama. Land held at a quit rent.

lā-khirāj bās, n. Ground on which a house is built, held rent-free.

lā-khirāj-dār, n. A holder of rent-free land.

lā-khirāj zamīn. Land exempted from payment of revenue; rent-free land.

lā-dāvā, lā-dāvī dastāvez, n. m. A deed or act of relinquishment; an acquittance; a withdrawal of claim; a deed of surrender; waiver; a deed foregoing a claim, or admitting that there is none.

lā-dāvā likhnā, yā likh denā, v. a.

To resign; forego, abandon, give up, or relinquish a claim. [tible.

lā-rad, adj. Irrefutable; irrefragable, incontes-

lā-ilm, adj. Ignorant; unknowing; unaware.

lā-alam, I dont know. [information.

lā-ilmī, n. f. Ignorance; want or absence of

lā-kalām, adj. 1. Certain; unquestionable; indisputabe; indubitable.

2. Unconditional; fixed.

lā-kalām, lā-raib, adv. Without fail; positively; absolutely; undoubtedly; most assuredly unquestionably; incontestibly.

lā-kalām bāqī, adj.

Undoubted balance or remainder.

lā-vāris, adj. Heirless; having no heir.

lā-vārisī, lā-vārisī māl, n. f. Property to which there is no heir, and which therefore escheats to the state; unclaimed property.

lā-vārisī khutūt, n. Unclaimed letters.

lā-valad, adj. Childless; without issue.

lā-valad marnā, v. n. To die without issue.

H لاٹهی लाठी *lāṭh'ī*; Rus. *laṭṭhī*, n. f. S. यष्टि Pr. *laṭṭhī*. A club; cudgel; bludgeon.

lāṭhī pāṭhī, n. Beating with clubs or sticks.

lāṭhī pongā k., v. a. To fight with clubs.

lāṭhī-vālā, n. m. A club-man.

A man armed with a bludgeon in the pay of *zamīndars*, indigo-planters, and others, employed to fight when serious affrays take place.

A لاحق *lā'haq, lāhiq*, adj. لحق joining.

Adjoining; touching; contiguous.

A لازم *lā'zim*, H. *chāhiye*, adj. لزم being necessary. Bound; compulsory (*lā-bud*, 1).

lāzim ātā hai. It necessarily follows.

lāzim ānā, yā paṛnā, v. n. 1. To become necessary; to follow of necessity.

2. To be incumbent on; to become a duty.

lāzim jānnā, v. n.

To consider necessary or indispensible.

lāzim malzūm, adj. 1. Reciprocal; correlative.

2. Necessary; inseparable. [gatory.

lāzim malzūm k. To make incumbent or obli-

ehtiyāt yā khabar lāzim huī. Was bound to see.

لازمی *lāz'mī*, adj.

Necessary; inevitable; what must be.

H لال پانی *lāl pānī*, n. m.

The menstrual discharge. [stocks.

H لال خاں لکڑا *lāl khāṅ lakṛā*, n. m. The

H لال گولا *lāl golā*, Bund, n. f.

Light reddish sandy soil.

P لام کاف *lām kāf, lām o kāf*; H. *gālī galauj*, n. Cont. of *lāf o gazāf*. Abusive language; abuse. [use bad language.

lām kāf k., v. a. To abuse; give abuse; revile;

H لانا लाना *lān'ā*, W.; *baṭāī-dār*, E.; *sājī-dār*, W. n. m. A confederation of cultivators for a fixed period, cultivating in common, and dividing the proceeds according to ploughs, bullocks, or men.

lānā gulāmoṅ kā gair-amaldārī se aur bechnā yā kharīdnā aise gulāmoṅ kā. G.G. Importation of slaves and sale or purchase of imported slaves. [import as a slave.

gair-mulk se gulām ke taur par lānā. G. G. To

لانابندي लानाबंदी *lānā-bandī*, n. f. Assessment of land according to the number of ploughs employed on it. [money from a debtor.

lānā lagānā, n. m. Taking cattle in lieu of

H لانک लांक *lāṅk, lān*; E. *lār*, n. f. Wheat or any small cereal cut in the straw.

H لاو लाव *lāo*, n. m. 1. The rope by which the leather bucket of a well is drawn up.

In some places the amount of land irrigated is reckoned by the *lāo*, instead of wells, being commonly 15 acres to a *lāo*.

2. The quantity of land irrigated by one *lāo* in a day. 3. The cable of a boat.

4. Demand; request.

5. A debt secured by a pledge.

lāo uṭhānā, v. n. To advance money to a cultivator for food, fodder, and seed.

lāo charas, n. Irrigation by water raised from wells in the bucket called *Charas*.

It is called *purhāī* when cattle are used, and *garrā* when manual labor is employed. *Carnegy.*

lāo chalānā, v. n. To irrigate from a well.

lāo lagānā, v. n. To assert a right to, and take over from a debtor property of any kind in satisfaction of a debt.

lāo lagānā, n.m. Payment in kind. [cut the crops.

H لاوا लावा *lāv'ā*, n.m. A laborer employed to

H لاوني लावनी *lāv'nī, lāonī, lāunī*, E. n. f. S. लू to cut. Pr. *lunaī*. 1. (W. *lāī*) Cutting the crops; reaping. 2. Wages in kind to reapers in harvest time.

3. Proceeds from land; rental; revenue.

lāonī k., E.; *lāī ko jānā*, W. v. a. To cut the crops; to reap.

A لايق *lā'yaq*, adj. لبق doing right. Worthy; competent; capable.

lāyaq-i-etibār, adj. Credible; worthy of credit.

lāyag banjar; Ped. for H. *honhār banjar*, Waste land fit for tillage. [tention.

lāyaq-i-pizīrāī, adj. Worthy of reception or at-

lāyaq-i-pasand, adj. Eligible; fit to be chosen.

lāyaq-i-phāṅsī h., Ped. for H. *phāṅsī ke kām k.*, v. n. 1. To deserve death.

2. To be liable to capital punishment.

lāyaq-i-tahsīn; H. *mān'ne-jog*, adj. Admissible; that may be accepted, granted, or conceded.

lāyaq-i-kafālat, G. G. adj. Bailable.

lāyaq-i-sazā; H. *shāshan-jog*, adj. Penal.

lāyaq-i-shādī; H. *bar-jog*, adj. Marriageable.

lāyaq taur se. Properly; suitably.

lāyaq-i-uzr, adj. 1. Excusable. 2. Objectionable; open to objection. [consideration.

lāyaq-i-iltifāt, iltifāt ke lāyaq, adj. Worthy of

lāyaq qubūl ke nahīṅ. Inadmissible; that which cannot be received or entertained.

lāyaq-mand, lāyaq-vālā, Illit. Worthy.

lāyaq h., v. n. 1. To deserve; merit; to be worthy of. 2. To become; suit; fit; answer.

qānūnan jurm ke lāyaq. G. G. Capable by law of committing an offence.

ghaṭāē jāne ke lāyaq, G. G. Liable to abate.

A لباس *libās'*, n. m. لبس clad. 1. Apparel; raiment; vestment; costume; habit.

ba-tagaiyur-i-libās jānā, G. G., H. *bhes badal-ke jānā*. To go in disguise. [apparent.

لباسي *libāsī*, adj. See *du-bhes*. 1. Formal; 2 Fictitious; counterfeit; sham (*jālī*, 2).

H لپاڈکي लप्पा डुक्की *lap'pā-ḍuk'kī*, n. f. Scratching and biting; a tussle; boxing; fighting.

lappā-ḍuk'kī k. To fight; have a set to.

H لٹنا लुटना *luṭ'nā*; Tir. *lūṭal geṭ*, v. n. S. लुट 1. To be plundered; robbed 2. To be cheated, defrauded. 3. To be ruined, undone

H لٹھ लठ *laṭh*, n. m. S. यष्टि or लष्टि 1. A club; cudgel. 2. A measuring rod or pole.

In the N.-W. P. the measuring chain (*jarīb*) is divided into 10 *laṭṭhās* or *gaṭṭhas*, and each *laṭṭhā* into 10 *karis* links. A *bīghā* is a square of 20 *laṭṭhās*.

laṭh-bāzī, n. Club-fighting.

laṭh chalnā, v. n. To fight with clubs.

لٹھیت लठैत *laṭhait'*, adj. Carrying a club. [man.

laṭhait', *laṭh-bāz*, n.m. A clubman; a bludgeon-

H لٹیرا लुटेरा *luṭer'ā*, n. m. S. लुट 1. A freebooter; highwayman. 2. A swindler.

H لجھڑي लिझड़ी *lijh'ṛī*, n.f. The after-birth; the *placenta*.

H: لچا लुच्चा *luch'chā*, n. m. *luchchī*, n. f. S. लुच्छ See بدمعاش 1. A libertine; a *roué* (اوباش).

2. A scamp: vagabond; reprobate.

3. A low abandoned fellow who leads a dissolute life and subsists by gambling, or by intimidating respectable persons to give him money.

A لحاظ *lihāz'*, n. m. لحظ looking through half shut eyes, or through the outer corner of the eye. See توجه 1. Notice. 2. Deference; importance; weight (ادب). 3. Shame.

lohāz-i-hākimānah k. To take judicial notice.
lihāz k., v. a. 1. To notice; take notice of; regard; mind; have regard to.
2. To defer or pay respect to.
3. To heed; carry out.
4. To be partial to; side with.
lihāz ke qābil, adj. Worthy of attention or consideration.
lihāz na k., v. n. To disregard; turn away from.
ba-lihāz. With advertence to.
ba-lihāz-i-zurūrat-i-vaqt. G. G. As occasion requires.
ba-lihāz-i-qānūn Quoad law; according to regulation.
bilā-lihāz. Without reference to; independently.

H لڈو کھلانا लड्डू खिलाना *laḍḍū khilānā.* To give bribes.

thag ke laḍḍū khā baiṭhnā, v. n. To be settled and done for, as by a Thug's *laḍḍū*.

The Thug's *laḍḍū* is a sweet ball containing a poison with which Thugs produce insensibility in travellers whom they rob.

H لڑاکا लड़ाका *laṛāk'ā, laṛākū, laṛo'kaṛ*, adj.
1. Wrangling; quarrelsome; pugnacious.
2. Factious; riotous.

لڑانا लड़ाना *laṛā'nā*, v. a. Caus. of لڑنا q.v.

لڑائي लड़ाई *laṛā'ī, laṛāī bhiṛāī*, n. f.
1. Contention; quarrel; brawl.
2. Conflict; contest; skirmish; affray; warfare.
3. Wrestling; boxing; pugilism; fight; fighting; combat. 4. Battle; war; campaign.
5. Hostility; enmity.

laṛāī bāndhnā, v. a. To make a quarrel.
laṛāī kā ghar, n. m. 1. A firebrand; an incendiary. 2. The cause of quarrel.

H لڑکا گود لينا *laṛkā god lenā*, To adopt (a son).
laṛke-bālon kī khabar na lenā. To neglect wife and children.
laṛke-bāle. Family; household.
laṛke-vālā, n. m. *laṛke-vālī*, n. f. The father of the bridegroom.
rāh bāṭ kā laṛkā. A foundling.

H لڑنا लड़ना *laṛ'nā, laṛnā bhiṛnā*, v. a.
1. To struggle; contend; contest.
2. To clash with; jar against; cope or vie with.
3. To wrangle; quarrel; fight.

P لشكر *lash'kar*, n. m. A. *askar*. 1. An army; a military force. 2. A camp.
3. An encampment.

lashkar ikhaṭṭā, yā jamā k. To collect a force.
lashkar-khalās, Slang, A trull; strumpet.
lashkar-kashī, n. f. 1. Collecting an army; a levy; mobilization. 2. Invasion.

A لعنت *lān'at*; Illit. *nālat, niyānat*, n. f.

In *Mah. Law*, the testimony confirmed by oath on the part of the husband and wife (where the testimony is strengthened by an imprecation of the curse of God on the part of the husband, and of the wrath of God on the part of the wife), in case of the former accusing the latter of adultery, if she be not innocent. In such case, however, divorce should follow.

A لفظ *lafz, lavz*; Illit. *lavaz*, n. m. A word; term.

لفظاً *lafz'an*, adv. Literally; expressly.
lafz-ba-lafz, adv. Verbatim; word for word.
lafz-ba-lafz aur harf-ba-harf. Verbatim et literatim.
lafz mustāmala yā rozmarrah. A word in current or daily use.

لفظي *lafz'ī*, adj. Literal.
lafzī tarjumah. A literal or word-for-word translation.
lafzī mā'nī, n. f. The literal meaning.
nizāë lafzī, n. f. A wordy dispute.

P لفنگ *lafang', lafangiyā*, n. m. A loose character.

A لقب *laq'ab*, n. m. A surname; title; appellation of honor.

A لقطة *luq'tā*, n. Treasure trove.

Property which a person finds on the ground and takes charge of as a trust until claimed, calling witnesses to his finding it, and announcing his intention of restoring it. If not claimed after a year he should dispose of it in charity, or he may keep it for the owner if the article be durable.

P لقندرا *luqan'drā, luqqā*, n. m. A transposition of *qalandar* a devotee. 1. A loose character; a profligate. 2. A scamp; cheat.

A لقيت *laqīt'*, n. f. لقي (Mah. law). A founding.

It is considered meritorious to take charge of a deserted child, and the finder becomes its guardian, but cannot make it a slave. The state is bound to provide for those foundlings of whom no charitable individual takes charge.

H لكڑياں دينا लकड़ियां देना *lakṛiyāṅ denā*, v. a. To place wood on the funeral pyre.

H *lakshmī pūjā*, n. 1. The Hin. worship of Lakshmī on the last day of the dark fortnight of Kārtik (Sept.—Oct.). 2. A ceremony in honor of the same, observed by a bride and bridegroom when the bride has been brought to the house of her husband.

H لكھا लिकखा *likkh'ā, likhā*, adj. Written; engrossed.

likkhā-paṛhā, n. m. One who can read and write; an educated person.
uske hāth kā likkhā. His own handwriting.

لكھاوٹ लिखावट *likhā'vaṭ*, n. f.

A writing; an inscription.

H لکھائي **लिखाई** *likhā'ī*, n. f.

1. The art or occupation of writing.
2. The remuneration for writing or copying.

H لکھنا **लिखना** *likh'nā*, v. n. S. लिख् to write, Pr. *lih*; Pālī, *lekheti*.

To write; put or set down.

likhnā ba-nām falāṅ. To draw (a bill) upon.
likkhī falāne kī. Drawn by one (a bill).
likkhī falāne ke ūpar. Drawn on one.

لکھت **लिखत** *likh'at, likhtam, likhant*.n.f. 1. Writing; penmanship. 2. Anything written; a letter; a note of hand; a deed; document.

likhat parhat h., v. n. To be reduced to writing (an agreement, etc.).
likhat sākshī, n. f. Written evidence; a deed.
pichhlī likhat, n. f. An endorsement.
likher'ā; Bhoj. *likhak*, n. m. A writer; copyist; [clerk.

H لگاتار **लगातार** *lagātār'*, adv.

1. Uninterruptedly; constantly. 2. *Seriatim.*

H لگان **लगान** *lagān'*, E. n. m.

1. Assessment on land (*partā*, 2).
2. Rent or revenue from land.

lagān khālis, n. Net rent.
lagān muravvajah, yā māmūlī, n. Customary [rent.
lagān muqarrarī, n. m. Fixed rent.
lagān vāqaī, n. Actual rent.
takhfīf-i-zar-i-lagān, G. G. Abatement of reve- [nue.
tasfīyā-i-lagān, Adjustment of rents.
muāfī-i-zar-ī-lagān, n. Remission of revenue.
be-lagāo, adj. 1. Disconnected; separate.
2. Disinterested; impartial.

لگاوٹ **लगावट** *lagāv'at*, n. f.

1. Connection; application; adherence.
2. Attachment; affection. 3. A *liaison.*
4. Sexual intercourse; unlawful union.

H لگائي **लुगाई** *lugā'ī*; Contemp. *lugaiyā*; Garh *lojnī*, n. f. *layā* attached to.

A woman (استری)

lugāī k., v. a. To marry a widow.
lugāī-vālā, n. m. A married man.

H لگ بھگ **लग भग** *lag bhag*, adj.

Approximate (قریب).

lag bhag, adv. Approximately; about.

H لگن **लगन** *lag'an*, n. m. S. लग्न, Pālī, *laggo*.

The letter addressed by the father of the bride to the father of the bridegroom fixing the date of the marriage.

lagan-kundlī, n. f. A horoscope.

H لگنت **लगन्त** *lagant'*, (*Slang*) Sexual inter- [course.

lagant k. To have sexual intercourse with.
lage lage, adv. Side by side; collaterally.

E لمبر *lam'bar; nambar*, n. m. Cor. of number.

1. Number. 2. Marks given at an examination. 3. Rank.

lambar ānā, v. a To come to one's turn.
lambar-dār, nambar-dār, sadar mālguzār, n. m.

The registered representative of a coparcenary community who is responsible for the Govt. revenue.

As the representative of the rest a *lambar-dār* may hold his office by descent, or by election.

lambar-dārī, nambar-dārī, n. f.

The office or duty of a *lambardār.*

lambar sābiq meṅ qāyam rakhnā,

To replace in the file.

lambar se khārij h., v. n. To be struck off [the file.
lambar khiṅchnā, v. n. 1. To be prolonged (a matter). 2. To be postponed (a case).
lambar-vār, adv. By turns; in order.
lamb'arī, adj. According to the number; in [order.
lam'brī, n. m. A standard measure.
lambrī muqaddama, yā nālish.

A regular suit, headed according to its number on the file of causes.

lambarī nālish, A regular suit.
sīga-i-lambarī, Numerical order.

H لنگاڑا **लुङ्गाड़ा** *luṅgār'ā, luṅgārā*; Tir. *lamphā*; Bhoj. *luṅgerā*, n. m.

A dissolute or abandoned wretch; a profligate; rip; loose fish (*badmāāsh*).

لنگاڑاپن **लुङ्गाड़ापन** *luṅgārā-pan, luṅgār-pan*, n.m.

1. Profligacy; libertinism (بدمعاشي).
2. Rascality; villainy.

P لنگر خرچ *langar kharch*; n. m. Provisions or expenses for the support of the poor.

H لنگواڑا **लङ्गवाड़ा** *laṅgvā'ṛā*, n. m.

(*Brokers*) One hundred.

H لنگوري **लङ्गूरी** *laṅgūr'ī*, n.f. A gratification taken to help one to recover stolen property.

A لواحق *lavāh'aq*, n. m. pl. 1. Relations; kindred. 2. Appurtenances.

A لوازم *lavāz'im, lavāzima, lavāzimāt*. n. m.

Necessaries; appurtenances; baggage.

lavāzim i-sanad The particulars necessary for the grant of a patent or *sanad.*

The vouchers from and to the different officers and departments requisite for the final issue of a grant of land or revenue under the Mah. government, as usually endorsed on the patent.

mulāzim-i-sarkārī ko apne lavāzim-i-mansabī ke anjām meṅ kisī tarah kī riāyat na karnī chāhiye. G. G. A public servant should show no favour in the exercise of his official functions.

lavāzim-i-mansabī. G. G. Official functions; [public duties.

H لوت लूट *lūṭ, luṭṭas*, n. f. S. लुण्ठ 1. Booty ; plunder ; prize. 2. Pillage ; rapine ; depredation ; spoliation. 3. Blackmail ; extortion ; robbery. 4. Unfair dealing ; high charges.
lūṭ parnā, yā h. To be plundered, pillaged.
lūṭ kā māl, n. m. Plunder ; booty.
lūṭ k., yā machānā, lūṭā khasoṭī k., v. a. To plunder ; pillage ; ravage ; loot.
lūṭ mār, lūṭ khasoṭ, n. f. Plundering and killing ; pillage ; havoc. [ravage.

لوتنا लूटना *lūṭ'nā*, v. a. 1. To plunder ; spoil ; 2. To extort ; rob ; make high charges.

H لوڑا लौड़ा *lauṛ'ā, lolā, lavvā*, n. m. Dim. *lolī, lolo*, n. f. *Membrum virile* ; *penis* (*lanḍ*).
lauṛā pelā k. (Obscene slang) v. a. To abuse ; to use smutty language.

H لوڑھنا लोढ़ना *loṛh'nā*, E., n. Gleanings.

H لوڑھي लोढ़ी *loṛ'hī, loḍhī*, n. f. The ceremony of burning fuel in the name of the goddess *Kālī. Panj. Khatrīs.*

A لوطي *lūt'ī*, n. m. A sodomite. [Lame.

H لولا लूला *lūlā*. 1. E. Without hands. 2. W.

H لون लोन *lon, lūn*, Rus. for *non*, n. m. S. लवण Salt.

لونار लोनार *lonār'*, n. m. A place where salt is produced ; salt land or pit.

لوني लोनी *lon'ī, lūnī, nonī, khār, reh, shor*, n. f. The salt that effloresces from walls, etc.

لونيا लोनिया *lon'iyā, lonā, noniyā*, adj. Saltish ; brackish.
lon'iyā, n. m. A caste of men employed in the manufacture of salt.

H P لونڈے باز *launḍe-bāz*, n. m. A sodomite.
launḍe-bāzī, n. f. Sodomy.

H A لوہامحال *lohā mahāl*, n. m. Revenue derived from iron mines, and melting and working the metal. [fore ; consequently.

A لہذا *lihāz'ā*, adv. *lit.* for this reason. There-

H لہولہان लहूलुहान *lahū luhān*, adj. Bloody ; weltering in blood (*khūn-ālūdah*).

A ليت و لعل *lait o lāl* ; n. f. See *ṭālā*. 1. Procrastination. 2. Evasion.
lait o lāl meṅ ḍālnā, lait o lāl k., v. a. To dally ; dilly dally.

A ليكن *lek'in* ; Sant. *menkhān*, conj. But ; on the contrary.
lekin agar, conj. But if. [n. f.

H ليكھ लेख *lekh, lekhan, likhant* ; Sant. *ol*, 1. A writing (*likhat*, 2). 2. Signature ; endorsement.

ليكھا लेखा *lekh'ā*, n. m. 1. (*lekhā jokhā*) An account ; a reckoning. 2. A ledger.
lekhā bahī, n. f. 1. Account books. 2. A ledger.
lekhā-patr, n. m. An account ; a bill.
lekhā pūrā, yā pharchā k., v. a. To settle or close an account ; discharge a balance.
lekhā ḍālnā, v. a. To open an account with.
lekhā ḍeoṛhā barābar k., v. a. To square accounts ; pay one's score.
lekh'e, adv. Concerning ; as to. [outstandings.

H لينا लेना *le'nā*, n. m. Money to be realised ;

لينا लेना *lenā*, v. a. To have sexual intercourse with.
lenā kisī chīz masrūqa yā magrūtah kā jān-būjh-ke. G.G. Receiving stolen or plundered property knowingly.
le-bhāgnā, uṛnā, yā saṭaknā, v. n. To be off with ; carry off ; run away with ; abduct.
le-pālak, n. m. An adopted child.
le-pālak k., le pālnā, v. n. To adopt as a son.
le-paṛnā, le sonā, v. n. 1. To lie or lay with. 2. To have sexual intercourse with.
le-jānā, v. n. 1. To carry ; take away ; convey. 2. To export. [calumniate.
le-marnā, līye marnā, v. n. To accuse falsely ;
len-den, lenā-denā, levā-deī, n. m. See بيوہار 1. Business. 2. Money dealings. 3. Communication.
len-den band k., v. a. To close a business.
len-den k., v. a. To deal with ; trade ; transact ; transact business.
jān kā levā. A mortal enemy.
livāl', n. m. A purchaser.
vālī-i-jāyaz ki hifāzat se insān ko le-bhāgnā, G.G. Kidnapping from a lawful guardian.
ğair mulk meṅ gulām kī tareh le-jānā, G. G. To export as a slave. [former husband.

H ليڻڈرا लेंडरा *lenḍ'rā*, n. m. A son by a

م

A ما *mā*, In comp. only. What ; which.
mā-bād. What comes after ; following.
mā-baqā, The rest ; remainder ; surplus.
mā-bahil ihtiyāj. Whatever is necessary.
mā-bahil-imtiyāz, The line of demarkation.
mā-bahil-nizā. The thing disputed.
mā-baēn, adv. Meantime ; in the interim.
mā-baēn tahqīqāt. During the proceedings.

mā-tahat, adj. 1. Subordinate; dependant. 2. Lower; inferior.
mā-hasal, n. m. 1. Harvest; produce. 2. Profit; income. 3. Inference; conclusion.
mā-hazar, adj. Present; ready at hand.
mā-sabaq. Preceding; aforesaid; before-mentioned.
mā-salaf, Passed; elapsed.
mā-sivā, *mā-varā*. Besides; over and above.
mā fī-uz-zamīr. Intent; intention.
mā-qabal. Prior; preceding; last.
dafāt mā-sabaq. G. G. The preceding sections.
dafa-i-māqabal, G. G. The last or preceding section.

H ما باپ *mā bāp*, n. m. Father and mother; parents.
mā-bahan. Mother and sister.
mā bahan k, v. a To abuse one's mother and sister.
mā-jāī, n. f. One's own sister.
mā-jāyā, n. m. One's own brother.
bin mā bāp kā; Sant. *tuar*, n. m. An orphan.
bin mā kā bachchā, n. m. A motherless child.

H ماپ माप *māp*, *mapat*, *nāp*; Sant. *song*, n. f. S. मा to measure. 1. Measurement; survey. 2. A standard of measure or capacity.
māp kā pūrā. Full or standard height.
ماپنا मापना *māp'nā*, *nāpnā*, *māp lenā*, v. a. To measure; survey.
ماپک मापक *māp'ak*, n. m. 1. A measure. 2. A surveyor.
H. *māthā godnā*, v. a. To tattoo the forehead of a life prisoner or a slave.
māthe rolī chāval chaṛhnā, v. a. To be anointed, installed.

A ماجرا *māj'rā*, n. m. ما what and جري happened. An event
mājrā ittīfāqīyah, A contingent or fortuitous event.

H ماجهي माझी *mājh'ī*, adj. (*Butchers*) Eight rupees.
mājhī āsir, (*Butchers*) Eighteen rupees.
mājhī mainā, (*Butchers*) Twentyeight rupees.

A ماخوذ *mā-khūz'*, adj. Involved; implicated.
mākhūz az ruē nālish. Stands charged.
mākhūz hone ke lāyaq. G.G. Liable (criminally).
mujrimon ko mākhūz karānā. G. G. To bring offenders to justice.
shakhs-i-mākhūz. G. G. The accused person.
mākhūz, *k.*, v. a. To criminate; bring to trial.
mākhūz'ī, n. Arrest.

P مادر *mād'ar*, n. f. Mother
mādar ba-khatā, *mādar-ba-khattā*, A bastard.
mādar-chod, Slang, One who goes wrong with his mother. (A term of abuse).
mādar-khāhī k., v. a. To abuse one's mother.
mād'arī, adj. Maternal.
haq-i-mādarī. Maternal right.

H مار मार *mār*, n. f. 1. Beating; striking. 2. Stiff clay or loamy soil with some sand and vegetable mould; (*Bundelkhand*) a rich black loam.
mār baiṭhnā, To strike; beat.
mār paṛnā, v. n. To be beaten.
mār-pīṭ, *mār-piṭāī*, *mār-dhāṛ*, *mār-kuṭāī*, n. f. Beating and bruising; fighting; assault and battery.
mār ḍālnā, v. a. To kill; slay; murder.
mār rakhnā, v. n, To keep back wrongfully.
mār khānā, v. n. 1. To get a beating. 2. To earn by robbery.
mār marnā, v. a. To commit suicide.
mārā jānā, v. n. 1. To be killed, slain.
mārā mār, *mār mār*, n. f. Scuffle; fray; broil.
مارنا मारना *mār'nā*, v. a. 1. To beat; strike; thrash; knock down. 2. To kill; slay. 3. To usurp; defraud; rob. 4. (*Slang*) To commit sodomy.
haq mārnā, v. a. To wrong; injure.
mār'e, adv. For; for the sake or behalf of.

H ماسک मासिक *mās'ik*, adj. Monthly.

H ماس کبار मासकबार *mās-kubār*, n. A monthly statement.
mās nimās, *lit.* mouth by month. Interest added to capital, and subject to compound interest.

H ماشہ माशा *māsh'ā*; Rus. *māsā*, n.m.S. माष 1. A weight equal to $\frac{1}{12}$th of a tolah or 8 *rattīs*, q.v. 2. (*Brokers*) Four annas.

H ماگهات माघात *māghāt'*, n. f. Land broken up in *Māgh* for next year's crops.
māghāt-kī-fasal. Crops sown between *Māgh* and the rains.

A مال *māl*, n. m. See اسباب (3—7). 1. (*māl ṭāl*) Property; money. 2. (*māl matāa*) Goods. 3. Revenue; finance. 4. A prize (in a lottery, etc.). 4. The granulated sediment in an Indigo vat after heating and drawing off the water. 5. The registered representative of the village community who enters into engagements at the settlement, and to whom Govt. looks for its demand.
māl amvāt, n. m. 1. Property left by the deceased. 2. Unappropriated or unclaimed property.
māl bar-āmad, n. m. 1. Export. 2. (*māl bar-āmdah*) Recovered property. 3. (*māl gurāsh-ta-i-mujrim*) Property left by a criminal.
māl bar-āmad aur dar-āmad kī vusūl-bāqī. Balance of trade.
māl be-khaṭke. Unencumbered property.
māl chīrnā, v. a. To embezzle.

māl hisse-dārī, n. f. Joint stock.
māl-khānā, n. m. A treasury ; store-house.
māl matrūkā, yā maurūsah. A bequest; legacy.
māl hazam kar-ke muflis bannā, māl mār-ke divālā nikālnā. Fraudulent insolvency.
مالدار *māl-dār*, adj. Wealthy
māl-dār, māl-vālā, n. m. A wealthy person.
مالداري *māl-dārī*, n. f. Opulence
māl-dār-i-amānat. A trustee.
māl-dhanī, māl-vālā, A. H. n. m. A proprietor.
māl-zādah, n. m. A whore son. (An abuse).
māl-zādī, n. f. A bawd ; whore.
māl-sāyar. Duties; miscellaneous revenue from customs and other sources, exclusive of land.
māl-sharākat. Joint, undivided property ; joint stock.
māl-zāmin, n. m. Opp. of *hāzir-zāmin*, q. v.
Surety (the person) ; a surety for the payment of a demand against the bailee.
māl-zāminī, n. f. Opp. of *hāzir-zāminī*, Pecuniary bail ; security in property.
māl-zāmnī dākhil k., v. a. To give security.
māl-zabtī, n. f. Attached property ; escheat.
māl-i-ganīmat, Plunder.
māl gair-manqūla ; H. *atal dhan*, n. m.
Real or immoveable property.
māl farod. Bonded goods ; warehouse goods.
māl kā band o bast, n. m.
Settlement of the revenue.
māl katnā, v. n. 1. To be stolen.
2. To be sold in large quantities.
māl ko sarqa-i-sugra se bachā rakhne kā istehqāq, G. G. Right of private defence of property against theft.
māl kī hifāzat-i-khud-ikhtiyārī kā istehqāq. G.G.
Right of private defence of property.
māl kī rasīd jo jahāz par charhā hai.
Bill of lading.
مالگزار *māl-guzār*, n. m. A manager of cultivation and village matters ; a landlord ; one who pays revenue to Govt. (*lambardār*).

The person who pays the revenue assessed on an estate or village, whether on his own behalf or as the representative of others, and whether he be sole or joint proprietor or a holder under a proprietor or the State, and whether he pay the revenue to a proprietor or *zamīndār* or to the officers of the Government.

مالگزاري *māl-guzārī*, n. f. The Government demand, or revenue ; the land-tax.
mālguzārī āimā. A grant or assignment of land paying a quit-rent, an assignment of a portion of the Government revenue of an estate for charitable purposes.

A grant of waste land upon a small rent to a cultivator, who thereby acquires a proprietary right in the soil.

mālguzārī tahsīl kul. The entire revenue collections ; the net revenue. [public revenue.
mālguzārī-i-sarkār, n. f. Government revenue ;
mālguzārī talab k., v. a. To claim revenue.
māl-guzārī kā dākhlā, dākhlā. G. G.
Revenue receipt (for land).
māl-i-lā-vāris, n. m.
1. Unclaimed property. 2. Escheat.
māl-i-lā-vāris jo zabtī meṅ āve. Escheat.
māl-mārū, A. H. adj. One who embezzles.
māl mārnā, v. a. 1. To fleece ; swindle ; abstract ; make off with ; sweep ; strip ; gut ; make away with one's property.
2. To embezzle (*khayānat k.*). [property.
māl mujrim ; H. *chor ḍhor*, A criminal with
māl-i-mahmūlah, G. G. Goods on board ; cargo.
māl-i-mardum-khor, n. m. A swindler ; one who embezzles. [covered.
māl-masrūqah barāmad. Stolen property re-
māl-masrūqah le rakhnā. Receiving stolen property. [perty.
māl-i-maqrūqah. Distrained or attached pro-
māl-i-manqūlah; H. *uṭhāū dhan*, n. m. Personal or moveable property. [poses.
māl-i-vaqf. Property devoted to religious pur-
sarishta-i-māl kā ohde-dār, G. G.
A revenue officer.
huzūrī yā sadar māl-guzār. One who pays his revenue to the public or principal treasury, without the intervention of a proprietor or farmer, or subordinate native Collector; the chief amongst a number of co-sharers through whom the revenue of the rest, or of a certain portion of them is paid, the same as *lambardār*.
mazkūrī mālguzār. A payer of revenue through the intervention of a subordinate native Collector, or a proprietor or contractor.
mutaalliq māl-guzārī. G. G. Fiscal.
murde kā māl. n. f. 1. Unclaimed property. 2. Anything bought cheap or got for nothing.
naqd-māl, n. m. 1. A valuable prize.
māl jo qarz kī illat meṅ javāzan māḳhūz ho saktā hai. G. G.
Property legally liable for debts.
مالک *māl'ik* ; Illit. *mālak*, n. m. ملک possessing.
1. Owner ; proprietor. 2. Master ; lord.
3. A husband.
4. One empowered ; an employer.
mālik arāzī, n. m. A landholder. [proprietor.
mālik az ruē qānūn. Proprietor de *jure*, legal
mālik-i-ālā. A superior proprietor.
mālik-ul-mulk, n. m. *lit.* lord of the country.
A title addressed to sovereigns, princes, prime ministers, etc.
mālik aur karāēdār, n.m. Landlord and tenant.
mālik-i-hissa. A shareholder. [owner.
mālik haqīqī. Proprietor *de facto* ; the real
mālik-i-deh. A village proprietor.
mālik-i-sharaī. Proprietor or owner *de jure*.
mālik-i-shikmī yā adnā. A subordinate proprietor. [tor.
mālik ġair-muzāre. A non-cultivating proprie-

mālik k., v. a.
To empower; give a claim to; entitle.
mālik-i-makān, yā zamīn,
Householder; landlord.
mālik-i-hunḍī, n. m. The holder of a bill or draft.
mālik-muzāre. A cultivating proprietor.
mālik muqarrarī-dār. A possessor of an estate or farm on a perpetual fixed rate of rent or revenue, apparently not the original proprietor but one who by long possession claims to be considered as proprietor.
mālik mundarjah-i-kāgzāt. A recorded proprietor.
mālik h., v. n. To own; have a title to.
مالکانہ *mālikāna*, adj. Proprietory.
mālikāna, adv. In the manner of an owner.
mālikāna, n. m. An allowance of 5 to 10 per cent to *zamīndārs* ousted from their estates.
mālikāna-i-khāngī, n. m.
Fees levied on cultivators by a landholder for his household expenses.
mālikāna rusūm. Proprietory dues.

مالکیت *mālikī'yat*; Pop. *mālkīyat*, n. f.
Ownership; proprietory right.

مالي *mālī*, adj. 1. Belonging to property.
2. Belonging to revenue; financial.
mālī peshkār, n. m. A revenue accountant.
mālī kām, n. m. Revenue matters.
hukkām-i-mālī. Revenue officers.

H مالي माली *māl'ī*, n.m. *mālan*; Poet. *mālanyā*, n. f. S. मालिक; Pālī, *māliko*.
A gardener; also the caste.

A ماليت *māl'iyat*, n.f. 1. Wealth.
2. Value; worth.
māliyat paidāvār arāzī, G. G. Value of the produce.
māliyat takhmīnah. Estimated value.
māliyat jāṅchnā, v. a. To value; estimate.
māliyat dāvā The value of a claim.
māliyat muqaddmah kī kamī.
Defective valuation of suit.

H مام माम *mām*, n. m. Power; money; means.

H ماما मामा *mā'mā*, Hin.; *māmūṅ*, Mah.; *māmo*, Sant. n. m. S. माम or मातुल Pr. *māuo*.
Maternal uncle.
māmī, māīṅ, Hin.; *mumānī*, Mah.n.f.S. मातुलानी Pālī, *mātulānī*. Maternal uncle's wife.

A مامور *māmūr'*, part pass. امر commanding.
Ordered; appointed.
māmūr k., v. a. To constitute; set; appoint.
māmūr h., v. n. To be appointed to an office.

H مان मान *mān*, n. m. A son-in-law.

H مانجھ मांज *māṅj, māṅjhā*, n. f.
Marshy or alluvial land.

H مانڈل मांडल *māṅḍ'al*, n. f. The iron-ring round the mouth of a *charas*, q. v.

A مانع *mān'e*, n. m. 1. Bar.
2. Hindrance. 3. Prohibition. 4. Objection. 5. One who forbids or hinders.
māne ijrāe ḍigrī.
A bar to the execution of a decree.
māne dāvā yā nālish. A bar to a claim or suit.
vajah-i-māne, n. f. G. G. Cause to the contrary.
māne hukm. Arrest of judgment.
māne h., v. n. See *bāz rakhnā*, 5, 6.
1. To be a bar to.
2. To prevent; prohibit.
3. To object to (*eterāz k.* 1).

H مانگ بھرنا *māṅg bharnā*, v. a. 1. To apply *sendūr*, etc. to the *māṅg*. 2. To marry one.
māṅg-bharī, Wom. n. f. 1. A *feme covert*.
māṅg-jalī, Wom. n. f. A widow (*bidhwā*).
māṅg chirnā, Slang., v. n. To be defloured.
māṅg khulnā, v. n.
To die (one's betrothed wife or husband).
māṅg honā, v. n. To be in request or demand.

H مانگنا मांगना *māṅg'nā*, v. a.
1. To ask; request; demand.
2. To solicit one's hand in marriage.
3. To crave; beg; pray; solicit.
4. To borrow.
māṅge denā, v. a. To lend.
māṅge-kī, adj. Borrowed.
maṅget'ar, n. One who has been betrothed.

H ماوسا मावसा *mā'osā, māṅosā, mausā*, Hin.; *māṅsā*, Panj. n. m. Uncle.
ماوسي मावसी *mā'osī, māṅosī, mausī*, Hin.; *māṅsī*, Panj.; *māsī*, Brij. n. f. Aunt.
موسيرا मौसेरा *mauser'ā*, adj. Belonging to *māosā*.
mauserā bhāī, n. m. A cousin (mother's sister's son).
mauserī bahan, n. f. A cousin (mother's sister's daughter).

P ماه *māh, mah*, n. m. Z. and S. *mās*.
1. The moon. 2. A month.
māh ba-māh, māh-vār, adv. Every month; monthly.
māh-i-shamshī, n. m. A solar month.
māh-i-qamrī, n. m. A lunar month.
ماهواري *māh-vārī*, adj. Monthly.

H ماهون माहून *māhūn'*, n. An insect destructive to cotton. *Carnegy*.

A مباح *mubāh'*; Illit. *mubbāh*, adj.
Allowable; lawful (جائز 2, 3).
mubāh rakhnā, v. n. To hold legal or lawful.

mubāh k., v. a. To legalize; make lawful.

A مبادله *mubād'lah*, n. m. Barter (*badal*, 2).
mubādle kā hisāb, An exchange transaction.
mubādlah, k., v. a.
To make an exchange (*badalnā*, 2).
mubādlah h., v. n. To be exchanged.

A مباشرت *mubāsh'rat*, n. f. بشر he enjoyed her skin. Coition.
mubāshrat bā-mujrimānā. G. G. Incest.
mubāshrat k., v. a. To cohabit.

A مبلغ *mub'lağ, mubliğ*; pl. *mubāliğ*, n. m.
A sum of money.

A مبني *mab'nī*, adj. Founded; based.
mabnī ūpar īzā-rasānī ke. G. G. Vexatious.
mabnī-bar-fasād, adj. G. G. Litigious.
mabnī-i-fasād. G. G. A ringleader; an aggressor.
mabnī h., v. n. To be based upon.

A مبهم *mub'ham*, H. *gol*, adj. بهم was confused.
Ambiguous; indistinct (*gol*, 3).

A مبيعه *mabī'ya h.*, adj. Sold.
jāëdād-i-mabīya, G. G. Property sold.

A متا ثر *mutaas'sir*, adj. اثر made an impression.
1. Producing effect or impression; effective (*kārgar*, 1, 2).
2. Touching; affecting; impressive.

A متبنى *mutaban'nā*; Rus. *mutannā*, n.m. بن a son. An adopted child (*le-pālak*).
mutabannā k., To adopt a child (*god lenā*, 2).

A متحد *mutta'had*, adj. Made one; united.
azlā-i-muttahad. United states.

A متحقق *mutahaq'qaq*, adj. حق was true.
Proved; verified; true (*tahqīq*).
mutahaqaq k., v. a. To verify; prove; establish.

A متخاصم *mutakhās'im*, n.
An opponent; a litigant.
متخاصمين *mutakhāsmīn'*, n. f. The parties concerned in a case. [instituted.

A متدايره *mutādā'ërah*. adj. Filed; lodged;
muqaddama-i-mutadāërah. G.G. A pending suit.

A متدعويه *mutadāv'iya*, adj.
Claimed; made the subject of a claim.
baqāyā-i-mutadāviyā, G. G. Arrears claimed.
dād-i-mutadāviya, G. G. Relief sought.

A متذكره *mutazok'kara*, adj. 1. Mentioned; stated. 2. Referred to. [aforesaid.
mutazak'kara-i-bālā, adj. Above-mentioned;

A متصاعده *mutasāīda*, adj. G. G. Ascending.
silsila mustaqīma mutasāida. G. G.
Upwards in the direct ascending line.

A متصدي *mutasad'dī*; Pop. *musaddī*, n. m.
A writer; clerk: an accountant.
mutasaddī-garī, n. f. The office of clerk.

A متصل *muttas'al*, adj. وصل joined. Contiguous; adjoining; joined; adjacent. [sidered.

A متصور *mutasav'var*, part pass. Imagined; con-

A متضاد *mutazād'*, adj. Contradictory.

A متضرر *mutazar'rar*, p. adj. Hurt; injured.
jism ke mutazarrar hone kā andeshā, G. G.
Apprehension of danger to the body.

A متضمن *mutazam'min*, ضمن contained.
Comprising; comprehending; including.
mutazammin tahsīl īsāl zar-i-qarza, G. G.
For facilitating the collection of debts.
mutazammin izhār ehtarāz, G. G.
Any act to express dissent.

A متعدد *mutaād'dad*, adj. عدد numbering.
Many; various. [action.
mutaddad binā-i-dāvā. Multifarious cause of

A متعلق *mutaal'liq*, adj. علق hung to.
1. Connected; annexed; appended; subjoined. 2. Depending on; dependant.
3 Appertaining; concerning (*sambandhī*).
4. Pertinent: relevant; applicable.
mutaalliq-i-zāt-i-khās, adj. Personal; private.
mutaālliq-i-zar. Pecuniary.
mutaālliq-sarishtah. Official.
mutaālliq i-ilāqah. Amenable to jurisdiction.
mutaalliq k., v. a. 1. To append; join.
2. To extend to; apply; make applicable.
3. To attribute; ascribe; impute. 4. To assign; make over to; to entrust; invest.
mutaalliq moharrir yā mutasaddī. Clerical.
mutaaliqāt', mutaalliqān, mutaalliqīn, n. m.
1. Children; family.
2. Domestics; dependents.
khuāh muqadamme se mutaālliq ho yā na ho.
Whether relevant to the case or not.

A متعه *mutāh'*, n. m. A temporary marriage.
A left-handed marriage allowed by the *Shias*, but considered illegal by the Sunnis. [time.
متعاهي *mutāāī*, adj. Married for a specified

A متعهد *mutā'hid*, n. m. from عهد commanding. Pl. متعاهدين 1. A contractor. 2. One who enters into an engagement for the revenue.
mutahid, adj. Covenanted.
afsarān i-mutahid. Covenanted officers.
shāhān-i-mutahid. Contemporary kings.
gair-mutahid. G. G. Uncovenanted.

A متعين *mutaāi'yun* ; Pop. *mutaaiyan*, adj. Appointed ; constituted.
mutaaiyun k., v. a. To appoint (to an office).
mutaaiyun h., v.n. To fill an office.

A متغير *mutağai'yar*, adj. غير became changed. Changed.

A متفرق *mutafar'raq*, adj. فرق separated.
1. Miscellaneous.
2. Scattered ; dispersed.
mutafarraq k. To separate ; scatter ; disperse ; dissolve.
متفرقات *mutafarraqāt'*, n.
1. Sundries ; miscellaneous articles.
2. The several items of an account.
3. Separate and scattered portions of land included in a village or an estate.

A متفق *muttafiq'*, adj. وفق suited. Agreeing ; conspiring ; united ; unanimous.
muttafiq-ur-rāe, adj. Agreeing in opinion.
muttafiq-alah, muttafiq-ul-lafz, adj. Unanimous ; *nem con.*
muttafiq h. To agree upon ; to concur ; to be unanimous.
متفقه *muttaf'aqa*, adj. Associated.
jamāāt muttafaqa, G.G. An association.

A متمرد *mutamar'rid*, adj. مرد Refractory ; sarkash.
mutamarrid log. Factious or refractory people.

A متنازع *mutanāz'ā*, adj. نزع
Contested (in law).
mutanāzea fīh. The matter in dispute.

A متناسب *mutanās'ib*, part. act. نسب Proportioned or proportionate to one another.
jurmāne kā hissa-i-mutānāsiba. G. G. Proportion of the fine.

A متواتر *mutavā'tir*, adv. Successively.
taqāzāē mutavātir, n. m. G. G. Importunity.

H متوالا मतवाला *matvā'lā, matvārā, matvālī, matvārī*, adj.
Intoxicated ; drunken ; drunk.
matvālā h., v. n. To be drunk.

A متوجه *mutavaj'jah, mutvajjah*, adj.
1. Turned towards ; attentive.
2. Favorable ; favoring.
mutavajjah h., v. n. To turn one's face towards ; to attend to.

A متوسط *mutavas'sit*, adj. وسط keeping in the middle. 1. Intermediate ; middling.
2. Ordinary ; common.
mutavassit-ul-qīmat, Average price.

A متوطن *mutavat'tin*, n. m. An inhabitant ; a native.

A متوفى *mutavaf'fī*, adj. وفي ended.
Dead ; deceased ; the late.

A متولي *mutaval'lī*, n. m. An incumbent or trustee of a Mah. religious endowment.

H متونا मतौना *matau'nā*, n. m. The grain *kodoṅ*, when it is intoxicating.

A متهم *muttah'am*, n. m. وهم suspected.
The accused party.
muttaham k., v. a. To accuse (*ilzām denā*).

S متهيا मिथ्या *mit'thyā*, n. m. Pr. *michchhā*.
An untruth ; a falsehood (*jhūṭh*).
mitthyā sākshī. False evidence.
mithyā nām. A misnomer.
mitthyā-vād. Calumny ; false charge.
mitthyā-vādī, mitthyātī. n. m. A liar.
mitthyātī. One who believes in a false faith.

H متي मिती *mit'ī*, n.f. 1. The day of the month (تاريخ 1). 2. Interest ; discount.
mitī pūgnā, v. a. To mature (a bill).
mitī charhānā, yā ḍālnā, v. a. 1. See *tārīkh charhānā*. 2. To finish a letter or writing.
mitī-kāṭā, The rule for calculating discount.
mitī kāṭnā, v. a. To discount.
mitī-vār, adv. According to date (*tārīkh-vār*).
pakkī mitī, n. f. Due date ; maturity.
Interest allowed by bankers on money received, dating from the day after the receipt.
pahlī mitī charhānā, v. a To antedate.

H متيئي मतेई *mate'ī*; Bhoj. *maēbhā*, n. f. From H. *mātā* mother. A stepmother.

H متري मुटरी *muṭ'rī.*
A tenure in the Benares district under which a tenant held different kinds of land, and cultivated various crops at one fixed rate of money rent to the *zamīndār*.

H متهوت मठौट *maṭhauṭ', maṭhaud, maṭhoṭ* n. m. S. मस्तक the head. Capitation ; poll-tax.
In Bengal an extra or occasional cess or tax imposed upon the cultivators for some special purpose, or under some incidental pretext, either by the state or the *zamīndār*, or the principal revenue officer of a district. These taxes were in part abolished and in part consolidated by Ben. Reg. VIII 1793.

H متهي گرم كرنا *muṭṭhī garm k.*, v.a. To bribe.

متهيا मुठिया *muṭh'iyā*, n. m. 1. The handle or stilt of a plough, etc. 2. The stick with which the carder strikes the string of his bow. 3. The thick end of a stick. 4. A lump of sugar. 5. The man who feeds the sugar mill with the chopped canes.
6. The first fistful of seed sown.

H متيار मटियार *maṭiyār', maṭiyārā*, n. f.

Clayey soil (first quality). [clay pit.

متيال मटियाल *maṭiyāl'*; Bhoj. *maṭikhān*, n. m. A

H متي ڈلوانا *miṭṭī ḍalvānā*, v. a. *lit.* to cause earth to be thrown. A contrivance for recovering stolen property.

Each of the suspected parties is required to throw some earth in a certain spot, and the thief is thus given the chance of depositing the stolen article under the heap of earth without being detected.

pāṅḍar, yā pāṅḍū miṭṭī, n. f. Light red soil.
potnī miṭṭī, piṅḍol, n. White soil.

A مثال *misāl'*, n. f. مثل being like.

1. Likeness; similitude; simile; analogy.
2. A specimen. 3. An example.
4. A case adduced as a precedent.

A مثبتة *musab'batah, musbitah*, adj. 1. Engrossed. 2. Stamped; bearing a stamp or seal.
musabbatah isṭām. Bearing a stamp; stamped.

A مثل *misl*; Illit. *misal.*

The papers or records (of a case).
misl-baṅd, A file of suits.
misl-baṅd, adj. Filed with the suit.
misl-i-baṅd o bast, n. Settlement record; settlement papers. [suit).
misl-khuāṅ, n. m. Reader of the records (of a
misl-khuānī, n. f. Reading of the whole proceedings (of a case).
misl-i-dīvānī, n. A civil suit. [dual.
misl-i-avām-un-nās. G. G. As a private indivi-
misl-i-faujdārī, n. f. A criminal suit.
misl kardah zāt apnī kī. As if he had been present and consenting.
misl mutafarraqa. Miscellaneous proceedings.
misl murattab k., v. a. 1. To file the proceedings (of a case). 2. To prepare the *misl* (of a case).
misl murattab h., yā bannā, v. n. To be prepared (the whole proceedings of a case).
misl-i-muqadma. The record or *Misl* of a case.
misl meṅ shāmil, yā shāmil-i-misl k., v. a.
To file with the record; place on record.
be-misl, adj. Unequalled (*lā-sānī*).
ruēdād-i-misl, The whole course of proceedings in a case; a collection of like or similar documents forming the body of public proceedings in a judicial or revenue matter.

مثلي *misl'ī*, n. m. An old offender.

In *Mah.* Law, an article which, being lent or sold, is to be replaced by another of a similar description.

A مثنى *musan'nā*, n. m.

A duplicate; counterpart; counterfoil.
musannā, adj. Double; binary; duplicate.
musannā-beh, n. The original (of a copy).

A مجاريه *majār'iyah*, adj. جري flowing. 1. Current; in force. 2. Enacted; passed into law.
qānūn-i-majārīā, G. G. Law passed.
qānūn majāriya-i-Hind. The code of laws current in India. [being in force.
qānūn majāriye vaqt meṅ. A law for the time

A مجاز *majāz'*, adj. جوز passed as valid.

Competent; legally competent; authorized; warranted.
majāz, n. m. Authority; competency.
majāz aur mukhtār h., v. n. To have authority, etc.; to be legally authorized.
majāz hai, Is empowered.
hākim-i-majāz, An authorized officer; one invested with full legal powers. [court.
robrū adālat-i-majāz, G. G. In any competent
qānūn kī rū se majāz, G. G. Justified by law.
gair-majāz, adj. Unwarranted; not authorized.

مجازاً *majāz'an*, adv. Legally; lawfully.

مجازي *majāz'ī*, adv. 1. Artificial; false; spurious.

A مجامعت *mujā'maát, mujameat*, n. f. جمع collecting. Carnal connection; coition; *coitus.*
mujāmeat k., To have carnal intercourse with.

A مجاهدين *mujāhadīn'*, n. m. pl. جهد strove.
Warriors (for the faith); crusaders.

A مجبور *majbūr'*, adj. جبر constrained.

Constrained; compelled; coerced.
majbūr k., v. a. To constrain; coerce; compel.
majbūr h., v. n. To be compelled.
majbūr'an, majbūrī se, adv.
Compulsorily; of necessity.
majbūran ikhtiyār k., v. n. To adopt compulsorily. [illegal act.
fel-i-nā-jāiz par majbūr k. Constraining to an
mehnat karne par nā-javāzan majbūr k. G. G. Unlawful compulsory labour.

مجبوري *majbūr'ī*, n. f. 1. Want of power.
2. Constraint; compulsion; coercion.

A مجرا *muj'rā*, n. m.

Deduction; allowance; a set-off.
mujrā pānā, v. n. To receive credit (for a sum).
mujrā-talbī. A counter-claim.
mujrā k., yā denā, v. a. 1. To allow abatement or deductions. 2. To give credit (for a sum).
mujrā lenā, v. n. To deduct; subtract.
mujrā h., v. n. To be deducted, retrenched.
mujrā yā chhūṭ chāhnā.
To claim a credit or set-off.

مجرای *mujrā'ī, mujraī*, n. m. 1. Remission of revenue; reduction in the assessment.
2. A credit given on account.

A مجرم *muj'rim*, n. m. جرم pl. *mujrimān.*
A criminal; delinquent; offender; felon.

mujrim ṭhairānā, yā qarār denā.
To convict; sentence.
mujrim ishtahārī. A proclaimed offender. [*denā.*
mujrimān-i-ishtehārī ko dīdah-o-dānistah jagah
Harbouring knowingly proclaimed offenders.
mujrim ko giriftār k. To apprehend a criminal.
mujrim farārī. An escaped convict or offender.
mujrimoṅ kī fehrist meṅ chhapnā.
To be published in the Gazette.
مجرمانه *mujrimāna'h.* adv. Criminally.
mujrim h., v. n. To commit an offence.

A مجروح *majrūh'*, adj. جرح wounding.
1. Wounded. 2. Smitten by love.
majrūhān-i-jang ke wāste shafā-khānā h.
A hospital for wounded men.
majrūhān-i-jang ke wāste farāhimī-i-chandah.
G. G. Subscriptions raised for the relief of the wounded.
majrūh k. To wound; inflict a wound. [murder.
majrūhī-bil-qasd. Wounding with intent to
majrūhī qarīb-ul-marg. Wounding attended with danger to life. [into law; in force.

A مجريه *majrī'yah*, adj. Enacted; passed
qānūn-i-majrīyah. The laws in force.

E مجستريت *majisṭreṭ'*; Illit. *majisṭar*, n. m. Cor. of Eng. Magistrate.
The committing officer.
majisṭreṭ ālā. A consul; chief magistrate.
anāṛī majisṭreṭ, An honorary magistrate.
majisṭreṭ az taraf malkah āliyah.
A justice of the peace. [a magistrate.
ikhtiyārāt-i-majisṭreṭ. The judicial powers of
ikhtiyārāt-i-majisṭreṭī milnā yā atā h. To be invested with the powers of a magistrate.
مجستريتي *majisṭreṭ'ī*, n. f.
The office of magistrate.

A مجلس *maj'lis*, n. f. جلس sat. 1. A party; council (جماعت 1, 2).
majlis barāë rifāh-i-ām.
A meeting in the public interest.
majlis meṅ sharīk h., v.n. To join an assembly; attend a meeting. [society.
mīr-majlis, n. m. The president or head of a

A مجمع *maj'mā*, n. m. جمع collecting.
1. A place of meeting or rendezvous.
2. An assembly.
majma-i-khilāf qānūn, yā nā-jāiz, G. G.
An unlawful assemblage.
majma-i-ām. A public assemblage or meeting.
majma-i-ām meṅ mukhil h., v. n. G. G.
To disturb a public assembly.
majma-i-mazhabī. A religious assembly.
majma-i-mufsidān. A riotous assembly.
kisī bad-nīatī se majma ikhaṭṭā k.
To assemble with evil intent.

A مجمل *muj'mal*, adj. جمل summed up.
Abstracted; summary; brief (*ijmālī*).
mujmal hisāb. An abstract account.
مجملا *mujmal'an*, adv. In the abstract; compendiously; summarily; in short; cursorily.

A مجموعه *majmū'āh*, جمع collected. 1. An aggregate (جمع 1). 2. A collection; compendium. 3. A body of laws; a code.
majmūa zavābit faujdārī. The Code of criminal procedure (Act XXV of 1861).
majmūah tāzīrāt Hind.
The Indian penal code (Act XLVIII).
majmūah zavābit. A code of procedure.
majmūah zavābit dīvānī. The code of civil procedure (Act XXV of 1859).
majmūah, p. adj. Brought together; collected.
majmūah-qavānīn. A code; constitution.
majmū'ī, adj. Collective; aggregate.
majmūī qīmat. Aggregate value.
majmūī nambar. An aggregate number.

A مجوزه *mujav'vazah*, adj. 1. Proposed.
2. Decided; determined.
3. Prescribed; laid down.
mujavvizān-i-qānūn, A legislative body; legislature; court of legislature; parliament.
afsar-i-mujavvaz-i-muqadmah. G. G.
The officer trying the case.

H مچكا मचका *mach'kā*, n.m. Dullness of the market; depression of trade. [(the market).
machkā paṛnā, yā khānā, v.n. To be depressed

T مچلكه *muchal'ka*, n. m. A recognizance; bond; penal recognizance; penalty bond.
An engagement exacted from thieves or suspected persons engaging to refrain from any illegal act.
muchalkah ba-ibārat-i-zābitah; muchalkah ba-qaid tāvāṅ. A penal recognizance.
muchalkah pairavī nālish yā adāë shahādat. G.G.
A recognizance to prosecute a complaint or to give evidence.
muchalkah hifz-i-aman. G. G.
A bond to keep the peace.
muchalkah hifz-i-aman bā yā bilā zāminān likhnā. To enter into a bond to keep the peace with or without sureties.
muchalkah likhnā. To execute a recognizance.
muchalkah lenā, yā likhānā, v. a.
To take a recognizance. [haviour.
muchalkah-i-nek-chalanī. A bond for good be-
muchalka karvānā, v.a. To cause one to execute a recognizance.

A محابات *muhāb'āt, muhābā*, Mah. law. n. m. حب was loved. An act by which a man wilfully incurs an additional charge or loss, as by adding to a stipulated dower, selling a thing under, or buying at an overvaluation, either from personal regard or with a view to some ultimate advantage.

A محاذي *mahāz'ī*, adj. حذو faced. Opposite; over against; in front. [page or column.
mahāzī meṅ likhnā, To write on the opposite

A محاربة *mahār'bah, muhārbah*, n. f.
1. A combat; duel. 2. Fight; battle.

A محاسب *muhās'ib*, n. m. حسب computed.
An accountant; an examiner or auditor of accounts. [accountant.
mahāsib-i-deh; n. m. H. *paṭvārī*, A village

محاسبة *muhās'aba*, n m. حسب computed.
Adjustment or settlement of accounts.
muhāsaba-talab. Demanding a settlement of accounts. [2. To call to account.
muhāsabah lenā, v. a. 1. To take an account;
muhāsaba k., v. a. To settle accounts.

A محاصل *mahās'il*, n. m. حصل produced.
Proceeds; usufruct; revenue (آمدني 1).
mahāsil-i-khām. Gross produce.
mahāsil jāēdād-i-marhūnah. The usufruct of a mortgaged property.
mahāsil-i-deh, n. Village rents.
mahāsil shaē marhūnah. The usufruct.
mahāsil yā nikāsī h. To yield; produce.

A محافظ *muhāfi'z*, n. m. حفظ preserving, guarding.
1. A watchman; guard; warden. 2. A keeper; guardian; curator. 3. A protector.
muhāfiz-i-tan. Bodyguard.
muhāfiz-khānah, Record room.
muhāfiz-daftar, A record keeper. [*khāna*).
muhāfiz-i-mahbas, G. G. A jailor (*dārogah-i-jel-*

محافظت *muhāf'azat*; Illit. *mahāozat*, n. f. حفظ preserved. 1. Guardianship; protection.
2. Custody; care.

A محال *muhāl,'* adj. Impossible.
muhāl mutlaq. Absolutely impossible.
shart-i-muhāl, An impossible condition.

A محال *mahāl'*; Illit *muhāl*, n. m. 1. Real or landed estate. 2. Parcels of land separately assessed with the public revenue, the whole property of the revenue-payers in the *mahāl* being held hypothecated to Government for the sum assessed upon it.
mahāl khālisā ya mahāl mālguzārī.
An estate paying revenue to Government, a revenue-paying estate.
mahāl sharākatī, A joint or coparcenary estate.
mahāl ğair-munqasimah, mahāl mushtaraka, mahāl mushtarikah ğair-munqasimah.
A joint undivided estate.
mahāl mashrūt. An estate held on certain stipulated conditions.
mahāl maqrūqā, An attached estate.
mahāl mi'ānī, n. A record kept in the Collector's office of the several shares of an estate.

A محبس *mah'bas*, n. m. حبس confined.
A jail; prison; dungeon.
mahbas-i-dīvānī. A civil jail.

محبوس *mahbūs'*, n. m. A captive. [mus.
mahbūs sanad. A warrant of committal; a mitti-

A محتاج *mohtāj'*, *mauhtāj*, adj.
1. Poor; indigent; necessitous; needy.
2. Defective; wanting.
mohtāj, n.m. 1. A beggar; pauper. 2. A cripple.
mohtāj-khānah. A poor house.
mohtāj k., v. a. To impoverish; make poor.
mohtāj h., v. n. 1. To have occasion for; to be in need of. 2. To be very poor.
mohtāj'gī, mohtājī, n. f.
Indigence; poverty; want of means..

A محترفة *muhtar'afa*, n. A tax or taxes levied on trades and professions, or on the artificers of a village or their implements, as upon the weaver's loom, upon tradesmen and their shops and stalls, and sometimes upon houses; a license tax. [A censor.

A محتسب *muhtasib'*, n.m. حسب calculating.
A superintendant of market and police; an officer appointed to take cognizance of improper behaviour, as of indecency, drunkenness, gambling, and of the sale of intoxicating drugs and liquors, and false weights and measures.

A محتمل *muhtamal'*, adj. حمل bore. 1. Suspected; doubtful; ambiguous. 2. Susceptible; liable. 3. Possible; probable.

A محجوب الارث *mahjūb-ul-irs*. Excluded from in heritance; incompetent to inherit.
mahjūb ul-irs k. To disinherit; to exclude from or cut off from an inheritance. [ered.

A محجور *mahjūr'*, adj. حجر Debarred; hind-
mahjūr, n. m. In Mah. law, an inhibited slave who is incompetent to buy, sell, or transact any business on his own account, as opposed to *māzūr* a licensed slave.

A محدود *mahdūd'*, adj. حد setting bounds.
1. Limited; bounded; definite.
2. Defined; definite.
mahdūd ba-hisas. G. G. Limited by shares.
mahdūd ba-tāhud. G. G. Limited by guarantee.
mahdūd k., v. a. 1. To limit; bound. 2. To define.

A محرر *muhar'rir, muharrar*, n. m.
A writer; clerk.

moharrir-i-naqshā. The returning officer.
moharrir-i-adālat, A court clerk.
moharrir-i-rajisṭarī. A registration clerk.
محررة *muhar'rarah*, adj. Written; engrossed.
muhar'rirī, n. f. The business of a clerk.

A محرف *muhar'raf*, adj. 1. Tampered with.
2. Perverted (the sense).

A محرك *muhar'rik*; H. *prerṇak*, n. m. حرك
1. A mover. 2. A promoter. 3. A ringleader.

A محرم *mah'ram*, *mahram-i-rāz*, n. m.
1. A confidant; bosom friend.
2. A consort. 3. A man who is admitted into the women's apartments.

A محروم الارث *mahrūm-ul-irs.* G. G. adj.
Disinherited.
mahrūmī-i-virsā. G. G. Disinheritance.

A محسوب *mahsūb'*, adj. حسب computing.
1. Computed; calculated; numbered.
2. Carried to account.
mahsūb h., v. n. To be carried to account.

A محصول *mahsūl'*; Rus. *māsūl*, *masūl*, n.m.
Taxes; duty; customs; toll; excise; postage; public income from any source (*āmdanī*, 3).
mahsūl-i-ābkārī. Taxes on spirits.
mahsūl ugāhne-vālā, n. m. A revenue collector.
mahsūl ba qadr-i-māliyat, *Ad valorem* duty.
mahsūl parmaṭ. Customs duty.
mahsūl chukānā, v. a. To pay duty or postage.
mahsūl-chor, n. m. A smuggler (*chaukī-mār*).
mahsūl-dār, *mahsūlī*, adj. 1. Dutiable.
2. Paying a tax or duty.
mahsūl-i-ḍāk. Postage.
mahsūl sāyar. Miscellaneous duties.
mahsūl-i-saṛak. A road cess; toll.
mahsūl kī āmdanī, n. f. Income from taxes.
mahsūl lagānā, v. a. To tax; levy a tax.
mahsūl mārnā, v. a. To smuggle.
mahsūl māl bār-āmad. Export duties.
mahsūl-i-nahr. Canal rents.
mahsūl'ī, n. f. Lands paying revenue.
mahsūlī, adj Dutiable; bearing postage.
be-mahsūl, adj. Post free; not dutiable.
fard-i-mahsūl. A tariff.
mahsūl ṛaunṭoṭī yā chungī. Octroi charges.

A محصلي *muhass'ilī*, n. f.
1. The duty or fee of a tax gatherer, bailiff, etc; commission on collections. 2. The office of a Collector of rents or taxes.

A محض *mahz*, adj. 1. Pure; unmixed.
2. Absolute; entire; mere. [(بالكل).
mahz, adv. Absolutely; utterly; downright

mahz dastkhat. A blank endorsement.
mahz dastkhat k., v. a. To endorse in blank; to give *carte blanche*.
mahz zimnan, Implied merely.
mahz gair-mumkin. Absolutely impossible.
mahz fiqreh-bāzī. Sheer device or trickery.
mahz qaid, G. G. Simple imprisonment.

A محضر *mah'zar*, *mahzar-nāmah*, n. f. حضر was present. A public attestation.
A general application or representation; a statement laid before a judge; a document attested by a number of persons professing to be cognizant of the circumstances of the case, and submitted with their signatures to the court.
mahzar-khānah. A police station or court.

A محفوظ *mahfūz'*, adj. حفظ preserving.
1. Guarded; protected; preserved.
2. Secure; safe.
mahfūz rakhnā, v. a. To guard; preserve.
mahfūz rahnā, v. n. 1. To be protected, preserved. 2. To be safe and sound.
māl-mahfūz-rakhnā, G. G. Custody of property.
mahfūz'ī, n. G. G. Protection.

A محقق *muhaq'qaq*, *muhaqqiquh*, adj. حق was right. 1. See تحقيق. [firmed.
2. Certified; verified; authenticated; con-
3. Decided; positive.

A محكمة *mah'kamah*, *mahkmah*, n. m. حكم restraining, exercising authority. 1. (*mahkamah-i-adālat*) A court of law, justice, or judicature; a tribunal; session; assize.
2. A department (*saristah*, 4).
mahkamah-i-ibtidāī. A court of original jurisdiction.
mahkamah-i-apīl. An Appellate court.
mahkamah-i-ālā, yā āliyah. A High court.
mahkamah-i-kamsaryaṭ.
The commissariat department.

A محكوم *mahkūm'*, adj. Subjected; under command or authority.
mahkūm', n.m. A subject; a subordinate officer.
محكومة *mahkūm'ah*, adj.
Ruled; governed; enforced.

A محل *mahl*, *mahal*, n. m. 1. Place. 2. Wife.
mahl-dār, n. m. The watchman of a division.
mahl-dārnī, n. f 1. The midwife of a mahal or division. 2. The head of a brothel; the mother bawd. 3. The female superintendent of a lock hospital.
محلة *mahal'lah*; Pop. *muhalla*, n. m.
A parish; ward; a division of a town.
muhalleh-dār, *mīr-mahallah*, n. m. 1. The head man of a parish. 2. An officer in charge of a particular quarter of the town, bound to give

information to the *Darogā* of the police of any disorderly conduct, or the presence of culprits.

A محلل *muhal'lil*, n. m. حل untied. 1. One who makes lawful that which was illegal.

2. A man who marries a divorced woman that he may put her away, and so enable her to be married again to her first husband.

A محمولة *mahmūl'ah*, adj. حمل 1. Laden.

2. Bearing (a meaning). 3. Applicable.
mahmūlah-i-jahāz, A cargo; a shipment.
māl-i-mahmūla, A load.

A محنتانة *mehnatā'nah*; Pop. *mahntāna*, n. m. Remuneration; fee.
mehnatānah ajūrah, The wages of labor.
mehnatānah ba-hisāb fī sadī. Percentage. [fees.
mehnatānah takhmīnī, Estimated amount of
mehnatānah-i vakīl, Pleader's or Counsel's fee.

A محولة *muhav'vala*. adj. Cited; mentioned.

A مخارج *ma*khār'ij*, n. pl. of مخرج from خرج issued. 1. Expenses; disbursements; outgoings, as revenue; 2. Alienations; assignments of portions of the Government claim; remissions of revenue due by the *zamīndārs* on account of lands dismembered or alienated.

A مخاصمت *mu*khās'amat*, n. f. خصم
Mutual enmity or hostility.
binā-e-mukhāsamat, Cause of action.

A مخاصة *mu*khās'ah*, n. خص appropriated.

A village or land assignment to an individual either rent-free or at a low quit-rent on condition of service; a village held *khās* by the State, the revenue being paid to the Government direct, or the share of the Government in a village, or the revenue paid by it.

A مخالف *mu*khā'lif*, n. m. خلف coming after.

An opponent; adversary.
mukhālif, adj. Opposite; adverse; contrary.
mukhālif h., v. n. 1. To oppose. 2. To contravene.
مخالفت *mu*khāl'ifat*, n. f. 1. Enmity; opposition; contrariety; hostility.
2. Disagreement; dissension.
mukhālifat k., v. a. To oppose; go against.

A مخبر *mu*kh'bir, jāsūs*; Illit. *mukhbar*, n.m. خبر An informer; emissary; a spy.
mukhbir'ī, jāsūsī. n. f. Secret information.
ashkhās-i-mukhbir. G. G. Informers.

A مخبوط الحواس *ma*khbūt-ul-havās*, Insane.

A مختار *mu*khtār'*; Illit. *mukhtiyār*, adj. خير chosen. Invested with power or authority; independent; at liberty; authorized; competent; having legal power.
mukhtār, n. m. 1. An agent; assignee; a procurator; proctor. 2. A delegate; representative. 3. An attorney; a solicitor; an attorney not generally authorized to plead.
mukhtāratan', adv. By attorney.
mukhtār-i-riyāsat, n. m. A bailiff; a general manager of an estate.
mukhtār-i-ām, n. m. A general agent.
mukhtār-kār, n. m. A director; superintendent; commissioner (*sarbarāh*, 1).
mukhtār-kārī, mukhtārī, n. f. Procuration (the act); attorneyship (*sarbarāhī*).
mukhtār k., v. a. To authorize; empower.
mukhtār-i-kul, yā mutlaq, n. One invested with full powers; a plenipotentiary.
mukhtār kothī bīmā,
A manager of an insurance office.
mukhtār-i-maqbūlā, A recognized agent.
mukhtār-nāmah-i-khās, A special power of attorney. [torney.
mukhtār-nāmah-i-ām, A general power of at-
mukhtār h. 1. To have authority. 2. To act for one; to represent; stand for.
3. To be competent.
mukhtārī k., v. a. 1. To act for; represent; administer. 2. To practise as an attorney.

A مختصر *mu*khtas'ar, mukhtasir*, adj. خصر abridged. Concise (*mujmal*).
mukhtasar, n. m. An abstract (اجمال 2) [*lāsah k.*).
mukhtasar k., v. a. To abridge; epitomize (*khu-*
مختصراً *mu*khtas'aran, mukhtasar taur par*, adv.
Briefly (*mujmalan*).

A مخفي *ma*kh'fī*, adj. خفي hidden.
Secret; clandestine (*poshīdah*).
makhfī kharch, yā akhrājāt, n. f.
Secret or underhand expenditure.
makhfī habs-i-be-jā,
Wrongful confinement in secret.
makhfī madākhilat-i-bejā ba-khānah waqt-i-shab.
G. G. Lurking house-trespass by night.
makhfī madākhilat-i-be-jā ba-khāna. Lurking house trespass. [ing that.
makhfī na rahe. Be it known; whereas; see-
shaë-i-makhfī, G. G. A thing concealed. [ment.
qasdan makhfī rakhnā. G. G. Wilful conceal-

A مخل *mu*kh'il*, n. m. part. act of خل pierced. A disturber; intruder.
mukhil-i-haisīyat, adj. Defamatory.
mukkil-i-aman, A disturber of the peace.
mukhil h., v. n. To disturb; derange; interfere with; intrude on.

A مخلوط *ma'khlūt'*, adj. خلط mixed. Lands recently annexed to an estate or a district.

A مخمور *ma'khmūr'*, adj. Inebriate (*matvālā*).

A مد *madd, mad*, n. f.
1. Article; column.
2. A sign denoting the commencement of a paragraph or the insertion of a new item.
3. A head of accounts. 4. A peculiar mode of writing certain words in accounts.
madd-i-amānat. Head of deposits.
Revenue additions to the revenue of a district, either from the annexation of other lands, or from the full asessment of lands which had been wholly or partially exempt from payment of revenue.
madd-i-muqābil. *Per contra*.
mad meṅ ānā, v n. To come under a heading.
is mad meṅ. G. G. Under this head. [(*bābat*).
mad'de; Pop. *maddhe*, adv. On account of

A مداخل *madā'khil*, n. m. دخل entered.
Opp. of *makhārij*. Rent; income.
Changes in the disposition of landed property, or in the arrangement of the shares in a village.
madākhil makhārij. Additions and diminutions.
مداخلت *mudā'kh'ilat*, n. f.
1. Occupancy. 2. Interference.
mudākhilat bilā-marzī. G. G. Intrusion.
mudākhilāt-i-bejā, G. G. Trespass. [trespass.
mudākhilat-i-bejā ba-khānah, n. Lurking house
mudākhilat-i-sarīh. A direct act of interference. [meddler.
mudākhilat karne-vālā. An intruder; inter-
madākhilat mustalzim-i-sazā. Criminal trespass.
madākhlat nā-jāiz ba-khānah. House-trespass.

A مدارالمہام *madār-ul-mahām*, n. m.
1. A prime minister; regent.
2. A principal manager of affairs.
madār-i-dāvā. Ground of claim or action.

A مدارج *madār'ij*, n. m. pl. of درجہ
The steps or stages of a business.

A مدام *mudām'*, adv. Always; for ever.

A مداین *mudāyan'*, n. m. دین a debt.
A debtor or creditor.

A مدانیت *madāëna't*, n. f. دین borrowing, asking in loan. Mutual credit; dealings as debtor and creditor.

A مدت *mud'dát*, n. f. مد extending. See عرصہ
1. Duration; usance. 2. A long time.
muddat-ul-umr. All one's life; during life.
muddat-kā, A. H. adj. Old; ancient.
muddat guzarnā, v. n. To elapse (a long time).
muddat-i-madīd. A long space of time.
muddat-i-muqarrarah. A specified term or period.
muddat-i-hunḍī, mitī kī hunḍī. A bill after date.
muddat huī, A long time ago.
ek muddat, A long time; an age.

A مدخلہ *mad'khal'ah*, adj. Deposited; filed.
madkhalah tauzī. Brought on the rent-roll.
مدخولہ *mad'khūl'ah*; H. *rakhnī*, n. f.
A kept-mistress

A مدد *mad'ad, madad-gārī*; Illit. *madat*, n. f. مد extending. 1. Aid; assistance (امداد).
2. Reinforcements.
3. Allowance; provision; relief; help.
4. Laborers, masons, etc. (helpers).
madad bāṅṭnā, To distribute wages (to laborers).
madad-kharch 1. Subscriptions; contributions.
2. Advances. [a suppliant.
madad-khuāh. n. m. One who applies for aid;
madad denā yā k., madadgār h., v. a.
To render or furnish assistance.
مددگار *madad-gār*, n. m.
1 A helper. 2. An accessory. 3. An assistant.
madadgār-i-jurm. An abettor.
madadgārī bād az vuqū. Subsequent abetment.
mudagārī qabl az vuqū, Previous abetment.
madadgārī kī targīb denā. G. G.
Enticement of an abetment.
madad-i-maāsh 1. A maintenance; pension.
2. An assignment of revenue for the support of learned or pious Mahomedans, or of benevolent institutions.
madad māṅgnā, v. a. To ask for help.

H مدرا मुदरा *mud'rā, mudrī*, n. f. S. मुद्रा
1. (*Rare*) A seal; signet. 2. A seal ring.
3. An impression; a stamp. 4. A coin; medal.
mudrā-shālā. A mint (*ṭaksāl*).

A مدعا *mud'dāā*; Illit. *muddā*, دعو demanding.
1. Object; meaning.
2. Property; stolen property. [claimed.
muddaā bihā, The thing or object sued for or
muddaā pakaṛnā, v. n.
To discover stolen property.
muddaā hāsil h., v. n. To gain one's object.
muddaā nikalnā, v. n.
To be recovered (stolen property, etc.).
muddaā yeh hai. The real object is this.
مدعاعلیہ *muddāā-ālaih*, n. m. A defendant in a case; the adverse party.
muddaā'alah par gālib ānā. To cast defendant.
muddaā'alah tartībī. n. A defendant *pro forma*.
muddaā alaih-sharīk, A co-defendant.
muddaā-alaih k., v. a. 1. (*muddaā-alaih gardānnā*) To make a defendant in a case.
2. To indict; charge.
muddaā-alaih kī jānib se, muddaā-alaih kī taraf, yā or se, For the defence.
مدعاعلیہم *muddāā-alaihim*. G. G.
The persons accused.

ahad-ul muddâä-alaihim. G. G.
One of the persons accused.
مدعي *muddâ'ī*, n. m. *muddaiyah*, n. f. دعو demanded. Complainant; prosecutor (*dāvedār*).
muddaī sharīk, n. m. A co-plaintiff.
muddaī muddaā-alaih, n. m. The parties in a case; the litigant parties.
muddaī h., v, n. To claim; sue for.
muddaī, yā muddaā-alaihoṅ meṅ dākhil k.,
To make a party in a suit.

H مدک मदक *mad'ak*, n. f.
An intoxicating pill or bolus.
It is made of chopped betel leaves and opium which may be swallowed or smoked in a pipe.

A مدلل *mudal'lal*, adj. 1. Supported by reasons or proofs. 2. Well-grounded; reasonable.

A مدہوش *mudhosh'*, adj. دہش was confounded.
1. (*matvālā*) Intoxicated.
2. Senseless; insensible; stupefied.
مدہوشي *madhosh'ī*, n. f. 1. Intoxication.
2. Insensibility. [A debtor.

A مديون *madyūn'*, n. دين asking, owing.
mudyūn ḍigrī. A judgment debtor.
madyūn muflis. An insolvent debtor.

H مڈھ मुढ *muḍh*, adj. H. *mūṅḍ* head.
Principal; chief; head.
muḍh, n. m. 1. A chief or headman (*sardār*, 1—4). 2. A ringleader. [tioned; said.

A مذکور *mazkūr'*, adj. ذکر remembered. Men-
mazkūr; pl. *mazkūrāt*, n. m.
A statement; the contents or substance of a written statement.
mazkūrāt' n. pl. Contingent expenses; items.
mazkūrah bālā, mazkūr-us-sadr, adv.
Aforesaid; above-mentioned.
mazkūr'ī, n. f. An independent *taalluqdār* paying rent to Government.
مذکوري *mazkūr'ī*, n. m. A process-server.
mazkūrī tāalluq yā mahāl, n.
A dependant *taluq* or estate of which the revenue is paid through the intervention of a *zamīndār* or other revenue payer.
mazkūrī māl-guzār, n. A subordinate payer of revenue, not paying direct.
mazkūrī raiyat, n. A nominal or migratory cultivator; a tenant-at-will having no hereditary right of occupancy.

A مذمت *mazam'mat*, n. f. ذم blamed. 1. Evil-speaking. 2. Satire; lampoon. [creed; faith.

A مذہب *maz'hab*, n. m. Religious belief;
mazhab badalnā, v. n. To change one's religion.
mazhab meṅ milānā, v. a.
To convert to a religion.
aqīdah-i-mazhab. G. G. Religious belief.
muāfī-i-mazhab. G. G. A religious grant.
مذہبي *maz'habī*, adj. Religious.
mazhabī; Illit. *mazbī*, n. m.
1. One who is a Sikh by religion.
2. A Sikh of the sweeper caste.
mazhabī jhagṛā, A religious dispute.
mazhabī laṛāī. A religious war; a crusade.
mazhabī muāmlā. A religious matter or dispute.
dars-i-mazhabī. Religious teaching; preaching.
masala-i-mazhabī. Religious tenets.

A مراتب *marāt'ib*, n. m. pl. of مرتبه 1. Gradations of rank; degrees; dignities.
2. Articles; points; particulars.
3. Matters; circumstances; affairs.
marātib-i-tamhīdī, yā ibtidāī, n. m. Preliminary measures. [ent stages.
marātib taë k., v. a. To pass through the differ-
marātib-i-mutanāzeh-fīh. The points at issue.
marātib mundarje arzī dāvā.
The subject matter of a plaint.
marātib-i-mundarje arzī dāve se vajeh nālish nahīṅ paidā hotī. The subject matter of the plaint does not constitute a cause of action.
marātib-i-vāqeāt. The facts.

A مراجعت *murāj'aat*, n. f. رجع returned.
Return; coming back.

A مراد *murād'*, n. f. رود seeking.
1. Object. 2. Tendency; tenor; drift.
3. A vow.
murād dāva. The object of a suit. [template.
murād rakhnā, v. n. To intend; imply; con-
murād lenā, v. n.
To understand; conclude; infer.
murād hai. Is intended.
is murād se. With this intent or object.
ba-murād-durustī-i-intizām-i-faujdārī. For regulating criminal procedure. [this Code.
hasb murād ahkām is majmūah. G. G. Under
ba-murād-i-fāsid. Maliciously; with evil intent; with ill-will.
murād'ī, n. A certain number of annas.

A مراسلات *murāsalāt'*, n. m. رسل sent a message. Correspondence.
مراسله *murās'lah*, Ped. for *chiṭṭhī*, n. m. A letter.

A مرافعه *murāf'a*, n. m. رفع raised.
An appeal; action.
murāfa-i-akhīr. Final appeal. [instance.
murāfa-i-avval, murafa-i-ūlā. Court of first
murāfā-i-sānī, yā doyam. Court of second instance; an Appellate court. [higher court.
murāfa k, v. a. To appeal; refer (a case) to a
murāfe ke qābil. Appealable.
muqadme kā murāfa k., v. a. To remove a suit.

H مرانا **मराना** *marā'nā, marvānā,* Slang, v. a. To suffer sodomy.

A مرتب *murat'tab, murattab-shudah,* adj. رتب settled. 1. Arranged; set in order; regulated. 2. Compiled; digested.
murattab k., v. a. 1. To put in order; arrange. 2. To draw up; compile; digest.
galat dast-āvez murattab k., G. G. Making an erroneous document.
gair-murattab, adj. Not in order.

A مرتبة *martab'ah,* n. m. 1. Rank; office (*padvī,* 1). 2. Time.
kaī martabah. Several times; repeatedly.
kaī martabah aisā huā. Several instances have occurred.

H مرتدھن **मृत धन** *mrit dhan.* The estate of the deceased.

A مرتشي *murtash'ī,* adj. Given to bribe-taking; corrupt.

A مرتکب *murtak'ib,* adj. رکب rode. 1. Committing; perpetrating. 2. Guilty.
murtakib-i-jurm. One who commits a crime.
murtakib-i-jurm h. G. G. To commit an offence.
murtakib madākhilāt-i-bejā. A trespasser.
murtakib-i-vārdāt. G. G. The doer of a criminal act.
murtakib h. To commit; perpetrate; do (a wrong act).
murtakib huā. Committed; perpetrated.
zinā-kārī kā murtakib h. G. G. To commit adultery.
fel kā murtakib. G.G. The person doing the act.
qatl-i-amad kā murtakib. G.G. Guilty of murder.

A مرتہن *murta'han,* adj. رہن fixed, put, deposited. Pledged; pawned.
murtah'in, n. m. A mortgagee.
murtahin-dakhīl, yā qābiz. A mortgagee in possession.
murtahan mā-bād. A subsequent mortgagee.

H مرجاد **मरजाद** *marjād',* n. f. S. मर्य्यादा 1. Custom 2. A social code.

A مرجوعة *marjū'ā,* adj. رجع instituted. Instituted; filed; appealed.
ba-haisyat-i-marjūah. As brought or instituted (a suit).

P مرحلهدار *marhala-dār.* A road watchman.

P مردار *murdār,* n.m. 1. A dead body; a corpse. 2. Carrion (*Mah.*). The carcase of an animal that has died a natural death, or which has not been killed in a lawful manner, and is therefore unfit for food.
murdah jalānā. Burning the dead; cremation.
murdah-shū. Mah. One who washes the dead.
murdah-farosh, Mah. n. m. A low caste whose business it is to carry the dead.

P مردي *murd'ī,* n. f. 1. Manhood; virility. 2. (Wom.) *Membrum virile.*

A مرقومة *marqūma', marqūma-i-bālā,* adj. Aforesaid (*mazkūrah-i-bālā*).
marqūm-ul-hāshiyā, Written on the margin.

H مرگھٹ **मरघट** *mar'ghaṭ, murd-ghaṭṭī;* Tir. *marchaur,* n. m. S. मृतघट्ट, H. *mar* die, *ghāṭ* ferry. The place where Hindus burn their dead.

A مرمت *maram'mat,* n. f. رم mending. Amending a plaint or plea.
marammat savāl. A supplemental plaint.

H مرو **मरू** *mar'ū, maru asthal,* n. m. S. मरु sandy. A dry or sandy and sterile tract.

H مروانا **मरवाना** *marvā'nā,* v. a. Caus. of مرانا q. v. To suffer sodomy or improper sexual intercourse.

H مروٹ **मरवट** *mar'vaṭ, maruaṭ,* n. m. H. *mārnā* to kill. Rent-free land given to the families of retainers killed in battle.

A مروج *murav'vaj, muravvajah;* Illit. *muravvij,* adj. روج was easily saleable. Current; usual (جاري 2, 3).
muravvaj k., v. a. To give currency to; to spread (*jārī k.* 2, 3, 4).
muravvaj h., v. n. To gain ground; to become prevalent; to prevail; to be in force (*jārī h.*).

A مرہون *marhūn', marhūnah,* adj. رہن Pawned; pledged; mortgaged.

H مری **मरी** *mar'rī,* n. f. Lands assigned in lieu of interest of loans. *Carnegy.*

A مزاحم *muzā'him,* adj. زحم straitened him. Hindering; obstructive.
muzāhim, n. m. One who brings a cross action, or interferes in a suit, esp. to obstruct proceedings.
muzāhim-dār, n. m. One whose rights or possessions are incidentally encroached upon.
muzāhim h., muzāhimat k., v. a. To obstruct; offer obstruction; oppose; resist; bar; hinder (*roknā,* 2, 3, 5).
مزاحمت *muzāh'imat,* n. f. Opposition; bar; interruption (آڑ 6, 7, 8).
muzāhimat-i-bil-jabr k. G. G. Resisting by force.
muzāhimat-i-bejā. Wrongful restraint.
muzāhimat-i-bejā k., v. a. To restrain wrongfully.
muzāhimat-i-bejā kī sazā. G. G. Punishment for wrongful restraint.

muzāhimat-i-jismānī. Personal restraint.
muzāhimat-i-qurqī. Breach of attachment.
bilā-muzāhimat. Undisturbed.
qasdan muzāhimat pahuṅchānā. G. G. To obstruct intentionally.

مزاحمي *muzāh'imī*, n. f. An action in bar of proceedings, a cross-suit.
muzāhimī natthī. Papers relating to a cross-suit or suit in hindrance of proceedings.

A مزار *mazār'*, n. m. A tomb; shrine.

A مزارع *muzār'ā*, n. m. زرع he sowed. A husbandman; a cultivator.
muzāra i-maurūsī, n. m. A permanent cultivator.
muzāra-i-ğair-maurūsī, A tenant-at-will.

A مزرعة *maz'rā*, n. m. 1. A hamlet. 2. A farm.

مزروعه *mazrū'āh*, adj. Cultivated; tilled.
mazrūah, n. m. Cultivated land; a field with a crop on it.

A مزيد *mazīd'*, n. m. زيد increased. Increase; augmentation.
shahādat-i-mazīd. G. G. Further evidence.
miyād-i-mazīd. G. G. Further time.

A مساوي *musāv'ī, masāvī, mutasāvī*, adj. Equal.
hissa-i-masāvī. G. G. Equal shares.

A مستاجر *mustā'jir*, n. m. اجر compensated. 1. A farmer or farm-holder. 2. A contractor.
mustājir-i-aslī, n. m. The original lessee.
mustājir khās sarkār kā. A farmer of land holding immediately of Government.
mustājir-i-sarkārī, n. m. A Government farmer or lessee.
mustājir-i-farzī, G. G. n. m. The ostensible farmer.

مستاجري *mustā'jirī*, n. f. 1. A lease of land; a holding; a farm. 2. A contract.
mustājirī denā, v. a. To let in farm; to lease.

A مستبين غير مرسوم *mustabīn ğair-marsūm.* A partially irregular deed, deficient in some formalities, and not admitted as legal evidence, but as intimation of the intention of the executor.
mustabīn marsūm. A regular deed or contract, executed in proper legal form.
ğair-mastabīn. A contract or deed wholly irregular and invalid.

A مستثني *mustas'nā*, adj. ثني doubled. 1. Excluded; excepted. 2. Except (*bajuz*).
mustasnīyāt-i-āmmā, G. G. General exceptions.
mustasnā k., v. a. To exclude; except.

A مستحق *mustah'aq*, adj. حق was right. 1. Entitled; having a claim. 2. Deserving; meritorious.
mustahaq k., v. a. To entitle; give a claim to.
mustahaq h., v. n. 1. To be entitled to. 2. To deserve.

A مستدعي *mustada'ī*, دعي claimed. An applicant (*dāvedār*).
mustadaī nīlām. G. G. Intending purchasers.

A مسترد *mustar'ad*, adj. 1. Repeated; revoked; overruled. 2. Reversed; set aside; annulled.
mustar'ad k., v. a. To cancel, abrogate; make void. (*tardīd k.*).

A مستطيع *mustatīā'*, n. m. A solvent person; one able to pay.

A مستعار *mustāār'*, adj. Taken on loan.
mustaār denā, v. a. To lend for use (*māṅge denā*).
mustaār lenā, v. n. To borrow (*māṅge lenā*).

A مستعفي *mustāf'ī*, adj. عفو begging to be released from an obligation. Resigned (an office).

A مستعمل *mustām'al*, adj. عمل did. Established; in use; common.
mustāmal h., v. n. To prevail; to be current or in force.
alfāz-i mustāmala dafa hāzā. G. G. The words used in this clause.
gair-mustāmal taur par. G. G. Unused manner.
gair-mustāmal, adj. Not in use; obsolete.

A مستغرق *mustağ'raq*, adj. غرق 1. Drowned; immersed. 2. Absorbed; occupied. 3. Hypothecated.

A مستغيث *mustağīs'*, n. m. غوث calling for aid. A complainant; prosecutor (*dāvedār*).
mustagīs-ilah. The accused; a defendant.

A H مستفيد هونا *mustafīd' h.* v. n. To gain or acquire any benefit.
mustafīd hone kā mustahaq. G. G. Entitled to the benefit (of).

A مستقل *mustaq'il*, adj. Permanent.
mustaqil āsāmī, n. f. A permanent post.
mustaq'lī. Fixed; confirmed, applied to hereditary tenants.

A مستقيم *mustaqīm'*, *mustaqīma*, adj. قوم stood. Erect; straight.
qarābat-i-mustaqīma. Lineal consanguinity.

A مستلزم سزا *mustalzim-i-sazā*, *mustaujib-i-sazā.* Penal; punishable.

A مستند *mustan'ad*, adj. سند supported. Authenticated; genuine.

A مستوجب *mustauj'ib*, adj. وجب was fitted. 1. Liable: fitting. 2. Deserving (*sazāwār*, 2).
mustaujib-ul-adā. Payable ; recoverable.

A مستورات *mastūrāt'*, n. f. ستر became veiled. 1. Women. 2. Respectable (i.e. veiled) women (*pardah-nashīn*).

A مسدود *masdūd'*, adj. Obstructed ; closed.
masdūd-i-chand-rozah. Barred temporarily.
masdūd h., v. n. 1. To fail ; cease.
2. To be obstructed.

A مسروقة *masrūq'ah*, *masrūq*, adj. سرق Stolen : robbed.
māl-i-masrūqah, n.m. Stolen property (*chorī kā māl*).

A مسطور *mastūr'*, *mastūrah*, adj. See *marqūm*.
1. Written ; expressed.
2. Aforesaid ; above-mentioned.

A مسكرات *muskirāt'*, n. m.
Intoxicating drugs as opium, etc. [ing.

A مسكن *mas'kan*, n. m. سكن rested. A dwelling.
maskan-i-māmūlī, n. m. Ordinary residence.
maskan-i-mustaqil. G. G. A domicile.

A مسكين *miskīn'*, adj. سكن was quiet, humble. Poor ; having no property.

A مسلح *musal'lah*, adj. سلح Armed.
musallah-jung, adj. Armed for fight.
musallah h., v. n. To arm. [shambles.

A مسلخ *mas'lakh*, n. f. Slaughter-house ;

A مسلسل *musal'sal*, *silsilevār*, adj. سل drew out. Concatenated ; successive.

A مسلم *musallam*, Entire ; whole.
musallam-alehī. The seller to whom the advance is paid in the kind of sale called *salām*.
musallam-fīhī.
The goods on which the advance is paid.
musallama-i-āmma, Universally admitted.

A مسلماني *musalmān'ī*, n. f.
Circumcision.
musalmānī k., v. a. To circumcise.

A مسلوب الحواس *maslūb-ul-havās*, n. m.
The senses weakened with age, etc.
maslūb-ul-havāsī, n. f. Mental imbecility ; unsoundness of mind.
maslūb-ul-aql, adj. Insane ; mad.

A مسئلة *mas'alah*, *masla*, n.m. 1. A maxim ; saw ; an aphorism. 2. A tenet ; doctrine.
3. A proposition. [of *caveat emptor*.
maslā mushtarī hoshiyār bāsh. The principle
masla wāqeāt amr-i-wāqaī. The principle or doctrine of *factum valeat*.

A مسماة *musammāt'*, n. f.
A title prefixed to the names of women.
musammāt, adj. Called (a lady).

A مسموعة *masmū'āh*, adj. سمع hearing. Heard.

A مسمى *musam'mā*, *musammī*, *musammāt*, adj. اسم Named ; called ; entitled.

H مسن मिसन *mis'an*, n. m.
A soil mixed of clay and sand.

A مسودة *masvad'ah* ; Pop. *masaudā*, n. m. سود. 1. The original or draught of a letter ; a rough. 2. A draft ; a bill. 3. (*Slang*) A son.
masvadah qānun-i maqsūdul-nifāz. G. G.
A draft of a law ; a bill,

P H مسي كرنا *mis'sī k.*, v. a. To deflour.
missī lagāī, n.f. A ceremony among prostitutes.
☞ A feast followed by a *nautch* is given by a newly initiated member to those of her profession, after which the novitiate is allowed the esteemed privilege of blackening her teeth.
missī h., v. n. To be defloured.

A مشاراليه *mushār'un-ilaih*, adj.
Above-mentioned ; aforesaid.

A مشتبة *mushtab'ah*, adj. شبه doubt.
Doubtful ; equivocal (احتمالي 3). [money.
mushtabah-ul-vusūl. Doubtful recoveries of
mushtabah-ul-vaza logoṅ kā ek giroh. G. G.
A gang of suspicious characters.
amr-i-mushtabah, G.G. The matter in question.

A مشترك *mushtar'ak*, adj.
Shared ; joint ; common ; coparcenary.
مشتركة *mushtar'ak ah*, adj. Incorporated ; held in common or partnership.
jāedād-i-mushtarakah, yā maurūsī, G. G.
Joint family property.
garaz-i-mushtarak, G. G. A common object.

A مشتري *mushtar'ī*, n. m. شري
A purchaser (خريدار 1).
mushtarī baē mashrūt. A conditional vendee.
mushtarī-i-digrī. G. G.
A purchaser of a judicial decree.
mushtarī farzī, n. m. A nominal purchaser.
mushtarī nīlām, n. m. An auction purchaser ; a purchaser at a judicial or public sale.

A مشتمل *mushtam'al*, adj.
Inclusive ; common (*shāmil*).

A مشتهر *mushta'har*, adj. شهر he made it commonly known. Proclaimed; advertised; promulgated ; made public.

mushtahar ba-nīlām h.
To be advertised for sale.
mushtahar kiyā jānā. G. G. To be notified by proclamation.
mushtahar k., v. a. To advertise (*ishtihār denā*).

A مشخصه *musha'kh'khasa, mushakhkhas,* adj. See *ma'khsūs.* 1. Specified.
2. Fixed; estimated; assessed.
The term is applied to land or districts for which a settlement of the revenue has been made, and to subordinate tenures for which the holders engage to pay a fixed rent annually upon the whole lot.
mushakhkhasī jamā, n. f. Stipulated revenue; net amount of the revenue.
mushakhkhasī jot, n. f. A farm or lands held at a stipulated rent.
mushakhkhasī-dār. A landholder with whom a settlement has been made.
mushakhkhas k., v. a. See *makhsūs k.*
1. To specify. 2. To fix; settle; estimate.

A مشروطا *mashrūt'*, adj. شرط stipulated. 1. Agreed upon; stipulated. 2. Defined; limited.
Conditional, as applied to assignments or grants of land revenue, importing that the grant was accompanied by certain stipulated conditions.
mashrūt, n. m. A settled revenue of 10 per cent, allowed to *zamīndārs.*
mashrūt-i thāne-jāt. Conditional assignments for the support of police or military stations under the Mah. Government.
mashrūt-i dīvānī, n. f. Conditional assignments for the remuneration of a fiscal functionary.
mashrūt-i-faujdārī. Assignments to military and police establishments.
mashrūt ba-imtihān, On condition of passing the prescribed examination.
مشروطاً *mashrūt'an*, adv. Conditionally.
مشروطي *mashrūt'ī*, adj. Stipulated; contracted.
mashrūtī tamassuk. An indemnity bond.

A مشقت *mashaq'qat*; Illit. & Rus. *masakkat*, n. f. شق Labor (محنت 1).
mashaqqat-i-tāzīrī. Penal servitude.
mashaqqat-i-tāzīrī ba-hālat-i-qaid.
Imprisonment with hard labor.
mashaqqat-i-shadīd, Hard labour.
bā-mashaqqat, With labor.
bā-mashaqqat va jaulān, With labor in irons.
bilā-mashaqqat, Without labor.

A مشکوک *mashkūk'*, adj. شک See احتمالي (3).
1. Ambiguous; uncertain.
2. Altered; tampered with.

H مشکیں باندهنا मुशकें बांधना *mushken bāndhnā, yā charhānā*, v.a. To tie the hands behind the back; to pinion; to tie one's arms.

A مشموله *mashmūl'ah*, part. pass. شمل tying a bag over a sheep's udder to prevent the lamb from sucking.
Incorporated with (*shāmil*, 1, 2, 3).
mashmūla muqaddamah. Filed with the case.

A مشورت *mashvar'at*, n. f. *mashvarah*, n. m. شور 1. Consultation; counsel.
2. A conspiracy; plot.
mashvarat, yā mashvarah k., v. a. To consult.
mashvarah mujrimāna, A criminal conspiracy.
mashvarah lenā, v. n. 1. To consult.
2. To take advice.
kisī mashvare nā-jāiz meṅ sharīk h., v. n.
To engage in a conspiracy. [Well-known.

A مشهور *mashhūr'*; Illit. *mānshur*, adj. شهر
mashhūr o mārūf, Noted; famous.
mashhūr bad-dyānatī, n. f. Notorious corruption.
mashhūr k., v. a. To proclaim (*ishtehār denā*).
mashhūr malik, G. G. n. m.
The acknowledged proprietor.
mashhūr h., v. n. 1. To become public.
2. To become notorious, famous.
mashhūr hai, It is currently reported.

A مشیئت *mashī'yat, mashīat,* n. f. شيأ willed. (*Mah. law*) Power or will.

A مشير *mashīr'*, *mushīr salāh-kār*; H. *mantrī*, n. m. A minister.
mashīr-i-jalsa, n. m. A member of council.
mashīr-i-khās, n. m. A privy counsellor.
mashīr-i-qaisar-i-Hind.
Knight companion of the Bath, K.C.B.
mashīrān-i-saltanat. Privy council. [an associate.

A مصاحب *musā'hib*, n. m. 1. A companion;
2. An aide-de-camp.
مصاحبت *musā'habat, musāhebī*, n. f. Companion.

A مصارف *masār'if*, n.m. pl. of صرف Expenses.
masārif-i-bejā, Unnecessary expenses.
masārif-i-shādī, Marriage expenses. [expenses.
masārif-i-zurūrī, n. m. Immediate or necessary
masārif-i-ārzī, yā gair-muqarrarī, n. m.
See *kharch-i-gair-māmūlī.*
masārif-i-mulk, State expenditure.

A مصدق *masad'daq, musaddaqa*, adj.
Verified; attested; authenticated. [court.
musaddaqa-i-adālat. Authenticated by the
naql-i-musaddaqa, G.G. An authenticated copy.

A مصدوره *masdūr'ah*, adj. صدر
Issued; enacted; passed into law.
masdūrah-bālā. Above-cited. [gūl).

A مصروف *masrūf'*, adj. صرف Employed (*mash-*

irtikāb men masrūf rahnā. G. G.
To continue in the commission of.

A مصلحت *masla'hat*, n. f. 1. Expedience; advisability. 2. Good policy. [consultation.
maslahat k., v. n. To consult together; hold a
maslahat mālūm h. To deem expedient.
maslahat nahīn, Not advisable. [the time.
maslahat-i-vaqt, adj. Seasonable; suited to
muqtazāë maslahat, G. G. Expedient. [opportune.
مصلحتاً *maslahatan'*, adv. Advisedly; *a propos*;

A مصمم *musam'mam*; H. *pakkā*, adj.
Fixed; determined.
musammam irādah, n. m. Fixed determination.

A مصنوعي *masnū'ī*, *masnū*, adj.
Fabricated (جعلي).
masnūī dastkhat, n. m. G. G. A false signature.
masnūī yā qalabī sikkā, n. m. Counterfeit coin.

A مضافات *muzāfāt'*, n. f. 1. Additions; annexations; appendages.
2. Environs; suburbs.

A مضر *muz'ir*, adj. ضرر q. v.
1. Deleterious; offensive; bad.
2. Obnoxious; injurious. [riously.
muzir h., v. n. To be pernicious; to affect inju-
havā ko muzir-i-sehat k. G. G. To make the atmosphere noxious to health.
مضرت *mazar'rat*, n. f. ضرر Injury (ضرر). [damage.
mazarrat pahunchānā, v. a. To injure; hurt;
mazarrat-rasānī, n.f. Injuring another. [prised.

A مضمن *muz'man*, adj. ضمن Included; com-

A مطابق *mutāb'iq*, adj. طبق Like; coinciding.
mutābiq, adv. In conformity or accordance with (حسب).
mutābiq-i-āīn, qānūn ke mutābiq. Lawful; legal; according to law.
mutābiq-i-tārīkh. According to the date.
mutābiq-i-hukm. G. G. Under the order of.
mutābiq sanad. Agreeably to a grant or title.
mutābiq qānūn ke pesh ānā, v. n.
To deal according to law.
mutābiq k, v. a. 1. To compare with.
2. To make like; reconcile. [cide.
mutābiq h., v. n. To agree; correspond; coin-
is ekat ke mutābiq. G. G. Under this act.
is dafa ke mutābiq. G. G. Under this section.
qānūn-i-hind ke mutābiq. G. G.
By the law of India. [ance
مطابقت *mutāb'iqat*, n, f. Conformity; accord-

A مطالبة *mutālaba*, n. m. طلب 1. A demand; requisition; call.
2. A claim; due (*dain*).
mutālaba-i-khāngī. G. G. A private demand.
mutālba-i-khafīf, n. m. Small causes.
mutālba khafīfah, A small Cause Court.
mutālba-i-sarkārī. n. f.
The Government demand.
mutālba-i-farebī, n. m. A fraudulent demand.
mutālba k., v. a. To demand; claim. [liability.
mutālba-i-muqaddam, A prior or preliminary
mutālba muakhkhar. A secondary liability.
mutālba-i-yāftanī. Unrealized assets.
ind-ul-mutālba. On demand.

A مطبع *mat'bā*, n. m. طبع stamped.
A press (*chhāpe-khānā*).
مطبوعة *matbū'ā*, adj. Printed; published.

A مطلب *mat'lab*; Illit. *matlib*, *matbal*, n. m.
Object. [ance of a work.
matlab-barārī, n. f. The discharge or perform-

A مطلق *mut'laq*, adj. طلق 1. Absolute; entire.
2. Independent; unchecked. [(بالكل).
mutlaq, *mut'laqan*, adv. Entirely; absolutely
mutlaq-ul-inān, 1. Independent; not subject.
2. Free; unconcerned.
mutlaq vakālat-nāmā, A full power; a document conveying absolute authority to an agent or representative.
mutlaq vakīl, G. G. An agent furnished with full and absolute powers.
razāmandī-i-mutlaq, G. G. Unconditional assent.

A مطلوب *matlūb'*, *matlūbā*, adj. 1. Desired; sought. 2. Demanded; called for.

A مطمئن *mutmain'*, adj. 1. Satisfied; contented. 2. Quiet; tranquil.
mutmain k., v. a. To encourage; give confidence.

A مطيع *mutī'*, adj. 1. Subject to; under.
2. Submissive; obedient; amenable.
mutī k., v. a. To subjugate; reduce to submission (*zer k.*).

A مظاهرت *muzā'harat*, n. f. ظہر
A formula of divorce, in which a man declares his wife indifferent to him.

A مظلوم *mazlūm'*, adj. ظلم Oppressed; injured.

A مظهر *muz'hir*, adj. ظہر A deponent.
muzhir, n. m. An informer.
muzhar-alaihī. The defendant.
shakhs-i-muzhir-i-razāmandī. G. G.
The person giving the consent.
muzhir h., To affirm; declare; report; depose.
مظہرہ *muz'hirah*, Stated; alleged.

A مع *māë*, adv. With (*sāth*). [(علاوه).
maā-hāzā, adv. Along with or in addition to

A معاش *māash* ; Pop. *māsh*, n.f. عيش 1. Livelihood (*ājīvkā*, 1). 2. Landed property.
maāsh-dār. The owner of an estate.
tarz-i-muāsh, *tarīqa-i-maāsherat*,
Way of life ; social condition.
maāsh'rat, n. f. Social life ; society.
sipāhiyān-i-māzūr kī madad-i-maāsh, G. G. Maintenance of sick soldiers. [of subsistence.
zāhirā sūrat i-maāsh. G. G. Ostensible means
nek-maāsh. One who earns an honest livelihood.

A معاف *mu'āf* ; Illit. *māf*, adj. عفو 1. Exempted (*barī*, 1). 2. Forgiven ; pardoned ; excused. 3. Rent-free (land).
muāf bil-shart, A conditional pardon.
muāf k., v. a. 1. To absolve ; dispense with. 2. To pardon ; excuse. 3. To remit.
muāf mutlaq, A free pardon.
muāf h., v. n. To be pardoned, excused.
معافي *muāf'ī*, *muāfī-i-zamīn*, *arāzī i-muāfī*, n. f. 1. (*muāfi*) A pardon ; exemption. 2. Remission of revenue. 3. A rent-free grant ; rent-free lands. 4. A grant from Government ; an estate given as pension.
muāfī istivā, n. f. A tenure by which waste land is held for a time rent-free, and for a further period at a quit-rent until the given term expires.
muāfī bāqī, n. f. Remission of a balance.
muāfī chāhnā, v. n.
To beg or ask pardon or remission.
muāfī chitthī, n. f.
A free pass ; exemption from payment of a toll or tax ; a warrant of remission.
It was formerly applied to certain classes of pilgrims, exempting them from payment of the pilgrim tax. [life.
muāfī hīn-hayāt, Released or exempted during
muāfī-dār, n. m. A holder of rent-free land ; a grantee. [perpetuity.
muāfī dāemī, *yā istamrārī*, n. f. Released in
muāfī-ravanna, n. m. An order or permit for the transit of merchandise free of duty.
muāfī-i-zar-i-lagān. G.G. Remission of revenue.
muāfī-i-sāl, n. m. A year of exemption from assessment on some special account. [pardon.
muāfī sazā kā mauūd k. G. G. To tender a
muāfī mujrāī. Land exempt from tax, assigned to various individuals.
muāfī-nāmā, n. m. A warrant or order of exemption from duty or assessment.
muāfī nazrānedār. Property exempt from revenue, but paying a fine or quit-rent.
muāfī māṅgnā, v. n. To beg pardon; apologize.
muāfī māmūlī, n. f.
Established or customary remissions.
muāfī nā-jāyaz, n. f. An illegal grant.

A معاملہ *muām'ala*, *muāmila* ; Illit. *māmlā*, n. m. عمل acted. See بيوپار 1, 2, & امر (1, 2). 1. Dealing. 2. Negotiation. 3. A contract ; bargain. 4. An affair ; matter ; concern. 5. Proceeding ; particular. 6. Cause or suit in law ; a case. 7. A lass. 8. Sexual intercourse.
muāmala-i-shikastagī, n. f. Impeachment of contract. [proceeding.
muāmala-i-adālat, n. m. A judicial matter or
muāmale ke jumlah qarāyan.
Probabilities of the case.
muāmala-bāzārī meṅ, In course of business.
muāmalah bannā, v. n. 1. To be settled (a business) ; struck (a bargain).
2. To gain one's end.
muāmala pukht-paz yā pakkā k.
To settle a matter ; conclude a bargain.
muāmala-pardāzī k. To act. [with.
muāmala parnā. v. n. To have to do or deal
muāmala khārijī, n. m. An irrelevant matter.
muāmala-dāṅ, *muāmala-shinās*, n. m.
A man of business.
muāmala-dānī, n. f. A knowledge of business.
muāmala saṅgīn, n. m.
A grave matter ; a serious business.
muāmala-i-fāsid, n. m. A dishonest transaction.
muāmale kā sachchā, *khush-muāmala*,
An honest person.
muāmale kā khoṭā, A dishonest person.
muāmala k., v. a. 1. To deal with ; to buy and sell (*len den k.*). 2. To treat with ; negotiate.
3. To contract ; bargain.
muāmale kī haqīqat-hāl, The merits of a case.
muāmala mukammal, *yā pakkā h.*, v. n.
To be completed (a transaction). [action.
muāmala naqdī. n. m. A ready-money trans-
muāmalāt-i-mulkī, *mulkī muāmalāt*, State affairs ; politics.
ind-ul-muāmala, At the time of the transaction.
binā-i-muāmala, Cause of action. [tion.
daqal fasal kā muāmalah. A doubtful transac-
khoṭā muāmala. A doubtful transaction ; an unprincipled action.

A معاوضہ *muāv'azah*, *muāvaz*, n. f. عوض
1. Consideration given (*badlah*, 1, 2, 3).
2. Exchange ; barter.
muāwazā islāhāt Compensation for unexhausted improvements (a common cause of action under the Rent Acts.) *Carnegy*. [(*badlah denā*).
muāvazah dilānā, v. a. To award compensation
muāvazah-i-naqdī, A money compensation.

A معاون *muāv'in*, n. m. 1. A helper ; supporter. 2. An assistant.
muāvin-i-jurm, An accessory; abetter. [(*sahāī*).
معاونت *muāv'inat*, n. f. Assistance ; help ; aid
muāvanat k., v. a. To help ; assist. [contract.

A معاہدہ *muā'hadah*, n. m. An agreement
muāhidah jāyaz, n. m. G. G. A lawful contract.

muāhidah k., v. a. To enter into a contract.
muāhadoṅ ke nuqs-i-mujrimānā, G. G. Criminal breach of contract. [tract.
tāmīl-i-muāhidah. The performance of a con-
tāmīl muāhidah-i-khās. Performance of a specific contract. [tract in writing.
jāyaz muāhidah tahrīrī, G. G. A lawful con-
shikastagī muāhidah yā ahd-shikanī yā nuqs muāhidah. A breach of contract.
qānūn-i-muāhadah, A tort act.

A معائنه *mūā'ēnah*, n. m. عين Inspection.

muāënah k., v. a. 1. To see; inspect. 2. To look into; examine.

A معتاد *mōtād'*, *mautād*; Illit. *mohtāj*, n. f. عود
A fixed allowance.

A معتبر *mōtabar'*; Illit. *mātbar*, adj. عبر
1. Reliable (*etbārī* 1). 2. True.
motabar ādmī, A trustworthy person.
motabar jānnā, To adopt, admit, or receive as true or genuine.
motabar-shahādat. Reliable testimony.
motabar khabar, Authentic news.
معتبري *motabar'ī*, *motbarī*; Illit. *mātbarī*, n. f. Credit; trustworthiness (اعتبار 1).

A معترض *mōtariz'*, n. m. عرض An objector.
motariz h., v. n. 1. To object; question (*etirāz k.*). 2. To hinder; obstruct; impede; come across. [acknowledges.

A معترف *mōtarif'*, part. act. عرف One who
mōtarif h., v. n. To acknowledge; confess.

A معتقد *mōtaqid'*, n. m.
A believer; follower of a creed or faith.
mōtaqid h., v. n. To believe or confide in.

A معتمد *mōtamad'*, *mōtamid*, adj.
Trustworthy; reliable.

A معدلت *mād'alat*, n. f. عدل justice; equity.
mādalat-i-haqīqī. Natural justice.
mādalat haqīqī ke usūl par.
On the principles of natural justice.
mādalat āmmā. Public justice.
jarāyam mukhālif mādalat āmmā.
Offences against public justice.

A معدود *mādūd'*, adj. عد counted.
1. Numbered; computed. 2. Limited.

A معدوم *mādūm'*, *mādām*, adj. عدم lacked.
Extinct; non-existent. [in abeyance.
kisī miyād tak mādūm yā multavī rahnā. To be

A معذور *māzūr'*, *māzūr*, adj. 1. Excused; excusable. 2. Dispensed with. 3. Unserviceable.
māzūr-ul-khidmat, adj. Pensioned; invalided.
معذور رکهنا *māzūr rakhnā*, v. n. To excuse; to hold excusable. 2. To dispense with.

A معرفت *mār'afat*; H *hāth*, prep. عرف
Through the medium of; by the hands of; care of (*duāre*).

A معزول *māzūl'*, adj. عزل
Deposed; dismissed (from office). [office).
māzūl k., v. a. To discharge; dismiss (from
māzūl h., v. n To be dismissed (*bartaraf h.*).
معزولي *māzūl'ī*, n. f. Dismissal (*bartarfī*).
māzūlī lāzim ānā, v. n. To involve dismissal.

A معصوم *māsūm'*, adj. عصم.
Innocent; guileless; simple. [abeyance.

A معطل *muāt'tal*, adj. عطل Suspended; in
muāt'tal k., v. a. To suspend (from office).
معطلي *muāt'talī*, n. f. Suspension from office.

A معقول *māqūl'*, adj. عقل
1. Reasonable. 2. Right. 3. Fair. 4. Good and sufficient; satisfactory. 5. Worthy. 6. Acceptable. 7. Appropriate. 8. Pertinent. 9. Expedient. 10. Liberal; good.
qarāiṅ-i-māqūl, G.G. Reasonable cause.

A معلق *muāl'laq*, adj. n. m.
Any transaction not closed, as a sale in which payment of the price is deferred.

A معمول *mā'mūl'*, n.m. See دستور A custom.
māmūl ke din, A recurring period (menses).
معمولي *māmūl'ī*, adj. Wonted; common.
māmūlī kharch, n. m. Current expenses.
māmūlī savālāt, n. m. The ordinary questions.
māmūlī kār ravāī, n.f. Ordinary practice or use.
aiyām-i-māmūlī, n. m. Due time.
dastūr-i-māmūlī, n. m. The ordinary course.

A معهود *māhūd'*, adj. Agreed on; stipulated.

A معيشت *māīsh'at*, n. f. 1. Livelihood.
2. Daily food; the necessaries of life.

A معين *muāi'yan*, *muāiyana*, adj. عين
Appointed; established; fixed.
muaiyan zābitā n. m. 1. An established rule. 2. Fixed or legal charges. 3. A table of wages or allowances. 4. A list of public servants of any establishment.

muaiyan k., v. a. To appoint; establish.
muaiyan h., v. n. To be appointed, established.
tā muddat-i-muaiyana-i-adālat. For such period as the court may direct. [course.
khilāf dastūr-i-muaiyana. Out of the ordinary
arsa-i-muaiyan, G. G. A specified time.
miyād-i-muaiyanā. The period allowed. [in cash.
naqd yā mublig-i-muaiyan. G. G. A certain sum

vaqt-i-muaiyan. The appointed time.

A مغالطة *muḡāl'atah, mugāltah,* n. m. غلط See *dhokā,* (1, 2). 1. Leading into error. 2. Deception; delusion. 3. Error (*bhūl,* 4).
mugāltah-dihī, n. G. G. Deception.
mugāltah-dihī k. To mistake; misreport.
mugāltah denā, v. a. 1. To misinform; mislead. 2. To practise deception; to balk; delude.
is muḡālteh meṅ, G. G. Under this misconception.
amr-i-qānūn kī mugālta-khurī, G. G. A mistake of law.
amar-i-vāqai kī muḡāltā-khurī. A mistake of (fact.

A مغلظات *muḡallazāt',* n. f. pl. of غليظ Foul or abusive language.
mugallazāt baknā, yā sunānā, v. a. To use foul [language.

A مغلوب *maḡlūb',* adj. غلب Overcome; subdued; defeated.
malgūb ḍigrī. The person against whom decree is issued; a judgment-debtor; the party cast; the defeated party.
maglūb-ul-gazab, Irascible; passionate.
maglūb k., v. a. To overcome; subdue.

A مفت *muft, muft meṅ;* Sant. *moslete,* adv. 1. Gratuitously; for nothing.
muft-khorā, n. m. A loafer.
muft meṅ kām karānā, v. a. 1. To get work done for nothing. 2. To press; impress.

A مفتري *muftar'ī,* adj. Knavish; tricky.
muftar'ī, n. m. A slander; a calumniator.

A مفتي *muft'ī,* n. m. فتو A Mah. jurist or law officer.

A مفرور *mafrūr', mafrūrah,* n. m. فر A run-away (*farārī*).

A مفروض *mafrūz',* adj. فرض 1. Supposed; hypothetical.

A مفسد *muf'sid,* adj. فسد Factious; mischievous (دنگئي 2, 3).
mufsid, n. m. An incendiary; a mischief-maker; ringleader (*āg-lagāu,* 2).
mufsidā'nah, adv. 1. Riotously. 2. Feloniously.
majmaë-mufsidān, A riotous assembly; mob.
مفسده *mufsad'ah, mufsidah,* n. m. A riot.
mufsadah barpā k., v. n. To set up a riot.

A مفصل *mufas'sal;* Pop. *mufassil,* adj. فصل cut. Detailed; circumstantial; full.
mufassal, mufassilan, adv. In detail; fully (*tafsīl-wār*).
mufassal, n. pl. *mufassilāt,* 1. Particular mention; specification. 2. The country, as distinguished from the town.
mufassal jamā, Opp. of *sadar jamā.* The gross amount of revenue payable to a *zamīndār* or *mālguzār,* by the subordinate cultivators.
mufassal taālluq, A subordinate division of a district or estate.
mufassal kharch, n. Charges of collection in [the provinces.
mufassal dīvānī adālat. A provincial court of appeal whose decrees were final in certain cases before 1793. These courts were then merged into the city and *zila* courts.
mufassal adālat, n. A provincial court of justice.
mufassal qānūṅgo. n. A district or provincial accountant and registrar.
mufassal kahnā, yā bayān k., To detail; particularize.
koī jurm minjumlah jarāim mufassalah-zail. G. G. Any of the following offences.

A مفقود *mafqūd',* adj. فقد Missing; lost; extinct; non-existing.
mafqūd, n. m. (*Mah. law*) One of whom it is not known whether he be living or dead.
mafqūd-ul-asar. G. G. adj. Void.
mafqūd-ul-khabar, An address not found.

A مفلس *muf'lis, muflis qallāṅch;* Illit. *mukhlis,* adj. فلس Penniless; indigent (*garīb,* 1).
muflis; Illit. *mukhlis,* n. m. 1. A pauper.
muflis k., kar denā, yā banā denā, v. a. To impoverish; make poor.
ba-sīgah muflisī. In forma pauperis.
مفلسي *muflis'ī,* n. f. Pauperism; poverty; indigence.

A مفوضه *mufav'vazah,* adj. فوض Committed to the care of; resigned; ceded; vested; entrusted. [understood.

A مفهوم *mafhūm',* adj. فهم Comprehended;
mafhūm, n. m. An object.
mafhūm-i-māqūl, G. G. A reasonable construction.
mafhūm h., v. n. To imply; to be understood.

A مفيد *mufīd', mufīd-i-matlab,* adj. فيد See *fāëdemand.* Good; advantageous.

A مقابل *muqāb'il,* adj. قبل 1. Confronting; opposing; against 2. Matching; corresponding; like.

A مقابله *muqāb'alah, muqāb'lah;* Illit. *muqālbah,* n. m. قبل went before. 1. Opposition. 2. Comparison. 3. Encounter.
muqāblah aur imtehān, Check; audit.
muqāble par mustaid h. G. G. To resist.
muqāblah chāhnā yā k., muqāble ānā, v. n. To challenge; call to combat; defy.
muqāblah k., v. a. 1. To confront; oppose; contend with. 2. To compete or cope with. 3. To compare; collate. 4. To balance; examine; check, compare (accounts, papers, etc.).

*ba-muqābl*ah *tarfain.*
In the presence of the parties.
fel ke muqābleh meṅ, G. G. Against an act.

A مقاسمه *muqās'amah*, n. قسم dividing.
Partition of the crop between the proprietor or cultivator, and the State, either in kind or value.

A مقام *maqām'* ; Illit. *muqām'*, n. m. pl. *maqāmāt*, قوم 1. Place; site.
2. A halt. 3. Occasion ; opportunity.
maqām bolnā, v. n. To order a halt.
maqām-i-pardah, yā makhsūs, n. Privities.
maqām denā ; Hin. Wom. *mukām denā*, v. a.
To go out to condole with.
maqām i-siyāsat, The house of correction.
maqām-i-shikāyat, Ground of complaint.
maqām k., To encamp ; halt ; stay ; put up.
maqām-i-muaiyan. G. G. A certain place.
maqām-i-muqarrarah,
The appointed place or column.
ba-maqām, adv. Instead ; in the place of.
مقامي *maqām'ī*, adj. 1. Stationary ; resident.
2. Local.

A مقبوضه *maqbūz'ah*, adj. قبض seized.
Seized ; taken possession of ; held ; possessed ; occupied.

A مقتضاء *muqtazā'ē, muqtizāē*, n. m. قضي
Requisition ; demand ; necessity.
muqtazāē insāf, The ends of justice.
muqtazāē-vaqt. Demanded at the time.
muqtazāē-vaqt, The nick of time.
ba-muqtazāē, adv. According to ; in conformity with ; in consequence of. [ing.
مقتضي *muqtaz'ī*, adj. قضي Demanding ; exact-

A مقتول *maqtūl'*, adj. Killed ; slain.
maqtūl o majrūh. Killed and wounded.

A مقدار *miqdār'*, n. m. قدر 1. Magnitude ; size ; dimension. 2. Quantity ; weight.
3. Amount (جمع 1). 4. Rate ; settled allowance. 5. Measure (اندازة 3).
miqdār-i-jamā. Amount of assessment.
miqdār-i-dāvā. Valuation or value of suit.
miqdār-i-muqarrarah.
A fixed amount or quantity.

A مقدم *muqad'dam*, adj. قدم preceding. See *pahlā*. 1. Antecedent ; before.
2. Prior ; preceding. 3. Superior ; chief.
muqaddam ; Illit. *muqdam* ; Rus. *mukdam*, n.m.
The head man of a village, a representative of co-sharers ; the founder of a village or his descendants.

In Hindustan, the *muqaddam* has in some places become solely responsible for the public revenue, having been suffered to assume the character of a petty proprietor, and being designated as *mālik-muqaddam*. Under the farmer system the title was not unfrequently given to the village *zamīndār*. In some places the term is applied to the hereditary occupant of an estate in a village, immovable as long as he paid a fixed rate to the *zamīndār* or the Rājah. The *muqaddam bisvedār* is usually a head man who holds an entire share of a village, and sometimes an entire village, but in some places he appears to have been reduced to the state of hereditary cultivator from having been part proprietor of the village in consequence of the title having been appropriated, through fraud or violence, by some individual proprietor.

muqad'dam ; Rus. *mukdam*, n. m. 1. A village head. 2. A title of respect among villagers.
muqaddam jānnā, v. n. To consider preferable.
muqaddam h., v. n. To be first or most binding.
tārīkh muqaddam kar-ke likhnā, G. G. H. *pahlī mitī dālnā yā charhānā*, v. n. To antedate.
hiba-i-muqaddam, G. G. A prior bequest.

A مقدمه *muqad'damah, muqaddimah* ; Pop. *muqadmah* ; Rus. *mukadmā*, n. m. قدم going before. 2. Preliminary ; preamble ; prelude ; introduction. 2. Subject (*bāb*, 2).
3. A law suit ; case ; proceedings ; prosecution (دعوي 3). [suit.
muqadmah ibtidāī, n. m. An original case or
muqadmah apīl, n. m. An appeal case.
muqadmah ijrāē digrī. An execution case ; a case of execution of decree. [ble of a law.
muqadmah ba-izhār manshāē qānūn. The pream-
muqadmah bigārnā, v.a. To spoil a case. [case.
muqadmah banānā, yā uthānā, v. a. To get up a
muqadmah phir qāim k. yā az sar-i-nau nambar par kharā k. To revive a suit.
muqadmah pesh karne kā tarīqah.
How a suit is to be brought.
muqadmah taqsīm. A case of partition.
muqadmah taiyār yā murattab huā, Case closed.
muqadmah jismī. A case of personal violence.
muqadmah jītnā. To cast a defendant or to win a case. [missed (a case).
muqadmah khārij yā dismis h., v. n. To be dis-
muqadmah khafīf. A small cause. [of a suit.
muqadmah dāyar hote hue. During the progress
muqadmah dīvānī. A civil case.
muqadmah sangīn, Severe wounding.
muqadmah-i-faujdārī, n. m. A criminal case.
muqadme kā murāfah k. To remove a suit.
muqadmah kharā k., To institute a suit ; pursue by law ; prosecute ; litigate.
muqadme kī pairavī. The prosecution of a cause.
muqadme kī darpeshī ke vaqt. On the trial.
muqadme kī kār-ravāī. The proceedings in a cause. [suit.
muqadmah gūnāgūṅ vajeh kā. A multifarious
muqadmah lambarī yā nambarī. A regular suit
muqadmah larānā, v.a. To go to law ; litigate ; conduct a suit. [suit.
muqadmah mālī lagān yā zar bhej. A revenue

muqadmah mutadāëra. A pending suit.
muqadmah mutafarrīqāt. A miscellaneous case.
muqadmah murāfah yā ibtidāī. An original suit.
muqadmah marjūah dar pesh yā mez par ijlās meṅ. A case under litigation or under trial.
muqadmah hārnā, v. n. To lose one's cause.
ek aur muqadme meṅ. In another case; in a case.
tasfīyah muqaddamah. The settlement of a case.
hālāt-i-muqadmah, G. G. The facts of a case.

مقدمات *muqaddamāt'* n. m. pl. of مقدمه 1. Affairs ; transactions. 2. Causes ; cases.
muqaddamāt-i-ābkārī, *Ābkārī* suits. [laws.
muqaddamāt-i-istāmp. Cases under the stamp
muqaddamāt-i-sangīn. Aggravated cases ; cases of an aggravated nature.
muqaddamāt-i-savānah. Boundary cases.

مقدمي *muqad'damī* ; Illit. *muqdamī,* n. f. Dues paid to a *muqaddam* by the cultivators.

A مقدور *maqdūr',* n. m. 1. Power ; capacity (*majāl*). 2. Means; resources. 3. Presumption.
muqdūr bhar, A. H. ; *tā-ba-maqdūr,* P. A. ; *hatt-al-maqdūr,* A. adv. To the best of one's power or ability ; with all one's might.
maqdūr na rakhnā, v. n. To be unable.
maqdūr-vālā, A. H. n. m. A rich or wealthy person ; a capitalist.
be-maqdūr, adj. 1. Helpless ; incompetent. 2. Penniless (غريب). 3. Insolvent.
be-maqdūr qarazdāroṅ kī rihāī ke āīn ke mutābiq mukhlisī hāsil k. G. G. To take the benefit of the insolvent act.

A مقر *muq'ir,* adj. قر Confessing ; admitting.
muqir, man-muqir, n.m. One who admits a claim, or confesses a crime ; one who pleads guilty.
muqir bihī. An admitted claim ; a crime confessed. [is admitted.
muqir-lahū. The person in whose favor a claim
muqir-i-jurm h., To plead guilty.
muqir h., To confess ; admit (*iqrār k.*).

A مقرر *muqar'rar* ; Illit. *mukar,* adj. قر [tain. 1. Fixed; established. 2. Appointed. 3. Cer-
muqarrar ; Illit. *mukar,* adv. Assuredly ; unquestionably (*zurūr,* 2).
muqarrar k., v. a. 1. To set ; settle (*taiyun k*). 2. To appoint ; constitute. 3. To impose ; levy (as a tax).
muqarrar karnā takrāroṅ kā. Settling the issues. [taxes.
tikas muqarrar k., v. a. To impose or assess
jamā muqarrar k., v. a. To assess revenue.
hissa muqarrar k., v.a. To assign or allot shares.

مقرره *muqar'rarah,* adj. 1. Fixed ; established ; determined ; prescribed ; laid down. 2. Defined. 3. Usual ; customary. 4. Permanent. [ed portion.
muqarrarah, n. m. A fixed allowance ; appoint-

مقرري *muqar'rarī,* n. f. 1. A fixed lease ; quit-rent. 2. A fixed stipend.
A tenure held at a fixed and permanent rent when payable to a proprietor, or revenue when payable to Government.
muqarrarī istimrārī.
A tenure held at a fixed rate of assessment, but applied, in the Upper Provinces, to tenures of which the revenue is permanent only for the life of the holder.
muqarrarī paṭṭā. A lease for a definite extent of land at a fixed sum, not liable to any extra charge.
muqarrarī jamā. Fixed revenue ; a fixed and permanent rate of assessment.
muqarrarī jagah. Assigned places.
muqarrarīdār'. The occupant of a farm or estate paying a fixed and permanent rate of rent or revenue.
dar-muqarrarī. An estate held under a holder of land at a fixed rate.

A مقروض *maqrūz',* adj. قرض Indebted.
maqrūz, n. m. A debtor ; an obligor.

A مقروقه *maqrūq'ah, maqrūq,* adj. Distrained, sequestered ; attached ; confiscated. [perty
maqrūqah, n. m. Distrained or attached pro-

A مقسوم *maqsūm',* adj. قسم dividing. Divided ; partitioned.
maqsūm, n. m. 1. A portion ; share ; allotment ; lot. 2. Fate ; destiny.

A مقفل *muqaf'fal,* Ped. adj. Locked.
muqaffal k., Ped. *tālā denā,* H. v. a. To lock up.

A مقيد *muqai'yad,* adj. قيد Imprisoned ; confined (*pāband*). [stationed.

A مقيم *muqīm',* adj. قام stood. Residing ;
muqīm ; Illit. *mukīm,* n. m. 1. An inhabitant ; a resident. 2. A wholesale greengrocer.
muqīm h., v. n. 1. To occupy. 2. To halt ; stay or put up at.

H مکا मुक्का *muk'kā* ; Sant. *kuhau,* n. m. S. मुष्टिका A blow with the fist.
mukkā chalnā, v. n. To come to blows.
mukkā lagnā, v. n. 1. To receive a blow. 2 To suffer a shock. [the ear.
mukkā mārnā, v. a. To give a blow or box on

A مکار *makkār',* adj. مکر 1. Pretending (*dubhāo*). 2. Artful ; crafty ; false.
makkār ; A. H. *makarhāyā, makarhāī, makkārah,* n. m. An impostor.
makkārī, makkār-pan, n. Craftiness; artfulness.

A مکان *makān'* ; Rus. *makkān,* n.m. کون being. A dwelling house ; a room.

makān-i-ijlās, G. G. A court of legislature.
makān-dār, n. m.
A householder or owner; a landlord.
makān denā, jagah denā, v. a. To lodge; put up.
makān farhat-gāh, G. G. A country residence.
makān karāë denā, v. a. To let a house.
makān karāë lenā, v. n. To rent a house. [house.
makān mutaãlliqah khāndān, G. G. A family
makān mushtaraka yā mutaãlliqah mushtarak.
A joint family house.
makān maskūnah. A dwelling house.

H مکتا मकता *mak'tā, mukatta, mugta, mokta, makta, makhta.* A contract. [rent.
maktā-dār, The holder of an estate at a quit-

A مکر *makr*; Pop. *makar, makar chakar*, n. m. *makkārī*, n. f. 1. Pretence; pretext; colour; sham; disguise.
2. Imposture; cheating; deceit.
makr k., yā gāṅṭhnā, v. a. To feign; pretend.

A مکرر *mukar'rar*, adv. کر repeating.
Twice; again.
mukarrar pesh k., To present again; re-submit.
mukarrar sikarrar. adv. A second and a third time; repeatedly; over and over again.
mukarrar sikarrar kahnā.
To press or urge repeatedly.
mukarrar talab k., G. G. To recall.
mukarrar kahnā, v. n. To repeat; reiterate.
mukarrar yeh hai, yā āṅki. A postscript.

H مکرنا मुकरना *mukar'nā*; Bhoj. *makral*, v.n.
A منکر See *inkār k.*, 1, 2, 4, 5.
To deny; belie; go back from one's word.

A مکروہ *makrūh'*, adj. کرہ
Disgusting; loathsome; offensive).
makrūh, n. m. Actions which the Mah. law condemns as wrong, but does not invalidate.

A مکفول *makfūl'*, adj. کفل Secured by bond; hypothecated; bailed (*marhūn*).
makfūl bihī. A claim for which surety is given.
makfūl ãnhu. The person or thing for whom or which surety is given.
makfūl-lahū. The person demanding bail.

A مکلف *mukal'laf*, n. m. One legally responsible or accountable for his actions.

H مگدھی مگھئیا मगधी *mag'dhī, maghai'yā*, n. m.
1. A native or resident of Maggha.
2. A tribe of agriculturists in Behar.

P مگر *mag'ar*; E. *mudā*, adv. Unless; except; if not; only; perhaps; in case.

H مگھم मुग्घम *mug'gham*, adj. Secret; hidden.
mugghum rahnā, ghar ke ghar rahnā, v. n.
(*Gamblers*) To be quits. [endoes.
mugghum meṅ kahnā, v. n. To speak in inu-

A ملا *mul'lā, mullāṅ*; Contemp. *mullānah*, n. m. Cor. of مولی. 1. A doctor; professor.
2. A Mah. jurist; parish priest.
3. A judge; the deputy of a Qāzī.
4. A Mah. village schoolmaster who has also charge of the village mosque, and sometimes acts as butcher.

A ملاحظہ *mulāh'izah*; Illit. *mulāhzā*, n.m. لحظ
1. Inspection; notice. 2. Regard (*lihāz*, 4).
mulāhizah k., v. a. 1. To view; inspect closely; examine. 2. To regard with favor.
mulāhize meṅ āyā, mulāhize se guzrā, Had under consideration. [examined.
mulāhizah, yā muqābluh shud. Seen; compared;
ba-mulāhizah, 1. For the inspection of.
2. With reference to (*ba-lihāz*).
bād mulāhezah subūt-i-tahrīrī. After a consideration of the documentary evidence.

A ملازم *mulāz'im*, n. m. لزم being necessary.
1. A servant; follower; an attendant.
2. A person employed to watch a debtor.
mulāzim-i-khās, A private servant. [mestics.
mulāzim khāngī, n. m. Domestic servants; do-
mulāzim-i-sarkārī, n.m. G. G. A Govt. or public servant. [public servant.
mulāzim-i-sarkārī bannā, G. G. Personating a
mulāzim k., yā banānā, v.a. To engage a servant.
ملازمت *mulāz'imat, mulāzmī*, n.f. 1. Attendance; service; duty. 2. Waiting on a superior.
Continued watch over an insolvent debtor by his creditors, although he has been discharged by the Qazī, to discover if he possess or acquire any property that may be applied to the liquidation of his debts.
mulāzimat ikhtiyār k., v. a. To take service.
mulāzimat hāsil k., v. n. To be permitted to wait upon; to be admitted to an audience.

A ملاقات *mulāqāt'*; Rus. *mulākhāt, mulkāt*, n.f. لقی visiting. 1. A meeting; visit (*bheṭ*, 1).
2. Carnal intercourse.

H ملان मिलान *milān'*, n. f. 1. Comparison.
2. Adjustment. 3. A supplementary or subsidiary statement.
milān jamā-bandi, n. An appendix or supplement to the account of the revenue of a village, shewing the varieties that occur in the extent of land under cultivation.
milān milānā, v. a. To adjust the accounts of land under cultivation.

ملاو मिलाव *milā'o*, n. m. 1. Mixture; admixture; commixture; composition. 2. Amalgamation; annexation. 3. Adulteration; alloy.
4. Accord; union.

5. Adjustment; reconciliation. [adulterate.
milāo k., v.a. 1. To mix; intermix. 2. To alloy;

H ملايں मलायन *malā'yan*; W. *bukhaur*; E. *ghoghā par h.*; Bhoj. *muāri.*
Rice which stops short without forming seed, owing to defective nourishment, etc.

H ملبا मलबा *mal'bā*, n.m. H. *mail* dirt. 1. Rubbish; dirt; sweepings. 2. Bricks, stones, earth, etc. of a broken house. 3. Village expenses.

These are—feeding the members of the community when absent on public duty, or those of other villages on a visit; feeding religious mendicants; payments to subordinate police and revenue officers; allowance to village watchmen; remuneration to individuals for losses incurred in supplying cattle and carts for the public service; loss on exchange on coins with which the revenue is paid; repairing tanks and wells; fines imposed for plundered property when traced within the boundary of the village; presents to dancers, singers, jugglers and the like, for the amusement of of the inhabitants; charitable gifts; interest on money borrowed on account of the community; expenses of religious worship and occasional ceremonies and festivals; expenses of the *Patvārī* or accountant; charges for lights for the place of assembly and the person in charge of it; expenses of *Panchāyats* collected on the business of the village; funeral expenses of a head man or any respectable member; marriage expenses of neighbours when passing through the village, etc. The total varies from 10 to 12 per cent. on the public assessment.

A ملبس *mulab'bis*, n. m. 1. An impostor.
2. Counterfeit coin.

A ملتمس *multam'is*, Ped. n. m. لمس touching.
A petitioner. [pending.

A ملتوي *multav'ī*, adj. Postponed; adjourned;

multavī rakhnā, yā k., v. a. 1. To suspend; intermit. 2. To postpone; adjourn; defer; put off. [left in abeyance.
multavī rahnā, yā h., v. n. To be deferred,
multaviyāt'; pl. of ملتوي Suits undecided or pending; adjournments.

A ملحق *mul'hiq, mulhaqah*, adj. Annexed (متصل).
mulhiq h., v. n. To be annexed. [glanced at.

A ملحوظ *malhūz'*, *malhūz-i-khātir*, adj. لحظ
Considered; contemplated; regarded.
malhūz rakhnā, v.a. To regard; mind; consider.

A ملزم *mul'zam, mulzim*, adj. Accused; charged.

mulzim k., ṭhairānā, yā qarār denā, v. n.
To charge; arraign; impeach.

A ملک *milk*; Illit. *milak*, n. f.

1. Landed property; rent free-land.
2. Lands given to certain classes, viz. (1) the learned and their pupils, (2) those who have abandoned the world, (3) the helpless and destitute, and (4) decayed gentry. Similar grants in money were styled *vazīfah.* *Carnegy.*

milk nisf-rīt. Lands paying half the Govt. revenue. [tuity.
milk muāfī-i-davām. Rent-free land in perpe-
milk-i-lā-khirāj, n. Proprietorship of lands exempt from revenue payment. [ship in land.

ملکي *milk'ī*, adj. Proprietary; relating to owner-
milkī, n. m. A landed proprietor.

ملکيت *milkī'yat, milkiyat*, n. f. 1. (*haqq-i-milkīyat*) Proprietary right in land.
2. Landed or real property.
milkīyat istamrārī. Proprietary right or possession in perpetuity.
milkīyat jo ba-sabab vafāt muāfīdār ke dākhil zābtah ho. Lapsed *muāfī* tenure.
milkīyat jo kisī khās shart virāsat se chalī ātī ho. G. G. Entail.
milkīyat zamīn. Land tenure. [of tenure.
milkīyat yā qabze kī sūrat yā haisīyat. Nature
mulk se khārij k.; H. *des-nikālā denā*, v. a.
To banish; exile.

ملکي *mulk'ī*, adj. 1. Belonging to one's country; national; provincial.
2. Political; civil. 3. Native; domestic.
mulkī, n. f. An era in use in some places, as in *Puranyā*, which is one month in advance of the Faslī year, beginning with the 1st of *Sāvan.* [General.
mulkī lāṭh, n. m. The Viceroy or Governor-

H ملکانا मलकाना *malkā'nā*, A caste of Hindūs forcibly converted to Mohammadanism.

A ملکه *mal'ikah*; Pop. *malkah*, n.f. 1. A queen.
2. (*malkā masūr*) The pulse *masūr*, q. v.
malkah moazzamah, The exalted queen.
malkah Vikṭūriā, n. f. Queen Victoria.

H ملماس मलमास *malmās'*, E.; *malh, laund*, W. n. m. S. मल impurity. मास month.
An intercalary month, in which no ceremonies are allowed.

H ملي بهگت मिली भगत *milī bhagat*, n. f.
A confederacy (*sāzish*).

A ممالک *mumāl'ik*, pl. of ملک q. v.
mumālik-i-gair-āīn, Non-regulation provinces.
mumālik-i-mahrūsah, Protected provinces.
mumālik-i-magrabī o shimālī.
The North-Western Provinces; N. W. P.
mumālik muffavvazah, adj. Ceded Provinces.

A ممانعت *mumān'aāt. mumāneat*, n. f. منع forbade. Prohibition; restriction.
mumāneat k., v. a. To prohibit (*manā k.*).
mumāniyat-i-qānūnī. A legal obstacle.

H ممانی मुमानी *mumān'ī, mumānī jān*, W.; *mavānī*, E. n. f. Mother's brother's wife (*māmī*); an aunt.

E ممبر *mim'bar*, n. m. Cor. of member. [cil.
kauṅsal kā mimbar, kauṅslī, A member of coun-

A ممتحن *mumta'hin*, n. m. محن striking.
An examiner; auditor. [examiner.
mumtahin-i-afyūn, n. m. G. G. An opuim

A ممتوعه *mamtū'āh*, n. f.
A temporary wife; a concubine.

A ممکن *mum'kin*; S. *sambhav*; H. *hone-jog*, adj; مکن being possible. Possible; practicable; feasible; can; liable; contingent. [table.
mumkin-ut-tabdīl; H. *palatne jog*, adj. Commu-
mumkin-ut-taqsīm; H. *bāṅṭ-jog*. adj.
Partitionable; liable to partition.
mumkin-ul-dakhūl, adj. Accessible. [culturable.
mumkin-uz-zirāāt; H. *khetī-jog*, adj Arable;
mumkin-ul-vusūl, yā husūl; H. *pāne-jog*, adj.
Attainable.
mumkin-ul-vuqū; H. *honhār*, adj. 1. Possible.
2. What is to happen. [sessed.

A مملوکه *mumlūk'ah, mumlūk*, adj. ملک Pos-
mamlūkah, n. f. (*Mah.*) 1. A purchased slave.
2. A child brought up in the house of another. [possessed.
mumlūkah o maqbūzah, adj. Purchased and

A ممنوع *mamnū', mamnūah*, adj. منع forbidding, repelling. 1. Prohibited; forbidden.
2. Illicit; contraband.
mamnū az qānūn. Malum prohibitum.[missible.
mamnu-us-samāat, n. Barred (hearing); inad-

H ممیا ساس ममिया सास *mamiyā sās*, Mah; *maulas*, Hin. n. f. The husband's or wife's maternal aunt.
mamiyā susar, Mah.; *maulasrā*, Hin. n. m.
The husband's or wife's maternal uncle.
mamerā bhāī, n. m. Mother's brother's son; a first cousin by the mother's side.
mamerī bahn, n. f. A niece of a maternal uncle.

A منادی *manād'ī, munādī*, n. f. pl. of ندا
Proclamation (*ḍauṅḍī*).
manādī k., yā pherṇā, v. a. To proclaim; promulgate. [tom-tom.
manādī karānā, Caus. To proclaim by beat of
manād'ā, The vocative case.

A مناسب *munās'ib*, adj. نسب Suitable.
munāsib jānnā, yā samajhnā, v. n.
To consider proper or suitable.
munāsib nahīṅ. G. G. Inapplicable.
munāsib, yā shāyāṅ h. To apply; suit.
munāsib jama, A reasonable assessment. [case.
munāsib hāl muqadmah ke. Applicable to the
hirāsat-i-munāsib. G. G. Safe custody.
nā-munāsib istifādah. G. G. Undue advantage.

A منافع *manāf'e*; Pop.*munāfā*,n.m.pl.of منفعت
1. Profits; gains (*prāpt*, 2). 2. The surplus proceeds or nett profits of an estate.
munāfā bāqī, munāfā zāid, n. Surplus profits.
munāfa-i-khām, n. m. Gross profits.
munāfa-i-mālikānah. Proprietary profits.
munāfa-i-miād mustājirī.
Profits of the term of a farm.

A مناہی *manā'hī*; Pop. *manāī*, n. f. نہی prohibiting. Prohibitions; things prohibited.

A من بعد *min bād*, adv.
Afterwards; hereafter. [(*joṅ-kā-toṅ*).
min-wa-in; Illit. *ain main*, adv. As it was
min jumlah, adv. From among; out of.
minjumlah chand jarāyam ke koī koī ek jurm.
G. G. One of the several offences.

A منتخب *munta'kh'ab*,نخب extracting,drawing. A table shewing at a glance the fields situate in different parts of the village owned or cultivated by the same person.
muntakhab asāmīvār. A list of proprietors and tenants and of all lands in the village, giving detailed statistics of each field and the total area of each holding, with the recorded rents.

A منتظر *muntaz'ir*, adj. نظر saw. Expectant.
muntazir-i-hukm, Awaiting orders.
muntazir rakhnā, v. a. To keep one in expectation or waiting.
muntazir rahnā, v.n. To expect; await; wait for.
hukm ke muntazir rahnā, v. n. To wait orders.
mauqe kā muntazir rahnā, v. n.
To wait for an opportunity.

A منتظم *muntazim'*, n. m. نظم strung. 1. A manager; superintendent. 2. An economist.

A منتقل *muntaq'al*, adj. نقل transporting.
Transferred; transported. [assignee.
muntaqal-alaih, n. m. A transferee; an alience;
muntaqal k., v. a. 1. To transfer; alienate; assign. 2. To dispose of; sell. 3. To endorse.
muntaqal karnā bād sakārne ke,
To negotiate after acceptance.

A منجانب *min-jān'ib*; H. *or se*, adv.
On the part of; for; on one's behalf.

A & H منحرف ہونا آئین سے *munharif h. āīn se*. Infringement of law.

H مندا **मन्दा** *man'dā, mandī*; Poet. *mand*, adj. S. **मन्द** Pālī, *mando*. 1. Dull (market) (*sust*,). 2. Moderate; low.
mandā, mandvārā, n. m. 1. Dullness of the market; depression of trade.
2. Decrease; diminution.
mandā bolnā, v. n. To become dull (a market).
mandā bechnā, yā lagānā, v. a. To sell cheap.
mandā parnā, yā h., mandānā v. n.
1. To be abated, lulled. 2 To become dull; to decline (a business).
mandī hai, (The trade) is depressed.

A مندرج *mundar'aj, mundarjah*, adj. درج enfolded. Inserted; included (داخل 3).
mundaraj k., v. a. To insert (*dākhil k.*, 3).
mundarjah-zail, adv. .
As follows; as below mentioned. [section.
mandaraj dafā hāzā. G. G. Mentioned in this

H مندھاونیوالا *mundhāone-vālā, barsāone-vālā*, E. One who receives the grain emptied out from the *chhāj* and carries it away to the heap to which it belongs.

H منڈ **मुण्ड** *mund, mūṅṛ*, n. m. *muṅḍiyā*, n. f. S. **मुण्ड**, Pālī, *mundo*. 1. The head.
2. (*muṅḍh, mudh*) Chief; head; principal.
mund-chirā, n. m. 1. A sect of mendicants who extort alms by threatening to wound themselves. 2. An extortioner.
mund-chirāpan, n. m. Extortion.

A منزلہ *manzil'ah, manzil'ā*, n. m. (*In Comp.*) A story (of a house).
ba-manzilah subūt-i-movaiyad. G.G. As corroborative evidence. [part of the will.
ba-manzilah-i-juzv vasīyat-nāmah. As additional

A منسلک *munsal'ak, munsal'ikah*, adj. سلک thrusting in. 1. Threaded; strung together.
2. Appended; annexed.
munsalik k., v. a. To append; file.
munsalak-shudah, A. P. adj. Attached; filed.

A منسوب *mansūb'*, adj. 1. Related; allied.
2. Betrothed.

A منسوخ *mansūkh'*, adj. نسخ make void. Cancelled; abolished; repealed (*mustaradd*).
mansūkh k. v. a. To rescind; cancel; abolish (*mustarad k.*); declare null and void.
منسوخي *mansūkh'ī*, n. f. Cancelment; abolition; annulment; repeal. [ment.
mansūkhī-i-bandobast. Annulment of settle-
ba-mansūkhī. In supercession of.

A منشا *man'shā*, n. m. Tenor; drift (ارتقا 1).
manshā-i-ekaṭ. G. G. The purpose of the act.
manshāē insāf, The ends of justice.
manshāe-dāvā. Cause of action; object of suit; the relief sought for in a suit.
manshaē qānūn, n. m. The purport of a law.
hasb-i-manshāē. G. G. In the sense of.

A منشور *manshūr'*; S. **वृत्तपत्र** A charter.

A منشي *manash'shī*. G. G. A. H. *nashe-vālī*, n. f. Intoxicating drugs. [intoxication.
manashshī hone ke bāis, G. G. By reason of

A منصب *man'sab*, n. m. نصب set up. 1. Post; function; station. 2. Dignity (*martabah*, 1).
mansab-dār, n. m. A functionary; an officer or official of rank.
mansab-i-sarkārī, An official post or position.
amal-i-mansabī, G. G. An official act.

A منصرم *munsar'im*, n. m. 1. Manager; administrator (*sarbarāhkār*, 1). 2. A subordinate settlement officer. 3. The head clerk of a court of settlement or judge's court.
4. A proxy; substitute. 5. The teacher of a school who teaches *Patwārīs*.

A منصف *mun'sif*, n. m. نصف half.
1. A just judge. 2. A subordinate judge.
منصفي *munsif'ī*, n. f. 1. Justice; equity.
2. A Munsif's Court.
munsifī k., v. a. 1. To preside over a court of justice. 2. To do justice.
munsifā'nah, adv. Equitably; justly.
taqsīm-i-munsifānah. G. G.
Proper or equitable distribution.

A منظر عام *manzar-i-ām*, G. G.
A conspicuous place.

A منظور *manzūr'*, adj. 1.Sanctioned; granted.
2. (*manzūr-i-nazar*) Approved; acceptable.
manzūr k., v. a. See *qubūl k.* and *mānnā* (4, 6, 7). 1. To admit. 2. To agree to.
3. To confirm: affirm.
peshgāh se manzūr kiyā gayā, G. G.
Received the assent of.
منظوري *manzūr'ī*, n. f. 1. Consent; permission; sanction. 2. Approval; choice (*qubūl*).
manzūrī bā-qarīnah, yā zimnan,
Tacit or implied consent.
manzūrī-i-bil. Audit of a bill.
manzūrī sānī. Re-admission.
manzūrī khās, Special sanction. [tion.
manzūrī kā muntazir rahnā, v. n. To wait sanc-
manzūrī kī āsāmī, G.G. A Government appointment conveying a retiring pension.
manzūrī nīlām, The confirmation of a sale.
ba-manzūrī, adv. With the consent, approval, or sanction of. [proval of.
ba-shart-i-manzūrī, G. G. Subject to the ap-

A منعقد *munʻaq'ad*, adj. عقد tied. 1. Bound (by contract, etc.). 2. Betrothed.

A H منع كرنا *manā k.*, v. a.
To prohibit; interdict.

A منفعت *munfā'at*, n. f. نفع gained.
Profit; gain; emolument (فايده).

A منقسم *munqas'am*, adj.
Divided; apportioned; distributed.

A H منقلب كرنا *munqal'ib k.* G. G.
To pervert; misrepresent; reverse; upset; convert; change.

A منقوله *manqūl'ah*; H. *uṭhāū dhan*, n. f.
Movable or personal property.
gair-manqūlah; H. *aṭal dhan*, n. f.
Real or immovable property.

A منكوحه *mankū'hā*, n. f. نكح *genitale arvum.*
A legally married wife; a married woman.

H منگني मंगनी *manġ'nī*, n. f. 1. (E.) A loan.
2. See *rūkan.* 3. (*Mah.*) Betrothal (*sagāī*).

H منوتي मनौती *manau'tī*, *īnch manautī*, n. f.
S. मानित. 1. Satisfaction.
2. Surety (ضامني). 3. An acceptance.
manautī-dār, n. m. One who becomes a surety for a consideration, esp. one who is a security to Government for a revenue payment.

A منها *min'hā*, adj. Subtracted; deducted.
minhā-dār, n. A holder of land exempted from revenue payment, or subject to a diminished assessment.
minhā-shudah. G. G. Deducted.
minhā k., v. a. To deduct; remit.
منهائي *minhā'ī*, n. f. 1. An abatement.
2. A reduction. 3. A reduction in the assessment; remission of rent or revenue.
4. A usufructuary loan. 5. A deduction from the assessed area of an estate or village on account of an unculturable tract of wood or water, wilderness or waste, etc. [money.

H منهه سينا *munh sīnā*, v. a. To give hush-

H منيم *munīm*, n. m. 1. A Hindi accountant or clerk.
2. (*munīm dīvān*) An agent; a manager.
munīm'ī, n. f. The office of a *munīm.*

A مواجب *mavāj'ib*, n. m. prop. ماوجب
Dues; allowances; salaries; pensions.

A مواخذه *muvāʻkh'izah*; Illit. *māʻkhzā*, *māẓ-zā*, n. m. اخذه taking. 1. Calling to account; impeachment. 2. Accountability (*javāb-dihī*).
3. Amends; damages.
muvākhze-dār, adj. Responsible; answerable.
mavākhize se barī k., v. a. To discharge from liability; relieve from responsibility. [law.
muvākhize se chhuṛānā, v. a. To redeem in
muvākhizah k., v. a. 1. To call to account; impeach. 2. To demand as a due; to claim.
mavākhize meṅ mubtilā h. G. G. 1. To be encumbered. 2. To be impeached. [G. G. n. m.

A موازنه رقبه بندي *muvāzina raqba-bandī*,
A list or statement of all the land belonging to a village.

A موازي *mavāzī*, adj. A sum; total.

A موافق *muāf'iq*; Illit. *māfiq'*; Rus. *māphak*, adj. وفق was appropriate.
1. Like; conformable; consonant.
2. Suitable. 3. Favorable; propitious.
muāfiq, adv. Agreeably to. [practice.
muāfiq sarishta. Conformably to procedure or
muāfiq sir kā, adj. 1. Fitting; appropriate.
2. Middling; not much. 3. Passable; adequate; neither more nor less (*bīch kī rās*).
muāfiq h., v. n.
To consist with; to be agreeable to.
موافقت *muāf'aqat*; Illit. *māfqat*; Rus. *māphkhat*, n. f. See اتفاق, 1—7. 1. Concordance; conformity. 2. Correspondence; fitness. 3. Propitiousness. 4. Affinity; friendship.
muāfaqat rakhnā, v. n. 1. To fit; suit; become.
2. (— *khānā*) To agree with (a person).
muāfaqat k., v. n. [into friendship.
1. To reconcile; conciliate anew; to enter
2. To comply with.

A موت *maut*, n. f. S. *mritu.* Death; mortality.
maut bilā-qatl, n. f. A violent death.
maut kī sūrat banānā, v. n. To feign death.
apnī maut marnā, v. n. To die a natural death.
ba-hālat-i-maraz-ul-maut. G. G. On his death bed.

H موتهالا मोथाला *mothāl'ā*, n. f.
Deficiency of moisture in the soil.

A H موثر اور كارآمد نهوگي *muassar aur kār-āmad na hogī.* G. G.
Shall cease to have effect. [reason.

A موجب *mūj'ib.* n. m. Pl. موجبات Cause;
mūjib shuba-i-fareb, G. G. Suspicious.
mūjibāt-i-apīl, n. f. Grounds of appeal, as set forth in the pleadings of the appellant.

A موجود *mauj'ūd'*, adj. وجد existed. See حاضر (1,2). 1. Present. 2. At hand; available.
3. Existing; extant. 4. Ready.
maujūd rahnā, v. n. 1. To subsist; continue.
2. To attend; wait on.

maujūd k., v. a. 1. To produce; bring before (*hāzir k.*). 2. To provide; supply.
maujūdgī men, adv. In presence of.
maujūd'ah, adj. 1. Present. 2. Extant. [stances.
hālat-i-maujūdah. The present state or circum-

A موجه *muvaj'jah*, adj. وجه turning the face to. Reasonable; valid. *Vajah mavajjah*.

A مودع *muvaddā*, n.m. A trustee; one to whom property is entrusted.

A موديع *mūdiā*, n. m. A depositor; one who leaves any thing in trust with another.

A مورث *mūr'is*, n. m.

The legator; the person from whom an inheritance is derived, whether in the descending or ascending line.
mūris-i-ālā yā muttahid, n.m. The common ancestor; a remote progenitor.
mūris-i-fāsid.

In Mah. law, a maternal grandfather and the mother of a maternal grandfather are termed false ancestors. They are not entitled to any specific share, nor included in the number of sharers or residuaries.

H مورچها मूरछा *mūr'chhā*, *mūrchhā-gat*, n. f. S. मूर्छा Pr. *muchchhā*. A swoon; stupefaction.
mūrchhā ānā, yā khānā, v. n. To swoon; faint.
مورچهت मूरछित *mūr'chhit*, adj. Fainted; in a swoon; insensible; entranced.

A مورخه *muvar'rakhah*, adj. 1. Written. 2. Dated; bearing date; under date.

A موروثي *maurūs'ī*; H. *bapautī*, adj.

Patrimonial; hereditary; ancestral.
maurūsī ijārah, n. m. A hereditary farm, held either at a fixed or variable rent, according to the terms of the lease, but descending from father to son as long as the stipulated rent is paid.
maurūsī asāmī yā raaiyat, n. f.

A cultivator in a village holding by hereditary descent although not one of the proprietary community. He cannot be dispossessed as long as he pays his rent and he cannot alienate his land by sale or mortgage without the consent of the parties of whom he holds.
maurūsī bilā-shartī. A ryot with absolute right of occupancy at fixed rates.
maurūsī shartī. A ryot with right of occupancy subject to future change (Sect. 6, Act X of 1859).
maurūsī-aima. Hereditary rent-free tenure.
maurūsī muqaddam. The head man of a village, holding his office by hereditary descent. In some places he is looked upon as the proprietor of the village lands.
ğair-maurūsī asāmī, yā raaiyat. A cultivator not holding by hereditary tenure, but for a stipulated term, or on lease, in contradistinction to the *Pāhī* or tenant at will.

H موسد मूसद *mūs'ad*, W.

The wooden scrapers for scraping out the boiled juice of the sugarcane.

A موسوم *mausūm'*, adj. Named; called; entitled. [crops by field mice.

P موش خوري *mūsh-khurī*, n. f. Injury to

A موصوف *mausūf'*; adj. وصف described.

1. Described; named; celebrated.
2. Before-mentioned; above-mentioned.
mausūf-ilaih. The afore-mentioned.

A موصي *mūs'ī*, n. m. *mūsiyā*, n. f. وصي bequeathed. A testator.
mūsā-bihī. Bequeathed, conveyed by a will.
mūsā lahū. A legatee; a devisee. [land.

A موضع *mauz'ā*, n. m. A parcel or parcels of
mauzā aslī, n. m. The chief village, or that originally settled; the homestead.
mauzā dākhilī,

All the villages and lands which are comprised in the assessment settled with the original or principal village.
mauza-i-sirf, G. G. An independent village.
mauzā mushtarikah, n. m.

A mauza held in common.
mauza-vār, By mauzās or villages.
mavāza mālguzārī, G. G. n. m.

Estates paying revenue to Government.
mauzīn'ā, n. m. A village register kept by the village accountant shewing the extent of the lands, the average rate of rent per *bīghā*, the amount of cultivated and waste land, and the persons paying or exempt from revenue.

H موہران मोहरान *mohrān'*,

A duty on wild fruit.

A موهوب *mauhūb'*, adj. وهب given.

Given, granted. [legatee.
mauhūb-ilaih, *mauhūb-lahū*, n. m. A grantee;
mauhūb-lahum. G. G. A class of legatees.[rative.

A موئيد *muai'yad*, adj. Confirmatory; corrobo-
ba-manzil-i-sabūt-i-muaiyad. G. G.

As corroborative evidence.
subūt-i-muaiyad. G. G. Corroborative evidence.

A مويشي *mavesh'ī*; H. *bheṛ bakrī'*, n. f. S. महिष buffalo. Goats and sheep; cattle.

maveshī charānā, v. n. To depasture cattle.
maveshī-khānā, n. m. 1. A cattle pen. 2. A pound.
maveshī kī pāëmālī, n. f. Trespass of cattle.
maveshī lā-vāris. Unclaimed cattle.

H مہا **महा** *mahā'*, adj. (*In comp.*) Great.

mahā aprādh, yā dosh, n. m. A heinous sin or crime. [ner or criminal.
mahā-aprādhī, mahā-pāpī, n. m. A great sin-
mahā-jan, n. m. 1. A merchant; banker.
2. A man of credit.
mahā-janī, adj. Commercial; mercantile.
mahā-janī, n. f. Banking business; exchange.
mahā-janī parchah, chiṭṭhī, yā hunḍī, n.
A cheque; bill of exchange.
mahā-janī rīt, n. f. Commercial usage. [credit.
mahā-janī sākh, n. f. Mercantile or commercial
mahā-janī lekhā, n. m. Mercantile accounts.
مہتا **महता** *mah'tā*, n. m.
A chief; the headman of a village.

A مہتمم *mohtamim'*, n. m. A manager; superintendent; an inspector; overseer.
mohtamim-i-akhbār, n. m.
An editor of a newspaper. [officer.
mohtamim-i-band o bast, n. m. A settlement
mohtamim-i-tarka-i-zī-haqq. G. G.
Rightful executor or administrator.
mohtamim kār-i-dīvānī. Remembrancer of legal affairs. [cargo.
mohtamim māl-i-saudāgrī dar jahāz. A super-
mohtamim-i-matba, A press manager.
mohtamim yā dāroga-i-pulis. A superintendent of police. [1, 2).
مہتممی *moh'tamimī*, n. f. Managership (اہتمام

H مہتو **महतू** *mah'tū*, n. m. A land bailiff.

P مہر *mohr*, n. f. 1. A seal.
2. The impression of a seal; a stamp.
3. A gold coin; gold mohar (*ashrafī*).
mohr-bar-dār, n. m. Keeper of the seal.
mohr-i-taqlīdī, G. G. A counterfeit seal. [seal.
mohr-i-hākim, mohr-mansabī, n. f. An official
mohr-i-khās, yā dastī, n. f. A signet.
mohr-i-shāhī, n.f. The privy seal; royal signet.
mohr-i-adālat, n. f. The court's seal.
mohr k. yā lagānā, v. a. To stamp; seal.
mohr-kan, n. m. A seal engraver; a lapidary.
mohr-kanī, n. f. Seal-engraving.
mohr lagānā, v. a. 1. To seal up; put a seal on.
2. To close; shut.
moh'rī, adj. 1. Sealed; sealed up.
2. Bearing one's signet.
mohrī parvānah, n. A sealed writ.
mohrī ruqqā, n. m. A note of hand bearing one's signet, or stamped with one's seal.
vasāyaq-i-ğair-mohrī. G. G.
Instruments not under seal.
vasāyaq-i-mohrī. G. G. Instruments under seal.

A مہر *mahr*, n. m. A marriage portion or gift settled by the husband upon the wife before marriage; jointure; alimony.
mahr-āna, n. m. The *Qāzī's* marriage fee. [wife.
mahr bāṅdhnā, v. a. To settle a portion on a
mahr bakhshnā, v.n. To give up a jointure. [tion.
mahr kā dāvā k., v.a. To claim a marriage por-
mahr misal. The customary marriage portion.
mahr majhūl, n. m. An unknown dower.
mahr muajjal, n. m.
A marriage portion paid inmediately.
mahr muaiyan. An express dower.
mahr movajjal, n. m. A marriage portion to be paid after a specified time.
mahr-nāmā, n. m. A marriage settlement.
mahr-i-fātmah. A small jointure.

A مہلت *moh'lat*, n. f. مہل
1. Delay; respite. 2. Intermission; cessation; armistice. 3. Time; leisure.
mohlat denā, v. a. To allow time; defer or postpone. [respite.
mohlat milnā, v. n. To be allowed time or a
mohlat-i-munāsib, G. G. Reasonable time.

A مہلک *moh'lik*, adj. Fatal (قاتل).
mohlik bīmārī, marz-i-mohlak, n.f. A fatal disease.
mohlik jagah, n. f. A vital part.
mohlik zakhm, n. m. A mortal wound.
mohlik h., v. n. To prove fatal.

H مہنت **महन्त** *mahant', mahanth*, n. m.
An abbot; a head of a religious order.

A مہیا *muhai'yā*, adj. Got ready; prepared.
muhaiyā k., v. a. To make ready; procure.

H مہینا **महीना** *mahī'nā*; Rus. *mhīnā*, n. m.
S. **मास** 1. A month.
2. Monthly wages; salary.
mahīnā bhar. The whole month.
mahīnā charhnā, v. n. 1. To be in arrears.
2. To pass (the time for menstruation).
mahīne-dār, n. m. A monthly servant.
mahīne se h., v. n. To be with menses.
mahīne ke mahīne, mahīne gail, mahīne-vār, chāṅd ke chāṅd; Sant. *chāndo chāndo*,
Monthly; every month.
mahīne kī hāṅḍī, n. f. Monthly obsequies.
mahīnār'ī, mahīne kī bīmārī, n. f. The menses.

H مئی **मै** *maī*, n.f. A barrow.

P H میاں بھائی *miyān bhāī*,
Two men living with one woman.

S میتھن **मैथुन** *mai'thun, maithun*, n. m.
Sexual intercourse; coition.

H میٹھا تیلیا *mīṭhā teliyā*,
A very active vegetable poison.

والے میٹھے *mīṭhe-vāle*, n. m. Thugs who kill travellers with a poison called *mīṭhā-telyā*.

P میر *mīr*, n. m. A chief; leader.
mīr-bahr, n. m. A collector of port duties.
mīr-bahrī, n. f. Port duties.
mīr-bakhshī, n. m. Paymaster-general.
mīr-deh. The head peon, or messenger of a *zamīndār*; the inspector or superintendent of a village; a native officer employed to preserve the village boundaries from encroachment; one employed to carry the measuring chain, or apply it to actual measurement in a survey.
mīr adl, n. m. Chief justice (*Mah.*).
A superintendent of the courts who revised the decisions of the *Qāzīs* and judges, and passed sentence.
mīr-majlis, n. m. 1. The master of the ceremonies. 2. A president or chairman. [of the town.
mīr-muhallah, n. m. The headman of a quarter
mīr-manzil, n. m. Quarter-master-general.
mīr-munshī, n. m. Chief secretary.

A میراث *mīrās'*, n. f. Hereditary estate or property; a bequest (*bapautī*).
میراثی *mīrās'ī*, adj. Inherited (*bapautī*).

H میڑا मैड़ा *mair'ā*; Tir. *ḍhel-ṛhoṛā*, n. m.
1. A harrow. 2. A ramp. [field.
mairā phernā, v. n. To break the clods of a

P میز بان *mez-bān*, n. m.
An entertainer; a host.
mez-bānī; Illit. *mijmānī*, n. f.
Hospitality; entertainment.

A میزان *mīzān'*, n. f. 1. A balance; a pair of scales. 2. (*Arith.*) Total. [cast up.
mīzān denā, lagānā, yā k., v. a. To total;
mīzān-i-kul, n. f. The grand total.

A میعاد *mīād'*, *miyād*, n. f. 1. Term; period. 2. Usance. 3. Imprisonment (*qaid*). [a term.
miyād barhānā, v. a. To extend or prolong
miyād bolnā, v. a. To sentence to imprisonment for a term (*qaid k.*).
miyād tamām, yā pūrī h., v. n. To expire (a term or period).
miyād ṭāl denā, To pass (a term).
miyād-i-sazā, n. f. A term of punishment.
miyād gair-munqaziyā. An unexpired term.
miyād qānūnī, A term prescribed by law.
miyād-i-qānūnī ke andar. Within the period or term prescribed by law.
miyād-i-qalīl. G. G. A short term.
miyād kāṭnā, v. n. To undergo imprisonment for the full term.
miyād-i mazīd. G. G. Further time.
miyād-i-mustājirī. The term of a farm.
miyād-i-muaiyanā yā muqarrarā, n. f.
A fixed period; the period allowed.
miyād mauūdah, A stipulated term.
miyād-i-nālish, n. f. Limitation statute. [time.
be-miyād, adj. Not confined to any stipulated
bain-ul-miyād. adv. Within the limit or term stipulated or required by law. [sonment.
qaid-kī-miyād. G. G. Limit of term of impri-
میعادی *mīād'ī*, *miyādī*, adj. Limited; terminable.
miyādī, n. f. A term prisoner (*qaidī*).
miyādī ijārah, n. f. A terminable lease; a farm or lease for a specified term.
mīyād-i-muqarrarah, A fixed period or term.
miyādī hunḍī. A bill after date.
naqshejāt-i-miyādī. G. G. Periodical returns.

H میکا मैका *mai'kā*; Brij. *māekā*; Panj. *nānkā*; E. *naihar*, n. m. S. मातृक
The bride's paternal home.
maikā basānā, Wom. v. n. To leave her father-in-law's and live with her parents.
maike-vāliyān, n. f. *maike-vāle*, n. m. [side.
The relations of the bride on the mother's

P میلان خسره *mīlān khasrā*,
Supplement to the *jamā-bandī*.

H مینا मीना *mīn'ā*, n. m. pl. *mīne*.
A caste of Hindu robbers of Rajpūtāna.

H مینار *mīnār'*, *minārā*; Illit. *munārā*, n. m.
1. A pillar; turret; steeple; minaret; tower of a mosque.
2. A boundary pillar; a mile stone.

H مینڈ मेंड *meṅḍ*, *meṅṛ*, n. f. A boundary mound (of a field); land-mark; a dam.
meṅḍ-bandī, n. f. A record of boundaries.

H A مینڈقول *meṅḍ qaul*. A rate assessed on land by the computation of the average rates of the surrounding fields. *Carnegy*.

H مینڈھی मेंढी *meṅ'ḍhī*, *meṅṛhī*.
A cess on the harvest of fields rented in kind, usually *aṛhaiyā* or $2\frac{1}{2}$ seers, equal to one ser *pakkā*, for the weigh-man. Oudh.

H میو मेव *meo*, *mevātī*, *mivātī*, n. m. *mivātan*, *meonī*, n. f. A thieving tribe inhabiting the mountainous parts of Delhi.
The Meos are now settling down into most respectable members of society.

ن

P نا *nā*; H. *nā*; A. *lā*; S. न No; not.
nā-insāf; H. *annyāī*, adj. Unjust.
nā-insāfī; H. *annyāo*, n. f. Injustice. [justice.
nā-insāfī k.; H. *annyāo k.*, v. a. To do in-

nā-bāliġ; H. *yānā*, adj. A minor; ward; youth.
nā-bāligī; H. *yān-pan*, n. f. Nonage; minority.
nā-bāligi-kī sūrat. During minority.
nā-pāk; H. *apavitr*, adj.
Polluted; unclean; impure (*gandah*, 2).
nā-pāk k., v. a. To defile; pollute.
nā-pākī; H. *apavitrtā*, n. f.
Pollution; impurity; foulness.
nā-jāiz ṭhairānā yā qarār denā, nā-jaiz rakhnā. v. a. To reject; refuse to allow.
nā-jāiz k., v. a. To invalidate; make null.
nā-jāiz māl, Contraband goods.
nā-jāiz vasīlah. G. G. Illegal means.
nā-javāzī. n. f. Illegality; invalidity.
nā-javāzī se bāz rakhnā. 1. To withhold wrongfully. 2. To defraud.
nā-haq phāṅsnā, v. a. To accuse falsely.
nā-haq-shinās, adj. Unjust.
nā-haq-shināsī, n. f. Injustice; wrong.
nā-haq k., v. a. To do an injustice; act unjustly.
nā-haq kushī, n. f. Unjustifiable homicide.
nā-haq kahnā, v. n. 1. To calumniate; slander. 2. To speak in vain.
nā-haq lenā, v. a. To take wrongfully; to usurp.
nā-dār; H. *nir-dhan*, n. m. A pauper.
nā-dār, adj. 1. Blank.
2. Impecunious; insolvent.
nā-dārī; H. *an-hot*, n. f. 1. Pauperism; insolvency.
2. Poverty (*muflisī*).
nā-dārī ba-rāh-i-fareb, nā-dārī ba-nīyat-i-fāsid. Fraudulent insolvency.
nā-dihand; H. *līchar, le-loṭ*, adj.
Not paying what is due.
nā-dihand, n. m. A defaulter.
nā-ravā, adj. Not right or proper (*nā-jāiz*).
nā-shāistah, adj. 1. Unbecoming. 2. Unmannerly. 3. Unworthy. 4. Improper; disreputable. 5. Inexpedient; injudicious.
nā-farmānī, n. f. 1. Disobedience of orders.
2. (*Law*) Contempt.
nā-farmānī k.; H. *āgyā na mānnā*, v. n.
To disobey; refuse to obey.
nā-qābil; H. *an-jog*, adj.
Incapable; incompetent; unfit.
nā-qābil i-etirāz, Indisputable.
nā-qābil-i-intiqāl; H. *an-palaṭ jog*, adj. Not transferable.
nā-qābil-i-taqsīm; H. *an-baṭāū.* Impartible.
nā-qābliyat, n. f. Incapacity; incompetence.
nā-mard; H. *napunsak*, adj. Impotent; imbecile.
nā-mard k., v. a. To emasculate.
nā-mardī, n. f. Impotency.
nā-mutābiq, adj. Inconsistent.
nā-motabar, adj. Incredible; untrustworthy.
nā-motabar ṭhairānā, v. a.
To pronounce unworthy of credit.
nā-māqūl, adj. 1. Irrational; unreasonable; absurd. 2. Improper (*nā-lāyaq*).
nā-māqūl hujjat. An absurd or untenable argument.
nā-masmū k., v. a.
To dismiss or non-suit (a case).

*nā-mumkin-ul-zarā*at.* adj. Uunculturable.
nā-manzūr, adj.
Refused; rejected; inadmissible.
nā-manzūr shud. Refused or rejected (an order written on an application). [nonsuit.
nā-manzūr k., v. a. To refuse; reject; disallow;
nā-manzūrī, n. f. Rejection; veto.
nā-muyassarī; Pop. *nā-maisarī*, Wom. n. f. Poverty.
adāē nā-jāiz. G. G. Corrupt payment.
abvāb yā mahsūl-i-nā-jāiz. G. G.
Unauthorized cess or impost.
tifl-i-nā bāliġ. G. G. A minor.
shakhs-i-nā-kardah-gunāh. G. G. An innocent person.

H ناپ नाप *nāp, napat, nāp tol*; Sant. *song*, n.f.
S. मापन, Measure; measurement; survey.
nāp kā pūrā, Of full measure, height, etc.
be-nāp, be-māp, adj. Unmeasured; not surveyed.
A lease in which it is agreed between the renter and the cultivator that the original measurement and average rates shall remain unaltered as long as the cultivator pays the stipulated rent.
jamī nāp, jamā paimāna, Standard or full measure.
chaltā paimāna, chaltī nāp, Somewhat below the standard measure.

H ناتا नाता *nāt'ā, nāta-rishtah*, n. m. S. ज्ञातेय
Relationship; relative; kindred (*rishtah*, 2).
nātā-jornā, v. n. To form a connection with.
nāte-dār, n. m. A relative; kinsman.
nāte-dārī, n. f. Relationship (*rishte-dārī*).

H ناتن नातिन *nāt'in*, E.; *dheotī*, W. n. f. S. नप्त्री
Daughter's daughter; granddaughter.
ناتي नाती *nāt'ī*, E. n. m. S. नप्तृ, Pālī, *nattā.*
A daughter's son; a grandson (W. *dheotā*).

H نار नार *nār*, W.; *hornādā*, Tir.; *duali*, Bhoj.
The large leathern thong by which the ox yoke is tied to the pole of the drag.

H نارو नारू *nār'ū*, n. Sowing by drills.

A ناطق *nāt'iq*, adj.
Definitive; positive; decisive (قطعي).

A ناظر *nāz'ir*, n. m. نظر saw.
1. An inspector a supervisor. 2. (*nāzir-i-adālat*). A sheriff; bailiff.
The officer of the court who is charged with the serving of process, or who is sent to take depositions, and make inquiry into any breach of law or the peace.
nazār'at, n. f. The office of a *nāzir.*

A ناظم *nāz'im*, n. m. نظم strung together.
An administrator; a governor; the superior officer or governor.

T ناغه *nāġ'ah*, adj. Vacant; blank; absent; nought.
nāgah, n. m. 1. Absence.
2. Adjournment; intermission; respite.

nāgah h., yā k. To be absent. [ways.
bilā-nāgah, adv. Without fail; regularly; al-
A نافذ *nāf'iz*, adj. 1. Issued; passed.
2. Operative; in force.
nāfi'zan, adj. Of good effect. [into law.
nāfiz-shudah yā huā, adj. Executed; passed
nāfiz k., v. a. 1. To issue; pass (an order).
2. To serve; execute; use, exercise (a right); put in execution; enforce.
nāfiz va muassir hogā. G. G. Shall take effect.
nafiz honā, v. n.
To issue; arise; become operative.
ikhtiyār nāfiz k., G. G. To exercise a right.
A ناقص *nā'qis*, adj. نقص diminishing, injuring. 1. Defective; wanting; mutilated.
2. Unsound; bad; vicious; worthless.
nāqis-ul-aql, adj. Of unsound mind. [mutilate.
nāqis k., v. a. To vitiate; render defective;
nāqis h., v. n. To deteriorate; to be vitiated.
H ناک کاٹنا *nāk kāṭnā utārnā, yā uṛānā*, v. a.
1. To cut off one's nose. 2. To disgrace one. To cut off a wife's nose is the traditional punishment of infidelity.
nāk kāṭne kā ḍar dikhānā. G. G. Duress by menaces or threats (*per minas*). [and ears.
nāk kān kāṭnā, v. a. To cut off one's nose
ناکا नाका *nāk'ā*, n. m. 1. A toll or customs' station. 2. A subordinate police station.
3. E. The post or beat of a constable 4. A gate or passage through the customs' line.
nākā-bandī, n. f. 1. Placing a picquet on a road. 2. Collections on account of land customs and transit duties. [transit duties.
nāke-dār, n. m. The receiver of customs or
P ناکدخدا *nā-kad'khudā'*, n. m. A bachelor.
nā-kadkhudāī', n. f. The unmarried state.
H ناگا नागा *nāg'ā*, n. m. S. नाग. A class of Hin. mendicants who go naked and carry arms.
H ناگل नागल *nāg'al, chirai'yā*, n. m. S. लङ्गल
The hooks of a yoke to which the ropes round the bullocks' necks are tied, and by which the draught is distributed.
P ناگہاں *nāgahān'*, adj. Sudden.
nā-gahānī tanāzā, n. G. G. A sudden fight.
nā-guhānī laṛāī, n. G. G. A sudden quarrel.
P نالش *nāl'ish*; Rus. *lānas, nānas*, n. f. 1. A complaint. 2. An action; a charge (دعوي).
nālish isbāt muā'khazah-dārī. A suit brought to establish an incumbrance. [one.
nālish az taraf-i-falān. An action in favor of
nālish istirdād-i-dāva.
A suit for the avoidance of a claim.
nālish istirdād matālabah izāfah lagān. A suit to contest a demand of enhanced rent.

nālish istiqrār-i-istehqāq. A suit for a declaratory right. [tious suit.
nālish barāē īzā-rasānī yā taklīf-dihī. A vexa-
nālish ba-nazar īzā-rasānī yā takhrīb.
A malicious prosecution.
nālish ba-nām-i-falān, G. G. *nālish falāne par.*
An action against one. [ter.
nālish be-dakhlī. A suit for ejectment or ous-
nālish baibāt. A foreclosure suit.
nālish-paṭṭī, Calendar of crimes.
nālish phir qāyam k. To revive a suit. [divāj.
nālish husūl huqūq-i-shauharī yā istehqāq iz-
A suit for restoration of conjugal rights.
nālish khārij yā kal-adum huī. The action was lost. [*nālish*).
nālish khilāf. G. G. A false complaint (*khilāf*
nālish dāyar karne ke qābil Actionable.
nālish dakhl-yābī. A suit for possession.
nālish darog ba-yaraz īzā-rasānī.
A false and malicious complaint.
nālish dīvānī, A civil suit.
nālish zātī, A personal action.
nālish zar-i-harjah, An action for damages.
nālish ziyādah lagān. A complaint of excessive demand of rent. [lent suit.
nālish sāzishī yā farebī. A collusive or fraudu-
nālish sāqit huī. G. G. Action abated.
nālish sarāsarī, n. A summary suit.
nālish sarāsarī az taraf-i-ṭhekahkār. G. G. Farmer's suit against vendors. [lar suit.
nālish silsilah yā ām, nālish lambarī. A regu-
nālish se dast-bardār h. To withdraw a suit.
nālish falāne ke nām se, nālish falāne kī taraf se. An action on the part of one. [cution.
nālish faujdārī. A criminal action or prose-
nālish fauj-dārī kī hidāyat k.
To direct a criminal prosecution.
nālish kā istehqāq, Right of action.
nālish k., nālishī h., To bring an action; institute proceedings. [for action.
nālish kī binā qāyam k. To furnish a ground
nālish ke māne h., To bar a suit.
nālish mabnī bar adāvat. A malicious charge.
nālish-i-mutafarraqah. A miscellaneous suit.
nālish muzāhamī. A cross suit; an action in bar of proceeding.
nālish muflisī. A suit in *forma pauperis.*
nālish vā-guzāsht qurqī. An action of replevin.
nālishī arzī, A plaint; the representation of the complaint.
ba-sabab tamādī aiyām muddaī ko istehqāq nālish bāqī na rahā. The plaintiff's right of action is barred by lapse of time. [document.
kisī dastāvez kī rū se nālish k. To sue upon a
mujaddadan nālish k. G.G. To bring a fresh suit.
mujaddadan nālish karne kā ikhtiyār na rakhna. To be precluded from bringing a fresh suit.
vajeh nālish. G.G. Cause of action. [prosecutor.
نالشي *nāl'ishī*, n. f. A complainant; a suitor;

H & P نام **नाम** *nām*; Rus. *nāoṅ*, n.m.S. नामन्.
A name; designation; title.
nām-burdah, P. adj. The above-named; aforementioned.
nām bigāṛnā, yā gaṅvānā, v. a. To spoil one's [name; defame.
nām-ba-nām, After each name; per head.
nām-patr, n. m. A list of persons.
nām pukārnā, v. a. To call over the names.
nām-zad; Illit. *nām-jād*, adj.
1. Named; entitled.
2. Nominated; appointed. 3. Betrothed.
4. Dedicated. 5. Noted; on men's tongues.
nām-zad, P. n. f. A betrothed damsel.
nām sākh, Character and credit.
nām se, adv. In the name of.
nām kā pahlā harf. The initials of one's name.
nām kā kharrā, yā lekh-fard, A list of names.
nām kī bhūl, yā chūk.
A wrong name; misnomer.
nām likhnā, chaṛhānā, yā dākhil k., v. a.
1. To enter or register one's name.
2. To affix one's signature.
nām lagnā, v. n. To be charged, accused.
nām o nishān, P. adj. 1. Sign; mark; trace.
2. Name and address.
ba-nām, ba-nām-i-falāṅ, P. adv.
1. To the address of.
2. In the name of; in favor of; against.
ba-nām nihād, G. G. Purporting to be.
jis-ke nām par, Against whom.

A ناموس *nāmūs'*, n. f. A. نمس concealing (a secret). Honor; grace. [dishonor.

H ناموسي *nāmos'ī, nāmūsī*, Illit. n. f. Disgrace;

P نامه *nām'ah*, n. m. 1. (*nāma o payām*)
A letter (*chiṭṭhī*, 1). 2. (*In Comp.*) A writing; written document; deed, as *iqrār-nāmah* a deed of agreement.
nāmah-bar, n. m. A messenger; letter-carrier.
nāma-nigār, A correspondent.

H نانا **नाना** *nān'ā*; Sant. *goṛom bābā*, n. m.
Maternal grandfather.

H نانٿھ **नांठ** *nāṅṭh*; A. *māl lā-vāris*.
The estate or property of a deceased person who leaves no heir after him.
nāṅṭh par baiṭhnā. To take possession of unclaimed property.
nāṅṭhā; A. *lā-vāris*, One who has no heirs.

P نانکار *nānkār, nānkār zamīn*, n. m.
An allowance; maintenance.
Land granted to servants for their subsistence; an assignment of a portion of the land or revenue of an estate made to the occupant or *zamīndār* as an allowance for his subsistence, usually amounting to about five, or sometimes, ten per cent on the assessment payable to the state; a rent-free grant of land for service in lieu of pay.

nānkār mujrāī, n. Deductions from the revenue or assignments from it, on account of *nānkār*, or subsistence allowance.
tankhuāhī nān-kār. An allowance for work done.

H نانواں **नांवां** *nān'vāṅ*; Illit. *nāmā*, n. m.
1. A name (*nām*, 1). 2. The price of an article. 3. Money due. 4. Small change.
nāṅvāṅ pakānā, v. a. To make up an account.
nāṅvāṅ chukānā, v. a.
To settle or discharge a balance.

P A نان و نفقه *nān o nafqah*, n. m.
Maintenance; alimony (*roṭī kapṛā*).
nān o nafqah denā, v. a. To give one a maintenance.
nān o nafqah na denā, v. a. To neglect one's [wife or children.

H ناني **नानी** *nān'ī*; Sant. *goṛom āyo*, n. f.
Mother's mother; maternal grandmother.

A نايب *nā'yab*; Pop. *nāib*, n. m. نوب being near. A deputy; delegate. [ant.
nāyab dīvān, The deputy treasurer or account-
nāyab munshī. An assistant writer or underclerk.
nāyab munīb, A deputy and his chief.
nayāb'at, nāēbī, n. f. Deputyship; agency.
ilāqeh kā nāyab. G. G. District delegate.

H نايک **नायक** *nā'yak, nāik*, n. m. S. नी to lead. 1. A leader; chief. 2. The head of a caravan. 3. A corporal. 4. An overseer of labourers. 5. A leader of a band of musicians.
نايکا **नायका** *nā'ēkā*, n. f. The mistress of a brothel; the mother-bawd.

P نبيره *nabīr'ah*, n.m. A grandson. [defloured.

H نتهني اترنا *nathnī utarnā*, v. n. To be

H نتهی **नत्थी** *nat'thī*, n. f. 1. The string with which papers are strung together.
2. The record or papers in a cause.
natthī k., v. a. To string together; annex; file.

A نتيجه *natīj'ah*, n. m.
End; conclusion; effect (انت)
natījah-i-tahqīqāt, G.G. The result of an enquiry.

H نج **निज** *nij, nij-kā*, adj. S. निज; Pālī, *nijo*.
1. One's own 2. Special (خاص 1, 2).
3. Not official.
nij-adhikār, A prerogative.
nij-bhāī, Own brother (*apnā bhāī*).
nij-putr, A legitimate son.
nij taalluq, One's own *taalluq* or estate.
In Bengal, a portion of land of which the proprietor or payer collects the rents from the cultivators direct, without any intermediate agency; the private lands of a *zamīndār*, or those cultivated by himself for his own benefit.

nij jot. The lessee's own cultivation or home farm.

Lands cultivated by the proprietors or revenue-payers themselves, and for their own benefit. Also, land allowed to be set apart for the private maintenance of a *zamīndār*, on whom before the decennial settlement in Bengal no revenue was assessed.

nij-jotā, yā kāsht, A cultivating proprietor.
nij dhām, One's own house.
nij-kharch, Private expenses.
nij kā hisāb, Private account.
nij kārī, n. f. Land paying rent in kind.
nij kā māl, Private property.
nij kā naukar, n. m. A private servant.
nij kī rāh, A private way.
نج निज *nij,* n. m. One's private house or office.

A نجس *naj'as,* Dirty; filthy.

āb-i-najas. G. G. Offensive matter (liquid).

A نجيب الطرفين *najīb-ul-tarfain.*
Noble on both sides.

H & P نخاس كي گهوڑي *nak'khās kī ghorī,* *lit.* a mare on public sale. A frail woman.

نخاس واليان *nakhās-vāliyān,* n. f. Prostitutes.

A نذر *nazr, naz'ar, nazrā'nah,* n. f.
1. A present from an inferior.
2. A fee paid to the state, or to its representative, on succeeding to an office or property.

نذرانه *nazrā'nā.* Commutation for service of an assignee of Government revenue.
nazar-i-aimma. A charitable gift or grant for the support of priests, etc, a benefice; charity lands.
nazar-i-dargāh. An assignment of revenue under the Mah. Government to a sacred shrine, or any religious establishment.
nazar-i-qatai, n. f. A present made to the farmer or revenue officer by the cultivators for permission to cut their corn.

S نر निर *nir,* A negative prefix.

nir-upāē; A. *lā-ilāj,* adj.
Without remedy; irretrievable.
*nir-aprādh, nir-aprādhī,*adj. Innocent;guiltless.
nir-uttar, n. m. Unanswerable; *nihil dicit*; making no defence.
nir-bans, adj. Without issue; extinct (a family).
nir-dosh thairānā, yā rakhnā, To exonerate; exculpate; absolve; acquit.
nir-dhan, n. m. A poor man; a pauper.
nir-dosh, nis-pāp, adj. Sinless; innocent; faultless. [man.

S & P نر नर *nar*; Sant. *herel,* n. m. A male;

nar-badh, nar-hinsā, Manslaughter; homicide.
aulād-i-narīnah, n. m. Male issue.

H نرا नरा *nar'ā,* A pit full of water in a field. [A king (*rājā,* 1.).

S نرپ नृप *nrip,* n. m. नृ man, पा preserve.
nrip-drohī, n. m. A king's foe; a traitor.
nrip-ghātik, n. A regicide.

P نرخ *nir'kh*; Pop. *nirakh*; Sant. *niruk,* n.m.
Market rate (*bāzār kā nirkh*); current price.
2. The standard rate at which the lands of a village or district are assessed.
nirkh-bandī. Adjustment or statement of rates.
nirkh dārogah, An officer who regulates the market rates.
nirkh muqqarrar k.; H *bhāo nikālnā,* v. a.
To fix the selling price.
nirkh-nāmah, A table of price currents.
nirkh-nāmah hundyān. Course of exchange.

P نرم *narm, naram,* adj. Light; easy.
band o bast-i-narm. Light assessment.

H نرنے निरनै *nirna'ē, nirne,* n. m. S. निर्णय
Adjudication; award.
nirne patr. The award; verdict.
nirne k., v. a. 1. To distinguish; discriminate.
2. To adjudge; decide. [tion.

A نزاع *nizā'ā, nizā,* n. m. Dispute; contention.
nizā-i-sarhad. A boundary dispute.
nizā-i-qanūnī, n. An issue of law.
nizā k. To dispute; litigate.
nizā men, In dispute.
nizā-i-muqadmah, An issue for decision.

P نزدات *nizdāt',* n. f. An inefficient balance; a suspense account.

P H نزديک هونا *nazdīk honā, yā jānā,* v.n.
1. To approach; draw near.
2. To have sexual intercourse with.
نزديكي *nazdīk'ī,* n. f. 1. Proximity (*qurbat*).
2. Propinquity. 3. Coition.

A نزول *nuzūl',* n. m. 1. Crown or government lands; escheated land property which falls to the state from default of heirs. 2. An office for investigating lapsed claims.

H نس नस *nas*; Sant. *sir,* n. f. S. स्नसा
1. A sinew; tendon; nerve.
2. The organ of generation. [mite.
nas-katā, n. m. 1. A eunuch (*khojā*). 2. A cata-
nas marānā, v. n. Slang.
To submit to sexual intercourse.

A نسبت *nis'bat,* n. f. 1. Relation (تعلق 1, 2).
2. Affinity; analogy. 3. Ratio; proportion.
4. Betrothal; relationship by marriage.
5. A relation; connection.

nisbat rakhnā, v. n.
To bear relation to (*taalluq rakhnā*).
nisbat k., v. a. 1. To ascribe; attribute; impute. 2. To refer or assign to. 3. To betroth; form an alliance with.
nisbat-nāmā, kursī-nāmah, nasab-nāmah, n. m. A genealogical table.
nisbat ho jānā, v. n. To be betrothed.
nisbat, adv. 1. With respect, relation, or reference to; respecting. 2. In comparison with; than; in proportion to.
نسبتي *nis'batī*, adj. 1. Related or having reference to. 2. Related by marriage.
nis'batī, nisbatī bhāī, Mah. n. m. A wife's brother; brother-in-law.

A نسخ *nas*ᵉ*kh*, n. m. Ped.
Abolition; abrogation; repeal.
naskh k., v. n. 1. To abrogate; annul; cancel. 2. To upset; set aside.
khat-i-naskh. G. G. Cancellation.

H نس سنتان **निससन्तान** *nis-santān*, adj.
Childess; without issue.

A نسل *nasl, nasal*, n. f. See بنس
نسلاً *nas'lan*, adv. Lineally.
nasl-i-pidarī, n. The paternal line.
nasl-i-mādrī. The maternal line.
naslan bād naslan, Generation after generation (*bans paramparā*).
nasl'ī, adj. Genealogical.

H نسيا **निसया** *nis'yā*, n. m. (*Brokers*) One pice.

A نشا *nash'ā*, n. m. 1. An intoxicating liquor. 2. Intoxication; drunkenness.
nashā pānī k. yā jamānā, v. n. 1. To liquor up. 2. To take bribes.
nashe-bāz, n. m. A drunkard.
nashe kī hālat men, nashe men, adv. In a state of intoxication.

P نشان *nishān'*, n. m. *nishānī*, n. f.
1. A mark; impression. 2. A signal. 3. A flag; colors. 4. A device. 5. Armorial bearings; coat of arms. 6. One's place of residence or address (*patā*, 2).
nishān-bardār, n. m. A standard bearer; an ensign.
nishān parnā, v. n. To be left (a mark, etc.).
nishān-paṭṭī, n. f. A descriptive list or roll (of fugitive slaves, deserters, etc.).
nishān-dihī, n.f. Specification; particular mention.
nishān-dihī k, nishān batānā, v. a.
To point out; indicate.
nishān-i-saudāgarī, n. m. A trade mark.
nishān k., yā ḍālnā, v. a. 1. To mark; sign; make a mark. 2. (*nishānī k.*) To sign; witness (a bond); to check. 3. To stamp; impress.
nishān multabis, n. m. A counterfeit mark.
nishān milkīyat, nishān-i-māl.
A property mark.
pānī par tairne-vālā nishān, G. G. A buoy.
samandrī nishān, G. G. Sea-mark.

S نشچے **निश्चय** *nishcha'ē*; H. *nische, nahche*, n. Certainty. See تحقيق.
nishchaē, adj. Certain (*tahqīq*).
nishchaē, adv. Truly (*tahqīq*).
nishchaē k., v. a. 1. To make sure (*tahqīq k.*). 2. To ratify; guarantee.

P نشست جمع *nishast-i-jama*, n. f.
Adjustment of rent with a tenant.
nishast-i-khirāj. Assessment; the act.

A نصف *nisf*, adj. Half.
nisf jamā par bandodāst k., To settle at half assessed rates.
nisf jama, rīt, yā khirāj. Half the revenue assessment, latterly levied on the holders of resumed rent-free tenures.
nisf-mukammal. Imperfect; unfinished.
nisf-tahsīl. Half the collections.
nisf rīt, n. f. Land paying half of the Government revenue.

A نطفه *nut'fā*, n.m. 1. Semen (بيج 4). 2. Son.
nutfa-i-bint-ul-inab, lit. the seed of the daughter of the grape. A bastard begotten in a drunken fit.
nutfa-i-be-tahqīq, nutfa-i-harām. Misbegotten; illegitimate.
nutfā jamā. Conceived (in the womb).

A نظامت *nazām'at, nizāmat*, n. f.
Administration.
nazāmat-i-adālat, n. f. A supreme court of criminal justice.
nizām shamsī, The solar system.

A نظر *naz'ar, nazr*; Sant. *benget*, n. f.
1. Sight. 2. Supervision.
nazar-andāzī, n. f. Valuation of land or estimate of a crop upon inspection.
nazar-bāz, n. m. 1.A detective. 2. An ogler.
nazar-band, n. m. 1. A spell; charm. 2. A state prisoner.
nazar-band, adv. Under arrest; on *parole*.
nazar-band rakhnā, v. a.
To detain a suspected person.
nazar-bandī, n. f. 1. Surveillance. 2. Confinement; arrest.
nazar parnā, v. n. To happen to see; to fall under one's notice.
nazar sānī, n. f. A review or second examination; revision.
ba-hirāsat-i- munāsib nazar-band rakkhā jānā. G. G. To be detained in safe custody.
ba-nazar, adv. In view of; in order to; according to.
ba-nazar iske, adv. Seeing that; whereas.
ba-nazar-i-amn o āsāyash, For keeping the peace; for the maintenance of the peace; for the public safety or interest.

ba-nazar insāf yā dād-dihī.
For the purpose or sake of justice.
ba-nazar āīn. Looking to the law ; *quoad* law ; in a legal point of view.
ba-nazar hālat-i-khās, With reference to the peculiar or special circumstances.
ba-nazar hālāt-i-muqaddamah. Under the circumstances of the case.
ba-nazar haqīqat hāl. With reference to the facts, circumstances, or merits of the case.
ba-nazar sarāsarī, On a hasty view ; on the face of ; summarily.
kaī nazar se, In many respects. [management.

A نظم ونسق *nazm o nasq,* 1. Administration ;
2. System of Government ; policy.
nazm o nasq k., v.a. To organize ; administer.
nazm o nasq mulāzimīn-i-sarkārī.
Mutation of establishment.

A نظير *nazīr',* n. f. A precedent.
nazīr denā yā lānā, v. n. 1. To cite ; quote.
2. To adduce a precedent or authority.
nazīr muhavvala. The precedent cited.

A P نعلبندي *nāl-bandī,* n. f. Tribute.

Under the Mah. government, a contribution exacted from petty princes or the peasantry on the plea of keeping up the cavalry of the state, or preventing the horsemen from devastating the country, subsequently converted into a permanent tribute.

nāl-bandī dene-vālā, n. m. A tributary.

A نفاذ *nifāz',* n.m. نفذ flowing. Passing (of an act,) ; issue (of an order.) ;
nifāz-i-istehqāq, G. G. The exercise of a right.
nifāz pānā, v. n. To be passed, enacted (a law) ; to be in force.
nifāz dastāvez. The execution of a deed.
nifāz qānūn. The passing of a law.
istehqāq-i-nifāz, haq-i-āmad raft. Right of way.

A نفاس *nafās',* n. m. 1. The afterbirth.
2. The forty days after childbirth.
3. Bringing forth *lochia* or the natural discharge of blood after childbirth.

A نفرت *naf'rat,* n. f. Disgust (*ghin*). [some.
nafrat-angez ; H. *ghināonā,* Disgusting ; loath-
nafrat k., yā khānā, v. n. To be disgusted.
nafrīn', n. f. Curse ; malediction. [truth or fact.

A نفس الامر *nafs-ul-amr,* n. m. The essential
نفس الحال *nafs-ul-hāl yā amr,*
The facts or merits of a case. [purport.
نفس المطلب *nafs-ul-matlab,* The substance ;
نفس قانوني *nafs-i-qānūnī.* The law itself.

A نفع *naf'ā, nafā* ; Rus. *naphā* ; Sant. *barphai,* n. m. Profit (فايده 1, 2).
nafa uṭhānā, v. n. To make a profit.
nafa o nuqsān. Profit and loss.

A نفقه *naf'qa, nafqā,* n.m. 1. Necessary means of subsistence ; supply of food, clothes and lodging which in law is obligatory upon certain relations, as the support of a wife by her husband, of a child by its parents, of a needy parent by its child, and of relatives and dependants in general.
2. The formal denial of his paternity to a child born of his wife ; rejection or abandonment of a child.

A H نقب دينا *naqab denā yā lagānā, naqab-zanī k,* v. a.
To break into (a house).
naqab-zan, n. m. A burglar.
naqab-zanī, n.f. House-breaking ; burglary.

A نقد *naqd, naqad* ; Illit. *nag̃ad, nagad, nakad,* n. m. 1. (*naqdī*) Ready money ; cash ; prompt or ready payment. 2. A son-in-law, so called because he receives money from his father-in-law when he visits him.
naqdā naqd, Prompt payment.
naqd o jins, Money and goods.
naqdī jinsī, Money rent, calculated on the value of the produce.
naqd'ī chiṭṭhā, khātā rokaṛ n. m. Cash account.
naqdī faislā, n. m.
A settlement of cash balances.
naqdī gumāshta, n.m. A cash-keeper.
naqdī mazkūrāt. Miscellaneous items in the revenue accounts allowed for and settled in money.
sarmāyā-naqdī, G. G. Funded property.

A نقش *naqsh,* n. m. An impression ; a stamp ; mark.
naqsha irsāl k. To make a return.
naqsha-i-intiqālī. A deed of conveyance or transfer of landed property.
naqsha-i-band o bast-i-sarsarī. A summary settlement statement.
naqsh-i-pā, n. m. A foot-print ; track.
naqsh karne kā ālā, G. G. An instrument for making an impression.
نقشه *naqsh'a,* n. m. 1. A delineation ; picture.
2. A plan ; design. 3. A form ; blank form ; exemplar. 4. A figured statement ; table ; return. 5. A register ; muster roll.
naqsha-i-tabdīlī. Record or transfer of shares in landed property.
naqsha-i-jāedād va qaraz. Statement of assets and liabilities paid or to be paid in ready money, applied esp. to the land-revenue which is paid in money, in contradistinction to that which is paid in kind.

naqsha juz o kul.
Details and particulars, small and great.

A report drawn up by the native collector or surveyor, furnishing details of cultivation, the condition of the cultivators, the quality of the lands, the mode of management, etc., so as to form a guide to the assessment. [ance.

naqsha-i-hāzrī o gair-hāzrī, A register of attend-
naqsha hadd o bast, A boundary map.
naqsha-i-huqūq va zimmedārī,
A statement of rights and liabilities.
naqsha-khām, n. m. A rough plan. [return.
naqsha-i-sālānā, n. m. An annual statement or
naqsha-i-shash-māhī ; H. *naqshā adhsālā,* n. m.
A half-yearly statement or return.
naqshe kā namūnā, An exemplar of a form.
naqsha-i-kishtvār. Field map ; a plan of fields according as they are assessed.
naqsha kampās, n. m. A survey map. [ment.
naqsha kamī-beshī, n. m. A comparative state-
naqsha khevat, n. m. The draft or transcript of the village register. [turn.
naqsha-i-mardum-shumārī, n. m. Census ; re-
naqsha mauzavār, n. m. A village statement.
naqsha miādī, A. Periodical return. [man.
naqsha-navīs. 1. A statistical writer. 2. A drafts-
naqshejāt gang barāmad vā gang shikastā.
Returns on fluvial action.
naqshejāt-i-miyādī. G. G. Periodical returns.

A نقص *nuqs,* n. m. 1. Defect. 2. Decrease ; diminution. 3. Infirmity (in a title).
nuqs taădud-i-dāva, Defect of misjoinder.
nuqs-i-jismānī, G. G.
Corporal or bodily defect; infirmity.
nuqs-i-khidmat, Breach of duty.
nuqs-i-azīm, n. m. A material defect. [mind.
nuqs-i-aql, Uusound mind ; unsoundness of
nuqs-i-faislah, Defect of judgment.
nuqs-i-qāte, n. m. A vital defect.
nuqs-i-qānūnī, n. m. A legal defect.
nuqs kamī-i-qīmat, n. m. Error of defective valuation. [tion of suit.
nuqs māliyat-i-muqaddamah. Error of valua-
nuqs-i-mujrimānā. G. G. Criminal breach.
nuqs-i-muāhada. A breach of contract.
nuqs nikālnā, v. a. To pick out faults. [(6, 7).

نقصان *nuqsān';* Sant. *lokasmān,* n. m. See توٹا
1. Harm ; damage ; injury ; detriment.
2. Loss ; waste. 3. Defect. [uṭhānā, 2.).
nuqsān uṭhānā, n. m. To suffer a loss (*ṭoṭā*
nuqsān bil-qasd. Voluntary waste or damage.
nuqsān-i-badanī yā mālī, G. G. Harm to person or property. [uṭhānā, 2).
nuqsān bharnā, v. n. To bear a loss (*ṭoṭā*
nuqsān pahuṅchānā, v. a.
To cause loss, injury, or damage.
nuqsān pahunchāne kī nīyat se. G. G. With intent to injure. [formity.
nuqsan-i-jismani-i-khilqī. G. G. Offensive de-
nuqsān-i-khās, n. m. Special damages. [or injury.
nuqsān-i-zātī, yā khās, n. m. Personal violence
nuqsān rasānī, Committing or doing a mischief.
nuqsān-i-ām, G. G. A common injury.
nuqsān-i-fāhish. A heavy loss.

Gross inadequacy of price of an article sold which, according to some lawyers, if effected by an agent, annuls the sale.

nuqsān-i-qānūnī, A legal injury.
nuqsān k., v. a. 1. To do harm to ; affect injuriously. 2. To destroy ; ruin.
nuqsān gavārā k., v. n. To abide loss.
nuqsān mutaălliq-i-jism yā māl. G. G.
Harm to person or property.
nuqsān gavārā karnā paṛā. Made to abide loss.

A نقل *naql, naqal,* n. f. 1. Change of place, removal. 2. Transfer, alienation (of property).
3. A copy ; transcript.
naql-ul-māl-bilā javāz. G. G. Smuggling.
naql-ul-naql. G. G. Copy of a copy.
naql ba jinsihī, naql mutābiq-i-asl. G. G.
An exact counterpart of the original ; a true copy.
naql paṭṭa yā paṭṭajāt. A record or register of leases or revenue engagements.

An account kept by the village accountant, giving, under the name of each cultivator, an abstract of his tenure, shewing the extent of his farm and amount of revenue, and the name, measurement, assessment, and revenue of each field. [tation.

naql khilāf, G. G. 1. A false copy. 2. A misquo-
naql k., v. a. 1. To make a copy. 2. To represent ; personate ; act. 3. To relate ; narrate. [copy.
naql musaddaq, An attested or authenticated
naql-navīs, n. m. A copyist.
naql-navīsī, n. f. Copying ; section-writing.
naql h., v. n. To be copied from.
نقلي *naql'ī,* adj. 1. Fabricated ; counterfeit ; false. 2. Traditional ; handed down.

H نکا नक्का *nak'kā, nakkī* ; Mār. *nāko,* n. m.
1. One *kaurī,* q. v. 2. The ace.
nakkā-dūā, nakkā-mūṭh, n. m. Gambling (*juā*).
nakkī par lagānā yā rakhnā, v. a.
To stake ; hazard.

A نکاح *nikāh',* n. m. Matrimony ; marriage ; nuptials ; a legal marriage.
nikāh-i-bevagān. G. G. Widow marriage.
nikāh-parhāī, Marriage fees.
nikāh paṛhānā, v. a. To tie the nuptial knot.
nikāh paṛhā jānā, v. n. To be married.
nikāh-i-sānī, n. m. A second marriage.
nikāh k., yā nikāh meṅ lānā, v. n.
To wed ; take in marriage.
nikāh-mutā. A marriage for a limited time in consideration of a present.
nikāh-i-muvaqqat. A temporary marriage.

The offspring of such marriages are legitimate.

nikāh-nāmā, A marriage contract.

nikāh'ī, nikāhtā, adj. Married (woman).
arkān-i-nikāh, The essentials of a marriage, viz. the proposal and consent.
sharāyat-i-nikāh, The conditions of marriage, viz. discretion, puberty, and freedom of the contracting parties.

H نکاس निकास *nikās'*, n. m. S. निष्कास See اصل 1—5, and ابتدا 1. Spring. 2. Extraction. 3. Issue; discharge; outgoing; outlet; vent. 4. (*nikāsī*) Net produce; income; outturn. 5. Sale; export. 6. (*nikāsī*) Transit duties. 7. Settlement of accounts. 8. The outer boundary of land attached to a town.
nikās-patr, yā tahsīl, n. m. A statement of adjusted accounts, or of the gross produce of an estate receivable from the cultivator.
nikāsī pakkī, nikāsī pukhtah, n. f. Net receipts, proceeds, or rents.
nikāsī hāl. n. f. Existing assets.
nikāsī khālis, Net assets.
nikāsī khām. Gross revenue of an estate or a village receivable from the cultivators by the *zamīndār*, according to the accounts of the *paṭvārī* or *gumāshta*.
nikāsī sālānā, Annual assets.
nikāsī kī chiṭṭhī, n. f. Certificate of clearance; a passport; permit.
نکال رکھنا *nikāl rakhnā*, v. n. To lay or put by.
nikāl lānā, v. a. To bring away; abduct.
nikāl lenā, yā le jānā, 1. To steal; make away with. 2. To abduct; run away with.
muṅh se nikālnā, v. n. To bring out (words); to speak.

H نکانا निकाना *nikā'nā*; Sant. *heṛet*, v.a. 1. To weed (*nalānā*). 2. To pick with the nails.
نکائي निकाई *nikā'ī*, n. f. Weeding, and its cost (*nalāī*).

P نگران *nigrān'*, part. act. Looking; watchful.
nigrān-i-hāl rahnā, nigrānī k. v. n. To look after; to be watchful.
nigrān'ī, n. f. Supervision; superintendence.

H نگڑ निगड़ *nig'aṛ*; Bhoj. *goṛ-kaṛī*; Tir. *paī-kār*, n. m. S. निगड 1. Fetters; an iron chain for the feet (esp. of an elephant). 2. The stocks.

H نلانا नलाना *nalā'nā, narā'nā*, v.a. To weed.

H نل پٹي *nal-paṭṭī*, n. f. A tax for keeping aqueducts in repair.

P نمايش *numā'yash*, n. f. See *dikhāvaṭ*.
numāyash jabr mujrimāna, G. G. A show of criminal force.

H نمٹے निमटे *nimṭ'e*, n. m. (*Brokers*) Eight annas (*ṭālī*).
نمک محال *namak-mahāl*, n.m. The salt revenue.
namak nā-jāyaz. G. G. Contraband salt. [ظاہر].

P نمودار *namūdār'*, adj. Visible; conspicuous
namūdār beshī. Increase of the rate entered on the vouchers exhibited.
namūdār-kamī. Defficiency or diminution of the exhibit rate.
namūdār'ī, n. f. Display; show.
Payment made by a cultivator on his field being exempted from actual measurement, settling his assessment by samples of the crop.

P نمونه *namūn'ah*, n. m. Pl. *namūnajāt*.
1. A pattern (*bāngī*).
2. A model (*naqsha*, 1, 2, 3).
namūnajāt band qarār dād-i-jurm. G. G. Forms of charge.

H نندا निन्दा *nind'ā*; W. Illit. *nindrā*; Mār. *nindiyā*, n. f. S. निंद Evil-speaking (*bad-goī*).
nindā-patr, nindā-lekh, n. m. A libel.
nindā k., nindnā, nindrā k., v. n. To speak ill of; backbite.
nind'at, adj. Slandered; calumniated.
nind'ak, n. m. A slanderer; calumniator.
نند کا بھائي *nand kā bhāī yā bīr*, n. m. (Hin. Wom.) *lit.* Sister-in-law's brother; husband.

H نندن नन्दन *nand'an*, n. m. A son.

H ننگا नङ्गा *nan'gā, nangī*, Bhoj. *langā*, Naked; bare.
nangā k., v. a. 1. To strip; take off one's clothing. 2. To bare; uncover.
nangā mādar-zād, nangā dhuṛangā, chum-nangā, adj. Naked as a newborn child; stark naked.
nangā h., v. n. To be naked.

P نو *nau*, adj. S. नव New.
nau-ābād, adj. Newly-settled, peopled, or colonized.
nau-ābād, n. Unsettled lands; clearing waste and forming a *maurūsī* right in the land reclaimed. A new tenant who settles in a village on the best terms he can make.
nau-barār, n. f. Land recently made subject to assessment.
nau-toṛ, P. H. adj. Newly broken (land).
nau-roz, n. m. 1. New year's day according to the Persian calendar, being that on which the sun enters *Aries*.
nau-shikast. Waste alluvial land newly cultivated.

H نو नौ *nau*; Sant. *āre*, adj.S. नव P. *noh*. Nine.
nau sāt, lit. nine and seven.
A division of the crop, in some parts of Bengal, between the *zamīndār* and the cultivator, the farmer taking nine-sixteenths and leaving seven-sixteenths to the latter.

A نواب *navvāb', navāb*; Illit. *nabāb*, n. m. نايب
1. A governor. 2. A lord.

نوابي *navvāb'ī*, n. f. 1. The office of a *navvāb*; viceroyalty. 2. Anarchy; misrule. [suburbs.

A نواح *navāh'*, *navāhī*, *gird navāh*, n.f. Environs;

H نواسہ नवासा *navās'ā*, *nanvāsā*; Sant. *ka-ṟartet*, n. m. *navāsī*, n. f.
A daughter's son (E. *nātī*).

E نوٹ *noṭ*, *loṭ*, n. m. Cor. of note.
1. Currency note. [sory note.
2. (*parmesarī noṭ*) Government promis-
noṭ sarkār-i-Inglistān. Exchequer bills. [ment.

P نوشت *navisht'*, *navishtah*, n.f. A writing; docu-

A نوع *nau'*, n. m. Manner.

nau-i-haqīyat. Tenure; manner of holding.
nauyat qabza yā haqīyat.
Nature of a tenure or interest.
nauīyat qabza yā haqīyat kī tasrīh k., v. a.
To specify or make a specification of the nature of a tenure or interest.

P نوکر *nauk'ar*, *naukar chākar*; Sant. *guti*, n.m.
1. A servant 2. A domestic; retainer; an attendant. [situation.

نوکري *naukr'ī*, n. f. Employment; a post;
naukrī-peshā, n. m. A public or private servant. [service.
naukrī se bhāgnā, *yā bhāg jānā*. Desertion from
naukrī k., v. a. To serve.
yāft kī naukrī, A lucrative office.

H نوليوا नौलेवा *naulev'ā*, n. m.
A deposit of mud after floods. *Carnegy.*

نونچہ *noncha'ě*, n. m. A factitious salt made of the ashes of burnt straw previously steeped in brine, and used to adulterate culinary salt.

H نونيا नोनिया *non'iyā*, *nonihār*, n. m.
1. One who makes or deals in salt.
2. A saltpetre manufacturer.

P نويسندہ *navīsin'dah*, n. m. 1. A writer; clerk; an accountant. 2. A correspondent.

P نہاں *nihāṅ'*, adj.
Concealed; private; clandestine.
andām-i-nihānī, The privities, esp. the *vulva*.

A نہايت *nihā'yat*, *nihāyat kā darjah*, n. f.
Excess (انتہا 1).
nihāyat, adj. and adv. See بہت adv. and adj.
nihāyat tang k., v. n. To press one very hard.
nihāyat ke darjah, adv. At least; at most.
be-nihāyat, adj. Boundless; unlimited.
nahr kā mahkmah, v. n. The canal department.
nahr kī āb-pāshī, *nahr-paṭāī*, n. f.
Canal irrigation.

nahr'ī, *nahrī zamīn*, n. f. Land irrigated from a canal. [from water courses.

H نہل *nih'al*, n. f. Alluvial land recovered

A نيابت *niyāb'at*, n. f. Deputyship; vicegerency; lieutenancy.

P نياز درگاہ *niyāz dargāh*, n. f. A grant of money or land to a Mah. shrine or mosque.

H نيام پتر नियामपत्र *niyām patr*, n. m.
1. A deed or contract.
2. A declaratory deed by a Hindū widow that she had adopted a son. *Carnegy.*

H نياو नियाऊ *niyā'ū*, Rus. adj. Bad; inferior.
niyāū rāj, Maladministration; bad government.

H نياو नियाव *niyā'o*; Tir. *niyāě*, n. m. S. न्याय
Justice (انصاف).
niyāo chukānā, v. a. 1. To administer justice.
2. To hear complaints.
3. To settle a dispute. [tice; bench.
niyāě sabhā, *yā kachahrī*, n. f. A court of jus-
niyāo ke het. For the purpose of justice.

A نيت *nī'yat*; Tir. *net*, n. f. Intent.
nīyat-i-mujrimānā, n. f. A criminal intent.
is nīyat se ki sarqa sugra hove. G. G. Intending to cause a theft to be committed.
burī nīyat se, *ba nīyat-i-fāsid*, adv. Maliciously; fraudulently; with a sinister object. [riot.
balvā karne kī nīyat. G. G. Intent to cause
dehish ba nīyat-i-bad. G. G. Corrupt payment.

P نيست *nest*, adj. S. नास्ति non-existence. *lit. non est.* Null; void. [*būd*).
nest yā nest o nābūd k. v. a. 1. To nullify (*nā-*
2. To abolish; annihilate; put an end to; to demolish.
nest o nabūd h., v. n. To perish; to be annihilated, ruined, destroyed; cease to be.

P نيکداري *nek-dārī*, n. f. Perquisites or fees received or collected from the *raiyats*, being shares of the produce of their lands appropriated to particular public officers or other persons in the village. *Carnegy.*

H نيگ नेग *neg*; Sant. *leg*, n. m. 1. Custom; usage; rule. 2. A privilege; exclusive right.

P & H نيل नील *nīl*; W. Illit. and Tir. *līl*, n. m. S. नील Pālī, *nīlo*. [marks or wales.
1. Indigo. 2. The indigo plant. 3. Blue
nīl-baṟī, n. f. An inferior kind of indigo.
nīl kī koṭhī, *nīl kā kār-khānā*, n. m.
An indigo factory. [vat.
nīl kī ghuṭāī, *yā mahāī*, Beating indigo in the
nīl-vālā; Tir. *līlhā*, n.m. An indigo-planter.

nīl'ā, n. m. The sediment or dried juice of the indigo plant.

Port. نیلام *nīlām'*; Illit. *īlām, lilām, lillām,* n. m. An auction; a public sale.
nīlām ba illat ijrāē ḍigrī. A sale in execution of a decree; an execution sale.
nīlām ba illat bāqī māl-guzārī. A sale for arrears of revenue.
nīlām ba illat-i-ḍigrī. An auction sale in execution of a decree.
nīlām khuāstah. 1. Balance of revenue short, realized by the public sale of lands. 2. A deficit on the sale.
nīlām-dār, n. m. An auction purchaser.
nīlām qataī, n. f. A peremptory auction sale.
nīlām kā tarīq. Sale process.
nīlām k., yā karānā, v. a. To sell by auction.
nīlām-ghar, n. m. An auction-room.
nīlām meṅ rakhnā, v. n. To send to an auction.
nīlām h., v. n. To be sold by public auction.
nīlām'ī, adj. For auction sale; auctionable.

P نیم *nīm*, adj. 1. Half.
nim-āne paṭvārī, n. m. Half an *ānā* on the Rupee given as a fee to the village accountant at the settlement of the assessment.
nem bāṅdhnā, k., yā lenā, v. n. 1. To bind oneself to; to vow. 2. To observe; practice.
nem-patr, n. m. A written agreement (اقرارنامه).

H نیو नेव *nev, neo*; Rus. *nīm*; Mār. *nīṅv*, n.f. See بنیاد (1). A foundation; basis.
neo dharnā, ḍālnā, yā jamānā, v. a. To found; lay the foundation of.

و

H وا वा *vā, athvā*; P. *yā*. Or. [again.

P واپس *vāp'us*; Pop. *vāpis*, adv. Back;
vāpis ānā, v. n. To come back; to return.
vāpis k. yā denā, v. a. 1. To refund; reimburse (*pherna*, 2). 2. To send back; remand.
vāpis lenā, v. n. To claim back (*pher lenā*).
vāpis milnā, v. a. To get back; to be restored.
واپسی *vāp'isī*, n. f. 1 Return; reversion. 2. Refund. 3. Remand. 4. A return ticket by ferry or dak.
vāpisī hukm-nāmah. Return (of a writ).
vāpisī zar fāzil. Refund of excess collections.
vāpisī muqad lamah. The remand of a case.

A واجب *vāj'ib*; *vājibī*, adj. وجب was right- 1. See جایز 2. Due; binding; obligatory; necessary.
vājib thā arz kīyā, I have set down what was right and proper. (Written at the end of a petition).
vājib jānnā, v. n. To deem right or incumbent.
vājib-ul-ittibā. Binding (upon one).
vājib-ul-adā, ya dain, adj. Due; payable.
vājib-ul-izhār, Fit to be represented. [*ne-jog*).
vājib-ul-taslīm, Acceptable; receivable (H. *mān-*
vājib-ul-tāzīr; H. *shāshan-jog*, adj. Punishable.
vājib-ul-tāmīl. What may be enforced or carried into execution.
vājib-ul-rahm, Deserving commiseration.
vājib-ul-riāyat, adj. 1. Worthy of attention. 2. Excusable.
vājib-ul-talab, adj. Claimable; receivable.
vājib-ul-arz, lit. fit to be represented. 1. A written representation or petition. 2. A settlement; agreement; administration paper.
vājib-ul-arz. This is also called an *iqrārnāmah* and is an engagement entered into by the *māl-guzārs* and coparceners. In coparcenary mahals this is the most important of all the papers, for it is intended to show the whole constitution of the village.
vājib-ul-arz-khās. A special village administration paper. [paper.
vājib-ul-arz ām. A general administration
vajib-ul-arz khevaṭ. A village administration paper; revenue engagement.
vājib-ul-qatl. Liable to capital punishment.
vājib-ul-qatl ṭhairānā. To sentence or condemn to death.
vājib-ul-qatl h. To be condemned to death.
vājib-ul-vusūl, adj. Capable of being realized; recoverable.
vājib samjho! Fail not!
vājib o lāzim. Right and proper.
vājib o lāzim ṭhairānā. To justify; vindicate.
vājib h., v. n. 1. To be necessary, expedient, proper; to become a duty. 2. To fall due.
karnā qānūnan vājib hai. G. G. Is bound by law to do.
واجبی *vāj'ibī*, n. f. pl. *vājibāt.* 1. Expediency; incumbency. 2. Wages; stipend (*tankhuāh*).
vājibī, vājbī, adj. Just; reasonable; moderate.
vājibī dāvā. A just claim.
vājibī-sā, adj. A little (*thoṛā-sā*).
vājibī se, adv. 1. Fitly; by fair means; equitably (*ṭhīk*, 2). 2. Deservedly.

A واحد *vāh'id*, adj. One.
jamāat-i-vāhid pulis. G. G. One police force.

A وارث *vār'is*, n. m. ورث inherited. 1. Heir; legatee. 2. Master; owner. 3. A husband.
vāris-i-āyiṅdah. A reversioner.
vāris baid. A remote heir.
vāris shartī. n. Presumptive heir. [direct heir.
vāris sulbī. An heir of one's own body; a
vāris mutlavvassit. An intermediate heir.

vāris h. To inherit; obtain as an inheritance.
be-vāris, be-vārisā, be-vārsī, adj. See *lā-vāris.*
lā-vāris k. To disinherit.

A واردات *vārdāt',* n. f. pl. of وارد. 1. Occurrences; events; incidents; accidents.
2. Affrays; crimes.
vārdāt-i-khafīf. A petty affray. [bloodshed.
vārdāt-i-sangīn. A serious affray; a riot with
jāë vārdāt, mauqa-i-vārdāt. The place where the affray occurred.
mauqa-i-vārdāt pe tahqīqāt k. v. a.
To make enquiry on the spot where the crime was committed.

A وارد صادر *vārid-sādir,* n. m. A traveller.
vārid h. 1. To descend; alight on.
2. To arrive. 3. To befal.
nau-vārid, n. m. A new-comer.

E وارنٹ *vār'ant;* Sant. *āront,* n. m. Cor. of Eng. warrant; a writ.
vārant-talāshī. A search-warrant.
vārant jārī k., v. a. To issue a warrant.
varant rihāī. A warrant of acquittal.
vārant supurdagī. A warrant of commitment.
vārant giriftārī. A warrant of arrest.

A واسطہ *vāst'a,* n. m. وسط intermediate.
1. A medium; an instrument. 2. Relationship (*taalluq,* 1). 3. Account; sake.
4. Business; concern. 5. A cause (باعث 1).
6. An agent; a broker; middleman.
vāstah taālluq. A dependent *taālluq,* one subordinate, not to a *zamīndār,* but to a superior *taālluqdār.*
vāstah-dār. 1. A relation by blood or marriage.
2. An interested party. [*rakhnā*).
vāsta rakhnā. To bear upon; concern (*taālluq*
vāsta-i-nāqisa. The missing link.
ba-vāstah, adv. 1. By means of; through (*ba-sabab*); in virtue of.
2. Intermediately; indirectly.

A واصل *vāsil,* n. m. Money paid; realisation of revenues, rents, etc.
vāsil-bāqī. 1. Receipts and balances.
2. An account of payments.
vāsil-bāqī k., v. a. To balance an account.
vāsil-bāqī kharch. An account formerly kept shewing the amount of revenue assessed, the portion realized, the balance outstanding, with the deductions for charges of collection drawn up at the close of the year at the settlement of the revenue accounts. [balances.
vāsil-bāqī navīs. A writer of receipts and
واصلات *vāsilāt',* pl. of واصل The proceeds of an estate; usufruct; mesne profits.
vāsilāt bajāë sūd. Usufruct in lieu of interest.
vāsilāt āyandah. Future mesne profits.

A واضح *vāz'eh,* adj. Manifest; clear; obvious.
vāzeh k. To make clear; explain.
vāzeh ho ki, vāze rāë sharīf ho,
Be it known that; seeing that; whereas
vāzeh hai. It is evident.

A واضع *vāz'e,* n. m. An inventor; a founder.
vāzeān-i-qānūn, G. G. Legislators.

A واقع *vāq'ā, vāqeā,* n. m. pl. واقعات (*waqū*).
An occurrence; event. [of fact.
amr-i-vāqah kī mugālta-khurī. G. G. A mistake
bināë dāvā vāqā huā. Cause of action accrued.
akhrājāt vāqaī. G. G. Actual expenses.
jang-i-vāqaī. G. G. Actual warfare.
واقعي *vaq'āī,* adj. Real, actual (حقيقي 1).
vāqe men, vāqaī, adv. In fact; really; *de facto.*
vāqa-navīs, n. m.
An intelligencer; a newswriter.

A واقف *vāq'if,* adj. وقف standing, stopping.
Aware of; acquainted with; privy to (آگاه).
vāqif-kār, vāqif-hāl, n. m. 1. An experienced person. 2. A connoisseur.
nā-vāqif, adj. 1. Unacquainted; unaware.
2. Ignorant; inexperienced.
واقفيت *vāqfī'yat, vāqif-kārī,* n. f. Knowledge; privity (آگاہی). [acquaintance with.
vāqfīyat paidā k. To acquire a knowledge of, or
vāqfīyat jismānī. Carnal knowledge.
vāqfīyat zātī. Personal knowledge.

P واگزاشت *vāguzāsht',* n. f. 1. (*vāguzāsht-i-qurqī*) Withdrawal or removal of attachment. 2. A grant. [land.
vāguzāsht-i-chand-rozah. A temporary grant of
vāguzāsht dāyamī. A perpetual grant of land.
vāguzāsht qurqī kī nālish. Action of replevin.
vāguzāsht karnā qurqī kā.
To withdraw an attachment.

A والا *va-illā,* adv. And if not (H. *nahīn to*).

A والد *vāl'id,* n. m. ولد offspring. Father.
والده *vāl'idah,* n. f. Mother; respected mother.
والدين *vālidain',* n. m. Parents.

A والي *vāl'ī,* n. m. ولي being near.
1. A guardian. 2. Owner; proprietor.
3. A ruler; chief; governor.
vālī varis. 1. Guardians. 2. Parents; patrons.
be-vālī-vāris, adj. Without a guardian or protector; unprotected; unclaimed.

H واندي वांदी *vān'dī.* A tenant-at-will living in another village. [legator.

A واہب *vāh'ib,* n. m. وہب A donor; grantor;

A وثيقه *vasīq'ah*, n. f. وثق made sure.

1. A document; deed (*dastāvez*).
2. Stock; Government Pro. note.

vasīqah intiqāl. A deed of transfer.
vasīqah jān-bīmā. A life assurance policy.
vasīqah hissah-dārī. Scrip.
vasīqe-dār, n. m. A holder of a Govt. Pro. note.
vasīqah sarkārī. Government paper.
vasīqah zamānat. A bail bond.
vāsīqah muāvazah. A bond for which full consideration has been given.
vasīqah musaddaqah. An authenticated deed.
vasīqah-i-waqf. A deed of endowment.

A وجوب *vujūb'*, n. m. وجب was necessary.

Necessity; obligation.

tārīkh vajūb qist mālguzārī. The date on which the revenue instalment is due.
وجوبيت *vujūb'iat*, n. f. 1. Validity.
2. Right; justice.

A وجود *vujūd'*, *vajūd*, n. m. وجد being.

1. Being. 2. Existence; entity; life.
3. Substance; body; material frame.
4. (Slang) *Membrum virile*.

vujūd pānā, yā pakarnā, v. n.
1. To come into existence; come to be.
2. To be embodied, incarnated.

vujūd adam-vajūd. Existence or non-existence.
vujūd men lānā. To give being; to create. [of.
bā-vujūd, bā vajūde ki. Notwithstanding; in spite
kisī tadbīr kā vujūd. G. G. The existence of a design. [face to.

A وجوه *vujū'h*, pl. of *vajah*, وجه turning the

Personal respectability; position; credit.

وجوهات *vujūhāt'*, n. f. pl. of وجه q. v.
vujūhāt-i- subūt. Proofs; evidence.
vujūhat-i-khafīf, vajūhāt khārjī. Secondary reasons. [case.
vujūhāt qavī pesh k. To make out a strong

A وجه *vaj'ah*, n. f. Court *amlah*, pl. *vajūhāt*.

1. A cause; reason; ground. 2. Means (ذريعه 1). 3. Way; manner (*dhang*, 1). 4. (*vajah subūt*) Plea (*dalīl*). 5. Wages; salary.

vajah-i-apīl. The grounds of an appeal.
vajah bayān, yā pesh k. To set forth reasons; state the grounds.
vajah tahrīk. G. G. A motive.
vajah tahrīk yā haq-ul-saī. A motive or reward.
vajah tar-dīd, Rebutter; counterproofs; evidence for the defence.
vajah tamhīdī. Preliminary grounds.
vajah subūt, Proof; evidence.
vajah subūt pesh-kardah, guzrānīdah, yā mudākhalah. Proofs adduced. [dence.
vajah subūt pesh k. To adduce proof or evi-
vajah subūt-tahrīrī. Documentary evidence,
vajah sūbūt taqrīrī. Oral evidence.
vajah subūt kāmil, Conclusive proof.
vajah subūt vāqeāt. Circumstantial evidence.
vajah se. By reason of; in consequence of.
vajah qavī. 1. An efficient cause.
2. A strong reason.
vajah kāfī. Sufficient cause, excuse, or ground.
vajah maāsh, qūt, yā guzrān.
1. A means of livelihood.
2. Subsistence money or allowance. [plea.
vajah māqūl, yā muvajjah. A good reason or
vajah muqarrirī. A fixed allowance.
vajah movajjah, A strong proof or reason.
vajah nālish, yā mukhāsmat.
Ground of complaint; cause of action.
is vajah se. G. G. By reason of.
ba-vajah, adv. 1. In a way; in such a way that. 2. By means of; on account of.
be-vajah, adv. Without reason (*be-sabab*).
kaī vajeh se. In many respects. [sit.

A وديعت *vadī'āt* n. f. ودع entrusted. A depo-

A وراثت *virās'at*, n. f. *virsah*, n. m. ورث inherited. 1. Inheritance; patrimony.
2. Hereditary right.

virāsat se, By inheritance or descent.
virāsat kī sanad, A certificate of heirship.
virāsat-nāmah, n. m.
A deed of inheritance or heirship.
وراثتا *virāsatan'*, adv. By way of inheritance.
virāsatan pahunchnā. To devolve by inheritance.
virsah batnā, v. n. To be divided (an inheritance).
virsah pānā, v. n. To acquire a property by inheritance or bequest.
virsah-dār, n. A joint or co-heir. [an ancestor.
virse men ānā, v. n. To descend; proceed from
hajb o takhāruj dar virsa, n. Exclusion from and partial surrender of inheritance.

S وردهي वृद्धि *vrid'dhi*, n. f. 1. Increase, especially the increase of money; interest.
2. *Kāyik vriddhī*. Bodily interest, the advantage arising from the body of an animal pledged as security for a loan.

1. *Karm*, Interest on money paid at stated periods.
2. *Kālikā vriddhi*, Periodical, payable usually, monthly. 3. *Chakra-vriddhi*, Compound interest.
4. *Kārila vriddhi* or *Kārikā vriddhi*. Interest at a stipulated rate higher than the usual rates.
5. *Shikhā-vriddhi* Interest at an usurious rate, payable daily. 6. *Bhoglābhā* The usufruct of land, gardens, etc. as *Dharam vriddhī*; Lawful interest; *anyāyā vriddhi*, Improper or usurious interest *Nidanā vriddhi*, Moderate interest; *Parma-vriddhi*, or *para vriddhi*, Interest at the highest legal rates; *Samani-vriddhī*, Interest at a usual or moderate rate, *Vastava* or *Vāstavikā vriddhi*, Established, just, or customary interest. [entice.

P H ورغلانا *varğalān'nā*, v. a. ورغلانيدن To

A وزن *vaz'an*; Rus. *ujan*, n. m. 1. Weight (*bojh*, 1). 2. A measure of weight. 3. Weight; influence. 4. Credit; weight.

A وسط *vast*, n. m. The middle; centre.

وسطى *vas'tī, vustā*, adj. See وسط.
1. Middling; middle. 2 Average.
vastī madarsah. G. G. A middle school.
vastī mumālik. The Central Provinces.
visāt'at, n. f. Medium; means.
bilā visātat, Without intervention; directly; not mediately.

A وسعت *vus'ăt, vasat*, n.f. وسع extended. 1. Extent; space; area. 2. Latitude; amplitude.
3. Dimensions; capacity. [large.
vusat d., vasī k., v. a. To extend; stretch; en-
vusat rakhnā, v. n. To occupy; contain; fall.
vusat na rakhnā, v. n.
To be unable to contain, pay, etc.
māl-i-kasīr-ul-vusat, G. G. Goods of bulk.

A وسيع *vasī'*, adj. وسع power, ability.
Wide; spacious; extensive.
vasī mānī. G. G. A wide sense.

A وسيله *vasīl'ah*, n. m. See ذريعه 1. Means.
2. Mediation; intervention; interposition.
3. Patronage; interest.
vasīlah paidā k., v. n. To make interest.
vasīlah rakhnā, v. n. To have interest. [means.
vasīlah fāsid, yā nā-jāyaz. Corrupt or illegal
vasīle se, ba-vasīla, ba-vasātat.
By means of; through; by.
vasīlah-yāftah. Supplied with means; enabled.
be-vasīlah, be-madad, adj. Without means or resources; unprovided; without interest.

A وصل *vasl, visāl*, n. m. 1. Union
2. Carnal or sexual intercourse.

وصول *vusūl'*, n. m. وصل joined.
Realization (of revenue, etc.); recovery; collections (*āmdanī*). [or balances.
vusūl bāqī. Realization or recovery of arrears.
vusūl pānā, v. n. To realize. [revenue.
vasūl jama, yā mālguzārī. Collection of the
vuzūl qarz Recovery of a debt. [assessment.
vusūl k., v. a. To collect; realize; raise by
vusūl karne-vālā. A receiver of collections.
vusūl nīlām. Sale proceeds; monies realized by public sale or auction.
vusūl huā. Realized; accrued.
zar-i-jurmānah vasūl k. G. G. To levy a fine.

وصولي *vusūl'ī*, n. f. That may be collected or realized; dues recoverable.

A وصي *vas'ī*, n. m. Administrator; executor
to a will; one appointed by will, in contradistinction to *wālī* or a natural guardian.
kār-i-vasī. Administration; executorship.

A وصيت *vasī'yat, vasīyat zabānī*, n. f.
A nuncupative will.
vasīyat k., vasīyat meṅ denā. To bequeath; leave by will. [testament.
vasīyat-nāmah, vasīyat tahrīrī. G. G. A written
vasīyat-nāmah riyāatī. A privileged will. Act X. of 1865. [will. Act X. of 1865.
vasīyat-nāmah ġair-riyāatī. An unprivileged
istehqāq-i-tarkah bar binaē vasīyat-nāmah.
Testamentary succession.
bilā-vasīyat, adj. Intestate; without a will.
bilā-vasīyat marnā. Dying intestate.
titimma-i-vasīyat-nāmah, G. G. A codicil. [perty.
tarkah bilā-vasīyat-nāmah, G. G. Intestate pro-
tarkah-i-shakhs bilā vasīyat. G. G.
An intestate's property.
hibah-vasīyatī. G. G. A testmentary disposition.

A وضع *vaz'ă*, n. f. See *chāl*, 6, 7.
1. Nature; tenor. 2. Behaviour. [(انداز).
3. Mode; fashion; appearance. 4. Style
5. Description; character; complexion.
6. Deduction; retrenchment (*kamī*, 4, 6).
vaza badalnā v. n. 1. To change one's dress.
2. To disguise oneself.
vază hamal; H. *jannā*. Child-birth.
vaza-dār. Stylish; elegant.
vaza-dārī, n. f. Style; manner; elegance.
vază k., v. a. 1. To make; form; model.
2. To deduct; subtract; except; allow.
vazī o sharīf, Low and high; nobles and plebeians.
khilā'-i-vazah fitrī. G. G. Unnatural lust. [ter.
mushtabah-ul-vază. G. G. A suspicious charac-

A وضيعه *vazī'at, vazia*, n. f.
Under the Mah government, authorized deductions from the gross revenue on account of dismembered territory and legal allowances to the *zamīndars*.

A وطن *vat'an*, n. m. وطن abiding, dwelling.
Hereditary property; village offices which descend according to the laws of succession.
vatan jāne kī rukhsat, ghar jāne kī chhuṭṭī.
Furlough.
vatan-dār. A possessor of *vatan* property or of hereditary offices. *Carnegy.*

A وظيفه *vazīf'ah*, n. m. pl. *vazāif*.
1. Mah. daily worship (*vird*). [sion.
2. A stipulated allowance; stipend; pen-
3. A gift of land for past services.
4. A scholarship.
vazīfah-dār, vazīfah-khuār. [sioner
A stipendiary; scholarship-holder; pen-
vazīfah-i-sālānah. G. G. An annuity.

A وعدہ *vād'ah, vāda*; Illit. *vāëdā*; Rus. *avādā*, n. m. A promise; agreement (اقرارنامہ 1).
vādah ṭālnā, v. n.
To evade a promise or agreement.
vādah-khilāf, vādah-shikan, n. m. A promise-breaker. [ment; default.
vādah-khilāfī. Breach of promise or engage-
vālah k., v. a. To promise; engage. [word.
vādah-vafā, vāde kā sachchā, adj. True to one's
vādah vafā k., v. a. To keep faith.
vādah vaīd. Evading a promise. [parole.
zabānī vādah, G. G. A verbal promise; a

A وقايع *vaqā'yā*, n. m. Events; occurrences.
vaqāyā-nigār yā navīs, n. m.
A newswriter; a correspondent. [ent.
vaqāyā-navīsī, n. f. The office of a correspond-

A وقت *vaqt*; Illit. *vakhat, bakhat*; Sant. *okte*, n. m. pl. *auqāt*. 1. Time; term.
vaqt dāyar hone muqaddamah, vaqt darpeshī muqaddamah. Pendente lite.
vaqt-i-muāmlah. At the time of the transaction.
ba vaqt adālat. Judicially; while the court was sitting; during the hearing.
khās vaqt meṅ, At the proper time. [office hours.
gair-vaqt meṅ, During leisure hours; after
muqarrarī vaqt. Fixed time. [time.
وقتا فوقتا *vaqtan fa-vaqtan*, adv. From time to

A وقف *vaqf*, n. m. 1. A religious or charitable endowment; a legacy for pious uses.
vaqf k., v. a. To make a grant for charitable or religious purposes. [endowment.
vaqf-kunindah. A person making a charitable
vaqf-nāmah, n. m. A deed of endowment.
وقفہ *vaqf'ah*, n. m. 1. Delay; pause. [ment.
2. An interval; interlude. 3. An adjourn-
4. A reprieve. [adjournment.
vaqfah denā, v. a. To grant an extension or

A وقوع *vuq'ū', vaqū*, n. m.
1. An occurrence; event.
2. An incident; a contingency. [red-handed.
vuqū-i-jurm, vaqū jurm ke vaqt. Flagrante delicto;
vuqū meṅ ānā, v. n. To commence; begin to be; ensue. [perpetrated.
vuqū meṅ āyā. 1. Happened. 2. Committed;
vuqū meṅ lānā, v. a. To cause; commit. [ed.
vuqū h., v. n. 1. To happen. 2. To be perpetrat-
jurm vaqū meṅ āyā. G. G.
The offence was committed.
koī amal vaqū meṅ lānā. G. G. To do anything.

A وكالت *vakāl'at*; Illit. *vikālat*; Rus. *vakīlāt, ukīlāt, ukālat*, n. f. وكل entrusted (an affair). The function of an advocate; practice at the bar. [advocate.
vakālat k., v. n. To practise as a pleader or
vakālat mufridāt. Special agency limited to a particular transaction.
vakālat-nāmah, n. m. A power of attorney.
kisī kī taraf se vakālat k., v. a. To advocate one's cause. [vocate.
وكالتا *vakālatan'*, adv. Through a *vakīl* or ad-
وكيل *vakīl'*; Rus. *ukīl*, n. m. [court of law.
1. An agent; an authorized pleader in a
2. An agent who represents an estate at the head quarters of another.
vakīl sarkārī, n. m. A Government pleader.
vakīl k., v. a. To appoint a *vakīl*.
vakīl mutlaq yā ām. 1. A plenipotentiary; a representative with absolute powers.
2. A permanently appointed pleader; a standing counsel.

A ولادت *valād'at*, n. f. ولد born. Birth.

A ولايت *valā'yat, vilāyat*, n.f. Guardianship.
valāyat kā istehqāq. Right of guardianship.
ولايتا *valā'yatan*, adv. In behalf of.

A ولد *val'ad, vald*, n. m. Son; offspring.
valad-ul-zinā, valad-ul-haiz, valad-ul-harām.
A bastard; whoreson.
valad-ul-halāl. Legitimate.
valad magrūr, n. The son of a person who has mistaken the condition of the mother, as begotten on a female within the prohibited degrees of relationship without his being aware of it, or on a female slave supposing her to be a free woman. In the latter case the child is the property of the master of the slave, but the father may redeem it.
lā-valad; H. *nāṭhā*, adj.
Having no children; heirless.
lā-valad marnā, v. n. To die without issue.
ولديت *valdī'yat*, n. f. Parentage; descent.

A ولي *val'ī*, n. m. *valīak*, n. f. 1. Lord; prince.
2. A guardian (of a ward).
valī aslī, n. A natural guardian.
valī-ud-dam. One entitled to exact retaliation, or the price of blood.
vālī baīd, (Mah. Law) A remote guardian.
Guardians of this description are the most distant paternal kindred, whose guardianship extends only to matters connected with education and marriage of their wards.
valī jabīr yā majbīr. An authoritative guardian recognised by the law.
valī jināyat. The next of kin, or other person entitled to exact retaliation for offences against the person of a relative, or of one under his charge.
valī qānūnī, n. m. A legal guardian.
ولي عہد *valī-ahd*, n. m. An heir apparent.
valī-ahd farzī, n. The heir presumptive.
valī-ahdī, n, f. The status of an heir-apparent.

valī qarīb. A near guardian.
In Mah. Law, fathers and paternal grandfathers and their executors and the executors of such executors. [guardian.
valī muqarrarī (*Mah. Law.*) A testamentary
valī va sar-parast-i-nā bāligān. Court of Wards.

A وهابي *vahāb'ī,* n. m. 1. A follower of the doctrines of an Arabian reformer of Mahomedanism, *Shaikh Abd-ul-vahāb.*

P ويران *vīrān';* Illit. and Wom. *vairān,* adj.
1. Waste; desolate. 2. Dreary; dismal.
vīrān jagah. A desert place.
vīrān k., v. a. To destroy; lay waste; depopulate. [village.
vīrān kheṛā, n. m. The deserted site of a
ويرانه *vīrān'ah,* n. m. 1. Waste; forest-land.
2. A solitude.
ويراني *vīrān'ī,* n. f. Depopulation.

H ويرنا वैरना *vair'nā,* n. m. A drill.
vairnā; Furrukh. *vīrnā,* v. a.
1. To sow by drill. 2. To grind.

ه

H هابوڑا हाबूड़ा *hābūṛ'ā,* Brij.
A freebooter; highwayman. [sugarcane.

H هاپر हापर *hāp'ar,* n. f. A nursery for

H هاتھ हाथ *hāth;* Sant. *tī,* n. m. S. हस्त Pr. *hattho;* A. *yad.* 1. The hand; arm.
2. A cubit measure; half a yard.
3. A hand (in an Office, etc.).
4. Reach. 5. Possession; clutches.
6. Protection; patronage. 7. Power.
hāth uṭhānā, v. n. 1. To raise or lift up one's hands; to salute. 2. To lift up the hands in prayer; to pray for one.
3. To lift one's hands against one.
hāth par Qurān, yā Gaṅgā jalī rakhnā, v. a. To make one swear by the Quran or on Ganges' water; administer an oath.
hāth pīle k., Hin. v. *n. lit.* to stain the hands with turmeric. To get one married; have a quiet or inexpensive wedding.
هاتھا پائي हाथा पाई *hāthā-pāī;* E. *hāthā-bāṅhī,* n. f. Pulling and hauling; fisticuffs; fighting.

H هاٹ हाट *hāṭ;* Panj. *haṭṭī;* Sant. *hāṭia,* n. f. S. हट्ट 1. A shop.
2. A mart. 3. A market day.
hāṭ k., v. n. 1. To open a shop. 2. To market.
hāṭ kholnā, To open a shop.

A هادي *hād'ī,* n. m. هدي directing.
1. A guide; director; leader. 2. A spiritual guide; a head of a religious order.

H هار हार *hār,* n. f. 1. Fatigue; weariness. 2. Defeat; discomfiture. 3. Forfeiture; loss.
4. Pasturage.
هارجيت हारजीत *hār-jīt,* n. f. 1. Loss and gain.
2. Gambling; hazard.
hār jīt k. To bet; gamble. [disturber

A هارج *hār'ij,* n. m. An intermeddler; a
hārij h., v. n. See *māne h.*

H هارنا हारना *hār'nā;* Tir. *hārab,* v. n. S. हारण To fail; lose.
hār-ke, hār jhak mār-ke, hār-ke, jhak mār-ke. When all's done; at last.
hār'ū; Brij. *hārūn,* n. m.
An unlucky gamester; a great loser.

H هار هاري हारहारी *hār-hārī,* n. f.
The division of a bankrupt's effects.

H هاڑنا हाड़ना *hāṛ'nā, hāṛ lenā;* Tir. *bhaṛārab,* v. a. To test the accuracy of weights and measures. [dealers) Two.

H هاز اسپينا हाज़ अ़सपीना *hāz aspīnā,* (Horse

H هالا हाला *hāl'ā,* n. m. H. *hal* a plough.
1. A tax on ploughs.
2. An instalment of revenue.

H هالي हाली *hāl'ī;* Tir. *harvāh,* n. m.
A ploughman. [نقصان

H هان हान *hān;* Tir. *hāni,* n. f. S. हानि See
1. Loss. 2. Injury; mischief. 3. Deficiency; blank. 4. Slaughter; murder.
hān-pūran. An indemnity.
hān pūran k., v. a. To indemnify; reimburse.
hān yā ṭoṭā uṭhānā, v.n. To suffer loss. [peding.

A هايل *hā'yal,* p. adj. Lying in the way; im-

A هبه *hib'a,* n. m. وهب giving; bestowing.
A gift; grant (عطا 2).
It is said to resemble a sale in the first stage only, i. e. before the consideration for which the gift is made has been received, and the seizin of the donor and donee is, therefore, a requisite consideration.
hibat-ul-akhz. A demonstrative legacy.
It is a legacy where a testator bequeaths a certain sum of money or a certain quantity of any commodity, and refers to a particular fund or stock out of which payment is to be made.
hibah aslī yā qarībah. An original bequest.
hibah bir-ragbat.
A voluntary gift or settlement.

hiba bil-evaz. A mutual or return gift.
hiba bil-kināyā. An implied gift.
hibah ba-hālat marz-ul-maut. A gift made on one's death bed. [for return.
hibah ba shart-ul-evaz. A gift with stipulation
hibah tamlīk. A gift or property.
hibah-i-baīdah. An ulterior bequest.
hibah sānī. A second bequest.
hibah khās, n. m. A specific legacy.

It consists in the bequest of a specified part of the testator's property, which is distinguished from all other parts of his property. The distinction between this and a *demonstrative* legacy consists in this, that where specified property is given to the legatee the legacy is *specific*, and where the legacy is directed to be paid out of specified property it is *demonstrative.*

hibah shartīyah, hibah mashrūt.
A conditional bequest which takes effect on the fulfilment of certain conditions specified in the will ; a conditional gift.
hibah-i-qataī yā mutlaq.
An absolute or unconditional gift.
hibah kal-ādam. Avoid bequest, i. e. one which is made to a person by particular description, and there is no person in existence at the testator's death who answers the description. [veyance.
hibah-nāmah. A deed of gift ; deed by con-
hibah mā-baqā. A residuary bequest.
hibah musha. A gift of undefined or undivided property, which is not valid until the property has been separated, and transferred to the donee. [contingent gift.
hibah mauqūf ba-vaqū dīgar amr. G. G. A
hibah vujūbī An onerous bequest, i. e. one which imposes an obligation on the legatee, who, unless he accept the obligation, cannot avail himself of the legacy.
hibah-i-vujūbī, An absolute gift.
hiba vasīyati. A testamentary disposition.

A ہتک *hat'ak*, n. f. ہتک rending (a veil, etc). Detraction ; defamation. [to defame.
hatak izzat k., v. a. To bring disgrace upon ;
hatak izzat yā hurmat, Defamation of character.

H ہتنا हतना *hat'nā, hannā*, v. a. S. हन kill.
To kill ; slaughter.

H ہتھ हथ *hath*, Cont. of ہاتھ Hand.
hath-udhār. See *dast-gardān*, 1.
hath udhār, yā hath pher denā. To lend for use.
hath-pher, n. f. 1. Sleight of hand (in a money changer) ; changing a good for a bad rupee.
2. E. Borrowing.
hath pher lenā, E. v. n. To borrow.
hath-ras, n. m. Amorous dalliance.
hath-karī, n. f. A handcuff ; manacle.
hath-levā, n. m. A part of the Hin. marriage ceremony.

The hands of the bride and bridegroom are joined palm to palm with some flour put between them, and tied with a red thread.

H ہتیا हत्या *hat'tyā* ; Illit. *hittyā*, n. f. S. हन kill. Slaughter ; murder.
hattyā k., v. a. To kill ; murder.
hattyārā, n. m. 1. A murderer ; assassin.

H ہتیار हतियार *hatiyār', hathyār*, n.m.S. हन to kill. An instrument ; implement.
hathiyār vāste shauq o shikār ke. G. G.
Arms for private use.

H ہتتال हटताल *haṭtāl', haṛtāl, hartāl*, n. f.
H. *hāṭ* shop, *tālā* lock. 1. Passive resistance.
2. Closing all the shops of a market as a passive resistance to exaction.

H ہٹوا हटुआ *haṭ'uā* ; Tir. *haṭṭoē*, n. m. H. *hāṭ* a shop. 1. A shopkeeper.
2. A weighman (*tolā*, 2).
haṭvā'ī, n. f. The office of a *haṭuā*, q. v.
haṭaiṭā, n. m. Goods.

A ہجری *hij'rī*, The Mah. era from the 15th July A. D. 622.

A ہجوم *hujūm', hajūm*, n. m. ہجم driving in. A mob ; concourse (*bhīṛ*).
hujūm k., v. n. To crowd ; make a crowd.

A ہدایت *hidā'yat*, n. f. ہدی guiding. 1. Direction (*rahnumāī*). 2. Injunction ; precept.
hidāyat tākīdī k., v. a. To enjoin strictly ; direct with urgency.
hidāyat-i-qānūn se inhirāf k. G. G.
Disobeying a direction of law.
hidāyat-i-qānūnī. A direction of law.
hidāyat k., v. a. 1. To guide ; direct.
2. To instruct ; enjoin ; charge. [a code.
hidāyat-nāmah, n. m. A book of instructions ;
hidāyat nāmah-i-band o bast.
Directions for settlement officers.
hidāyat-nāmah-i-mālguzāri, n. Directions for collectors of Land-revenue ; a body of instructions for revenue officers.
hukm yā hidāyat-i-jāiz. G. G. Lawful orders or directions. [ernment shall direct.
hasb-i-hidāyat-i-gavarmenṭ. As the Local Gov-

A ہذا *hāz'ā* ; H. *yeh*, dem. pron. This.
majmuā hāzā. G. G. This code.
ba-mūjib ekaṭ hāzā. G. G. By this act.

H ہر हर *har, hal* ; Sant. *nahel*, n.m. A plough.
harā'ī, n. f. The furrows made by the plough.
ہرواہا हरवाहा *harvā'hā, hal-bāhā, hariyā*, n. m.
A ploughman.

ہرَوری हरौरी *haraur'ī*; Tir. *harourī*; Bhoj. *harvāhī*, n. f. 1. (*hālī*) The occupation of ploughing, or the place where ploughing is going on. 2. (*harval*) Money lent by a cultivator to a ploughman bearing no interest as long as he serves.

ہرول हरवल *har'val*; Bhoj. *harvarhi*, n. m. Advances made to ploughmen without interest.

ہرہا हरहा *har'hā,haryā*; Tir. *harak barad*, n.m.
1. Bullocks used in the plough.
2. Unbroken or vicious cattle. [ing of fields.

har'ī, n. f. Voluntary or compulsory plough-
har'iyar, n. m. The end of the sowing season.

H ہربونگ हरबोंग *harbaung'*, *harbang*, *har bhong*, *harbong kā rāj*, *harbam*, n. m. *lit.* the rule of Harbaug. Civil disorders; maladministration; anarchy.

H ہرٹھیا हरठिया *harath'iyā*, *rahatiyā*. The driver of the bullocks at a Persian wheel.

A حرج *harj*, *haraj*, n. m. See نقصان
1. An interruption. 2. A nuisance.
3. (*haraj maraj*) Interruption; delay.

harj āyandah. Prospective injury or loss.

harj k., v. a. 1. (*harj ḍālnā*) To interrupt; disturb. 2. To obstruct; delay; retard.
3. To damage; injure.

ہرجہ *har'jah*, n. m. 1. Demurrage.
2. Damages; compensation (تاوان 1).

harja tashkhīs k. To assess damages.

harja-i-zātī, n. m. Personal damages.

H ہردا हरदा *hard'ā*, n. m. 1. (*harā*) Weeds (in a field). 2. Mildew; smut (in corn).
3. A disease of the cerealia, in which the plant withers and assumes a yellow tinge.

H ہرس हरस *har'as*, *haris*, n. f. S. हलीषा 1. The ploughshare. 2. The beam of a plough.

H ہرسنگھ हरसिंघ *harsingh'a*. A right of cutting brush-wood. *Carnegy.*

harsingha o ghar-singhā. Wood for making implements of husbandry and houses.

H ہرن हरन *har'an*, n. m. S. हरण from हृ take. (*In Comp. only*) 1. Taking away; removing. 2. Theft; plunder.

ہرنا हरना *har'nā*, v. a. 1. To take; seize. 2. To steal; plunder. 3. To take away; remove.

H ہرواہا हरवाहा *harvā'hā*, n. m.

An agricultural bondsman, who has sold his services for an advance, and is bound, together with his descendants, to serve until the advance is repaid.

H ہری بولنا *harī bolnā*, n. m. The barbarous practice in Bengal of forcing a dying man to call on God (*Harī bolo*) with a view to hasten his death by breaking his bones.

H ہریانہ हरयाना *hariyā'nā*, n.

A certain division of a crop.

The cultivator retains nine parts and the *zamīndār* receives seven.

H ہڑکنی हुड़कनी *huṛak'nī*, n. f.

1. A dancing girl. 2. A harlot.

H ہڑنا हड़ना *har'nā*, v. n. To be tested (the accuracy of a weight).

H ہزار *hazār'*; Rus. *hajjār*, adj. A thousand.

P ہست وبود *hast o būd*. An estimate of the assets of a tract of land; also, when corrupted into *hastnābūd*, it signifies a remission granted by *zamīndārs* for the portion of land failing in produce. *Elliot.*

hast o būd jama. An account shewing the total amount of revenue under all heads of assessment to which any estate is liable.

hast o būdī. Land which has been assessed on the basis of a comparative valuation of its produce.

P ہفتگانہ *haftgā'na*, n. m. A register of revenue claims and payments kept in the Collector's office; village papers prepared by the village accountant.

H ہل हल *hal*, *har*, n. m. S. हल A plough.

halā'ētā, *halwāṭ*, *harauṭī*, *halsot*.
The first ploughing of the season.

It is generally preceded by the taking of omens, and other superstitious ceremonies. A commencement is made at the N.-W. corner and facing the S.-E., and the plough is then driven towards the middle of the field. *Carnegy.*

hal-barār, *hal-sārī*, n. f. Assessment according to the number of ploughs. [cultivation.

hal-bandī, n. f. The quantity of land under

hal-taḍḍī, n. f. A drill-plough (?).

hal jotnā, *chalānā*, *yā phernā*, v. a. To plough.

hal chalnā, v. n. To be ploughed.

hal-dār, n. m. The possessor of a plough.

hal-sajjā, *har-sajjā*, n. m. 1. Mutual assistance in ploughing. 2. A sharer in a plough.

hal-sajjā aur jotā, n. The three shares in a plough, viz. the ploughman's, and his two bullocks'. [lands of a village.

hal-ghasīṭ, *har-ghasīṭ*, n. f. The cultivated

hal-jotā, *hālī*, *hal-vāhī*, *hal-bāhā*, A ploughman.

haliā'ū, n. m. A division of crops in which the *zamīndār* gets seven, and the *asāmī* nine parts. *Carnegy.*

A هلاکت *halāk'at*; Illit. *hilākat*, n.f. 1. Homicide; manslaughter. 2. Death; execution.
halākat kā bāis h. G. G., *halāk karānā*, v. a. To cause death.
halākat lāzim-malzūm. G. G. Justifiable homicide.
halāk k., v. a. To kill; put to death.
halākat-i-nafs k. To lay violent hands on one's self.

H هلکا हलका *hal'kā, halkī*; Tir. and Bhoj. *halluk*; Rus. *halvā*; Sant. *rawāl*, adj. S. लघु light. Opp. of *bhārī*.
1. Light; not heavy. 2. Poor; not fertile. 3. Shallow. 4. Small. 5. Trifling. 6. Moderate; low. 7. Cheap; low-priced. 8. Depressed (trade). 9. Easy; light.
halkā mol lagānā, v. a. To put a low or moderate price upon.
halkī jamā. Light assessment.
halkī chorī; Ped. *sarqa-i-khafīf*, n. f. Petty theft.

H هلگرا हलगरा *hal-garā*, n. S. हालगरा
Land retaining moisture.

P ہم بستر *ham-bistar yā ham-khuāb h.*, v. n.
To sleep or cohabit with one.
ham-bistarī, n. f. Sleeping together; cohabitation.
ham-rāhiyān-i-lashkar. G. G. Camp followers.
ham-shīrah; H. *bahan*, n. f. A sister.
ham-shīrah-zād; H. *bhānjā*, n.m. A sister's son; nephew.

H ہننا हना *han'nā, hatnā*, S. हन kill.
To kill; slay.

H ہنڈا بھاڑا हुंडा भाड़ा *hunḍā bhāṛā*, n. m.
A contract for the transportation of goods, including the payment of duties.

H ہنڈاون हुण्डावन *hunḍāv'an*; Tir. *hunḍiāvan*, n. m. 1. Exchange; rate of exchange. 2. Discount.

H ہنڈی हुण्डी *hunḍ'ī, hinḍvī, hunḍvī*, n. f. S. हुण्डिका from हुण्ड to collect.
A bill of exchange; draft; cheque.
hunḍī bahī, n. f. A cheque-book; bill-book.
hunḍī bhejnā. To make a payment by a bill.
hunḍī paṭnā, To be cashed (a bill).
hunḍī jo na pate. A dishonored bill.
hunḍī sakārnā, v. a. To honor a bill.
hunḍī kā behvār. Exchange.
hunḍi k., v. a. To draw a bill or cheque.
hunḍī-karnevālā. The drawer of a cheque.
hunḍī miādī. A bill payable after date.
hunḍī-vālā. A native banker.
kisī par hunḍī k., v. a. To draw on a person.

H ہنکاری हुंकारी *hunkār'ī*, n. f. H. *āṅkṛā* a hook. A curved line round figures in *sārrāfī* accounts. ۱ ॥—॥) = 1—9—6.

P ہنگامہ *haṅgām'ah*, n. m. 1. Tumult; uproar. 2. An affray; a disturbance.
haṅgāma-pardāz, adj. Tumultuous; riotous.
haṅgāma-pardāzī, Making a tumult or riot.
haṅgāma-i-shadīd. A riot.
haṅgāma k., v. a. To raise a disturbance; make a riot.
haṅgāme kā murtakab h. To commit a riot.
sazā-i-irtikāb-i-haṅgāma. G. G.
Punishment for committing a riot.

A ہئیت نکاح *haiat-i-nikāh*, n. f. Coverture.

H ہیٹھا हीठा *hīṭh'ā*, n. m. A person appointed to take care of standing crops. *Carnegy.*

H ہیرانا हीराना *hīrā'nā.* Manuring a field by penning cattle or sheep in it.
In the Kangra District the farmers pay wandering shepherds for penning their flocks in their fields, and if after two or three winters the shepherd goes to another farmer's field, the first farmer generally brings an action for damages against the shepherd. Barnes. Kangra Settlement Report.

H ہیکڑی *hek'ṛī*, n. f.
Force; power; authority.
hekṛī se, adv. Perforce; by force.
hekṛī k., yā jatānā, v. n. To use force; to menace.

ي

PH یابندہ ہونڈی *yābindah-i-hunḍī*, Ped. for H. *hunḍī-pānevālā*, n. m.
The holder of a draft or bill.

P یادداشت *yād-dāsht*, n. f. 1. A memorandum; memo. 2. A reminder. 3. A souvenir.
yād-dāsht-i-apīl. A memorandum of appeal.
yād-dāsht-i-sharākat.
A memorandum of association.
yād-dāsht-i-zohrī, n. f. An endorsement; a writing on the back of a paper. [(*paida*).

P یافت *yāft*, n. f. Income; emoluments
yāft kī naukrī, A lucrative post.
یافتنی *yāftan'ī*, n. f. Opp. of *dādanī.*
Dues; bills receivable; credits.

S یتھارتھ यथार्थ *yathārth'*, adv. Exactly.

S یتھاسکت यथाशक्त *yathā sakt.*
According to one's means.

A یتیم *yatīm'ī*; Sant. *ṭuar*, n. m. An orphan.
یتیمی *yatīm'ī*, n. m.
The state or pupilage of an orphan.

P یک *yak*, adj. One.
yak bāchhi, A distribution of any sum or cess, levied upon all lands at an equal rate.

yak-jaddī, ham-jaddī, adj. Lineal ; direct.
yak-digar, One another ; mutually.
yak-sālā, n. m. A cess levied originally for but one year.
yakun jama, n. f. A statement of the total rent of each piece of land in the village accounts.
yakum zamīn, A statement of the total land measured to each Ryot for the current year.
yakun kamī, Total remission or deficiency.

P یگانگت *yagān-gat, yagāngī,* n. f. Kinship.

A یومیہ *yaumī'ya*; **P.** *rozānah,* adv. Daily.
yaumīya, n. m. Daily allowance or wages (*rozīna*).
yaumīya-dār, n. m. A daily pensioner (*rozínah-dār*).

H یہہ **यह** *yeh,* pron. This.
yeh muqaddama sāhibān kalaktar kī mārfat bākhūbī anjām ho saktā hai. G. G.
The Collector is an efficient instrument for the purpose.

THE END.

ERRATA.

Page.	Col.	Line.	For	Read
4	1.	7	*Apīlāt*	*apīlāṅṭ*
5	2	45	अतिविपा	अतिविपा
5	2	46	*feror.*	*ferox.*
6	2	44	*ija'rāh*	*ijā'rah*
9	1	23	*-kār'nā*	*-karnā*
12	2	15	*khilaf-i-adab*	*khilāf-i-adab*
12	2	17	*khilaf-i*	*khilāf-i*
12	2	19	*idkhal*	*idkhāl*
12	2	34	*admī*	*ādmī*
13	1	27	*aṭa'rī*	*aṭā'rī*
13	2	6	*īzn-na'mah*	*izn-nā'mah*
14	1	15	*-kasht*	*-kāsht*
15	1	4	*irsal*	*irsāl*
16	2	23	*-i-ta līf*	*-i-taklīf*
16	2	32	*aljaz-i*	*alfāz-i*
18	1	15	*-ha'lat*	*-hā'lat*
18	2	8	असागोत्रा	आसागोत्रा
20	1	37	*-i-hīfāzat-i-*	*-i-hifāzat-i-*
21	1	40	*rāṅd*	*rāṅḍ*
21	2	14	*-i-t blī*	*-i-tablī*
21	2	15	*istiswab*	*istiswāb*
24	1	18	*āsratai*	*āsratāī*
27	2	37	*-mujib-i-*	*-mūjib-i-*
27	2	37	*khalāyak.*	*-khalāyaq.*
31	2	23	*āftab-*	*āftāb-*
32	2	3	*Ramzām.*	*Ramzān.*
32	2	8	*nā munasib*	*nā munāsib*
34	1	3	*iqrār-namah*	*iqrār-nāmah*
35	2	15	*decapetatum*	*decapetalum*
41	2	32	[*craft*	*dele*
44	2	37	*amr-t-nāzuk*	*amr i-nāzuk*
46	1	21	*amānāt-dār*	*amānat-dār*
48	1	5	rapture	rupture
51	1	9	*andkosh*	*anḍ kosh*
51	1	27	*mānkhā-deh*	*mankhā-deh*
53	2	30	*ṭaṭṭi*	*ṭaṭṭī*
60	1	47	*Āhl-kār*	*Ahl-kār*
61	1	41	*īfā-i-digrī*	*ifā-i-ḍigrī*
77	1	7	*mushāhāra*	*mushāhara*
78	1	22	*bar-qārār*	*bar-qarār*
78	2	35	*na-jawāzī*	*nā-jawāzī*
79	1	33	*bārtāo*	*bartāo*
84	1	1	*khārīj*	*khārij*
90	2	Last	previtive	primitive
91	2	53	*khilaf*	*khilāf*
92	1	39	*byāth'tā*	*byāh'tā*
92	2	44	बज्ज	बीज
93	2	22	*sazae*	*sazāë*
95	1	16	*māzīd*	*mazīd*
96	2	31	*dāiṅ*	*ḍāin*
96	2	39	*bābāt*	*bābat*
99	1	11	*patṛā*	*paṭṛā*
101	2	1	*parwāṅ-i*	*parwāna-i*
107	1	Last	*-haiyat*	*-haiyāt*
109	2	26	*mauqā*	*mauqe*
111	2	2	*-mulāzāmat*	*-mulāzamat*
112	2	9	[of Anatomy.	*dele*
112	2	52	*zāmīn*	*zāmin*
114	2	13	*-munsab*	*-mansab*
114	2	17	*tamīl*	*tāmīl*
114	2	24	*tavīq*	*tāvīq*
118	1	46	*urṭī*	*uṛṭī*
118	2	35	*talīm yāftā*	*tālīm-yāfta*
121	1	11	*-tagrīrī*	*-taqrīrī*
129	2	41	more	move
131	1	9	چرسال	چتسال
131	1	38	*haras*	*charas*
133	2	40	*chhinalā*	*chhinālā*
135	1	7	*chīj*	*chhīj*
135	1	15	چتر	چترا
135	2	28	omnipresent ;	omnipresent and
135	2	37	absquatuated	absquatulated
136	1	56	*hal-i*	*hāl-i*
136	2	43	[Exclusion.	*dele*
136	2	44	حجت	حجب
138	1	5	*sāb*	*hisāb*
139	1	13	خصول	حصول
139	2	7	*hīszah*	*hissa*
139	2	11	*hīssah-*	*hissah-*
140	1	52	*haq-bhet*	*haq-bheṭ*
141	1	21	*bīnā-i*	*binā-i*
141	1	23	*-shara-i*	*-sharai*

Page.	Col.	Line.	For	Read
141	2	29	*muttaălliqat*	*muttaălliqāt*
141	2	55	tennre.	tenure.
142	1	1	*qīsm, yā qīsm*	*qism, yā qism*
142	1	33	*zāmiṅdār's*	*zamiṅdār's*
142	1	45	*bhaī*	*bhāī*
143	1	Last	*āmal*	*āmad*
143	2	13	*barīnda-*	*barinda-*
144	2	32	*hāzīrī*	*hāzirī*
144	2	45	*khārījah*	*khārijah*
146	1	5	*-āmad*	*-amad*
146	2	53	خويدن	خریدن
147	1	20	*ḍigrī*	*ḍigrī*
148	1	27	*khīlaf-i*	*khilāf-i*
149	1	48	*khārīj*	*khārij*
150	2	8	*vāsīlāt*	*vāsilāt*
151	2	8	*sābīq*	*sābiq*
152	2	15	*-baībat*	*-baibāt*
152	2	18	*khārīj*	*khārij*
154	2	16	*paṭrariyāṅ,*	*paṭvāriyān*
154	2	51	*na-jāiz*	*nā-jāiz*
156	1	23	*kachā*	*kachchā*
157	2	Line 10, with bracketed continuation, and line 30 should come next to line 31.		
157	2	38	دهار اباچهه	دهار باچهه
158	1	24	जान *dharā jā-na*	जाना *dharā jā-nā*
160	2	28	*garoh*	*giroh*
160	2	34	*isbat-i*	*isbāt-i*
161	1	15	*ijra*	*ijrā*
162	1	31	*khilānā*	*khilāne*
163	2	12	*-bad*	*-bād*
163	2	15	*raz-*	*rāz*
164	1	23	*zakūt*	*zakāt*
164	2	7	رب السلام	رب السلّم
165	1	35	*rezīl*	*razīl*
165	1	43	Fees ;	5. Fees ;
165	2	21	*khazana*	*khazāna*
166	1	19	*nātā*	*nātī*
166	1	50	*khātīr*	*khātir*
166	2	23	*riāyātī*	*riāyatī*
167	1	13	رفع	رفع

Page.	Col.	Line.	For	Read
167	1	30	*-pashī*	*-pāshī*
170	2	4	*rahān-*	*rahan-*
171	1	5	*-ikhtiydr*	*-ikhtiyār*
179	2	20	v. a.	v. n.
180	2	4	*mustaqīl*	*mustaqil*
183	2	34	*sudā·*	*saudā*
191	1	Line 40 should come after line 29.		
191	2	16	*salāhiyāt*	*salāhiyat*
192	1	12	*ke*	*kī*
200	1	26	*alāh'dagī-*	*alah'dagī*
202	2	32	*azādah*	*āzād*
204	2	8	*fātva-i*	*fatva-i*
204	2	9	*fātva-i*	*fatva-i*
205	2	After line 44 read To be deceived or cheated.		
208	2	25	*qabil*	*qābil*
208	2	49	*qārīq*	*qāriq*
209	1	35	*tamīl*	*tāmīl*
209	2	35, etc.	*muaqām*	*maqam*
211	1	50	*qad*	*qadr*
212	1	53	*mumkīn*	*mumkin*
214	1	39	*qullah*	*qulbah*
217	1	53	*kītāb*	*kitāb*
218	1	41	*kachhuā*	*kachhue*
218	2	53	cast	caste
224	2	5	*ta*	*tā*
225	2	40	*gatthā*	*gaṭṭhā*
227	2	36	*-shikāst*	*-shikast*
232	1	9	*lohāz*	*lihāz*
239	1	30	*mutānāsiba*	*mutanāsiba*
243	1	39	*bār-*	*bar-*
245	2	5	*rakhnī*	*karī*
246	1	40	*taluq*	*taălluq*
249	1	25	*-jung*	*-jang*
255	2	30	*muqadmak*	*muqadmah*
268	2	13	*muqqarrar*	*muqarrar*
269	1	22	Childess ;	Childless ;
269	2	15	*bandodast*	*bandobast*
277	1	42	*vuzūl*	*vusūl*
277	2	10	*binae*	*bināë*
278	1	Last.	[aduocate.	[advocate.
282	2	26	هوندی	ہندی

FALLON'S NEW ENGLISH AND HINDUSTĀNĪ DICTIONARY, a companion volume to the Author's Hindustānī and English Dictionary, to be completed in about 9 to 12 parts, each part to consist of 48 pages super-royal 8vo. One part will be issued every two to three months. Price to Subscribers One rupee eight annas for each Part.

In the New Dictionary will be found

First.—A greater degree of fullness and accuracy than have yet been attained.

Second.—A considerable number of English phrases and idioms, with idiomatic Hindustānī translations.

Third.—Technical terms in European Arts, Science, and Philosophy rendered for the first time in popular Hindustānī, in addition to the Arabic and Sanskrit terms in present use in Government Colleges and Schools.

Fourth.—The primary and secondary English meanings with their Hindustānī equivalents arranged in logical order.

Fifth.—The Hindustānī equivalents so arranged that the more commonly used or colloquial phrase shall come before the less used or pedantic phrase.

Sixth.—Examples, chiefly colloquial, with idiomatic translations.

Seventh.—The examples will sometimes consist of English Proverbs, with idiomatic Hindustānī translations and parallel Native proverbs when there are any.

Eighth.—Affinities between Sanskrit, Hindī, Persian, and Arabic words, and their equivalents in Anglo-Saxon, English (with its dialects), and other European languages of the Arian group.

FALLON'S NEW HINDUSTĀNĪ-ENGLISH DICTIONARY, with illustrations from Hindustānī Literature and Folk-lore, 1,216 pages, super-royal 8vo., Rs. 52, with Packing and Postage One Rupee.

FALLON'S HINDUSTĀNĪ-ENGLISH LAW & COMMERCIAL DICTIONARY, comprising many Law phrases and notes in addition to the Law phrases given in the general Dictionary, about 283 pages super-royal 8vo., Rs 10, with Packing and Postage As. 8. This is the Author's English-Hindustānī Law and Commercial Dictionary, enlarged and reversed.

In course of compilation.

FALLON'S HINDUSTĀNĪ PROVERBS, being a collection of above twelve thousand proverbs, with English translations, and parallel English Proverbs when there are any.

Preparing for the Press.

FALLON'S ENGLISH-HINDUSTĀNĪ LAW & COMMERCIAL DICTIONARY, comprising the technical terms only, 2nd Edition, revised and enlarged, super-royal 8vo., 120 to 150 pp. Rs. Four, with Packing and Postage As. 6.

Subscribers registered by the compiler at Delhi.